MACROECONOMICS

MACROECONOMICS

SEVENTH EDITION

RUDIGER DORNBUSCH
Massachusetts Institute of Technology
Ford Professor of Economics and
International Management

STANLEY FISCHER
International Monetary Fund
on Leave from Massachusetts Institute of Technology

RICHARD STARTZ
University of Washington

**Irwin
McGraw-Hill**

Boston, Massachusetts   Burr Ridge, Illinois   Dubuque, Iowa
Madison, Wisconsin   New York, New York   San Francisco, California   St. Louis, Missouri

Irwin/McGraw-Hill

*A Division of The **McGraw·Hill** Companies*

Macroeconomics

Copyright © 1998, 1994, 1990, 1987, 1984, 1981, 1978 by The McGraw-Hill Companies, Inc. All rights reserved. Printed in the United States of America. Except as permitted under the United States Copyright Act of 1976, no part of this publication may be reproduced or distributed in any form or by any means, or stored in a data base or retrieval system, without the prior written permission of the publisher.

This book is printed on acid-free paper.

domestic 1 2 3 4 5 6 7 8 9 0 VNH VNH 9 0 0 9 8 7 6
international   3 4 5 6 7 8 9 0 VNH VNH 9 0 0 9

ISBN 0-07-017985-9

Editorial Director: Michael Junior
Publisher; Gary Burke
Sponsoring editor: Lucille Sutton
Editorial Assistant: Jeff Begley
Marketing Manager: Nelson Black
Project manager: Natalie Durbin
Production supervisor: Tanya Nigh
Designer: Ed Butler
Cover designer: Brad Thomas
Compositor: York Graphic Services, Inc.
Typeface: Times Roman
Printer: Von Hoffmann Press

Cover illustration: Vasily Kandinsky, *Composition 8,* July 1923
Photographer: David Heald, © The Solomon R. Guggenheim Foundation, New York

Library of Congress Cataloging-in-Publication Data
Dornbusch, Rudiger.
    Macroeconomics.—7th ed./Rudiger Dornbusch, Stanley Fischer, Richard Startz.
        p. cm.
    Includes bibliographical references and index.
    ISBN 0-07-017985-9
    1. Macroeconomics. I. Fischer, Stanley. II. Startz, Richard, 1952–   . III. Title.
HB172.5.D67 1998
    339—dc21   97-30777
                                        CIP

International Edition
Copyright © 1998. Exclusive rights by The McGraw-Hill Companies, Inc., for manufacture and export. This book cannot be re-exported from the country to which it is consigned by The McGraw-Hill Companies, Inc. The International Edition is not available in North America.

When ordering this title, use ISBN 0-07-115232-6.

http://www.mhhe.com

ABOUT THE AUTHORS

RUDI DORNBUSCH is Ford Professor of Economics and International Management at MIT. He did his undergraduate work in Switzerland and holds a Ph.D. from the University of Chicago. He has taught at Chicago, at Rochester, and since 1975 at MIT. His research is primarily in international economics, with a major macroeconomic component. His special research interests are the behavior of exchange rates, high inflation and hyperinflation, and the problems and opportunities that high capital mobility poses for developing economies. He visits and lectures extensively in Europe and in Latin America, where he takes an active interest in problems of stabilization policy, and has held visiting appointments in Brazil and Argentina. His writing includes *Open Economy Macroeconomics* and, with Stanley Fischer and Richard Schmalensee, *Economics*. His interests in public policy take him frequently to testify before Congress and to participate in international conferences. He regularly contributes newspaper editorials on current policy issues here and abroad.

STANLEY FISCHER is First Deputy Managing Director of the International Monetary Fund, on leave from the Department of Economics at MIT. He was an undergraduate at the London School of Economics and has a Ph.D. from MIT. He taught at the University of Chicago while Rudi Dornbusch was a student there, starting a long friendship and collaboration. He has been a member of the faculty of the MIT Economics Department since 1973. During that period he has taken leaves at the Hebrew University in Jerusalem and at Stanford. From 1988 to 1990 he was Chief Economist at the World Bank. He joined the IMF in 1994. His main research interests are economic growth and development; international economics and macroeconomics, particularly inflation and its stabilization; and the economics of transition.

RICHARD STARTZ is Professor of Economics, and currently department chair, at the University of Washington. He was an undergraduate at Yale University and received his Ph.D. from MIT, where he studied under Stanley Fischer and Rudi Dornbusch. He taught at the Wharton School of the University of Pennsylvania before moving on to the University of Washington, and he has taught, while on leave, at the University of California–San Diego, the Stanford Business School, and Princeton. His principal research areas are macroeconomics, econometrics, and the economics of race. In the area of macroeconomics, much of his work has concentrated on the microeconomic underpinnings of macroeconomic theory. His work on race is part of a long-standing collaboration with Shelly Lundberg. In addition to his work in economics, he is the author of two books on personal computing.

To Fine, Rhoda, and Shelly

CONTENTS
In Brief

CONTENTS

PART

3

FIRST MODELS *187*

PART

4

PART

5

PREFACE

In 1977, the first edition of this text opened with these words:

> Our aim in writing this book has been to explain how modern macroeconomics is used in understanding important economic issues, and to help the reader analyze macroeconomic problems for her or himself.... The book is policy- and issue-oriented.

These words remain true today. But both the economy and the study of economics have changed in 20 years. This new edition reflects those changes. Indeed, about 40 percent of the material in this edition is new or has been revised in the 4 years since the sixth edition. What has remained constant is the authors' conviction that the best textbook is one written with an abiding respect for both student and instructor. We have not shied away from difficult material, although we emphasize straightforward explanation. Further, where scientific questions about the economy remain unsettled, we state so frankly. At the same time, we are clear about which channel is occupied by the mainstream of the profession.

We have taken the position that the best teaching reflects the instructor's own scholarship, interests, and research and that a textbook must facilitate this. While the text is organized around our own quite strongly held views as to what is important, we have also provided numerous points of departure for deeper exploration of particular topics. While we doubt that anyone will follow all these branches, we hope everyone will explore one or more.

This seventh edition differs from its predecessors in two important ways. First, we have given far greater emphasis to the long-run behavior of the economy than we did in previous editions. This emphasis is reflected in the greatly expanded coverage of economic growth and in an extended discussion of the intergenerational aspects of budget deficits and of social security. Second, we have, in keeping with our respect for student and instructor, included more material exploring state-of-the-art research than is customary in undergraduate texts. At the same time, we have reduced the book's level of difficulty by emphasizing concepts over technique. We have also changed the text in two more subtle ways: by adding many more international examples and by providing many more illustrations based on real-world data. These changes are in response to the increasing need for taking a global perspective and to students' desire to have ideas and concepts confirmed by real data.

Our book is used today not only in the United States but around the world, in many languages and far more countries, from Canada to Argentina to Australia; all over Europe; in India, Indonesia and Japan; from China and Albania to Russia. Even before the Czech Republic gained independence from communism, an underground translation was secretly used in macroeconomics seminars at Charles University in Prague. There is no greater pleasure for teachers and textbook authors than to see their efforts succeed so concretely around the world.

PLANS OF ATTACK

We provide here several alternative paths through the book to fit a variety of course goals and student needs. We think the best plan is to begin at the beginning and work through the entire book (which is why, of course, we organized the material the way we did), but there are a number of approaches that can be taken to give a different emphasis or simply to reduce the breadth of material covered:

- **An Overview Course:** The course can be shortened substantially by omitting the chapters that focus on the microeconomic detail beneath macroeconomic theory. Omit Chapters 8 and 13 through 17. In the United States, you might also choose to omit Chapters 12 and 21, on international interdependence, and perhaps Chapter 4, on growth and policy.
- **A Traditional Aggregate Demand–Oriented Course:** Chapters 3 and 4, on growth, can be moved to the end of the course. Chapter 18, on stabilization policy, can be moved up in front of Chapter 13. Omit most of Chapter 8, with the possible exception of the material on New Keynesian economics.
- **A "Supply-Side" Course:** The IS-LM material in Chapters 9 through 11 can be deemphasized. Greater emphasis might be given to the discussion of hyperinflations in Chapter 19. For students ready for challenging material, explore Chapter 8's sections on the random walk of GDP and on real business cycles.
- **A Business School Course:** Omit Chapter 8. Emphasize Chapters 16 and 17 on the Fed and on financial markets.

Throughout the book, we have labeled some material "optional" and some even "superoptional." This material is technically difficult. Many of the optional sections will be fun for students who enjoy a technical challenge, but the instructor should specify clearly which of these sections are required and which are truly optional.

ACKNOWLEDGMENTS

We have in the past acknowledged our debts to correspondents, colleagues, and students individually. There is no longer room to do that, but we have to depart from our new rule to thank Avery Tillet Ke, Jessica Rutledge, and Jennifer Ward-Batts for their superb assistance in preparing this seventh edition.

In addition, we and McGraw-Hill would like to thank the reviewers of this edition: Berhanu Abegaz, College of William and Mary; Gerald Adams, University of Pennsylvania; Niels G. Bolwig, University of Aarhus; Paul Burkett, Indiana State University; Stephen Cassler, Allegheny College; David DeJong, University of Pittsburgh; Jim Gale, Michigan Technical University; James Howell, Stanford University; John James, University of Virginia; Manfred Keil, Northeastern University; Robert Murphy, Boston College; Julie Nelson, University of California–Davis; Thomas Pogue, University of Iowa; and Douglas Wooley, Radford University.

SUPPLEMENTARY MATERIAL

An *Instructor's Manual* and *Test Bank* to accompany the text have been prepared by Professor Juergen Fleck of Hollins College. The *Instructor's Manual* has been substantially updated and includes chapter summaries, learning objectives, solutions to the end-of-chapter problems, and many additional problems (and their solutions) that can be used for class discussion, homework assignments, or examination questions. The *Test Bank* has been expanded and now includes more than 750 questions.

The *Study Guide,* by Jessica Rutledge of the University of Washington–Seattle, that accompanies the text has again been revised and brought up to date. It contains a wide range of questions, starting from the very easy and progressing in each chapter to material that will challenge the more advanced student. The *Study Guide* is a great help in studying, particularly since active learning is so important in mastering new material.

Learning can be made more active yet with the help of the software program *PC-Macroeconomics,* developed by Professors F. Gerard Adams of the University of Pennsylvania and Eugene Kroch of Villanova University. It is available with the text as well as separately. The program follows the sequencing in the text and patiently builds the analytical framework by using empirical data that allow students to understand macroeconomics in a step-by-step integration of text, data, and graphics. Students can either view the analysis in a demonstration mode, choose to interact within the parameters set in the program, or change the parameters as desired. There is also a "Policy Game" that gives students meaningful experience in analyzing various policy options. *PC-Macroeconomics* is a standard Windows application and is entirely self-explanatory.

Rudiger Dornbusch
Stanley Fischer
Richard Startz

MACROECONOMICS

1

Introduction and National Income Accounting

CHAPTER 1

Introduction

CHAPTER HIGHLIGHTS

◆ Each chapter starts off with "Chapter Highlights," giving you a guide to the chapter's most important points. In this chapter, we emphasize three linked models which collectively describe the macroeconomy.

◆ The long-run behavior of the economy is the domain of growth theory, which focuses on the growth of productive capacity.

◆ Over horizons of moderate length, the productive capacity of the economy can be treated as largely fixed. Output is thus fixed by aggregate supply, and prices depend on both aggregate supply and aggregate demand. Large-scale inflation is always the result of changing aggregate demand.

◆ In the short run, the price level is fixed and changes in aggregate demand generate changes in output, resulting in booms and recessions.

Macroeconomics is concerned with the behavior of the economy as a whole—with booms and recessions, the economy's total output of goods and services, the growth of output, the rates of inflation and unemployment, the balance of payments, and exchange rates. Macroeconomics deals with both long-run economic growth and the short-run fluctuations that constitute the business cycle.

Macroeconomics focuses on the economic behavior and policies that affect consumption and investment, the dollar and the trade balance, the determinants of changes in wages and prices, monetary and fiscal policies, the money stock, the federal budget, interest rates, and the national debt.

In brief, macroeconomics deals with the major economic issues and problems of the day. To understand these issues, we have to reduce the complicated details of the economy to manageable essentials. *Those essentials lie in the interactions among the goods, labor, and assets markets of the economy and in the interactions among national economies that trade with each other.*

In dealing with the essentials, we go beyond details of the behavior of individual economic units, such as households and firms, or the determination of prices in particular markets, which are the subject matter of microeconomics. In macroeconomics we deal with the market for goods as a whole, treating all the markets for different goods—such as the markets for agricultural products and for medical services—as a single market. Similarly, we deal with the labor market as a whole, abstracting from differences between the markets for, say, unskilled labor and doctors. We deal with the assets market as a whole, abstracting from differences between the markets for IBM shares and for Rembrandt paintings. The benefit of the abstraction is that it facilitates increased understanding of the vital interactions among the goods, labor, and assets markets. The cost of the abstraction is that omitted details sometimes matter.

It is only a short step from studying how the macroeconomy works to asking how to make it perform better. The fundamental questions are, *Can* the government and *should* the government intervene in the economy to improve its performance? The great macroeconomists have always enjoyed a keen interest in the application of macrotheory to policy. This was true in the case of John Maynard Keynes and is true of American leaders in the field, including members of the older Nobel laureate generation such as Milton Friedman of the University of Chicago and the Hoover Institution, Franco Modigliani and Robert Solow of M.I.T., and James Tobin of Yale University. The next generation's leaders, such as Robert Barro, Martin Feldstein, and N. Gregory Mankiw of Harvard University, Nobel laureate Robert Lucas and Thomas Sargent of the University of Chicago, Olivier Blanchard of M.I.T., and Robert Hall and John Taylor of Stanford University, despite being more—and in some cases altogether—skeptical about the wisdom of active government policies, also have strong views on policy issues.

Because macroeconomics is closely related to the economic problems of the day, it does not yield its greatest rewards to those whose primary interest is abstract. Macrotheory is a little untidy at the edges. But then the world is a little untidy around the edges. This book uses macroeconomics to illuminate economic events from the Great Depression through the 1990s. We refer continually to real-world events to elucidate the meaning and the relevance of the theoretical material.

There is a simple test for determining whether you understand the material in this book: Can you apply the material to understand current discussions about the national and international economy? Macroeconomics is an applied science. It is rarely beautiful, but it is overwhelmingly important to the well-being of nations and peoples.

1-1

MACROECONOMICS ENCAPSULATED IN THREE MODELS

The study of macroeconomics is organized around three models that describe the world, each model having its greatest applicability in a different time frame. The *long-run* behavior of the economy is the domain of growth theory, which focuses on the growth of productive capacity. In the *medium run,* we treat productive capacity as given. The level of productive capacity determines output, and fluctuations in demand relative to this level of supply determine prices and inflation. In the *short run,* fluctuations in demand determine how much of the available capacity is used and thus the level of output and unemployment. It is in the realm of the short-run model that we find the greatest role for government policy. Nearly all macroeconomists subscribe to these three models, but opinions differ as to the time frame in which each model is best applied. Everyone agrees that behavior over decades is best described by the growth theory model. There is less agreement over the applicable time scope for the medium-run versus the short-run model.

This chapter is largely devoted to outlining the three models with a broad brush. The remainder of the text paints in the details.

LONG-RUN GROWTH

The long-run behavior of the economy is the domain of *growth theory*. Figure 1-1*a* illustrates the growth of income per person in the United States over more than a century. We see a fairly smooth growth curve, averaging 2 or 3 percent a year. In studying growth theory, we ask how the accumulation of inputs—investment in machinery, for example—and improvements in technology lead to an increased standard of living. We ignore recessions and booms and related short-run fluctuations in employment of people and other resources. We assume that labor, capital, raw materials, and so on, are all fully employed.

How can a model that ignores fluctuations in the economy possibly tell us anything sensible? Fluctuations in the economy—the ups and downs of unemployment, for example—tend to average out over the years. Over very long periods, all that matters is how quickly the economy grows on average. Growth theory seeks to explain growth rates averaged over many years or decades. Why does one nation's economy grow at 2 percent a year while another nation's grows at 4 percent a year? Can we explain growth miracles such as the 8 percent annual growth in Japan in the early postwar period? What accounts for growth debacles such as Bangladesh's half percent annual postwar growth?

Chapters 3 and 4 examine the causes of economic growth and of differences in growth rates among nations. In industrialized countries, changes in the standard of living

BOX 1-1 Models and the Real World

Models are simplified representations of the real world. A good model accurately explains the behaviors that are most important to us and omits details that are relatively unimportant. The notion that the earth revolves around the sun on an elliptical path and that the moon similarly revolves around the earth is an example of a model. The exact behavior of sun, earth, and moon is much more complicated, but this model enables us to understand the phases of the moon. For this purpose, it is a good model. Even though the real orbits are not simple ellipses, the model "works."

In economics, the complex behavior of millions of individuals, firms, and markets is represented by one, two, a dozen, a few hundred, or a few thousand mathematical relations in the form of graphs or equations or computer programs. The intellectual problem in model building is that humans can understand the interactions between, at most, only a handful of relations. So usable macrotheory relies on a toolbox of models, each consisting of two or three equations. A particular model is a tool based on a set of assumptions—for example, that the economy is at full employment—that are reasonable in some real-world circumstances. Understanding the macroeconomy requires a rich toolbox and the application of sound judgment regarding when to deploy a particular model.

FIGURE 1-1   PER CAPITA GNP, 1873–1994 (THOUSANDS OF 1987 DOLLARS).

The diagram includes an exploded view of the period 1973–1983. (Note that the scales of the two panels differ.) (Source: U.S. Department of Commerce, Statistical Abstract of the United States, 1994.)

BOX 1-2 Aggregate Supply and Aggregate Demand

- The *level of aggregate supply* is the amount of output the economy can produce given the resources and technology available.
- The *aggregate supply tradeoff* between price and output represents firms' decisions to raise or lower prices when demand for output rises or falls.
- The *level of aggregate demand* is the total demand for goods to consume, for new investment, for goods purchased by the government, and for net goods to be exported abroad.

depend primarily on the development of new technology and the accumulation of capital—broadly defined. In developing countries, the development of a well-functioning infrastructure is more important than the development of new technology, as the latter can be imported. In all countries, the rate of saving is a key determinant of future well-being. Countries that are willing to sacrifice today have higher standards of living in the future.

Do you really care whether the economy grows at 2 percent a year rather than 4 percent? Over a lifetime you'll care a great deal: at the end of one 20-year generation, your standard of living will be 50 percent higher under 4 percent growth than under 2 percent. (Over 100 years a 4 percent growth rate produces a standard of living *seven* times higher than does a 2 percent growth rate.)

THE ECONOMY WITH FIXED PRODUCTIVE CAPACITY

What determines the inflation rate—the change in the overall price level? Why are prices in some countries stable for many years, while prices in other countries double every month? *To study inflation and to study the short- to medium-run determination of output, we introduce the aggregate supply–aggregate demand model.* In the long run, the level of output is determined solely by supply-side considerations. Essentially, output is determined by the productive capacity of the economy. The price level is determined by the level of demand relative to the output the economy can supply.

Figure 1-2 shows a medium-run aggregate supply–aggregate demand diagram—the overall price level (P) in the economy is shown on the vertical axis, and total output (Y) is shown on the horizontal axis. The aggregate supply and aggregate demand schedules each give one relation between the overall price level in the economy and total output. The *aggregate supply (AS) curve* depicts, for each given price level, the quantity of output firms are willing to supply. The position of the aggregate supply curve depends on the productive capacity of the economy. The *aggregate demand (AD) curve* presents, for each given price level, the level of output at which the goods markets and

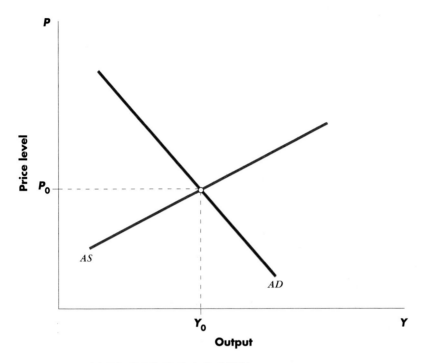

FIGURE 1-2   AGGREGATE DEMAND AND SUPPLY.

money markets are simultaneously in equilibrium. The position of the aggregate demand curve depends on monetary and fiscal policy and the level of consumer confidence. The intersection of aggregate supply and aggregate demand determines price and quantity.[1]

Figure 1-2 illustrates an aggregate supply curve with intermediate slope, neither vertical nor horizontal. The question "How steep is the aggregate supply curve?" is the main controversy in macroeconomics. In the long run, the aggregate supply curve is vertical. (Economists argue over whether the long run is a period of a few quarters or of a decade.) Figure 1-3 shows a vertical aggregate supply curve. Output is pegged to the position where this supply curve hits the horizontal axis. The price level, in contrast, can take on any value.

Mentally shift the aggregate demand schedule to the left or right. You will see that the intersection of the two curves moves up and down (the price changes), rather than horizontally (output doesn't change). It follows that *in the long run* output is determined by aggregate supply alone and prices are determined by both aggregate supply and aggregate demand. This is our first substantive finding.

The growth theory and long-run aggregate supply models are intimately linked: the position of the vertical aggregate supply curve in a given year equals the level

---

[1]You should be warned that the economics underlying the aggregate supply and aggregate demand schedules is very different from the economics of the ordinary, garden-variety supply and demand that you may remember from studying microeconomics.

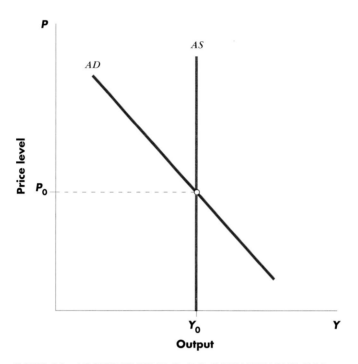

FIGURE 1-3   AGGREGATE DEMAND AND SUPPLY: THE LONG RUN.

of output for that year from the very long run model, as shown in Figure 1-4. Since economic growth over the very long run averages a few percent a year, we know that the aggregate supply curve typically moves to the right by a few percent a year.[2]

We are ready for our second conclusion: Very high inflation rates—that is, episodes with rapid increases in the overall price level—are always due to changes in aggregate demand. The reason is simple. Aggregate supply movements are on the order of a few percent; aggregate demand movements can be either small or large. So the only possible source of high inflation is large movements of aggregate demand sweeping across the vertical aggregate supply curve. In fact, as we will eventually learn, the only source of really high inflation rates is government-sanctioned increases in the money supply.[3]

Much of macroeconomics can be capsulized as the study of the position and slope of the aggregate supply and aggregate demand curves. You now know that in the long run the position of the aggregate supply curve is determined by very long run economic growth and that the slope of aggregate supply is simply vertical.

---

[2]Sometimes there are shocks which temporarily disrupt the orderly rightward progression of the aggregate supply schedule. These shocks are rarely larger than a few percent of output.

[3]Temporary price increases of 10 or 20 percent can be due to supply shocks—for example, the failure of the monsoon to arrive in an agricultural economy. However, ongoing double-digit annual price increases are due to printing too much money.

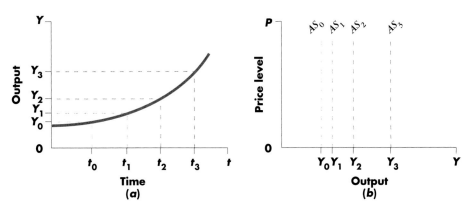

FIGURE 1-4   DETERMINATION OF AGGREGATE SUPPLY: THE VERY LONG RUN.

THE SHORT RUN

Examine panel *(b)* of Figure 1-1. When we take a magnified look at the path of output, we see that it is not at all smooth. Short-run output fluctuations are large enough to matter a great deal. Accounting for short-run fluctuations in output is the domain of aggregate demand.[4]

[4]Mostly. Supply shocks—the OPEC oil embargo is an example—sometimes matter too.

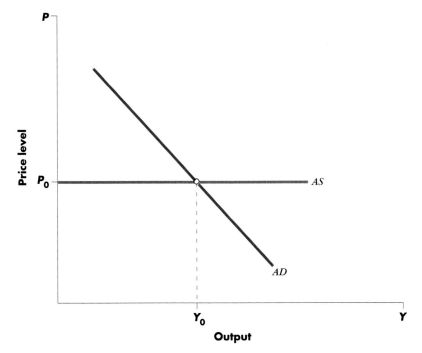

FIGURE 1-5   AGGREGATE DEMAND AND SUPPLY: THE SHORT RUN.

The mechanical aggregate supply–aggregate demand distinction between the long run and the short is straightforward. *In the short run, the aggregate supply curve is flat.* The short-run aggregate supply curve pegs the price level at the point where the supply curve hits the vertical axis. Output, in contrast, can take on any value. The underlying assumption is that the level of output does not affect prices in the short run. Figure 1-5 shows a horizontal short-run aggregate supply curve.

Repeat the exercise above and mentally shift the aggregate demand schedule to the left or right. You will see that the intersection of the two curves moves horizontally (output changes), rather than up and down (the price level doesn't change). It follows that *in the short run* output is determined by aggregate demand alone and prices are unaffected by the level of output. This is our third substantive finding.[5]

Much of this text is about aggregate demand alone. We study aggregate demand because in the short run aggregate demand determines output and, therefore, unem-

---

[5]As we said in the last footnote, "mostly." This is an example of what we mean when we say that applying a model requires judgment. There have certainly been historical periods when supply shocks outweighed demand shocks in the determination of output.

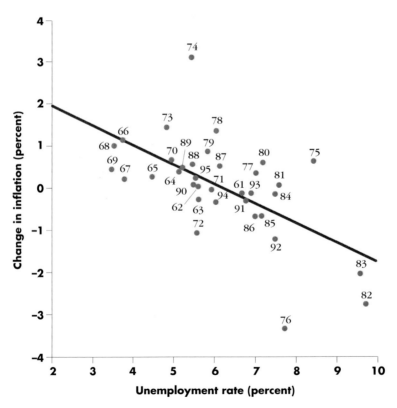

FIGURE 1-6 UNEMPLOYMENT AND THE CHANGE IN INFLATION, 1961–1995.

(Source: DRI/McGraw-Hill Macroeconomic Database.)

ployment. When we study aggregate demand in isolation, we are not really ignoring aggregate supply; rather, we are assuming that the aggregate supply curve is horizontal, implying that the price level can be taken as given.

THE MEDIUM RUN

We need one more piece to complete our outline of how the economy works: How do we describe the transition between the short run and the long run? In other words, what's the process which tilts the aggregate supply curve from horizontal to vertical? The simple answer is that when high aggregate demand pushes output above the level sustainable according to the very long run model, firms start to raise prices and the aggregate supply curve begins to move upward. The medium run looks something like the situation shown in Figure 1-2; the aggregate supply curve has a slope intermediate between horizontal and vertical.

The speed with which prices adjust is a critical parameter for our understanding of the economy. At a horizon of 15 years, not much matters except the rate of very long run growth. At a horizon of 15 seconds, not much matters except aggregate demand. What about in between?

It turns out that prices usually adjust pretty slowly; thus, over a 1-year horizon, changes in aggregate demand give a good, though certainly not perfect, account of the behavior of the economy. The speed of price adjustment is summarized in the *Phillips curve,* one version of which is shown in Figure 1-6.

In Figure 1-6, the change in the inflation rate is plotted against the unemployment rate. Pay careful attention to the numbers attached to the horizontal and vertical scales. A 2 point drop in unemployment is a very large change. You can see that such a drop, say, from 6 to 4 percent, will increase the inflation rate by only about 1 point over a period of a year. So over a 1-year horizon, the aggregate supply curve is quite flat and aggregate demand will provide a good model of output determination.

1-2

TO REITERATE . . .

The remainder of the text just fills in the details.

More seriously, nearly everything you will learn about macroeconomics can be fit into the growth theory, aggregate supply, and aggregate demand framework. This intellectual outline is so vital that it is worth the time to repeat parts of the previous section in slightly different words.

GROWTH AND GDP

The *growth rate* of the economy is the rate at which the gross domestic product (GDP) is increasing. On average, most economies grow by a few percentage points per year over long periods. For instance, U.S. real GDP grew at an average rate of 3.1 percent per year from 1960 to 1996. But this growth has certainly not been smooth, as Figure 1-1*b* confirms.

TABLE 1-1   Per Capita Real Income Growth Rates, 1913–1990
(Average Annual Growth Rate, Percent)

COUNTRY	GROWTH RATE	COUNTRY	GROWTH RATE
Argentina	.6	India	1.0
Brazil	2.4	Japan	3.5
China	2.2	Spain	2.0
France	2.1	United Kingdom	1.6
Ghana	.1	United States	1.7

Source: A. Maddison, "A Comparison of GDP Per Capita Income Levels in Developed and Developing Countries, 1700–1980," *Journal of Economic History,* March 1983, table 2, updated for 1981–1990 by the authors, from the World Bank, *World Tables,* 1992.

What causes GDP to grow over time? The first reason GDP changes is that the available amount of resources in the economy changes. The principal resources are capital and labor. The labor force, consisting of people either working or looking for work, grows over time and thus provides one source of increased production. The capital stock, including buildings and machines, likewise rises over time, providing another source of increased output. Increases in the availability of factors of production—the labor and capital used in the production of goods and services—thus account for part of the increase in GDP.

The second reason GDP changes is that the efficiency of factors of production may change. Efficiency improvements are called *productivity increases.* Over time, the same factors of production can produce more output. Productivity increases result from changes in knowledge, as people learn through experience to perform familiar tasks better.

Table 1-1 compares the growth rates of real per capita income in different countries. Studies of the sources of growth across countries and history seek to explain the reasons that a country like Brazil grew very rapidly (at least until the late 1980s) while Ghana, for example, has had very little growth. Ghana's income in 1980 was only 20 percent higher than in 1913, while Brazil's income had increased more than fivefold. Obviously, it would be well worth knowing what policies, if any, can raise a country's average growth rate over long periods of time.

THE BUSINESS CYCLE AND THE OUTPUT GAP

Inflation, growth, and unemployment are related through the *business cycle.* The business cycle is the more or less regular pattern of expansion (recovery) and contraction (recession) in economic activity around the path of trend growth. At a cyclical *peak,* economic activity is high relative to trend; at a cyclical *trough,* the low point in economic activity is reached. Inflation, growth, and unemployment all have clear cyclical patterns. For the moment we concentrate on measuring the behavior of output or GDP relative to trend over the business cycle.

The red line in Figure 1-7 shows the *trend path* of real GDP. The trend path of GDP is the path GDP would take if factors of production were fully employed. Over time, GDP changes for the two reasons we already noted. First, more resources become available: the size of the population increases, firms acquire machinery or build

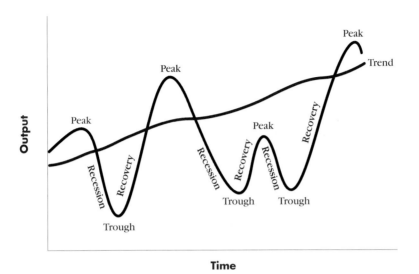

FIGURE 1-7   THE BUSINESS CYCLE.

plants, land is improved for cultivation, the stock of knowledge increases as new goods and new methods of production are invented and introduced. This increased availability of resources allows the economy to produce more goods and services, resulting in a rising trend level of output.

But, second, factors are not fully employed all the time. Full employment of factors of production is an economic, not a physical, concept. Physically, labor is fully employed if everyone is working 16 hours per day all year. In economic terms, there is full employment of labor when everyone who wants a job can find one within a reasonable amount of time. Because the economic definition is not precise, we typically define full employment of labor by some convention, for example, that labor is fully employed when the unemployment rate is 5.5 percent. Capital similarly is never fully employed in a physical sense; for example, office buildings or lecture rooms, which are part of the capital stock, are used only part of the day.

Output is not always at its trend level, that is, the level corresponding to (economic) full employment of the factors of production. Rather, output fluctuates around the trend level. During an *expansion* (or *recovery*) the *employment* of factors of production increases, and that is a source of increased production. Output can rise above trend because people work overtime and machinery is used for several shifts. Conversely, during a *recession* unemployment increases and less output is produced than could in fact be produced with the existing resources and technology. The wavy line in Figure 1-7 shows these cyclical departures of output from trend. Deviations of output from trend are referred to as the *output gap*.

The output gap measures the gap between actual output and the output the economy could produce at full employment given the existing resources. Full-employment output is also called *potential output*.

$$\text{Output gap} \equiv \text{potential output} - \text{actual output} \qquad (1)$$

The output gap allows us to measure the size of the cyclical deviations of output from potential output or trend output (we use these terms interchangeably). Figure 1-8 shows actual and potential output for the United States; the shaded lines represent recessions.[6]

The figure shows that the output gap grows during a recession, such as in 1982. More resources become unemployed, and actual output falls below potential output. Conversely, during an expansion, most strikingly in the long expansion of the 1960s, the gap declines and ultimately even becomes negative. A negative gap means that there is overemployment, overtime for workers, and more than the usual rate of utilization of machinery. It is worth noting that the gap is sometimes very sizable. For example, in 1982 it amounted to as much as 10 percent of output.

INFLATION AND THE BUSINESS CYCLE

Increases in inflation are inversely related to the output gap. Expansionary aggregate demand policies tend to produce inflation, unless they occur when the economy is at high levels of unemployment. Protracted periods of low aggregate demand tend to re-

[6]Dating of the business cycle is done by the National Bureau of Economic Research (NBER). The NBER is a private, nonprofit research organization based in Cambridge, Massachusetts.

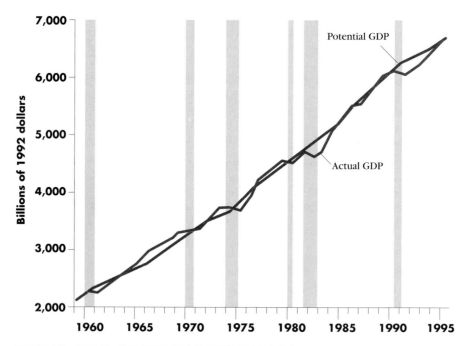

FIGURE 1-8   ACTUAL AND POTENTIAL OUTPUT, 1959–1995.

(Source: Congressional Budget Office, The Economic and Budget Outlook, *July 1996, and DRI/McGraw-Hill Macroeconomic Database.)*

FIGURE 1-9   THE RATE OF INFLATION IN CONSUMER PRICES, 1960–1996.

(Source: DRI/McGraw-Hill Macroeconomic Database.)

duce the inflation rate. Figure 1-9 shows one measure of inflation for the U.S. economy for the period since 1960. The inflation measure in the figure is the rate of change of the *consumer price index (CPI),* the cost of a given basket of goods representing the purchases of a typical urban consumer.

Figure 1-9 shows inflation, the *rate of increase* of prices. We can also look at the *level* of prices. All the inflation of the 1960s and 1970s adds up to a large increase in the price level. In the period 1960–1996, the price level more than quintupled. On average, a product that cost $1 in 1960 cost $5.27 by 1996. Most of that increase in prices took place after the early 1970s.

Inflation, like unemployment, is a major macroeconomic concern. However, the costs of inflation are much less obvious than those of unemployment. In the case of unemployment, potential output is going to waste, and it is therefore clear why the reduction of unemployment is desirable. In the case of inflation, there is no obvious loss of output. It is argued that inflation upsets familiar price relationships and reduces the efficiency of the price system. Whatever the reasons, policy makers have been willing to increase unemployment in an effort to reduce inflation—that is, to trade off some unemployment for less inflation.[7]

---

[7]For a very readable account of inflation, see Milton Friedman, "The Causes and Cures of Inflation," in his *Money Mischief* (New York: Harcourt Brace Jovanovich, 1992).

1-3

OUTLINE AND PREVIEW OF THE TEXT

We have sketched the major issues we shall discuss in this book. We now outline our approach to macroeconomics and the order in which the material will be presented. The key overall concepts, as already noted, are growth, aggregate supply, and aggregate demand. Growth depends on the accumulation of economic inputs and on improvements in technology. Aggregate supply depends primarily on growth but also on disturbances such as changes in the supply of oil. Aggregate demand is influenced by monetary policy, primarily via interest rates and expectations, and by fiscal policy.

The coverage starts in Chapter 2 with national income accounting, emphasizing data and relationships that are used repeatedly later in the book. The crucial long-run issue of growth is developed in Chapters 3 and 4. Chapter 5 introduces the aggregate supply–aggregate demand framework and discusses how aggregate supply and demand interact to determine both real GDP and the price level. Chapter 6 explores the aggregate supply curve in more detail. Chapter 7 looks further at the causes of, costs of, and tradeoffs between inflation and unemployment. Chapter 8, "The New Macroeconomics," takes a side trip from the dissection of the economy to examine the frontiers of economic research. (Much of this chapter is optional material. Not everyone will want to work through it on a first reading.) Chapters 9 through 11 present the underpinnings of aggregate demand—the *IS-LM* model. Chapter 12 adds international trade to the aggregate demand model. Chapters 13 through 17 examine the individual sectors that together make up the whole economy. Chapters 18 through 20 further explore government policy, including both successes and failures. Chapter 20 extends Chapter 12's discussion of the role of international trade in macroeconomics.

1-4

PREREQUISITES AND RECIPES

In concluding this introductory chapter, we offer a few words on how to use this book. Note that the material requires no mathematical prerequisite beyond high school algebra. We use equations when they appear helpful, but they are not an indispensable part of the exposition. Nevertheless, they can and should be mastered by any serious student of macroeconomics.

The technically harder chapters or sections can be skipped or dipped into. Many sections are identified as "optional" to denote difficult material. We either present them as supplementary material or provide sufficient nontechnical coverage to help you get on without them later in the book. The reason we present more advanced material or treatment is to afford complete and up-to-date coverage of the main ideas and techniques in macroeconomics. Even though you may not be able to grasp every point of such sections on first reading—and should not even try to—we suggest that you read this material to get the main message and gain an intuitive appreciation of the issues that are raised.

The hard part of understanding our complex economy is trying to comprehend the interaction of several markets and many variables, as the direct and feedback effects in the economy constitute a quite formidable system. How can you ensure that you will progress efficiently and with some ease? The most important thing is to ask questions. Ask yourself, as you follow an argument: Why is it that this or that variable should affect, say, aggregate demand? What would happen if it did not? What is the critical link?

There is no substitute whatsoever for active learning. Are there simple rules for active study? The best way to study is to use pencil and paper and work through each argument by drawing diagrams, experimenting with flowcharts, writing out the logic of the argument, working out the problems at the end of each chapter, and underlining key ideas. Using the *Study Guide,* which contains summaries of each chapter and many practice problems, will also help in your studies. Another valuable approach is to take issue with an argument or position or to spell out the defense for a particular view on policy questions. Beyond that, if you get stuck, read on for half a page. If you are still stuck, go back five pages.

As a final word, this chapter is designed for reference purposes. You should return to it whenever you want to check where a particular problem "fits" or what concepts a particular topic is relevant to. The best way to see the forest is from Chapter 1.

SUMMARY

1. Models are simplified depictions which attempt to capture just the essential elements of how the world works. We use a variety of models to focus on a variety of economic questions.
2. We use the concepts of growth theory, aggregate supply, and aggregate demand to focus our discussion.
3. Growth theory explains the long-run behavior of the economy through understanding how productive capacity grows.
4. In the medium run, productive capacity can be taken as given. Output depends on aggregate supply, and prices depend on both aggregate supply and aggregate demand.
5. In the short run, the price level is fixed and output is determined by the level of aggregate demand.

KEY TERMS

long run	aggregate supply curve	output gap
medium run	aggregate demand curve	potential output
short run	Phillips curve	inflation
growth theory	growth rate	consumer price index (CPI)
aggregate supply–aggregate demand model	business cycle	
	trend path of output	

CHAPTER 2

National Income Accounting

CHAPTER HIGHLIGHTS

◆ Gross domestic product is the value of the goods and services produced within the country. In equilibrium, the amount of output produced equals the amount demanded.

◆ Output is paid out primarily to labor and capital.

◆ Output is demanded for private consumption and investment, for government expenditure, and for international trade.

◆ The dollar value of gross domestic product depends on both physical production and the price level. Inflation is the change over time in the price level.

Good accounting turns data into information. We study national income accounting for two reasons. First, the national income accounts provide the formal *structure* for our macrotheory models. We divide output in two ways. On the production side, output is paid out to labor in the form of wages and to capital in the form of interest and dividends. On the demand side, output is consumed or invested for the future. The division of output into factor payments (wages, etc.) on the production side provides a framework for our study of growth and aggregate supply. The division of income into consumption, investment, and so on, on the demand side provides the framework for studying aggregate demand. The input and output, or demand and production, accountings are necessarily equal in equilibrium. In addition to looking at real output, the national income accounts provide measures of the overall price level. This provides a basis for our discussions of inflation.

The second reason for studying national income accounts is to learn a few ballpark numbers which help characterize the economy. If we spread annual U.S. output equally across the population, would each person control $3,000, $30,000, or $300,000? Is a dollar today worth a 1947 penny, dime, or dollar? Is income paid mostly to labor or mostly to capital? While memorizing exact statistics is a waste of time, knowing rough magnitudes is vital for linking theory to the real world. And macroeconomics is very much about the world we live in.

We begin our study with the basic measure of output—*gross domestic product,* or *GDP.* GDP is the value of all final goods and services produced in the country within a given period. It includes the value of goods produced, such as houses and CDs, and the value of services, such as airplane rides and economists' lectures. The output of each of these is valued at its market price, and the values are added together to get GDP. In 1996 the value of GDP in the U.S. economy was about $7,500 billion, or something over $7.5 trillion. Since the U.S. population was about 265 million, *per capita GDP* (GDP per person) was roughly $28,000 per year (= $7,500 billion/ 265 million).

2-1

THE PRODUCTION OF OUTPUT AND
PAYMENTS TO FACTORS OF PRODUCTION

The production side of the economy transforms inputs, such as labor and capital, into output, GDP. Inputs such as labor and capital are called *factors of production,* and the payments made to factors, such as wages and interest payments, are called *factor payments.* Imagine a student pie-baking economy with you as the entrepreneur. You hire several friends to roll dough, and you rent a kitchen from another friend. Your factor inputs are friends (labor) and kitchens (capital). Output is measured as the number of pies. With some experience, you could predict the number of pies that can be produced with a given number of friends and so many kitchens. You could express the relation as a mathematical formula called a *production function,* which is written in this case as

$$\text{Pies} = f(\text{friends, kitchens}) \tag{1}$$

We will, of course, be interested in a somewhat more general production function relating GDP (Y) to inputs of labor (N) and capital (K), which we'll write as $Y = f(N,K)$. The production function will be a focal point for our study of growth in Chapters 3 and 4, where we will also elaborate on the role of technology and on the use of inputs other than labor and capital.

Once the pies are baked, it's time to make factor payments. Some of the pies you give to your friends as payment for their labor. These pies are wage income. You also need to set aside one slice from each pie (about 8 percent of the pie in the United States) to send to the government as a contribution for social security. This slice is also considered a payment to labor, since the payment is made on behalf of the worker. You should also take a pie for yourself as a fair return for your management skills. This pie, too, is a payment to labor. A few pies you leave for the kitchen owner. These are payments to capital. Any remaining pies are true profit.

All the factor payments, including profit, if any, add up to the total number of pies produced. We can express this as an equation:

$$\text{Pies} = \text{labor payments} + \text{capital payments} + \text{profit} \qquad (2)$$

More generally, we might write that labor payments equal the wage rate (w) times the amount of labor used and that capital payments equal the interest rate (i) times the amount of capital borrowed and write $Y = (w \times N) + (i \times K) + \text{profit}$.

Panel (*b*) of Figure 2-1 shows the GDP pie broken down into factor payments plus a few complicating items.

GDP AND GNP

The first complication is that factor payments include receipts from abroad made as factor payments to domestically owned factors of production. Adding these payments to GDP gives *gross national product,* or *GNP.* For instance, part of U.S. GDP corresponds to the profits earned by Honda from its U.S. manufacturing operations. These profits are part of Japan's GNP, because they are the income of Japanese-owned capital. In the United States the difference between GDP and GNP is only about 1 percent and can be ignored for our purposes, but the difference can be more important in some other countries.

GDP AND NDP

The second complication is quite important but also quite straightforward. Capital wears out, or *depreciates,* while it is being used to produce output. *Net domestic product (NDP)* is equal to GDP minus depreciation. NDP thus comes closer to measuring the net amount of goods produced in the country in a given period: it is the total value of production minus the value of the amount of capital used up in producing that output. Depreciation is typically about 11 percent of GDP, so NDP is usually about 89 percent of GDP.

NATIONAL INCOME

The third complication is that businesses pay indirect taxes which must be subtracted from NDP before making factor payments. These payments are large, amounting to

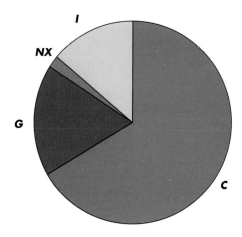

(a) Components of demand for output

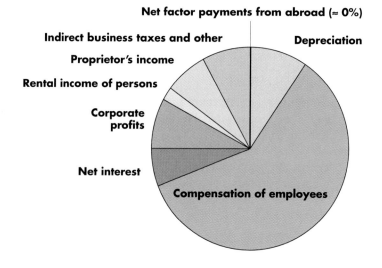

(b) Payments to factors of production

FIGURE 2-1   COMPOSITION OF GDP.

(Source: DRI/McGraw-Hill Macroeconomic Database.)

nearly 10 percent of NDP, so we need to mention them here. (Having done so, we won't mention them again.) What's left for making factor payments is *national income,* equaling about 80 percent of GDP.

You should remember that about three-fourths of factor payments are payments to labor. Most of the remainder goes to pay capital. Only a small amount goes for other factors of production or true profits. The same allocation is very roughly the case in most industrialized countries. (There are a small number of resource-extraction economies based on oil, copper, or guano where natural resources are a dominant factor of production.)

RECAP

From this section you should remember:

- GDP is the value of all final goods and services produced in the country within a given period.
- In the United States, per capita GDP is around $28,000 per year. Per capita GDP is roughly the same in other wealthy countries.
- GDP is the sum of all factor payments.
- Labor is the dominant factor of production.

2-2

OUTLAYS AND COMPONENTS OF DEMAND

In this section we look at the demand for output, and we discuss the *components* of the aggregate demand for domestically produced goods and services, the different purposes for which GDP is demanded.

Total demand for domestic output is made up of four components: (1) consumption spending by households (*C*), (2) investment spending by businesses and households (*I*), (3) government (federal, state, and local) purchases of goods and services (*G*), and (4) foreign demand (*NX*). These four categories account, definitionally, for all spending. The fundamental *national income accounting identity* is

$$Y \equiv C + I + G + NX \tag{3}$$

Memorize this identity. You will use it repeatedly in this course and in organizing your thinking about the macroeconomy.

We now look more closely at each of the four components.

CONSUMPTION

Table 2-1 presents a breakdown of the demand for goods and services in 1996 by components of demand. The table shows that the chief component of demand is *consumption spending* by the household sector. This includes spending on anything from food to golf lessons, but it also involves, as we shall see in discussing investment, consumer spending on durable goods such as automobiles—spending that might be regarded as investment rather than consumption.

Figure 2-2 shows the percentage of GDP accounted for by consumption in both Japan and the United States. Note that the consumption share is not constant by any means. Observe, too, that Japan consumes a far smaller share of its GDP than is the case in the United States. The rising share of consumption in the United States in the 1980s is considered one of the important reasons for poor economic performance.

TABLE 2-1   GDP and Components of Demand, 1996, Second Quarter

	$ BILLIONS	PERCENT
Personal consumption expenditures	5,139	68.1
Gross private domestic investment	1,096	14.5
Government purchases of goods and services	1,409	18.7
Net exports of goods and services	−99	−1.3
Gross domestic product	7,545	100.0

Source: DRI/McGraw-Hill.

Higher consumption (or lower saving), as we will see in a moment, means either less investment or larger trade deficits.

GOVERNMENT

Next in size we have *government purchases* of goods and services. This component of GDP includes such items as national defense expenditures, costs of road paving by state and local governments, and salaries of government employees.

We draw attention to the use of certain words in connection with government spending. We refer to government spending on goods and services as *purchases* of goods and services. In addition, the government makes *transfer payments,* payments

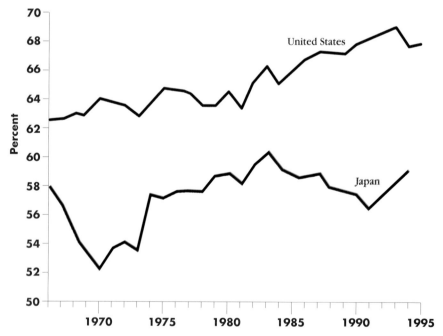

FIGURE 2-2   CONSUMPTION AS A SHARE OF GDP: UNITED STATES AND JAPAN, 1960–1995.

(Source: International Monetary Fund, International Financial Statistics Yearbook, *1996.)*

that are made to people without their providing a current service in exchange. Typical transfer payments are social security benefits and unemployment benefits. Transfer payments are *not* counted as part of GDP; this is to avoid double counting, since the consumption or investment by the recipients of the payments is counted in *C* or *I*. We speak of *transfers plus purchases* as *government expenditure.* The federal government budget, on the order of $1,700 billion ($1.7 trillion), refers to federal government expenditure. Less than one-third of that sum is spent on federal government purchases of goods and services; most of it is used for transfers.

INVESTMENT

Gross private domestic investment requires some definitions. First, throughout this book, "investment" means additions to the physical stock of capital. As we use the term, investment does *not* include buying a bond or purchasing stock in General Motors. Investment includes housing construction, building of machinery, construction of factories and offices, and additions to a firm's inventories of goods.

If we think of investment more generally as any current activity that increases the economy's ability to produce output in the future, we would include not only physical investment but also what is known as investment in human capital. *Human capital* is the knowledge and ability to produce that is embodied in the labor force. Investment in education can be regarded as investment in human capital, but the official accounts treat personal educational expenditures as consumption and public educational expenditures as government spending.[1]

The classification of spending as consumption or investment is to a significant extent a matter of convention. From the economic point of view, there is little difference between a household's building up an inventory of peanut butter and a grocery store's doing the same. Nevertheless, in the national income accounts, the individual's purchase is treated as a personal consumption expenditure, whereas the store's purchase is treated as inventory investment. Although these borderline cases clearly exist, we can apply a simple rule of thumb: Investment is associated with the business sector's adding to the physical stock of capital, including inventories.[2] Officially, however, all household expenditures are counted as consumption spending. This is not quite so bad as it might seem, since the accounts do separate households' purchases of *durable goods* like cars and refrigerators from their other purchases.

In passing, we note that in Table 2-1 investment is listed as "gross." It is *gross investment* in the sense that depreciation is not deducted. *Net investment* is gross investment minus depreciation.

---

[1]In the total incomes system of accounts (TISA), referred to in footnote 7 on page 32, the definition of investment is broadened to include investment in human capital, which means that total investment in that system is more than one-third of GDP. But in this book and in the official national income accounts investment counts only additions to the physical capital stock.

[2]The GDP accounts record as investment *business sector* additions to the stock of capital. Some government spending, for instance, for roads or schools, also adds to the capital stock. Estimates of the capital stock owned by government are available in *Fixed Reproducible Tangible Wealth in the United States, 1925–92* (Washington, D.C.: U. S. Bureau of Economic Analysis, forthcoming).

NET EXPORTS

The item "Net exports" appears in Table 2-1 to account for domestic spending on foreign goods and foreign spending on domestic goods. When foreigners purchase goods we produce, their spending adds to the demand for domestically produced goods. Correspondingly, that part of our spending that purchases foreign goods has to be subtracted from the demand for domestically produced goods. Accordingly, the difference between exports and imports, called *net exports,* is a component of the total demand for our goods. U.S. net exports have been negative since the 1980s, as shown in Figure 2-3, reflecting a high level of imports and a low level of exports; note, though, that net exports have been close to zero in some years (trade has been nearly balanced) and very negative in others (the United States has had a large balance-of-trade deficit).

The role of net exports in accounting for GDP can be illustrated with an example. Assume that personal sector spending was higher by $20 billion. How much higher would GDP be? If we assume that government and investment spending remained unchanged, we might be tempted to say that GDP would have been $20 billion higher. That is correct if all the additional spending had fallen on domestic goods. The other extreme, however, is that all the additional spending had fallen on imports. In that event, consumption would have been up $20 billion *and* net exports would have been down $20 billion, with *no* net effect on GDP.

FIGURE 2-3 U.S. NET EXPORTS, 1960–1995.

(Source: DRI/McGraw-Hill Macroeconomic Database.)

RECAP

From this section you should remember:

- Demand for GDP is split into four sectors: consumption, investment, government, and net exports, according to the identity of the purchaser.
- $Y \equiv C + I + G + NX$
- The relative sizes of the demand sectors vary across countries and across time, but rough numbers to remember for the United States are consumption, 68 percent; investment, 15 percent; government purchases of goods and services, 18 percent; and net exports, slightly negative.

2-3

SOME IMPORTANT IDENTITIES

In this section we summarize the discussion of the preceding sections by presenting a set of national income relationships that we use extensively in Chapter 9 and beyond. We introduce here some notation and conventions that we follow throughout the book.

For analytical work in the following chapters, we simplify our analysis by making assumptions that ensure that disposable income is equal to GDP. For the most part, we disregard depreciation and thus the difference between GDP and NDP as well as the difference between gross investment and net investment. We refer simply to investment spending. We also disregard indirect taxes and business transfer payments. With these conventions in mind, *we refer to national income and GDP interchangeably as income or output.* These simplifications have no serious consequences and are made only for convenience. Finally, just in the next subsection, we omit both the government and foreign sector.

A SIMPLE ECONOMY

We denote the value of output in our simple economy, which has neither a government nor foreign trade, by Y. Consumption is denoted by C and investment spending by I. The first key identity is that output produced equals output sold. Output sold can be expressed in terms of the components of demand as the sum of consumption and investment spending. Accordingly, we can write

$$Y \equiv C + I \qquad (4)$$

What happens to unsold output? *We count the accumulation of inventories as part of investment* (as if the firms sold the goods to themselves to add to their inventories), and therefore all output is either consumed or invested.

The next step is to establish a relation among saving, consumption, and GDP. How will income be allocated? Part will be spent on consumption, and part will be saved.[3] Thus we can write

$$Y \equiv S + C \qquad (5)$$

---

[3]Decisions about saving are made by businesses as well as directly by consumers. It is convenient to ignore the existence of corporations and consolidate, or add together, the entire private sector.

where S denotes private sector saving. Identity (5) tells us that the whole of income is allocated to either consumption or saving. Next, identities (4) and (5) can be combined to read

$$C + I \equiv Y \equiv C + S \qquad (6)$$

The left-hand side of identity (6) shows the components of demand, and the right-hand side shows the allocation of income. The identity emphasizes that output produced is equal to output sold. The value of output produced is equal to income received, and income received, in turn, is spent on goods or saved.

Identity (6) can be slightly reformulated to show the relation between saving and investment. Subtracting consumption from each part of identity (6), we have

$$I \equiv Y - C \equiv S \qquad (7)$$

Identity (7) shows that in this simple economy *investment is identically equal to saving.*

One can think of what lies behind this relationship in a variety of ways. In a very simple economy, the only way the individual can save is by undertaking an act of physical investment—for example, by storing grain or building an irrigation channel. In a slightly more sophisticated economy, one could think of investors financing their investing by borrowing from individuals who save.

REINTRODUCING THE GOVERNMENT AND FOREIGN TRADE

We now reintroduce the government sector and the external sector.[4] We denote government purchases of goods and services by G and all taxes by TA. Transfers to the private sector (including interest) are denoted by TR. Net exports (exports minus imports) are denoted by NX.

We return to the identity between output produced and sold, taking account now of all components of demand, including G and NX. Accordingly, we restate the fundamental identity:

$$Y \equiv C + I + G + NX \qquad (8)$$

Next we turn to the derivation of the very important relation between output and disposable income. Now we have to recognize that part of income is spent on taxes and that the private sector receives net transfers (TR) in addition to national income. Disposable income (YD) is thus equal to income plus transfers less taxes:

$$YD \equiv Y + TR - TA \qquad (9)$$

Disposable income, in turn, is allocated to consumption and saving:

$$YD \equiv C + S \qquad (10)$$

Combining identities (9) and (10), we have

$$C + S \equiv YD \equiv Y + TR - TA \qquad (11)$$

or

$$C \equiv YD - S \equiv Y + TR - TA - S \qquad (11a)$$

---

[4]"Government" here means the federal government plus state and local governments.

Identity (11*a*) states that consumption is disposable income less saving or, alternatively, that consumption is equal to income plus transfers less taxes and saving. Now we use the right-hand side of equation (11*a*) to substitute for *C* in identity (8). With some rearrangement, we obtain

$$S - I \equiv (G + TR - TA) + NX \tag{12}$$

SAVING, INVESTMENT, THE GOVERNMENT BUDGET, AND TRADE

Identity (12) cannot be overemphasized. The first set of terms on the right-hand side $(G + TR - TA)$ is the *government budget deficit (BD)*. $G + TR$ is equal to total government expenditure, consisting of government purchases of goods and services (*G*) plus government transfer payments (*TR*). *TA* is the amount of taxes received by the government. The difference $(G + TR - TA)$ is the excess of the government's spending over its receipts, or its budget deficit. The second term on the right-hand side is the excess of exports over imports, or the *net exports of goods and services,* or net exports for short.

Thus, identity (12) states that the excess of saving over investment $(S - I)$ in the private sector is equal to the government budget deficit plus the trade surplus. The identity suggests, correctly, that there are important relations among the excess of private saving over investment $(S - I)$, the government budget (*BD*), and the external sector (*NX*). For instance, if, for the private sector, saving is equal to investment, then the government's budget deficit (surplus) is reflected in an equal external deficit (surplus).

Table 2-2 shows the significance of identity (12). To fix ideas, suppose that private sector saving *S* is equal to $1,000 (billion). In the first two rows we assume that exports are equal to imports, so the trade surplus is zero. In row 1, we assume the government budget is balanced. Investment accordingly has to equal $1,000 billion. In the next row we assume the government budget deficit is $150 billion. *Given the level of saving* of $1,000 billion and a zero trade balance, it has to be true that investment is now lower by $150 billion. Row 3 shows how this relationship is affected when there is a trade surplus.

Any sector that spends more than it receives in income has to borrow to pay for the excess spending. The private sector has three ways of disposing of its saving. It can make loans to the government, which thereby pays for the excess of its spending over the income it receives from taxes. Or the private sector can lend to foreigners, who are buying more from us than we are buying from them. They therefore are earning less from us than they need in order to pay for the goods they buy from us, and we have

TABLE 2-2 The Budget Deficit, Trade, Saving, and Investment
(Billions of Dollars)

SAVING (S)	INVESTMENT (I)	BUDGET DEFICIT (BD)	NET EXPORTS (NX)
1,000	1,000	0	0
1,000	850	150	0
1,000	900	0	100
1,000	950	150	−100

to lend to cover the difference. Or the private sector can lend to business firms, which use the funds for investment. In all three cases, households will be paid back later, receiving interest or dividends in addition to the amount they lent.

The last row of Table 2-2 is relevant to the change in the U.S. budget and trade deficits during the eighties. Early in the decade, the government budget deficit increased. Private saving did not increase much, and private investment did not fall. Accordingly, as a matter of arithmetic, the United States had to be importing more than it was exporting. That is what happened, as shown in Figure 2-3.

2-4

MEASURING GROSS DOMESTIC PRODUCT

There are a number of subtleties in the calculation of GDP. There are also a number of nonsubtle problems. We start with the straightforward points.

FINAL GOODS AND VALUE ADDED

GDP is the value of *final* goods and services produced. The insistence on final goods and services is simply to make sure that we do not double-count. For example, we would not want to include the full price of an automobile in GDP and then also include as part of GDP the value of the tires that were sold to the automobile producer for use on the car. The components of the car that are sold to the manufacturers are called *intermediate* goods, and their value is not included in GDP. Similarly, the wheat that goes into pie is an intermediate good. We count only the value of the pie as part of GDP; we do not count the value of the wheat sold to the miller and the value of the flour sold to the baker.

In practice, double counting is avoided by working with *value added*. At each stage of the manufacture of a good, only the value added to the good at that stage is counted as part of GDP. The value of the wheat produced by the farmer is counted as part of GDP. Then the value of the flour sold by the miller minus the cost of the wheat is the miller's value added. If we follow this process along, we will see that the sum of the value added at each stage of processing is equal to the final value of the bread sold.

CURRENT OUTPUT

GDP consists of the value of output *currently produced*. It thus excludes transactions in existing commodities, such as old masters or existing houses. We count the construction of new houses as part of GDP, but we do not add trade in existing houses. We do, however, count the value of Realtors' fees in the sale of existing houses as part of GDP. The Realtor provides a current service in bringing buyer and seller together, and that is appropriately part of current output.

PROBLEMS OF GDP MEASUREMENT

GDP data are, in practice, used not only as a measure of how much is being produced but also as a measure of the welfare of the residents of a country. Economists and politicians talk as if an increase in real GDP means that people are better off. But GDP data

BOX 2-1 Light and Truth

To shed light on just how much quality change can matter, William Nordhaus, of Yale University, has calculated how much better room lighting is now than in the past, based on estimates of energy requirements per lumen. The improvements—very few of which show up in the official statistics—are enormous. Today's electric light is about 25 times as efficient as Edison's first electric light was in 1883.

Unmeasured quality improvements are not new. Nordhaus calculates that 5 liters of sesame oil cost a Babylonian worker about 1/2 shekel (roughly 2 weeks' wages). Light equivalent to two candles burning for an hour cost a Babylonian about an hour's wages.*

*For other serious, but fun, comparisons, see William D. Nordhaus, "Do Real Output and Real Wage Measures Capture Reality? The History of Lighting Suggests Not," Cowles Foundation Discussion Paper 1078, 1994.

---

are far from perfect measures of either economic output or welfare. There are, specifically, three major problems:

- Some outputs are poorly measured because they are not traded in the market. If you bake homemade pie, the value of your labor isn't counted in official GDP statistics. If you buy a (no doubt inferior) pie, the baker's labor is counted. This means that the vastly increased participation of women in the labor force has increased official GDP numbers with no offsetting reduction for decreased production at home. (We officially measure the value of commercial day care, but taking care of your own kids is valued at zero.)

  Note, too, that government services aren't directly priced by the market. The official statistics assume that a dollar spent by the government is worth a dollar of value.[5] GDP is mismeasured to the extent that a dollar spent by the government produces output valued by the public at more or less than a dollar.

- Some activities measured as adding to GDP in fact represent the use of resources to avoid or contain "bads" such as crime or risks to national security. Similarly, the accounts do not subtract anything for environmental pollution and degradation. This issue is particularly important in developing countries. For instance, one study of Indonesia claims that properly accounting for environmental degradation would reduce the measured growth rate of the economy in recent years by 3 percent.[6]

- It is difficult to account correctly for improvements in the quality of goods. This has been the case particularly with computers, whose quality has improved dramatically while their price has fallen sharply. But it applies to almost all goods, such as cars, whose quality changes over time. The national income accountants

---

[5]You probably have the immediate reaction that a dollar spent by the government on higher education is worth far more than a dollar—we hope.

[6]R. Repetto, W. Magrath, M. Wells, C. Beer, and F. Rossini, *Wasting Assets: Natural Resources in the National Income Accounts* (Washington, D.C.: World Resources Institute, June 1989).

attempt to adjust for improvements in quality, but the task is not easy, especially when new products and new models are being invented.

Attempts have been made to construct an *adjusted GNP* series that takes account of some of these difficulties, moving closer to a measure of welfare. The most comprehensive of these studies, by Robert Eisner of Northwestern University, estimates an adjusted GNP series in which the level of real GNP is about 50 percent higher than the official estimates.[7]

2-5

INFLATION AND PRICE INDEXES

GDP would be easy to measure if all we consumed was pie. One year GDP would be 1,000 pies; the next year 1,005. Unfortunately, life is beer and skittles. You can't add a pint of beer to a game of skittles, but if the price of a pint is a dollar and a game of skittles costs 50 cents, you can say that a pint and a game adds $1.50 to GDP. Now suppose that next year all prices double: a pint and a game add $3 to GDP, but clearly nothing *real* has changed. While *nominal GDP* has doubled, *real GDP*—which is what we care about—is unchanged.

Real GDP measures changes in *physical* output in the economy between different time periods by valuing all goods produced in the two periods *at the same prices,* or in *constant dollars.* Real GDP is now measured in the national income accounts at the prices of 1992.[8] This means that, in calculating real GDP, today's physical output is multiplied by the prices that prevailed in 1992 to obtain a measure of what today's output would have been worth had it been sold at the prices of 1992.

Nominal GDP measures the value of output in a given period in the prices of that period, or, as it is sometimes put, in *current dollars.*[9] Thus 1998 nominal GDP measures the value of the goods produced in 1998 at the market prices prevailing in 1998, and 1929 nominal GDP measures the value of goods produced in 1929 at the market prices that prevailed in 1929. Nominal GDP changes from year to year for two reasons. First, the physical output of goods changes, and, second, market prices change. Changes in nominal GDP that result from price changes do not tell us anything about the performance of the economy in producing goods and services. That is why we use real rather than nominal GDP as the basic measure for comparing output in different years.

---

[7]Eisner presents his data in his book, *The Total Incomes System of Accounts* (Chicago: University of Chicago Press, 1989). In appendix E, he reviews a variety of other attempts to adjust the standard accounts for major inadequacies. Eisner estimated an adjusted GNP rather than a GDP series mainly because he did his work at the time when GNP was used as the basic measure of output.

[8]The Bureau of Economic Analysis now produces "chain-weighted" estimates of real GDP. These estimates use 1992 prices but each year shift the weights given to various goods in measuring real GDP. See *Survey of Current Business,* January–February 1996.

[9]National income account data are regularly reported in the *Survey of Current Business (SCB).* Historical data are available in the September issue of *SCB;* in the Commerce Department's *Business Statistics,* a biennial publication; and in the annual *Economic Report of the President.* On the Internet, a wealth of information and data is presented on the Bureau of Economic Analysis web site, http://www.bea.doc.gov/.

TABLE 2-3   Real and Nominal GDP, an Illustration

	1992 NOMINAL GDP	1998 NOMINAL GDP	1998 REAL GDP*
Beer	1 at $1.00 $1.00	2 at 2.00 $4.00	2 at $1.00 $2.00
Skittles	1 at $0.50 0.50	3 at $0.75 2.25	3 at $0.50 1.50
	$1.50	$6.25	$3.50

*Measured in 1992 prices.

If all prices change in fixed proportion, say, every price doubles, then any reasonable price index will also change in that proportion. When some prices rise more than others, different price indexes will differ modestly according to how the different prices are weighted. Such differences are generally inconsequential for understanding macrotheory.

In Table 2-3 we present a simple example that illustrates the calculation of nominal and real GDP. The hypothetical outputs and prices of beer and skittles in 1992 and 1998 are shown in the first two columns of the table. Nominal GDP in 1992 was $1.50 and in 1998 was $6.25. However, much of the increase in nominal GDP is purely the result of the increase in prices and does not reflect an increase in physical output. When we calculate real GDP in 1998 by valuing 1998 output at the prices of 1992, we find that real GDP is $3.50. Since beer consumption doubled and skittle consumption tripled, we know that real GDP more than doubled and less than tripled. The fourfold increase in nominal GDP does not measure real value.

INFLATION AND PRICES

Inflation is the rate of change in prices, and the price level is the cumulation of past inflations. If P_{t-1} represents the price level last year and P_t represents today's price level, then the inflation rate over the past year can be written as

$$\pi \equiv \frac{P_t - P_{t-1}}{P_{t-1}} \tag{13}$$

where π stands for the inflation rate. Correspondingly, today's price level equals last year's price level adjusted for inflation:

$$P_t = P_{t-1} + \pi \times P_{t-1} \tag{14}$$

In the United States in the mid-1990s, the inflation rate was relatively low, around 2 or 3 percent per year, even though prices were much higher than they were 20 years earlier. High inflation rates in the 1970s had pushed up the price level. Once raised, the price level doesn't fall unless the inflation rate is negative—in other words, unless there is a *deflation.*

PRICE INDEXES

No single price index is perfect. The three main price indexes are the GDP deflator, the consumer price index, and the producer price index. Figure 2-4 shows the historical behavior of the GDP deflator, *p,* as well as the purchasing power of the dollar, 1/*p.*

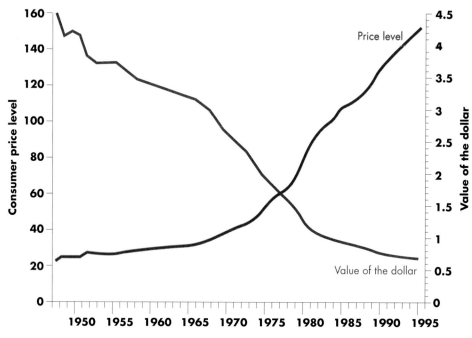

FIGURE 2-4   THE CONSUMER PRICE INDEX AND VALUE OF THE DOLLAR.

(Source: DRI/McGraw-Hill Macroeconomic Database.)

The GDP Deflator

The calculation of real GDP gives us a useful measure of inflation known as the *GDP deflator.* The GDP deflator is the ratio of nominal GDP in a given year to real GDP of that year. The deflator measures the change in prices that has occurred between the base year and the current year. Using the fictional example in Table 2-3, we can get a measure of inflation between 1992 and 1998 by comparing the value of 1998 GDP in 1998 prices and 1992 prices. The ratio of nominal to real GDP in 1993 is 1.79 (= 6.25/3.50). We ascribe the 79 percent increase to price increases, or inflation, over the 1992–1998 period.

Since the GDP deflator is based on a calculation involving all the goods produced in the economy, it is a widely based price index that is frequently used to measure inflation.

The Consumer and Producer Price Indexes

The *consumer price index (CPI)* measures the cost of buying a fixed basket of goods and services representative of the purchases of urban consumers. The CPI differs in three main ways from the GDP deflator. First, the deflator measures the prices of a much wider group of goods than the CPI does. Second, the CPI measures the cost of a given basket of goods which is the same from year to year. The basket of goods included in the GDP deflator, however, differs from year to year, depending on what is produced in the economy in each year. When corn crops are large, corn receives a relatively large weight in the computation of the GDP deflator. By contrast, the CPI measures the cost of a fixed basket of goods that does not vary over time. Third, the

BOX 2-2   Measuring Inflation: An "Academic" Exercise?

Price indexes are imperfect, in part because market baskets change and in part because quality changes are very hard to quantify. The resulting errors, on the order of a percent or so a year, have mostly been of interest to the economists who create and study price indexes. Recently, "correcting" price indexes has become a hot political topic. Many payments are "indexed to inflation," meaning that the nominal payment is adjusted for inflation to keep the real value constant. In the United States, social security is one such payment.

Because the U.S. social security system is in long-run financial danger, many politicians would like to reduce its costs. But the same politicians are loath to reduce benefits. Well, here's a clever solution: Suppose we announce that the official price index overstates inflation and legislate a "correction" of 1 percent per year. Then we can claim to be paying the same real benefits while spending 1 percent less the first year, 2 percent less the second year, and so forth.

Current price indexes probably overstate inflation. But as you can imagine, the economists who study price indexes would like to find a scientifically based correction rather than one based on current political trends. One careful study of the bias in the CPI, by Matthew Shapiro and David Wilcox, gives a range of estimates for how much the official CPI overstates inflation. The estimates center around 1 percent per year but could be as low as .6 or as high as 1.5 percent per year.[*]

The discussion of inflation mismeasurement is an example of how scientific work in economics has an immediate policy impact. To reduce the kind of criticism about political decision making hinted at above, in 1996 the Senate appointed a panel of blue-ribbon economists to review measurements of the CPI.[†] The panel reported that current CPI measurements overstate inflation by about 1.1 percent a year. As a dramatic example of how CPI measurement affects real benefit levels, the panel estimated that a 1 percent overestimate of cost-of-living increases would, between 1996 and 2008, increase the national debt by $1 trillion through overindexing of tax and benefit programs.

A 1 percent mismeasurement of the price level would matter less if the errors didn't build up year after year. Cumulative mismeasurement at the 1 percent annual level makes a very large difference. Leonard Nakamura gives a good example in terms of real wages.[‡] According to official statistics, between 1970 and 1995 the average real (measured in 1982 dollars) wage in the economy declined from about $8 an hour to just under $7.50. Correcting for a 1 percent annual bias in inflation would change this picture from a drop to an increase, from $8 to about $9.50 an hour.

[*]Matthew D. Shapiro and David W. Wilcox, "Mismeasurement in the Consumer Price Index: An Evaluation," NBER Working Paper 5590, 1996.

[†]Advisory Commission to Study the Consumer Price Index, "Final Report to the Senate Finance Committee," Dec. 5, 1996.

[‡]Leonard Nakamura, "Measuring Inflation in a High-Tech Age," Federal Reserve Bank of Philadelphia *Business Review*, November–December 1995. See also, by the same author, "Is U.S. Economic Performance Really That Bad?" Federal Reserve Bank of Philadelphia working paper, April 1996.

CPI directly includes prices of imports, whereas the deflator includes only prices of goods *produced* in the United States.[10]

The GDP deflator and the CPI differ in behavior from time to time. For example, at times when the price of imported oil rises rapidly, the CPI is likely to rise faster than the deflator. However, over long periods the two produce quite similar measures of inflation.

The *producer price index (PPI)* is the third price index that is widely used. Like the CPI, the PPI is a measure of the cost of a given basket of goods. However, it differs from the CPI partly in its coverage, which includes, for example, raw materials and semifinished goods. It differs, too, in that it is designed to measure prices at an early stage of the distribution system. Whereas the CPI measures prices where urban households actually do their spending—that is, at the retail level—the PPI is constructed from prices at the level of the first significant commercial transaction.

This makes the PPI a relatively flexible price index and one that frequently signals changes in the general price level, or the CPI, some time before they actually materialize. For this reason, the PPI and, more particularly, some of its subindexes, such as the index of "sensitive materials," serve as one of the business cycle indicators that are closely watched by policy makers.

SUMMARY

1. GDP is the value of all final goods and services produced in the country within a given period.
2. On the production side, output is paid out as factor payments to labor and capital. On the demand side, output is consumed or invested by the private sector, used by the government, or exported.
3. $Y \equiv C + I + G + NX$
4. $C + G + I + NX \equiv Y \equiv YD + (TA - TR) \equiv C + S + (TA - TR)$
5. The excess of the private sector's saving over investment is equal to the sum of the budget deficit and net exports.
6. Nominal GDP measures the value of output in a given period in the prices of that period, that is, in current dollars.
7. Inflation is the rate of change in prices, and the price level is the cumulation of past inflations.

KEY TERMS

gross domestic product (GDP)	gross national product (GNP)	consumption spending
factors of production	net domestic product (NDP)	government purchases
factor payments	depreciation	transfer payments
production function	national income accounting identity	government expenditure

[10]Detailed discussion of the various price indexes can be found in the Bureau of Labor Statistics' *Handbook of Methods* and in the Commerce Department's biennial *Business Statistics*.

gross private domestic investment	investment	real/nominal GDP
	saving	inflation
durable goods	government budget deficit	deflation
gross/net investment	final/intermediate goods	GDP deflator
net exports	value added	consumer price index (CPI)
national income	adjusted GNP	producer price index (PPI)

PROBLEMS

Conceptual

1. What would happen to GDP if the government hired unemployed workers, who had been receiving amount $TR in unemployment benefits, as government employees and now paid them $TR to do nothing? Explain.

2. In the national income accounts, what is the difference between:
   a. A firm's buying an auto for an executive and the firm's paying the executive additional income to buy the automobile herself?
   b. Your hiring your spouse (who takes care of the house) rather than having him or her do the work without pay?
   c. Your deciding to buy an American car rather than a German car?

3. What is the difference between GDP and GNP? Is one a better measure of income/output than the other? Why?

4. What is NDP? Is it a better or worse measure of output than GDP? Explain.

5. Increases in real GDP are often interpreted as increases in welfare. What are some problems with this interpretation? Which do you think is the biggest problem with it, and why?

6. The CPI and PPI are both measures of the price level. How are they different, and when might you prefer one of these measures over the other?

7. What is the GDP deflator, and how does it differ from the consumer and producer price indexes? Under what circumstances might it be a more useful measure of price than the CPI and PPI?

8. If you woke up in the morning and found that nominal GDP had doubled overnight, what statistic would you need to check before you began to celebrate? Why?

Technical

1. In the text, we calculated the change in real GDP in the hypothetical economy of Table 2-3, using the prices of 1992. Calculate the change in real GDP between 1992 and 1998 using the same data but *the prices of 1998*. Your answer should demonstrate that the prices that are used to calculate real GDP do affect the calculated growth rate, but typically not by very much.

2. Show from national income accounting that:
   a. An increase in taxes (while transfers remain constant) must imply a change in net exports, government purchases, or the saving-investment balance.
   b. An increase in disposable personal income must imply an increase in consumption or an increase in saving.
   c. An increase in both consumption and saving must imply an increase in disposable income.

   [For both (b) and (c) assume there are no interest payments by households or transfer payments to foreigners.]

3. The following is information from the national income accounts for a hypothetical country:

GDP	$6,000
Gross investment	800
Net investment	200
Consumption	4,000
Government purchases of goods and services	1,100
Government budget surplus	30

What is:
a. NDP?
b. Net exports?
c. Government taxes minus transfers?
d. Disposable personal income?
e. Personal saving?

4. Assume that GDP is $6,000, personal disposable income is $5,100, and the government budget deficit is $200. Consumption is $3,800, and the trade deficit is $100.
a. How large is saving (*S*)?
b. How large is investment (*I*)?
c. How large is government spending (*G*)?

5. If a country's labor is paid a total of $6 billion, its capital is paid a total of $2 billion, and profits are zero, what is the level of output? (*Hint:* see equation 2.)

6. Consider an economy which consists only of those who bake bread and those who produce its ingredients. Suppose that this economy's production is as follows: 1 million loaves of bread (sold at $2 each); 1.2 million pounds of flour (sold at $1 per pound); and 100,000 pounds each of yeast, sugar, and salt (all sold at $1 per pound). The flour, yeast, sugar, and salt are sold only to bakers, who use them exclusively for the purpose of making bread.
a. What is the value of output in this economy (i.e., nominal GDP)?
b. How much value is added to the flour, yeast, sugar, and salt when the bakers turn them into bread?

7. Suppose a country's CPI increased from 2.1 to 2.3 in the course of 1 year. Use this fact to compute the rate of inflation for that year. Why might the CPI overstate the rate of inflation?

2

Growth, Aggregate Supply and Demand, and the New Macroeconomics

CHAPTER 3

Growth and Accumulation

CHAPTER HIGHLIGHTS

- Economic growth is due to growth in inputs, such as labor and capital, and to improvements in technology.

- Capital accumulates through saving and investment.

- The long-run level of output per person depends positively on the savings rate and negatively on the rate of population growth.

- The neoclassical growth model suggests that the standard of living in poor countries will eventually converge to the level in wealthy countries.

We have enormously higher incomes than did our great grandparents. People in industrialized nations are far wealthier than people living in less developed countries. In fact, Americans and many Europeans had higher incomes a century ago than people in poor countries do today. What accounts for these vast differences? What will determine our standard of living in the future? *Growth accounting* and *growth theory* answer these questions. Growth accounting explains what part of growth in total output is due to growth in different factors of production (capital, labor, etc.). Growth theory helps us understand how economic decisions control the accumulation of factors of production, for example, how the rate of saving today affects the stock of capital in the future.

Figure 3-1 shows GDP for four countries over more than a century and a half. The graph has four striking characteristics. First, the long-term growth record of the United States is remarkable, with average income increasing more than sixteenfold over the nineteenth and twentieth centuries. Second, Japan has gone from being a moderately poor country before World War II to being a wealthy country with a standard of living roughly equal to that of the United States. Third, Norwegian income has spurted in the last 25 years. Fourth, Bangladesh was miserably poor 150 years ago and—growthless—remains that way today.

Our goal in this chapter and the next is to explain Figure 3-1. Why is income in the United States so much higher today than it was a century ago? Why has Japan largely caught up with the United States, and why has Bangladesh not? We will learn that economic growth results from the accumulation of factors of production, particularly capital,

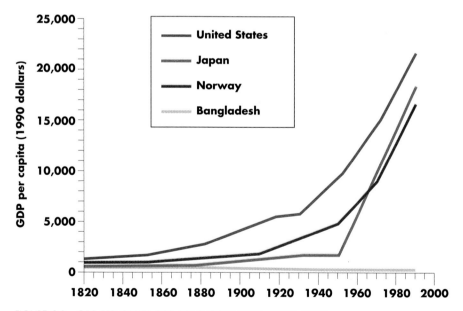

FIGURE 3-1 GDP PER CAPITA FOR FOUR COUNTRIES, 1820–1992.

The United States, Japan, and Norway have experienced growth in real GDP, while Bangladesh has had virtually zero growth.
(Source: Angus Maddison, Monitoring the World Economy 1820–1992, *1995)*

and from increased productivity. In this chapter, we see how these two factors account for economic growth and how savings rates and population growth determine capital accumulation. In the next chapter we turn to the question of why productivity increases.

3-1

GROWTH ACCOUNTING

In this section we use the production function to study two sources of growth. Output grows through increases in inputs and through increases in productivity due to improved technology and a more able work force. The *production function* provides a quantitative link between inputs and outputs. As a simplification, we first assume that labor (N) and capital (K) are the only important inputs. Equation (1) shows that output (Y) depends on inputs and the level of technology (A). (We say that A represents the level of technology because the higher A is, the more output is produced for a given level of inputs. Sometimes A is just called "productivity," a more neutral term than "technology.")

$$Y = AF(K,N) \tag{1}$$

More input means more output. In other words, the *marginal product of labor,* or *MPN* (the increase in output generated by increased labor), and the *marginal product of capital,* or *MPK* (the increase in output generated by increased capital) are both positive.

Equation (1) relates the level of output to the level of inputs and the level of technology. It is frequently easier to work with growth rates than with levels. The production function in equation (1) can be transformed into a very specific prediction relating input growth to output growth. This prediction is summarized by the *growth accounting equation* (derived in the appendix to this chapter):[1]

$$\Delta Y/Y = [(1 - \theta) \times \Delta N/N] + (\quad \theta \quad \times \Delta K/K) + \Delta A/A$$
$$\begin{matrix} \text{Output} \\ \text{growth} \end{matrix} = \begin{pmatrix} \text{labor} & \\ \text{share} & \times & \text{labor} \\ & & \text{growth} \end{pmatrix} + \begin{pmatrix} \text{capital} & \\ \text{share} & \times & \text{capital} \\ & & \text{growth} \end{pmatrix} + \begin{matrix} \text{technical} \\ \text{progress} \end{matrix} \tag{2}$$

where $(1 - \theta)$ and θ are weights equal to labor's share of income and capital's share of income.[2]

Equation (2) summarizes the contributions of input growth and of improved productivity to the growth of output:

- Labor and capital each contribute an amount equal to their individual growth rates *multiplied by the share of that input in income.*
- The rate of improvement of technology, called *technical progress,* or the *growth of total factor productivity,* is the third term in equation (2).

---

[1]Two assumptions, a competitive economy and constant returns to scale, are required to move from equation (1) to equation (2). These assumptions are discussed in the appendix. Box 3-1 begins an example using the Cobb-Douglas production function (the example continues in the appendix), but equation (2) in no way requires this specific production function.

[2]"Labor's share" means the fraction of total output that goes to compensate labor—in other words, wages, salaries, and so on, divided by GDP.

BOX 3-1   The Cobb-Douglas Production Function

The generic formula for the production function is $Y = AF(K,N)$. If you prefer to follow the discussion with a specific formula, you can use the *Cobb-Douglas production function*, $Y = AK^\theta N^{1-\theta}$. At least for the United States, $\theta \approx .25$ makes the Cobb-Douglas function a very good approximation to the real economy, so the Cobb-Douglas function can be written as $Y = AK^{.25}N^{.75}$. Economists like the Cobb-Douglas functional form because it provides a relatively accurate description of the economy and is very easy to work with algebraically. For example, the marginal product of capital is

$$MPK = \theta AK^{\theta-1}N^{1-\theta} = \theta A(K/N)^{-(1-\theta)} = \theta Y/K.$$

The growth rate of total factor productivity is the amount by which output would increase as a result of improvements in methods of production, with all inputs unchanged. In other words, there is growth in total factor productivity when we get more output from the same factors of production.[3]

Example: Suppose capital's share of income is .25 and that of labor is .75. These values correspond approximately to the actual values for the U.S. economy. Furthermore, let labor force growth be 1.2 percent and growth of the capital stock be 3 percent, and suppose total factor productivity grows at the rate of 1.5 percent per annum. What is the growth rate of output? Applying equation (2), we obtain a growth rate of $\Delta Y/Y = (.75 \times 1.2 \text{ percent}) + (.25 \times 3 \text{ percent}) + 1.5 \text{ percent} = 3.15 \text{ percent}$.

An important point in equation (2) is that the growth rates of capital and labor are weighted by their respective income shares. Because labor's share is higher, a 1-percentage-point increase in labor raises output by more than a 1-percentage-point change in capital. Because the weights add to 1, if capital and labor *both* grow by an extra 1 percent, so does output.

This point—that growth in inputs is weighted by factor shares—turns out to be quite critical when we ask how much extra growth we get by raising the rate of growth of the capital stock, say, by implementing supply-side policies. Suppose that in the example above, capital growth had been twice as high—6 percent instead of 3 percent. Using equation (2), we find that output growth would increase from 3.15 to 3.9 percent, rising by less than a percentage point even though capital growth rose by an additional 3 percentage points.

ACCOUNTING FOR GROWTH IN PER CAPITA OUTPUT

Equation (2) describes growth in total output. But do we really care about total national income or about the income of an average person, *GDP per capita?* Switzerland is a "rich" country and India is a "poor" country even though aggregate Indian GDP is higher. Our notion of "standard of living" refers to individual well-being.

---

[3]There is a distinction between *labor productivity* and total factor productivity. Labor productivity is just the ratio of output to labor input, *Y/N*. Labor productivity certainly grows as a result of technical progress, but it also grows because of the accumulation of capital per worker.

Per capita GDP is the ratio of GDP to population. In studying growth, it's traditional to use lowercase letters for per capita values, so we define $y \equiv Y/N$ and $k \equiv K/N$. The growth rate of GDP equals the growth rate of per capita GDP plus the growth rate of the population: $\Delta Y/Y = \Delta y/y + \Delta N/N$, and $\Delta K/K = \Delta k/k + \Delta N/N$. To translate the growth accounting equation into per capita terms, subtract population growth, $\Delta N/N$, from both sides of equation (2) and rearrange the terms:

$$\Delta Y/Y - \Delta N/N = \theta \times [\Delta K/K - \Delta N/N] + \Delta A/A \qquad (3)$$

Equation (3) is rewritten in per capita terms as:

$$\Delta y/y = \theta \times \Delta k/k + \Delta A/A \qquad (4)$$

The number of machines per worker, k, also called the *capital-labor ratio,* is a key determinant of the amount of output a worker can produce. Since θ is around .25, equation (4) suggests that a 1 percent increase in the amount of capital available to each worker increases per capita output by only about a quarter of 1 percent. The quantitative link is less than one to one because of *diminishing marginal returns.*

THE POSTWAR CONVERGENCE OF THE U.S AND JAPANESE ECONOMIES

The process of one economy's catching up with another economy is called *convergence.* Since the end of World War II, the standard of living in Japan has caught up with that in the United States. How much of the remarkable postwar convergence between the United States and Japan can be explained by an accounting relation as simple as equation (4)? Table 3-1 presents the necessary data.

Figure 3-1 shows that the rate of Japanese catch-up with the United States was greater in the early than in the late postwar period, so we split the analysis into two periods, 1950–1973 and 1973–1992. We look first at the second period, in which the greater rate of capital accumulation in Japan accounts for much of the difference in output growth.

Between 1973 and 1992 (the second row of Table 3-1), Japan outpaced the United States in growth of GDP per capita by 1.65 percent per year. In just under 20 years, output in Japan grew 36 percent more than did output in the United States. What accounts for this achievement? Putting the numbers from Table 3-1 into equation (4), the difference of 3.16 percent per year in capital per capita growth ($\Delta k/k$) in the last column of Table 3-1 predicts a .79 percent ($.79 = \Delta y/y = \theta \times \Delta k/k = 0.25 \times 3.16$) GDP per capita growth differential. In other words, something as simple as equation

TABLE 3-1   Postwar Annual Growth Rates
(Percent)

	GDP PER CAPITA			CAPITAL PER CAPITA		
	UNITED STATES	JAPAN	DIFFERENCE	UNITED STATES	JAPAN	DIFFERENCE
1950–1973	2.42	8.01	5.59	2.48	7.94	5.46
1973–1992	1.38	3.03	1.65	2.89	6.05	3.16
1950–1992	1.94	5.73	3.79	2.66	7.09	4.43

Source: Angus Maddison, *Monitoring the World Economy, 1820–1992.* (Paris: Organization for Economic Cooperation and Development, 1995.)

(4) accounts for about half (.79 out of 1.65) of the observed difference in growth rates.

During the early postwar period, Japanese growth was an amazing 5.59 points higher than U.S. growth. We can show that this difference is too great to be explained by relative capital accumulation. Putting the data in the first row of Table 3-1 into equation (4) explains only 1.37 ($1.37 = \Delta y/y = \theta \times \Delta k/k = 0.25 \times 5.46$) points of the difference. This leaves 4.22 points to be explained by relative differences in technological change,[4] $\Delta A/A$. During the early postwar period, Japan actively imported technology from the West. Starting from a lower base level of technology, a huge amount of growth was possible through "technology catch-up." In the later postwar period, technology transfer became much more of a two-way street. Today, Japanese-American differences in $\Delta A/A$ are much less important than in the past.

Calculations such as these show that while capital accumulation is not the only determinant of GDP, it is a very important one. Therefore, we would like to know what determines the rate of capital accumulation. When we turn to growth theory later in the chapter, we examine how the savings rate determines capital growth.

3-2

EMPIRICAL ESTIMATES OF GROWTH

The calculations in the previous section showed the importance of capital accumulation for growth but also suggested that technical progress can be even more important. An early and famous study by Nobel Prize winner Robert Solow of M.I.T. examined the period 1909–1949 in the United States, using a more sophisticated version of the calculations we just made.[5] Solow's surprising conclusion was that over 80 percent of the growth in output per labor hour over that period was due to technical progress.

Specifically, Solow estimated a U.S. GDP growth equation similar to equation (2) that identifies capital and labor growth along with technical progress as the sources of output growth. Between 1909 and 1949, the average annual growth of total GDP was 2.9 percent per year. Of that, Solow concluded that .32 percent was attributable to capital accumulation, 1.09 percent was due to increases in the input of labor, and the remaining 1.49 percent was due to technical progress. Per capita output grew at 1.81 percent per year, with 1.49 percentage points of that increase resulting from technical progress.

Solow found that the important determinants of GDP growth are technical progress, increased labor supply, and capital accumulation—in that order. The important determinants of growth in GDP per capita are technical progress and capital accumulation.

Increased population actually decreases GDP per capita even though it increases GDP. While this may sound confusing, both conclusions follow directly from equation (2). More workers means more output, but output increases less than proportionately. Equation (2) tells us that each percentage point of growth in the labor force leads to a $1-\theta$ percentage-point increase in output, specifically, about three-quarters of a point. Because the increase is less than one for one, output grows less quickly than the num-

[4]As we will see below, improvements in human capital also play a role.

[5]R. Solow, "Technical Change and the Aggregate Production Function," *Review of Economics and Statistics,* August 1957.

BOX 3-2   The Solow Residual

How is technical progress measured? By definition, changes in A account for all productivity changes not due to changes in factor inputs. Changes in A are sometimes called changes in total factor productivity, or *TFP*—a more neutral term than "technical progress." Since inputs and outputs are directly observable but A is not, economists measure $\Delta A/A$ by turning equation (2) inside out:

$$\Delta A/A = \Delta Y/Y - [(1 - \theta) \times \Delta N/N] + (\theta \times \Delta K/K)$$

and attributing everything left over to changes in *TFP*. Measured this way, changes in *TFP* are called the *Solow residual*.

ber of workers and output per worker (GDP per capita) falls. There is another way to say all this: If you increase the number of workers without proportionately increasing the number of machines, the average worker will be less productive because she has less equipment to work with.

FACTORS OTHER THAN CAPITAL AND LABOR

The production function and therefore equations (2) and (4) omit a long list of inputs other than capital and labor—in part because capital and labor are the most important inputs and in part just as a simplification. Of course, in specific times and in specific places inputs other than labor and capital matter a great deal. Two other important inputs are natural resources and human capital.

Natural Resources

Much of the early prosperity of the United States was due to the nation's abundant, fertile land. Between 1820 and 1870, the land area of the United States grew at 1.41 percent per year (contributing greatly to growth), although in modern times U.S. land growth has been negligible. The opening of the Russian east roughly coincided with the opening of the American west and similarly contributed to Russian economic growth.

For a more recent example of the occasional importance of natural resources, consider the recent sharp increase in Norwegian GDP (see Figure 3-1). Between 1970 and 1990, Norway's per capita GDP rose from 61 percent of U.S. per capita GDP to 77 percent. Much of this Norwegian growth spurt was due to the discovery and development of massive oil reserves.[6]

Human Capital

In industrialized countries, raw labor is less important than the skills and talents of workers. Society's stock of such skills is increased by investment in *human capital*

---

[6]Although possession of rich natural resources should contribute to a higher standard of living, some empirical evidence suggests that countries with more natural resources on average do *worse*. One explanation is that such countries squander their wealth. See Jeffrey D. Sachs and Andrew M. Warner, "Natural Resource Abundance and Economic Growth," Harvard Institute for International Development working paper, October 1995.

through schooling, on-the-job training, and other means in the same way that physical investment leads to increased physical capital. (In poor countries, investments in health are a major contributor to human capital. In times of extreme poverty, the critical investment can be providing workers with enough calories to enable them to bring in the harvest.) Adding human capital, H, we can write the production function as

$$Y = AF(K,H,N) \tag{5}$$

The factor share of human capital is large in industrialized countries. An influential article by Mankiw, Romer, and Weil suggests that the production function is consistent with factor shares of one-third each for physical capital, raw labor, and human capital.[7] Differential growth in these three factors can explain about 80 percent of the variation in GDP per capita across a wide sample of countries, emphasizing the critical role of factor accumulation in the growth process.

According to the previous section a large physical capital stock, the result of a high investment ratio, should lead to high GDP. Panel *(a)* of Figure 3-2 plots (the logarithm of) per capita GDP against investment (as a fraction of GDP) for a cross section of countries. It's apparent that high investment does lead to high income. But is there a similar relationship between human capital and output? Human capital is difficult to measure precisely, but average years of schooling can serve as a proxy for human capital. In panel *(b)* we see that the evidence strongly supports the positive relationship between human capital and output. In the next chapter we will see that human capital, like physical capital, can continue to accumulate and therefore can be a contributor to permanent growth.

Any change in a major factor of production will affect output. GDP in some tropical countries depends greatly on the arrival of monsoons. Immigration boosts per capita output when skilled workers enter the country, a fact which has frequently benefited the United States. In contrast, immigration consisting of war refugees typically depresses per capita output in the short run. However, a factor of production adds to output growth only so long as the supply of the factor itself is growing. Such fluctuations in factor input may last for several years, but they rarely last for several decades (although the opening of the American west and the Russian east would be exceptions).

Short-run fluctuations in input factors—everything from monsoons to refugee flows—are sometimes quite important. Nonetheless, over great sweeps of history the two important factors are capital accumulation (physical and human) and technological progress. Our study of growth theory concentrates on these two factors.

3-3

GROWTH THEORY: THE NEOCLASSICAL MODEL

There have been two periods of intense work on growth theory, the first in the late 1950s and the 1960s and the second 30 years later, in the late 1980s and early 1990s. Research in the first period created *neoclassical growth theory.* Neoclassical growth

---

[7]N. G. Mankiw, D. Romer, and D. Weil, "A Contribution to the Empirics of Economic Growth," *Quarterly Journal of Economics,* May 1992.

FIGURE 3-2   RELATIONSHIP OF (*a*) INVESTMENT RATIO AND (*b*) AVERAGE YEARS OF SCHOOLING TO GDP.

The higher the rate of investment—in physical or human capital—the higher the GDP. (Source: Data taken from R. Barro and J. Lee, "International Comparisons of Educational Attainment," NBER working paper, 1993.)

theory focuses on capital accumulation and its link to savings decisions and the like. The best-known contributor is Robert Solow.[8] Endogenous growth theory, studied in the next chapter, focuses on the determinants of technological progress.

---

[8]R. Solow, "A Contribution to the Theory of Economic Growth," *Quarterly Journal of Economics,* February 1956. The collection of papers in Joseph Stiglitz and Hirofumi Uzawa (eds.), *Readings in the Theory of Economic Growth* (Cambridge, Mass.: M.I.T. Press, 1969), contains many of the most important papers of that period.

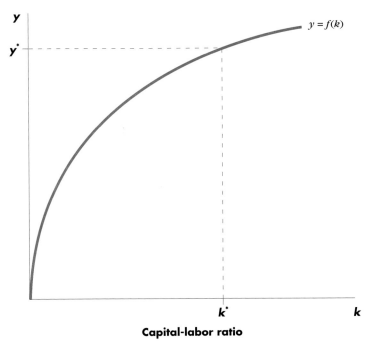

FIGURE 3-3   PER CAPITA PRODUCTION FUNCTION.

The production function y = f(k) is the relationship between per capita output and the capital-labor ratio.

Neoclassical growth theory begins with a simplifying assumption. We start our analysis by pretending that there is no technological progress. This implies that the economy reaches a long-run level of output and capital called the *steady-state equilibrium.* The steady-state equilibrium for the economy is the combination of per capita GDP and per capita capital where the economy will remain at rest, that is, where per capita economic variables are no longer changing, $\Delta y = 0$ and $\Delta k = 0$. Much of growth theory involves studying the transition from the economy's current position to this steady state. As a final step, we add technological progress to the model. (Perhaps this seems a bit roundabout. But this trick allows us to use simple graphs for the analysis and still get to the right answer.)

Figure 3-3 presents the production function in terms of GDP per capita graphed against the capital-labor ratio.[9] The production function in per capita terms is written

$$y = f(k) \tag{6}$$

[9]The production function defined in equation (1) gave output as a function of both labor and capital. We wish to work in per capita variables. Divide both sides of the production function in (1) by N: $Y/N = AF(K,N)/N$. Next use the fact of constant returns to scale (discussed in the appendix to this chapter) to write $AF(K,N)/N = AF(K/N,N/N)$. Remembering that $K/N \equiv k$ (and since $N/N \equiv 1$), we write $AF(K/N,N/N) = AF(k,1)$. To remind us that we are working in per capita terms, it is conventional to define $f(k) \equiv AF(k,1)$.

The Cobb-Douglas in Per Capita Terms

Following through on the Cobb-Douglas example, we write

$$Y/N = AK^{\theta}N^{1-\theta}/N = AK^{\theta}N^{-\theta}N/N = A(K/N)^{\theta} \text{ or } y = f(k) = Ak^{\theta}$$

Note the shape of the production function in Figure 3-3. As capital rises, output rises (the marginal product of capital is positive), but output rises less at high levels of capital than at low levels (diminishing marginal product of capital). Each additional machine adds to production, but adds less than did the previous machine.[10] We will see below that "diminishing marginal product" is the key explanation of why the economy reaches a steady state rather than growing endlessly.

STEADY STATE

An economy is in a *steady state* when per capita income and capital are constant. The steady-state values of per capita income and capital,[11] denoted y^* and k^*, are those values where the investment required to provide capital for new workers and to replace machines which have worn out is just equal to the saving generated by the economy. If saving is greater than this investment requirement, then capital per worker rises over time and therefore output does as well. If saving is less than this investment requirement, then capital and output per worker fall. The steady-state values y^* and k^* are the levels of output and capital at which saving and required investment balance.

Once we have y^* and k^* as a point of reference, we can examine the transition path of the economy from an arbitrary point to the steady state. For example, if the economy starts with less capital than k^* and income below y^*, we examine how capital accumulation moves the economy over time toward y^* and k^*.

INVESTMENT AND SAVING

The investment required to maintain a given level, k, of capital per capita depends on population growth and the depreciation rate, the rate at which machines wear out. We assume first that the population grows at a constant rate $n \equiv \Delta N/N$. Therefore, the economy needs an investment, nk, to provide capital for new workers. Second, we assume that depreciation is a constant d percent of the capital stock. Concretely, we might assume that depreciation is 10 percent per year, so every year 10 percent of the capital stock needs to be replaced to offset wear and tear. This adds dk to the requirement for new machinery. Thus, the investment required to maintain the level of capital per capita is $(n + d)k$.

Now we examine the link between saving and growth in capital. We are assuming there is no government sector and no foreign trade or capital flows. We also assume that saving is a constant fraction, s, of income, so per capita saving is sy. Since income equals production, we can also write $sy = sf(k)$.

The net change in capital per capita, Δk, is the excess of saving over required investment:

$$\Delta k = sy - (n + d)k \qquad (7)$$

The *steady state is defined by* $\Delta k = 0$ and occurs at the values of y^* and k^* satisfying

$$sy^* = sf(k^*) = (n + d)k^* \qquad (8)$$

---

[10]The diminishing curvature is the graphical equivalent of $\theta < 1$ in equation (2).

[11]For income *per head* and capital *per head* to remain unchanging even though population is growing, income and capital must grow at the same rate as population. As a symbol for the rate of population growth, we define $n \equiv \Delta N/N$, so in the steady state $\Delta Y/Y = \Delta N/N = \Delta K/K = n$.

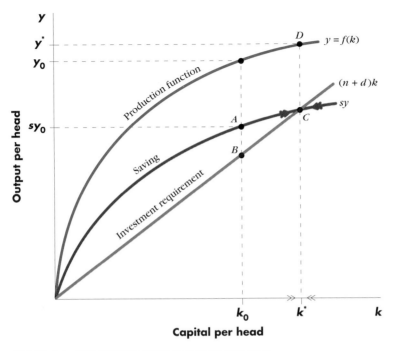

FIGURE 3-4   STEADY-STATE OUTPUT AND INVESTMENT.

Figure 3-4 presents a graphical solution for the steady state. With individuals sav-ing a constant fraction of their income, the curve sy, which is a constant proportion of output, shows the level of saving at each capital-labor ratio. The straight line $(n + d)k$ shows the amount of investment that is needed at each capital-labor ratio to keep the capital-labor ratio constant by supplying machines both as replacements for those that have worn out and as additions for workers newly entering the labor force. Where the two lines intersect, at point C, saving and required investment balance with steady-state capital k^*. Steady-state income is read off the production function at point D.

THE GROWTH PROCESS

In Figure 3-4 we study the adjustment process that leads the economy from some initial capital-labor ratio over time to the steady state. The critical element in this transition process is the rate of saving and investment compared with the rate of depreciation and population growth.

The key to understanding the neoclassical growth model is that when saving, sy, exceeds the investment requirement line, then k is increasing, as specified by equation (7). Accordingly, when sy exceeds $(n + d)k$, k must be increasing, and over time the economy is moving to the right in Figure 3-4. For instance, if the economy starts at capital-output ratio k_0, then with saving at A exceeding the investment needed to hold k constant at B, the horizontal arrow shows k increasing.

The adjustment process comes to a halt at point C. Here we have reached a cap-ital-labor ratio, k^*, for which saving and investment associated with that capital-labor

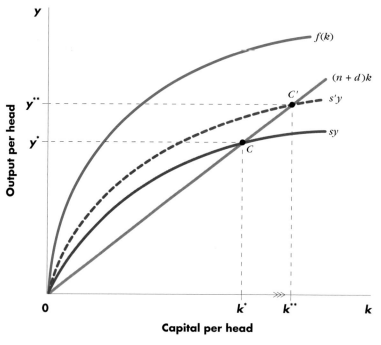

FIGURE 3-5   INCREASE IN SAVINGS RATE MOVES THE STEADY STATE.

If the savings rate increases, the steady-state capital-labor ratio increases.

ratio exactly match the investment requirement. Given the exact matching of actual and required investment, the capital-labor ratio neither rises nor falls. We have reached the steady state.

Note that this adjustment process leads to point *C* from any initial level of income. An important implication of neoclassical growth theory is that countries with equal savings rates, rates of population growth, and technology (that is, the same production function) should eventually converge to equal incomes, although the convergence process may be quite slow.

At that steady state, both *k* and *y* are constant. With per capita income constant, aggregate income is growing at the same rate as population, that is, at rate *n*. *It follows that the steady state growth rate is not affected by the savings rate.* This is one of the key results of neoclassical growth theory.

AN INCREASE IN THE SAVINGS RATE

Why should the long-run growth rate be independent of the savings rate? Aren't we always being told that one of the main reasons Japan grows faster than the United States is that the Japanese save more than Americans? Shouldn't it be true that an economy in which 10 percent of income is set aside for additions to the capital stock is one in which capital and therefore output grow faster than in an economy in which only 5 percent of income is saved? According to neoclassical growth theory, the savings rate does not affect the growth rate *in the long run*.

In Figure 3-5 we show how an increase in the savings rate affects growth. In the short run, an increase in the savings rate raises the growth rate of output. It does not affect the *long-run growth rate* of output, but *it raises the long-run level of capital and output per head.*

In Figure 3-5, the economy is initially in steady-state equilibrium at point *C*, at which saving precisely matches the investment requirement. Now people want to save a larger fraction of income. This causes an upward shift of the savings schedule, to the dashed schedule.

At point *C*, at which we initially had a steady-state equilibrium, saving has now risen relative to the investment requirement; as a consequence, more is saved than is required to maintain capital per head constant. Enough is saved to allow the capital stock per head to increase. The capital stock per head, *k*, will keep rising until it reaches point *C'*. At *C'*, the higher amount of saving is just enough to maintain the higher stock of capital. At point *C'*, both capital per head and output per head have risen.

However, at point *C'*, the economy has returned to its steady-state growth rate of *n*. Thus, with this constant-returns-to-scale production function, an increase in the sav-

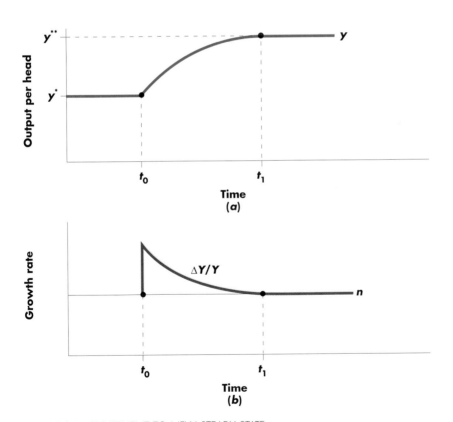

FIGURE 3-6   ADJUSTMENT TO NEW STEADY STATE.

Panels (a) and (b) show the adjustment of output and of the output growth rate following the increase in the savings rate depicted in Figure 3-5.

ings rate will in the long run raise only the level of output and capital per head, and not the growth rate of output per head.

In the transition process, however, the higher savings rate increases the growth rate of output and the growth rate of output per head. This follows simply from the fact that the capital-labor ratio rises from k^* at the initial steady state to k^{**} in the new steady state. The only way to achieve an increase in the capital-labor ratio is for the capital stock to grow faster than the labor force (and depreciation).

Figure 3-6 summarizes the effects of an increase in the savings rate, paralleling the shift shown in Figure 3-5. Figure 3-6a shows the level of per capita output. Starting from an initial long-run equilibrium at time t_0, the increase in the savings rate causes saving and investment to increase, the stock of capital per head grows, and so does output per head. The process will continue at a diminishing rate. Figure 3-6b shows the growth rate of output, plotting the rate of change of the level of output in panel (a). The increase in the savings rate immediately raises the growth rate of output because it implies faster growth in capital and therefore in output. As capital accumulates, the growth rate decreases, falling back toward the level of population growth.

POPULATION GROWTH

The preceding discussion of saving and the influence of the savings rate on steady-state capital and output makes it easy to discuss the effects of increased population growth. An increase in the population growth rate affects the $(n + d)k$ line in the diagram, rotating it up and to the left. In the end-of-chapter problems we ask you to show the following results:

- An increase in the rate of population growth *reduces* the steady-state *level* of capital per head, k, and output per head, y.
- An increase in the rate of population growth *increases* the steady-state rate of growth of *aggregate* output.

The decline in output per head as a consequence of increased population growth points up the problem faced by many developing countries, as discussed in Chapter 4.

◆ OPTIONAL ◆

GROWTH WITH EXOGENOUS TECHNOLOGICAL CHANGE

Figure 3-2, and the analysis which followed, set $\Delta A/A = 0$ as a simplification. This simplification helped us understand steady-state behavior, but it eliminated the long-term-growth part of growth theory. We reinstate growth in GDP per capita by allowing technology to improve over time, that is, $\Delta A/A > 0$.

The production function in Figure 3-2 can be thought of as a snapshot of $y = Af(k)$ taken in a year in which A is normalized to 1. If technology improves at 1 percent per year, then a snapshot taken a year later will be $y = 1.01 f(k)$; 2 years later, $y = (1.01)^2 f(k)$; and so forth. In general, if the rate of growth is defined as $g = \Delta A/A$, then the production function rises at g percent per year, as shown in Figure 3-7. The savings function grows in a parallel fashion. As a result, in growth equilibrium y and k both grow over time.

The technology parameter A can enter the production function in any of several positions. For mathematical analysis, it is frequently assumed that technology is *labor-*

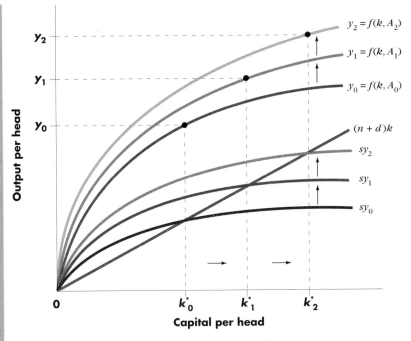

FIGURE 3-7   EXOGENOUS TECHNOLOGICAL CHANGE.

An exogenous increase in technology causes the production function and savings curve to rise. The result is a new steady-state point at a higher per capita output and higher capital-labor ratio. Thus, increases in technology over time result in growth of output over time.

augmenting, so the production function can be written $Y = F(K,AN)$. ("Labor augmenting" means that new technology increases the productivity of labor.) In this formulation, equation (4) is modified to $\Delta y/y = \theta \times \Delta k/k + (1 - \theta) \times \Delta A/A$. In growth equilibrium y and k both grow at the rate of technological progress, g. (Y and K both grow at the rate of technical progress plus the rate of population growth, $g + n$.) In this model, real wages also grow at rate g (see the appendix at the end of this chapter).

We can estimate the rate of technical progress in the postwar United States using the data in Table 3-1 and the formula

$$g \approx (\Delta y/y - \theta \times \Delta k/k)/(1 - \theta) \qquad (4')$$

From the first line in Table 3-1 we can calculate $g \approx (2.42 - 0.25 \times 2.48)/(0.75) = 2.40$. Since growth in technology and in GDP and capital per capita all come out about the same, the data suggest that the United States had reached a growth steady state. (The numbers should all be equal to g.) The assumption that the economy was in a growth steady state works less well in the later postwar period, as capital growth is notably higher than GDP growth. This difference is consistent with the idea of a *productivity slowdown.* Repeating the same arithmetic but using the second line of Table 3-1 gives only $g \approx (1.38 - 0.25 \times 2.89)/(0.75) = 0.88$.

BOX 3-3 The Cobb-Douglas Production Function with Labor-Augmenting Technical Progress

Putting labor-augmenting technical progress into the Cobb-Douglas production function gives us the production function

$$Y = K^{\theta}(AN)^{1-\theta} = A^{1-\theta}K^{\theta}N^{1-\theta}$$

Note that the leading factor, A, now has an exponent of $1 - \theta$ instead of an implicit exponent of 1. This corresponds to the modification of equation (4) in the text to include $(1 - \theta) \times \Delta A / A$ in place of $\Delta A / A$.

The second popular place to insert technology in the production function is, as it was at the beginning of the chapter, right out front, $Y = AF(K,N)$. Written this way, A is called *total factor productivity* because it augments all factors, not just labor. Here, equation (4) works as originally specified, so $g \approx (\Delta y/y - \theta \times \Delta k/k)$. (The difference between equations (4) and (4′) is really just a difference in units of measurement.) Specified in this way, g is called the *Solow residual,* indicating that total factor productivity really measures all the changes in production that we can't account for by changes in input factors.

Return again to Figure 3-1. We have used growth theory to explain the long upward trend in the standard of living in the United States (technical progress and the accumulation of physical and human capital); the convergence of Japanese and U.S. standards of living (transitional capital accumulation and technology transfer); and the Norwegian growth spurt (oil!).

RECAP

There are four key results of neoclassical growth theory.
- First, the growth rate of output in steady state is exogenous; in this case it is equal to n. It is therefore independent of the savings rate, s.
- Second, although an increase in the savings rate does not affect the steady-state growth rate, it does increase the steady-state *level* of income by increasing the capital-output ratio.

- Third, when we allow for productivity growth, we can show that if there is a steady state, the steady-state growth rate of output remains exogenous. The steady-state rate of growth of per capita income is determined by the rate of technical progress. The steady-state growth rate of aggregate output is the sum of the rate of technical progress and the rate of population growth.
- The final prediction of neoclassical theory is that of *convergence:* If two countries have the same rate of population growth, the same savings rate, and access to the same production function, they will eventually reach the same level of income. In this framework, poor countries are poor because they have less capital, but if they save at the same rate as rich countries and have access to the same technology, they will eventually catch up.

Further, if countries have different savings rates, then according to this simple neoclassical theory, they will reach different *levels* of income in the steady state, but if their rates of technical progress and population growth are the same, their steady-state growth rates will be the same.

SUMMARY

1. Neoclassical growth theory accounts for growth in output as a function of growth in inputs, particularly capital and labor. The relative importance of each input depends on its factor share.
2. Labor is the most important input.
3. Long-run growth results from improvements in technology.
4. Absent technological improvement, output per person will eventually converge to a steady-state value. Steady-state output per person depends positively on the savings rate and negatively on the rate of population growth.

KEY TERMS

growth accounting	marginal product of capital	Solow residual
growth theory	(*MPK*)	human capital
production function	total factor productivity	neoclassical growth theory
Cobb-Douglas production function	GDP per capita	steady-state equilibrium
marginal product of labor (*MPN*)	capital-labor ratio	
	diminishing marginal returns	
	convergence	

PROBLEMS

Conceptual

1. What information does a production function provide?
2. Can the Solow growth model help to explain the phenomenon of convergence?
3. Consider a production function which omits the stock of natural resources. When, if ever, will this omission have serious consequences?
4. If, in the context of a standard production function, $Y = F(K,N)$, where K represents physical capital and N represents raw labor, we were to interpret the Solow residual ($\Delta A/A$) as "technological progress," we would be in error. What, besides technological progress, would this residual catch? How could you expand the model to eliminate this problem?

5. Figure 3-4 provides a basic illustration of the Solow growth model. Interpret it, being careful to explain the meaning of the saving and investment requirement lines. Why does the steady state occur where they cross?

6. What factors determine the growth rate of steady-state per capita output? Are there other factors which could affect the growth rate of output in the *short run?*

Technical

1. In a simple scenario with only two factors of production, suppose that capital's share of income is .4 and labor's share is .6 and that annual growth rates of capital and labor are 6 and 2 percent, respectively. Assume there is no technical change.
   a. At what rate does output grow?
   b. How long will it take for output to double?
   c. Now suppose technology grows at a rate of 2 percent. Recalculate your answers to (a) and (b).

2. Suppose output is growing at 3 percent per year and capital's and labor's shares of income are .3 and .7, respectively.
   a. If both labor and capital grow at 1 percent per year, what would the growth rate of total factor productivity have to be?
   b. What if both the labor and the capital stocks are fixed?

3. Suppose again that capital's and labor's shares of income are .3 and .7.
   a. What would be the effect (on output) of increasing the capital stock by 10 percent?
   b. What would be the effect of increasing the pool of labor by 10 percent?
   c. If the increase in labor is due entirely to population growth, will the resulting increase in output have an effect on people's welfare?
   d. What if the increase in labor is due, instead, to an influx of women into the workplace?

4. Suppose an earthquake destroys one-quarter of the capital stock. Discuss the adjustment process of the economy, and using Figure 3-5, show what happens to growth in the short run and in the long run.

5. Suppose there is an increase in the population growth rate.
   a. Show graphically how this affects the growth rate of both output per capita and total output in the short and the long run. (*Hint:* Use a diagram like Figure 3-5.)
   b. Chart the time paths of per capita income and the per capita capital stock following this change. (*Hint:* Use a diagram like Figure 3-6.)

6. Consider a production function of the form $Y = AF(K,N,Z)$, where Z is a measure of natural resources used in production. Assume this production function has constant returns to scale and diminishing returns in each factor.
   a. What will happen to output per head if capital and labor both grow but Z is fixed?
   b. Reconsider (a), but add technical progress (growth in A).
   c. In the 1970s there were fears that we were running out of natural resources and that this would limit growth. Discuss this view using your answers to (a) and (b).

7. Consider the following production function: $Y = K^{.5}(AN)^{.5}$, where both the population and the pool of labor are growing at a rate $n = .07$, the capital stock is depreciating at a rate $d = .03$, and A is normalized to 1.
   a. What are capital's and labor's shares of income?
   b. What is the form of this production function?
   c. Find the steady-state values of k and y when $s = .20$.

    d. At what rate is per capita output growing at the steady state? At what rate is total output growing? What if total factor productivity is increasing at a rate of 2 percent per year ($g = .02$)?

8. Suppose the level of technology is constant. Then it jumps to a new, higher constant level.

    a. How does this technological jump affect output per head, holding the capital-labor ratio constant?

    b. Show the new steady-state equilibrium. What has happened to per capita saving and the capital-labor ratio? What happens to output per capita?

    c. Chart the time path of the adjustment to the new steady state. Does the investment ratio rise during transition? If so, is this effect temporary?

9.* For a Cobb-Douglas production function $Y = AK^\theta N^{(1-\theta)}$, verify that $1 - \theta$ is labor's share of income. [*Hint:* Labor's share of income is the piece of income which results from that labor ($MPL*N$) divided by total income.]

APPENDIX

In this appendix we briefly show how the fundamental growth equation [equation (2) in this chapter] is obtained. We start with the production function $Y = AF(K,N)$ and ask how much output changes if labor changes by ΔN, capital changes by ΔK, and technology changes by ΔA. The change in output will be

$$\Delta Y = MPN \times \Delta N + MPK \times \Delta K + F(K,N) \times \Delta A \qquad (A1)$$

where MPN and MPK are the marginal products of labor and capital, respectively. Dividing both sides of the equation by $Y = AF(K,N)$ and simplifying yields

$$\frac{\Delta Y}{Y} = \frac{MPN}{Y} \Delta N + \frac{MPK}{Y} \Delta K + \frac{\Delta A}{A} \qquad (A2)$$

Now we multiply and divide the first term by N and the second term by K:

$$\frac{\Delta Y}{Y} = \left(\frac{MPN \times N}{Y}\right) \frac{\Delta N}{N} + \left(\frac{MPK \times K}{Y}\right) \frac{\Delta K}{K} \times \frac{\Delta A}{A} \qquad (A3)$$

    These transformations follow from rules of mathematics. To get the rest of the way to equation (2), we need to make two strong, but very reasonable, assumptions: The production function exhibits *constant returns to scale,* and the economy is *competitive.*

    The phrase "constant returns to scale" (CRTS) means that if all inputs increase in equal proportion, output increases in that same proportion. (Mathematically, if we multiply both inputs by a constant c, output will also be multiplied by c: $AF(cK,cN) = cAF(K,N) = cY$.) CRTS is a believable assumption because of the *replication argument:* If one factory using X workers produces output Y, then two factories using X workers each should produce output $2Y$, three factories using X workers each should produce output $3Y$, and so forth. In addition to this attractive logical argument, empirical evidence also suggests that returns to scale are roughly constant.

    In a competitive economy, factors are paid their marginal products. Thus $MPN = w$, where w is the real wage. Total payment to labor is the wage rate times the amount of labor, $w \times N$; the total payment to labor as a fraction of all payments—which is to say, "labor's share"—is

---

*An asterisk denotes a more difficult problem.

BOX A3-1 Following Along with the Cobb-Douglas

To show that the Cobb-Douglas has constant returns to scale, multiply both K and N by c:

$$A(cK)^{\theta}(cN)^{1-\theta} = A(c^{\theta}K^{\theta})(c^{1-\theta}N^{1-\theta}) = c^{\theta}c^{1-\theta}AK^{\theta}N^{1-\theta} = c^{\theta+(1-\theta)}Y = cY$$

To show that capital's share is θ, multiply the marginal product of capital from Box 3-1 on page 45 (which is what a unit of capital gets paid in a competitive market) by the number of units of capital and divide by total output:

$$MPK \cdot K/Y = (\theta Y/K) \cdot K/Y = \theta$$

And yes, the exponent θ in the Cobb-Douglas is the same θ that appears in the growth accounting equation [equation (2)].

$MPN \times N/Y$. (The argument for capital is analogous.) Now substitute $1 - \theta \equiv$ labor's share for $MPN \times N/Y$ and $\theta \equiv$ capital's share for $MPK \times K/Y$ into equation (A3) to reach equation (2):

$$
\begin{aligned}
\Delta Y/Y &= [(1 - \theta) \times \Delta N/N] + (\theta \times \Delta K/K) + \Delta A/A \\
\text{Output growth} &= \left(\begin{array}{c}\text{labor} \\ \text{share}\end{array} \times \begin{array}{c}\text{labor} \\ \text{growth}\end{array}\right) + \left(\begin{array}{c}\text{capital} \\ \text{share}\end{array} \times \begin{array}{c}\text{capital} \\ \text{growth}\end{array}\right) + \begin{array}{c}\text{technical} \\ \text{progress}\end{array}
\end{aligned}
\tag{2}
$$

CHAPTER 4
Growth and Policy

CHAPTER HIGHLIGHTS

◆ Rates of economic growth vary widely across countries and across time.

◆ Endogenous growth theory attempts to explain growth rates as functions of societal decisions, in particular savings rates.

◆ Income in poor countries appears to be converging toward income levels of rich countries, but at extraordinarily slow rates.

Can we grow faster? The previous chapter explained how GDP and GDP growth are determined by the savings rate, the rate of population growth, and the rate of technical progress. How do society's choices affect these parameters? In countries on the leading edge of technology, the advance of knowledge is a key determinant of growth. Invention of new technology is much less important for poorer countries, because poorer countries can grow by "borrowing" technology, as well as by investing in physical and human capital. In the first part of this chapter we look at how society's choices lead to technical progress—the subject called *endogenous growth theory*. Paul Romer and Robert Lucas are responsible for much of the early development of this concept.[1] In the second part of the chapter we turn to an examination of a variety of social policies affecting growth.[2]

4-1

GROWTH THEORY: ENDOGENOUS GROWTH

Neoclassical growth theory dominated economic thought for three decades because it does a good job of explaining much of what we observe in the world and because it is mathematically elegant. Nonetheless, by the late 1980s dissatisfaction with the theory had arisen on both theoretical and empirical grounds.[3] Neoclassical growth theory attributes long-run growth to technological progress but leaves unexplained the economic determinants of that technological progress. Empirical dissatisfaction developed over the prediction that economic growth and savings rates should be uncorrelated in the steady state. The data make it clear that savings rates and growth are positively correlated across countries.[4]

THE MECHANICS OF ENDOGENOUS GROWTH

The solution to both the theoretical and the empirical problems with neoclassical theory lies in modifying the assumed shape of the production function in a way that allows for self-sustaining—*endogenous*—growth. In this section we look at the difference between endogenous growth and the previous chapter's neoclassical theory in a bit of a me-

---

[1]Robert E. Lucas, Jr., "On the Mechanics of Economic Development," *Journal of Monetary Economics,* July 1988; Paul Romer, "Increasing Returns and Long-Run Growth," *Journal of Political Economy,* October 1986. The volume edited by Alwyn Young, *Readings in Endogenous Growth* (Cambridge, Mass.: M.I.T. Press, 1993), contains many of the key papers.

[2]N. Gregory Mankiw provides an accessible overview of issues of growth in "The Growth of Nations," *Brookings Papers on Economic Activity, No. 1* (1995). The best state-of-the-art examination of both the theory of and the empirical evidence on growth is the graduate-level text by Robert J. Barro and Xavier Sala-i-Martin, *Economic Growth* (New York: McGraw-Hill, 1995).

[3]For an especially readable discussion, see Paul Romer, "The Origins of Endogenous Growth," *Journal of Economic Perspectives,* Winter 1994. Two other excellent references are Mancur Olsen, "Big Bills on the Sidewalk: Why Are Some Nations Rich and Others Poor?" *Journal of Economic Perspectives,* Spring 1996, and Bennett McCallum, "Neoclassical versus Endogenous Growth: An Overview," Federal Reserve Bank of Atlanta *Economic Quarterly,* Fall 1996.

[4]More recent work raises questions as to whether this observation is really an important argument against the neoclassical model. Mankiw ("Growth of Nations") writes, "The inability of saving to affect steady-state growth . . . might appear inconsistent with the strong correlation between growth and saving across countries. But this correlation could reflect the transitional dynamics that arise as economies approach their steady states."

BOX 4-1 A Nobel Laureate's Words

I do not see how one can look at figures like these without seeing them as possibili-
ties. Is there some action a government of India could take that would lead the In-
dian economy to grow like Indonesia's or Egypt's? If so, what, exactly? If not, what
is it about the "nature of India" that makes it so? The consequences for human wel-
fare involved in questions like these are simply staggering: Once one starts to think
about them, it is hard to think about anything else. *

TABLE 1 GDP Per Capita

	1990 DOLLARS		CUMULATIVE GROWTH, %
	1950	1992	
United States	9,573	21,558	125.20
Bangladesh	551	720	30.67
China	614	3,098	404.56
Egypt	517	1,927	272.73
India	597	1,348	125.80
Indonesia	874	2,749	214.53
Mexico	2,085	5,112	145.18
South Korea	876	10,010	1,042.69
Taiwan	922	11,590	1,157.05
Tanzania	427	604	41.45
Thailand	848	4,694	453.54
U.S.S.R.	2,834	4,671	64.82
Zaire	636	407	−36.01

Source: Angus Maddison, *Monitoring the World Economy 1820–1992,* Paris: Organization for Economic Cooperation and Development, 1995.

*Robert E. Lucas, Jr., "On the Mechanics of Economic Development," *Journal of Monetary Economics,* July 1988.

chanical way. With the mechanical part under our belt, we flesh out the economics in the section following.

Figure 4-1*a* reproduces the basic Solow growth diagram from Chapter 3. You will remember that the steady state occurs at point *C*, where the savings and investment requirement lines cross. Anywhere the savings line is above the investment requirement line, the economy is growing because capital is being added. Starting at point *A*, for example, the economy moves, over time, to the right. How do we know that this process eventually comes to a halt (i.e., reaches a steady state)? Because of the *diminishing marginal product of capital,* the production function and parallel savings curve eventually flatten out. Since the investment requirement line has a constant positive slope, the investment requirement line and savings curve are guaranteed to cross.

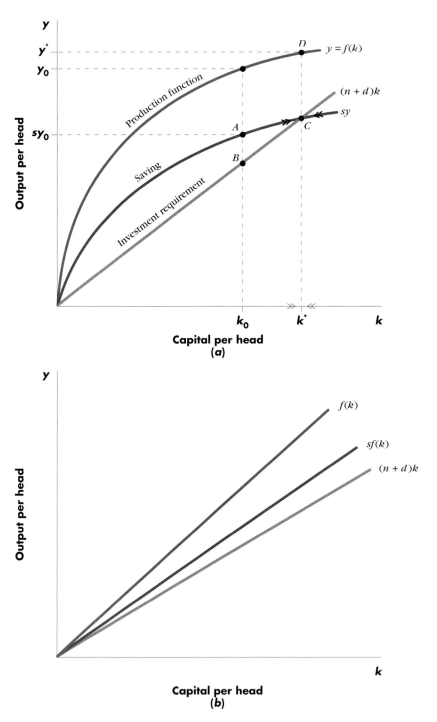

FIGURE 4-1   *(a)* SOLOW GROWTH MODEL VS. *(b)* ENDOGENOUS GROWTH.

Contrast Figure 4-1*b,* where we have changed the assumed shape of the production function to show a *constant marginal product of capital.* The production function, and parallel savings curve, is now a *straight line.* Since the savings curve no longer flattens out, saving is everywhere greater than required investment. The higher the savings rate, the bigger the gap of saving above required investment and the faster is growth.

The economy described in Figure 4-1*b* can be illustrated with a simple algebraic model leading to endogenous growth. Assume a production function with a constant marginal product of capital and with capital as the only factor. Specifically, let

$$Y = aK \tag{1}$$

that is, output is proportional to the capital stock. The marginal product of capital is simply the constant *a.*

Assume that the savings rate is constant at *s* and that there is neither population growth nor depreciation of capital. Then all saving goes to increase the capital stock. Accordingly,

$$\Delta K = sY = saK \tag{2}$$

or

$$\Delta K / K = sa$$

The growth rate of capital is proportional to the savings rate. Further, since output is proportional to capital, the growth rate of output is

$$\Delta Y / Y = sa \tag{3}$$

In this example, the higher the savings rate, the higher the growth rate of output.

THE DEEPER ECONOMICS OF ENDOGENOUS GROWTH

If a simple change to the assumed shape of the production function provides a satisfactory, albeit oversimplified, solution to the problems with neoclassical growth theory, what took 30 years to figure out? It turns out that eliminating diminishing marginal returns violates deep microeconomic principles. The changed assumption implies constant returns to scale for capital; in other words, a firm with twice as much machinery will produce twice as much output. But if doubling capital doubles output, then doubling all factors of production—that is, labor as well as capital—will more than double output. If there are constant returns to scale to capital alone, there will be *increasing returns to scale* to all factors taken together. This suggests that larger and larger firms are ever more efficient, so we should see a single firm come to dominate the entire economy. Since nothing remotely like this happens, we ought to rule out the possibility of increasing returns to scale to all factors and constant returns to a single factor, at least for a single firm.

Suppose, however, that an individual firm doesn't capture all the benefits of capital: some of the benefits are *external* to the firm. In this case, when a firm increases capital, the firm's production rises but so does the productivity of other firms. As long as the *private* return has constant returns to all factors, there will be no tendency to monopolization.

Paul Romer's intellectual breakthrough was to partially separate private returns to capital from social returns.[5] Investment produces not only new machines but new ways of doing things as well—sometimes because of deliberate investment in research and sometimes because of serendipitous spin-offs. While firms do capture the production benefits of new machines, it is much harder to capture the benefits of new methods and new ideas because methods and ideas are easy to copy.

◆ OPTIONAL ◆

We turn now to a more fully developed endogenous growth model, a model with labor as well as capital. The key assumption is that better technology is produced as a by-product of capital investment. Specifically, assume that technology is proportional to the level of capital per worker in the economy overall, $A = \alpha K/N = \alpha k$, and that technology is labor-augmenting, so the production function can be written as $Y = F(K,AN)$.[6] The growth equations are like those of Chapter 3, except that technology growth, instead of being exogenously specified, now depends on capital growth, $\Delta A/A = \Delta K/K - \Delta N/N$.

Working through the algebra requires two steps. First, we show that output and capital grow at equal rates, implying that y/k is a constant. Then we use this fact to work backward to the growth rates. For the first step, put the technology growth formula, $\Delta A/A = \Delta K/K - \Delta N/N = \Delta k/k$, into the GDP growth equation [equation (4) in Chapter 3] to show that output and capital grow at the same rate:

$$g = \Delta y/y = \theta \times \Delta k/k + (1 - \theta) \times \Delta A/A$$
$$g = \Delta y/y = \theta \times \Delta k/k + (1 - \theta) \times \Delta k/k$$
$$g = \Delta y/y = \Delta k/k$$

Since the numerator and denominator of y/k grow at an equal rate, y/k is constant. We find this constant by dividing the production function by K and simplifying:

$$y/k = F(K,AN)/K = F(K/K,AN/K) = F(1,\alpha) \equiv a$$

From Chapter 3 we know that the equation for capital accumulation can be written $\Delta k/k = sy/k - (n + d)$. Making the substitution for y/k, we have

$$\Delta y/y = \Delta k/k = g = sy/k - (n + d) = sa - (n + d)$$

The growth rate of GDP per capita is $sa - (n + d)$. A high savings rate generates a high growth rate. High rates of population growth and depreciation lead to a low growth rate.

All this hinges on the notion that there are substantial *external* returns to capital. Is this reasonable? If capital is physical machinery, probably not. After all, the benefits of a drill press are pretty much captured by the owner of the drill press. In contrast, consider the role of *human capital,* particularly investment knowledge. It is expensive to create a new drill press or a new idea. However, a copy of a drill press costs as much as the first one, while an idea can be copied at little or no expense. Since the contri-

---

[5]See Paul Romer, "Increasing Returns and Long-Run Growth."

[6]To be clear about notation, note that a is the marginal product of capital and that α governs the way capital and labor combine to produce technology, A.

BOX 4-2 One Idea Leads to the Next

Paul Samuelson wrote, in *Foundations of Economic Analysis**, "And most college graduates in physics know more than Isaac Newton: for as Newton himself said, a scientist sees further than his predecessors because he stands on the shoulders of earlier giants." The source of Samuelson's famous dictum is, "If I have seen further it is by standing on the shoulders of Giants" (Newton to Hooke, Feb. 5, 1676).

*(Cambridge, Mass.: Harvard University Press, 1947.)

bution of new knowledge—new inventions and discoveries—is only partially captured by the creator, there can be substantial external benefits. Further, each new idea makes the next idea possible, so knowledge can grow indefinitely. Thus economists think that investment in human capital in general and research and development specifically is the key to understanding long-run growth.

CONVERGENCE

The question of "convergence" centers on whether economies with different initial levels of output eventually grow to equal standards of living.

Neoclassical growth theory predicts *absolute convergence* for economies with equal rates of savings and population growth and with access to the same technology. In other words, they should all reach the same steady-state income. (If Figure 4-1a is the same for two economies, they eventually reach the same steady state even if one economy begins farther to the left.) *Conditional convergence* is predicted for economies with different rates of savings or population growth; that is, steady-state incomes will differ as predicted by the Solow growth diagram, but *growth rates* will eventually equalize.

Contrast conditional convergence with the prediction of endogenous growth theory that a high savings rate leads to a high growth rate. In a series of papers, Robert Barro has shown that while countries that invest more tend to grow faster, the impact of higher investment on growth seems to be transitory:[7] countries with higher investment will end in a steady state with higher per capita income but not with a higher growth rate. This suggests that countries do converge *conditionally,* and thus endogenous growth theory is not very important for explaining international differences in growth rates, although it may be quite important for explaining growth in countries on the leading edge of technology.

Barro's evidence suggests that conditional convergence is taking place at a rate of 2 percent per year. For instance, if India's income level is now 5 percent of that of the

---

[7]See, for example, Robert Barro's "Economic Growth in a Cross Section of Countries," *Quarterly Journal of Economics,* May 1991, and his "Determinants of Economic Growth: A Cross-Country Empirical Study," NBER Working Paper 5698, August 1996.

United States, in 35 years it would be approximately 10 percent of the U.S. level[8]—provided that the other variables that affect the level of income, such as the savings rate, are the same between the two countries. This convergence is very slow; it means that people in India today cannot look forward to catching up anytime soon with the United States merely by relying on the "natural" neoclassical force of convergence.

RECAP

- Endogenous growth theory relies on constant returns to scale to accumulable factors to generate ongoing growth.
- The microeconomics underlying endogenous growth theory emphasizes the difference between social and private returns when firms are unable to capture some of the benefits of investment.
- Current empirical evidence suggests that endogenous growth theory is not very important for explaining international differences in growth rates.

[8]It takes 35 years for an economy growing at 2 percent to double its size. In this case the doubling is relative to another economy.

◆ OPTIONAL ◆

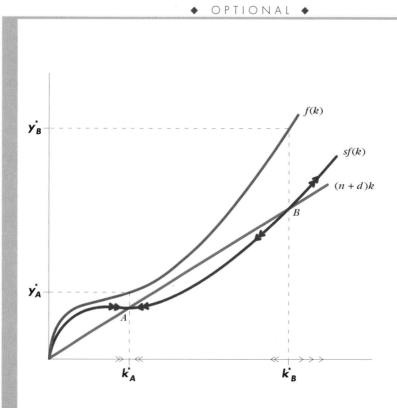

FIGURE 4-2 A CHOICE BETWEEN A STEADY STATE AND CONTINUED GROWTH.

A production function such as this could explain a world with both no-growth and high-growth countries.

GROWTH TRAPS AND TWO-SECTOR MODELS

Explaining high or low growth isn't the same as explaining *no* growth. Little or no growth is the most accurate description of Bangladesh since 1820—and of most of humankind for most of history. To explain a world with both no-growth and high-growth countries, we would like a model in which there is a possibility of both a no-growth, low-income equilibrium and a positive-growth, high-income equilibrium. In other words, something that combines elements of neoclassical and endogenous growth theories.

Suppose there are two kinds of investment opportunities, those with diminishing marginal product (as in the neoclassical growth model) and those with constant marginal product (as in the endogenous growth model). The production function will begin with a curved section (as in Figure 4-1*a*) and end with an upward-sloping line (as in Figure 4-1*b*).

Figure 4-2 shows an example. This model has a "neoclassical growth equilibrium" at point *A* but acts like an endogenous growth model to the right of point *B*. At low income and capital, the capital requirement line strikes the savings line in the neoclassical region (point *A*), leading to a no-growth steady state. At high income and capital (past point *B*), the savings line is above the capital requirement line, leading to ongoing growth.

One remaining piece is omitted from Figure 4-2. With two outlets for investment, society must choose not only total investment but also the division between the two kinds. Societies that direct investment toward research and development will have ongoing growth. Societies that direct investment toward physical capital may have higher output in the short run at the cost of lower long-run growth.

4-2

GROWTH POLICY

The previous section focused on the determinants of the rate of technical progress, a problem of most interest to countries on the cutting edge of new technology. In this section we focus on the problems of population growth and the process by which some countries move from underdeveloped to developed status.

POPULATION GROWTH AND MALTHUS

One of the oldest ideas in economics is that population growth works against the achievement of high incomes. The Solow growth model predicts that high population growth, n, means lower steady-state income because each worker will have less capital to work with. However, over a wide range of incomes, population growth itself depends on income. Extremely poor countries in modern times have very high birth rates and very high death rates, resulting in moderately high population growth. As incomes rise, death rates fall (especially through reductions in infant mortality) and population growth rises. At very high incomes, birth rates fall. Indeed, many of the wealthier countries in the world are approaching zero population growth (ZPG).

◆ O P T I O N A L ◆

A simple version of a Solow model with endogenous population growth can be shown graphically. If we were to graph *n* against *y*, it would rise, fall, and then level off near zero. The slope of the investment requirement line depends on *n*, but since *n* is no longer constant, the investment requirement line becomes a curve. Modifying the investment requirement line on the Solow diagram to account for changing *n* gives a picture which looks something like Figure 4-3.

The investment requirement line with variable population growth in Figure 4-3, $[n(y) + d]k$, rises slowly, then sharply, and eventually flattens out. As shown, the investment requirement line crosses the savings curve at points *A*, *B*, and *C*. Point *A* is a poverty trap with high population growth and low income. The equilibrium at *C* has low population growth and high income. Note the arrows showing the direction of movement toward the steady state. Points *A* and *C* are said to be *stable equilibria* because the economy moves toward these points. *B* is an *unstable equilibrium* since the economy tends to move away from *B*.

How can an economy escape from the low-level equilibrium? There are two possibilities. If a country can put on a "big push" which raises income past point *B*, the economy will continue on its own the rest of the way to the high-level point *C*. Alternatively, a nation can effectively eliminate the low-level trap by moving the savings curve up or the investment requirement line down so that they no longer touch at *A* and *B*. Raising productivity or raising the savings rate raises the savings line. Population control policies lower the investment requirement line.

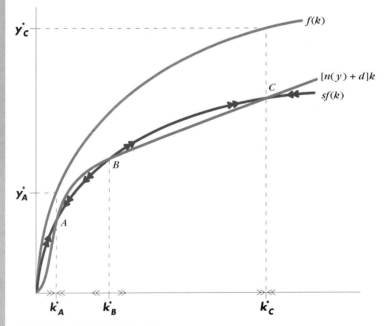

FIGURE 4-3   THE POVERTY TRAP.

In this model with two steady-state equilibria, a high rate of population growth results in a low level of per capita income.

Some governments are beginning to recognize the need to reduce population growth—in some countries, by trying to persuade people to use contraceptives; in other countries, by instituting policies that have even included forced sterilization. But it is often difficult to reduce the rate of population growth in very poor countries, where large families may serve as a social security system, since having children ensures that the parents are taken care of in their old age.

LESSONS FROM THE ASIAN TIGERS

Growth in Hong Kong, Singapore, South Korea, and Taiwan has been so remarkable that the four nations are sometimes called the "Asian Tigers." They have been held up as examples of effective development to the rest of the world. It has been argued—especially by some political leaders from these nations—that they have learned a special trick worthy of emulation. However, the best current evidence is that the principal "special trick" is old-fashioned hard work and sacrifice. In other words, these countries have not had remarkable increases in total factor productivity, A; they've saved and invested, put more people to work, and concentrated on education in order to raise human capital. What can we learn by examining the experience of the Asian Tigers?

Table 4-1 is taken from a very careful study of East Asian growth by Alwyn Young. All four countries have remarkably high growth, but their growth is mostly explained by increased input, not by higher productivity. Growth in total factor productivity, a measure of output per unit of input, is high, but not remarkable, in Hong Kong, South Korea, and Taiwan. Singapore's *TFP* growth is notably small. All four countries have had a drastic increase in the fraction of the population that works, largely due to increased labor force participation by women. Each country also greatly increased its human capital, moving educational attainment to levels close to those of the leading industrialized nations.

The Asian Tigers have several other characteristics in common. All four have relatively stable governments. The four share an outward-looking economic policy, encouraging their industries to export, compete, and learn to survive in the world market.

The near-zero productivity growth in Singapore is nonetheless noteworthy. In an influential article comparing Singapore and Hong Kong, Alwyn Young draws attention to the fact that Hong Kong has had an essentially *laissez-faire,* free-market government

TABLE 4-1 Growth in the Asian Tigers
(Percent)

	HONG KONG (1966–1991)	SINGAPORE (1966–1990)	SOUTH KOREA (1966–1990)	TAIWAN (1966–1990)
GDP per capita growth	5.7	6.8	6.8	6.7
TFP growth	2.3	0.2	1.7	2.6
Δ % labor force participation	38→49	27→51	27→36	28→37
Δ % secondary education or higher	27.2→71.4	15.8→66.3	26.5→75.0	25.8→67.6

Source: Alwyn Young, "The Tyranny of Numbers: Confronting the Statistical Realities of the East Asian Growth Experience," *Quarterly Journal of Economics,* August 1995.

BOX 4-3 Is High Income Good?
The Golden Rule

If this seems a strange question, remember that we're interested in high income insofar as it leads to high *consumption*. The higher the savings rate chosen by a society, the higher the steady-state capital and income. But the higher is k, the greater the investment required just to maintain the capital-labor ratio, as opposed to being used for current consumption. So too high a savings rate can lead to high income but low consumption.

Steady-state consumption, c^*, equals steady-state income, $y^* = f(k^*)$, minus steady-state investment, $(n + d)k^*$:

$$c^* = f(k^*) - (n + d)k^*$$

Steady-state consumption is maximized at the point where a marginal increase in capital produces just enough extra output to cover the increased investment requirement, $MPK(k^{**}) = (n + d)$. Capital k^{**}, the *golden-rule capital stock*, corresponds to the highest permanently sustainable level of consumption, the level at which we can "do unto future generations as we hope previous generations did unto us." Above the golden-rule level, we can cut back on saving and consume more both now and later. Below this level, we can increase future consumption only by making the choice to consume less today. The empirical evidence is that we are below the golden-rule level of saving.

while Singapore's government maintains tight control over the economy, with most of the economy's investments being indirectly directed by the government.[9] He argues that the government of Singapore has tried to force the pace of development, relying on foreign investment to bring in new technologies, but has moved on too rapidly to ever more sophisticated goods before local entrepreneurs and workers have mastered the current technology.

The fact remains that the Tigers have achieved something extraordinary in human history: they have been growing at rates that will transform them from being among the poorest of countries to having income levels that—already in Singapore, soon in the others—match those of the rich industrial countries. It is reassuring to see that this can be done the old-fashioned way, through saving, hard work, and competition.

REFORM AND GROWTH IN EASTERN EUROPE

In the 1990s, the formerly communist countries of eastern Europe and of the former Soviet Union are facing an economic growth and reform challenge of unprecedented nature and scale. Each of these economies had been run through a highly centralized planning system. In most of them, nearly all property and all industry were owned by

[9]A. Young, "A Tale of Two Cities: Factor Accumulation and Technical Change in Hong Kong and Singapore," *NBER Macroeconomics Annual*, 1992.

TABLE 4-2   GDP Declines in Formerly Socialist Economies, 1989–1994

COUNTRY	YEAR OF LOWEST OUTPUT	DECLINE, %
Albania	1992	39.9
Bulgaria	1993	27.4
Czech Republic	1993	21.4
Poland	1991	17.8
Russia	1994	48.3

Source: S. Fischer, R. Sahay, and C. Végh, "Stabilization and Growth in Transition Economics," *Journal of Economic Perspectives,* Spring 1996.

the state, and unemployment was virtually unknown. Several of them, including the former Soviet Union and Poland, ended the communist period with massive budget deficits and large external debts.

As the countries themselves, agencies such as the International Monetary Fund and the World Bank, and academic economic advisers to the new governments wrestled with the question of how to reform, a basic reform strategy was developed:[10]

1. Restore macroeconomic stability by bringing the budget close to balance and pursuing tight monetary and credit policies.
2. Liberalize prices by removing price controls and allowing markets to begin operating.
3. Privatize government-owned firms by selling them, or even by giving them away to the citizens.
4. Liberalize foreign trade, allowing domestic firms and consumers to have access to world markets.
5. Establish a social safety network so that people who become unemployed do not become destitute.
6. Develop, as rapidly as possible, the legal framework that a market economy needs in order to operate (e.g., contract and bankruptcy laws).

This agenda is overwhelming; accomplishing its directives will take decades. It includes such things as the necessity to develop banks and train business managers and accountants. Since the changes are interdependent, ideally they should all take place at once. However, no government can operate that fast—least of all a new government made up of people who have spent their working lives in a very different type of economy. That is why the reform process is bound to look chaotic at the outset and will take time.

The initial stages of reform are very difficult. Table 4-2 shows estimates of the decline in output during the period 1989–1994. These data are rough, but they show a massive decline in each country. For comparison, note that real output in the United States declined by 30 percent in the Great Depression, between 1929 and early 1933. The drop in per capita GDP in the former U.S.S.R. pushed living standards to the levels of 1960. In some parts of what had been the Soviet Union, the economy essentially stopped working.

---

[10]See "Symposium on Economic Transition in the Soviet Union and Eastern Europe," *Journal of Economic Perspectives,* Fall 1991.

East Germany is a special case. Since its unification with West Germany, it has been receiving massive subsidies from the western part of the country. The unification made the adjustment more difficult in some respects, for wages in the east have risen very fast, and eastern Germans are therefore less employable than they otherwise would be. The German government is spending massively on retraining, on subsidizing investment in the eastern part of Germany, and on making welfare payments to eastern Germans. The estimate is that half the income of eastern Germans comes from the German government. Still, there is no doubt that the living standards of eastern Germans have risen and will continue to rise far more rapidly than the standards of citizens of other countries that had been behind the iron curtain.

How long will it take for the situation to turn around? The answer varies from country to country. There are some signs that the bottom was reached in Poland in 1991 or 1992. In Russia the bottom will probably occur in 1996 or 1997; in some of the slower-reforming countries of the former Soviet Union there may be more years of decline to come. Even after these economies reach the bottom, it will take some time—possibly a decade—to get back to the level they were at when the revolutions began. In the much longer run, the standard of living in these countries will be higher than it would have been under the old system.

THE TRULY POOR COUNTRIES

The growth line for Bangladesh (see Figure 3-1) and the nation's GDP data (see the table in Box 4-1) illustrate a striking problem. Compared to the rest of the world, Bangladesh hasn't had any economic growth! (Bangladesh is used as an example. The same holds true for a number of other countries.) Income is so low that much of the population lives at the border of subsistence.

Have we explained Bangladesh? In part yes. Saving in Bangladesh is very low. Barro and Sala-i-Martin report that between 1960 and 1985, investment in Bangladesh averaged 4.6 percent of GDP, as compared to 36.6 percent and 24 percent in Japan and the United States, respectively.[11] Population growth in Bangladesh, and other extremely poor countries, was also much higher than in Japan or the United States. So the effect of both saving and population growth is as theory would predict. The poorest countries are hard-pressed to invest in human capital. Many of the poorest countries also have hostile climates for foreign investment, either because of deliberate policies which attempt to encourage domestic production instead or simply because the economic and legal environment is uncertain and the nations are unwilling or unable to guarantee investors the ability to repatriate profits.

NATURAL RESOURCES: LIMITS TO GROWTH?

Production uses up natural resources, in particular energy. Is it true, as is sometimes alleged, that exponential growth in the economy will eventually use up the fixed stock of resources? Well yes, it is true in the limited sense that current theories suggest the universe will one day run down. However, this seems more of a concern for a course in astrophysics, or perhaps theology, than for a course in economics. Over any interesting horizon, the economy is protected from resource-depletion disasters by two factors. First,

[11]Barro and Sala-i-Martin, *Economic Growth*, table 10.1.

technical progress permits us to produce more using fewer resources. For example, the energy efficiency of room lighting has increased by a factor of 4,500 since Neolithic times.[12] Second, as specific resources come into short supply, their prices rise, leading producers to shift toward substitutes.

Environmental protection is important, however. Even here, technology can be directed to assist us. For example, the conversion of urban transportation systems from horses to internal combustion engines has eliminated most of the pollution associated with transportation.[13] As incomes rise and populations move away from the edge of survival, people and governments choose to spend more on protecting the environment. Unlike other consumption choices, environmental protection is often "bought" through political choices rather than in the marketplace. Because the benefits of environmental protection flow across property boundaries, there is greater reason for the government to intervene on environmental issues than there is with respect to purely private goods.

SUMMARY

1. Economic growth in the most developed countries depends on the rate of technological progress. According to endogenous growth models, technological progress depends on saving, particularly saving directed toward human capital.
2. International comparisons support conditional convergence. Adjusting for differences in savings and population growth rates, developing countries advance toward the income levels of the most industrialized countries.
3. There are extraordinarily different growth experiences in different countries. High saving, low population growth, outward-looking orientation, and a predictable economic environment are all important progrowth factors.

KEY TERMS

endogenous growth	conditional convergence	golden-rule capital stock
increasing returns to scale	stable equilibrium	
absolute convergence	unstable equilibrium	

PROBLEMS

Conceptual

1. What is endogenous growth? How do endogenous growth models differ from the neoclassical models of growth presented in Chapter 3?
2. Why doesn't the constant marginal product of capital assumed in this chapter's simple model of endogenous growth create a situation in which a single large firm dominates the economy, as traditional microeconomic reasoning would suggest?
3. How do the implications of an increase in saving with regard to both the level and the growth rate of output differ between the neoclassical growth model outlined in Chapter 3 and the basic endogenous growth model outlined in this chapter?

[12]Actually, people in Neolithic times probably didn't have "rooms" per se. For a more recent benchmark, the energy efficiency of room lighting has improved by a factor of 20 since 1900. See William D. Nordhaus, "Do Real Output and Real Wage Measures Capture Reality? The History of Lighting Suggests Not," Cowles Foundation Discussion Paper 1078, 1994.

[13]Think about it for a minute.

4. *(Optional)*
    a. What sorts of capital investment does this chapter suggest are most useful for explaining long-run equilibrium growth?
    b. Discuss the long-run growth potential of each of the following government programs:
        i.   Investment tax credits
        ii.   R&D subsidies and grants
        iii. Policies intended to increase saving
        iv.   Increased funding for primary education
5. What is the difference between absolute and conditional convergence, as predicted by the neoclassical growth model? Which seems to be occurring, empirically?
6. Can endogenous growth theory help explain international differences in growth rates? If so, how? If not, what can it help explain?
7. Suppose a society can invest in two types of capital—physical and human. How can its choice regarding the distribution of investment affect its long-term growth potential?
8. a. Consider once more the neoclassical model with a steady-state level of per capita output. Suppose a society can choose its rate of population growth. How can this choice affect the steady-state per capita output? Could such a policy help the country avoid falling into a poverty trap?
    b. Now suppose we have an endogenous growth model. How will a lower population growth rate affect the society's long-term growth potential?
9. What elements of neoclassical and endogenous growth models can help us explain the remarkable growth of the group of countries known as the Asian Tigers?
10. Economies in transition from communist to capitalist regimes have experienced and, in some cases, are still experiencing painful, if temporary, declines in output and in living standards. What factors lie behind the declines in output? Can elements of the neoclassical or endogenous growth models help explain them?
11. Does growth in per capita output, among both more and less industrialized countries, have the potential to increase indefinitely? Explain.

Technical

(All optional)

1. Consider a two-sector model of growth, with two kinds of investment opportunities—one with a diminishing marginal product and one with a constant marginal product. (*Hint:* See Figure 4-2.)
    a. What does the production function for this problem look like?
    b. Characterize the set of equilibria for this model. Does output in any of the equilibria have nonzero per capita growth?
    c. What can this model help us explain that strict endogenous and neoclassical growth models cannot?
2. Now suppose we have a one-sector model with a variable rate of population growth. (*Hint:* See Figure 4-3.)
    a. What does the investment requirement line look like for this model?
    b. Characterize the set of equilibria, being sure to discuss their stability or lack thereof. Does output in any of these equilibria have nonzero per capita growth?
    c. Suppose your country is in a "poverty trap"—at the equilibrium with the very lowest level of output per person. What could the country do to move toward a point with higher income?

**3. Suppose you add a variable rate of population growth to a two-sector model of growth. (*Hint:* Combine Figures 4-2 and 4-3.)

    a. What do the production function, investment requirement line, and savings line look like?

    b. Characterize the set of equilibria for this model. Does output in any of the equilibria have nonzero per capita growth?

    c. Does the addition of the variable rate of population growth to this model help you explain anything that a simpler two-sector model with a fixed rate of growth, or a one-sector model with variable population growth, cannot?

*4. Consider an economy whose production function is $Y = K^{\theta}(AN)^{1-\theta}$, with $A = 4\ K/N$. Suppose that it has a savings rate of .1, a population growth rate of .02, and an average depreciation rate of .03 and that $\theta = .5$.

    a. Reduce the production function to the form $y = ak$. What is a?

    b. What are the growth rates of output and capital in this model?

    c. Interpret a. What are we really saying when we assume that the labor-augmenting technology, A, is proportional to the level of capital per worker?

    d. What makes this an endogenous growth model?

5. Consider an economy in which production is characterized by the neoclassical function $Y = K^{.5}N^{.5}$. Suppose, again, that it has a savings rate of .1, a population growth rate of .02, and an average depreciation rate of .03.

    a. Write this production function in per capita form, and find the steady-state values of k and y.

    b. At the steady-state value of K, is there more or less capital than at the golden-rule level?

    c. Determine what savings rate would yield the golden-rule level of capital in this model.

    d. In the context of this neoclassical growth model, can a country have *too much* saving?

---

*One asterisk denotes a more difficult problem. Two asterisks means the problem is *really* hard.

CHAPTER 5

Aggregate Supply and Demand

CHAPTER HIGHLIGHTS

◆ Output and prices are determined by aggregate supply and aggregate demand.

◆ The slope of the aggregate supply curve reflects the economy's price adjustment mechanism. In the short run, the aggregate supply curve is flat. In the long run, the aggregate supply curve is vertical.

◆ Changes in aggregate demand, the result of changes in fiscal and monetary policy as well as individual decisions about consumption and investment, change output in the short run and change prices in the long run.

Macroeconomics is concerned with the behavior of the economy as a whole—with booms and recessions, the economy's total output of goods and services, and the rates of inflation and unemployment. Having explored long-run economic growth in the preceding chapters, we turn to the short-run fluctuations that constitute the business cycle.

Business cycle swings are *big!* In the Great Depression, output fell by nearly 30 percent; between 1931 and 1940 the unemployment rate averaged 18.8 percent. The Great Depression was the defining event for a generation. Post-World War II recessions have been much milder, but they still dominated the political scene when they occurred.

Inflation rates vary widely. A dollar stuffed under your mattress in 1974 would have bought less than 34 cents' worth of goods in 1997. In contrast, during the Great Depression prices *dropped* by one-fourth.

The aggregate supply–aggregate demand model is the basic macroeconomic tool for studying output fluctuations and the determination of the price level and the inflation rate. We use this tool to understand why the economy deviates from a path of smooth growth over time and to explore the consequences of government policies intended to reduce unemployment, smooth output fluctuations, and maintain stable prices.

Figure 5-1 shows a supply and demand model. The *aggregate supply (AS) curve* describes, for each given price level, the quantity of output firms are willing to supply. The *AS* curve is upward-sloping as firms are willing to supply more output at higher prices. The *aggregate demand (AD) curve* shows the combinations of the price level and level of output at which the goods and money markets are simultaneously in equilibrium. The *AD* curve is downward-sloping as higher prices reduce the value of the money supply, which reduces the demand for output. The intersection of the *AD* and *AS* schedules at *E* determines the equilibrium level of output, Y_0, and the equilibrium price level, P_0. Shifts in either schedule cause the price level and the level of output to change.

Before we go deeply into the factors underlying the aggregate demand and supply curves, we show how the curves will be used. Suppose that the Fed increases the money supply. What effects will that have on the price level and on output? In particular, does

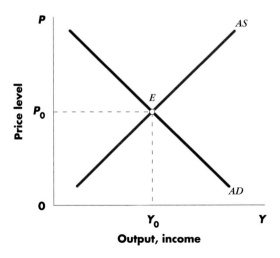

FIGURE 5-1   AGGREGATE SUPPLY AND DEMAND.

Their intersection at point E jointly determines the level of output, Y_0, and the price level, P_0.

BOX 5-1 "Aggregate Supply" and "Aggregate Demand"—What's in a Name?

Figure 5-1 has the friendly, familiar appearance that you probably remember from your study of microeconomics. What's more, the mechanical workings of the model (demand shifts up . . . prices and quantities both rise . . . etc.) are the same as the workings of a microeconomic supply and demand diagram. However, the economics underlying the aggregate supply–aggregate demand diagram is unrelated to the microeconomic version. (It's too bad that our macroeconomic version wasn't given a different name.) In particular, "price" in microeconomics means the ratio at which two goods trade: I'll give you two bags of candy in exchange for one economics lecture, for example. In contrast, in macroeconomics "price" means the nominal price level, the cost of a basket of all the goods we buy measured in money terms.

One particular item from macroeconomics provides a special opportunity for confusion. In microeconomics, supply curves are relatively more elastic in the long run than in the short run, at least as a rough rule of thumb. The behavior of aggregate supply is just the opposite. The aggregate supply curve is vertical in the long run and horizontal in the short run. (We will, of course, discuss why this is so.)

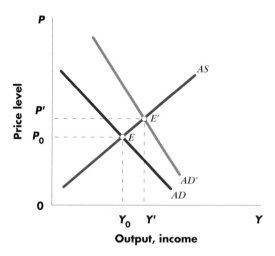

FIGURE 5-2   AN INCREASE IN THE NOMINAL MONEY STOCK SHIFTS AGGREGATE DEMAND TO THE RIGHT.

The equilibrium point moves from E to E'.

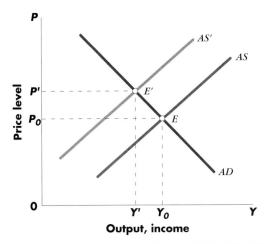

FIGURE 5-3   A LEFTWARD SHIFT OF AGGREGATE SUPPLY.

A shift to AS' moves the equilibrium point from E to E'.

an increase in the money supply cause the price level to rise, thus producing inflation? Or does the level of output rise? Or do both output and the price level rise?

Figure 5-2 shows that an increase in the money supply shifts the aggregate demand curve, *AD,* to the right, to *AD'.* We will see later in this chapter why this should be so. The shift of the aggregate demand curve moves the equilibrium of the economy from *E* to *E'.* The price level rises from P_0 to P', and the level of output from Y_0 to Y'. Thus an increase in the money stock causes both the level of output and the price level to rise. It is clear from Figure 5-2 that the amount by which the price level rises depends on the slope of the aggregate supply curve and the extent to which the aggregate demand curve shifts. Much of the text is devoted to exploring the slope of the aggregate supply curve and the causes of shifts in the aggregate demand curve.

Figure 5-3 shows the results of an adverse (upward and leftward) aggregate supply shock (the 1973 OPEC oil embargo is a classic example of such a shock). The leftward shift of the aggregate supply curve cuts output and raises prices.

5-1

THE AGGREGATE SUPPLY CURVE

The aggregate supply curve describes, for each given price level, the quantity of output firms are willing to supply. In the short run the *AS* curve is horizontal (the *Keynesian* aggregate supply curve); in the long run the *AS* curve is vertical (the *classical* aggregate supply curve). Figure 5-4 shows the two extreme cases. We begin by examining the long-run case.

THE CLASSICAL SUPPLY CURVE

The *classical aggregate supply curve* is vertical, indicating that the same amount of goods will be supplied whatever the price level. The classical supply curve is based on

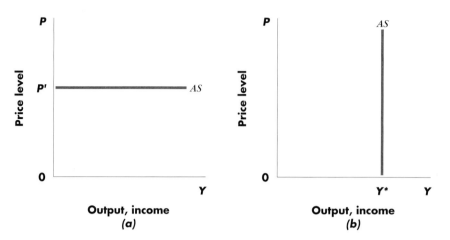

FIGURE 5-4   KEYNESIAN AND CLASSICAL AGGREGATE SUPPLY FUNCTIONS.

(a) The horizontal Keynesian AS curve implies that any amount of output will be supplied at the existing price level. (b) The vertical classical supply function is based on the assumption that there is always full employment of labor, and thus that output is always at the corresponding level, Y*.

the assumption that the labor market is in equilibrium with full employment of the labor force. We call the level of output corresponding to full employment of the labor force *potential GDP, Y**. Potential GDP grows over time as the economy accumulates resources and as technology improves, so the position of the classical aggregate supply curve moves to the right over time, as shown in Figure 5-5. In fact, the level of potential GDP in a particular year is determined largely as described by the growth theory models we have just studied.

It is important to note that while potential GDP changes each year, the changes *do not depend on the price level*. We say that potential GDP is "exogenous with respect to the price level"; what's more, changes in potential GDP over a short period are usually relatively small, a few percent a year. We can draw a single vertical line at potential GDP and call it "long-run aggregate supply" without needing to worry much about the rightward movement due to potential GDP growth.

THE KEYNESIAN AGGREGATE SUPPLY CURVE

The *Keynesian aggregate supply curve* is horizontal, indicating that firms will supply whatever amount of goods is demanded at the existing price level. The idea underlying the Keynesian aggregate supply curve is that because there is unemployment, firms can obtain as much labor as they want at the current wage. Their average costs of production therefore are assumed not to change as their output levels change. They are accordingly willing to supply as much as is demanded at the existing price level.

It is important to note that on a Keynesian aggregate supply curve, the price level *does not depend on GDP*. In most countries prices rise in most years; in other words, there is some ongoing, though perhaps small, inflation. This price increase is associated with an upward shift of the aggregate supply curve—not a shift along the curve. Rather than simply saying that the Keynesian *AS* curve is horizontal, it would be more

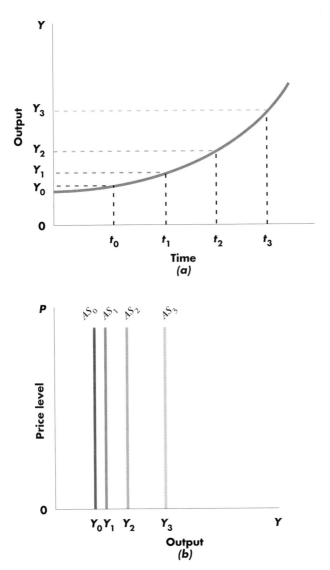

FIGURE 5-5   GROWTH OF OUTPUT OVER TIME, TRANSLATED INTO SHIFTS IN AGGREGATE SUPPLY.

accurate to say that the Keynesian *AS* curve is horizontal at the "expected" price level and that the expected price level may shift over time. We explore the consequences of this shift below. For simplicity of exposition, we assume—for the moment—that we are in an economy with no expected inflation. The key point is that in the short run the price level is unaffected by current levels of GDP.

FRICTIONAL UNEMPLOYMENT AND THE NATURAL RATE OF UNEMPLOYMENT

Taken literally, the classical model implies that there is no unemployment. In equilibrium, everyone who wants to work is working. But there is always some unemployment.

BOX 5-2 Vertical or Horizontal: Is It All a Matter of Timing?

The text describes the aggregate supply curve as vertical in the long run, horizontal in the short run, and implicitly having an intermediate slope in the midterm. This picture over-simplifies in a way that can be very important for policy. The truth is that the aggregate supply curve, even in the short run, is really a curve and not a straight line.

Figure 1 shows that at low levels of output, below potential output Y^*, the aggregate supply curve is quite flat. When output is below potential, there is very little tendency for prices of goods and factors (wages) to fall. Conversely, where output is above potential, the aggregate supply curve is steep and prices tend to rise continuously. The effects of changes in aggregate demand on output and prices therefore depend on the level of actual relative to potential output.

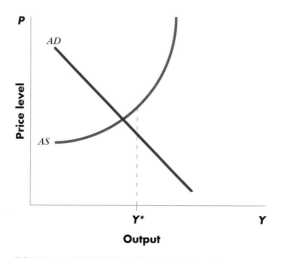

FIGURE 1   AGGREGATE DEMAND AND NONLINEAR AGGREGATE SUPPLY.

In a recession we are on the flat part of the aggregate supply curve, so demand management policies can be effective at boosting the economy without having much effect on the price level. However, as the economy approaches full employment, policy makers must be wary of too much stimulus to avoid running the aggregate demand curve up the vertical portion of the aggregate supply curve shown in the figure.

That level of unemployment is accounted for by labor market frictions, which occur be-cause the labor market is always in a state of flux. Some people are moving and chang-ing jobs; other people are looking for jobs for the first time; some firms are expanding and hiring new workers; others have lost business and have to reduce employment by firing workers.

Because it takes time for an individual to find the right new job, there will always be some *frictional unemployment* as people search for jobs. Frictional unemployment is the unemployment that exists as a result of individuals' shifting between jobs and looking for new jobs.

There is some amount of frictional unemployment associated with the full-employment level of employment and the corresponding full-employment (or potential) level of output, Y^*. That amount of unemployment is called the *natural rate*. The *natural rate of unemployment* is the rate of unemployment arising from normal labor market frictions that exist when the labor market is in equilibrium. Current estimates are that the natural rate in the United States is about 5.5 percent.

5-2

THE AGGREGATE DEMAND CURVE

The aggregate demand curve shows the combinations of the price level and level of output at which the goods and money markets are simultaneously in equilibrium. Expansionary policies—such as increases in government spending, cuts in taxes, and increases in the money supply—move the aggregate demand curve to the right. Consumer and investor confidence also affects the aggregate demand curve. When confidence increases, the *AD* curve moves to the right. When confidence drops, the *AD* curve moves to the left.

The aggregate demand relation between output and prices is quite sophisticated. Indeed, Chapters 9, 10, and 11 are devoted to developing the *IS-LM* model, which is the underpinning of aggregate demand. Here we give a brief introduction.

The key to the aggregate demand relation between output and prices is that aggregate demand depends on the *real money supply*. The real money supply is the *value* of the money provided by the central bank (the Federal Reserve in the United States) and the banking system. If we write the number of dollars in the money supply (the *nominal money supply*) as $\overline{M}$ and the price level as P, we can write the real money supply as $\overline{M}/P$. When $\overline{M}/P$ rises, interest rates fall and investment rises, leading overall aggregate demand to rise. Analogously, lowering $\overline{M}/P$ lowers investment and overall aggregate demand.

For a given level of the nominal money supply, $\overline{M}$, high prices mean a low real money supply, $\overline{M}/P$. Quite simply, high prices mean that the value of the number of available dollars is low. As a result, a high price level means a low level of aggregate demand, and a low price level means a high level of aggregate demand. Thus the aggregate demand curve in Figure 5-1 slopes down.

More formally, we can express the aggregate demand curve algebraically as

$$Y = \gamma \overline{A} + \beta \frac{\overline{M}}{P} \tag{1}$$

where $\overline{A}$ represents the state of fiscal policy and consumer confidence. Increases in $\overline{A}$ or $\overline{M}$ shift the aggregate demand curve to the right. Increases in P are movements *along*

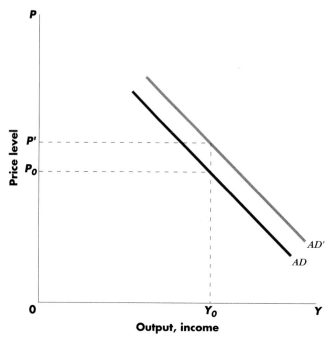

FIGURE 5-6   AN INCREASE IN THE MONEY SUPPLY SHIFTS AGGREGATE DEMAND UPWARD.

A 10 percent increase in the money supply shifts AD up by 10 percent.

the aggregate demand curve, with higher P corresponding to movements up and to the left along the AD curve in Figure 5-1.[1]

It is important for what follows to see that *an increase in the nominal money stock shifts the AD schedule up exactly in proportion to the increase in nominal money.* Why? Look at Figure 5-6 and at equation (1). Suppose that $\overline{M}_0$ leads to the AD curve shown in the figure and that the value P_0 corresponds to output Y_0. Now suppose $\overline{M}$ increases 10 percent to $\overline{M}'$ (= $1.1 \times \overline{M}$). This shifts the aggregate demand curve up and to the right to AD'. The value of P corresponding to Y_0 must be exactly P' (= $1.1 \times P_0$). At this value of P, the new *real* money supply equals the old real money supply ($\overline{M}'/P'$ = $(1.1 \times \overline{M}_0)/(1.1 \times P_0) = \overline{M}_0/P_0$). The right-hand side of equation (1) is unchanged, so Y, the left-hand side, must also be unchanged.

5-3

FISCAL AND MONETARY POLICY UNDER

ALTERNATIVE SUPPLY ASSUMPTIONS

In Figure 5-1 we showed how the aggregate supply and demand curves together determine the equilibrium level of income and prices in the economy. Now we use the aggregate demand and supply model to study the effects of monetary and fiscal policy in the two extreme supply cases—Keynesian and classical.

---

[1]Note that, strictly speaking, the aggregate demand curve should be drawn as a hyperbola and not a straight line. We show it as a straight line for convenience.

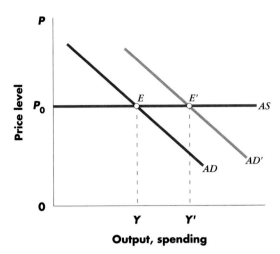

FIGURE 5-7   FISCAL EXPANSION: THE KEYNESIAN CASE.

Given perfectly elastic supply, a fiscal expansion, shifting AD to the right, will increase output but leave the equilibrium price level unchanged.

THE KEYNESIAN CASE

In Figure 5-7 we combine the aggregate demand schedule with the Keynesian aggregate supply schedule. The initial equilibrium is at point E, where AS and AD intersect. At that point the goods and assets markets are in equilibrium.

Consider now a fiscal expansion. Increased government spending, or a cut in tax rates, shifts the AD schedule out and to the right, from AD to AD'. The new equilibrium is at point E', where output has increased. Because firms are willing to supply *any* amount of output at the level of prices P_0, there is no effect on prices. The only effect of higher government spending in Figure 5-7 is an increase in output and employment.

In the Keynesian case, an increase in the nominal quantity of money likewise leads to an expansion in equilibrium output. With a horizontal AS schedule there is again no impact on prices.

THE CLASSICAL CASE: FISCAL POLICY

In the classical case, the aggregate supply schedule is vertical at the full-employment level of output. Firms will supply the level of output Y^* whatever the price level. Under this supply assumption we obtain results very different from those reached using the Keynesian model. Now the price level is not given but, rather, depends on the interaction of supply and demand.

In Figure 5-8 we study the effect of a fiscal expansion under classical supply assumptions. The aggregate supply schedule is AS, with equilibrium initially at point E. Note that at point E there is full employment because, by assumption, firms supply the full-employment level of output at any level of prices.

The fiscal expansion shifts the aggregate demand schedule from AD to AD'. At the initial level of prices, P_0, spending in the economy would rise to point E'. At price level P_0 the demand for goods has risen. But firms cannot obtain the labor to produce

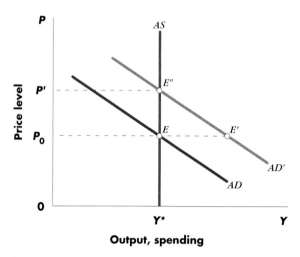

FIGURE 5-8   FISCAL EXPANSION: THE CLASSICAL CASE.

Given perfectly inelastic supply, a fiscal expansion shifts AD to the right, resulting in an increase in the price level but no change in output.

more output, and output supply cannot respond to the increased demand. As firms try to hire more workers, they bid up wages and their costs of production, so they must charge higher prices for their output. The increase in the demand for goods therefore leads only to higher prices, and not to higher output.

The increase in prices reduces the real money stock and leads to a reduction in spending. The economy moves up the AD' schedule until prices have risen enough, and the real money stock has fallen enough, to reduce spending to a level consistent with full-employment output. That is the case at price level P'. At point E'' aggregate demand, at the higher level of government spending, is once again equal to aggregate supply.

CROWDING OUT

Note what has happened in Figure 5-8: Output is unchanged at the full-employment level, $Y*$, but government spending is higher. That must mean the private sector is spending less—its spending must have fallen by precisely the amount that government spending has risen. There is thus *full,* or complete, *crowding out. Crowding out occurs when an increase in government spending results in less spending by the private sector.* With a classical supply curve, every dollar increase in real government spending is offset by a dollar reduction in private spending, so crowding out is complete.

MONETARY EXPANSION UNDER CLASSICAL CONDITIONS

Under Keynesian supply conditions, with prices given, a rise in the nominal money stock means a rise in the real money stock—so output rises. Consider, by contrast, the adjustments that occur in response to a monetary expansion when the aggregate supply curve is vertical and the price level is no longer fixed.

In Figure 5-9 we study an expansion in the nominal money stock under classical supply conditions. The initial full-employment equilibrium is at point E, where the AD

BOX 5-3 Keynesian and Classical— Short Run and Long

We have repeatedly used the terms "Keynesian" and "classical" to describe assumptions of a horizontal or vertical aggregate supply curve. Note that these are *not* alternative models providing alternative descriptions of the world. Both models are true: the Keynesian model holds in the short run, and the classical model holds in the long run. Economists do have contentious disagreements over the time horizons in which either model applies. Almost all economists (*almost* all) agree that the Keynesian model holds over a period of a few months or less and the classical model holds when the time frame is a decade or more. Unfortunately, the interesting time frame for policy relevance is several quarters to a few years. The speed with which prices adjust—that is, how long it takes the aggregate supply curve to rotate from horizontal to vertical—is an area of active research.

and *AS* schedules intersect. Now the nominal money stock is increased, and accordingly, the aggregate demand schedule shifts up and to the right to AD'. If prices were fixed, the economy would move to E', the Keynesian equilibrium. But now output is in fixed supply. The increase in aggregate demand leads to an excess demand for goods. Firms that attempt to expand hire more workers, thereby bidding up wages and costs. Prices increase in response, which means the real money stock falls back toward its initial level. In fact, prices keep rising until the excess demand for goods disappears. Thus they must increase until the economy reaches

FIGURE 5-9   MONETARY EXPANSION: THE CLASSICAL CASE.

point E'', where AS intersects the new aggregate demand schedule, AD'. Only when aggregate demand is again equal to full-employment supply does the goods market clear and the pressure for prices to rise disappear.

Consider now the adjustment that takes place in moving from E to E''. There is no change in output, only a change in the price level. We know from the previous section that expansion of the nominal money stock causes the aggregate demand curve to move upward in proportion to the increase in money. Thus at point E'' the real money stock, $\overline{M}/P$, is back to its initial level. At E'' both nominal money and the price level have changed in the same proportion, leaving real money and hence aggregate demand unchanged. We thus have an important implication of the classical model: Under classical supply conditions, an increase in nominal money raises the price level in the same proportion but leaves real output unchanged.

Ongoing Money Growth and Inflation

Figure 5-9 shows that an increase in the money supply leads to an eventual increase in the price level. What happens if the money supply grows, say, 10 percent a year? Every year the AD curve in Figure 5-9 would move up another 10 percent and the intersection of the aggregate demand and classical aggregate supply curves would move up 10 percent. In the long run, prices would rise 10 percent annually, so we would see ongoing 10 percent money growth leading to 10 percent annual inflation.[2]

THE NEUTRALITY OF MONEY

Money is *neutral* when changes in the money stock lead only to changes in the price level, with no real variables (output, employment, and interest rates) changing.

We saw above that the classical supply curve has the powerful and important implication that fiscal policy cannot affect output. The neutrality of money likewise has strong policy implications. For instance, if money were neutral, there would be an easy way to reduce the inflation rate if we ever wanted to do that. All we would have to do would be reduce the rate at which the money stock is growing.

In practice, it is very difficult to change the inflation rate without producing a recession, as in the 1979–1983 period in the United States. When a lower growth rate of money leads first to unemployment, and only later to lower inflation, as it did in the recession in 1982, we know that money is not neutral. Changes in the quantity of money have real effects; monetary policy affects the level of output. This means that the aggregate supply curve cannot be vertical in the short run.

5-4

SUPPLY-SIDE ECONOMICS

All economists are in favor of policies which move the aggregate supply curve to the right by increasing potential GDP. Such supply-side policies as removing unnecessary

---

[2]Well, approximately. We know from growth theory that the aggregate supply curve moves rightward 2 or 3 percent a year. This partially offsets money growth. You can think of increased potential GDP as "absorbing" some part of the extra money. So inflation would be a little bit less than the 10 percent money growth.

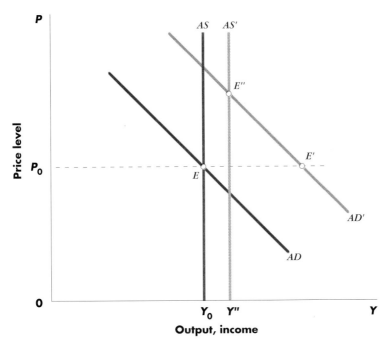

FIGURE 5-10   EFFECTS OF CUTTING TAX RATES ON AGGREGATE DEMAND AND SUPPLY.

regulation, maintaining an efficient legal system, and encouraging technological progress are all desirable, although not always easy to implement. However, there is a group of politicians and pundits who use the term "supply-side economics" in reference to the idea that cutting tax rates will increase aggregate supply enormously—so much, in fact, that tax collections will rise, rather than fall. Even political allies (George Bush before he was president, for instance) of the supply-siders refer to this notion as "voodoo economics." We use the aggregate supply–aggregate demand diagram in Figure 5-10 to show what happens when tax rates are cut.

Cutting tax rates has effects on both aggregate supply and aggregate demand. The aggregate demand curve shifts right from AD to AD'. The shift is relatively large. The aggregate supply curve also shifts to the right, from AS to AS', because lower tax rates increase the incentive to work. However, economists have known for a very long time that the effect of such an incentive is quite small, so the rightward shift of potential GDP is small. The large shift in aggregate demand and small shift in aggregate supply are illustrated in Figure 5-10.

What should we expect to see? In the short run, the economy moves from E to E'. GDP does rise substantially. As a result, total tax revenues fall proportionately less than the fall in the tax rate.[3] However, this is purely an aggregate demand effect. In the long run, the economy moves to E''. GDP is higher but only by a very small amount.

---

[3] In principle, GDP *might* even rise so much that tax collections rise. In practice, it appears that the effect is not this strong.

As a result, total tax collections fall and the deficit rises. In addition, prices are permanently higher.

The United States experimented with supply side economics in the 1981 1983 tax cuts. The results were just as predicted.

Not *all* supply-side policies are silly. In fact, *only* supply-side policies can permanently increase output. Important as they are, demand management policies are useful only for short-term results. For this reason, many economists strongly favor supply-side policies—they just don't believe in the magic of cutting tax rates. Many conservative economists favor cutting tax rates for the small, but real, incentive effect. However, these economists also believe in cutting government spending at the same time. Tax collections would fall, but so would government spending, so the effect on the deficit would be nearly neutral.

SUMMARY

1. The aggregate supply and demand model is used to show the determination of the equilibrium levels of *both* output and prices.
2. The aggregate supply schedule, *AS,* shows at each level of prices the quantity of real output firms are willing to supply.
3. The Keynesian supply schedule is horizontal, implying that firms supply as many goods as are demanded at the existing price level. The classical supply schedule is vertical. It would apply in an economy that has full price and wage flexibility. In such a frictionless economy, employment and output are always at the full-employment level.
4. The aggregate demand schedule, *AD,* shows at each price level the level of output at which the goods and assets markets are in equilibrium. This is the quantity of output demanded at each price level. Along the *AD* schedule fiscal policy is given, as is the nominal quantity of money. The *AD* schedule is derived using the *IS-LM* model.
5. Moving down and along the *AD* schedule, lower prices raise the real value of the money stock. Equilibrium interest rates fall, and that increases aggregate demand and equilibrium spending.
6. A fiscal expansion shifts the *AD* schedule outward and to the right. An increase in the nominal money stock shifts the *AD* curve up by the same proportion as the money stock increases.
7. Under Keynesian supply conditions, with prices fixed, both monetary and fiscal expansion raise equilibrium output. A monetary expansion lowers interest rates, while a fiscal expansion raises them.
8. Under classical supply conditions, a fiscal expansion has no effect on output. But a fiscal expansion raises prices, lowers real balances, and increases equilibrium interest rates. That is, under classical supply conditions there is full crowding out. Private spending declines by exactly the increase in government demand.
9. A monetary expansion, under classical supply conditions, raises prices in the same proportion as the rise in nominal money. All real variables—specifically, output and interest rates—remain unchanged. When changes in the money stock have no real effects, money is said to be neutral.
10. Supply-side economics makes the claim that reducing tax rates generates very large increases in aggregate supply. In truth, tax cuts produce very small increases in aggregate supply and relatively large increases in aggregate demand.

KEY TERMS

aggregate supply (AS) curve

aggregate demand (AD) curve

classical aggregate supply curve

Keynesian aggregate supply curve

frictional unemployment

natural rate of unemployment

real money supply

nominal money supply

full crowding out

neutrality of money

PROBLEMS

Conceptual

1. What do the aggregate supply and aggregate demand curves describe?
2. Explain why the classical supply curve is vertical. What are the mechanisms that ensure continued full employment of labor in the classical case?
3. What relationship is captured by the aggregate supply curve? Can you provide an intuitive justification for it?
4. How does the Keynesian aggregate supply curve differ from the classical one? Is one of these specifications more appropriate than the other? Explain, being careful to state the time horizon to which your answer applies.
5. The aggregate supply and demand model looks, and sounds, very similar to the standard supply and demand model of microeconomics. How, if at all, are these models related?
6. When is money neutral?

Technical

1. When the goods market is in equilibrium in a closed economy, $S + TA - TR = I + G$. Using this fact, explain why, in the classical case, a fiscal expansion must lead to full crowding out.
2. **a.** If the government were to reduce income taxes, how would the reduction affect output and the price level in the short run? In the long run? Show how the aggregate supply and demand curves would be affected, in both cases.

   b. What is supply-side economics? Is it likely to be effective, given your answer to part (a)?
3. Suppose that the government increases spending from G to G' while simultaneously raising taxes in such a way that, at the initial level of output, the budget remains balanced.

   a. Show the effect of this change on the aggregate demand schedule.

   b. How does this affect output and the price level in the Keynesian case?

   c. How does this affect output and the price level in the classical case?

CHAPTER 6

Aggregate Supply: Wages, Prices, and Unemployment

CHAPTER HIGHLIGHTS

◆ The aggregate supply curve describes the price adjustment mechanism of the economy.

◆ The Phillips curve links inflation and unemployment. The aggregate supply curve links prices and output. The Phillips curve and aggregate supply curve are alternative ways of looking at the same phenomena.

◆ According to the modern Phillips curve, inflation depends on expectations of inflation, as well as unemployment.

In this chapter we further develop the aggregate supply side of the economy. *The aggregate supply curve describes the price adjustment mechanism of the economy.* In the very short run, we know the aggregate supply curve is horizontal; and in the long run, we know the aggregate supply curve is vertical. In this chapter we examine the dynamic adjustment process which carries us from the short run to the long run.

We begin with an examination of the mechanics of the aggregate supply curve. We then look at some of the economics that underlie the mechanics. The price-output relation along the aggregate supply curve is built up from the links among wages, prices, employment, and output. The link between unemployment and inflation is called the *Phillips curve.* We translate between unemployment and output and also translate between inflation and price changes. These translations allow us to use the Phillips curve and the aggregate supply curve as alternative ways to picture the economy's price adjustment mechanism. We also use the aggregate supply curve to study how the economy adjusts to *supply shocks* such as the sudden, sharp increases in oil prices in 1973–1974, in 1979–1980, and, briefly, following the Iraqi invasion of Kuwait in 1990. Finally, we add the role of *price expectations* into the aggregate supply curve. Understanding the price expectations mechanism provides the explanation of *stagflation*—the simultaneous presence of high unemployment and high inflation.

Before we get down to business, some words of warning, and some of encouragement: The warning is that the theory of aggregate supply is one of the least settled areas in macroeconomics. We do not fully understand why wages and prices are slow to adjust, although we do have a number of reasonable theories. In practice the labor market seems to adjust slowly to changes in aggregate demand, the unemployment rate is clearly not always at the natural level, and output does change when aggregate demand changes. The words of encouragement are that although there is a variety of models of aggregate supply, the basic phenomenon that has to be explained—the apparent slow adjustment of output to changes in demand—is widely agreed upon. All modern models, however different their starting points, tend to reach a similar result: that in the short run the aggregate supply curve is flat, but in the long run it is vertical.

6-1

THE AGGREGATE SUPPLY CURVE AND
THE PRICE ADJUSTMENT MECHANISM

Figure 6-1a shows the flat short-run aggregate supply curve in green and the vertical long-run curve in orange. It also illustrates an entire spectrum of intermediate-run curves. Think of the aggregate supply curve as rotating, counterclockwise, from horizontal to vertical with the passage of time. The aggregate supply curve which applies at, say, a 1-year horizon is light blue and medium-sloped. If aggregate demand is greater than potential output, Y^*, then this intermediate curve indicates that after a year's time prices will have risen enough to partially, but not completely, push GDP back down to potential output.

Figure 6-1a gives a useful, but static, picture of what is really a dynamic process. We focus on the aggregate supply curve as a description of the mechanism by which prices rise or fall over time. Equation (1) gives the aggregate supply curve

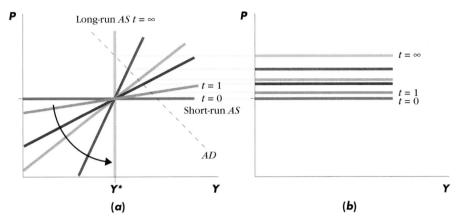

FIGURE 6-1   THE DYNAMIC RETURN TO LONG-RUN AGGREGATE SUPPLY.

$$P_{t+1} = P_t[1 + \lambda(Y - Y^*)] \tag{1}$$

where P_{t+1} is the price level next period, P_t is the price level today, and Y^* is potential output. Equation (1) embodies a very simple idea: If output is above potential output, prices will rise and be higher next period; if prices are below potential output, prices will fall and be lower next period.[1] What's more, prices will continue to rise or fall over time until output returns to potential output. Tomorrow's price level equals today's price level if, and only if, output equals potential output.[2]

The upward-shifting horizontal lines in Figure 6-1b correspond to successive snapshots of equation (1). We start with the horizontal green line at time $t = 0$. If output is above potential, then the price will be higher—that is, the aggregate supply curve will move up—by time $t = 1$, as shown by the light blue line. According to equation (1), and as shown in Figure 6-1b, the price keeps moving up until output is no longer above potential output.

---

[1]Sometimes equation (1) is written to show P_t adjusting from P_{t-1} rather than P_{t+1} adjusting from P_t. This alternative puts a little slope in even the shortest-run AS curve, where our version has the shortest-run curve horizontal. Nothing substantive rests on the difference.

[2]For the moment, we leave out the very important role of price expectations. If you look ahead to the last section of the chapter, you will see that including price expectations in the aggregate supply curve is necessary to explain inflation when the economy is at $Y = Y^*$.

Box 6-1 Aggregate Supply Lines and Curves

Both equation (1) and Figure 6-1 portray the aggregate supply curve as a straight line. You will remember from Chapter 5 that this isn't entirely correct: when output is well above potential, aggregate supply curves up more sharply. You can think of this curvature as λ becoming higher if the economy is in a very large boom.

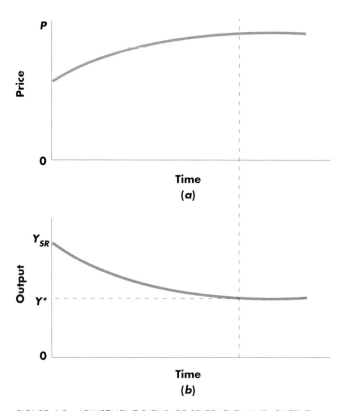

FIGURE 6-2   ADJUSTMENT PATHS OF PRICE LEVEL AND OUTPUT.

Note that panels (*a*) and (*b*) of Figure 6-1 are alternative descriptions of the same process. Panel (*a*) illustrates the dynamics of price movements. Panel (*b*) shows snapshots after a given amount of time has elapsed. For example, the light blue schedule shows the cumulative effect of price movements after perhaps a year's time. Figure 6-2 presents another way of looking at the adjustment process: plotting the equilibrium points from Figure 6-1 against elapsed time.

The *speed of price adjustment* is controlled by the parameter λ in equation (1). If λ is large, the aggregate supply curve moves quickly, or, equivalently, the counterclockwise rotation in Figure 6-1*a* occurs over a relatively short time period. If λ is small, prices adjust only very slowly. Quite a bit of the disagreement among economists about the best course for macroeconomic policy centers on λ. If λ is large, the aggregate supply mechanism will return the economy to potential output relatively quickly; if λ is small, we might want to use aggregate demand policy to speed up the process.

RECAP

We summarize the description of the aggregate supply schedule:

- The aggregate supply schedule is flatter the smaller the impact of output and employment changes on current prices. If prices respond very little to changes in unemployment, the *AS* schedule in Figure 6-1 will be very flat. The coefficient λ in equation (1) captures this output–price-change linkage.

• The position of the short-run *AS* schedule depends on the level of prices. The schedule passes through the full-employment level of output, Y^*, at $P_{t+1} = P_t$. At higher output levels there is overemployment, and hence prices next period will be higher than those this period. Conversely, when unemployment is high, prices next period will be lower than those this period.

• The short-run *AS* schedule shifts over time. If output is maintained above the full-employment level, Y^*, prices will continue to rise over time.

6-2

WAGES, PRICES, AND OUTPUT: THE FACTS

The classical model of macroeconomics holds that the economy is *always* at full employment. Any unemployment that is observed is purely frictional—workers moving from one job to another. Moreover, because there is no unemployment in the model, there can also be no relation between the state of the labor market and the behavior of wages: wages are determined by productivity and the impact of money on prices, not at all by unemployment.

But the economy is not always at full employment. Two major facts about the labor market need to be placed at the center of a realistic macroeconomic model. First, the rate of unemployment fluctuates far more than is consistent with the view that all unemployment is frictional. Figure 6-3 shows the unemployment rate for the period since 1959. It cannot be that the 10.8 percent unemployment rate at the end of 1982 was equal to the natural rate, much less that the 25 percent unemployment rate in 1933, in the depths of the Great Depression, can have been equal to the natural rate. Thus it cannot be that the labor market is always in equilibrium at the full-employment level of employment.

The second fact that is inconsistent with the classical theory is that there appears to be a systematic relationship between the rate of change of wages and unemployment.

THE PHILLIPS CURVE

In 1958 A. W. Phillips, then a professor at the London School of Economics, published a comprehensive study of wage behavior in the United Kingdom for the years 1861–1957.[3] The main finding is summarized in Figure 6-4, reproduced from his article: The *Phillips curve* is an inverse relationship between the rate of unemployment and the rate of increase in money wages. The higher the rate of unemployment, the lower the rate of wage inflation. In other words, there is a tradeoff between wage inflation and unemployment.

---

[3]A. W. Phillips, "The Relation between Unemployment and the Rate of Change of Money Wages in the United Kingdom, 1861–1957," *Economica*, November 1958.

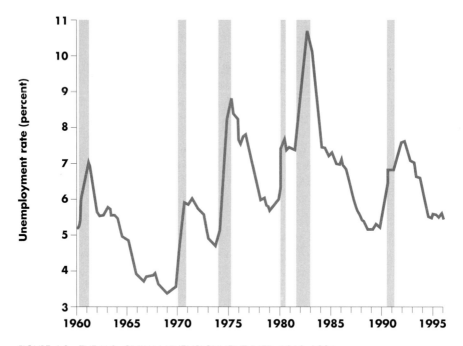

FIGURE 6-3   THE U.S. CIVILIAN UNEMPLOYMENT RATE, 1960–1996.

(Source: DRI/McGraw-Hill Macroeconomic Database.)

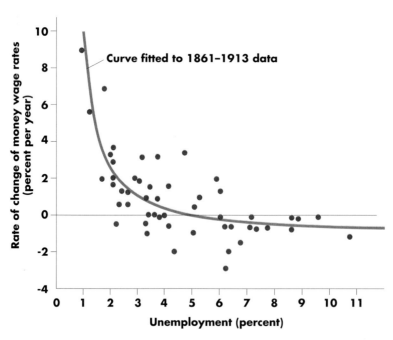

FIGURE 6-4   THE ORIGINAL PHILLIPS CURVE FOR THE UNITED KINGDOM.

(Source: A. W. Phillips, "The Relation between Unemployment and the Rate of Change of Money Wages in the United Kingdom, 1861–1957," Economica, *November 1958.)*

The Phillips curve shows that the rate of wage inflation decreases with the unemployment rate. Letting W_t be the wage this period, and W_{t+1} the wage next period, the rate of wage inflation, g_w, is defined as

$$g_w = \frac{W_{t+1} - W_t}{W_t} \tag{2}$$

With u^* representing the natural rate of unemployment,[4] we can write the simple Phillips curve as

$$g_w = -\epsilon(u - u^*) \tag{3}$$

where ϵ measures the responsiveness of wages to unemployment. This equation states that wages are falling when the unemployment rate exceeds the natural rate, that is, when $u > u^*$, and rising when unemployment is below the natural rate.

The Phillips curve implies that wages and prices adjust slowly to changes in aggregate demand. Why? Suppose the economy is in equilibrium with prices stable and unemployment at the natural rate. Now there is an increase in the money stock of, say, 10 percent. Prices and wages both have to rise by 10 percent for the economy to get back to equilibrium. But the Phillips curve shows that for wages to rise by an extra 10 percent, the unemployment rate will have to fall. That will cause the rate of wage increase to go up. Wages will start rising, prices too will rise, and eventually the economy will return to the full-employment level of output and unemployment. This point can be readily seen by rewriting equation (2), using the definition of the rate of wage inflation, in order to look at the level of wages today relative to the past level:

$$W_{t+1} = W_t[1 - \epsilon(u - u^*)] \tag{3a}$$

For wages to rise above their previous level, unemployment must fall below the natural rate.

Although Phillips's own curve relates the rate of increase of wages or wage inflation to unemployment, as in equation (3) above, the term "Phillips curve" gradually came to be used to describe either the original Phillips curve *or* a curve relating the rate of increase of *prices*—the rate of inflation—to the unemployment rate. Figure 6-5 shows inflation and unemployment data for the United States during the 1960s that appear entirely consistent with the Phillips curve.

THE POLICY TRADEOFF

The Phillips curve rapidly became a cornerstone of macroeconomic policy analysis. It suggested that policy makers could choose different combinations of unemployment and inflation rates. For instance, they could have low unemployment as long as they put up with high inflation—say, the situation in the late 1960s in Figure 6-5. Or they could maintain low inflation by having high unemployment, as in the early 1960s.

You already know that the idea of a permanent unemployment-inflation tradeoff must be wrong because you know that the long-run aggregate supply curve is vertical. The piece of the puzzle that is missing in the simple Phillips curve is the role of price

[4](1) You will see below that there is a close connection between the natural rate of unemployment, u^*, and potential output, Y^*. (2) Many economists prefer the term "NAIRU" ("Nonaccelerating Inflation Rate of Unemployment") to the term "natural rate."

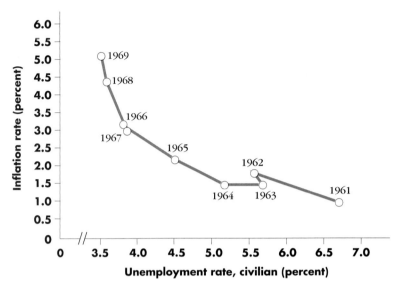

FIGURE 6-5   RELATIONSHIP OF INFLATION AND UNEMPLOYMENT: UNITED STATES, 1961–1969.
(Source: DRI/McGraw-Hill.)

expectations. We will examine this critical element below, but first we explore why wages do not adjust instantaneously and how to translate between the Phillips curve and the aggregate supply curve.

6-3

THE WAGE-UNEMPLOYMENT RELATIONSHIP: WHY ARE WAGES STICKY?

In the neoclassical theory of supply, wages adjust instantly to ensure that output is always at the full-employment level. But output is not always at the full-employment level, and the Phillips curve suggests that wages adjust slowly in response to changes in unemployment. The key question in the theory of aggregate supply is why the nominal wage adjusts slowly to shifts in demand, or why wages are *sticky*. Wages are sticky, or wage adjustment is sluggish, when wages move slowly over time, rather than being fully and immediately flexible, so as to ensure full employment at every point in time.

To clarify the assumptions that we make about wage stickiness, we translate the Phillips curve in equation (3) into a relationship between the rate of change of wages, g_w, and the level of employment. We denote the full-employment level of employment by N^* and the actual level of employment by N. We then define the unemployment rate as the fraction of the full-employment labor force, N^*, that is not employed:[5]

---

[5]Equation (4) implies that the unemployment rate is zero at full employment, when $N = N^*$. In fact, there is positive frictional unemployment even when the economy is at full employment. We are implicitly defining the unemployment rate in equation (4) relative to the natural rate of unemployment. You might wish to mentally substitute $u - u^* = \dfrac{N^* - N}{N^*}$ for equation (4).

$$u = \frac{N^* - N}{N^*} \tag{4}$$

Substituting equation (4) into (3), we obtain the Phillips curve relationship between the level of employment and the rate of change in wages:

$$g_w = \frac{W_{t+1} - W_t}{W_t} = -\epsilon\left(\frac{N^* - N}{N^*}\right) \tag{3b}$$

or, rewriting the equation, we show the Phillips curve as a relationship between the wage this period, the wage last period, and the actual level of employment:

$$W_{t+1} = W_t\left[1 + -\epsilon\left(\frac{N^* - N}{N^*}\right)\right] \tag{5}$$

Equation (5), the wage-employment relation, *WN,* is illustrated in Figure 6-6. The wage next period (say, next quarter) is equal to the wage that prevailed this period but with an adjustment for the level of employment. At full employment ($N = N^*$), next period's wage is equal to this period's. If employment is above the full-employment level, the wage next period increases above this period's wage. If employment is below the full-employment level, the wage next period falls below this period's wage. The extent to which the wage responds to employment depends on the parameter ϵ. If ϵ is large, unemployment has large effects on the wage and the *WN* line is steep.

The Phillips curve relationship in equation (5) also implies that the *WN* relationship shifts over time, as shown in Figure 6-6. If there is overemployment this period, the *WN* curve will shift upward next period to *WN'*. If there is less than full employment this period, the *WN* curve will shift downward next period to *WN"*. Thus, changes in aggregate demand that alter the rate of unemployment this period will have effects on wages in subsequent periods. The adjustment to a change in employment is dynamic; that is, it takes place over time.

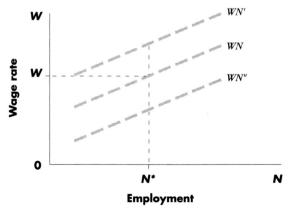

FIGURE 6-6 THE WAGE-EMPLOYMENT RELATION.

WAGE STICKINESS

Although there are different approaches to macroeconomics, each school of thought has had to try to explain why there is a Phillips curve or, equivalently, the reasons for wage stickiness. The explanations are not mutually exclusive, and we shall therefore briefly mention several of the leading approaches.

Imperfect Information—Market Clearing

Some economists have sought to explain the Phillips curve in a context in which markets clear: wages are fully flexible but adjust slowly because expectations are temporarily wrong. In the 1960s, Milton Friedman and Edmund Phelps developed models in which, when nominal wages go up because prices have risen, workers mistakenly believe their real wage has risen and so are willing to work more.[6] Thus, in the short run, until workers realize that the higher nominal wage is merely a result of a higher price level, an increase in the nominal wage is associated with a higher level of output and less unemployment. In these models, the slow adjustment of wages arises from workers' slow reactions to or *imperfect information* about changes in prices.

This explanation was put in an explicit *rational expectations* context by Robert Lucas. In the Lucas model (developed in Chapter 8), workers do not know the current price level at the time they have to decide whether to work at the going nominal wage.[7] When the wage they are paid rises, they realize it may have risen either because the overall price level has increased *or* because the wage for their type of labor has risen. If the cause of the wage increase is a higher price level, then their real wage has not changed, and they should not increase the amount of work they offer. But if the wage for their type of labor has risen, then the real wage is up, and they should work more. Since the workers cannot know the cause of the increase when they have to decide whether to work more or not, they compromise, working a bit more but not as much more as they would if they were *sure* the real wage had risen. In this way, Lucas develops a short-run tradeoff between higher wages and higher employment that depends on workers' being imperfectly informed.

Coordination Problems

The *coordination approach* to the Phillips curve focuses more on the process by which firms adjust their prices when demand changes than on wages.[8] Suppose that there is an increase in the money stock. Ultimately, as we know from Chapter 5, prices will go up in the same proportion as the money supply, and output will be unchanged. But if any one firm raises its price in proportion to the increase in the money stock, and no other firm does, then the single firm that has raised its price will lose business to the others. Of course, if all firms raised their prices in the same proportion, they would move immediately to the new equilibrium. But because the firms in an economy can-

---

[6]Milton Friedman, "The Role of Monetary Policy," *American Economic Review,* March 1968; Edmund S. Phelps, "Phillips Curves, Expectations of Inflation, and Optimal Unemployment over Time," *Economica,* August 1967. See also Edmund Phelps, "A Review of Unemployment," *Journal of Economic Literature,* September 1992.

[7]Robert E. Lucas, "Some International Evidence on Output-Inflation Tradeoffs," *American Economic Review,* June 1973.

[8]See the papers under the heading "Coordination Failures" in N. Gregory Mankiw and David Romer (eds.), *New Keynesian Economics,* vol. 2 (Cambridge, Mass.: M.I.T. Press, 1991).

not get together to coordinate their price increases, each will raise prices slowly as the effects of the change in the money stock are felt through an increased demand for goods at the existing prices.

Coordination problems can also help explain why wages are sticky downward, that is, why they do not fall immediately when aggregate demand declines. Any firm cutting its wages while other firms do not will find its workers both annoyed and leaving the firm. If firms coordinated, they could all reduce wages together; but since they generally cannot coordinate, wages go down slowly as individual firms cut the nominal wages of their employees, probably with those firms whose profits have been hardest hit moving first.[9]

Efficiency Wages and Costs of Price Change

Efficiency wage theory focuses on the wage as a means of motivating labor. The amount of effort workers make on the job is related to how well the job pays relative to alternatives. Firms may want to pay wages above the market-clearing wage to ensure that employees work hard to avoid losing their good jobs.

Efficiency wage theory offers an explanation for slow changes in real wages but by itself does not explain why the average *nominal* wage is slow to change, although it does help explain the existence of unemployment. However, taken in combination with the fact that there are costs of changing prices, efficiency wage theory can generate some stickiness in nominal wages even if the costs of resetting prices are quite small.[10] Combining that stickiness with problems of coordinating, this theory can help account for nominal wage stickiness.

CONTRACTS AND LONG-TERM RELATIONSHIPS

In developing the explanation of wage stickiness, we build on the above theories and on one central element—the fact that the labor market involves long-term relations between firms and workers. Most members of the labor force expect to continue in their current job for some time. Working conditions, including the wage, are renegotiated periodically, but not frequently, because it is costly to negotiate frequently. Even in cases where the wage is supposed to be set by market conditions, obtaining the information needed about alternative wages is costly. Typically, firms and workers reconsider wages and adjust them no more than once a year.[11]

---

[9]A very similar explanation for downward wage rigidity was presented by Keynes in his *General Theory* (New York: Macmillan, 1936). Some recent work suggests that wage cutting has become more common in the United States in recent years. See, for instance, Alan S. Blinder and Don H. Choi, "A Shred of Evidence on Theories of Wage Stickiness," *Quarterly Journal of Economics,* November 1990.

[10]See George A. Akerlof and Janet L. Yellen, "A Near-Rational Model of the Business Cycle, with Wage and Price Inertia," *Quarterly Journal of Economics,* Supplement, 1985, and, edited by the same authors, *Efficiency Wage Models of the Labor Market* (New York: Cambridge University Press, 1986). See, too, the papers on "Costly Price Adjustment" in N. Gregory Mankiw and David Romer (eds.), *New Keynesian Economics,* vol. 1 (Cambridge, Mass.: M.I.T. Press, 1991), and the discussion in Richard Layard, Stephen Nickell, and Richard Jackman, *Unemployment: Macroeconomic Performance and the Labor Market* (New York: Oxford University Press, 1991).

[11]The frequency with which wages (and prices) are reset depends on the stability of the level of output and prices in the economy. In extreme conditions, such as hyperinflations, wages might be reset daily or weekly. The need to reset prices and wages frequently is one of the important costs of high and unstable rates of inflation.

Wages are usually set in nominal terms in economies with low rates of inflation.[12] Thus the agreement is that the firm will pay the worker so many dollars per hour or per month for the next quarter or year. Most formal union labor contracts last 2 or 3 years and may fix nominal wages for the period of the contract. Frequently, labor contracts include separate wage rates for overtime hours; this implies that the wage rate paid by firms is higher when more hours are worked. That is one reason the *WN* curve in Figure 6-6 is positively sloped.

At any moment of time, firms and workers will have agreed, explicitly or implicitly, on the wage schedule that is to be paid to currently employed workers. There will be some base wage that corresponds to a given number of hours of work per week and depends on the type of job, with perhaps a higher wage for overtime. The firm then sets the level of employment each period.

Now consider how wages adjust when the demand for labor shifts and firms increase the hours of work. In the short run, wages rise along the *WN* curve. With demand up, workers will press for an increase in the base wage at the next labor negotiation. However, it will take some time before all wages are renegotiated. Further, not all wages are negotiated simultaneously. Rather, wage-setting dates are *staggered;* that is, they overlap.[13] Assume that wages are set for half the labor force in January and for the other half in July. Suppose the money stock goes up in September. Prices will be slow to adjust because no wage will be adjusted until 3 months after the change in the money stock. And when the time comes to renegotiate half the contracts, in January, both the firms and the workers negotiating know that other wages will not change for the next 6 months.

Workers do not seek to adjust their base wage all the way to the level that will take the economy to the long-run equilibrium. If they did, their wages would be very high relative to other wages for the next 6 months, and firms would prefer to employ those workers whose wages have not yet risen. There is thus a danger of unemployment to the January wage-setting workers if the renegotiated wages go too high. Wages are therefore adjusted only partway toward equilibrium.

Then in July, when the time comes to reset the other half of the wages, those too are not driven all the way to the equilibrium level because the January wages would then be relatively lower. So the July wages go above the January wages, but still only partway to the full-employment equilibrium base wage.

This process keeps on going, with the supply curve rising from period to period as wages leapfrog each other while first one wage and then another is renegotiated. The position of the aggregate supply curve in any period will depend on where it was last period because each unit that is renegotiating wages has to consider the level of its wage relative to the wages that are not being reset. And the level of the wages that are not being reset is reflected in last period's wage rate.

---

[12]In economies with high inflation, wages are likely to be *indexed* to the price level; that is, they adjust automatically when the price level changes. Even in the United States, some long-term labor contracts contain indexing clauses under which the wage is increased to compensate for past price increases. The indexing clauses typically adjust wages once a quarter (or once a year) to compensate for price increases in the past quarter (or year).

[13]The adjustment process we present here is based on John Taylor, "Aggregate Dynamics and Staggered Contracts," *Journal of Political Economy,* February 1980.

During the adjustment process, firms will also be resetting prices as wages (and thus firms' costs) change. The process of wage and price adjustment continues until the economy is back at the full-employment equilibrium with the same real balances. The real-world adjustment process is more complicated than our January-July example because wages are not reset quite as regularly as that and, also, because both wage and price adjustment matter.[14] But the January-July example gives the essence of the adjustment process.

This account of slow wage and price adjustment raises at least two serious questions. First, why do firms and workers not adjust wages more frequently when clearly understandable disturbances affect the economy? If they did, perhaps they could adjust wages so as to maintain full employment. Recent research emphasizes that even comparatively small costs of resetting wages and prices can keep adjustment processes from operating quickly.[15] Further, the problems of coordinating wage and price adjustments so that wages and prices move back rapidly to equilibrium are formidable in a large economy in which there are many different forces affecting supply and demand in individual markets.

Second, when there is high unemployment, why do firms and unemployed workers not get together on wage cuts that create jobs for the unemployed? The main reason, addressed by efficiency wage theory, is that such practices are bad for the morale and therefore the productivity of those in the labor force who are on the job.[16]

To summarize, the combination of wages that are preset for a period of time and wage adjustments that are staggered generates the gradual wage and output adjustment we observe in the real world. This accounts for the gradual vertical movement of the short-run aggregate supply curve.

INSIDER-OUTSIDER MODELS

Finally, we draw attention to an approach that emphasizes the implications for the wage behavior–unemployment link that result from this simple fact: The unemployed do not sit at the bargaining table.[17] While the unemployed would prefer firms to cut wages and create more jobs, firms effectively negotiate with the workers who have jobs, not with the people who are unemployed. That has an immediate implication. It is costly for firms to turn over their labor force—firing costs, hiring costs, training costs—and, as a result, *insiders* have an advantage over outsiders. More important, threatening insiders that they will be unemployed unless they accept wage cuts is not very effective. People who are threatened may have to give in, but they will respond poorly in terms

[14]For an interesting study of the frequency of price adjustments (for newspapers), see Stephen G. Cecchetti, "Staggered Contracts and the Frequency of Price Adjustment," *Quarterly Journal of Economics,* Supplement, 1985.

[15]See the references in footnote 10.

[16]See Robert M. Solow, *The Labor Market as a Social Institution* (Cambridge, England: Basil Blackwell, 1990), for a discussion of the relation between pay and productivity.

[17]See Assar Lindbeck and Dennis Snower, *The Insider-Outsider Theory of Employment and Unemployment* (Cambridge, Mass.: M.I.T. Press, 1988), and Assar Lindbeck, "Macroeconomic Theory and the Labor Market," *European Economic Review,* vol. 36 (1992).

of their morale, effort, and productivity. Far better to reach a deal with the insiders and pay them good wages even if there are unemployed workers who would be eager to work for less.

The *insider-outsider model* predicts that wages will not respond substantially to unemployment and thus offers another reason why we do not quickly return to full employment once the economy experiences recession.

6-4

FROM PHILLIPS CURVE TO THE AGGREGATE SUPPLY CURVE

Now we are ready to derive the aggregate supply curve. The derivation will take four steps. First, we translate output to employment. Second, we link the prices firms charge to their costs. Third, we use the Phillips curve relationship between wages and employment. Fourth, we put the three components together to derive an upward-sloping aggregate supply curve.

THE PRODUCTION FUNCTION

The production function links the level of labor employment to the level of output. The simplest production function is one in which output is proportional to the input of labor:

$$Y = aN \tag{6}$$

Here Y is the level of output produced, and N is the amount of labor input or employment (measured in hours of work, for example). The coefficient a is called the input coefficient, or *labor productivity*. Labor productivity is the ratio of output to labor input, Y/N, that is, the amount of output produced per unit of labor employed. For instance, if a is equal to 3, then 1 unit of labor (1 hour of work) will produce 3 units of output.[18]

COSTS AND PRICES

The second step in developing the theory of supply is to link firms' prices to their costs. Labor costs are the main component of total costs. The guiding principle here is that a firm will supply output at a price that at least covers its costs. Of course, firms would like to charge more than cost, but competition from existing firms and firms that might enter the industry to capture some of the profits prevents prices from getting far out of line from costs.

We assume that firms base price on the labor cost of production. Since each unit of labor produces a units of output, the labor cost of production per unit is W/a. For

---

[18]We assume labor productivity is constant for simplicity, even though in practice it changes over the business cycle and over time. Productivity tends to grow over long periods, as workers become better trained and educated and are equipped with more capital. It also changes systematically during the business cycle. Productivity tends to fall before the start of a recession and to recover during the recession and at the beginning of the recovery.

instance, if the wage is \$15 per hour and a is 3, the labor cost is \$5 per unit. The ratio W/a is called the *unit labor cost*. Firms set price as a *markup, z,* on labor costs:

$$P = \frac{(1 + z)W}{a} \tag{7}$$

The markup over labor costs covers the cost of other factors of production that firms use, such as capital and raw materials, and includes an allowance for the firms' normal profits. If competition in the industry is less than perfect, the markup will also include an element of monopoly profit.[19]

EMPLOYMENT AND WAGES AND THE AGGREGATE SUPPLY CURVE

The three components of the aggregate supply curve are the production function (6), the price-cost relation (7), and the Phillips curve (5). The price level is proportional to the wage [from equation (7)]. But tomorrow's wage is linked through the Phillips curve (5) to the level of employment and to today's wages. Using the pricing rule in equation (7), we replace both wages in equation (5) with prices to obtain a link between the level of employment and the price level:

$$P_{t+1}\left(\frac{1 + z}{a}\right) = P_t\left(\frac{1 + z}{a}\right)\left[1 + \epsilon\left(\frac{N - N^*}{N^*}\right)\right] \tag{8}$$

which reduces to

$$P_{t+1} = P_t\left[1 + \epsilon\left(\frac{N - N^*}{N^*}\right)\right] \tag{8a}$$

Further, the level of output is proportional to employment [from the production function, equation (6)]. Thus we can replace N and N^* in equation (8a) by Y/a and Y^*/a. Making those changes, we obtain

$$P_{t+1} = P_t\left[1 + \epsilon\left(\frac{Y - Y^*}{Y^*}\right)\right]$$

Finally, defining $\lambda \equiv \epsilon/Y^*$, we reach the *aggregate supply curve:*

$$P_{t+1} = P_t[1 + \lambda(Y - Y^*)] \tag{9}$$

Figure 6-7 shows the aggregate supply curve implied by equation (9). The supply curve is upward-sloping. Like the WN curve on which it is based, the AS curve shifts over time. If output this period is above the full-employment level, Y^*, then next period the AS curve will shift up to AS'. If output this period is below the full-employment level, the AS curve next period will shift down to AS''. Thus the properties of the AS curve are those of the WN curve. This results from two assumptions: that the markup is fixed at z, and that output is proportional to employment.

---

[19]In a competitive industry, the price is determined by the market, rather than set by firms. That is quite consistent with equation (7), for if the industry were competitive, z would cover only the costs of other factors of production and normal profits, and the price would thus be equal to the competitive price. Equation (7) is slightly more general, because it allows also for price setting by firms in industries that are less fully competitive.

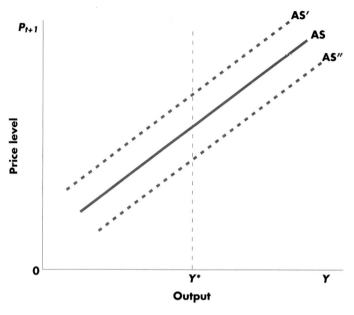

FIGURE 6-7   THE AGGREGATE SUPPLY CURVE.

The AS curve is derived from the WN curve, with the added assumptions that the markup is fixed and that output is proportional to employment.

The *AS* curve is the aggregate supply curve under conditions in which wages are less than fully flexible. Prices increase with the level of output because increased output implies increased employment, reduced unemployment, and therefore increased labor costs. The fact that prices in this model rise with output is entirely a reflection of the adjustments in the labor market, in which higher employment increases wages.

6-5

THE EFFECTS OF A MONETARY EXPANSION

Having presented the underpinnings of the aggregate supply curve, we revisit the effects of a monetary expansion.

In Figure 6-8 we show the economy in full-employment equilibrium at point *E*. The aggregate supply schedule, *AS*, is drawn for a given price level, *P*. It passes through the full-employment output level, Y^*, at the price level *P* because when output is at the full-employment level, there is no tendency for wages to change, and hence prices are also constant from period to period. The aggregate supply schedule is drawn relatively flat, suggesting a small effect of output and employment changes on wages.

SHORT-RUN EFFECTS

Suppose now that the nominal money stock is increased. At each price level real balances are higher, interest rates are lower, and hence the demand for output rises. The *AD* schedule shifts upward, proportionately, as we saw in Chapter 5, to *AD'*. At the

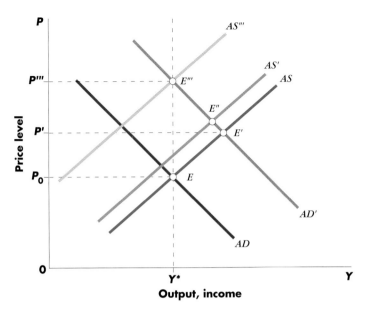

FIGURE 6-8   THE SHORT-RUN EFFECT OF AN INCREASE IN THE MONEY STOCK.

initial price level, P, there is now an excess demand for goods. Firms find that their inventories are running down and accordingly hire more labor and raise output until the economy reaches E', the short-run equilibrium point. Note that at E' both output and next period's prices have risen. A monetary expansion has led to a short-run increase in output. The rise in prices is due to the increase in labor costs as production and employment rise.

Compare now the short-run result with the Keynesian and classical models of Chapter 5. Our new equilibrium at E' has a feature of each: output is higher, and prices have risen. Whether we are more nearly in the classical or Keynesian situation depends entirely on the slope of the aggregate supply schedule, that is, on the coefficient λ, which translates employment changes into wage changes.

MEDIUM-TERM ADJUSTMENT

The short-run equilibrium at point E' is not the end of the story. At E' output is above normal. Therefore, as equation (9) indicates, prices *will keep on rising*. Consider what happens next in Figure 6-8. Looking back, the price in the preceding period was P' at point E'. Therefore, the new supply curve passes through the full-employment output level at a price equal to P'. We show this by shifting the aggregate supply schedule up to AS', reflecting the increase in wages that has taken place since last period in response to the high level of employment.

With the new aggregate supply schedule, AS', and with the aggregate demand schedule unchanged at the higher level AD', the new equilibrium is at E''. Comparing E' and E'', we note that output now has fallen compared with that of the first period and prices have risen further. The increase in wages has been passed on by firms as an upward shift of the AS schedule, and the resulting price increase reduces real balances, raises interest rates, and lowers equilibrium income and spending. Thus, we enter a phase of the adjustment process in which the initial expansion begins to be reversed—although output is still above the full employment level, Y^*.

LONG-TERM ADJUSTMENT

As long as output is above normal, employment is above normal, and therefore wages are rising. Because wages are rising, firms experience cost increases, and these are passed on, at each output level, as an upward shift of the aggregate supply schedule. As long as the short- and medium-term equilibrium positions of the economy (points E', E'', etc.) lie to the right of Y^*, the AS schedule is shifting upward and to the left. As a result, output will be declining toward the full-employment level and prices will keep rising.

Figure 6-8 shows that the upward-shifting AS schedule gives us a series of equilibrium positions on the AD schedule, starting with E' and moving up toward E'''. During the entire adjustment process, output is above the full-employment level and prices are rising. The AS curve keeps shifting up, until the aggregate supply curve, AS''', intersects the aggregate demand curve at E''', at which point the economy has returned to full employment.

At E''', prices have risen in the same proportion as the nominal money stock, and so the real money stock, M/P, is again at the initial level. When real balances and therefore interest rates are again at the initial level, so are aggregate demand, output, and employment.

THE NEUTRALITY OF MONEY

In the long run, once wages and prices have had time to adjust fully, the model has the same predictions as the classical case of Chapter 5: an increase in the money stock has no real effects. In the long run, according to our dynamic model of aggregate supply, *money is neutral*—it has no real effects and raises only prices.

But there is a crucial difference: *In this more realistic model of aggregate supply, money is neutral in the long run but not in the short run.* In the classical case a monetary expansion leads immediately to an equiproportionate rise in prices with no real expansion. Here, *both* output and prices rise in the short and medium terms, and only in the long run do we reach the classical case. By assumption, though, *the real wage remains constant in the adjustment process.* In the short run the predictions of our model more closely resemble the Keynesian case of Chapter 5, and the more slowly wages adjust to changes in employment, the greater the resemblance. Because the adjustments of wages and prices are, in fact, slow, the short- and medium-term adjustments are an essential aspect of macroeconomics. This is a point on which nearly all groups of macroeconomists agree.

6-6

SUPPLY SHOCKS

From the 1930s to the late 1960s, it was generally assumed that movements in output and prices in the economy were caused by shifts in the aggregate demand curve—by changes in monetary and fiscal policy (including wars as fiscal expansions) and investment

FIGURE 6-9   THE REAL PRICE OF OIL, 1974–1996.

(Source: DRI/McGraw-Hill Macroeconomic Database.)

demand. But the macroeconomic story of the 1970s was largely a story of *supply shocks.*

A supply shock is a disturbance to the economy whose first impact is a shift in the aggregate supply curve. In the 1970s, the aggregate supply curve was shifted by two major oil price shocks, which increased the cost of production and therefore increased the price at which firms were willing to supply output. In other words, the oil price shocks shifted the aggregate supply curve, in a way we shall soon show.

Figure 6-9 shows the real, or relative, price of oil.[20] The first OPEC shock, which quadrupled the real price of oil between 1971 and 1974, helped push the economy into the 1973–1975 recession, until then the worst recession of the post-World War II period. The second OPEC price increase, in 1979–1980, doubled the price of oil and sharply accelerated inflation. The high inflation led, in 1980–1982, to a tough monetary policy to fight the inflation, with the result that the economy went into even deeper recession than in 1973–1975. After 1982 the relative price of oil fell throughout the 1980s, with a particularly sharp decline in 1985–1986. There was a brief oil price shock in the second half of 1990, as a result of the Iraqi invasion of Kuwait. That temporary shock played a part in worsening the recession of 1990–1991, though the recession is dated as having begun in July, before Kuwait was invaded.

The two oil price shock–related recessions of the 1970s leave no doubt that supply shocks matter. We analyze their effect by incorporating prices of raw materials into the aggregate supply curve.

---

[20]The *relative* price of oil is defined here as the world crude-oil price deflated by the U.S. GDP deflator.

INCORPORATING MATERIALS PRICES INTO THE ANALYSIS

In equation (7) labor costs (and the markup) were the only determinants of output prices. Materials such as energy or copper or cotton were not explicitly included. But these goods are used as inputs, and their prices, too, have an impact on the prices of final goods.

We incorporate materials prices into our analysis by modifying the price equation to include not only labor costs and the markup but also *materials prices,* which we denote by P_m:

$$P = \frac{W(1 + z)}{a} + \Theta P_m \tag{10}$$

In equation (10) the term Θ denotes the materials requirement per unit of output, and hence ΘP_m is the component of unit costs that comes from materials inputs.

The wage rate, we recall, increases with the level of output. Hence from equation (10) we still get an upward-sloping supply curve. Further, any increase in the price of materials will increase the price level at a given W. Thus an increase in P_m shifts the AS curve upward, as in Figure 6-10.

Alternatively, we can write the price equation in terms of the relative, or real, price of materials, which we denote by lowercase p_m. The relative price is given by

$$p_m = \frac{P_m}{P} \tag{11}$$

Substituting from equation (11) into (10) gives us a modified equation linking wages and prices:

$$P = \frac{1 + z}{1 - \Theta p_m}\left(\frac{W}{a}\right) \qquad 1 > \Theta p_m \tag{12}$$

Equation (12) shows that for given wages, profit margins, and labor productivity, an increase in the real price of materials will increase prices simply because it raises costs.

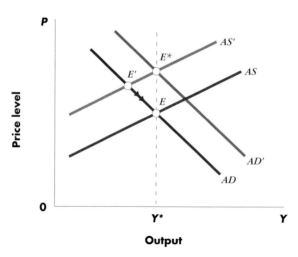

FIGURE 6-10   ADVERSE SUPPLY SHOCK RESULTING FROM AN INCREASE IN THE PRICE OF OIL.

The impact of a change in real materials prices, therefore, is an upward shift in the aggregate supply schedule at each level of output, as in Figure 6-10.

AN ADVERSE SUPPLY SHOCK

An *adverse supply shock* is one that shifts the aggregate supply curve up. Figure 6-10 shows the effects of such a shock—an increase in the price of oil—reflecting an increase in p_m in equation (12). The AS curve shifts upward to AS', and the equilibrium of the economy moves from E to E'. The immediate effect of the supply shock is thus a rise in the price level and a reduction in the level of output. An adverse supply shock is doubly unfortunate: it causes *higher* prices and *lower* output.

There are two points to note about the impact of the supply shock. First, the shock shifts the AS curve upward because each unit of output now costs firms more to produce. Second, we are assuming that the supply shock does not affect the level of potential output, which remains at $Y*$.[21]

What happens after the shock has hit? In Figure 6-10, the economy moves from E' back to E. The unemployment at E' forces wages and thus the price level down. The adjustment is slow because wages are slow to adjust. The adjustment takes place along the AD curve, with wages falling until E is reached.

At E the economy is back at full employment, with the price level the same as it was before the shock. But the nominal wage rate is lower than it was before the shock because the unemployment in the meantime has forced the wage down. Thus the *real* wage, too, is lower than it was before the shock: the adverse supply shock reduces the real wage.

ACCOMMODATION OF SUPPLY SHOCKS

Both fiscal and monetary policy barely responded when the first oil price shock hit the economy at the end of 1973. Because supply shocks were then a new phenomenon, neither economists nor policy makers knew what, if anything, could be done about them. But when the unemployment rate went above 8 percent at the end of 1974, both monetary and fiscal policy turned stimulatory in 1975–1976. These policies helped the economy recover from the recession more rapidly than it otherwise would have.

But why not always respond to an adverse supply shock with stimulatory policy? To answer that question, we look again at Figure 6-10. If the government had, at the time of the oil price increase, increased aggregate demand enough, the economy could have moved to $E*$ rather than E'. Prices would have risen by the full extent of the upward shift in the aggregate supply curve. Money wages would have remained unchanged, and the economy would have stayed at full employment. Of course, the real wage would have been lower, but in the end it was lower anyway.

The monetary and fiscal policies that shift the AD curve to AD' in Figure 6-10 are known as *accommodating policies*. There has been a disturbance that requires a fall in the real wage. Policy is adjusted to make possible, or accommodate, that fall in the real wage *at the existing nominal wage*.

---

[21]The increase in the price of oil in the 1970s both shifted up the AS curve and reduced the level of potential output because firms reduced their use of oil and could not use capital as efficiently as before. For simplicity, we are assuming in Fig. 6-10 that the supply shock does not affect $Y*$.

So the question now is why accommodating policies were not undertaken in 1973–1975. The answer is that there is a tradeoff between the inflationary impact of a supply shock and its recessionary effects. The more accommodation there is, the greater the inflationary impact of the shock and the smaller the unemployment impact. The policy mix actually chosen resulted in an intermediate position—some inflation (quite a lot) and some unemployment.

6-7

STAGFLATION, EXPECTED INFLATION, AND THE

INFLATION-EXPECTATIONS-AUGMENTED PHILLIPS CURVE

The Phillips curve is the cornerstone of macroeconomic policy analysis, and we have now established theoretical underpinnings for the empirical Phillips curve shown in Figure 6-5. But that *simple* Phillips curve relationship fell apart after the 1960s, both in Britain and in the United States. Figure 6-11 shows the behavior of inflation and unemployment in the United States over the period since 1960. The data for the 1970s and 1980s do not fit the simple Phillips curve story.

Something is missing from the simple Phillips curve; that something is *expected, or anticipated, inflation.* When workers and firms bargain over wages, they are concerned

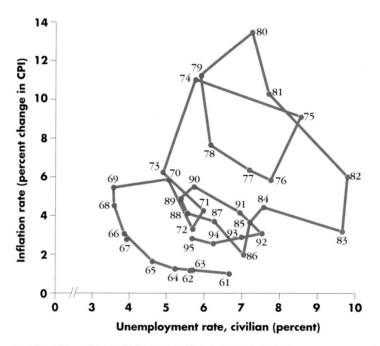

FIGURE 6-11   RELATIONSHIP OF INFLATION AND UNEMPLOYMENT: UNITED STATES, 1961–1995.

(Source: DRI/McGraw-Hill Macroeconomic Database.)

with the real value of the wage, so both sides are more or less willing to adjust the level of the nominal wage for any inflation expected over the contract period. Unemployment depends not on the level of inflation but, rather, on the excess of inflation over what was expected.

A little introspection illustrates the issue. Suppose that on the first of the year your employer announces a 3 percent across-the-board raise for you and your coworkers. While not massive, 3 percent is a nice increase, and you and your colleagues might be reasonably pleased. Now suppose we tell you that inflation has been running 10 percent a year and is expected to continue at this rate. You will understand that if the cost of living rises 10 percent while your nominal wage rises only 3 percent, your standard of living is actually going to fall, by about 7 (= 10 − 3) percent. In other words, you care about wage increases *in excess* of expected inflation.

We can rewrite equation (3), the original wage-inflation Phillips curve, to show that it is the excess of wage inflation over expected inflation that matters:

$$(g_w - \pi^e) = - \epsilon(u - u^*) \tag{13}$$

where π^e is the level of expected price inflation.

Maintaining the assumption of a constant real wage, actual inflation, π, will equal wage inflation. Thus the equation for the modern version of the Phillips curve, the *(inflation-) expectations-augmented Phillips curve,* is

$$\pi = \pi^e - \epsilon(u - u^*) \tag{14}$$

Note two critical properties of the modern Phillips curve:

- Expected inflation is passed one for one into actual inflation.
- Unemployment is at the natural rate when actual inflation equals expected inflation.

We have now an additional factor determining the height of the short-run Phillips curve (and the corresponding short-run aggregate supply curve). Instead of intersecting the natural rate of unemployment at zero, the modern Phillips curve intersects the natural rate at the level of expected inflation. Figure 6-12 shows stylized Phillips curves for the early 1960s (when inflation had been running at about 2 percent) and the early 1980s (when inflation had been running 6 to 8 percent).

Firms and workers adjust their expectations of inflation in light of the recent history of inflation.[22] The short-run Phillips curves in Figure 6-12 reflect the low level of inflation that was expected in the early 1960s and the much higher level that was expected in the early 1980s. The curves have two properties you should note. First, the curves have the same short-run tradeoff between unemployment and inflation; that is to say, the *slopes are equal.* Second, in the early 1960s full employment was compatible with roughly 2 percent annual inflation; in the early 1980s full employment was compatible with roughly 7 percent inflation.

The height of the short-run Phillips curve, the level of expected inflation, π^e, moves up and down over time in response to the changing expectations of firms and workers. *The role of expected inflation in moving the Phillips curve adds another au-*

---

[22]How quickly firms and workers adjust and the extent to which they look to the future rather than to recent history are matters of some dispute.

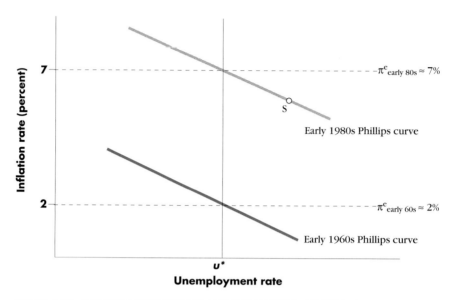

FIGURE 6-12   INFLATION EXPECTATIONS AND THE SHORT-RUN PHILLIPS CURVE.

tomatic adjustment mechanism to the aggregate supply side of the economy. When high aggregate demand moves the economy up and to the left along the short-run Phillips curve, inflation results. If the inflation persists, people come to expect inflation in the future (π^e rises) and the short-run Phillips curve moves up.

STAGFLATION

Stagflation is a term coined to mean high unemployment ("stagnation") and high inflation. For example, in 1982 unemployment was over 9 percent and inflation approximately 6 percent. Point *S* in Figure 6-12 is a stagflation point. It is easy to see how stagflation occurs.[23] Once the economy is on a short-run Phillips curve that includes significant expected inflation, a recession will push actual inflation down below expected inflation (e.g., a movement to the right on the 1980s Phillips curve in Figure 6-12), but the absolute level of inflation will remain high. In other words, inflation will be lower than expected but well above zero.

DOES THE AUGMENTED PHILLIPS CURVE FIT THE DATA?

We have seen in Figure 6-11 that when we leave out expected inflation, the empirical relation between inflation and unemployment is a mess. We would like some *evidence* that adjusting for expected inflation gives us a reliable Phillips curve. Unlike inflation and unemployment, which are directly measurable and regularly reported by the official statistics agencies, expected inflation is an idea in the heads of everyone engaged in setting prices and wages. There can be no meaningful official measure of expected

[23]For some reason, journalists delight in reporting that economists don't understand stagflation. This was probably true in the 1960s and early 1970s, before the role of inflation expectations was fully appreciated. The 1960s were a long time ago. As you see, stagflation is no longer a puzzle.

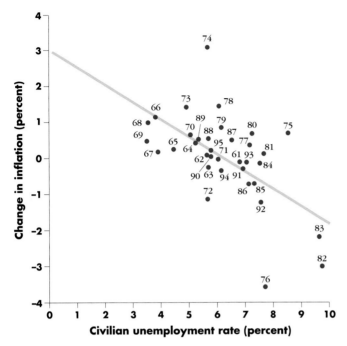

FIGURE 6-13   RELATIONSHIP OF CHANGES IN INFLATION TO UNEMPLOYMENT RATES.

inflation, although there are surveys taken in which economic forecasters are asked what they expect inflation to be over the coming year. Nonetheless, we get surprisingly good results from the naive assumption that people expect inflation this year to equal whatever inflation was last year—we assume $\pi_t^e = \pi_{t-1}$. So to check on the modern Phillips curve, we plot $\pi - \pi^e \approx \pi - \pi_{t-1} = -\epsilon(u - u^*)$ in Figure 6-13.

The figure shows that even this very simple model of expected inflation works quite well, although certainly not perfectly. What's more, the line through the data in Figure 6-13 gives us a number for the slope of the short-run Phillips curve. One extra point of unemployment reduces inflation by only about one-half of a percentage point; in other words; $\epsilon \approx .5$. One point of unemployment is a lot. One-half point of inflation is rather little. So the figure shows that the short-run Phillips curve (and the corresponding short-run aggregate supply curve) is quite flat,[24] even though we know that the long-run Phillips curve (and the corresponding long-run aggregate supply curve) is vertical.

RECAP
_____

Points to remember:

- The Phillips curve shows that output is at its full employment level when actual inflation and expected inflation are equal.

_____

[24]The short-run aggregate supply curve corresponding to the inflation-expectations-augmented short-run Phillips curve can be written $P_{t+1} = P_{t+1}^e + P_t[1 + \lambda(Y - Y^*)]$, where P_{t+1}^e is the price level expected next period, $P_{t+1}^e = P_t(1 + \pi^e)$.

- The modern Phillips curve states that inflation exceeds expected inflation when actual unemployment is below full employment.
- Stagflation occurs when there is a recession along a short-run Phillips curve based on high expected inflation.
- Adjustments to expected inflation add a further automatic adjustment mechanism to the supply schedule and speed the progression from the short-run to the long-run aggregate supply curve.
- The short-run Phillips curve is quite flat.

SUMMARY

1. The aggregate supply curve describes the price adjustment mechanism of the economy.
2. The labor market does not adjust quickly to disturbances. Rather, the adjustment process takes time. The Phillips curve shows that nominal wages change slowly in accordance with the level of employment. Wages tend to rise when employment is high and fall when employment is low.
3. The frictions that exist as workers enter the labor market and look for jobs or shift between jobs mean that there is always some frictional unemployment. The amount of frictional unemployment that exists at the full-employment level of unemployment is the natural rate of unemployment.
4. The theory of aggregate supply is not yet settled. Several explanations have been offered for the basic fact that the labor market does not adjust quickly to shifts in aggregate demand: the imperfect-information–market-clearing approach; coordination problems; efficiency wages and costs of price changes; and contracts and long-term relationships between firms and workers.
5. In deriving the supply curve in this chapter, we emphasize the long-run relationships between firms and workers and the fact that wages are generally held fixed for some period, such as a year. We also take into account the fact that wage changes are not coordinated among firms.
6. The short-run aggregate supply curve is derived from the Phillips curve in four steps: output is assumed proportional to employment; prices are set as a markup over costs; the wage is the main element of cost and adjusts according to the Phillips curve; and the Phillips curve relationship between the wage and unemployment is therefore transformed into a relationship between the price level and output.
7. The short-run aggregate supply curve shifts over time. If output is above (below) the full-employment level this period, the aggregate supply curve shifts up (down) next period.
8. A shift in the aggregate demand curve increases the price level and output. The increase in output and employment increases wages somewhat in the current period. The full impact of changes in aggregate demand on prices occurs only over the course of time. High levels of employment generate increases in wages that feed into higher prices. As wages adjust, the aggregate supply curve shifts until the economy returns to equilibrium.
9. The aggregate supply curve is derived from the underlying assumptions that wages (and prices) are not adjusted continuously and that they are not all adjusted together. The positive slope of the aggregate supply curve is a result of some wages being adjusted in response to market conditions and of previously agreed-upon overtime rates coming into effect as employment changes. The slow movement of the sup-

ply curve over time is a result of the slow and uncoordinated process by which wages and prices are adjusted.

10. Materials prices, along with wages, are determinants of costs and prices. Changes in materials prices are passed on as changes in prices and, therefore, as changes in real wages. Materials price changes have been an important source of aggregate supply shocks.

11. Supply shocks pose a difficult problem for macroeconomic policy. They can be accommodated through an expansionary aggregate demand policy, with increased prices but stable output. Alternatively, they can be offset, through a deflationary aggregate demand policy, with prices remaining stable but with lower output.

12. Expectations of inflation are built into the Phillips curve. When actual inflation and expected inflation are equal, the economy is at the natural rate of unemployment. Expectations of inflation adjust over time to reflect the recent levels of inflation.

13. Stagflation occurs when there is a recession plus a high inflation rate. That is, stagflation occurs when the economy moves to the right along a Phillips curve that includes a substantial component of expected inflation.

KEY TERMS

price adjustment mechanism	coordination approach	monetary and fiscal accom-
speed of price adjustment	efficiency wage theory	modation
Phillips curve	staggered price adjustment	anticipated inflation
sticky wages	insider-outsider model	augmented Phillips curve
imperfect information	supply shock	stagflation
rational expectations	adverse supply shock	

PROBLEMS

Conceptual

1. Explain how the aggregate supply and Phillips curves are related to each other. Can any information be derived from one that cannot be derived from the other?

2. How do short- and long-term Phillips curves differ? (*Hint:* in the long run, we return to a classical world.)

3. This chapter has discussed a number of different models which can be used to justify the existence of sticky wages, and hence the ability of aggregate demand to affect output. What are they? What are their similarities and differences? Which of these models do you find the most plausible?

4. **a.** What is stagflation?
   b. Describe a situation which could produce it. Could the situation you've described be avoided? Should it be avoided?

5. Explain how the ability of inflation expectations to shift the Phillips curve helps the economy to adjust, automatically, to aggregate supply and demand shocks.

Technical

1. Analyze the effects of a reduction in the nominal money stock on the price level, on output, and on the real money stock when the aggregate supply curve is positively sloped and wages adjust slowly over time.

2. What happens to prices, output, and the real wage in the long run and short run when labor's productivity [the parameter a in equation (6)] increases?

3. **a.** Show, in an aggregate supply and demand framework, the long- and short-run effects of a decline in the real price of materials.
   b. Describe the adjustment process, assuming that output began at its natural (full-employment) level.

CHAPTER 7

The Anatomy of Inflation and Unemployment

CHAPTER HIGHLIGHTS

- The costs of unemployment, largely forgone output, are very large.

- The cost of anticipated inflation is very small, at least at the moderate levels experienced in industrial countries.

- The cost of unanticipated inflation, which can be quite large, is mainly distributional. There are big winners and big losers.

- Unemployment rates, both the natural rate and the rate of cyclical unemployment, vary widely among different groups and countries.

The Gallup Organization regularly conducts opinion polls asking, What is the most important problem facing the country? Possible answers include drugs, crime, pollution, and the threat of nuclear war. In 1981, with the inflation rate in double digits, a majority of those polled named inflation as the most important problem facing the country. In 1996, neither inflation nor unemployment was regarded as a major issue. As Table 7-1 shows, when inflation or unemployment (or both) is high, it is seen as *the* national issue, but when either is low, it practically disappears from the list of concerns.

Both inflation and unemployment should be avoided as much as possible. But since short-run tradeoffs between inflation and unemployment exist, it is also important to get a better understanding of the relative economic costs of inflation and unemployment. This information provides the input for policy makers' evaluation of the tradeoffs.

In an ideal world, policy makers would pick the lowest-cost combination of unemployment and inflation. But how do policy makers deal with the tradeoff in practice? One answer is given by the theory of the *political business cycle,* described at the end of the chapter. According to this theory, policy makers try to make the inflation and unemployment results come out just right at the time of elections. Of course, the inflation (or the recession to stop it) will come later, after the election.

This chapter focuses on the details of the costs of unemployment and inflation. Before diving into the details, we remind you of the "big-picture" costs:

TABLE 7-1 The Most Important Problem Facing the Country?

	INFLATION		UNEMPLOYMENT	
	RATE, %	NUMBER-ONE PROBLEM, % OF RESPONDENTS	RATE, %	NUMBER-ONE PROBLEM, % OF RESPONDENTS
1981	10.4	73	7.5	8
1982	6.2	49	9.6	28
1983	3.2	18	9.5	53
1984	4.4	10	7.5	28
1985	3.6	7	7.2	24
1986	1.9	4	7.0	23
1987	3.7	5	6.2	13
1988	4.1	—*	5.5	9
1989	4.8	3	5.3	6
1990	5.4	—	5.5	3
1991	4.2	—	6.8	23
1992	2.8	—	7.4	25
1993	3.1	—	7.1	13
1994	2.5	1	6.6	11
1995	2.8	1	5.5	9
1996	2.7	—	5.6	5

*"—" indicates less than 1 percent.

Source: Gallup Report, various issues; DRI/McGraw-Hill Macroeconomic Database, various reports.

BOX 7-1 The "Sacrifice Ratio"— An International Perspective

In the short run, governments can reduce inflation only at the cost of increased unemployment and reduced output. The *sacrifice ratio* is the percentage of output lost for each 1 point reduction in the inflation rate. The sacrifice ratio varies depending on the time, place, and methods used to reduce inflation. Nonetheless, it is useful to have a ballpark estimate for making choices about policy. Table 1 provides estimates for a number of countries.

TABLE 1   Estimated Average Sacrifice Ratios

COUNTRY	RATIO, %
Australia	1.00
Canada	1.50
France	.75
Germany	2.92
Italy	1.74
Japan	.93
Switzerland	1.57
United Kingdom	.79
United States	2.39

Source: Laurence Ball, "How Costly Is Disinflation? The Historical Evidence," *Business Review,* Federal Reserve Bank of Philadelphia, November–December 1993.

- There are two main costs of unemployment: lost production and undesirable effects on the distribution of income.
- The costs of anticipated inflation are small. The costs of unanticipated inflation are probably small on net, but unanticipated inflation may cause significant redistributions of wealth within the economy.

UNEMPLOYMENT

The largest single cost of unemployment is lost production.[1] People who can't work don't produce—high unemployment makes the social pie smaller.[2] The cost of lost output is very high: a recession can easily cost 3 to 5 percent of GDP, amounting to losses

---

[1]But see, as well, William Darity and Arthur Goldsmith, "Social Psychology, Unemployment and Macroeconomics," *Journal of Economic Perspectives,* Winter 1996.

[2]The unemployed do receive increased leisure, which ought to be counted as an offsetting benefit. When unemployment is *involuntary,* the value of leisure is less than the value of work.

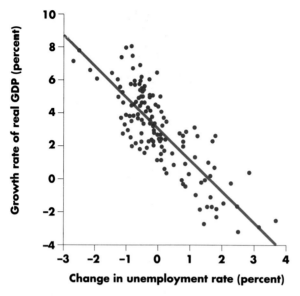

FIGURE 7-1   OKUN'S LAW: THE RELATION BETWEEN UNEMPLOYMENT AND GDP GROWTH.
(Source: DRI/McGraw-Hill Macroeconomic Database.)

measured in hundreds of billions of dollars. The late Arthur Okun codified an empirical relation between unemployment and output over the business cycle. *Okun's law* states that 1 extra point of unemployment costs 2 percent of GDP. Figure 7-1 plots real GDP growth against the change in unemployment, showing that Okun's law gives an excellent account of the unemployment-output relation in the United States.

The costs of unemployment are borne very unevenly. There are large *distributional consequences*. In other words, the costs of a recession are borne disproportionately by those individuals who lose their jobs.[3] For example, college students who have the bad luck to graduate during a recession face enormous difficulty in starting a career. The same students, if they had had the good fortune to graduate during a boom, would have gotten off to a much quicker start. Workers just entering the labor force, teenagers, and residents of urban ghettos are among the groups most vulnerable to increased unemployment.

INFLATION

The costs of extremely high inflation are easy to see. Money lubricates the economy. In countries where prices double every month, money stops being a useful medium of exchange, and, sometimes, output drops dramatically. But at the low, single-digit levels of inflation typical in the United States the costs of inflation are more difficult to identify. *Unexpected* inflation has an easily seen distributional cost: debtors benefit by

---

[3]There is an old, rather pointed, joke about this: Person 1: "What's the difference between a 'recession' and a 'depression'?" Person 2: "A 'recession' is when you lose your job. A 'depression' is when I lose *my* job."

BOX 7-2 Okun's Law, the Short-Run Phillips Curve, and the Sacrifice Ratio

We've presented several ballpark numbers which bear directly on measuring the short-run tradeoff between output and inflation. How well do they fit together? At the end of Chapter 6 we put a number to the slope of the short-run Phillips curve. We concluded that 1 extra point of unemployment reduces inflation by .5 point—holding inflation expectations constant. Turning this around, a 1-point reduction in inflation costs 2 points of unemployment. According to Okun's law, 2 points of unemployment cost 4 percent of output. Thus the implied sacrifice ratio is about 4, somewhat higher than Ball's estimate of 2.39.

Part of the difference reflects the fact that these rough estimates are just that—rough. But Ball's estimate of the sacrifice ratio includes an important element omitted when we paste together the Phillips curve and Okun's law. During a disinflation, expected inflation falls. The drop in expected inflation causes a downward *shift* of the Phillips curve on top of the movement *along* the Phillips curve. This extra drop lowers the sacrifice ratio. Ball's method of estimating the sacrifice ratio implicitly included this extra kick. So the sacrifice ratio is probably closer to 2.39 than 4. Either number indicates that the output cost of disinflation is very high.

repaying in cheaper dollars, and creditors suffer by being repaid in cheaper dollars. Economists have a hard time understanding why low levels of more-or-less predictable inflation are more than a minor nuisance. However, economists aside, it is clear that the public has a very strong dislike of inflation that policy makers ignore at their own peril.

7-1

THE ANATOMY OF UNEMPLOYMENT

Research on the U.S. labor market has revealed five key characteristics of unemployment:

- There are large variations in unemployment rates across groups defined by age, race, or experience.
- There is high turnover in the labor market. Flows into and out of employment and unemployment are high relative to the numbers of employed or unemployed.
- A significant part of this turnover is cyclical: layoffs and separations are high during recessions, and voluntary quits are high during booms.
- Most people who become unemployed in any given month remain unemployed for only a short time.
- Much of U.S. unemployment consists of people who will be unemployed for quite a long time.

TABLE 7-2 U.S. Labor Force and Unemployment, 1996
(Millions of persons 16 years and over)

Working-age population	200.8
Labor force	133.9
Employed	127.1
Unemployed	6.8
Not in labor force	67.0

Source: DRI/McGraw-Hill.

These facts are critical to understanding what unemployment means and what can or should be done about it.[4]

The starting point for a discussion of unemployment is Table 7-2. The working-age (16 or older) population of the United States in 1996 was 201 million people, of whom 66.7 percent were *in the labor force.* The size of the labor force is determined from surveys. The labor force consists of people who respond that they are unemployed as well as those who say they are employed. An *unemployed person* in these surveys is defined as one who is out of work *and* who (1) has actively looked for work during the previous 4 weeks, or (2) is waiting to be recalled to a job after having been laid off, or (3) is waiting to report to a new job within 4 weeks. The condition of having looked for a job in the past 4 weeks tests that the person is *actively* interested in working.[5]

THE UNEMPLOYMENT POOL

At any point in time there is a given number, or *pool,* of unemployed people, and there are flows in and out of the *unemployment pool.* A person may become unemployed for one of four reasons:

1. He or she may be a new entrant into the labor force—someone looking for work for the first time—or may be a reentrant—someone returning to the labor force after not having looked for work for more than 4 weeks.
2. The person may quit a job in order to look for other employment and may register as unemployed while searching.
3. The person may be laid off. The definition of *layoff* is a suspension without pay lasting or expected to last more than 7 consecutive days, initiated by the employer "without prejudice to the worker."[6]
4. The worker may lose her job, either by being fired or because the firm closes down.

---

[4]For reviews, see Kevin Murphy and Robert Topel, "The Evolution of Unemployment in the United States," *NBER Macroeconomics Annual,* 1987, and Chinhui Juhn, Kevin Murphy, and Robert Topel, "Why Has the Natural Rate of Unemployment Increased over Time?" *Brookings Papers on Economic Activity* 2 (1991).

[5]Those who are of working age but not in the labor force are not counted as unemployed. "Out of the labor force" includes retired persons, homemakers, and full-time students. It also includes *discouraged workers*—people who would like to work but have given up looking.

[6]The qualification means that the worker was not fired but, rather, will return to the old job if demand for the firm's product recovers. Until the 1990–1991 recession, over 75 percent of laid-off workers in manufacturing typically returned to jobs with their original employers. The proportion in 1990–1991 was much lower.

BOX 7-3 The Changing Hours of Work

Figure 1 shows average hours worked per week in the United States. Several facts stand out:

- Hours per week showed a secular decline during the postwar period that continued until the 1980s.
- Hours worked dropped more quickly during recessions (the shaded areas) and picked up temporarily at the beginning of recoveries.
- The decline in hours worked came to an end in the 1990s, and the length of the average workweek has even increased a bit.

FIGURE 1   AVERAGE HOURS WORKED PER WEEK IN THE UNITED STATES, 1947–1994.

(Source: DRI/McGraw-Hill Macroeconomic Database.)

There are essentially three ways of moving out of the unemployment pool:

1. A person may be hired into a new job.
2. Someone laid off may be recalled to his or her employer.
3. An unemployed person may stop looking for a job and thus, by definition, leave the labor force.

FIGURE 7-2   U.S. UNEMPLOYMENT RATES, POOLED, AND BY SEX, AGE, AND RACE, 1947–1996.

Note the different scales in panels (a) and (b) versus panels (c) and (d). (Source: DRI/McGraw-Hill Macroeconomic Database; Bureau of Labor Statistics, Economic Indicators.)

The concept of the unemployment pool gives a good way of thinking about changes in unemployment. Unemployment is rising when more people are entering the pool than leaving. Thus, other things equal, increases in quits and layoffs increase unemployment, as does an increase in the flow of new entrants into the labor market. Job loss accounts for about half of new unemployment. Voluntary separations, new entrants, and reentrants into the labor force together account for the other half.

The contemporaneous link between unemployment and output embodied in Okun's law and Figure 7-1 is an accurate first approximation, but the dynamics of the output-unemployment link are somewhat more complicated. Consider the typical adjustment pattern of labor use during a recession. Employers first adjust hours per worker—for example, by cutting overtime—and only then trim their workforce. Next, layoffs and firings increase, increasing the flow into unemployment. But, at the same time, quits decrease, as workers sensibly decide to hold on to their current job. During a prolonged recession, many of the unemployed become discouraged and leave the labor force, making the *reported* unemployment rate lower than it would otherwise be. As a result of all these effects, unemployment changes usually lag behind output changes.

VARIATION IN UNEMPLOYMENT ACROSS GROUPS

At any point in time there is a given aggregate level of unemployment or, expressed as a fraction of the labor force, an unemployment rate. For example, in August 1996, the unemployment rate was 5.1 percent. But this aggregate number conceals wide variations across various segments of the population. Figure 7-2 shows the unemployment rates for several groups. Teenagers have much higher unemployment rates than do older workers. Black unemployment is typically double the rate of white unemployment. Female unemployment was higher than male unemployment up through the late 1970s, but today the unemployment rate for women is about the same as—or perhaps a bit lower than—the rate for men.

The variation of unemployment rates across different groups in the labor force can be examined using the relationship between the overall unemployment rate, u, and the unemployment rates, u_i, of groups within the labor force. The overall rate is a weighted average of the unemployment rates of the groups:

$$u = w_1 u_1 + w_2 u_2 + \ldots + w_n u_n \tag{1}$$

The w_i weights are the fraction of the civilian labor force that falls within a specific group, say, black teenagers.

Equation (1) shows that the overall unemployment rate can change for two reasons: (1) the unemployment rate changes for all groups; or (2) the weights shift toward a group with higher- (or lower-) than-average unemployment. For example, in the last half of the 1990s and the early years of the twenty-first century, the number of teenagers relative to the number of older workers will rise. Since teenagers have above-average unemployment, we would expect the national unemployment rate to rise even if neither the unemployment rate for teenagers nor that for older workers changed.

CYCLICAL AND FRICTIONAL UNEMPLOYMENT

There is an important distinction between cyclical and frictional unemployment. *Frictional unemployment* is the unemployment that exists when the economy is at full employment.

TABLE 7-3   Labor Turnover Rates in Manufacturing, 1981
(Per 100 employees; average of monthly data)

ACCESSIONS			SEPARATIONS			
NEW HIRES	RECALLS	TOTAL†	QUITS	LAYOFFS	OTHER*	TOTAL†
2.0	1.0	3.2	1.3	1.8	.7	3.6

*Includes involuntary separations.

†Components do not add to totals due to averaging and rounding.

Source: Employment and Earnings, March 1982.

Frictional unemployment results from the structure of the labor market—from the nature of jobs in the economy and from the social habits and labor market institutions (e.g., unemployment benefits) that affect the behavior of workers and firms. The frictional unemployment rate is the same as the natural unemployment rate, which we discuss in more detail below. *Cyclical unemployment* is unemployment in excess of frictional unemployment: it occurs when output is below its full-employment level.

With this preliminary discussion in mind, we now turn to a closer examination of unemployment.

LABOR MARKET FLOWS

Labor market *turnover,* flows into and out of unemployment and employment and between jobs, is large.[7] Table 7-3 shows the average of monthly flows in 1981 into and out of employment. These data (which, unfortunately, are no longer collected) show the movement, or turnover, in the labor market by splitting net employment changes into their different components.

Table 7-3 presents a remarkable picture of the movement in the labor force. In 1981, in each month, manufacturing companies on average added 3.2 names to their payrolls per 100 employees and, at the same time, removed on average 3.6 names from their payrolls per 100 employees. These data show that people are taking *and* leaving jobs even during times of high unemployment. Even though the unemployment rate in 1981 was 7.5 percent, firms were hiring new people and calling back workers who had been laid off—despite the high unemployment rate. Perhaps even more surprising, 1.3 percent of the workers in manufacturing quit their jobs voluntarily.

DURATION OF UNEMPLOYMENT

A second way of looking at flows into and out of unemployment is to consider the *duration of spells of unemployment*. A spell of unemployment is a period in which an individual remains continuously unemployed. The duration of unemployment is the average length of time a person remains unemployed.

---

[7]The important papers in this area include Robert E. Hall, "Why Is the Unemployment Rate So High at Full Employment?" *Brookings Papers on Economic Activity* 3 (1970); Kim B. Clark and Lawrence H. Summers, "Labor Market Dynamics and Unemployment: A Reconsideration," *Brookings Papers on Economic Activity* 1 (1979); and George Akerlof, Andrew Rose, and Janet Yellen, "Job Switching, Job Satisfaction and the U.S. Labor Market," *Brookings Papers on Economic Activity* 2 (1988).

TABLE 7-4 Unemployment by Duration

LENGTH OF UNEMPLOYMENT, WEEKS	PERCENT OF UNEMPLOYED	
	1992*	1996*
Less than 5	34.8	37.8
5–14	31.4	30.9
15–26	15.7	15.3
27 and over	15.3	16.0
Mean number of weeks	16.7 wk.	16.6 wk.
Unemployment rate	7.4%	5.5%

*February.
Source: DRI/McGraw-Hill.

By looking at the duration of unemployment, we get an idea of whether unemployment is typically short-term, with people moving quickly into and between jobs, and whether long-term unemployment is a major problem. Table 7-4 shows data on the duration of unemployment for 1992 and 1996, years of high and low unemployment. Historically, the duration of unemployment was high when the unemployment rate was high.[8] The table shows that this relation fell apart during the 1990s recovery, when unemployment fell but the duration of unemployment remained high. It is an open question whether this change represents a temporary aberration or a permanent shift in the behavior of unemployment.

7-2

FULL EMPLOYMENT

The notion of full employment, or the natural rate, or frictional rate, of unemployment, plays a central role in macroeconomics and also in macroeconomic policy. We start by discussing the theory of the natural rate, and then turn to examine estimates of the rate.

DETERMINANTS OF THE NATURAL RATE

The determinants of the natural rate of unemployment, u^*, can be thought of in terms of the *duration* and *frequency* of unemployment. The duration of unemployment (the average length of time a person remains unemployed) depends on cyclical factors and, in addition, on the following structural characteristics of the labor market:

- The organization of the labor market, including the presence or absence of employment agencies, youth employment services, and the like
- The demographic makeup of the labor force

---

[8]Michael Baker, in "Unemployment Duration: Compositional Effects and Cyclical Variability," *American Economic Review,* March 1992, shows that historically the duration of unemployment for all labor market groups tended to increase when unemployment went up.

- The ability and desire of the unemployed to keep looking for a better job, which depends in part on the availability of unemployment benefits

The last point deserves special notice. A person may quit a job to have more time to look for a new and better one. We refer to this kind of unemployment as *search unemployment.* If all jobs are the same, an unemployed person will take the first one offered. If some jobs are better than others, it is worthwhile searching and waiting for a good one. The higher the unemployment benefits, the more likely people are to keep searching for a better job, and the more likely they are to quit their current job to try to find a better one. Thus an increase in unemployment benefits will increase the natural rate of unemployment.

The behavior of workers who have been laid off is also important when considering the duration of unemployment. Typically, a worker who has been laid off returns to her original job and does not search much for another job. The reason is quite simple: A worker who has been with a firm for a long time has special expertise in the way that firm works and may have built up seniority rights, including a pension. Hence, such an individual is unlikely to find a better-paying job by searching. The best course of action may be to wait to be recalled, particularly if the individual is eligible for unemployment benefits while waiting. However, as discussed in Box 7-4, this return-to-original-job pattern appears to have broken down in the early 1990s.

FREQUENCY OF UNEMPLOYMENT

The *frequency of unemployment* is the average number of times, per period, that workers become unemployed. There are two basic determinants of the frequency of unemployment. The first is the variability of the demand for labor across different firms in the economy. Even when aggregate demand is constant, some firms are growing and some are contracting. The contracting firms lose labor, and the growing firms hire more labor. The greater the variability of the demand for labor across different firms, the higher the unemployment rate. The second determinant is the rate at which new workers enter the labor force: the more rapidly new workers enter the labor force—that is, the faster the growth rate of the labor force—the higher the natural rate of unemployment.

The three factors affecting duration and the two factors affecting frequency of unemployment are the basic determinants of the natural rate of unemployment. These factors obviously change over time. The structure of the labor market and the labor force can change. The variability of the demand for labor by differing firms can shift. As Edmund Phelps has noted, the natural rate is *not* "an intertemporal constant, something like the speed of light, independent of everything under the sun."[9]

ESTIMATES OF THE NATURAL RATE OF UNEMPLOYMENT

Estimates of the natural rate keep changing, from about 4 percent in the 1960s to 6 percent in the early 1980s to 5.5 percent in the early 1990s. The estimates are made pragmatically, using as a benchmark some period when the labor market was thought to be in equilibrium.

[9]See E. S. Phelps, "Economic Policy and Unemployment in the Sixties," *Public Interest,* Winter 1974.

BOX 7-4 Downsizing, Unemployment Duration, and the Recovery of the 1990s

One possible explanation for the increase in unemployment duration is the wave of corporate "downsizing" that swept the United States in the early 1990s. In a typical recovery, unemployed workers return to their old jobs or find similar work at other firms. After the 1991–1992 recession, many jobs, particularly many management jobs, were permanently eliminated. As a consequence, unemployed workers had to undertake much lengthier searches and were unemployed for long periods.

Figure 1 shows that the average duration of unemployment remained high through the first half of the 1990s. This further illustrates the uneven distributional consequences of unemployment. By 1996, relatively few workers were unemployed, but those who were had been jobless for a long time.

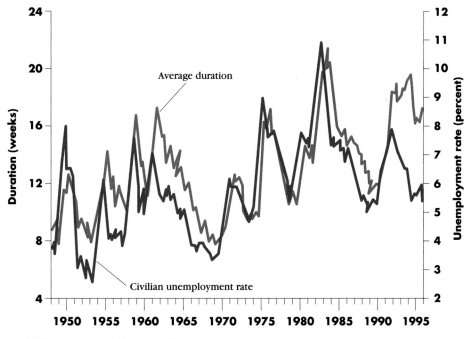

FIGURE 1   UNEMPLOYMENT RATES AND DURATION, 1948–1996.

(Source: DRI/McGraw-Hill Macroeconomic Database.)

The basis for the estimate is an equation for the natural rate (which we denote u^*) that is very similar to equation (1):

$$u^* = w_1 u_1^* + w_2 u_2^* + \ldots + w_n u_n^* \tag{2}$$

Equation (2) says that the natural rate is the weighted average of the natural rates of unemployment of the subgroups in the labor force. The estimate usually starts from a period like the mid-1950s, when the overall unemployment rate was 4 percent. It is then adjusted for changes in the composition of the labor force (i.e., the w weights) and for changes in the natural rates for the different groups (i.e., the u^* for each group).

The first set of adjustments, for the changing composition of the labor force, takes into account such changes as the increasing share of teenagers, for whom the natural rate of unemployment appears to be higher, in the labor force. These adjustments increase the natural rate, but very little.[10] The second set of adjustments tries in a variety of ways to take account of changes in the fundamental determinants of the natural rate, such as unemployment benefits.

Until the 1980s, there was an official full-employment–unemployment rate estimate. In the 1960s it was 4 percent. Adjustments for changes in the composition of the labor force raised the estimate to 4.9 percent in the early 1970s. Extrapolating to the 1980s and 1990s, the 4 percent rate of the 1960s corresponds to a range of 5 to 6 percent. It is important to recognize that the full-employment rate, u^*, is nothing but a benchmark and should properly be viewed as a band at least 1 percentage point wide.[11]

There is agreement that the natural rate of unemployment varies over time. The problem of measuring the natural rate has again become an area of active research. Some researchers, notably Douglas Staiger, James Stock, and Mark Watson, believe that the range of possible values for the natural rate is so broad as to be nearly useless for policy making. Others, Robert Gordon in particular, believe that while the natural rate varies over time, the value of the natural rate on a particular date can be estimated with considerable precision.[12]

HYSTERESIS AND THE RISING NATURAL RATE OF UNEMPLOYMENT

From 1973 to 1988 the U.S. unemployment rate stayed well above the natural rate estimated using the demographic adjustment method. Even more strikingly, unemployment

---

[10]See, for example, the demographic adjustments in Brian Motley, "Has There Been a Change in the Natural Rate of Unemployment?" Federal Reserve Bank of San Francisco *Economic Review,* Winter 1990.

[11]There is an important alternative estimate of the natural rate of unemployment: the *nonaccelerating inflation rate of unemployment* (NAIRU). This terrible terminology arises from the use of a Phillips curve like $\pi = \pi_{-1} + \epsilon(u - u^*)$, where π_{-1} may represent the expected inflation rate. It is then possible to get an estimate of u^*—the natural rate, or NAIRU—by looking for the unemployment rate at which inflation is neither accelerating nor decelerating (i.e., where $\pi = \pi_{-1}$). These estimates also tend to show an increasing NAIRU over time.

[12]Douglas Staiger, James H. Stock, and Mark W. Watson, "How Precise Are Estimates of the Natural Rate?" in C. Romer and D. Romer (eds.) *Reducing Inflation: Motivation and Strategy* (Chicago, Ill. University of Chicago Press, 1997). The Winter 1997 *Journal of Economic Perspectives* has a careful discussion of the controversy; see in particular Robert J. Gordon, "The Time-Varying NAIRU and Its Implications for Economic Policy," Joseph Stiglitz, "Reflections on the Natural Rate Hypothesis," and Olivier Blanchard and Lawrence Katz, "What We Know and Do Not Know about the Natural Rate of Unemployment."

rates in Europe averaged 4.2 percent in the 1970s and nearly 10 percent in the 1980s. Some economists argue that the unemployment rate over long periods cannot move too far from the natural rate and, therefore, that the natural rate in both the United States and Europe must have risen a lot in the 1980s.

One possible explanation is that extended periods of high unemployment raise the natural rate, a phenomenon known as *unemployment hysteresis.*[13] There are various ways in which this could happen. The unemployed might become accustomed to not working. They might find out about unemployment benefits, how to obtain them and how to spend the day doing odd jobs. Or the unemployed may become discouraged and apply less than full effort to locating a job.

The problem may be reinforced by the actions of potential employers. For instance, they may believe that the longer a person has been unemployed, the more likely it is that the person lacks either the energy or the qualifications to work. Long unemployment spells thus *signal* to firms the possibility (not the certainty!) that the worker is undesirable, and, accordingly, firms shy away from hiring such workers. Hence, the higher the unemployment rate (and therefore the longer the unemployment spells), the more unbreakable the vicious circle lengthening unemployment spells.

REDUCING THE NATURAL RATE OF UNEMPLOYMENT

Discussion of methods for reducing the natural rate of unemployment tends to focus on the high unemployment rates of teenagers and on the very high proportion of total unemployment accounted for by the long-term unemployed.

We start with teenage unemployment. Teenagers enter and leave the labor force in part because the jobs they hold are not particularly attractive. To improve jobs, the emphasis in some European countries, especially Germany, is to provide technical training for teenagers and thus make holding on to a job more rewarding. The European apprenticeship system, in which young people receive on-the-job training, is also widely credited not only with providing serious jobs for the young but also with making youths productive workers for the long term.

Teenagers' wages (on average) are closer to the minimum wage than are those of more experienced workers. Many teenagers earn the minimum wage, and some would earn less if that were permissible. Accordingly, reducing the minimum wage might be one way of reducing the teenage unemployment rate. However, programs allowing "subminimum" wages for teenagers appear to have had little impact.[14]

Unemployment Benefits

We come next to the implication of unemployment benefits for unemployment. A key concept is the *replacement ratio.* The replacement ratio is the ratio of after-tax income while unemployed to after-tax income while employed.

---

[13]See James Tobin, "Stabilization Policy Ten Years After," *Brookings Papers on Economic Activity* 1 (1980), and Olivier Blanchard and Lawrence Summers, "Hysteresis in the Unemployment Rate," *NBER Macroeconomics Annual,* 1986.

[14]For example, Charles Brown, in "Minimum Wages Laws: Are They Overrated?" *Journal of Economic Perspectives,* Summer 1988, finds little evidence that these measures have affected teenage unemployment.

BOX 7-5 Unemployment in International Perspective

In the early postwar period—indeed, through the 1960s—European unemployment was typically far less than unemployment in the United States. But this is no longer the case, as can be seen in Table 1. European unemployment in the 1980s averaged more than twice its 1970s level, which in turn was almost twice the 1960s level and was still very high in the 1990s.

With the European unemployment rate averaging more than 9 percent for a decade, it became a prime public issue and topic of academic research.* Many reasons have been advanced for the continuation of high unemployment, among them the hysteresis theory discussed in the text.

Other prominent explanations include the *inflexibility* of European labor markets, specifically the downward inflexibility of real wages and the high firing costs imposed by law. The argument is that firms were reluctant to hire workers because it would be so expensive to fire them if necessary later.†

The strength of European unions receives part of the blame. The *insider-outsider theory* of the labor market says that firms bargain with the insiders (the already employed) and have no reason to take account of the outsiders, the unemployed. Of course, if unions were not so strong, the firms might be willing to hire the outsiders at lower wages, or new firms would be set up to take advantage of the cheap labor.‡ High European unemployment benefits also contribute to high unemployment, with some potential workers being better off unemployed than in a job.

European unemployment is a problem especially because of its incidence. The share of youth among the unemployed is very high, as is the share of the unemployed who experience long-term unemployment. The long-term unemployment has for many gone on so long that most have greatly reduced their lifetime earnings potential. For example, in 1993 the long-term unemployment rate was about one-tenth the overall unemployment rate in the United States but was more than half the overall unemployment rate in much of Europe.

What can be done? One view is that aggregate demand should be increased. Another is that structural labor market policies, including training and reductions in unemployment benefits, would help cut unemployment. The idea of *work sharing*—everybody working fewer hours per day so that more people have jobs—has also been proposed.§

Notice that unemployment rates in Europe vary widely and are especially low in

*An extensive study of the European labor market appears in *The OECD Jobs Study: Evidence and Explanations* (Paris: OECD, 1995).

†See Edmond Malinvaud, *Mass Unemployment* (Oxford: Basil Blackwell, 1988), and Charles Bean, Richard Layard, and Stephen Nickell (eds.), *Unemployment* (Oxford: Basil Blackwell, 1987).

‡See Assar Lindbeck and Dennis Snower, *The Insider-Outsider Theory* (Cambridge, Mass.: M.I.T. Press, 1989). For a recent discussion of the linkages between the economics and the politics of European unemployment, see Gilles Saint-Paul, "Exploring the Political Economy of Labour Market Institutions," *Economic Policy*, October 1996.

§Jacques Dreze, "Work Sharing: Some Theory and Recent European Experience," *Economic Policy*, October 1986.

TABLE 1 Unemployment Rates and Long-Term Unemployed, Selected Countries, 1983 and 1993

	UNEMPLOYMENT RATE, PERCENT		UNEMPLOYED MORE THAN 1 YEAR, PERCENT OF TOTAL UNEMPLOYMENT*	
	1983	1993	1983	1993
North America				
Canada	11.2	10.3	7.8	11.4
United States	7.4	6.0	13.3	11.7
Japan	2.7	2.9	12.9	17.2
Central and western Europe				
Belgium	12.1	9.7	64.8	52.9
France	9.7	12.5	42.2	34.2
Germany (western)	7.1	6.9	41.6	40.3
Ireland	15.5	14.7	36.7	59.1
Netherlands	11.8	7.2	48.8	52.3
United Kingdom	11.7	9.6	45.6	42.5
Southern Europe				
Italy	9.4	12.0	69.8	57.7
Spain	19.7	23.8	52.4	56.1
Nordic countries				
Finland	5.2	18.2	19.2	30.6
Norway	3.1	5.4	6.3	27.2
Sweden	3.1	8.0	10.3	10.9
Australia	8.9	9.7	25.4	36.5

*The unemployment measure attempts to standardize across countries and so may differ from official statistics. For further discussion and an earlier version of this table, see R. Ehrenberg and J. Smith, *Modern Labor Economics*, 6th ed. (Reading, Mass.: Addison-Wesley, 1997).

Source: OECD, *Employment Outlook*, July 1995, tables L and Q.

Sweden and Norway. In part, this reflects the relatively robust state of the Scandinavian economies in 1983 and 1993. But Sweden, in particular, has a very activist policy for finding jobs for the unemployed—including public sector employment when necessary.

The European experience stands in sharp contrast to the minimal unemployment in Japan. Japanese workers typically receive part of their income in the form of a *bonus*, once or twice a year. This means, in effect, that firms can cut wages (i.e., the bonus) when times are bad, thus creating wage flexibility. Martin Weitzman has proposed a *profit-sharing* scheme for Europe and the United States, which would make the wage more flexible, but profit sharing has not caught on.[¶]

In economics, where experiments are not usually possible, any extreme experience—like the Great Depression or European unemployment—provides an opportunity to test and develop theories. That, along with the need to deal with a severe social problem, is why so much attention has been paid to the European unemployment of the 1980s. Unfortunately, that experience has extended into the 1990s as well.

[¶]Martin Weitzman, "Macroeconomic Implications of Profit Sharing," *NBER Macroeconomics Annual*, 1986.

Unemployment benefits increase the rate of unemployment in two ways. First, unemployment benefits allow longer job search. The higher the replacement ratio, the less urgent it is for an unemployed person to take a job. Feldstein and Poterba have shown that high replacement ratios significantly affect the *reservation wage,* the wage at which a person receiving unemployment benefits is willing to take a new job.[15]

The issue of the effects of unemployment benefits on unemployment is particularly lively in Europe. Many observers argue that high levels of European unemployment result from the very high replacement ratios there. Patrick Minford states: "The picture presented is a grim one from the point of view of incentives to participate in employment. The replacement ratios are such that, should a person 'work the system,' incentives to have a job are, on the whole, rather small for a family man."[16]

The second channel is *employment stability.* With unemployment insurance, the consequences of being in and out of jobs are less severe.[17] Accordingly, it is argued, workers and firms do not find it as much in their interest to create highly stable employment, and firms are more willing to lay off workers temporarily than to attempt to keep them on the job. The employment stability effect is mitigated by *experience rating.* The unemployment insurance tax is raised on firms whose employees have high unemployment rates, giving firms an incentive toward more stable employment. However, experience rating does not make firms bear the entire cost of unemployment insurance, so the mitigation is only partial.

In addition to changes in real unemployment, unemployment benefits raise the *measured* unemployment rate through *reporting effects.* To collect unemployment benefits, people have to be "in the labor force," looking for work even if they do not really want a job. They therefore get counted as unemployed. One estimate suggests that reporting effects raise the unemployment rate by about half a percentage point.

There seems to be little doubt that unemployment compensation does add to the natural rate of unemployment.[18] This does not imply, though, that unemployment compensation should be abolished. Unemployment insurance may increase economic efficiency by subsidizing the job search process, which results in improved worker-employer matches. Of greater importance, there is considerable randomness in who becomes unemployed and who does not, and fairness argues for sharing the burden of unemployment. In designing unemployment benefits, there is a tradeoff between

---

[15]Martin Feldstein and James Poterba, "Unemployment Insurance and Reservation Wages," *Journal of Public Economics,* February–March 1984.

[16]Patrick Minford, *Unemployment, Causes and Cures* (Oxford: Blackwell, 1985), p. 39.

[17]Randall Wright argues that European insurance compensates for short work hours rather than just total unemployment, as is the case in the United States and Canada. He concludes that the European system results in less variability of employment, though higher variability in hours per worker. See his "The Labor Market Implications of Unemployment Insurance and Short-Time Compensation," Federal Reserve Bank of Minneapolis *Quarterly Review,* Summer 1991.

[18]Among the most convincing evidence is the finding that unemployment spells tend to end, with the worker going back to a job, at precisely the time that unemployment benefits run out (typically after 26 or 39 weeks of unemployment). See Lawrence Katz and Bruce Meyer, "Unemployment Insurance, Recall Expectations, and Unemployment Outcomes," *Quarterly Journal of Economics,* November 1990.

reducing the distress suffered by the unemployed and the likelihood that higher bene-fits raise the natural rate.[19]

7-3

THE COSTS OF UNEMPLOYMENT

The unemployed as individuals suffer both from their income loss while unemployed and from the related social problems that long periods of unemployment cause. Soci-ety on the whole loses from unemployment because total output is below its potential level.

This section provides some estimates of the costs of forgone output resulting from unemployment, and it clarifies some of the issues connected with the costs of unem-ployment and the potential benefits from reducing unemployment. We emphasize the costs of cyclical unemployment, which is associated with short-run deviations of the unemployment rate from the natural rate.

THE COSTS OF CYCLICAL UNEMPLOYMENT

A first measure of the costs of cyclical unemployment is the output lost because the economy is not at full employment. We can obtain an estimate of this loss by using Okun's law, illustrated in Figure 7-1.

According to Okun's law, the economy loses about 2 percent of output for each 1 percent that the unemployment rate exceeds the natural rate. Consider 1991's mild recession. Using a Data Resources, Inc. (DRI) estimate that the natural rate in 1991 was 5.5 percent and noting that the actual rate was 6.6 percent, we conclude that the recession caused a loss of 2.2 percent of GDP in 1991. That amounts to about $130 billion. As the recession deepened into 1992, the unemployment rate averaged 7.4 percent. DRI estimates a 1992 natural rate of 5.4 percent, so the output loss was about 4 percent of GDP, or about $250 billion.

These very large costs invite the question of why policy makers should tolerate such high unemployment.

Distributional Impact of Unemployment

While the Okun's law estimate provides the basic measure of the overall costs of cycli-cal unemployment, the distributional impact of unemployment also has to be taken into account. Typically a 1-percentage-point increase in the overall unemployment rate is accompanied by a 2-percentage-point increase in the unemployment rate among blacks (see Figure 7-2). In general, unemployment hits poorer people harder than it hits the rich, and this aspect should increase concern about the problem.

---

[19]This tradeoff was at the center of an argument between Congress and the Reagan and Bush administra-tions during recent recessions: Congress generally voted to extend the payment of unemployment benefits by 3 months, in order to help the unemployed, while the administration sometimes argued that this would raise unemployment.

The Okun's law estimate encompasses *all* the lost income, including that of all individuals who lose their jobs. That total loss could, in principle, be distributed among different people in the economy in many different ways. For instance, one could imagine that the unemployed would continue to receive benefit payments totaling close to what their income had been while employed, with the benefit payments financed through taxes on working individuals. In that case, the unemployed would not suffer an income loss from being unemployed, but society would still lose from the reduction in total output. The unemployment compensation system partially, but by no means fully, spreads the burden of unemployment.

Other Costs and Benefits

Are there any other costs of unemployment or, for that matter, any offsetting benefits? A possible offsetting benefit occurs because the unemployed, by not working, have more leisure. However, the value that can be placed on that leisure is small. In the first place, much of it is unwanted leisure.

Second, because people pay taxes on their wages, society in general receives a benefit in the form of tax revenue when workers are employed. When a worker loses her job, society bears the additional cost of lost tax revenue on top of the worker's lost wages. This is an additional reason that the benefit of increased leisure provides only a partial offset to the Okun's law estimate of the cost of cyclical unemployment.

7-4

THE COSTS OF INFLATION

There is no direct loss of output from inflation, as there is from unemployment. In considering the costs of inflation, it is important to distinguish between inflation that is *perfectly anticipated,* and taken into account in economic transactions, and *imperfectly anticipated,* or unexpected, inflation. We start with perfectly anticipated inflation.

PERFECTLY ANTICIPATED INFLATION

Suppose that an economy has been experiencing a given rate of inflation, say, 5 percent, for a long time and that everyone correctly anticipates that the rate of inflation will continue to be 5 percent. In such an economy, all contracts would build in the expected 5 percent inflation.

Borrowers and lenders would know and agree that the dollars in which a loan is repaid will be worth less than the dollars given up by the lender when making the loan. Nominal interest rates would be raised 5 percent to compensate for the inflation. Long-term labor contracts would increase wages at 5 percent per year to take account of the inflation and would then build in whatever changes in real wages are agreed to. Long-term leases would take account of the inflation. In brief, any contracts in which the passage of time is involved would take the 5 percent inflation into account. In that category we include the tax laws, which we are assuming would be indexed. The tax brackets themselves would be increased at the rate of 5 percent per year.[20]

In such an economy, inflation has no real costs—except for two qualifications. The first qualification arises because no interest is paid on currency—notes and coins—not least because it is very difficult to do so. This means that the costs of holding currency rise along with the inflation rate.

The cost to the individual of holding currency is the interest forgone by not holding an interest-bearing asset.[21] When the inflation rate rises, the nominal interest rate rises, the interest lost by holding currency increases, and the cost of holding currency therefore increases. Accordingly, the demand for currency falls. Individuals have to make do with less currency, making more trips to the bank to cash smaller checks than they did before. The costs of these trips to the bank are often described as the "shoe-leather" costs of inflation. They are related to the amount by which the demand for currency is reduced by an increase in the anticipated inflation rate, and they are estimated to be small.

The second qualification is the "menu costs" of inflation. These arise from the fact that with inflation—as opposed to price stability—people have to devote real resources to marking up prices and changing pay telephones and vending machines as well as cash registers. Those costs are there, but one cannot get too excited about them.

We should add that we are assuming here reasonable inflation rates, say, in the single or low double digits, that are low enough not to disrupt the payments system. At such low to moderate inflation rates, the costs of fully anticipated inflation are small.[22]

The notion that the costs of fully anticipated inflation are small does not square well with the strong aversion to inflation reflected in policy making and politics. The most important reason for that aversion is that the inflationary experience of the United States is one of varying, imperfectly anticipated inflation, the costs of which are substantially different from those discussed in this section.

---

[20]The taxation of interest would have to be on the *real* (after-inflation) return on assets for the tax system to be properly indexed.

[21]Note that cash holders are effectively making an interest-free loan to the government. The direct effect of higher interest rates is a transfer of revenue from the private to the public sector. This is sometimes called an "inflation tax."

[22]There is clear cross-country evidence that high rates of inflation are associated with low rates of sustained growth. The negative link is not due to costs of inflation per se. Rather, "The inflation rate serves as an indicator of the overall ability of the government to manage the economy. Since there are no good arguments for very high rates of inflation, a government that is producing high inflation is a government that has lost control." (Stanley Fischer, "Macroeconomic Factors in Growth," *Journal of Monetary Economics,* December 1993.) See also V. V. Chari, Larry E. Jones, and Rodolfo E. Manuelli, "Inflation, Growth, and Financial Intermediation," Michael Bruno and William Easterly, "Inflation and Growth: In Search of a Stable Relationship," and Robert J. Barro, "Inflation and Growth," all in Federal Reserve Bank of St. Louis *Review,* May–June 1996, and M. Bruno, "Does Inflation Really Lower Growth," *Finance and Development,* September 1995.

ЁЁō5⁵ō5$‑

BOX 7-6 Surely, Anticipated Inflation Isn't Really Costless?

It mainly is, but the view of the average citizen seems to be closer to "5 percent inflation costs me 5 percent." Probably the misperception arises from a viewpoint something like the following: We understand that in a 5 percent anticipated inflation nominal prices and nominal wages both rise 5 percent and so real wages are unchanged. Workers, however, see the 5 percent wage increase and attribute it to their own hard work, to the bargaining power of their unions, or to the success of their companies. The increase in prices is seen as eroding these "earned" gains.

While students of economics understand that the increases in nominal wages and prices are linked consequences of the inflation rate, it is hard to convince the general public of this view.

IMPERFECTLY ANTICIPATED INFLATION

The idyllic scenario of full adjustment to inflation does not describe economies in the real world. Modern economies include a variety of institutional features representing different degrees of adjustment to inflation. Economies with long inflationary histories, such as those of Brazil and Israel, have made substantial adjustments to inflation through the use of indexing. Those in which inflation has been episodic, such as the U.S. economy, have not.

Wealth Redistribution Through Inflation

One important effect of inflation is a change in the real value of assets fixed in nominal terms. Between 1966 and 1996 the price level in the United States rose almost fivefold, cutting the purchasing power of all claims or assets fixed in money terms to one-fifth their initial value.[23] Thus, someone who bought a 30-year government bond in 1966 and expected to receive principal of, say, $100 in constant purchasing power at the 1996 maturity date actually wound up with a $100 principal that had a purchasing power of $20 in 1966 dollars. Similarly, a worker who retired on a fixed dollar pension in 1966 finds that her income will buy only about one-fifth of what it did at retirement. The near quintupling of the price level has—if it was unanticipated—transferred wealth from the creditors or holders of bonds to the borrowers and from pensioners to firms.

This redistribution effect operates with respect to all assets fixed in nominal terms, in particular, money, bonds, savings accounts, insurance contracts, and some pensions. It implies that *realized real interest rates* are lower than nominal interest rates on assets, and even possibly negative. Obviously, it is an extremely important effect, since

---

[23]Remember from Chap. 2 that measured inflation probably overstates true inflation. A rough guess might be that prices over this period rose to 3.5, rather than to 5, times their original level.

TABLE 7-5 Real Asset Returns
(Percent per year)

	1960–1969	1970–1979	1980–1989	1990–1995
Currency	− 2.3	− 7.1	− 5.6	− 3.5
Treasury bills	1.6	− 0.8	3.3	1.3
Bonds	2.3	0.4	5.0	3.7

Source: DRI/McGraw-Hill Macroeconomic Database.

it can wipe out the purchasing power of a lifetime's saving that is supposed to finance retirement consumption. Table 7-5 shows real returns on various assets. We note that currency earns negative real returns whenever inflation is positive.

Table 7-6 shows the asset and liability positions by sector in the U.S. economy. The *net* nominal creditor status of a sector is just equal to nominal assets less nominal liabilities. Under this definition, the household sector is a creditor in nominal terms, with the government and nonfinancial and financial business the offsetting major monetary debtors. Unanticipated inflation therefore erodes the real value of households' net nominal creditor position. Nonfinancial corporations are net monetary debtors, reflecting their debt-financed capital structure. Financial corporations, too, are net monetary debtors.

In 1991 the total value of assets fixed in nominal terms held by households was $5.4 trillion. An increase of 1 percentage point in the price level would reduce the real value of these assets by $54 billion. Thus a change in the price level brings about a major *redistribution of wealth*. In particular, with government as the major net nominal debtor, the main redistribution is between the government sector and the private sector.

We must go beyond Table 7-6 in two respects. First, the table does not tell us to what extent inflation was anticipated when the contracts behind the figures in the table were drawn up. Inflation might have been correctly anticipated, so the wealth transfers occurring as a result of the inflation would not cause any surprises or upset.

TABLE 7-6 Net Nominal Creditor Status, Year End 1991
(Billions of dollars)

	ASSETS			LIABILITIES,
		FINANCIAL		
	TANGIBLE	NOMINAL	REAL	NOMINAL
Households	9,102	5,371	9,819	4,190
Farm and unincorporated business	866	49		163
Nonfinancial corporate business	5,061	2,238		3,433
Financial business	508	10,189	1,844	11,553
Public sector (net)*				2,815

*Financial liabilities.

Source: Federal Reserve Board, *Balance Sheets for the U.S. Economy, 1960–1991*.

Second, the gains and losses from the redistributions of wealth among sectors and individuals that takes place as a result of unanticipated inflation basically cancel out over the economy as a whole. When the government gains from inflation, the private sector pays lower taxes. When the corporate sector gains from inflation, owners of corporations benefit at the expense of others. If we really did not care about redistributing wealth among individuals, the costs of unanticipated inflation would be negligible. Included in the individuals of the previous sentence are those belonging to different generations, since the current owners of the national debt might be harmed by inflation—to the benefit of future taxpayers.

Who gains and who loses from unanticipated inflation? There is a popular belief that the old are more vulnerable to inflation than the young in that the old own more nominal assets. Offsetting this, however, is the fact that social security benefits are indexed, so a substantial part of the wealth of retirees is protected from unanticipated inflation. Common political rhetoric also alleges that the poor are especially vulnerable to unanticipated inflation. There appears to be little evidence supporting this view for the United States.[24]

Inflation redistributes *wealth* between debtors and creditors. It could also redistribute *income*. A popular line of argument has always been that inflation benefits capitalists or recipients of profit income at the expense of wage earners. Unanticipated inflation, it is argued, means that prices rise faster than wages and therefore allow profits to expand. For the United States in the post-World War II period, there is no persuasive evidence to this effect. There is evidence that the real return on common stocks—that is, the real value of dividends and capital gains on equity—is reduced by unanticipated inflation. Thus, equity holders are hurt by unanticipated inflation.[25]

The last important distributional effect of inflation concerns the real value of tax liabilities. A failure to index the tax structure implies that inflation moves the public into higher tax brackets and thus raises the real value of its tax payments or reduces real disposable income. Absent indexed tax brackets, inflation is effectively the same as a congressionally voted increase in tax schedules. Tax brackets in the United States have been indexed since 1985.[26]

The fact that unanticipated inflation serves mainly to redistribute wealth has led to some questioning of the reasons for public concern over inflation. The gainers, it seems, do not shout as loudly as the losers. Since some of the gainers (future taxpayers) have yet to be born, this is hardly surprising. There is also a notion that the average wage earner misperceives the connection between the nominal wage and price-level increases (see Box 7-6).

---

[24]See Rebecca Blank and Alan Blinder, "Macroeconomics, Income Distribution and Poverty," in Sheldon Danziger and Daniel Weinberg (eds.), *Fighting Poverty* (Cambridge, Mass.: Harvard University Press, 1986).

[25]See Charles R. Nelson, "Inflation and Rates of Return on Common Stocks," *Journal of Finance,* May 1976, for one of the earliest articles with this result—which has stood up to repeated testing. See also Franco Modigliani and Richard Cohn, "Inflation, Rational Valuation and the Market," *Financial Analysts Journal,* March–April 1979, for a controversial view of the reasons inflation affects the stock market.

[26]Inflation also affects the real rate of taxation of interest and other asset returns when taxes are not adjusted for inflation. U.S. tax laws do not adjust the taxation of asset returns for inflation.

7-5

INFLATION AND INDEXATION: INFLATION-PROOFING THE ECONOMY

In this section we look briefly at two kinds of contracts that are especially affected by inflation, long-term loan contracts and wage contracts. We then discuss the possibility of reducing people's vulnerability to inflation by *indexation,* which ties the terms of contracts to the behavior of the price level.

INFLATION AND INTEREST RATES

There are many long-term nominal loan contracts, including 30-year government bonds and 25 or 30-year mortgages. For example, a firm may sell 20-year bonds in the capital markets at an interest rate of 8 percent per year. Whether the *real* (after-inflation) interest rate on the bonds turns out to be high or low depends on what the inflation rate will be over the next 20 years. The rate of inflation is thus of great importance to long-term lenders and borrowers, and this is especially true in housing.

Inflation and Housing

The typical U.S. or Canadian household buys a home by borrowing from a bank or a savings and loan institution. The interaction of inflation and taxes has a big impact on the real cost of borrowing. Traditionally, U.S. mortgages—this is the term for the home loan—set a fixed nominal interest rate for a duration of 25 or 30 years. The interest payments are deductible in calculating U.S. federal income taxes,[27] thereby reducing the effective interest cost of the loan. For instance; suppose the marginal tax rate is 30 percent; then the nominal interest cost is 70 percent of the actual mortgage rate.[28]

Now consider the economics of investing in a home, for example, for someone buying a home in 1963 and financing it with a 25-year fixed-interest mortgage. The mortgage rate in 1963 was 5.9 percent, and the rate of inflation over the next 25 years averaged 5.4 percent. Thus the pretax actual real interest cost of borrowing was .5 percent. In addition, the home buyer could deduct the interest paid on the mortgage from his or her taxable income. At an interest rate of 5.9 percent and a tax rate of 30 percent, the tax reduction was worth 1.77 percent a year (30 percent of 5.9 percent), so the after-tax real cost of borrowing was *minus* 1.3 percent—not a bad deal! But of course inflation could have turned out to be lower than expected, and then the borrower would have done worse than she expected and the lender would have made, rather than lost, money.

Uncertainty about the outlook for inflation was one of the reasons a new financial instrument made its appearance: the *adjustable rate mortgage (ARM),* which is a particular example of a *floating rate* loan. This is a long-term loan with an interest rate that is periodically (every year, for example) adjusted in line with prevailing short-term interest rates. To the extent that nominal interest rates roughly reflect inflation trends,

---

[27]In an interesting difference between two fairly similar tax codes, interest payments on home mortgages are not deductible in Canada.

[28]A table of worked-out examples appears in Chap. 14.

adjustable rate mortgages reduce the effects of inflation on the long-term real costs of financing home purchases. Both adjustable rate and long-term fixed-interest mortgages are now in use in the United States. Interestingly, mortgage loans in Canada have been variants of ARMs for many years.

Indexed Debt

In countries where inflation rates are high and uncertain, long-term borrowing using nominal debt becomes impossible: lenders are simply too uncertain about the real value of the repayments they will receive. In such countries, governments typically issue *indexed debt.* A bond is indexed (to the price level) when either the interest or the principal or both are adjusted for inflation.[29]

The holder of an indexed bond will typically receive interest equal to the stated real interest rate (e.g., 3 percent) plus whatever the inflation rate turns out to be. Thus, if inflation is 18 percent, the bondholder receives 21 percent; if inflation is 50 percent, the *ex post* nominal interest payment is 53 percent. That way the bondholder is compensated for inflation.

Many economists have argued that governments should issue indexed debt so that citizens can hold at least one asset with a safe real return. However, it is generally only governments in high-inflation countries, such as Brazil, Argentina, and Israel, that issue such debt, and they do it because they could not otherwise borrow.

Among low-inflation countries, the U.K. government has been issuing indexed bonds since 1979. The U.S. Treasury began issuing indexed debt in 1997, hoping that the value of "inflation insurance" would lower the real interest rate the government pays. Of course, since social security payments in many countries are effectively indexed, the citizens of those countries do hold an asset that protects them against inflation. However, the stream of social security payments is not an asset they can buy and sell.

We will consider the arguments for and against indexation below.

INDEXATION OF WAGES

Formal labor contracts sometimes include automatic *cost-of-living adjustment (COLA)* provisions. COLA provisions link increases in money wages to increases in the price level. COLA clauses are designed to allow workers to recover, wholly or in part, purchasing power lost through price increases since the signing of the labor contract.

This form of indexation is a quite common feature of labor markets in many countries. Indexation strikes a balance between the advantages of long-term wage contracts and the interests of workers and firms in not having *real* wages get too far out of line.

Because wage bargaining is time-consuming and difficult, wages are not negotiated once a week or once a month but, rather, in the form of 1- or 3-year contracts. But since prices will change over the term of these contracts, some adjustment has to be made for inflation. Broadly, there are two possibilities. One is to index wages to the CPI or the GDP deflator and, through periodic, say, quarterly, reviews, to increase wages by the increase in prices over the period. The other is to schedule periodic, preannounced wage increases based on the expected rate of price increase. If inflation

---

[29]It is also common to index debt to the value of a foreign currency, frequently the U.S. dollar.

were known with certainty, the two methods would produce the same result. But since inflation can differ from expectations, there will be discrepancies.

We should expect to find indexation, rather than preannounced wage increases, when uncertainty about inflation is high. Inflation is more uncertain when the inflation rate is high than when it is low, and therefore wage indexation is more prevalent in high-inflation than low-inflation countries.

In the U.S. economy more than 50 percent of workers who were covered in major collective bargaining agreements in the mid-1980s had contract provisions for automatic cost-of-living adjustments. These provisions were much more common after 1973, when inflation became higher and more variable, than they were before. They have again declined as inflation has stayed low. However, while COLA clauses are an important part of many collective bargaining contracts, relatively few American workers are covered because of the decline in unionization. By 1985, for example, only about 10 million workers out of a total labor force pool of 110 million were covered by COLA provisions.

Supply Shocks and Wage Indexation

Suppose real materials prices increase, and firms pass these cost increases on as higher prices of final goods. Consumer prices will rise, and under a system of wage indexation, wages will rise. This leads to further price, materials-cost, and wage increases. Indexation here feeds an inflation spiral that would be avoided under a system of prefixed wage increases, because then real wages could fall as a consequence of higher materials prices.

The example makes it clear that we must distinguish two possibilities in considering the effects of wage indexing: demand shocks and supply shocks. In the case of a demand shock, there is a "pure" inflation disturbance, and firms can afford to pay the same real wages and therefore will not be adversely affected in real terms by 100 percent indexation. In the case of an adverse supply shock, however, real wages must fall, and full indexation prevents that happening.

Wage indexation thus greatly complicates the adjustment of an economy to supply shocks. In the 1970s and 1980s, the U.S. economy adjusted more easily to the oil shocks than did countries in Europe, where full indexation is more common. The limited extent of wage indexing in the United States helped bring this easier adjustment about.[30]

WHY NOT INDEX?

Economists have often argued that governments should adopt indexation on a broad scale, indexing bonds, the tax system, and everything else they control. That way, inflation would be much easier to live with, and most of the costs of unanticipated inflation would disappear. Governments, by contrast, have been very reluctant to index.

There are three good reasons. First, as we see in the case of wage indexation, indexing makes it harder for the economy to adjust to shocks whenever changes in relative prices are needed. Second, indexing is in practice complicated, adding another

---

[30]See Michael Bruno and Jeffrey Sachs, *The Economics of Worldwide Stagflation* (Cambridge, Mass.: Harvard University Press, 1985).

layer of calculation to most contracts. Third, governments are scared that by making inflation easier to live with, indexation will weaken the political will to fight inflation, lead to higher inflation, and possibly make the economy worse off since indexation can never deal perfectly with the consequences of inflation.[31]

This last argument is one of political economy, the subject we discuss in the last section of the chapter.

7-6

IS A LITTLE INFLATION GOOD FOR THE ECONOMY?

Nominal wage cuts are rare. More than 25 years ago, James Tobin argued that a small amount of inflation is good for the economy—and reduces the natural rate of unemployment—because it provides a necessary mechanism for lowering real wages without cutting nominal wages.[32] The idea has recently been revived in an influential article by George A. Akerlof, William T. Dickens, and George L. Perry.[33]

The argument is as follows: In a changing world, some real wages need to go up and some need to go down in order to achieve economic efficiency and low unemployment. It is easy to raise real wages by simply raising nominal wages faster than inflation. To cut real wages, firms must hold nominal wage increases below the rate of inflation. For example, at a 10 percent inflation rate, a 3 percent real wage cut can be accomplished by holding the nominal wage increase to 7 percent. But at zero inflation, firms would have to cut paychecks by 3 percent.

Except when a firm is known to be in dire straits, workers are extraordinarily resistant to cuts in nominal pay. Such cuts, therefore, are very costly to firms. The recommendation, then, is to maintain inflation at something like 3 percent so that the real wage adjustment can be achieved without nominal pay cuts.

Nominal pay cuts have been relatively rare.[34] It is certainly true that workers and firms *say* they have a strong dislike for nominal pay cuts.[35] It is argued, on the other hand, that in an environment of steady zero inflation workers and firms would come to regard a 3 percent nominal cut in the same way they had previously viewed a 7 percent nominal wage increase during a 10 percent inflation.

The idea that positive inflation has a significant benefit is very controversial. The very existence of this controversy is a departure from the traditional view that zero is the best inflation target.

---

[31]Indexation cannot be perfect because there are lags in measuring the price level and making payments.

[32]See James Tobin, "Inflation and Unemployment" (American Economic Association presidential address), *American Economic Review,* March 1972.

[33]See G. A. Akerlof, W. T. Dickens, and G. L. Perry, "The Macroeconomics of Low Inflation," *Brookings Papers on Economic Activity* 1 (1996).

[34]See David Card and Dean Hyslop, "Does Inflation 'Grease the Wheels of the Labor Market'?" NBER Working Paper 5538, April 1996, for some evidence on the frequency of wage cuts.

[35]It is interesting to note that many universities have regulations that effectively forbid nominal wage cuts for individual faculty, although across-the-board cuts sometimes occur.

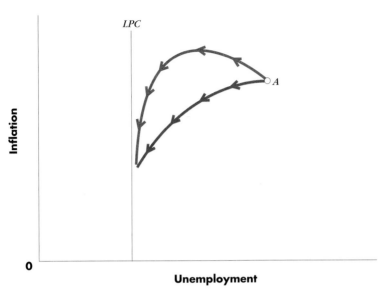

FIGURE 7-3 ALTERNATE PATHS OF INFLATION AND UNEMPLOYMENT.

7-7

THE POLITICAL ECONOMY OF INFLATION AND UNEMPLOYMENT

While the best of all worlds is one with neither inflation nor excess unemployment, that world is not available. In the short run, policy makers frequently have to decide how hard to fight an inflationary shock, knowing that the less they accommodate it, the more unemployment they will have. In the long run, policy makers have to decide whether to aim for a very low, or even zero, inflation rate or be willing to live with positive inflation.

ALTERNATIVE POLICY PATHS

Figure 7-3 shows a long-run Phillips curve, *LPC,* which indicates that in the long run there is no tradeoff between inflation and unemployment. Suppose now that as a consequence of a disturbance, say, an oil shock, the economy finds itself at point *A,* with high inflation and high unemployment. We show two possible adjustment paths. The red path shows higher inflation rates in the transition and corresponds to a policy choice of rapid restoration of low unemployment levels and then a long period of decelerating inflation. An alternative is the blue path, which shows an immediate reduction in inflation. Along this path inflation is falling, but the cost is that the reduction in unemployment is more gradual.

Figure 7-3 makes the point that policy makers do not choose between inflation and unemployment but, rather, between *adjustment paths* that differ in the inflation-unemployment mix. The red path corresponds to a gradualist disinflation policy; the blue path is closer to a "cold-turkey" policy.

How do policy makers actually choose between paths such as those shown in Figure 7-3? There are two ways of thinking about this problem. One is to assume that policy makers are "benevolent dictators" who act in the interests of society. They form estimates of the social costs associated with alternative paths of inflation and unemployment and choose the path that minimizes the total cost of stabilization to society.

The second approach to policy choices recognizes the political nature of the decisions. In a democracy, policy makers respond to the electorate and choose policies that will maximize their chances of being kept in office. This approach has given rise to an extensive literature in economics and political science that is classified as *political business cycle theory.*

POLITICAL BUSINESS CYCLE THEORY

Political business cycle theory studies the interactions between economic policy decisions and political considerations. The best-known prediction of the theory is that the business cycle mirrors the timetable of the election cycle.

We now review the building blocks of this theory.[36] We have already discussed the first, the tradeoffs from which a policy maker can choose. There are two more building blocks: how voters rate the issue (of inflation versus unemployment), and the optimal timing for influencing election results.

Rating the Issues

Table 7-1 showed results of Gallup opinion polls. We noted there that voters worry about inflation and unemployment when they are high. More careful study of the polls reveals a further important lesson: Voters worry about both the *level* and the *rate of change* of the inflation and unemployment rates. *Rising* unemployment increases the public's concern over unemployment. Concern over inflation depends on the expectation of rising inflation as well as on the level of inflation. These facts influence the types of policies politicians will choose.

Timing

The policy maker wants to be sure that at election time the economy is pointed in the right direction in order to garner maximum voter approval. The inflation rate and unemployment rate should be falling if possible—and should not be too high, if that can be managed. The problem is how to use the period from inauguration to election to bring the economy to just the right position.

The political business cycle hypothesis suggests the following: Politicians use restrictive policies early in an administration, raising unemployment to reduce inflation. The need for restraint can often be blamed on a previous administration. But as the election approaches, expansion takes over to ensure that falling unemployment brings voter approval even while the level of unemployment still checks inflation. According

---

[36]For a survey, see Alberto Alesina, "Macroeconomics and Politics," *NBER Macroeconomics Annual,* 1988, and William Nordhaus, "Alternative Approaches to the Political Business Cycle," *Brookings Papers on Economic Activity* 2 (1989). For a critical view, see K. Alec Chrystal and David A. Peel, "What Can Economics Learn from Political Science, and Vice Versa," *American Economic Review,* May 1986.

BOX 7-7 The Misery Index

The public dislikes both unemployment and inflation. One attempt to measure the political effect of unemployment and inflation is called the *misery index*, which is simply the sum of unemployment and inflation:

$$\text{misery index} = u + \pi$$

One version of political business cycle theory suggests that the party in power will do well if the misery index is low or falling and will do poorly if the misery index is high or rising. Figure 1 shows the misery index in the United States, as well as the percentage of the presidential vote received by the candidate of the incumbent party.

The data behind Figure 1 show a weak negative relation between the change in the misery index and the fortunes of the incumbent's party. But as you can gather from the figure, the evidence for the relation is hardly overwhelming. In part, this is because so many other factors also drive voters' decisions. In addition, voters probably do not weigh unemployment and inflation equally—as the misery index does implicitly.

FIGURE 1 THE MISERY INDEX AND THE PERCENTAGE OF THE PRESIDENTIAL VOTE TO THE INCUMBENT.

(Source: DRI/McGraw-Hill Macroeconomic Database.)

to this hypothesis, there should be a systematic cycle in unemployment, rising in the first part of a presidential term and declining in the second.

The empirical evidence on the political business cycle remains mixed.[37] The U.S. data do not show as clear a pattern over the 4-year presidential cycle as the theory would lead us to expect. Every now and then, though, as in 1969–1972, 1981–1984, and in 1988, the model seems to work to perfection.

In any event, there are factors that work against the political business cycle. In general, we know that the ability of the government to fine-tune the economy is limited. There are also difficulties specific to the implementation of politically motivated manipulations. One is that the president cannot use the business cycle fully because of midterm congressional elections. The second is that a president cannot indulge too openly in staging recessions and recoveries timed solely with a view to the election. There are risks to being caught in cynical manipulation of macroeconomic policies. Third, large macroshocks—oil shocks and wars—may on occasion overshadow the election cycle. Fourth, the executive does not control the full range of instruments. Specifically, the Fed is in large part independent and therefore need not accommodate an attempt to move the economy in an election cycle. In fact, though, the Fed has not always spoiled the game. At least on one occasion, in 1972, the Fed very obviously provided expansion just at the right time.[38] Fifth, if expectations are rational, monetary policy expansions staged just for the elections will have only small real effects and will mainly produce inflation.

Thus we should not be surprised that the electoral cycle is not completely regular. Nonetheless, the hypothesis should not be dismissed. No doubt, every administration would like to have the economy strongly expanding, with declining inflation, at election time. Some are skilled or lucky, and they are reelected. Others are less skilled, or unlucky, and they lose the election.

SUMMARY

1. The anatomy of unemployment in the United States reveals frequent short spells of unemployment. Nonetheless, a substantial fraction of U.S. unemployment is accounted for by those who are unemployed for a large portion of time.

2. There are significant differences in unemployment rates across age groups and race. Unemployment among black teenagers is highest, and that among white adults is lowest. The young and minorities have significantly higher unemployment rates than middle-aged whites.

3. The concept of the natural, or frictional, rate of unemployment singles out that part of unemployment which would exist even at full employment. This unemployment arises from the natural frictions of the labor market, as people move between jobs. The natural rate is hard to measure, but the consensus is to estimate it at about 5.5 percent, up from the 4 percent of the mid-1950s.

4. Policies to reduce the natural rate of unemployment involve structural labor market policies. Disincentives to employment and training, such as minimum wages, and incentives to extended job search, such as high unemployment benefits, tend

[37]See Ray Fair, "Econometrics and Presidential Elections," *Journal of Economic Perspectives,* Summer 1996.

[38]See Chap. 16 for a more extensive discussion of central bank independence.

to raise the natural rate. It is also possible that unemployment displays hysteresis, with extended periods of high unemployment raising the natural rate.

5. The costs of unemployment are the psychological and financial distress of the unemployed, as well as the loss of output. In addition, higher unemployment tends to hit the poorer members of society disproportionately.

6. The economy can adjust to perfectly anticipated inflation by moving to a system of indexed taxes and to nominal interest rates that reflect the expected rate of inflation. If inflation were perfectly anticipated and adjusted to, the only costs of inflation would be shoe-leather and menu costs.

7. Imperfectly anticipated inflation has important redistributive effects among sectors. Unanticipated inflation benefits monetary debtors and hurts monetary creditors. The government gains real tax revenue, and the real value of government debt declines.

8. In the U.S. housing market, unanticipated increases in inflation, combined with the tax deductibility of interest, made housing a particularly good investment during the 1960–1980 period.

9. In the U.S. economy, indexation is neither very widespread nor complete. The absence of strong indexation probably eased the adjustment to supply shocks.

10. While very high inflation rates are bad, there is some evidence that a small positive inflation rate lubricates the economy by reducing real wage rigidity.

11. The political business cycle hypothesis emphasizes the economy's direction of change. For incumbents to win an election, the unemployment rate should be falling and the inflation rate not worsening.

KEY TERMS

sacrifice ratio	search unemployment	reporting effects
Okun's law	frequency of unemployment	indexation
labor force	unemployment hysteresis	cost-of-living adjustment
unemployed person	replacement ratio	(COLA)
unemployment pool	reservation wage	political business cycle
frictional unemployment	insider-outsider theory	theory
cyclical unemployment	employment stability	misery index
spell of unemployment	experience rating	

PROBLEMS

Conceptual

1. Discuss strategies whereby the government (federal, state, or local) could reduce unemployment in or among (a) depressed industries, (b) unskilled workers, (c) depressed geographical regions, (d) teenagers. Include comments on the type of unemployment you would expect to see in these various groups, as well as on the relative duration of unemployment spells that should exist among these groups.

2. Discuss how the following changes would affect the natural (or frictional) rate of unemployment:
   a. Elimination of unions
   b. Increased participation of teenagers in the labor market
   c. Larger fluctuations in the level of aggregate demand

    d. Increase in unemployment benefits

    e. Elimination of minimum wages

    f. Larger fluctuations in the composition of aggregate demand

3. Discuss the differences in the unemployment patterns of adults and teenagers. What does this imply about the types of jobs (on average) that the groups are seeking?

4. A reduction in minimum wages during the summer months would reduce the cost of labor to firms, but it would also reduce the wage that minimum-wage earners receive.

    a. Who would benefit from this measure?

    b. Who would lose?

    c. Would you support this program?

5. Some people say that since inflation can be reduced in the long run without an increase in unemployment, we should reduce inflation to zero. Others believe that a steady rate of inflation at, say, 3 percent, should be our goal. What are the pros and cons of these two arguments? What, in your opinion, are good long-run goals for reducing inflation and unemployment?

6. Define the sacrifice ratio. At what horizons is it not zero? Explain.

7. State Okun's law. How does it help us evaluate the cost (to society) of unemployment?

8. What costs are associated with perfectly anticipated inflation? Do these costs change as the rate of inflation changes?

9. What costs are associated with imperfectly anticipated inflation? Discuss them carefully. Who loses, and who gains, when inflation is higher than we expect?

10. Should the United States index its wages and prices? Detail the pros and cons of such a plan. How would your answer differ if you expected that the nation would face a period of extremely high inflation (say, 300 percent)?

Technical

1. The following information is to be used for calculations of the unemployment rate: Suppose there are two major groups, adults and teenagers, with adults divided into men and women. Teenagers account for 10 percent of the labor force; adults account for 90 percent. Women make up 35 percent of the adult labor force. Suppose also that the unemployment rates for these groups are as follows: teenagers, 19 percent; men, 7 percent; women, 6 percent.

    a. Calculate the aggregate unemployment rate.

    b. What if the share of teenagers in the labor force increases from 10 to 15 percent. How will this affect the aggregate unemployment rate?

2. *(Optional)* Use the *Economic Report of the President* to find unemployment data for the years 1986, 1991, and 1996. Use four labor force groups: males, and females, in each case 16 to 19 years of age, versus 20 years of age or over. What would 1986 and 1996 unemployment have been if the unemployment rates of the four groups had been at their 1991 level? Interpret your result.

3. *(Optional)* Use the *Economic Report of the President* to find data on the duration of unemployment in 1991 and 1995. Compare the distribution of unemployment by duration over these years. What relationship (if any) do you find?

CHAPTER 8

The New
Macroeconomics

CHAPTER HIGHLIGHTS

◆ We discuss four new ideas that have revolutionized macroeconomics. Each idea has changed the way we think about the macroeconomy, but each also remains controversial.

◆ In a rational expectations model, people form expectations that are consistent with the way the economy operates. Anticipated monetary policy has no real effects in the short run or the long run.

◆ The random walk theory of GDP argues that most shifts in output are permanent, as opposed to transitory booms and recessions, and that changes in aggregate demand are much less important than changes in aggregate supply.

◆ Real business cycle theory argues that money is very unimportant and that economic fluctuations are due largely to changes in technology.

◆ The New Keynesian models of price stickiness offer new "microfoundations," explaining why the price level does not always adjust quickly to changes in the money supply.

This chapter offers advanced material presenting the revolution in macroeconomics that has developed over the last 25 years. These ideas are exciting and controversial. When introduced, each seemed as if it would forever change macroeconomics in both teaching and practice. Some of the dramatic impact has failed to materialize, in part because empirical support for these challenging ideas has not been as full and convincing as had been hoped by their proponents. What's more, the ideas in part contradict each other—as well as the traditional aggregate supply–aggregate demand model. Even so, the impact of these concepts on both research and policy has been revolutionary. And while the ideas continue to be contested, each remains an active component of the economics research agenda.

We look at four new theories in this chapter:

- Rational expectations
- The random walk of GDP
- Real business cycle theory
- New Keynesian models of price stickiness

These models yield contrasting conclusions about the conduct of monetary policy, but they are alike in their emphasis on the importance of consistency between macroeconomic and microeconomic theory.

These theories are at the forefront of research, and their exposition is necessarily more technical than is most of the text. For this reason, we begin with an informal overview.

8-1

AN OVERVIEW OF THE NEW MACROECONOMICS

RATIONAL EXPECTATIONS

In a *rational expectations equilibrium,* markets clear and there is nothing systematic that monetary policy can do to affect output or unemployment. The rational expectations approach is most closely associated with Nobel laureate Robert Lucas of the University of Chicago.

The term "rational expectations equilibrium" identifies two key features of this approach. First, it places weight on the role of expectations and specifically *rational* expectations. Economic agents do not know the future with certainty and therefore have to base their plans and decisions, including price setting, on their forecasts or expectations of the future. If these expectations are made in a rational fashion, agents use all available information as well as possible to come out with the best possible forecasts. Second, the rational expectations model insists on *equilibrium:* markets clear immediately. Phenomena such as insider-outsider effects, as seen in the preceding chapter, simply do not come into play.

The full neoclassical theory of aggregate supply asserts that unemployment is always at the natural rate, output is always at the full-employment level, and any unemployment is purely frictional. Changes in the price level—for example, as a result of an increase in the money stock—leave output and employment unchanged. Money wages will rise, but since the real wage is unchanged, neither the quantity of labor supplied nor that demanded will change. The analysis of the classical case in Chapter 5 applies in full: neither monetary nor fiscal policy changes will have any effect on output. The rational expectations equilibrium approach, first presented in "the Lucas model," offers a qualified departure from that conclusion.

Lucas presents a neoclassical model with one changed assumption: some people do not know the aggregate price level but do know the nominal (dollar) wage or price at which they can buy and sell. For instance, at a given moment in time, a worker knows that the going nominal wage rate is $12 per hour but does not know the aggregate price level, and thus does not know the real wage (the nominal wage divided by the price level, equal to the amount of goods the wage will buy). Suppose all nominal prices and wages rise in proportion. The real wage is unchanged, but if workers do not realize that prices have also risen, they will think that the real wage has risen and will supply more labor, so output will rise.

We turn now to the *rational expectations* aspect of this approach. How are firms and workers to form expectations of the price level? The rational expectations approach assumes that people use all relevant information in forming expectations of economic variables. In particular, it assumes that workers and firms will think through the economic mechanisms underlying the determination of the actual price level and then use the implied value of the actual price level as the expected price level.

Households' and firms' best guess is that full employment will prevail, although they recognize that this guess may be wrong in either direction. The expected price level, p^e, will be the price level consistent with full employment, or the price level which equates aggregate demand and supply, that is, $AS = AD$. The central implication of the rational expectations approach is that people may not always get forecasts right but they do not make *systematic* errors.

We are now ready to see the central implication of the Lucas approach, namely, *the differential reaction of the economy to anticipated versus unanticipated changes in the money supply.* In response to an anticipated change in the money supply, agents will expect an equiproportionate change in the price level. Both p and p^e will change in proportion to the change in the money supply, the real money supply will remain unchanged, and the economy will remain at full employment. In contrast, an unanticipated change in money will have its full AS–AD effect—precisely because an unanticipated change will not affect p^e. Of course, agents will discover any change in the money supply relatively quickly, so even "unanticipated" changes will have real effects only in the very short run.

Policy Irrelevance

At first sight, the Lucas model seems to be almost the same as the classical model: both models predict *policy irrelevance*—that neither monetary nor fiscal policy can affect the equilibrium level of income in the long run. The Lucas model is more interesting than the classical model, though, because it allows at least *transitory* deviations from full employment. However, these transitory deviations are the result of expectational errors, and they last only as long as the errors last—and that cannot be very long.

Moreover, there is no room for monetary policy in this world of rational expectations and market clearing. Suppose agents believe that the price level is lower than it actually is. The government need simply announce the correct statistics, and the market will, by itself, immediately go back to full employment. There is no need for accommodating monetary or fiscal policy to hasten the return to full employment. Thus policy does not matter. In fact, in some versions of this approach, policy responses are problematic because they make it more complicated for economic agents to determine exactly what is happening in the economy and how best to adjust to it. This is a radically different perspective from a Keynesian world, where policy offers relief from unemployment.

THE RANDOM WALK OF GDP

Are fluctuations in output mainly transitory or mainly permanent? If fluctuations are primarily permanent, changes in aggregate demand—the heart of Keynesian macroeconomics—must be of relatively little importance. The logic is as follows: (1) According to the *AS–AD* model, the effect of aggregate demand shocks wears off with time because the long-run aggregate supply curve is vertical. (2) Therefore, if the effect of shocks is permanent, their source must be something other than aggregate demand.

This argument was first advanced by Charles Nelson and Charles Plosser, who presented careful statistical evidence in favor of the dominant role of permanent shocks.[1] Nelson and Plosser's work does not suggest that the *AS–AD* model is theoretically flawed, but it does argue that the aggregate demand side is simply not very important. Their work serves as the inspiration for much of the real business cycle literature, discussed below.

The idea that changes in output are permanent is sometimes described by saying that GDP follows a *random walk,* meaning that, having wandered up or down, GDP has no tendency to return to trend. This contrasts with the implicit model in the text. We think of the path of output over time as following a growth trend, explained largely by technological improvement and capital accumulation, plus a business cycle of transitory fluctuations, explained by our aggregate supply–aggregate demand model. Since the fluctuations are transitory, output in our model tends to revert to the growth trend.

Inevitably, there has been a counterreaction to the random-walk argument. The evidence is clear that large permanent changes to output are important, but a number of economists have argued that these permanent changes are infrequent and that in between such changes aggregate demand is the primary source of fluctuations.

REAL BUSINESS CYCLE THEORY

Equilibrium *real business cycle (RBC) theory* asserts that fluctuations in output and employment are the result of a variety of real shocks that hit the economy, with markets

---

[1]Charles R. Nelson and Charles I. Plosser, "Trends and Random Walks in Macroeconomic Time Series: Some Evidence and Implications," *Journal of Monetary Economics,* September 1982.

adjusting rapidly and remaining always in equilibrium.[2] *Real business cycle theory is the natural outgrowth of the theoretical implication of the rational expectations approach*—that anticipated monetary policy has no real effect—and of the empirical implication of random-walk theory—that aggregate demand shocks are not an important source of fluctuations.[3]

With monetary causes of the business cycle assumed out of the way, real business cycle theory is left with two tasks. The first is to explain the shocks, or disturbances, that hit the economy, causing fluctuations in the first place. The second is to explain the *propagation mechanisms*. A propagation mechanism is a mechanism through which a disturbance is spread through the economy. In particular, the aim is to explain why shocks to the economy seem to have long-lived effects. We start with propagation mechanisms.

Propagation Mechanisms

The propagation mechanism that is most associated with equilibrium business cycles is the *intertemporal substitution of leisure.* Any theory of the business cycle has to explain why people work more at some times than at others: during booms employment is high and jobs are easy to find; during recessions employment is lower and jobs are hard to find. A simple, but unsatisfactory, equilibrium explanation would be that people voluntarily supply more labor in response to a higher wage. (Remember that the equilibrium approach requires that people be on their supply and demand curves at all times.) However, the empirical evidence does not support this explanation. The elasticity of the labor supply with respect to the real wage is very small, and the real wage changes very little over the business cycle.

RBC models explain large movements in output with small movements in wages as follows: There is a high elasticity of labor supply in response to *temporary* changes in the wage. Or, as the argument is put, people are very willing to substitute leisure intertemporally. The argument is that people care about their total work effort but care very little about *when* they work. Suppose that within a 2-year period they plan to work 4,000 hours at the going wage (50 weeks each year at 40 hours a week). If wages are equal in the 2 years, they would work 2,000 hours each year. But if wages were just 2 percent higher in one year than the other, they might prefer to work, say, 2,200 hours in one year, forgoing vacations and working overtime, and 1,800 hours in the other. By substituting between years, they work the same total amount but earn more total

---

[2]To read more about the real business cycle approach, see S. Rao Aiyagari, "On the Contribution of Technology Shocks to Business Cycles," Federal Reserve Bank of Minneapolis *Quarterly Review,* Winter 1994; John H. Cochrane, "Shocks," *Carnegie-Rochester Conference Series on Public Policy,* Spring 1994; and Mark W. Watson, "Measures of Fit for Calibrated Models," *Journal of Political Economy,* December 1993. For a forceful negative view of real business cycle theory, see Lawrence Summers, "Some Skeptical Observations on Real Business Cycle Theory," Federal Reserve Bank of Minneapolis *Quarterly Review,* Fall 1986. See also Charles Plosser, "Understanding Real Business Cycles," and N. Gregory Mankiw, "Real Business Cycles: A New Keynesian Perspective," both in *Journal of Economic Perspectives,* Summer 1989.

[3]Real business cycle theory also has some methodological differences from other areas of macroeconomics with regard to the best way to identify underlying economic parameters. For a methodological and historical perspective on some of these differences, see Robert G. King, "Quantitative Theory and Econometrics," Federal Reserve Bank of Richmond *Economic Quarterly,* Summer 1995. For a somewhat more catholic view on methodology in empirical macroeconomics, see Christopher A. Sims, "Macroeconomics and Methodology," *Journal of Economic Perspectives,* Winter 1996.

income. Note that the intertemporal substitution of leisure does not mean that the labor supply is sensitive to *permanent* changes in wages. If the wage rises, and will stay higher, there is nothing to be gained by working more this period than next. So it is quite possible for the response of labor supply to a permanent change in wages to be very small, even though the response to a temporary wage change is large.

This intertemporal substitution of leisure is clearly capable of generating large movements in the amount of work done in response to small shifts in wages—and thus could account for large output effects in the cycle accompanied by small changes in wages. However, there has not been strong empirical support for this view.

Disturbances

The mechanisms that propagate business cycles are set in motion by events or *disturbances* that change the equilibrium levels of output and employment in individual markets and the economy as a whole. The most important disturbances isolated by equilibrium business cycle theorists are shocks to *productivity,* or supply shocks, and shocks to *government spending.* A *productivity shock* changes the level of output produced by given amounts of inputs. Changes in the weather and new methods of production are examples. Suppose there is a temporary favorable productivity shock this period. Individuals will want to work harder to take advantage of the higher productivity. In working more this period, they raise output. They also invest more, thus spreading the productivity shock into future periods by raising the stock of capital. If the effect of the intertemporal substitution of leisure is strong, even a small productivity shock could have a relatively large effect on output.

Real business cycle theory has been, and continues to be, a major area of research for many macroeconomists. However, proponents of this view have been less successful at converting the rest of the profession to their view than they had once hoped. In part, this is because the evidence for the importance of money seems persuasive. Most policy makers continue to rely on the aggregate supply–aggregate demand model we have studied throughout the book.

NEW KEYNESIAN MODELS OF PRICE STICKINESS

The models described above are all in the equilibrium–market-clearing tradition. These models have become important in part because of their merits but also in part because economists have found rational decision making and market clearing to be a sound guiding principle. However, these models are inconsistent with the aggregate supply–aggregate demand behavior that many economists believe characterizes the real world. *New Keynesians* accept the premise of individual rational behavior, but develop models in which markets do not quickly reach the full classical equilibrium and prices do not always adjust to changes in the money supply.[4]

---

[4]For recent overviews of this literature, see Jean-Pascal Bénassy, "Classical and Keynesian Features in Macroeconomic Models with Imperfect Competition," Huw D. Dixon and Neil Rankin, "Imperfect Competition and Macroeconomics: A Survey," and Richard Startz, "Notes on Imperfect Competition and New Keynesian Economics," all in Huw D. Dixon and Neil Rankin (eds.), *The New Macroeconomics: Imperfect Markets and Policy Effectiveness* (Cambridge, England: Cambridge University Press, 1995). See also Robert J. Gordon, "What Is New Keynesian Economics?" *Journal of Economic Literature* 28 (1990), and Jacquim Silvestre, "The Market-Power Foundations of Macroeconomic Policy," *Journal of Economic Literature* 31 (1993). See footnote 33 for more readings.

We focus on a particular model of *price stickiness* developed by Greg Mankiw. Suppose that the money supply increases. According to equilibrium theories, firms should all increase prices proportionately. But suppose there is a small cost, a *menu cost,* of actually making the price change. Might firms choose to leave their price at its old—now "wrong"—value? The traditional answer is no, because the benefit of getting the price right surely outweighs any very small cost of changing it.

Mankiw invoked *imperfect competition* to show that the losses to a firm from having the "wrong" price may be a very small fraction of the value to society of having the correct price. This suggests that menu costs can be quite small compared to fluctuations in output but still be large enough that no single firm is willing to incur the costs and change prices. So an increase in the nominal money supply may leave prices unchanged, and the resulting increase in real money increases output.

We turn now to more detailed—and more technically challenging—considerations of these ideas.

◆ O P T I O N A L ◆

8-2

THE RATIONAL EXPECTATIONS REVOLUTION

In this section, we work through a basic rational expectations model in several steps. First, we give a simplified version of our *AS–AD* model and solve it with exogenously given price expectations. We show that, except by coincidence, the price predicted by the model will be inconsistent with the price that people expected. We turn then to a perfect-foresight model—a model in which we assume that people use the model's own predictions to form their price expectations. Finally, we change the perfect-foresight assumption to the weaker assumption of rational expectations, where agents do use the model to form price expectations but do so with only partial information. In both the perfect-foresight and rational expectations models, anticipated monetary policy will have no real effects. This is a direct consequence of the fact that actual and expected prices are consistent with one another and that the expectations-augmented Phillips curve asserts that deviations of unemployment from the natural rate are tied to the difference between realized inflation and expected inflation.

In each step of the model's development, you should focus on the link between the specification of expectations and the monetary policy multiplier. In the simplified *AS–AD* model with exogenous expectations, the monetary policy multiplier is relatively large. In the perfect-foresight model, where expectations adjust perfectly, the monetary policy multiplier is *zero.* Finally, the rational expectations model combines the assumptions of the *AS–AD* and perfect-foresight models. Expectations adjust perfectly with respect to anticipated changes in the money supply, but not at all to unanticipated changes; the monetary policy multiplier is zero with respect to anticipated changes in the money supply and relatively large with respect to unanticipated changes.

A SIMPLE AGGREGATE SUPPLY–AGGREGATE DEMAND MODEL

We begin with a simplified version of the aggregate supply–aggregate demand model, stripping out much of the detail developed in earlier chapters. We begin by specifying a simple aggregate demand schedule:

$$AD: \quad m + v = p + y \tag{1}$$

Equation (1) is called the *quantity theory equation:* m is (the log of) the money supply; v is "velocity" and is assumed to be constant; p is the price level; and y is GDP.[5]

We next specify a simple short-run aggregate supply curve, one which emphasizes the role of price expectations:

$$p = p^e + \lambda(y - y^*) \tag{2}$$

where p is again the price level, p^e is the *expected* price level, y is again GDP, and y^* is potential GDP. The parameter λ gives the slope of the aggregate supply curve. If λ is large, an increase in output above potential output causes a steep rise in prices above what had been expected. If λ is small, the short-run response of prices to output is small.

The aggregate demand and aggregate supply equations can be combined to solve for output [equation (3)] and prices [equation (4)] in terms of the money supply and other variables:[6]

$$y = \frac{1}{1+\lambda}m + \frac{1}{1+\lambda}(v - p^e) + \frac{\lambda}{1+\lambda}y^* \tag{3}$$

$$p = \frac{\lambda}{1+\lambda}(m + v - y^*) + \frac{1}{1+\lambda}p^e \tag{4}$$

Together, equations (3) and (4) tell us the equilibrium output and prices in our model economy. If the money supply rises 1 percent, output rises $1/(1 + \lambda)$ percent and prices rise $\lambda/(1 + \lambda)$ percent. To be concrete, suppose λ is ½: then a 1 percent increase in the money supply causes a ⅔ percent increase in output and a ⅓ percent increase in the price level.

Now we use equations (3) and (4) to illustrate the standard approach to making an economic "forecast." (Be warned that this forecast will be subject to the Lucas critique, below.) For our fabricated example, suppose that λ equals ½ and the values for the money supply, velocity, and potential GDP are $m = 2$, $v = 3$, $y^* = 4$, respectively. Most particularly, we assume that *agents in the economy expect* the price level to be $p^e = 5$. *What do you expect the price level to be?* What do you expect output to be? Try working out the answers for yourself. Our answers appear in the next paragraph.

Plugging the values given into equation (3), we find output is $y = 1\frac{1}{3} = \frac{2}{3}(2) + \frac{2}{3}(3 - 5) + \frac{1}{3}(4)$. From equation (4) we expect the price to be $p = 3\frac{2}{3} = \frac{1}{3}(2 + 3 - 4) + \frac{2}{3}(5)$.

---

[5]We employ here a quite technical, but quite useful, "trick." Equation (1), and the equations that follow, are written using the natural logarithms of the indicated variables. The quantity equation is usually written $MV = PY$, where M is the money supply, P is the price level, and so on. We use lowercase letters to represent logarithms, so $m = \ln(M)$, and so on. Thus we get to equation (1) by writing $\ln(MV) = \ln(PY) = \ln M + \ln V = \ln P + \ln Y = m + v = p + y$. Using logarithms has the advantage that a change in m can be interpreted as the *percentage* change in M. Having said all this, if you aren't comfortable with logarithms, no noticeable harm will be done if you just think of m as the money supply. Note that we call m "the money supply" in the text without continually qualifying the definition by saying "the logarithm of."

[6]If you want to work through the algebra yourself, a useful first step is to rewrite equation (1) with price on the left, as in $p = m + v - y$. Use this expression to substitute out for the price level in equation (2), giving an equation with y on both sides, $m + v - y = p^e + \lambda(y - y^*)$. Collecting terms and solving for output gives equation (3). Putting equation (3) back into $p = m + v - y$ and solving for the price level gives equation (4).

So the output from our model is that we expect the price to be 3⅔, taking as an input to the model that the expected price is 5! Shouldn't rational agents, who have a great deal at stake, make forecasts that are consistent with the way the economy (represented here by our simple model) actually operates? This is the essence of the *Lucas critique:* The standard aggregate supply–aggregate demand model assumes that economic agents make predictions for the economy that are inconsistent with the predictions the model itself makes.

Suppose that economic decision makers accept our forecast and change their expectation of the price level to $p^e = 3⅔$. Reworking equations (3) and (4) would then lead to predicting $y = 2⅔ = ⅔(2) + ⅔(3 − 3⅔) + ⅓(4)$ and $p = 2⅔ = ⅓(2 + 3 − 4) + ⅔(3⅔)$. Now the expected price input to and the price predicted as output from the model are closer, but they're still not the same. Modifying the model so that the predicted value of p and the input value p^e are equal leads to the idea of a perfect-foresight model.

A PERFECT-FORESIGHT MODEL

We now assume that agents *do* use the *AS–AD* model to forecast prices and that they have all the information necessary to make the forecast. Agents are said to have *perfect foresight.* Rather than assuming p^e is given from outside the model, we assume agents use the model itself to compute p^e. In other words, agents compute p based on m, v, p^e, and so forth. Agents then set their predicted price at $p^e = p$. Since p itself depends on p^e, the two must be solved for simultaneously.

Assume that our model correctly describes the economy, so economic decision makers use equation (4) to *predict prices and compute p^e, so $p^e = p$:*

$$p^e = p = \frac{\lambda}{1 + \lambda}(m + v - y^*) + \frac{1}{1 + \lambda}p^e \tag{5}$$

Collecting terms containing p^e,[7] we can rearrange equation (5) to give the perfect-foresight forecast and solution for the price level and the corresponding solution for output:

$$p^e = p = m + v - y^* \tag{6}$$

$$y = y^* \tag{7}$$

The perfect-foresight predictions in equations (6) and (7) are quite different from the original *AS–AD* predictions embodied in equations (4) and (3). The latter assume *exogenously* given price expectations; the former assume that price expectations are formed *endogenously* and, specifically, that expectation formation is consistent with the predictions of the model.

The switch to such consistently formed expectations has dramatic implications for the effectiveness of monetary policy. According to equation (4), a 1 percent increase in the money supply increases prices by $\lambda/(1 + \lambda)$ percent, but under perfect foresight a 1 percent increase in the money supply leads to exactly a 1 percent increase in the price level. According to equation (3), a 1 percent increase in the money supply increases output by $1/(1 + \lambda)$ percent, but under perfect foresight a 1 percent increase in the money supply leads to no increase at all in output. Notice that these perfect-foresight

---

[7]Write $p^e\left(1 - \dfrac{1}{1 + \lambda}\right) = \dfrac{\lambda}{1 + \lambda}(m + v - y^*)$, and then multiply through by $1 + \lambda$.

short-run results are the same as the long-run *AS–AD* results. Under perfect foresight, prices rise not only as a direct result of the increase in the money supply but also because of the increase in price expectations. This extra boost raises prices just enough to completely offset the increase in the money supply.

Under perfect foresight, monetary policy is neutral in the short run as well as in the long run.

A perfect-foresight model has two important shortcomings. First, it requires that economic decision makers know everything about the economy. Second, it implies that the economy is always at full employment.[8] Neither of these shortcomings is really critical, as we will see when we consider a rational expectations model in the next section.

A RATIONAL EXPECTATIONS MODEL

A *rational expectations model* assumes that agents make the best use of whatever information is available to them and that expectations are formed in a manner consistent with the way the economy actually operates. A rational expectations model is much like a perfect-foresight model in which some of the key variables are uncertain. To illustrate, suppose that before the money supply is known, economic decision makers expect the money supply to equal m^e. If the money supply actually turns out to be m, we can define the difference between the agents' expectation and the actual money supply,

$$\epsilon_m = m - m^e$$

as the agents' money forecast error. (Analogously, suppose agents expect potential output to be y^{*e}. Since potential output is actually y^*, the agents' potential output forecast error is $\epsilon_{y*} = y^* - y^{*e}$.) We show below that the monetary policy multiplier with respect to *anticipated* money, m^e, is zero, just as in the perfect-foresight model. The monetary policy multiplier with respect to *unanticipated* money, ϵ_m, is positive, just as in the *AS–AD* model.

The forecast errors in a particular quarter may be either positive (the money supply, for instance, turned out to be larger than anticipated) or negative (the money supply turned out to be smaller than anticipated), but on average rational forecast errors equal zero. The argument here is straightforward. Suppose ϵ_m averaged 7. In this case we could improve our forecasts by just raising every forecast m^e by 7. So while rational forecast errors may be either large or small, depending on the quality of information available, they average zero. Another way to express this is $(\epsilon_m)^e = 0$.

We next ask what the price level will be in equilibrium. We begin by repeating equation (4) but substituting $m^e + \epsilon_m$ for m and $y^{*e} + \epsilon_{y*}$ for y^*:

$$p = \frac{\lambda}{1 + \lambda}\left[\left(m^e + \epsilon_m\right) + v - (y^{*e} + \epsilon_{y*})\right] + \frac{1}{1 + \lambda}p^e \qquad (8)$$

We assume that agents form their expectations, p^e, on the basis of the price forecast in equation (8). However, we recognize that forecasts are based only on the information the agents have:[9]

---

[8] You can see in equation (2) that $p^e = p$ implies $y = y^*$.

[9] The expectation of ϵ_m, for instance, is zero, and the expectation of m^e is m^e. We assume, for simplicity of illustration, that v and λ are known exactly.

BOX 8-1 Rational Expectations Forecast Errors Are Unpredictable

Rational expectations differs from perfect foresight in that rational expectations forecasts are imperfect. They may be too high or too low, although the forecast is right on average. Rational expectations forecasts make the best use of the information available to the agents making the forecasts. As a consequence, the best guess of the forecast error, based on the information available when the forecast is made, is zero.

Suppose agents forecast p to be p^e. The forecast error, ϵ, is the difference between the realized value of p and the forecast:

$$\epsilon = p - p^e \tag{B1}$$

It's straightforward to show that the expected value of the forecast error, call it ϵ^e, is zero. The expected forecast error is the difference between the average value of p and the average value of p^e. But these two are equal on average, precisely because agents adjust p^e to make them equal on average. If p^e were higher on average than p, agents could improve their guesses just by lowering p^e.

$$p^e = \frac{\lambda}{1 + \lambda}(m^e + v - y^{*e}) + \frac{1}{1 + \lambda}p^e \tag{9}$$

Simplifying equation (9) gives

$$p^e = m^e + v - y^{*e} \tag{10}$$

Notice that the expected price under rational expectations, in equation (10), is the same as that under perfect foresight, in equation (6), except that it is based only on the limited information available to those making the forecast: m^e rather than m, for example. The equilibrium solutions for price and output are[10]

$$y = y^{*e} + \frac{1}{1 + \lambda}\epsilon_m + \frac{\lambda}{1 + \lambda}\epsilon_{y*} \tag{11}$$

$$p = m^e + v - y^{*e} + \frac{\lambda}{1 + \lambda}(\epsilon_m - \epsilon_{y*}) \tag{12}$$

What is the effect of an increase in the money supply under rational expectations? The question must now be broken down into two parts: What is the effect of an anticipated

---

[10]If you're working out the algebra for yourself, replace p^e in the price-level equation, (8), with the value from equation (10) to find

$$p = \frac{\lambda}{1 + \lambda}\left[\left(m^e + \epsilon_m\right) + v - \left(y^{*e} + \epsilon_{y*}\right)\right] + \frac{1}{1 + \lambda}\left(m^e + v - y^{*e}\right)$$

Simplify and make the analogous substitutions for output in equation (3) to derive equations (11) and (12).

increase in the money supply? What is the effect of an unanticipated increase in the money supply?

From examination of equation (11), we see that under rational expectations an anticipated increase in money supply has no effect at all on output but an unanticipated increase in the money supply increases output, by $1/(1 + \lambda)$. Notice that anticipated changes operate just as predicted by the perfect-foresight model above and that unanticipated changes operate just as predicted by our initial, exogenous price expectation, AS–AD model. In effect, anticipated monetary policy is neutral; unanticipated policy has its full AS–AD effects.

You should use equations (11) and (12) to check the effects of supply shocks (y^{*e} and ϵ_{y*}) and of shocks on the price level to see that these also behave as in the perfect-foresight model when anticipated and as in the AS–AD model when unanticipated.

THE RATIONAL EXPECTATIONS EQUILIBRIUM APPROACH: EMPIRICAL EVIDENCE

The rational expectations model has the very strong prediction that anticipated monetary policy should have no effect on output. Early studies seemed consistent with this view, finding evidence that only unanticipated changes in the money stock increase output.[11] However, these results did not stand up to further testing.[12]

We give here the flavor of these empirical tests. We wish to ask whether anticipated money growth increases output, as the AS–AD model predicts, or whether there is no effect, as suggested by rational expectations models. The test involves two steps. First, we have to estimate anticipated money growth. Second, we compare anticipated money growth to changes in output.

Figure 8-1 shows quarterly M2 growth from 1960 through 1996 in red. The actual growth rate is split into anticipated growth, in blue, and unanticipated growth, in green. In other words, we show three lines: $m = m^e + \epsilon_m$. Anticipated money growth is a statistical forecast based on the preceding four quarters of money growth.[13] Unanticipated growth is the difference between the forecast and the growth that actually occurred.

We plot output growth against our estimate of anticipated money growth in Figure 8-2, showing also the line that best fits the data. Two aspects of Figure 8-2 are salient: (1) Anticipated money growth by no means explains all output growth (many of the data points are far from the line); and (2) there is a strong positive relation between anticipated money growth and output growth (the line slopes upward). The estimated relation between output growth and anticipated money growth is

$$\Delta y = -0.0004 + 0.46\Delta m^e \tag{13}$$

---

[11]See, for instance, Robert Barro, "Unanticipated Money, Output, and the Price Level in the United States," *Journal of Political Economy,* August 1978.

[12]Two influential, if difficult, articles are John Boschen and Herschel Grossman, "Tests of Equilibrium Macroeconomics with Contemporaneous Monetary Data," *Journal of Monetary Economics,* November 1982, and Frederic Mishkin, "Does Anticipated Monetary Policy Matter? An Econometric Investigation," *Journal of Political Economy,* February 1982.

[13]For the statistically curious, the forecast is based on a least-squares regression of M2 growth on four lags of M2 growth.

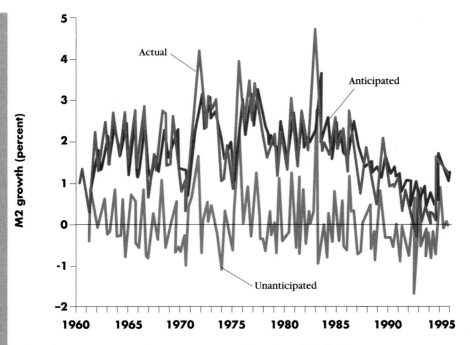

FIGURE 8-1   ACTUAL, ANTICIPATED, AND UNANTICIPATED M2 GROWTH.

(Source: DRI/McGraw-Hill Macroeconomic Database and authors' calculations.)

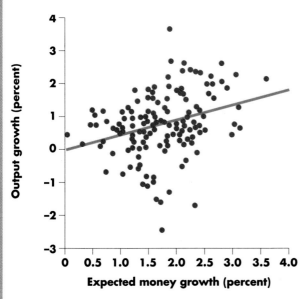

FIGURE 8-2   EXPECTED MONEY GROWTH AND GROWTH OF OUTPUT.

(Source: DRI/McGraw-Hill Macroeconomic Database and authors' calculations.)

suggesting that a 1 percent increase in money growth leads to about a .5 percent increase in output growth.[14]

Thus the statistical evidence is not very supportive of a strict interpretation of the rational expectations model. This view is bolstered by careful historical research on Federal Reserve records: Christina Romer and David Romer found six episodes of shifts in monetary policy that were intended to lower inflation, and they found that each such instance of contractionary monetary policy was followed by a recession.[15]

RECAP

- Rational expectations models predict that anticipated changes to the money supply change the overall price level proportionately, leaving output unchanged.
- With respect to anticipated money growth, rational expectations models operate as if the long-run aggregate supply curve applied instantaneously, not just in the long run.
- While the intellectual appeal of rational expectations models is very strong, the empirical evidence is less supportive.

◆ ◆   D O U B L E   O P T I O N A L   ◆ ◆

8-3

THE MICROECONOMICS OF THE IMPERFECT
INFORMATION AGGREGATE SUPPLY CURVE[16]

An important feature of the inflation-expectations-augmented aggregate supply curve is that output is high ($y > y^*$) when the nominal price level is higher than expected ($p > p^e$). This feature plays a central role in both the aggregate supply–aggregate demand model of Chapter 5 and the rational expectations model just presented. In this section, we examine Lucas's *imperfect-information model* of the aggregate supply curve.[17,18]

Why does output sometimes rise when the overall price level rises? Lucas's answer is that firms usually observe prices only in their own market. A high price might be due to high demand, or it might just reflect an increase in the overall price level. In the former case, the firm would like to increase production; in the latter case, the price

---

[14]Again, for the statistically curious, the *t* statistic of the coefficient in equation (13) is 3.9.

[15]Christina D. Romer and David H. Romer, "Does Monetary Policy Matter? A New Test in the Spirit of Friedman and Schwartz," *NBER Macroeconomics Annual*, 1989.

[16]This section and Sec. 8-5 are by far the most technically difficult in the book. You may wish to skip them.

[17]See Robert E. Lucas, Jr., "Expectations and the Neutrality of Money," *Journal of Economic Theory*, April 1972. Also see Edmund S. Phelps, "Introduction," in Edmund S. Phelps et al., *Microeconomic Foundations of Employment and Inflation Theory* (New York: Norton, 1970).

[18]We strip many of the details from Lucas's original presentation. For a more thorough presentation, see David Romer, *Advanced Macroeconomics* (New York: McGraw-Hill, 1995), chap. 6.

change should be neutral and production should be unchanged. But information is imperfect: when the firm sees a high price for its product, it doesn't know whether the cause is high demand or high overall prices. The firm, rationally, acts as if each cause were partially responsible and raises production a small amount. At the aggregate level, an unanticipated overall price increase is "misinterpreted" by every firm as a possible signal of higher demand, so the overall price increase leads to increased output. This connection gives us the Phillips curve relation we see in real-world data. We turn now to a simplified version of Lucas's original model.

Suppose the economy is composed of distinct markets—Lucas originally suggested a parable in which each market was on an isolated island. Inhabitants of each island produce goods and then meet at a central location to trade. People on island i are willing to work longer hours when the output from their island is expected to fetch a price, p_i, which is high relative to the overall price level in the economy, p. The supply of output produced on island i would be

$$y_i = \alpha(p_i - p) \tag{14}$$

if island i's inhabitants knew the overall price level.[19] We assume, instead, that they have to make a guess as to the overall price level. Call this guess the expectation of the price level given the information available on island i, $E(p|\text{island}\,i)$, so the supply is

$$y_i = \alpha[p_i - E(p|\text{island}\,i)] \tag{15}$$

The price which will be paid for goods produced on island i depends on the overall price level p and on a demand shock specific to the particular kind of goods made on island i, z_i. We suppose the inhabitants of the island know their local price, p_i, but observe neither the demand shock nor the overall price level. They must therefore infer the overall price level from p_i. High p_i might mean that z_i is high *or* that p is high. So when the inhabitants observe a high p_i, they increase their estimate of p, but not by too much, because sometimes high p_i is due to high z_i and normal levels of p. The best guess of p is

$$E(p|p_i) = k_0 + \frac{1}{a}\beta p_i, \quad 0 < \beta < 1 \tag{16}$$

where $E(p|p_i)$ indicates that the only information used in making a guess is the local price,[20] and a is a constant reflecting the slopes of the supply and demand curves.[21] If most changes in local prices, p_i, are due to changes in the overall price level, p, then β will be close to 1; if most changes are due to local demand shocks, z_i, then β will be close to zero.[22] *The value of β is the key to the slope of the aggregate supply curve—we see below that if $\beta = 1$, the aggregate supply curve will be vertical.*

---

[19]As before, lowercase y and p really represent logarithms of output and price. Nothing of any importance rests on this point.

[20]Since we don't permit the islanders any aggregate information, we must be implicitly assuming the anticipated inflation rate is zero.

[21]The intercept k_0 is not of any particular interest. It appears for technical reasons.

[22]Engineers will recognize this as a signal extraction problem where p is the signal and z_i is the noise; β will be close to 1 if there is a high signal-to-noise ratio.

BOX 8-2 A Visual Example of Forming an Expectation

Expectations formation plays a key role in the derivation of the imperfect-information aggregate supply curve. Equation (16) can be derived algebraically by using statistical theory, but we present here a more visual approach. Figure 1 shows three possible relations between observed p_i and the rational guess $E(p)$. Suppose the value of p_i contains no information about p. As shown on the red horizontal line, a rational person would guess p independently of the value of p_i. (This is the $\beta = 0$ case.) If all movements in p_i were movements in p, the best guess would be along the green 45° line. (This is the $\beta = 1$ case.) With imperfect information, as shown in blue, the optimal guess lies partway between the no-information and the perfect-information cases.

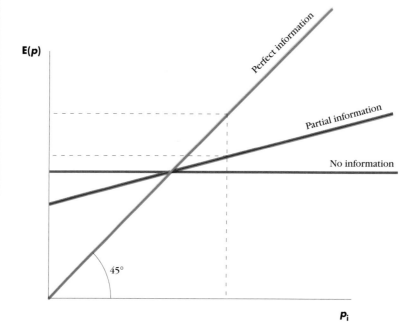

FIGURE 1   VISUAL EXAMPLE OF FORMING AN EXPECTATION.

We can use equation (16) to express supply as

$$y_i = \alpha\left[p_i - \left(k_0 + \frac{1}{a}\beta p_i\right)\right] = \alpha\left[\left(1 - \frac{\beta}{a}\right)p_i - k_0\right] \tag{17}$$

Demand for the product of island i depends on aggregate GDP, y, on the demand shock for the product of the island, z_i, and on the relative price of the island's product, $p_i - p$. That is,

$$y_i = y + z_i - \gamma(p_i - p) \tag{18}$$

The equilibrium price on an island is found by equating supply [equation (17)] and demand [equation (18)]:

$$\alpha\left[\left(1 - \frac{\beta}{a}\right)p_i - k_0\right] = y + z_i - \gamma(p_i - p) \tag{19}$$

Equation (19) gives the equilibrium relation between shocks, prices, and output for a particular island. But any one island is *representative* of the economy as a whole. Islands differ from one another because of idiosyncratic shocks, but the aggregate economy is just the average of the economies on the individual islands. Specifically, this means that aggregate output y is the average of the y_i's, that the overall price level p is the average of the p_i's, and that the z_i's average out to zero. If we average both sides of equation (19), we get

$$y = \alpha\left[\left(1 - \frac{\beta}{a}\right)p - k_0\right] \tag{20}$$

Equation (20) is the aggregate supply curve for the economy. With some further algebra, we can show that $a = 1,$[23] so the final expression for the aggregate supply curve is

$$p = \frac{1}{\alpha(1 - \beta)} \times (y + \alpha k_0) \tag{21}$$

The slope of the aggregate supply curve depends on both the slope of individual supply curves, α, and the relative importance of aggregate versus idiosyncratic shocks, β. If shocks to the overall price level play a dominant role, β will be close to 1 and the aggregate supply curve will be relatively steep. Thus, when most price shocks are attributed to changes in the overall price level, price shocks will be largely neutral, with little effect on output.

RECAP

- Agents forecast the overall price level on the basis of imperfect information. Agents are uncertain whether a price increase in an individual market is due to increased aggregate demand or to increased market-specific demand. As a result, increases in market-specific prices are attributed partially to increases in the overall price level and partially to increases in real demand.
- Unanticipated increases in the overall price level, p, generate partial increases in the anticipated price level, p^e, and partial increases in output, y. The positive associations between increases in p and y become the Phillips curve that we see in the data.

---

[23]If you want to do the algebra, use equation (20) to substitute for y in equation (19). Collect terms and simplify to show that

$$p_i = \frac{1}{\gamma + (1 - \beta)\alpha} z_i + p.$$

The generic expression for p_i is $p_i = a_0 + a_1 z_i + ap$, and the implicit coefficient of p in the expression just given shows that $a = 1$.

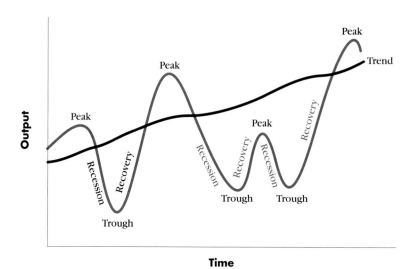

FIGURE 8-3   THE BUSINESS CYCLE.

8-4

THE RANDOM WALK OF GDP: DOES AGGREGATE DEMAND MATTER, OR IS IT ALL AGGREGATE SUPPLY?

In the orthodox model of the economy the business cycle is presented as fluctuations of GDP around a smooth trendline. These fluctuations last from a few quarters to several years. Shocks to aggregate demand are presumed to be the primary cause of these transitory fluctuations. In 1982, Charles Nelson and Charles Plosser offered a heterodox challenge by suggesting that the trend is not so smooth but, rather, is subject to large and frequent shocks that have a permanent effect on the level of GDP.[24] If the Nelson and Plosser view is correct, aggregate demand shocks—which are transitory in nature—are less important than aggregate supply shocks—which may be permanent.

Think of output as composed of a *trend,* or *secular, component,* perhaps the result of the growth processes discussed in Chapters 3 and 4, and a *cyclical component,* representing perhaps the business cycle. Figure 8-3 presents a stylized view of trend growth and fluctuations around the trend. In studying business cycles, we are interested in the fluctuations. So the first step in most studies of the economy is to create a *stationary* picture of the economy, that is, to *detrend* the data. Nelson and Plosser showed that the method used to model the trend plays a critical role in identifying shocks.

---

[24]Charles R. Nelson and Charles I. Plosser, "Trends and Random Walks in Macroeconomic Time Series: Some Evidence and Implications," *Journal of Monetary Economics,* September 1982. See also Stephen Beveridge and Charles R. Nelson, "A New Approach to Decomposition of Economic Time Series into Permanent and Transitory Components with Particular Attention to Measurement of the Business Cycle," *Journal of Monetary Economics,* March 1981; John Y. Campbell and N. Gregory Mankiw, "Are Output Fluctuations Transitory," *Quarterly Journal of Economics,* November 1987; and John H. Cochrane, "How Big Is the Random Walk in GNP?" *Journal of Political Economy,* October 1988.

TWO EQUIVALENT REPRESENTATIONS OF TREND AND SHOCK

Suppose the trend in y can be represented by a literal time trend, as in

$$y_t = \alpha + \beta t \tag{22}$$

Equation (22) states that y rises by β in each time period. By subtracting $y_{t-1} = \alpha + \beta(t-1)$ from each side of equation (22), we get

$$y_t - y_{t-1} = [\alpha + \beta t] - [\alpha + \beta(t-1)] \tag{23}$$

or

$$y_t = y_{t-1} + \beta \qquad or \qquad \Delta y_t = \beta \tag{24}$$

where Δy is defined as $y_t - y_{t-1}$. Equation (24) also states that y rises by β in each time period.

IS THE EFFECT OF SHOCKS PERMANENT OR TRANSITORY?

Equations (22) and (24) are precisely equivalent to one another. But suppose we add an output shock, u_t, to equation (22) or to equation (24)? If we add the shock to equation (22), we have

$$y_t = \alpha + \beta t + u_t \qquad or \qquad \Delta y_t = \beta + u_t - u_{t-1} \tag{25}$$

If we, instead, add the shock to equation (24), we have

$$y_t = y_{t-1} + \beta + u_t \qquad or \qquad y_t = \alpha + \beta t + u_t + u_{t-1} + u_{t-2} \ldots + u_0 \tag{26}$$

According to equation (25), the effect of a shock lasts one period, or, said differently, shocks to the change in y reverse themselves after one period. In sharp contrast, according to equation (26), the effect of a shock on the level of y is permanent, or, said differently, shocks to y accumulate over time. A variable that behaves as described by equation (25), that can be made stationary by taking out a time trend, is called *trend stationary*. A variable that behaves as described by equation (26), that can be made stationary by differencing, is called *difference stationary*. A difference-stationary process is dominated by permanent shocks; a trend-stationary process is dominated by transitory shocks.

Whether GDP is better described by equation (25) or by equation (26) sounds at first like a question of arcane statistical interest only. But the distinction strikes to the heart of the relevance of aggregate demand theory. According to the *AS–AD* model, business cycles caused by aggregate demand fluctuations are relatively short-lived, a matter of a few quarters or, at most, a few years. In contrast, shocks to aggregate supply might be permanent if they derived from permanent productivity improvements.

Nelson and Plosser showed that GDP includes both permanent and transitory shocks but that the GDP process is dominated by permanent shocks. Their evidence struck a blow arguing against the importance of aggregate demand in explaining the economy.

Figure 8-4 illustrates the importance of permanent shocks. The blue line is U.S. real GDP since 1947. The red line shows the trend of GDP estimated from 1947 through 1972 and then projected forward. The left side of the figure, covering years

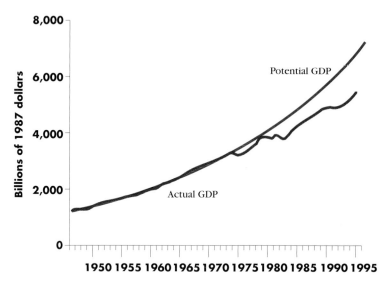

FIGURE 8-4   ACTUAL AND POTENTIAL GDP.

(Source: DRI/McGraw-Hill Macroeconomic Database and authors' calculations.)

prior to 1973, appears quite consistent with the idea of fluctuations around a trend. But if we project the same trend to the present, it is clear that something has shifted output permanently downward. It is hard to believe that the gap between output and the projected trend on the right-hand side of Figure 8-4 represents the actions of aggregate demand.

The idea that shocks with long-lasting impact are important to the economy is now generally accepted. The inference that aggregate demand is relatively unimportant remains controversial. An alternative view is that large and relatively permanent aggregate supply shocks occur, but only on rare occasions; in between, aggregate demand shocks dominate. Pierre Perron is the original exponent of this point of view.[25] Perron argues that while there are occasional permanent breaks in trend, within decades-long subperiods the economy does have important short-run fluctuations around trend. In Figure 8-5, we estimate separate trends for output before 1973 (in red) and after 1973 (in green). Within each subperiod, output appears to be well modeled as transitory fluctuations around trend. This view of the world argues that there are large, permanent, but infrequent, aggregate supply shocks and that, in between these shocks, aggregate demand shocks dominate year-to-year fluctuations.

Because the dispute between believers in difference stationary and believers in *trend stationary with breaks* rests on measurements of long-lasting phenomena, the dispute can't be easily settled by statistical analysis of the relatively short data periods currently available. The importance of aggregate demand shocks is likely to remain a controversial area.

---

[25]Evidence for this view is given in an influential, but difficult, article by Pierre Perron, "The Great Crash, the Oil Shock and the Unit Root Hypothesis," *Econometrica,* November 1989.

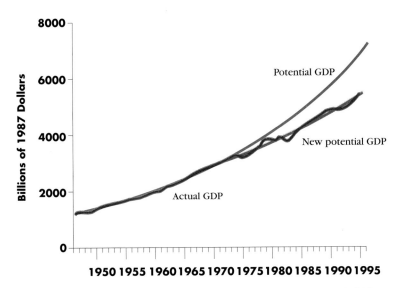

FIGURE 8-5   ACTUAL AND POTENTIAL GDP AND THE NEW POTENTIAL GDP.

Note that the newly calculated potential GDP is closer to actual GDP than the original forecast.
(Source: DRI/McGraw-Hill Macroeconomic Database and authors' calculations.)

RECAP

- There is significant empirical evidence that macroeconomic fluctuations are dominated by shocks with permanent effects. Since aggregate demand shocks do not have permanent effects, this evidence argues that aggregate demand fluctuations are less important than aggregate supply fluctuations. Changes due to aggregate supply shocks, in particular shocks to technology, could well be permanent.
- An alternative view of the evidence is that there are occasional episodes of large, permanent aggregate supply shocks, but that between these episodes aggregate demand shocks predominate.

◆◆ DOUBLE OPTIONAL ◆◆

8-5

REAL BUSINESS CYCLE THEORY

Rational expectations provided a theoretical basis for the notion that monetary policy should not have terribly important effects. The work of Nelson and Plosser cast doubt on the empirical importance of aggregate demand shocks. These ideas supported the development of *equilibrium real business cycle theory.*[26] RBC theory asserts that fluctuations in output and employment are the result of a variety of real shocks that hit the economy, with markets adjusting rapidly and remaining always in equilibrium.

---

[26]See footnote 2 for further readings.

RBC theorists also differ from more traditional macroeconomists on how to measure the economic parameters which govern a model's behavior. RBC theorists generally prefer using *calibration* or *quantitative theory* techniques. In practice, this means choosing a small number of parameters that are crucial to the behavior of a model and estimating the value of each parameter from microeconomic studies, rather than from the macroeconomic data itself. We explore here a very simple RBC model which focuses attention on a single parameter, the *intertemporal elasticity of substitution of labor.*

A SIMPLE REAL BUSINESS CYCLE MODEL

Real business cycle theorists create models in which firms choose optimal investment and hiring plans and individuals make optimal consumption and labor supply choices—all choices being made in a dynamic, uncertain environment. The resulting models are technically complex. In fact, they can be solved only by use of relatively sophisticated mathematics combined with computer simulation. We present here a simple model which gives the flavor of real business cycle models and focuses on the question of the intertemporal substitution of labor. In this simple model, the firm buys labor and produces output in each of the many periods. The representative worker sells her labor and buys consumption goods each period. If she wishes, she can save her consumption goods for another period.[27]

Each period, the representative firm buys labor L_t and uses it to produce output Y_t according to the production function

$$Y_t = a_t L_t \tag{27}$$

where a_t is the marginal product of labor in period t. (Looking ahead, we know the real wage rate will end up equaling a_t because in a competitive market the real wage rate equals the marginal product of labor.) Changes in the marginal product of labor are the source of real shocks in this simple model.

The representative worker has up to $\overline{L}$ hours available to sell in each period. Her leisure is $\overline{L}$ hours less the time she sells, so leisure equals $\overline{L} - L_t$. Each period the representative worker receives utility from leisure and from consumption, C_t. We assume that the worker's utility function in a given period can be expressed as[28]

$$U(C_t, \overline{L} - L_t) = C_t^{\gamma}(\overline{L} - L_t)^{\beta} \tag{28}$$

The worker's lifetime budget constraint states that the sum of lifetime consumption must equal the sum of lifetime earnings:[29]

$$C_t + C_{t+1} + C_{t+2} + \ldots = w_t L_t + w_{t+1} L_{t+1} + w_{t+2} L_{t+2} + \ldots \tag{29}$$

where w_t is the real wage rate in period t. The worker chooses consumption and leisure each period in amounts that will maximize the sum of lifetime utility subject to the budget constraint in equation (29).

---

[27]The pattern of capital investment and shifts in interest rates play important roles in real business models. We are omitting both in the interest of simplicity.

[28]We assume that γ and β are both positive.

[29]Note again that we are implicitly assuming a zero interest rate.

It will prove helpful to note that the marginal utility of leisure is

$$MU_{\text{leisure}} = \beta C_t^{\gamma}(\bar{L} - L_t)^{\beta - 1} = \frac{\beta U_t}{\bar{L} - L_t} \qquad (30)$$

How do we find the worker's optimal tradeoff defining her intertemporal substitution of leisure? If the worker reduces leisure 1 hour this period, she earns w_t more, which permits her to add w_t/w_{t+1} hours of leisure the following period. It follows that the marginal utility of leisure this period must equal w_t/w_{t+1} times the marginal utility of leisure next period:

$$MU_{\text{leisure}_t} = (w_t/w_{t+1}) \times MU_{\text{leisure}_{t+1}} \qquad (31)$$

Equating the values of the marginal utilities of present and future leisure—using equation (30) twice in equation (31)—gives us the worker's intertemporal substitution of leisure:

$$\frac{\bar{L} - L_t}{\bar{L} - L_{t+1}} = \left(\frac{w_{t+1}}{w_t}\right)^{\frac{1 - \gamma}{1 - \gamma - \beta}} \qquad (32)$$

Equation (32) tells us that if the wage in period $t + 1$ increases 1 percent while the wage in other periods remains constant, leisure in period $t + 1$ will fall by $(1 - \gamma)/(1 - \gamma - \beta)$. Depending on the values of β and γ, leisure might be very responsive or quite unresponsive to temporary changes in the wage rate.

Our model needs to be consistent with the empirical observation that *permanent* wage changes have little effect on labor supply. We can check this by computing the long-run response of leisure to a permanent wage change. Suppose the wage were constant over time, say, w^*. In this case consumption and labor supply would also be constant over time, say, C^* and L^*. From the budget constraint [equation (29)], it must be true that $C^* = w^*L^*$. Combine this with the worker's *consumption-leisure tradeoff*, $\bar{L} - L_t = (\beta/\gamma)(C_t/w_t)$ to derive the long-run labor supply, and we find

$$\bar{L} - L^* = \frac{(\beta/\gamma)(w^*L^*)}{w^*} \qquad or \qquad L^* = \frac{\gamma}{\beta + \gamma}\bar{L} \qquad (33)$$

Equation (33) shows that the long-run response of labor to the wage rate is zero, since w^* drops out of equation (33) entirely. So in this aspect our model is in accord with the facts.[30]

Consider now the effect of intertemporal substitution of labor as a *propagation mechanism*. Suppose there is a transitory technology shock in period t and thus the marginal product of labor rises by $\%\Delta a$. We know that the wage rate equals the marginal product of labor, so the wage rate will increase along with the increase in a. The total change in output will be

$$\%\Delta Y = \%\Delta a + \%\Delta L \qquad (34)$$

The propagation mechanism is the "extra kick" to output $\%\Delta L$. We know from equation (32) that leisure will decrease by $[(1 - \gamma)/(1 - \gamma - \beta)] \times \%\Delta a$. Since leisure

---

[30]Empirically, the long-run supply of labor is slightly backward-bending. In the long run, higher wages reduce labor supply somewhat as people prefer to spend some of their higher income on increased leisure.

hours are roughly three times labor hours,[31] the percentage increase in labor should be approximately $\%\Delta L = 3 \times [(1 - \gamma)/(1 - \gamma - \beta)] \times \%\Delta a$. The total change in output will be

$$\%\Delta Y = \left(1 + 3 \times \frac{1 - \gamma}{1 - \gamma - \beta} \right) \times \%\Delta a \qquad (35)$$

The parameters β and γ are examples of what are called *deep parameters* in the real business cycle literature. RBC theorists argue that our models should depend on the parameters which describe the preferences of consumer-workers and the parameters which describe the production function of firms. These parameters can be identified from microeconomic studies. In our very simple model, if $\beta + \gamma$ is close to 1, the intertemporal substitution of leisure will be very strong and the propagation mechanism in equation (35) will translate relatively small technology shocks into much larger output shocks. In contrast, if the intertemporal substitution of leisure is weak, this propagation mechanism will be relatively unimportant. The empirical evidence, based on microeconomic data, favors the view that intertemporal substitution is relatively weak.[32]

RECAP

- Real business cycle theory models the macroeconomy through the optimizing decisions about work and consumption made by individuals and the optimizing decisions about production made by firms. The model presented above is a simple version of the nonlinear, dynamic models deployed by RBC theorists.
- Real business cycle theory minimizes the role of nominal fluctuations and money.
- RBC theorists try to identify deep parameters which can be measured in microeconomic studies. The elasticity of the intertemporal substitution of leisure is a key example. The conclusions from the measurement of such parameters are not always favorable to the RBC models.

◆ O P T I O N A L ◆

8-6

A NEW KEYNESIAN MODEL OF STICKY NOMINAL PRICES

The introduction of rational expectations theory and real business cycle theory instituted a *New Classical* revolution against the Keynesian orthodoxy of the aggregate supply–aggregate demand model. New Classical theories are grounded in rational, maximizing behavior, characteristics which economists, by training, greatly prefer. On the other hand, these theories leave little or no role for the kind of sluggish nominal price adjustment that Keynesian economists believe they see in the real economy. Beginning

---

[31]Suppose one works 2,000 out of 8,760 = 24 × 365 hours.

[32]See Joseph Altonji, "Intertemporal Substitution in Labor Supply: Evidence from Micro Data," *Journal of Political Economy,* June 1986, and David Card, "Intertemporal Labor Supply: An Assessment," NBER Working Paper 3602, January 1991.

in the mid-1980s, and continuing today, a *New Keynesian* counterrevolution has arisen. New Keynesian models try to play by the intellectual rules of the New Classicists—that is, reflect rational, maximizing behavior—while still giving *AS–AD*-like results.

New Keynesian models generally rely on an assumption of imperfect competition. Under perfect competition, the individual actions of firms and consumers lead society to an "efficient" equilibrium. But under imperfect competition, individual decisions need not lead to efficient social outcomes. New Keynesian models explain how individually rational decisions under imperfect competition lead to socially undesirable booms and busts. In this section we examine one New Keynesian model, Mankiw's model of nominal price stickiness. Mankiw's model explains why individual, imperfectly competitive firms might leave nominal prices unchanged ("sticky") in the face of a change in the nominal money supply.

The intellectual problem that Mankiw faced is that according to economic theory, *nominal* prices are just measures based on an arbitrary unit of account. Microeconomic theory makes clear that only *relative* prices matter. In fact, microeconomic theory makes a very clear prediction related to the neutrality of money. Suppose that the economy initially has money supply $\overline{M}$ and that, through the supply and demand process, it reaches equilibrium with prices p_1, p_2, p_3, and so forth, for an average price level p. Now suppose that the money supply is $2\overline{M}$ instead. Microeconomic theory predicts that markets will reach the identical equilibria as previously, this time with prices $2p_1$, $2p_2$, $2p_3$, and an average price level $2p$. Nothing *real* has changed. The real money supply remains $2\overline{M}/2p = \overline{M}/p$, and the ratio of prices in any pair of markets, say, markets 1 and 3, remains unchanged, $2p_1/2p_3 = p_1/p_3$. So the Keynesians faced the question of how to reconcile rational, microeconomically justified economic theory with the idea that the nominal price level might not immediately reflect changes in the nominal money supply.

The beginning of the answer lay in recognizing that setting and changing prices is itself an economic activity. Since changing prices uses economic resources, firms will change prices only when the benefits from the price change outweigh the costs. On the surface, this seems a reasonable explanation for leaving prices unchanged in the face of a change in the money supply. The problem with this argument is that the cost of changing prices is surely very small and swings in the economy are on the order of several percent of GDP. It would seem that the benefits of a price change would nearly always outweigh the cost.

In 1985, Greg Mankiw solved this conundrum by using very basic microeconomic theory to show that the *private* benefits of changing a price can be much smaller than the *social* benefits if there is substantial monopoly power in the economy.[33] Firms base their decisions on the private benefit only, so it is possible that in the face of changed demand each firm will decide to hold constant the price it charges, even though the

---

[33]N. Gregory Mankiw, "Small Menu Costs and Large Business Cycles: A Macroeconomic Model of Monopoly," *Quarterly Journal of Economics,* May 1985. See also George A. Akerlof and Janet L. Yellen, "A Near Rational Model of the Business Cycle, with Wage and Price Inertia," *Quarterly Journal of Economics,* Supplement, 1985. These and a number of related articles are reprinted in N. Gregory Mankiw and David Romer (eds.), *New Keynesian Economics* (Cambridge, Mass.: M.I.T. Press, 1991). For an overview, see Laurence Ball and N. Gregory Mankiw, "A Sticky-Price Manifesto," *Carnegie-Rochester Conference Series on Public Policy,* December 1994.

social benefit of changing the price outweighs the social cost. We present a simplified version of Mankiw's analysis.

Suppose the production side of the economy consists of many small firms, each with some element of monopoly power in its own market. Indexing the markets by i, we can write the demand facing firm i as

$$Y_i = \left(\frac{P_i}{P}\right)^{-\epsilon} \frac{M}{P} \qquad (36)$$

where P_i is the price charged by firm i, P is the overall price level, and ϵ $(\epsilon > 1)$ is the elasticity of demand. Suppose that labor is the only input, the marginal product of labor is a, and the nominal wage is W. A monopolist sets its price as a markup over costs. Since marginal cost is W/a, the firm will charge[34]

$$P_i = \left(\frac{\epsilon}{\epsilon - 1}\right)\frac{W}{a} \qquad (37)$$

and the firm's nominal profit will be

$$\left(P_i - \frac{W}{a}\right)Y_i \qquad (38)$$

To provide a base of comparison for looking at sticky prices, we first ask what happens in the neoclassical model when the money supply increases by, say, 2 percent. Since money is neutral in a neoclassical model, we know that all nominal prices and wages will rise by 2 percent. We see that both the left and the right sides of equation (37) rise by 2 percent. Since M, P, and all the P_i's rise by 2 percent, real demand in equation (36) is unchanged. From equation (38), nominal profits rise 2 percent, but since overall prices have risen, real profits are unchanged. So everything in our model is consistent with the neutrality of money.

Suppose now that each firm has to undertake a small expenditure, z, called a "menu cost," if it raises its price. Each firm will compare the cost of maintaining its now "too low" price with the potential increase in profit if it raises prices 2 percent. Mankiw showed that the potential profit can be very small—literally "second order"—when two conditions hold:

- If the deviation between optimal price and existing price is small, the profit opportunity is *very* small.
- If the elasticity of firm demand is low, profit is relatively less sensitive to getting the price exactly right.

As an example, Figure 8-6 shows profit losses, measured as a percentage of optimal output, on the vertical axis and the percentage deviation of price from optimal price on the horizontal axis. The blue line shows profit losses for a modestly monopolistic firm (as it happens, one with a demand elasticity of 20). Suppose the firm's current price is 2 percent below optimal. Then, reading across on the blue line, we see that the firm is forgoing potential profit equal to .5 percent of output. If the menu cost

---

[34]Equation (36) can be derived from solving the monopolist's profit maximization problem. If you have had an intermediate microeconomics course, you may have seen the formula there.

FIGURE 8-6   MANKIW'S BREAKTHROUGH.

is more than this, the firm will leave its price unchanged. Since other firms face similar choices, they too leave prices unchanged. The net effect is that all nominal prices remain fixed, the overall price level remains fixed, the real money supply increases, and aggregate demand rises along with the real money supply. From equation (36), we see that the real money supply (M/P) and output will rise 2 percent. Note that the 2 percent gain in societal output is 4 times the privately forgone firm profits.

The key to Mankiw's breakthrough is the assumption that firms face a downward-sloping demand curve. In a perfectly competitive market, every firm faces a horizontal (infinitely elastic) demand curve, even though the demand curve for the market as a whole can have an arbitrary slope. If the demand curve facing an individual firm is horizontal, or nearly so, a small deviation of price from the optimal price causes a huge swing in demand and a correspondingly huge swing in profits. So in a competitive market, the private profit from getting prices right always outweighs a small menu cost.[35] In contrast, with a downward-sloping demand curve facing each firm, a small menu cost may well be bigger than potential profit changes.

Mankiw's work provides a rigorous microeconomic justification for nominal price stickiness. Since New Classical economists attack the rigor of the underpinnings of

---

[35]The red line in Fig. 8-6 shows potential profits for a relatively more competitive firm. The same 2 percent mispricing here costs more than 2 percent of output, about 4 times the cost in the less competitive, blue, case. By manipulating the elasticity, ϵ, one can make the contrast between the red and blue lines as large or small as desired.

Keynesian models, such justification is a key piece of the Keynesian response to rational expectations and real business cycle models. Not everyone agrees on the empirical significance of Mankiw's formulation, but the work is certainly a milestone in the New Keynesian counterrevolution.

RECAP

- The New Keynesians try to build models based on maximizing behavior which result in aggregate supply–aggregate demand-like behavior.
- Most New Keynesian models rely on imperfect competition.
- Prices can be sticky, even though the menu costs of adjustment are quite small, because the increased profit from resetting prices is even smaller.

SUMMARY

1. Modern theories emphasize the consistency of macroeconomic and microeconomic theories.
2. The rational expectations approach emphasizes the consistency of public expectations about the behavior of the economy.
3. Rational forecasts make errors, but not predictable ones.
4. The rational expectations approach suggests that anticipated monetary policy is neutral even in the short run.
5. An imperfect-information approach will explain a short-run upward-sloping aggregate supply curve, but one in which the tradeoff between output and inflation cannot be exploited through anticipated monetary policy.
6. The random-walk model of output suggests that economic fluctuations are highly persistent—and therefore not due to changes in aggregate demand.
7. The real business cycle approach builds models of a dynamic economy in which real shocks are propagated. These models minimize the role of the monetary sector.
8. New Keynesian models attempt to reintegrate aggregate demand, especially sticky prices, with solid microeconomic foundations.

KEY TERMS

rational expectations equilibrium	productivity shock	trend (secular) component of GDP
rational expectations	New Keynesian economics	cyclical component of GDP
policy irrelevance	price stickiness	trend stationary
random walk of GDP	menu cost	difference stationary
real business cycle (RBC) theory	imperfect competition	trend stationary with breaks
propagation mechanism	Lucas critique	deep parameters
intertemporal substitution of leisure	perfect foresight	New Classical economics
	imperfect-information model	

PROBLEMS

Conceptual

1. This chapter covers four broad classes of research—rational expectations theory, random walk in output, real business cycle theory, and models which endeavor to explain why output can diverge, in the short run, from its full-employment level. To what extent do these models complement or contradict each other? Discuss.

*2. What are rational expectations? How do rational expectations differ from perfect foresight? Is monetary policy neutral under both assumptions?

3. Describe a propagation mechanism used in real business cycle theory. Explain, briefly, how it works.

*4. What are the similarities and differences between Mankiw's menu-cost model of aggregate supply and Lucas's imperfect-information one? Classify each as New Keynesian or New Classical.

*5. What is the key assumption in Mankiw's menu-cost model of aggregate supply?

*6. What are deep parameters, in the sense used by proponents of real business cycle theory?

*7. In Lucas's imperfect-information model of aggregate supply, when will aggregate shocks (shocks to the economy at large, rather than to particular regions or markets) have the strongest effect on output? Explain.

*8. **a.** What is the difference between trend-stationary and difference-stationary processes?

 b. Why is this an important distinction, and how does our belief regarding which of these best characterizes output affect our forecasting strategy?

 c. Perron suggested that output might best be characterized as trend stationary with breaks. How does this help resolve the question of the importance of shocks to aggregate demand?

Technical

*1. **a.** Use equations (3) and (4) to forecast both the price level and the level of output which result from the simple *AS–AD* model of Section 8-2. You may assume that the slope of the aggregate supply curve is 2/3; that the values of the money supply, velocity, and potential GDP are 9, 8, and 7, respectively; and that the expected price level is 5.

 b. Evaluate your forecast in light of the Lucas critique.

 c. How does this forecast differ from that which would result from a perfect-foresight model?

 d. Is this forecast better or worse? Explain.

*2. Use equations (11) and (12) to check the effects of anticipated and unanticipated supply shocks on the level of output. Show that they behave as they would in a perfect-foresight model when anticipated and as they would in the standard *AS–AD* model when unanticipated.

3. Does empirical evidence support the rational expectations result that anticipated monetary policy should have no effect on output? Explain.

4. **a. Suppose, in the simple RBC model developed in Section 8-5, that $\gamma = .35$ and $\beta = .05$. How much of an output increase will result from a 10 percent increase in the marginal product of labor, given these parameter values? [*Hint:* Use equation (35).]

*One asterisk denotes a more difficult problem. Two asterisks means the problem is *really* hard.

    b. Would there be strong intertemporal substitution of leisure in using the parameters given in part (a)? Why or why not?

*5.   **a.** What does empirical evidence suggest regarding the extent to which people substitute leisure over time?

    b. What does this suggest regarding the role of intertemporal substitution in propagating shocks throughout the economy and regarding the ability of small technology shocks to generate large output shocks?

*6. This question relates to expectations formation in the Lucas imperfect-information model of aggregate supply.

    a. If $\alpha = 1$ and $\beta = .75$, what is the expected change in the overall price level when local prices, p_i, rise to 4 times their original level? [*Hint:* Use equation (19).]

    b. If α (the slope of the "local" supply function) is ½ for a particular region, by how much will output increase in the region as a result of this increase in its local prices?

    c. How would this result change if β were .25 instead of .75, and what would it mean for β to have such a small value?

    d. What if β were 1?

PART

3

First Models

CHAPTER 9

Income and Spending

CHAPTER HIGHLIGHTS

- In the most basic model of aggregate demand, spending determines output and income, but output and income also determine spending. In particular, consumption depends on income, but increased consumption increases aggregate demand and therefore output.

- Increases in autonomous spending increase output more than one for one. In other words, there is a multiplier effect.

- The size of the multiplier depends on the marginal propensity to consume and on tax rates.

- Increases in government spending increase aggregate demand and, therefore, tax collections. But tax collections rise by less than the increase in government spending, so increased government spending increases the budget deficit.

One of the central questions in macroeconomics is why output fluctuates around its potential level. Growth is highly uneven. In business cycle booms and recessions, output rises and falls relative to the trend of potential output. Over the last 25 years there have been four recessions, in which output declined relative to trend—even falling in some years, including 1991—and then recoveries, in which output rose relative to trend.

This chapter offers a first theory of these fluctuations in real output relative to trend. The cornerstone of this model is the mutual interaction between output and spending: spending determines output and income, but output and income also determine spending.

The *Keynesian* model of income determination that we develop in this chapter is very simple; it will be elaborated in later chapters. The central simplification is that we assume for the time being that prices do not change at all and that firms are willing to sell *any* amount of output at the given level of prices. Thus the aggregate supply curve, shown in Chapter 7, is assumed to be entirely flat. This chapter develops the theory of the aggregate demand schedule.

The key finding in this chapter is that because of the feedback between spending and output, increases in autonomous spending—increased government purchases, for example—generate further increases in aggregate demand. Other chapters introduce dynamic links between spending and output and allow for offsetting effects due to changes in prices and interest rates, but these more sophisticated models of the economy can be seen as elaborations of this chapter's model.

9-1

AGGREGATE DEMAND AND EQUILIBRIUM OUTPUT

Aggregate demand is the total amount of goods demanded in the economy. Distinguishing among goods demanded for consumption (C), for investment (I), by the government (G), and as net exports (NX), aggregate demand (AD) is determined by

$$AD = C + I + G + NX \qquad (1)$$

Output is at its *equilibrium level* when the quantity of output produced is equal to the quantity demanded. Thus an economy is at equilibrium output when

$$Y = AD = C + I + G + NX \qquad (2)$$

When aggregate demand—the amount people want to buy—is not equal to output, there is unplanned inventory investment or disinvestment. We summarize this as

$$IU = Y - AD \qquad (3)$$

where IU is unplanned additions to inventory. If output is greater than aggregate demand, there is unplanned inventory investment, $IU > 0$. As excess inventory accumulates, firms cut back on production until output and aggregate demand are again in equilibrium. Conversely, if output is below aggregate demand, inventories are drawn down until equilibrium is restored.

9-2

THE CONSUMPTION FUNCTION AND AGGREGATE DEMAND

With the concept of equilibrium output firmly defined, we now focus on the determinants of aggregate demand, and particularly on consumption demand. We focus on consumption in part because the consumption sector is so large and in part because it is easy to see the link between consumption and income. For simplicity, we omit the government and foreign trade, therefore setting both G and NX equal to zero.

The demand for consumption goods is not, in practice, constant but, rather, increases with income: families with higher incomes consume more than families with lower incomes, and countries where income is higher typically have higher levels of total consumption. The relationship between consumption and income is described by the *consumption function.*

THE CONSUMPTION FUNCTION

We assume that consumption demand increases with the level of income:

$$C = \overline{C} + cY \qquad \overline{C} > 0 \qquad 0 < c < 1 \tag{4}$$

This consumption function is shown by the green line in Figure 9-1. The variable $\overline{C}$, the *intercept,* represents the level of consumption when income is zero.[1] For every dollar increase in income, the level of consumption increases by $\$c$. For example, if c is .90, then for every $1 increase in income, consumption rises by 90 cents. The *slope* of the consumption function is c. Along the consumption function the level of consumption rises with income. Box 9-1 shows that this relationship holds in practice.

The coefficient c is sufficiently important to have a special name, the *marginal propensity to consume.* The marginal propensity to consume is the increase in consumption per unit increase in income. In our case, the marginal propensity to consume is less than 1, which implies that out of a dollar increase in income, only a fraction, c, is spent on consumption.

CONSUMPTION AND SAVING

What happens to the rest of the dollar of income, the fraction $(1 - c)$, that is not spent on consumption? If it is not spent, it must be saved. Income is either spent or saved; there are no other uses to which it can be put. It follows that any theory that explains consumption is equivalently explaining the behavior of saving.

More formally, look at equation (5), which states that income that is not spent on consumption is saved:

$$S \equiv Y - C \tag{5}$$

---

[1]Two points need to be made about the consumption function, equation (4). First, individuals' consumption demands are related to the amount of income they have available to spend, that is, their disposable income (YD), rather than just to the level of output. However, in this section, where we are ignoring the role of government and foreign trade, disposable income is equal to the level of income and output. Second, the real role of the intercept is to represent factors affecting consumption other than income—ownership of assets, such as stocks, bonds, and houses.

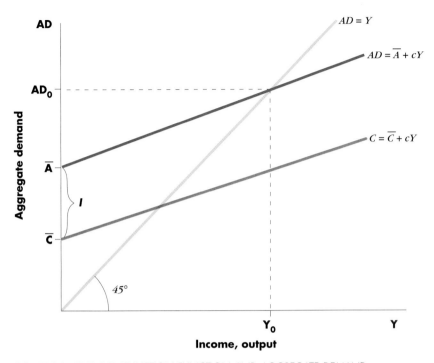

FIGURE 9-1   THE CONSUMPTION FUNCTION AND AGGREGATE DEMAND.

Equation (5) tells us that, by definition, *saving is equal to income minus consumption.*

The consumption function in equation (4) together with equation (5), which we call the *budget constraint,* implies a savings function. The savings function relates the level of saving to the level of income. Substituting the consumption function in equation (4) into the budget constraint in equation (5) yields the savings function:

$$S \equiv Y - C = Y - \overline{C} - cY = -\overline{C} + (1 - c)Y \qquad (6)$$

From equation (6), we see that saving is an increasing function of the level of income because the *marginal propensity to save,* $s = 1 - c$, is positive.

In other words, saving increases as income rises. For instance, suppose the marginal propensity to consume, c, is .9, meaning that 90 cents out of each extra dollar of income is consumed. Then the marginal propensity to save, s, is .10, meaning that the remaining 10 cents of each extra dollar of income is saved.

CONSUMPTION, AGGREGATE DEMAND, AND AUTONOMOUS SPENDING

We have specified one component of aggregate demand, consumption demand, and its link to income. Now we add investment, government spending and taxes, and foreign trade to our model, but we assume for the moment that each is *autonomous,* that is, determined outside the model and specifically assumed to be independent of income. Later chapters consider investment, the government, and foreign trade in detail. Here we just assume that investment is $\overline{I}$, government spending is G, taxes are $\overline{TA}$ and net

BOX 9-1 The Consumption-Income Relationship

The consumption function of equation (4), $C = \overline{C} + cY$, provides a good initial description of the consumption-income relationship. Annual per capita consumption and disposable personal income data for the United States for the years since 1960 are plotted in Figure 1. Recall from Chapter 2 that disposable personal income is the amount of income households have available for either spending or saving after paying taxes and receiving transfers.

The figure reveals a very close relationship between consumption and disposable income. The actual relationship is

$$C = -478 + .94YD$$

where C and YD are each measured in 1992 dollars per person. Although the relationship between consumption and disposable income is close, not all the points in Figure 1 lie exactly on the line. This means that something other than disposable income is affecting consumption in any given year. We turn our attention to the other factors determining consumption in Chapter 13. Meanwhile, it is reassuring that equation (4) is a quite accurate description of the real world's consumption-income relationship.

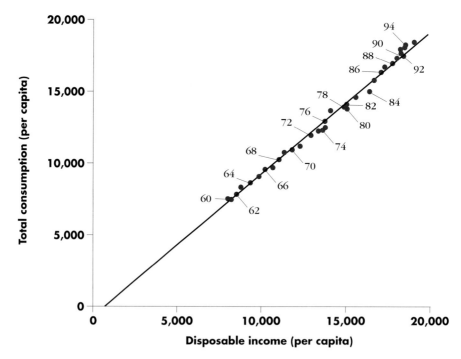

FIGURE 1   RELATIONSHIP OF TOTAL CONSUMPTION TO DISPOSABLE INCOME.

(Source: DRI/McGraw-Hill Macroeconomic Database.)

exports are $\overline{NX}$. Consumption now depends on *disposable income, YD = Y − $\overline{TA}$* as in $C = \overline{C} + c(Y − \overline{TA})$. Aggregate demand is the sum of the consumption function, investment, government spending, and net exports:

$$AD = C + I + G + NX$$
$$= \overline{C} + c(Y − \overline{TA}) + \overline{I} + G + \overline{NX}$$
$$= (\overline{C} − c\overline{TA} + \overline{I} + G + \overline{NX}) + cY$$
$$= \overline{A} + cY \tag{7}$$

The aggregate demand function, equation (7), is shown in Figure 9-1. Part of aggregate demand, $\overline{A} \equiv \overline{C} − c\overline{TA} + \overline{I} + G + \overline{NX}$, is independent of the level of income, or autonomous. But *aggregate demand also depends on the level of income.* It increases with the level of income because consumption demand increases with income. The aggregate demand schedule is obtained by adding (vertically) the demands for consumption, investment, government spending, and net exports at each level of income. At the income level Y_0 in Figure 9-1, the level of aggregate demand is AD_0.

EQUILIBRIUM INCOME AND OUTPUT

The next step is to use the aggregate demand function, *AD,* from Figure 9-1 and equation (7) to determine the equilibrium levels of output and income. We do this in Figure 9-2.

Recall the basic point of this chapter: The equilibrium level of income is such that aggregate demand equals output (which in turn equals income). The 45° line, *AD = Y,* in Figure 9-2 shows points at which output and aggregate demand are equal. Only at point *E* in Figure 9-2, and at the corresponding equilibrium levels of income and output (Y_0), does aggregate demand exactly equal output.[2] At that level of output and income, planned spending precisely matches production.

The arrows in Figure 9-2 indicate how the economy reaches equilibrium. At any income level below Y_0, firms find that demand exceeds output and inventories are declining, and they therefore increase production. Conversely, for output levels above Y_0, firms find inventories piling up and therefore cut production. As the arrows show, this process leads to the output level Y_0, at which current production exactly matches planned aggregate spending and unintended inventory changes are therefore equal to zero.

THE FORMULA FOR EQUILIBRIUM OUTPUT

The determination of equilibrium output in Figure 9-2 can also be expressed algebraically by using equation (7) and the equilibrium condition in the goods market, which is that output is equal to aggregate demand:

$$Y = AD \tag{8}$$

The level of aggregate demand, *AD,* is specified in equation (7). Substituting for *AD* in equation (8), we have the equilibrium condition:

$$Y = \overline{A} + cY \tag{9}$$

Since we have *Y* on both sides of the equilibrium condition in equation (9), we can collect the terms and solve for the equilibrium level of income and output, denoted by Y_0:

---

[2]We frequently use the subscript "0" to denote the equilibrium level of a variable.

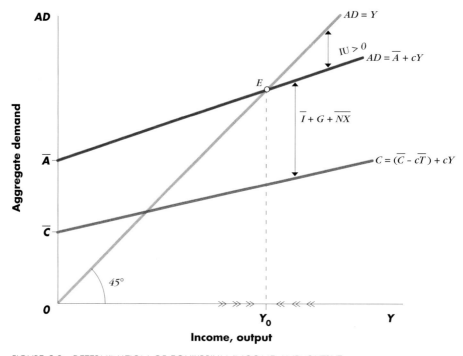

FIGURE 9-2   DETERMINATION OF EQUILIBRIUM INCOME AND OUTPUT.

$$Y_0 = \frac{1}{1-c}\overline{A} \qquad (10)$$

Figure 9-2 sheds light on equation (9). The position of the aggregate demand schedule is characterized by its slope, c (the marginal propensity to consume), and intercept, $\overline{A}$ (autonomous spending). Given the intercept, a steeper aggregate demand function—as would be implied by a higher marginal propensity to consume—implies a higher level of equilibrium income. Similarly, for a given marginal propensity to consume, a higher level of autonomous spending—in terms of Figure 9-2, a larger intercept—implies a higher equilibrium level of income. These results, suggested by Figure 9-2, are easily verified using equation (10), the formula for the equilibrium level of income.

Thus, the equilibrium level of output is higher the larger the marginal propensity to consume, c, and the higher the level of autonomous spending, $\overline{A}$.

Equation (10) shows the *level* of output as a function of the marginal propensity to consume and autonomous spending. Frequently, we are interested in knowing how a change in some component of autonomous spending would *change* output. Starting from equation (10), we can relate changes in output to changes in autonomous spending through

$$\Delta Y = \frac{1}{1-c}\Delta \overline{A} \qquad (11)$$

For example, if the marginal propensity to consume is .9, then $1/(1-c) = 10$, so a \$1 billion increase in government spending increases output by \$10 billion, since the recipients of the increased government spending increase their own spending, the recipients of that spending increase theirs, and so on. (We investigate the underpinnings of equation (11) more thoroughly in Section 9-3.) Note that we can compute the change in output without specifying the level of output either before or after the change.

SAVING AND INVESTMENT

There is a useful alternative formulation of the equilibrium condition that aggregate demand is equal to output. *In equilibrium, planned investment equals saving.* This condition applies only to an economy in which there is no government and no foreign trade.

To understand this relationship, return to Figure 9-2. Without government and foreign trade, the vertical distance between the aggregate demand and consumption schedules in the figure is equal to planned investment spending, $\bar{I}$. Note also that the vertical distance between the consumption schedule and the 45° line measures saving ($S = Y - C$) at each level of income.

The equilibrium level of income is found where AD crosses the 45° line, at E. Accordingly, at the equilibrium level of income, and only at that level, the two vertical distances are equal. Thus, at the equilibrium level of income, saving equals (planned) investment. By contrast, above the equilibrium level of income, Y_0, saving (the distance between the 45° line and the consumption schedule) exceeds planned investment, while below Y_0, planned investment exceeds saving.

The equality between saving and investment can be seen directly from national income accounting. Since income is either spent or saved, $Y = C + S$. Without government and foreign trade, aggregate demand equals consumption plus investment, $Y = C + I$. Putting the two together, we have $C + S = C + I$, or $S = I$.

If we include government and foreign trade in the analysis, we get a more complete picture relating investment to saving and also to net exports. Now income can either be spent, saved, or paid in taxes, so $Y = C + S + TA$ and complete aggregate demand is $Y = C + I + G + NX$. Therefore,

$$C + I + G + NX = C + S + TA$$
$$I = S + (TA - G) - NX \tag{12}$$

That is, investment equals private savings (S) plus the government budget surplus ($TA - G$) minus net exports (NX) or plus net imports, if you prefer.

Rather than using algebra, some people prefer to think of equation (12) in terms of a "corn economy": Investment is the corn left over that will be planted for next year's crop. The sources of corn investment are corn saved by individuals, any corn left over from government tax collections net of government spending, and any net corn imported from abroad.

9-3

THE MULTIPLIER

In this section we develop an answer to the following question: By how much does a $1 increase in autonomous spending raise the equilibrium level of income? There appears

TABLE 9-1   The Multiplier

ROUND	INCREASE IN DEMAND THIS ROUND	INCREASE IN PRODUCTION THIS ROUND	TOTAL INCREASE IN INCOME (ALL ROUNDS)
1	$\Delta\overline{A}$	$\Delta\overline{A}$	$\Delta\overline{A}$
2	$c\Delta\overline{A}$	$c\Delta\overline{A}$	$(1 + c)\Delta\overline{A}$
3	$c^2\Delta\overline{A}$	$c^2\Delta\overline{A}$	$(1 + c + c^2)\Delta\overline{A}$
4	$c^3\Delta\overline{A}$	$c^3\Delta\overline{A}$	$(1 + c + c^2 + c^3)\Delta\overline{A}$
. . .	. . .	. . .	. . .
. . .	. . .	. . .	. . .
. . .	. . .	. . .	$\dfrac{1}{1 - c}\Delta\overline{A}$

to be a simple answer. Since, in equilibrium, income equals aggregate demand, it would seem that a \$1 increase in (autonomous) demand or spending should raise equilibrium income by \$1. That answer is wrong. Let us now see why.

Suppose first that output increased by \$1 to match the increased level of autonomous spending. This increase in output and income would in turn give rise to further *induced* spending as consumption rises because the level of income has risen. How much of the initial \$1 increase in income would be spent on consumption? Out of an additional dollar of income, a fraction (c) is consumed. Assume, then, that production increases further to meet this induced expenditure, that is, that output and thus income increase by $1 + c$. That will still leave us with an excess demand, because the expansion in production and income by $1 + c$ will give rise to further induced spending. This story could clearly take a long time to tell. Does the process have an end?

In Table 9-1 we lay out the steps in the chain more carefully. The first round starts off with an increase in autonomous spending, $\Delta\overline{A}$. Next, we allow an expansion in production to meet exactly that increase in demand. Production accordingly expands by $\Delta\overline{A}$. This increase in production gives rise to an equal increase in income and, therefore, via the marginal propensity to consume, c, gives rise in the second round to induced expenditures of size $c\Delta\overline{A}$. Assume again that production expands to meet this increase in spending. The production adjustment this time is $c\Delta\overline{A}$, and so is the increase in income. This gives rise to a third round of induced spending equal to the marginal propensity to consume times the increase in income, $c(c\Delta\overline{A}) = c^2\Delta\overline{A}$. Since the marginal propensity to consume, c, is less than 1, the term c^2 is less than c, and therefore induced expenditures in the third round are smaller than those in the second round.

If we write out the successive rounds of increased spending, starting with the initial increase in autonomous demand, we obtain

$$\Delta AD = \Delta\overline{A} + c\Delta\overline{A} + c^2\Delta\overline{A} + c^3\Delta\overline{A} + \dots$$
$$= \Delta\overline{A}(1 + c + c^2 + c^3 + \dots) \tag{13}$$

For a value of $c < 1$, the successive terms in the series become progressively smaller. In fact, we are dealing with a geometric series, so the equation simplifies to

$$\Delta AD = 1/(1 - c)\Delta\overline{A} = \Delta Y_0 \tag{14}$$

From equation (14), therefore, we find that the cumulative change in aggregate spending is equal to a multiple of the increase in autonomous spending—just as we deduced from equation (10). The multiple $1/(1 - c)$ is called the *multiplier*.[3] The multiplier is the amount by which equilibrium output changes when autonomous aggregate demand increases by 1 unit.

The concept of the multiplier is sufficiently important to create new notation. The general definition of the multiplier is $\Delta Y/\Delta \overline{A}$, the change in equilibrium output when autonomous demand increases by 1 unit. In this specific case, omitting the government sector and foreign trade, we define the multiplier as α, where

$$\alpha \equiv \frac{1}{1 - c} \qquad (15)$$

Inspection of the multiplier in equation (15) shows that the larger the marginal propensity to consume, the larger the multiplier. For a marginal propensity to consume of .6, the multiplier is 2.5; for a marginal propensity to consume of .8, the multiplier is 5. This is because a high marginal propensity to consume implies that a larger fraction of an additional dollar of income will be consumed, and thus added to aggregate demand, thereby causing a larger induced increase in demand.

Why focus on the multiplier? The reason is that we are developing an explanation of fluctuations in output. The multiplier suggests that output changes when autonomous spending (including investment) changes *and* that the change in output can be larger than the change in autonomous spending. The multiplier is the formal way of describing a commonsense idea: If the economy for some reason—for example, a loss in confidence that reduces investment spending—experiences a shock that reduces income, people whose incomes have gone down will spend less, thereby driving equilibrium income down even further. The multiplier is therefore potentially part of the explanation of why output fluctuates.[4]

THE MULTIPLIER IN PICTURES

Figure 9-3 provides a graphical interpretation of the effects of an increase in autonomous spending on the equilibrium level of income. The initial equilibrium is at point E, with an income level Y_0. Now autonomous spending increases from $\overline{A}$ to $\overline{A}'$. This is represented by a parallel upward shift of the aggregate demand schedule to AD'. The upward shift means that now, at each level of income, aggregate demand is higher by an amount $\Delta \overline{A} \equiv \overline{A}' - \overline{A}$.

[3]Table 9-1 and equation (14) derive the multiplier using the mathematics of geometric series. If you are familiar with calculus, you will realize that the multiplier is nothing other than the derivative of the equilibrium level of income, Y_0, in equation (10) with respect to autonomous spending. Use calculus on equation (10) to check the statements in the text.

[4]Two warnings: (1) The multiplier is necessarily greater than 1 in this very simplified model of the determination of income, but as we shall see in the discussion of "crowding out" in Chap. 10, there may be circumstances in which it is less than 1. (2) The term "multiplier" is used more generally in economics to mean the effect on some endogenous variable (a variable whose level is explained by the theory being studied) of a unit change in an exogenous variable (a variable whose level is not determined within the theory being examined). For instance, one can talk of the multiplier for a change in the money supply on the level of unemployment. However, the classic use of the term is as we are using it here—the effects of a change in autonomous spending on equilibrium output.

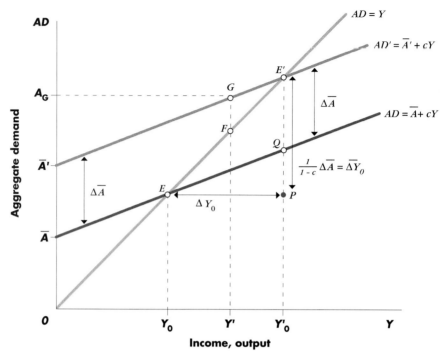

FIGURE 9-3   DERIVATION OF THE MULTIPLIER.

Aggregate demand now exceeds the initial level of output, Y_0. Consequently, inventories begin to run down. Firms will respond to the increase in demand and declining inventories by expanding production, say, to income level Y'. This expansion in production gives rise to induced expenditure, increasing aggregate demand to level A_G. At the same time, the expansion reduces the gap between aggregate demand and output to the vertical distance FG. The gap between demand and output is reduced because the marginal propensity to consume is less than 1.

Thus, with marginal propensity to consume less than unity, a sufficient expansion in output will restore the balance between aggregate demand and output. In Figure 9-3 the new equilibrium is indicated by point E', and the corresponding level of income is Y'_0. The change in income required is therefore $\Delta Y_0 = Y'_0 - Y_0$.

The magnitude of the income change required to restore equilibrium depends on two factors. The larger the increase in autonomous spending, represented in Figure 9-3 by the parallel shift in the aggregate demand schedule, the larger the income change. Furthermore, the larger the marginal propensity to consume—that is, the steeper the aggregate demand schedule—the larger the income change.

RECAP

There are three points to remember from this discussion of the multiplier:

- An increase in autonomous spending raises the equilibrium level of income.
- The increase in income is a multiple of the increase in autonomous spending.

- The larger the marginal propensity to consume, the larger the multiplier arising from the relation between consumption and income.

9-4

THE GOVERNMENT SECTOR

Whenever there is a recession, people expect and demand that the government do something about it. What can the government do? The government directly affects the level of equilibrium income in two separate ways. First, government purchases of goods and services, G, are a component of aggregate demand. Second, taxes and transfers affect the relation between output and income, Y, and the *disposable income*—income available for consumption or saving—that accrues to the household, YD. In this section, we are concerned with the way in which government purchases, taxes, and transfers affect the equilibrium level of income.

Disposable income (YD) is the net income available for spending by households after they receive transfers from and pay taxes to the government. It thus consists of income plus transfers minus taxes, $Y + TR - TA$. The consumption function is now

$$C = \overline{C} + cYD = \overline{C} + c(Y + TR - TA) \tag{4a}$$

The final step is a specification of *fiscal policy.* Fiscal policy is the policy of the government with regard to the level of government purchases, the level of transfers, and the tax structure. We assume that the government purchases a constant amount, $\overline{G}$; that it makes a constant amount of transfers, $\overline{TR}$; and that it imposes a *proportional income tax,* collecting a fraction, t, of income in the form of taxes:

$$G = \overline{G} \qquad TR = \overline{TR} \qquad TA = tY \tag{16}$$

With this specification of fiscal policy, we can rewrite the consumption function, after substituting from equation (16) for TR and TA in equation (4a), as

$$C = \overline{C} + c(Y + \overline{TR} - tY)$$
$$= \overline{C} + c\overline{TR} + c(1 - t)Y \tag{17}$$

Note in equation (17) that the presence of transfers raises autonomous consumption spending by the marginal propensity to consume out of disposable income, c, times the amount of transfers.[5] Income taxes, by contrast, lower consumption spending at each level of income. That reduction arises because households' consumption is related to *disposable* income rather than income itself, and income taxes reduce disposable income relative to the level of income.

While the marginal propensity to consume out of disposable income remains c, the marginal propensity to consume out of income is now $c(1 - t)$, where $1 - t$ is the fraction of income left after taxes. For example, if the marginal propensity to consume,

---

[5]We are assuming no taxes are paid on transfers from the government. As a matter of fact, taxes are paid on some transfers, such as interest payments on the government debt, and not paid on other transfers, such as welfare benefits.

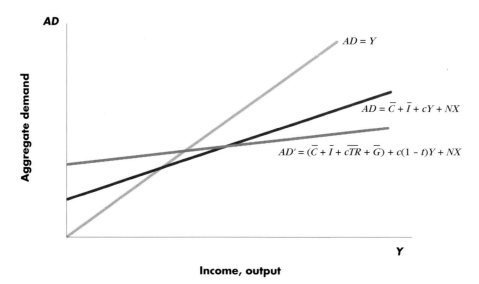

FIGURE 9-4   GOVERNMENT AND AGGREGATE DEMAND.

c, is .8 and the tax rate is .25, the marginal propensity to consume out of income, $c(1 - t)$, is .6 [= .8 × (1 − .25)].

Combining the aggregate demand identity with equations (16) and (17), we have

$$
\begin{aligned}
AD &= C + I + G + NX \\
&= [\overline{C} + c\overline{TR} + c(1 - t)Y] + \overline{I} + \overline{G} + \overline{NX} \\
&= (\overline{C} + c\overline{TR} + \overline{I} + \overline{G} + \overline{NX}) + c(1 - t)Y \\
&= \overline{A} + c(1 - t)Y
\end{aligned}
\tag{18}
$$

The effects of the introduction of government on the aggregate demand schedule are shown in Figure 9-4. The new aggregate demand schedule, denoted AD' in the figure, starts out higher than the original schedule, AD, but has a flatter slope. The intercept is larger because it now includes both government spending, $\overline{G}$, and the part of consumption resulting from transfer payments by the government, $c\overline{TR}$. The slope is flatter because households now have to pay part of every dollar of income in taxes and are left with only $1 - t$ of that dollar. Thus, as equation (18) shows, the marginal propensity to consume out of income is now $c(1 - t)$ instead of c.

EQUILIBRIUM INCOME

We are now set to study income determination when the government is included. We return to the equilibrium condition for the goods market, $Y = AD$, and using equation (17), write the equilibrium condition as

$$
Y = \overline{A} + c(1 - t)Y
$$

We can solve this equation for Y_0, the equilibrium level of income, by collecting terms in Y:

$$Y[1 - c(1 - t)] = \overline{A}$$

$$Y_0 = \frac{1}{1 - c(1 - t)}(\overline{C} + c\overline{TR} + \overline{I} + \overline{G})$$

$$Y_0 = \frac{\overline{A}}{1 - c(1 - t)} \tag{19}$$

In comparing equation (19) with equation (10), we see that the government sector makes a substantial difference. It raises autonomous spending by the amount of government purchases, $\overline{G}$, and by the amount of induced spending out of net transfers, $c\overline{TR}$; in addition, the presence of the income tax lowers the multiplier.

INCOME TAXES AND THE MULTIPLIER

Income taxes lower the multiplier, as can be seen from equation (19). If the marginal propensity to consume is .8 and taxes are zero, the multiplier is 5; with the same marginal propensity to consume and a tax rate of .25, the multiplier is cut in half, to $1/[1 - .8(1 - .25)] = 2.5$. Income taxes reduce the multiplier because they reduce the induced increase of consumption out of changes in income. Thus in Figure 9-4 the inclusion of taxes flattens the aggregate demand curve and hence reduces the multiplier.

INCOME TAXES AS AUTOMATIC STABILIZERS

The proportional income tax is one example of the important concept of *automatic stabilizers*. An automatic stabilizer is any mechanism in the economy that automatically— that is, without case-by-case government intervention—reduces the amount by which output changes in response to a change in autonomous demand.

One explanation of the business cycle is that it is caused by shifts in autonomous demand, especially investment. Sometimes, it is argued, investors are optimistic and investment is high—and so, therefore, is output. But sometimes they are pessimistic, and so both investment and output are low.

Swings in investment demand have a smaller effect on output when automatic stabilizers—such as a proportional income tax, which reduces the multiplier—are in place. This means that in the presence of automatic stabilizers we should expect output to fluctuate less than it would without them.

The proportional income tax is not the only automatic stabilizer.[6] Unemployment benefits enable the unemployed to continue consuming even though they do not have a job, so *TR* rises when *Y* falls. This means that demand falls less when someone becomes unemployed and receives benefits than it would if there were no benefits. This, too, makes the multiplier smaller and output more stable. Higher unemployment benefits and income tax rates in the post-World War II period are reasons that the business cycle fluctuations have been less extreme since 1945 than they were earlier.

EFFECTS OF A CHANGE IN FISCAL POLICY

We now consider the effects of changes in fiscal policy on the equilibrium level of income. Consider first a change in government purchases. This case is illustrated in

---

[6]Automatic stabilizers are discussed by T. Holloway, "The Economy and the Federal Budget: Guide to Automatic Stabilizers," *Survey of Current Business,* July 1984.

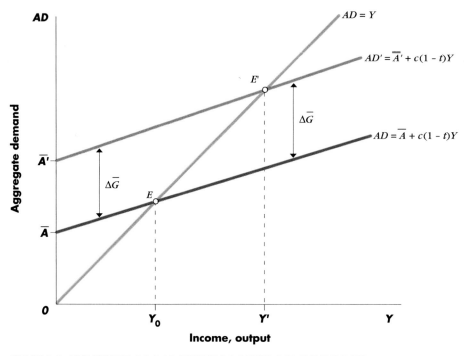

FIGURE 9-5   THE EFFECTS OF AN INCREASE IN GOVERNMENT PURCHASES.

Figure 9-5, where the initial level of income is Y_0. An increase in government purchases is a change in autonomous spending; therefore, the increase shifts the aggregate demand schedule upward by an amount equal to the increase in government purchases. At the initial level of output and income, the demand for goods exceeds output, and accordingly, firms expand production until the new equilibrium, at point E', is reached.

By how much does income expand? Recall that the change in equilibrium income will equal the change in aggregate demand, or

$$\Delta Y_0 = \Delta \overline{G} + c(1 - t)\Delta Y_0$$

where the remaining terms $(\overline{C}, \overline{TR}, \overline{I}, \text{ and } \overline{NX})$ are constant by assumption. Thus, the change in equilibrium income is

$$\Delta Y_0 = \frac{1}{1 - c(1 - t)}\Delta \overline{G} = \alpha_G \Delta \overline{G} \qquad (20)$$

where we have introduced the notation α_G to denote the multiplier in the presence of income taxes:

$$\alpha_G = \frac{1}{1 - c(1 - t)} \qquad (21)$$

Thus a \$1 increase in government purchases will lead to an increase in income in excess of a dollar. With a marginal propensity to consume of $c = .8$ and an income tax rate of $t = .25$, we would have a multiplier of 2.5: a \$1 increase in government spending raises equilibrium income by \$2.50.

Suppose that instead of raising government spending on goods and services, G, the government increases transfer payments, $\overline{TR}$. Autonomous spending, $\overline{A}$, will increase by only $c\Delta \overline{TR}$, so output will rise by $\alpha_G \times c\Delta \overline{TR}$. The multiplier for transfer payments is smaller than that for government spending—by a factor c—because part of any increase in $\overline{TR}$ is saved.

RECAP

- Government purchases and transfer payments act like increases in autonomous spending in their effects on income.
- A proportional income tax reduces the proportion of each extra dollar of output that is received as disposable income by consumers, and thus it has the same effects on income as a reduction in the propensity to consume.
- A proportional income tax is an automatic stabilizer.
- A reduction in transfers lowers output.

IMPLICATIONS

Since the theory we are developing implies that changes in government spending and taxes affect the level of income, it seems that fiscal policy can be used to stabilize the economy. When the economy is in a recession, or growing slowly, perhaps taxes should be cut or spending increased to get output to rise. And when the economy is booming, perhaps taxes should be increased or government spending cut to get back down to full employment. Indeed, fiscal policy is used actively to try to stabilize the economy, as in 1993, when the Clinton administration created a short-term stimulus.

9-5

THE BUDGET

Government budget deficits are now the norm in the United States, and surpluses are not yet in sight. But it was not always so, and it is not so now in some other countries. For most of its history, the U.S. *federal* government ran surpluses in peacetime and deficits during wars. It is only in the last 25 years that peacetime deficits have become standard in the United States.[7] An example of a country where the budget has been in surplus is Singapore, which in 1993 ran a budget surplus of approximately 15 percent of GDP![8]

The budget deficit on which the media and politicians focus is the federal budget deficit, which in 1995 was \$161 billion, or around 2 percent of GDP.[9] "Government"

---

[7]We deal with the budget in more detail in later chapters.

[8]Other countries with recent government budget surpluses are, for example, Jordan (1 percent of GDP in 1995) and New Zealand (.7 percent of GDP in 1994).

[9]The fiscal year starts on October 1 of the previous year.

in the national income accounts consists of all levels of government—federal, state, and local. State and local governments tend to run small (less than 1 percent of GDP) surpluses in boom years and small deficits in recession years. In 1995, the state and local surplus was $95 billion, about 1.3 percent of GDP.

Why the concern over the budget deficit? The fear is that the government's borrowing makes it difficult for private firms to borrow and invest, and thus slows the economy's growth. Full understanding of this concern has to wait until later chapters, but this section serves as an introduction, dealing with the government budget, its effects on output, and the effects of output on the budget.

The first important concept is the *budget surplus,* denoted by *BS.* The budget surplus is the excess of the government's revenues, taxes, over its total expenditures, consisting of purchases of goods and services and transfer payments:

$$BS \equiv TA - \overline{G} - \overline{TR} \tag{22}$$

A negative budget surplus, an excess of expenditure over revenues, is a *budget deficit.*

Substituting in equation (22) the assumption of a proportional income tax that yields tax revenues $TA = tY$ gives us

$$BS = tY - \overline{G} - \overline{TR} \tag{22a}$$

Figure 9-6 plots the budget surplus as a function of the level of income for given $\overline{G}$, $\overline{TR}$, and income tax rate, t. At low levels of income, the budget is in deficit (the surplus is negative) because government spending, $\overline{G} + \overline{TR}$, exceeds income tax collection. At high levels of income, by contrast, the budget shows a surplus, since income tax collection exceeds expenditures in the form of government purchases and transfers.

Figure 9-6 shows that the budget deficit depends not only on the government's policy choices, reflected in the tax rate (t), purchases ($\overline{G}$), and transfers ($\overline{TR}$), but also on anything else that shifts the level of income. For instance, suppose there is an increase in investment demand that increases the level of output. Then the budget deficit

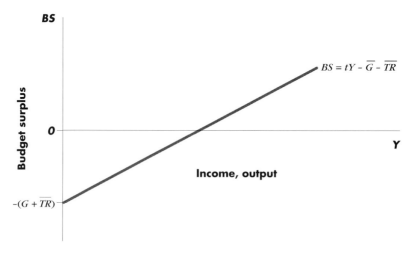

FIGURE 9-6   THE BUDGET SURPLUS.

will fall or the surplus will increase because tax revenues have risen. But the government has done nothing that changed the deficit.

We should, accordingly, not be surprised to see budget deficits in recessions, periods when the government's tax receipts are low. And in practice, transfer payments, through unemployment benefits, also increase during recessions, even though we are taking $\overline{TR}$ as autonomous in our model.

EFFECTS OF GOVERNMENT PURCHASES AND
TAX CHANGES ON THE BUDGET SURPLUS

Next we show how changes in fiscal policy affect the budget. In particular, we want to find out whether an increase in government purchases must reduce the budget surplus. At first sight, this appears obvious, because increased government purchases, from equation (22), are reflected in a reduced surplus or an increased deficit. On further thought, however, the increased government purchases will cause an increase (multiplied) in income and, therefore, increased income tax collection. This raises the interesting possibility that tax collection might increase by more than government purchases.

A brief calculation shows that the first guess is right: increased government purchases reduce the budget surplus. From equation (20) we see that the change in income due to increased government purchases is equal to $\Delta Y_0 \equiv \alpha_G \Delta G$. A fraction of that increase in income is collected in the form of taxes, so tax revenue increases by $t\alpha_G \Delta G$. The change in the budget surplus, using equation (21) to substitute for α_G, is therefore

$$\begin{aligned} \Delta BS &= \Delta TA - \Delta \overline{G} \\ &= t\alpha_G \Delta \overline{G} - \Delta \overline{G} \\ &= \left[\frac{t}{1 - c(1 - t)} - 1 \right] \Delta \overline{G} \\ &= -\frac{(1 - c)(1 - t)}{1 - c(1 - t)} \Delta \overline{G} \end{aligned} \qquad (23)$$

which is unambiguously negative.

We have, therefore, shown that an increase in government purchases will reduce the budget surplus, although in this model by considerably less than the increase in purchases. For instance, for $c = .8$ and $t = .25$, a \$1 increase in government purchases will create a \$0.375 reduction in the surplus.

In the same way, we can consider the effects of an increase in the tax rate on the budget surplus. We know that the increase in the tax rate will reduce the level of income. It might thus appear that an increase in the tax rate, keeping the level of government spending constant, could reduce the budget surplus. In fact, an increase in the tax rate increases the budget surplus, despite the reduction in income that it causes, as you are asked to show in the problem set at the end of this chapter.[10]

---

[10]The theory that tax rate cuts would increase government revenue (or tax rate increases reduce government revenue) is associated with Arthur Laffer, formerly at the University of Chicago and University of Southern California. Laffer's argument, however, did not depend on the aggregate demand effects of tax cuts but, rather, on the possibility that a tax cut would lead people to work more. This is a strand in supply-side economics, which we examined in Chap. 5.

We signal here another interesting result known as the *balanced budget multiplier.* Suppose government spending and taxes are raised in equal amounts and thus in the new equilibrium the budget surplus is unchanged. By how much will output rise? The answer is that for this special experiment the multiplier is equal to 1—output rises by the increase in government spending and no more.

9-6

THE FULL-EMPLOYMENT BUDGET SURPLUS

The final topic to be treated here is the concept of the full-employment budget surplus.[11] Recall that increases in taxes add to the surplus and that increases in government expenditures reduce the surplus. Increases in taxes have been shown to reduce the level of income; increases in government purchases and transfers, to increase the level of income. It thus seems that the budget surplus is a convenient, simple measure of the overall effects of fiscal policy on the economy. For instance, when the budget is in deficit, we would say that fiscal policy is expansionary, tending to increase GDP.

However, the budget surplus by itself suffers from a serious defect as a measure of the direction of fiscal policy. The defect is that the surplus can change because of changes in autonomous private spending—as can be seen in Figure 9-5. Thus, an increase in the budget deficit does not necessarily mean that the government has changed its policy in an attempt to increase the level of income.

Since we frequently want to measure the way in which fiscal policy is being used to affect the level of income, we require some measure of policy that is independent of the particular position of the business cycle—boom or recession—in which we may find ourselves. Such a measure is provided by the *full-employment budget surplus,* which we denote by BS^*. The full-employment budget surplus measures the budget surplus at the full-employment level of income or at potential output. Using Y^* to denote the full-employment level of income, we can write

$$BS^* = tY^* - \overline{G} - \overline{TR} \tag{24}$$

There are other names for the full-employment surplus. Among them are the *cyclically adjusted surplus* (or deficit), the *high-employment surplus,* the *standardized employment surplus,* and the *structural surplus.* These new names all refer to the same concept as the full-employment surplus, but they avoid implying that there is a unique level of full-employment output that the economy has not yet reached. They suggest, reasonably, that the concept is merely a convenient measuring rod that fixes a given level of employment as the reference point.

To see the difference between the actual and the full-employment budgets, we subtract the actual budget surplus in equation (22a) from the full-employment budget surplus in equation (24) to obtain

$$BS^* - BS = t(Y^* - Y) \tag{25}$$

---

[11]The concept has a long history; it was first used by E. Cary Brown, "Fiscal Policy in the Thirties: A Reappraisal," *American Economic Review,* December 1956.

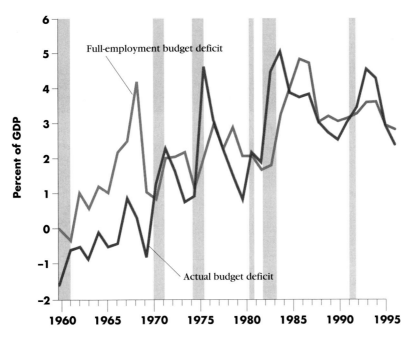

FIGURE 9-7   ACTUAL AND FULL-EMPLOYMENT BUDGET DEFICIT.

(*Source:* DRI/McGraw-Hill Macroeconomic Database; and Congressional Budget Office, *The Economic and Budget Outlook: Fiscal Years 1997–2006,* May 1996.)

The only difference arises from income tax collection.[12] Specifically, if output is below full employment, the full-employment surplus exceeds the actual surplus. Conversely, if actual output exceeds full-employment (or potential) output, the full-employment surplus is less than the actual surplus. The difference between the actual and the full-employment budget is the *cyclical* component of the budget. In a recession the cyclical component tends to show a deficit and in a boom there may even be a surplus.

We next look at the full-employment budget deficit shown in Figure 9-7. Public concern about the deficit mounted in the 1980s. For many economists, the behavior of the deficit during the high-unemployment years 1982 and 1983 was not especially worrisome. The actual budget is usually in deficit during recessions. But the shift toward deficit of the full-employment budget was regarded as an entirely different matter.

Two final words of warning: First, there is no certainty as to the true full-employment level of output. Various assumptions about the level of unemployment that corresponds to full employment are possible. The usual assumptions now are that full employment means an unemployment rate of about 5 to 5.5 percent, although when the actual unemployment rate was higher, there were some estimates as high as 7 percent.

---

[12]In practice, transfer payments, such as welfare and unemployment benefits, are also affected by the state of the economy, so *TR* also depends on the level of income. But the major cause of differences between the actual surplus and the full-employment surplus is taxes. Automatic movements in taxes caused by a change in income are about five times the size of automatic movements in spending. (See T. M. Holloway and J. C. Wakefield, "Sources of Change in the Federal Government Deficit, 1970–86," *Survey of Current Business,* May 1985.)

Estimates of the full-employment deficit or surplus will differ depending on the assumptions made about the economy at full employment.

Second, the high-employment surplus is not a perfect measure of the thrust of fiscal policy. There are several reasons for this: a change in spending with a matching increase in taxes, leaving the deficit unchanged, will raise income; expectations about future fiscal policy changes can affect current income; and in general, because fiscal policy involves the setting of a number of variables—the tax rate, transfers, and government purchases—it is difficult to describe the thrust of fiscal policy perfectly with a single number. But the high-employment surplus is nevertheless a useful guide to the direction of fiscal policy.[13]

SUMMARY

1. Output is at its equilibrium level when the aggregate demand for goods is equal to the level of output.

2. Aggregate demand consists of planned spending by households on consumption, by firms on investment goods, and by government on its purchases of goods and services and also includes net exports.

3. When output is at its equilibrium level, there are no unintended changes in inventories and all economic units are making precisely the purchases they had planned to. An adjustment process for the level of output based on the accumulation or rundown of inventories leads the economy to the equilibrium output level.

4. The level of aggregate demand is itself affected by the level of output (equal to the level of income) because consumption demand depends on the level of income.

5. The consumption function relates consumption spending to income. Consumption rises with income. Income that is not consumed is saved, so the savings function can be derived from the consumption function.

6. The multiplier is the amount by which a $1 change in autonomous spending changes the equilibrium level of output. The greater the propensity to consume, the higher the multiplier.

7. Government purchases and government transfer payments act like increases in autonomous spending in their effects on the equilibrium level of income. A proportional income tax has the same effect on the equilibrium level of income as a reduction in the propensity to consume. A proportional income tax thus reduces the multiplier.

8. The budget surplus is the excess of government receipts over expenditures. When the government is spending more than it receives, the budget is in deficit. The size of the budget surplus (or deficit) is affected by the government's fiscal policy variables—government purchases, transfer payments, and tax rates.

9. The actual budget surplus is also affected by changes in tax collection and transfers resulting from movements in the level of income that occur because of changes

---

[13]For further discussion of the full-employment deficit and alternative measures of fiscal policy, see Congressional Budget Office, *The Economic Outlook,* February 1984, appendix B; and Darrel Cohen, *A Comparison of Fiscal Measures Using Reduced Form Techniques,* Board of Governors of the Federal Reserve System, 1989. Early each year the Congressional Budget Office publishes *The Economic and Budget Outlook,* which contains an analysis of current fiscal policy and estimates of the full-employment budget.

in private autonomous spending. The full-employment (high-employment) budget surplus is used as a measure of the active use of fiscal policy. The full-employment surplus measures the budget surplus that would exist if output were at its potential (full-employment) level.

KEY TERMS

aggregate demand	budget constraint	automatic stabilizer
equilibrium level of output	marginal propensity to save	budget surplus/deficit
consumption function	disposable income	balanced budget multiplier
marginal propensity to	multiplier	full-employment budget
consume	fiscal policy	surplus

PROBLEMS

Conceptual

1. We call the model of income determination developed in this chapter a *Keynesian* one. What makes it Keynesian, as opposed to classical?
2. What is an autonomous variable? What components of aggregate demand have we specified, in this chapter, as being autonomous?
3. Using your knowledge of the amount of time required for the many components of the federal government to agree upon and implement changes in policy (i.e., tax codes, the welfare system), can you think of any problems with using fiscal policy to stabilize the economy?
4. Why do we call mechanisms such as proportional income taxes and the welfare system "automatic stabilizers"? Choose one of these mechanisms and explain carefully how and why it affects fluctuations in output.
5. What is the full-employment budget surplus, and why might it be a more useful measure than the actual, or unadjusted, budget surplus? The text provides other names for this measure, such as cyclically adjusted surplus and structural surplus. Why might we prefer to use these other terms?

Technical

1. Here we investigate a particular example of the model studied in Sections 9-2 and 9-3 with no government. Suppose the consumption function is given by $C = 100 + .8Y$, while investment is given by $I = 50$.
   a. What is the equilibrium level of income in this case?
   b. What is the level of saving in equilibrium?
   c. If, for some reason, output is at the level of 800, what will the level of involuntary inventory accumulation be?
   d. If I rises to 100 (we discuss what determines I in later chapters), what will the effect be on the equilibrium income?
   e. What is the value of the multiplier, α, here?
   f. Draw a diagram indicating the equilibria in both (**a**) and (**d**).
2. Suppose the consumption behavior in problem 1 changes so that $C = 100 + .9Y$, while I remains at 50.
   a. Is the equilibrium level of income higher or lower than it was in problem 1(**a**)? Calculate the new equilibrium level, Y', to verify this.

    b. Now suppose investment increases to $I = 100$, just as in problem 1(**d**). What is the new equilibrium income?

    c. Does this change in investment spending have more or less of an effect on Y than it did in problem 1? Why?

    d. Draw a diagram indicating the change in equilibrium income in this case.

3. Now we look at the role taxes play in determining equilibrium income. Suppose we have an economy of the type in Sections 9-4 and 9-5, described by the following functions:

$$C = 50 + .8YD$$
$$\bar{I} = 70$$
$$\bar{G} = 200$$
$$\overline{TR} = 100$$
$$t = .20$$

    a. Calculate the equilibrium level of income and the multiplier in this model.

    b. Calculate also the budget surplus, BS.

    c. Suppose that t increases to .25. What is the new equilibrium income? The new multiplier?

    d. Calculate the change in the budget surplus. Would you expect the change in the surplus to be more or less if $c = .9$ rather than .8?

    e. Can you explain why the multiplier is 1 when $t = 1$?

4. Suppose the economy is operating at equilibrium, with $Y_0 = 1,000$. If the government undertakes a fiscal change whereby the tax rate, t, increases by .05 and government spending increases by 50, will the budget surplus go up or down? Why?

5. Suppose Congress decides to reduce transfer payments (such as welfare) but to increase government purchases of goods and services by an equal amount. That is, it undertakes a change in fiscal policy such that $\Delta G = -\Delta TR$.

    a. Would you expect equilibrium income to rise or fall as a result of this change? Why? Check your answer with the following example: Suppose that, initially, $c = .8$, $t = .25$, and $Y_0 = 600$. Now let $\Delta G = 10$ and $\Delta TR = -10$.

    b. Find the change in equilibrium income, ΔY_0.

    c. What is the change in the budget surplus, ΔBS? Why has BS changed?

CHAPTER 10

Money, Interest, and Income

CHAPTER HIGHLIGHTS

- ◆ The model we introduce in this chapter, the *IS-LM* model, is the core of short-run macroeconomics.

- ◆ The *IS* curve describes the combinations of income and interest rates at which the goods market is in equilibrium.

- ◆ The *LM* curve describes the combinations of income and interest rates at which the money market is in equilibrium.

- ◆ Together, the *IS* and *LM* curves give aggregate demand.

- ◆ Increases in government spending raise output and interest rates.

- ◆ Increases in the money supply raise output and lower interest rates.

Money plays a central role in the determination of income and employment. Interest rates are a significant determinant of aggregate spending, and the Federal Reserve, which controls money growth and interest rates, is the first institution to be blamed when the economy gets into trouble. However, the stock of money, interest rates, and the Federal Reserve seem to have no place in the model of income determination developed in Chapter 9.

This chapter introduces money and monetary policy and builds an explicit framework of analysis within which to study the interaction of goods markets and assets markets. This new framework leads to an understanding of the determination of interest rates and of their role in the business cycle and introduces an avenue by which monetary policy affects output. Figure 10-1 shows the interest rate on Treasury bills. The interest rate on Treasury bills represents the payment received by someone who lends to the U.S. government. An interest rate of 5 percent means that someone who lends $100 to the government for 1 year will receive 5 percent, or $5, in interest. Figure 10-1 shows that interest rates are typically, but not always, high just before a recession, drop during the recession, and rise during the recovery. Figure 10-2 shows money growth and output growth. There is a strong, but not absolute, link between money growth and output growth. This chapter explores the link from money to interest rates to output.

The model we introduce in this chapter, the *IS-LM* model, is the core of short-run macroeconomics. It maintains the spirit and, indeed, many details of the model of the

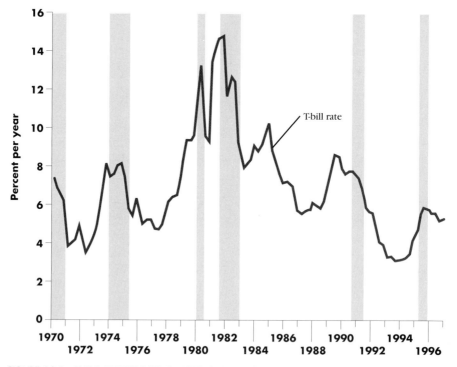

FIGURE 10-1   THE INTEREST RATE ON TREASURY BILLS.

(Source: DRI/McGraw-Hill Macroeconomic Database.)

BOX 10-1 Seemingly Difficult Material Alert

Let us be blunt. This is *the* chapter which students find most difficult to master.

We study two markets—the goods market and the money market—and their linkage through two economic variables—interest rates and income. Many students find it hard to link the formal two-market–two-variable model with verbal discussion of the economic operation of each market. So before diving into the substance of the chapter, we'll briefly explain here how things will connect up by the time we're done.

In the previous chapter we looked at a simple model of the goods market and found the value of GDP at which equilibrium output equaled aggregate demand. We had one market—goods—cleared by one variable—GDP (Y). The first thing we do in this chapter is introduce the interest rate into the goods market (via investment demand), leaving us with one market and two variables, GDP and the interest rate (i). We will eventually call the goods market equation the *IS curve*.

Next we introduce the money market, where equilibrium is determined when the demand for money equals the supply of money. The demand for money depends on income and interest rates. The supply of money is set by the central bank (the Federal Reserve in the United States). Solving for equilibrium in the money market again gives us one market and two variables, GDP and the interest rate. We will eventually call the money market equation the *LM curve*.

Finally, we put the goods and money markets together, giving us two markets—goods and money—and two variables—GDP and the interest rate. The *IS-LM model* finds the values of GDP and the interest rate which simultaneously clear the goods and money markets.

As we put all this together, be certain to keep a mental marker on whether we are talking about just the goods market, just the money market, or the linkage of the two. (Use different-color highlighters if it helps.) If you can do this, you should find the chapter not too difficult after all.

previous chapter. The model is broadened, though, by introducing the interest rate as an additional determinant of aggregate demand. In Chapter 9, autonomous spending and fiscal policy were the chief determinants of aggregate demand. Now we add the interest rate as a determinant of investment and therefore aggregate demand. We then have to ask what determines the interest rate. That question extends our model to include the money markets and forces us to study the interaction of goods and money markets. The Federal Reserve enters the picture through its role in setting the supply of money. Interest rates and income are jointly determined by equilibrium in the goods and money markets. As in the previous chapter, we maintain the assumption that the price level does not respond when aggregate demand shifts.

Understanding the money market and interest rates is important for three reasons:

1. Monetary policy works through the money market to affect output and employment.
2. The analysis qualifies the conclusions of Chapter 9. Consider Figure 10-3, which lays out the logical structure of the model. So far we have looked at the box

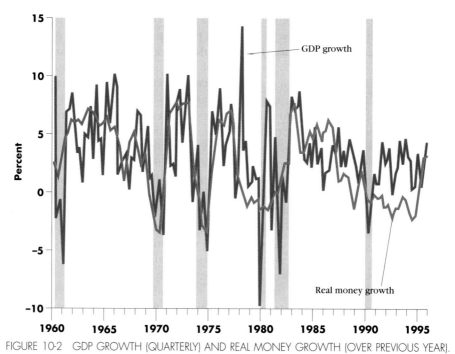

FIGURE 10-2   GDP GROWTH (QUARTERLY) AND REAL MONEY GROWTH (OVER PREVIOUS YEAR).

(Source: DRI/McGraw-Hill Macroeconomic Database.)

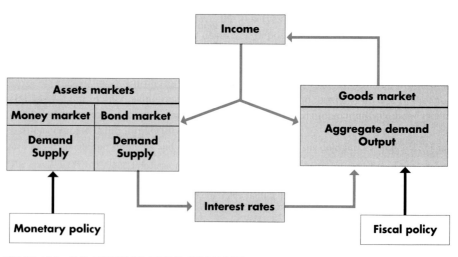

FIGURE 10-3   THE STRUCTURE OF THE *IS-LM* MODEL.

The IS-LM model emphasizes the interaction between the goods and assets markets. Spending, interest rates, and income are determined jointly by equilibrium in the goods and assets markets.

labeled "Goods market." By adding the assets markets, we provide a fuller analysis of the effect of fiscal policy, and we introduce monetary policy. We shall see, for instance, that an expansionary fiscal policy generally raises interest rates, thereby dampening its expansionary impact. Indeed, under certain conditions, the increase in interest rates may be sufficient to offset *fully* the expansionary effects of fiscal policy.

3. Interest rate changes have an important side effect. The *composition* of aggregate demand between investment and consumption spending depends on the interest rate. Higher interest rates dampen aggregate demand mainly by reducing investment. Thus, an expansionary fiscal policy tends to raise consumption through the multiplier but tends to reduce investment because it increases interest rates. Because the rate of investment affects the growth of the economy, this side effect of fiscal expansion is a sensitive and important issue in policy making.

OUTLINE OF THE CHAPTER

We use Figure 10-3 once more to lay out the structure of this chapter. We start in Section 10-1 with a discussion of the link between interest rates and aggregate demand. We use the model of Chapter 9 directly, augmented to include the interest rate as a determinant of aggregate demand. We derive a key relationship—the *IS* curve—that shows combinations of interest rates and levels of income at which the goods markets clear. In Section 10-2, we turn to the assets markets, particularly the money market. We show that the demand for money depends on interest rates and income and that there are combinations of interest rates and income levels—the *LM* curve—at which the money market clears.[1] In Section 10-3, we combine the two schedules to study the joint determination of interest rates and income. In Section 10-4, which is optional, we give a formal algebraic presentation of the full *IS-LM* model.

The *IS-LM* model continues to be used today, 60 years after it was introduced, because it provides a simple and appropriate framework for analyzing the effects of monetary and fiscal policy on the demand for output and on interest rates.[2] This chapter is long, so we reserve policy applications of the model for Chapter 11.

10-1

THE GOODS MARKET AND THE *IS* CURVE

In this section we derive a *goods market equilibrium schedule,* the *IS curve.* The *IS* curve (or schedule) shows combinations of interest rates and levels of output such that

[1]The terms *IS* and *LM* are shorthand representations, respectively, of the relationships investment (*I*) equals saving (*S*)—the goods market equilibrium—and money demand (*L*) equals money supply (*M*)—the money market equilibrium. The classic article that introduced this model is J. R. Hicks, "Mr. Keynes and the Classics: A Suggested Interpretation," *Econometrica,* April 1937, pp. 147–159.

[2]For a modern perspective on the usefulness of the *IS-LM* model, see Bennett T. McCallum and Edward Nelson, "An Optimizing *IS-LM* Specification for Monetary Policy and Business Cycle Analysis," Carnegie-Mellon University working paper, September 1996.

planned spending equals income. The *IS* curve is derived in two steps. First, we explain why investment depends on interest rates. Second, we insert the investment demand function in the aggregate demand identity—just as we did with the consumption function in the last chapter—and find the combinations of income and interest rates that keep the goods market in equilibrium.

THE INVESTMENT DEMAND SCHEDULE

So far, investment spending (*I*) has been treated as *entirely* exogenous—some number like $1,000 billion, determined altogether outside the model of income determination. Now, as we make our macromodel more complete by introducing interest rates as a part of the model, investment spending, too, becomes endogenous. The desired or planned rate of investment is lower the higher the interest rate.

A simple argument shows why. Investment is spending on additions to the firm's capital, such as machines or buildings. Typically firms borrow to purchase investment goods. The higher the interest rate for such borrowing, the lower the profits that firms can expect to make by borrowing to buy new machines or buildings, and therefore the less they will be willing to borrow and invest. Conversely, firms will want to borrow and invest more when interest rates are lower.

INVESTMENT AND THE INTEREST RATE

We specify an investment spending function of the form[3]

$$I = \bar{I} - bi \qquad b > 0 \tag{1}$$

where *i* is the rate of interest and the coefficient *b* measures the responsiveness of investment spending to the interest rate. $\bar{I}$ now denotes autonomous investment spending, that is, investment spending that is independent of both income and the rate of interest.[4] Equation (1) states that the lower the interest rate, the higher is planned investment. If *b* is large, then a relatively small increase in the interest rate generates a large drop in investment spending.

Figure 10-4, the investment schedule of equation (1), shows for each level of the interest rate the amount which firms plan to spend on investment. The schedule is negatively sloped to reflect the assumption that a reduction in the interest rate increases the profitability of additions to the capital stock and therefore leads to a larger rate of planned investment spending.

The position of the investment schedule is determined by the slope—the coefficient *b* in equation (1)—and by the level of autonomous investment spending, $\bar{I}$. If investment

---

[3]Here and in other places in the book, we specify linear (straight-line) versions of behavioral functions. We use the linear form to simplify both the algebra and the diagrams. The linearity assumption is not misleading as long as we confine ourselves to talking about small changes in the economy.

[4]In Chap. 9, investment spending was defined as autonomous with respect to income. Now that the interest rate appears in the model, we have to extend the definition of "autonomous" to mean independent of both the interest rate and income. To conserve notation, we continue to use $\bar{I}$ to denote autonomous investment, but we recognize that the definition has broadened. In fact, investment responds positively when income increases, for reasons discussed in Chap. 14. Here, we omit the responsiveness of investment to income as a simplification.

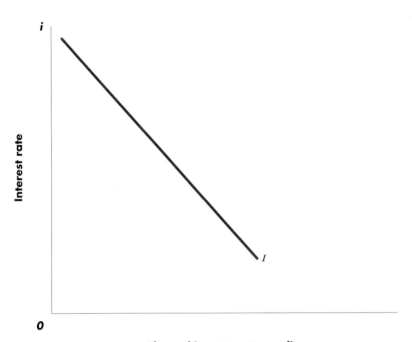

Planned investment spending

FIGURE 10-4   THE INVESTMENT SCHEDULE.

The investment schedule shows the planned level of investment spending at each rate of interest.

is highly responsive to the interest rate, a small decline in interest rates will lead to a large increase in investment, so the schedule is almost flat. Conversely, if investment responds little to interest rates, the schedule will be more nearly vertical. Changes in autonomous investment spending, $\bar{I}$, shift the investment schedule. An increase in $\bar{I}$ means that at each level of the interest rate, firms plan to invest at a higher rate. This would be shown by a rightward shift of the investment schedule.

THE INTEREST RATE AND AGGREGATE DEMAND: THE *IS* CURVE

We now modify the aggregate demand function of Chapter 9 to reflect the new planned investment spending schedule. Aggregate demand still consists of the demand for consumption, investment, government spending on goods and services, and net exports, only now investment spending depends on the interest rate. We have

$$AD \equiv C + I + G + NX$$
$$= [c\overline{TR} + c(1-t)Y] + (\bar{I} - bi) + \overline{G} + \overline{NX}$$
$$= \overline{A} + c(1-t)Y - bi \tag{2}$$

where

$$\overline{A} \equiv c\overline{TR} + \bar{I} + \overline{G} + \overline{NX} \tag{3}$$

From equation (2) we see that an increase in the interest rate reduces aggregate demand for a given level of income because a higher interest rate reduces investment spending. Note that $\overline{A}$, which is the part of aggregate demand unaffected by either the level of income or the interest rate, does include part of investment spending, namely, $\overline{I}$. As noted earlier, $\overline{I}$ is the *autonomous* component of investment spending, which is independent of the interest rate (and income).

At any given level of the interest rate, we can still proceed as in Chapter 9 to determine the equilibrium level of income and output. As the interest rate changes, however, the equilibrium level of income changes. We derive the *IS* curve using Figure 10-5.

For a given level of the interest rate, say, i_1, the last term of equation (2) is a constant (bi_1), and we can, in Figure 10-5a, draw the aggregate demand function of Chapter 9, this time with an intercept, $\overline{A} - bi_1$. The equilibrium level of income obtained in the usual manner is Y_1 at point E_1. Since that equilibrium level of income was derived for a given level of the interest rate (i_1), we plot that pair (i_1, Y_1) in the bottom panel as point E_1. This gives us one point, E_1, on the *IS* curve—that is, one combination of interest rate and income which clears the goods market.

Consider next a lower interest rate, i_2. Investment spending is higher when the interest rate falls. In terms of Figure 10-5a, that implies an upward shift of the aggregate demand schedule. The curve shifts upward because the intercept, $\overline{A} - bi$, has increased. Given the increase in aggregate demand, the equilibrium shifts to point E_2, with an associated income level Y_2. At point E_2, in panel (b), we record the fact that interest rate i_2 implies the equilibrium level of income Y_2—equilibrium in the sense that the goods market is in equilibrium (or that the goods market *clears*). Point E_2 is another point on the *IS* curve.

We can apply the same procedure to all conceivable levels of the interest rate and thereby generate all the points that make up the *IS* curve. They have in common the property that they represent combinations of interest rates and income (output) at which the goods market clears. That is why the *IS* curve is called the *goods market equilibrium schedule*.

Figure 10-5 shows that the *IS* curve is negatively sloped, reflecting the increase in aggregate demand associated with a reduction in the interest rate. We can also derive the *IS* curve by using the goods market equilibrium condition, that income equals planned spending, or

$$Y = AD = \overline{A} + c(1 - t)Y - bi \tag{4}$$

which can be simplified to

$$Y = \alpha_G(\overline{A} - bi) \qquad \alpha_G = \frac{1}{1 - c(1 - t)} \tag{5}$$

where α_G is the multiplier from Chapter 9. Note from equation (5) that a higher interest rate implies a lower level of equilibrium income for a given $\overline{A}$, as Figure 10-5 shows.

The construction of the *IS* curve is quite straightforward and may even be deceptively simple. We can gain further understanding of the economics of the *IS* curve by asking and answering the following questions:

• What determines the slope of the *IS* curve?

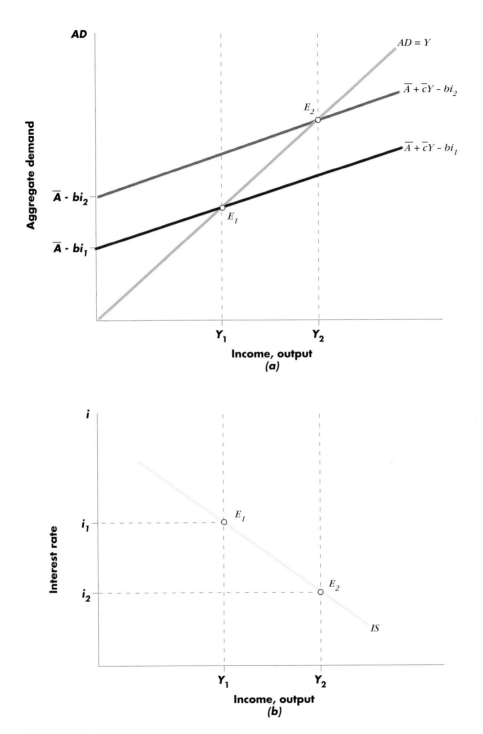

FIGURE 10-5   DERIVATION OF THE *IS* CURVE.

At a particular interest rate, equilibrium in panel (a) determines the income level. A decrease in the interest rate raises aggregate demand. The IS *curve shows the resulting negative relationship between interest rates and income.*

- What determines the position of the *IS* curve, given its slope, and what causes the curve to shift?

THE SLOPE OF THE *IS* CURVE

We have already noted that the *IS* curve is negatively sloped because a higher level of the interest rate reduces investment spending, thereby reducing aggregate demand and thus the equilibrium level of income. The steepness of the curve depends on how sensitive investment spending is to changes in the interest rate and also depends on the multiplier, α_G, in equation (5).

Suppose that investment spending is very sensitive to the interest rate, and so *b* in equation (5) is large. Then, in terms of Figure 10-5, a given change in the interest rate produces a large change in aggregate demand, and thus shifts the aggregate demand curve in Figure 10-5*a* up by a large amount. A large shift in the aggregate demand schedule produces a correspondingly large change in the equilibrium level of income. If a given change in the interest rate produces a large change in income, the *IS* curve is very flat. This is the case if investment is very sensitive to the interest rate, that is, if *b* is large. Correspondingly, if *b* is small and investment spending is not very sensitive to the interest rate, the *IS* curve is relatively steep.

The Role of the Multiplier

Consider next the effects of the multiplier, α_G, on the steepness of the *IS* curve. Figure 10-6 shows aggregate demand curves corresponding to different multipliers. The coefficient *c* on the solid blue aggregate demand curves is smaller than the corresponding coefficient *c′* on the dashed blue aggregate demand curves. The multiplier is accordingly larger on the dashed aggregate demand curves. The initial levels of income, Y_1 and Y'_1, correspond to the interest rate i_1 in panel (*b*).

A given reduction in the interest rate, to i_2, raises the intercept of the aggregate demand curves by the same vertical distance, as shown in panel (*a*). However, the implied change in income is very different. On the dashed curve, income rises to Y'_2, while it rises only to Y_2 on the solid line. The change in equilibrium income corresponding to a given change in the interest rate is accordingly larger as the aggregate demand curve is steeper; that is, the larger the multiplier, the greater the rise in income. As we see from panel (*b*), the larger the multiplier, the flatter the *IS* curve. Equivalently, the larger the multiplier, the larger the change in income produced by a given change in the interest rate.

We have thus seen that the smaller the sensitivity of investment spending to the interest rate and the smaller the multiplier, the steeper the *IS* curve. This conclusion is confirmed using equation (5). We can turn equation (5) around to express the interest rate as a function of the level of income:

$$i = \frac{\overline{A}}{b} - \frac{Y}{\alpha_G b} \tag{5a}$$

Thus, for a given change in *Y*, the associated change in *i* will be larger in size as *b* is smaller and as α_G is smaller.

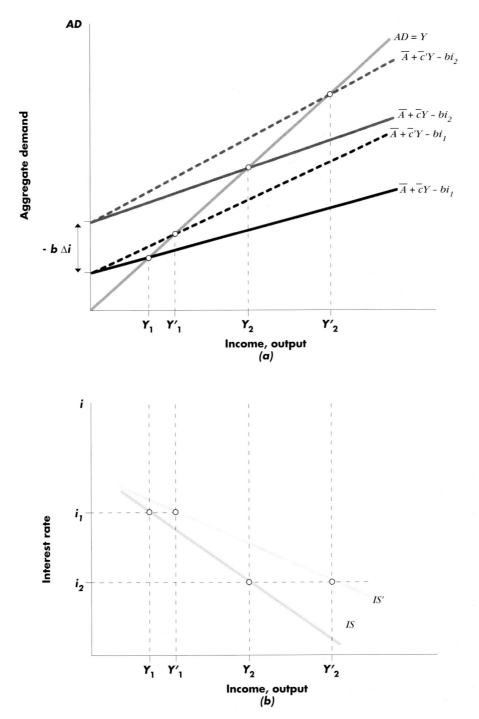

FIGURE 10-6 EFFECT OF THE MULTIPLIER ON THE SLOPE OF THE *IS* CURVE.

A higher marginal propensity to spend results in a steeper aggregate demand curve and, consequently, a flatter IS *curve.*

Given that the slope of the *IS* curve depends on the multiplier, fiscal policy can affect that slope. The multiplier, α_G, is affected by the tax rate: an increase in the tax rate reduces the multiplier. Accordingly, the higher the tax rate, the steeper the *IS* curve.[5]

THE POSITION OF THE *IS* CURVE

Figure 10-7 shows two different *IS* curves, the lighter one of which lies to the right and above the darker *IS* curve. What might cause the *IS* curve to be at *IS'* rather than at *IS?* The answer is an increase in the level of autonomous spending.

In Figure 10-7*a* we show an initial aggregate demand curve drawn for a level of autonomous spending $\overline{A}$ and for an interest rate i_1. Corresponding to the initial aggregate demand curve is the point E_1 on the *IS* curve in Figure 10-7*b*. Now, at the same interest rate, let the level of autonomous spending increase to $\overline{A}'$. The increase in autonomous spending increases the equilibrium level of income at the interest rate i_1. The point E_2 in panel (*b*) is thus a point on the new goods market equilibrium schedule, *IS'*. Since E_1 was an arbitrary point on the initial *IS* curve, we can perform the exercise for all levels of the interest rate and thereby generate the new curve, *IS'*. Thus, an increase in autonomous spending shifts the *IS* curve out to the right.

By how much does the curve shift? The change in income as a result of the change in autonomous spending can be seen from panel (*a*) to be just the multiplier times the change in autonomous spending. This means that the *IS* curve is shifted horizontally by a distance equal to the multiplier times the change in autonomous spending, as in panel (*b*).

The level of autonomous spending, from equation (3), is

$$\overline{A} \equiv c\overline{TR} + \overline{I} + \overline{G} + \overline{NX}$$

Accordingly, an increase in government purchases or transfer payments shifts the *IS* curve out to the right, with the extent of the shift depending on the size of the multiplier. A reduction in transfer payments or in government purchases shifts the *IS* curve to the left.

RECAP

Here are the major points about the *IS* curve:

- The *IS* curve is the schedule of combinations of the interest rate and level of income such that the goods market is in equilibrium.
- The *IS* curve is negatively sloped because an increase in the interest rate reduces planned investment spending and therefore reduces aggregate demand, thus reducing the equilibrium level of income.
- The smaller the multiplier and the less sensitive investment spending is to changes in the interest rate, the steeper the *IS* curve.
- The *IS* curve is shifted by changes in autonomous spending. An increase in autonomous spending, including an increase in government purchases, shifts the *IS* curve out to the right.

Now we turn to the money market.

---

[5]In the problem set we ask you to relate this fact to the discussion of automatic stabilizers in Chap. 9.

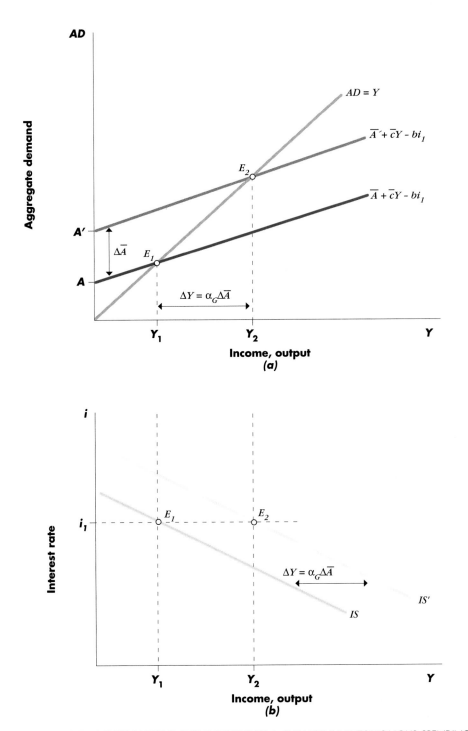

FIGURE 10-7   A SHIFT IN THE *IS* CURVE CAUSED BY A CHANGE IN AUTONOMOUS SPENDING.

An increase in autonomous spending increases aggregate demand and increases the income level at a given interest rate. This is represented by a rightward shift of the IS *curve.*

BOX 10-2 Real and Nominal Money Demand

At this stage we have to reinforce the crucial distinction between *real* and *nominal* variables. The nominal demand for money is the individual's demand for a given number of dollars. Similarly, the nominal demand for bonds is the demand for a given number of dollars' worth of bonds. The real demand for money is the demand for money expressed in terms of the number of units of goods that money will buy: it is equal to the nominal demand for money divided by the price level. If the nominal demand for money is $100 and the price level is $2 per good—meaning that the representative basket of goods costs $2—the real demand for money is 50 goods. If the price level later doubles to $4 per good and the demand for nominal money likewise doubles to $200, the real demand for money is unchanged at 50 goods.

Real money balances—real balances, for short—are the quantity of nominal money divided by the price level. The real demand for money is called the *demand for real balances*.

10-2

THE MONEY MARKET AND THE *LM* CURVE

In this section we derive a *money market equilibrium schedule,* the *LM curve.* The *LM* curve (or schedule) shows combinations of interest rates and levels of output such that money demand equals money supply. The *LM* curve is derived in two steps. First, we explain why money demand depends on interest rates and income, emphasizing that because people care about the purchasing power of money, the demand for money is a theory of *real* rather than *nominal* demand. Second, we equate money demand with money supply—set by the central bank—and find the combinations of income and interest rates that keep the money market in equilibrium.

THE DEMAND FOR MONEY

We turn now to the money market and initially concentrate on the demand for real balances.[6] The demand for money is a demand for *real* balances because people hold money for what it will buy. The higher the price level, the more nominal balances a person has to hold to be able to purchase a given quantity of goods. If the price level doubles, an individual has to hold twice as many nominal balances in order to be able to buy the same amount of goods.

The demand for real balances depends on the level of real income and the interest rate. It depends on the level of real income because individuals hold money to pay for their purchases, which, in turn, depend on income. The demand for money

---

[6]The demand for money is examined in depth in Chap. 15; here we present the arguments underlying the demand for money only briefly.

depends also on the cost of holding money. The cost of holding money is the interest that is forgone by holding money rather than other assets. The higher the interest rate, the more costly it is to hold money and, accordingly, the less cash will be held at each level of income.[7] Individuals can economize on their holdings of cash when the interest rate rises by being more careful in managing their money and by making transfers from money to bonds whenever their money holdings become large. If the interest rate is 1 percent, there is very little benefit from holding bonds rather than money. However, when the interest rate is 10 percent, it is worth some effort not to hold more money than is needed to finance day-to-day transactions.

On these simple grounds, then, the demand for real balances increases with the level of real income and decreases with the interest rate. The demand for real balances, which we denote as L, is accordingly expressed as

$$L = kY - hi \qquad k,h > 0 \tag{6}$$

The parameters k and h reflect the sensitivity of the demand for real balances to the level of income and the interest rate, respectively. A \$5 increase in real income raises money demand by $k \times 5$ real dollars. An increase in the interest rate of 1 percentage point reduces real money demand by h real dollars.

The demand function for real balances, equation (6), implies that for a given level of income, the quantity demanded is a decreasing function of the rate of interest. Such a demand curve is shown in Figure 10-8 for a level of income Y_1. The higher the level of income, the larger the demand for real balances and, therefore, the further to the right the demand curve. The demand curve for a higher level of real income, Y_2, is also shown in Figure 10-8.

THE SUPPLY OF MONEY, MONEY MARKET EQUILIBRIUM, AND THE *LM* CURVE

To study equilibrium in the money market, we have to say how the supply of money is determined. The nominal quantity of money, M, is controlled by the Federal Reserve System ("the Fed") in the United States. The *central bank* has other names in other countries, and of course through much of history the nominal quantity of money was determined by gold discoveries or similar events. We take the nominal quantity of money as given at the level $\overline{M}$. We assume the price level is constant at the level $\overline{P}$, so the real money supply is at the level $\overline{M/P}$.[8]

In Figure 10-9, we show combinations of interest rates and income levels such that the demand for real balances exactly matches the available supply. Starting with the level of income, Y_1, the corresponding demand curve for real balances, L_1, is shown in Figure 10-9b. It is drawn, as in Figure 10-8, as a decreasing function of the interest rate. The existing supply of real balances, $\overline{M/P}$, is shown by the vertical line, since it is given and therefore is independent of the interest rate. At interest rate i_1, the demand for real balances equals the supply. Therefore, point E_1 is an equilibrium point in the

[7]Some types of money, including most bank deposits, earn interest, but at a lower rate than bonds. Several sizable parts of money holding—including currency—earn no interest; so, overall, money earns less interest than other assets. Thus there is an interest cost to holding money.

[8]Since, for the present, we are holding constant the money supply and price level, we denote that fact by a bar.

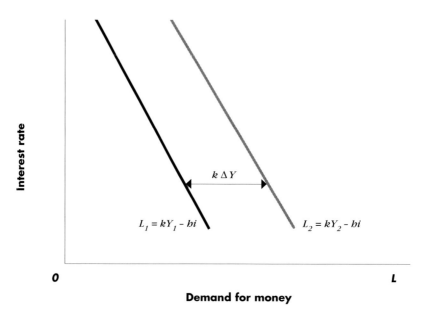

FIGURE 10-8   DEMAND FOR REAL BALANCES AS A FUNCTION OF THE INTEREST RATE AND
REAL INCOME.

*The higher the rate of interest, the lower the quantity of real balances demanded, given
the level of income. An increase in income raises the demand for money, as shown by
the rightward shift in the money demand schedule.*

money market. That point is recorded in Figure 10-9*a* as a point on the money market
equilibrium schedule, or the *LM* curve.

Consider next the effect of an increase in income to Y_2. In Figure 10-9*b*, the higher
level of income causes the demand for real balances to be higher at each level of the interest rate, so the demand curve for real balances shifts up and to the right, to L_2. The interest rate increases to i_2 to maintain equilibrium in the money market at that higher level
of income. Accordingly, the new equilibrium point is E_2. In Figure 10-9*a*, we record point
E_2 as a point of equilibrium in the money market. Performing the same exercise for all income levels, we generate a series of points that can be linked to give us the *LM* schedule.

The *LM* schedule, or *money market equilibrium* schedule, shows all combinations
of interest rates and levels of income such that the demand for real balances is equal
to the supply. Along the *LM* schedule, the money market is in equilibrium.

The *LM* curve is positively sloped. An increase in the interest rate reduces the demand for real balances. To maintain the demand for real balances equal to the fixed supply, the level of income has to rise. Accordingly, money market equilibrium implies that
an increase in the interest rate is accompanied by an increase in the level of income.

The *LM* curve can be obtained directly by combining the demand curve for real
balances, equation (6), and the fixed supply of real balances. For the money market to
be in equilibrium, demand has to equal supply, or

$$\frac{\overline{M}}{P} = kY - hi \qquad (7)$$

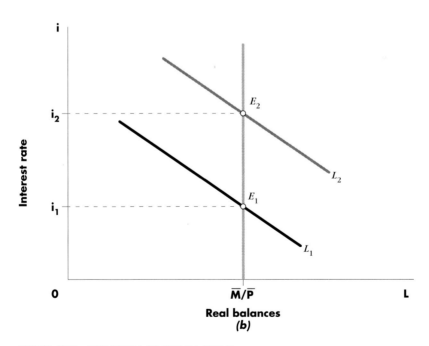

FIGURE 10-9 DERIVATION OF THE *LM* CURVE.

Panel (b) shows the money market. The supply of real balances is the vertical line $\overline{M}/\overline{P}$. L_1 and L_2 represent money demand at different levels of income (Y_1 and Y_2).

Solving for the interest rate,

$$i - \frac{1}{h}\left(kY - \frac{\overline{M}}{\overline{P}}\right) \tag{7a}$$

The relationship $(7a)$ is the *LM* curve.

Next we ask the same questions about the properties of the *LM* schedule that we asked about the *IS* curve.

THE SLOPE OF THE *LM* CURVE

The greater the responsiveness of the demand for money to income, as measured by k, and the lower the responsiveness of the demand for money to the interest rate, h, the steeper the *LM* curve will be. This point can be established by experimenting with Figure 10-9. It can also be confirmed by examining equation $(7a)$, where a given change in income, ΔY, has a larger effect on the interest rate, i, the larger is k and the smaller is h. If the demand for money is relatively insensitive to the interest rate and thus h is close to zero, the *LM* curve is nearly vertical. If the demand for money is very sensitive to the interest rate and thus h is large, the *LM* curve is close to horizontal. In that case, a small change in the interest rate must be accompanied by a large change in the level of income in order to maintain money market equilibrium.

THE POSITION OF THE *LM* CURVE

The real money supply is held constant along the *LM* curve. It follows that a change in the real money supply will shift the *LM* curve. In Figure 10-10, we show the effect of an increase in the real money supply. Panel (b) shows the demand for real money balances for a level of income Y_1. With the initial real money supply, $\overline{M/P}$, the equilibrium is at point E_1, with the interest rate i_1. The corresponding point on the *LM* schedule is E_1.

Now the real money supply increases to $\overline{M'/P}$, which we represent by a rightward shift of the money supply schedule. To restore money market equilibrium at the income level Y_1, the interest rate has to decline to i_2. The new equilibrium is, therefore, at point E_2. This implies that in Figure 10-10a, the *LM* schedule shifts to the right and down to LM'. At each level of income the equilibrium interest rate has to be lower to induce people to hold the larger real quantity of money. Alternatively, at each level of the interest rate the level of income has to be higher to raise the transactions demand for money and thereby absorb the higher real money supply. These points can be noted, too, from inspection of the money market equilibrium condition in equation (7).

RECAP

The following are the major points about the *LM* curve:

- The *LM* curve is the schedule of combinations of interest rates and levels of income such that the money market is in equilibrium.
- The *LM* curve is positively sloped. Given the fixed money supply, an increase in the level of income, which increases the quantity of money demanded, has to be

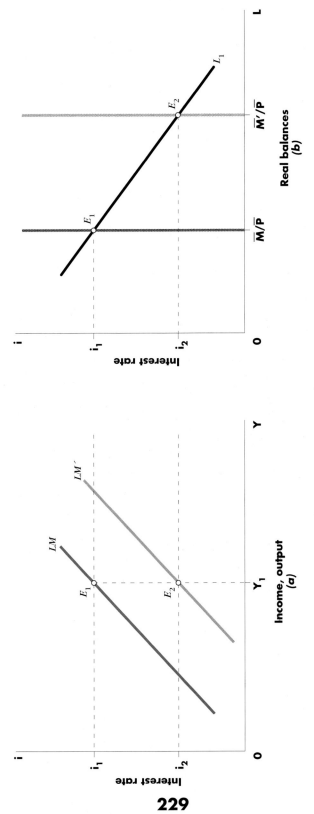

FIGURE 10-10   AN INCREASE IN THE SUPPLY OF MONEY SHIFTS THE *LM* CURVE TO THE RIGHT.

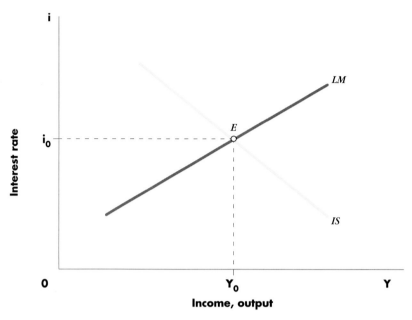

FIGURE 10-11   GOODS AND MONEY MARKET EQUILIBRIUM.

At point E, interest rates and income levels are such that the public holds the existing money stock and planned spending equals output.

accompanied by an increase in the interest rate. This reduces the quantity of money demanded and thereby maintains money market equilibrium.

- The *LM* curve is shifted by changes in the money supply. An increase in the money supply shifts the *LM* curve to the right.

We are now ready to discuss the joint equilibrium of the goods and assets markets. That is to say, we can now discuss how output and interest rates are determined.

10-3

EQUILIBRIUM IN THE GOODS AND MONEY MARKETS

The *IS* and *LM* schedules summarize the conditions that have to be satisfied in order for the goods and money markets, respectively, to be in equilibrium. The task now is to determine how these markets are brought into *simultaneous* equilibrium. For simultaneous equilibrium, interest rates and income levels have to be such that both the goods market *and* the money market are in equilibrium. This condition is satisfied at point *E* in Figure 10-11. The equilibrium interest rate is therefore i_0 and the equilibrium level of income is Y_0, given the exogenous variables, in particular the real money supply and fiscal policy.[9] At point *E*, both the goods market and the money market are in equilibrium.

---

[9]In general, exogenous variables are those whose values are not determined within the system being studied.

Figure 10-11 summarizes our analysis: The interest rate and the *level* of output are determined by the interaction of the money (*LM*) and goods (*IS*) markets.

It is worth stepping back now to review our assumptions and the meaning of the equilibrium at *E*. The major assumption is that the price level is constant and that firms are willing to supply whatever amount of output is demanded at that price level. Thus, we assume that the level of output Y_0 in Figure 10-11 will be willingly supplied by firms at the price level $\bar{P}$. We repeat that this assumption is one that is temporarily needed for the development of the analysis; it corresponds to the assumption of a flat, short-run aggregate supply curve.

CHANGES IN THE EQUILIBRIUM LEVELS OF INCOME AND THE INTEREST RATE

The equilibrium levels of income and the interest rate change when either the *IS* or the *LM* curve shifts. Figure 10-12, for example, shows the effects of an increase in the rate of autonomous investment on the equilibrium levels of income and the interest rate. Such an increase raises autonomous spending, $\bar{A}$, and therefore shifts the *IS* curve to the right. That results in a rise in the level of income and an increase in the interest rate at point E'.

Recall that an increase in autonomous investment spending, $\Delta \bar{I}$, shifts the *IS* curve to the right by the amount $\alpha_G \Delta \bar{I}$, as we show in Figure 10-12. In Chapter 9, where we dealt only with the goods market, we would have argued that $\alpha_G \Delta \bar{I}$ would be the change

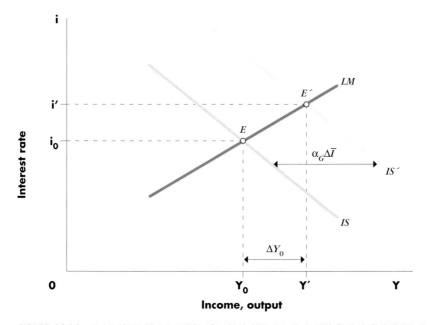

FIGURE 10-12   AN INCREASE IN AUTONOMOUS SPENDING SHIFTS THE *IS* CURVE TO THE RIGHT.

The equilibrium interest rate and level of income both rise.

in the level of income resulting from the change of $\Delta \bar{I}$ in autonomous spending. But it can be seen in Figure 10-12 that the change in income here is only ΔY_0, which is clearly less than the shift in the *IS* curve, $\alpha_G \Delta \bar{I}$.

What explains the fact that the increase in income is smaller than the increase in autonomous spending, $\Delta \bar{I}$, times the simple multiplier, α_G? Diagrammatically, it is clear that the explanation is the slope of the *LM* curve. If the *LM* curve were horizontal, there would be no difference between the extent of the horizontal shift of the *IS* curve and the change in income. If the *LM* curve were horizontal, the interest rate would not change when the *IS* curve shifts.

But what is the economics of what is happening? The increase in autonomous spending does tend to increase the level of income. But an increase in income increases the demand for money. With the supply of money fixed, the interest rate has to rise to ensure that the demand for money stays equal to the fixed supply. When the interest rate rises, investment spending is reduced because investment is negatively related to the interest rate. Accordingly, the equilibrium change in income is less than the horizontal shift of the *IS* curve, $\alpha_G \Delta \bar{I}$.

We have now provided an example of the use of the *IS-LM* apparatus. That apparatus is very helpful for studying the effects of monetary and fiscal policy on income and the interest rate, and we use it to do so in Chapter 11. To anticipate what is coming, you might want to experiment with how equilibrium income and interest rates change when expansionary fiscal policy moves the *IS* curve to the right or expansionary monetary policy moves the *LM* curve to the right.

10-4

DERIVING THE AGGREGATE DEMAND SCHEDULE

In earlier chapters we used the aggregate demand–aggregate supply apparatus. Here we derive the *aggregate demand schedule.* The aggregate demand schedule maps out the *IS-LM* equilibrium holding autonomous spending and the nominal money supply constant and allowing prices to vary. In other words, in learning to use the *IS-LM* model, you've already learned everything about deriving the aggregate demand schedule. Put simply, a higher price level means a lower *real* money supply, an *LM* curve shifted to the left, and lower aggregate demand.

Suppose the price level in the economy is P_1. Panel (*a*) of Figure 10-13 shows the *IS-LM* equilibrium. Note that the real money supply, which determines the position of the LM_1 curve, is $\overline{M/P_1}$. The intersection of the *IS* and LM_1 curves gives the level of aggregate demand corresponding to price P_1 and is so marked in the lower panel. Suppose, instead, that the price is higher, say P_2. The curve LM_2 shows the *LM* curve based on the real money supply $\overline{M/P_2}$. LM_2 is to the left of LM_1 since $\overline{M/P_2} < \overline{M/P_1}$. Point E_2 shows the corresponding point on the aggregate demand curve. Repeat this operation for a variety of price levels, and connect the points to derive the aggregate demand schedule.

(a)

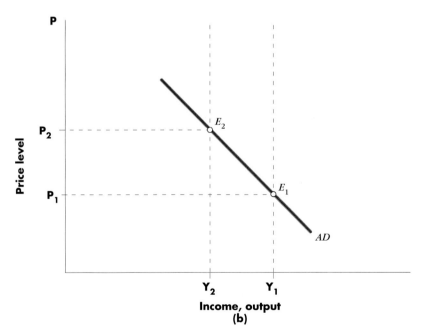

(b)

FIGURE 10-13 DERIVATION OF THE AGGREGATE DEMAND SCHEDULE.

10-5

A FORMAL TREATMENT OF THE *IS-LM* MODEL

Our exposition so far has been verbal and graphical. We now round off the analysis with a more formal, algebraic, treatment of the *IS-LM* model.

EQUILIBRIUM INCOME AND THE INTEREST RATE

The intersection of the *IS* and *LM* schedules determines equilibrium income and the equilibrium interest rate. We now derive expressions for these equilibrium values by using the equations of the *IS* and *LM* schedules. Recall from earlier in the chapter that the goods market equilibrium equation is

$$IS \text{ schedule:} \quad Y = \alpha_G(\overline{A} - bi) \tag{5}$$

and that the equation for the money market equilibrium is

$$LM \text{ schedule:} \quad i = \frac{1}{h}\left(kY - \frac{\overline{M}}{P}\right) \tag{7a}$$

The intersection of the *IS* and *LM* schedules in the diagrams corresponds to a situation in which both the *IS* and the *LM* equations hold: the *same* interest rate and income levels ensure equilibrium in both the goods *and* the money market. In terms of the equations, that means we can substitute the interest rate from the *LM* equation, (7*a*), into the *IS* equation, (5):

$$Y = \alpha_G\left[\overline{A} - \frac{b}{h}\left(kY - \frac{\overline{M}}{P}\right)\right]$$

Collecting terms and solving for the equilibrium level of income, we obtain

$$Y = \gamma\overline{A} + \gamma\frac{b}{h}\frac{\overline{M}}{P} \tag{8}$$

where $\gamma = \alpha_G/(1 + k\alpha_G b/h)$. Equation (8) shows that the equilibrium level of income depends on two exogenous variables: autonomous spending ($\overline{A}$), including autonomous consumption and investment ($\overline{C}$ and $\overline{I}$) and fiscal policy parameters (G, TR), and the real money stock ($\overline{M}/P$). Equilibrium income is higher the higher the level of autonomous spending, $\overline{A}$, and the higher the stock of real balances.

Equation (8) is the aggregate demand schedule. It summarizes the *IS-LM* relation, relating Y and P for given levels of $\overline{A}$ and $\overline{M}$. Since P is in the denominator, the aggregate demand curve slopes downward.

The equilibrium rate of interest, i, is obtained by substituting the equilibrium income level, Y_0, from equation (8) into the equation of the *LM* schedule, (7*a*):

$$i = \frac{k}{h}\gamma\overline{A} - \frac{1}{h + kb\alpha_G}\frac{\overline{M}}{P} \tag{9}$$

Equation (9) shows that the equilibrium interest rate depends on the parameters of fiscal policy captured in the multiplier and the term $\bar{A}$ and on the real money stock. A higher real money stock implies a lower equilibrium interest rate.

For policy questions we are interested in the precise relation between changes in fiscal policy or changes in the real money stock and the resulting changes in equilibrium income. Monetary and fiscal policy *multipliers* provide the relevant information.

THE FISCAL POLICY MULTIPLIER

The *fiscal policy multiplier* shows how much an increase in government spending changes the equilibrium level of income, holding the real money supply constant. Examine equation (8) and consider the effect of an increase in government spending on income. The increase in government spending, $\Delta \bar{G}$, is a change in autonomous spending, so $\Delta \bar{A} = \Delta \bar{G}$. The effect of the change in $\bar{G}$ is given by

$$\frac{\Delta Y}{\Delta \bar{G}} = \gamma \qquad \gamma = \frac{\alpha_G}{1 + k\alpha_G \dfrac{b}{h}} \qquad (10)$$

The expression γ is the fiscal or government spending multiplier once interest rate adjustment is taken into account. Consider how this multiplier, γ, differs from the simpler expression α_G that applied under constant interest rates. Inspection shows that γ is less than α_G since $1/(1 + k\alpha_G b/h)$ is less than 1. This represents the dampening effect of increased interest rates associated with a fiscal expansion in the *IS-LM* model.

We note that the expression in equation (10) is almost zero if h is very small and that it is equal to α_G if h approaches infinity. This corresponds, respectively, to vertical and horizontal *LM* schedules. Similarly, a large value of either b or k serves to reduce the effect of government spending on income. Why? A high value of k implies a large increase in money demand as income rises and hence a large increase in interest rates required to maintain money market equilibrium. In combination with a high b, this implies a large reduction in private aggregate demand.

THE MONETARY POLICY MULTIPLIER

The *monetary policy multiplier* shows how much an increase in the real money supply increases the equilibrium level of income, keeping fiscal policy unchanged. Using equation (8) to examine the effects of an increase in the real money supply on income, we have

$$\frac{\Delta Y}{\Delta (\overline{M/P})} = bh\gamma \qquad (11)$$

The smaller h and k and the larger b and α_G, the more expansionary the effect of an increase in real balances on the equilibrium level of income. Large b and α_G correspond to a very flat *IS* schedule.

SUMMARY

1. The *IS-LM* model presented in this chapter is the basic model of aggregate demand that incorporates the money market as well as the goods market. It lays particular stress on the channels through which monetary and fiscal policy affect the economy.

2. The *IS* curve shows combinations of interest rates and levels of income such that the goods market is in equilibrium. Increases in the interest rate reduce aggregate demand by reducing investment spending. Thus, at higher interest rates, the level of income at which the goods market is in equilibrium is lower: the *IS* curve slopes downward.

3. The demand for money is a demand for *real* balances. The demand for real balances increases with income and decreases with the interest rate, the cost of holding money rather than other assets. With an exogenously fixed supply of real balances, the *LM* curve, representing money market equilibrium, is upward-sloping.

4. The interest rate and level of output are jointly determined by simultaneous equilibrium of the goods and money markets. This occurs at the point of intersection of the *IS* and *LM* curves.

5. Monetary policy affects the economy first by affecting the interest rate and then by affecting aggregate demand. An increase in the money supply reduces the interest rate, increases investment spending and aggregate demand, and thus increases equilibrium output.

6. The *IS* and *LM* curves together determine the aggregate demand schedule.

7. Changes in monetary and fiscal policy affect the economy through the monetary and fiscal policy multipliers.

KEY TERMS

IS-LM model	*LM* curve	fiscal policy multiplier
goods market equilibrium schedule	real money balances	monetary policy multiplier
IS curve	demand for real balances	
money market equilibrium schedule	central bank	
	aggregate demand schedule	

PROBLEMS

Conceptual

1. How does the *IS-LM* model developed in this chapter relate to the model of aggregate demand developed in Chapter 9?

2. **a.** Explain in words how and why the multiplier α_G and the interest sensitivity of aggregate demand affect the slope of the *IS* curve.

    b. Explain why the slope of the *IS* curve is a factor in determining the working of monetary policy.

3. Explain in words how and why the income and interest sensitivities of the demand for real balances affect the slope of the *LM* curve.

4. **a.** Why does a horizontal *LM* curve imply that fiscal policy has the same effects on the economy as those derived in Chapter 9?

    b. What is happening in this case in terms of Figure 10-3?

    c. Under what circumstances might the *LM* curve be horizontal?

5. It is possible that the interest rate might affect consumption spending. An increase in the interest rate could, in principle, lead to increases in saving and therefore a reduction in consumption, given the level of income. Suppose that consumption is, in fact, reduced by an increase in the interest rate. How will the *IS* curve be affected?

*6. Between January and December 1991, while the U.S. economy was falling deeper into its recession, the interest rate on Treasury bills fell from 6.3 to 4.1 percent. Use the *IS-LM* model to explain this pattern of declining output and interest rates. Which curve must have shifted? Can you think of a reason—historically valid or simply imagined—that this shift might have occurred?

Technical

1. The following equations describe an economy. (Think of *C, I, G,* etc., as being measured in billions and *i* as a percentage; a 5 percent interest rate implies $i = 5$.)

$$C = 0.8(1 - t)Y \tag{P1}$$
$$t = 0.25 \tag{P2}$$
$$I = 900 - 50i \tag{P3}$$
$$\overline{G} = 800 \tag{P4}$$
$$L = 0.25Y - 62.5i \tag{P5}$$
$$\overline{M}/\overline{P} = 500 \tag{P6}$$

   a. What is the equation that describes the *IS* curve?
   b. What is the general definition of the *IS* curve?
   c. What is the equation that describes the *LM* curve?
   d. What is the general definition of the *LM* curve?
   e. What are the equilibrium levels of income and the interest rate?

2. Continue with the same equations.
   a. What is the value of α_G which corresponds to the simple multiplier (with taxes) of Chapter 9?
   b. By how much does an increase in government spending of ΔG increase the level of income in this model, which includes the money market?
   c. By how much does a change in government spending of ΔG affect the equilibrium interest rate?
   d. Explain the difference between your answers to parts (**a**) and (**b**).

3. **a.** How does an increase in the tax rate affect the *IS* curve?
   b. How does the increase affect the equilibrium level of income?
   c. How does the increase affect the equilibrium interest rate?

*4. **a.** Show that a given change in the money stock has a larger effect on output the less interest-sensitive is the demand for money. Use the formal analysis of Section 10-5.
   b. How does the response of the interest rate to a change in the money stock depend on the interest sensitivity of money demand?

5. Discuss, using the *IS-LM* model, what happens to interest rates as prices change along a given *AD* schedule.

6. Show, using *IS* and *LM* curves, why money is neutral in the classical supply case.

7. Suppose there is a decline in the demand for money. At each output level and interest rate the public now wants to hold lower real balances.
   a. In the Keynesian case, what happens to equilibrium output and to prices?
   b. In the classical case, what is the effect on output and on prices?

---

*An asterisk denotes a more difficult problem.

CHAPTER 11

Monetary and Fiscal Policy

CHAPTER HIGHLIGHTS

◆ Both fiscal and monetary policy can be used to stabilize the economy.

◆ The effect of fiscal policy is reduced by crowding out: increased government spending increases interest rates, reducing investment and partially offsetting the initial expansion in aggregate demand.

◆ As illustrative polar cases: In the case of the liquidity trap the LM curve is horizontal, fiscal policy has its maximum strength, and monetary policy is ineffective. In the classical case the LM curve is vertical, fiscal policy has no effect on output, and monetary policy has its maximum strength.

In fall 1991, the United States seemed headed for a double-dip recession, as the economic recovery that many had thought was well under way showed signs of running out of steam. Figure 11-1 shows how the economy went into recession in the third quarter of 1990, seemed to be emerging from it in the second quarter of 1991, and then faltered again at the end of 1991.

The fear of a double-dip recession pushed politicians and policy makers into extensive debate and some action. The Fed cut interest rates sharply: the average Treasury bill rate in the first quarter of 1992 was only 3.9 percent, well below the 6 percent of a year earlier, as can be seen in Figure 11-1. And Congress began discussing a fiscal package that would help the recovery by cutting taxes and increasing government spending. In his State of the Union address in January 1993, the president proposed his own set of stimulatory fiscal changes. Before the president and Congress could agree on a fiscal package, however, the data for the first quarter of 1993 came out and the recovery seemed once more to be back on track.

In this chapter we use the *IS-LM* model developed in Chapter 10 to show how monetary policy and fiscal policy work. These are the two main macroeconomic policy tools the government can call on to try to keep the economy growing at a reasonable rate, with low inflation. They are also the policy tools the government uses to try to shorten recessions, as in 1991, and to prevent booms from getting out of hand. As Figure 11-2 shows, fiscal policy has its initial impact in the goods market, and monetary policy has

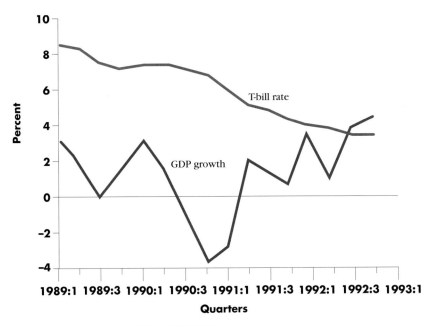

FIGURE 11-1 THE 1990–1992 RECESSION.

The recession began in the third quarter of 1990 and seemed to be ending in the second quarter of 1991. Then, at the end of that year, the recovery weakened, and a double-dip recession seemed possible. The Fed kept cutting interest rates as it attempted to get the recovery back on track.

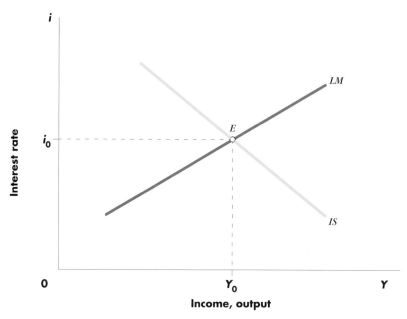

FIGURE 11-2   *IS-LM* Equilibrium.

its initial impact mainly in the assets markets. But because the goods and assets markets are closely interconnected, both monetary and fiscal policies have effects on both the level of output and interest rates.

Figure 11-2 will refresh your memory of our basic framework. The *IS* curve represents equilibrium in the goods market. The *LM* curve represents equilibrium in the money market. The intersection of the two curves determines output and interest rates in the short run, that is, for a given price level. Expansionary monetary policy moves the *LM* curve to the right, raising income and lowering interest rates. Contractionary monetary policy moves the *LM* curve to the left, lowering income and raising interest rates. Expansionary fiscal policy moves the *IS* curve to the right, raising both income and interest rates. Contractionary fiscal policy moves the *IS* curve to the left, lowering both income and interest rates.

11-1

MONETARY POLICY

In Chapter 10, we showed how an increase in the quantity of money affects the economy, increasing the level of output by reducing interest rates. In the United States, the Federal Reserve System, a quasi-independent part of the government, is responsible for monetary policy.

The Fed conducts monetary policy mainly through *open market operations,* which we study in more detail in Chapter 16. In an open market operation, the Federal Reserve buys bonds in exchange for money, thus increasing the stock of money, or it sells

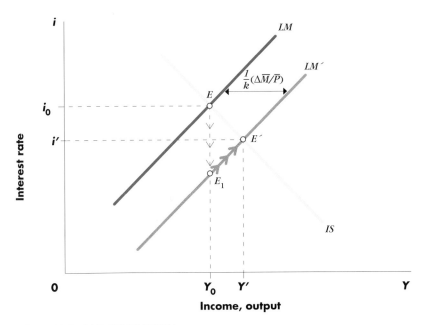

FIGURE 11-3   MONETARY POLICY.

An increase in the real money stock shifts the LM curve to the right.

bonds in exchange for money paid by the purchasers of the bonds, thus reducing the money stock.

We take here the case of an open market purchase of bonds. The Fed pays for the bonds it buys with money *that it can create*. One can usefully think of the Fed as printing money with which to buy bonds, even though that is not strictly accurate, as we shall see in Chapter 16. When the Fed buys bonds, it reduces the quantity of bonds available in the market and thereby tends to increase their price, or lower their yield— only at a lower interest rate will the public be prepared to hold a smaller fraction of its wealth in the form of bonds and a larger fraction in the form of money.

Figure 11-3 shows graphically how an open market purchase works. The initial equilibrium at point E is on the initial LM schedule that corresponds to a real money supply, $\overline{M/P}$. Now consider an open market purchase by the Fed. This increases the nominal quantity of money and, given the price level, the real quantity of money. As a consequence, the LM schedule will shift to LM'. The new equilibrium will be at point E', with a lower interest rate and a higher level of income. The equilibrium level of income rises because the open market purchase reduces the interest rate and thereby increases investment spending.

By experimenting with Figure 11-3, you will be able to show that the steeper the LM schedule, the larger the change in income. If money demand is very sensitive to the interest rate (corresponding to a relatively flat LM curve), a given change in the money stock can be absorbed in the assets markets with only a small change in the interest rate. The effects of an open market purchase on investment spending would then be small. By contrast, if the demand for money is not very sensitive to the interest rate (corresponding to a relatively steep LM curve), a given change in the money supply will cause a large change in the interest rate and have a big effect on investment de-mand. Similarly, if the demand for money is very sensitive to income, a given increase in the money stock can be absorbed with a relatively small change in income and the monetary multiplier will be smaller.[1]

Consider next the process of adjustment to the monetary expansion. At the initial equilibrium point, E, the increase in the money supply creates an excess supply of money to which the public adjusts by trying to buy other assets. In the process, asset prices increase and yields decline. Because money and asset markets adjust rapidly, we move immediately to point E_1, where the money market clears and where the public is willing to hold the larger real quantity of money because the interest rate has de-clined sufficiently. At point E_1, however, there is an excess demand for goods. The de-cline in the interest rate, given the initial income level Y_0, has raised aggregate demand and is causing inventories to run down. In response, output expands and we start mov-ing up the LM' schedule. Why does the interest rate rise during the adjustment process? Because the increase in output raises the demand for money, and the greater demand for money has to be checked by higher interest rates.

Thus the increase in the money stock first causes interest rates to fall as the pub-lic adjusts its portfolio and then—as a result of the decline in interest rates—increases aggregate demand.

THE TRANSMISSION MECHANISM

Two steps in the *transmission mechanism*—the process by which changes in monetary policy affect aggregate demand—are essential. The first is that an increase in real bal-ances generates a *portfolio disequilibrium;* that is, at the prevailing interest rate and level of income, people are holding more money than they want. This causes portfolio holders to attempt to reduce their money holdings by buying other assets, thereby chang-ing asset prices and yields. In other words, the change in the money supply changes interest rates. The second stage of the transmission process occurs when the change in interest rates affects aggregate demand.

These two stages of the transmission process appear in almost every analysis of the effects of changes in the money supply on the economy. The details of the analy-ses will often differ—some analyses will have more than two assets and more than one interest rate; some will include an influence of interest rates on other categories of de-mand, in particular consumption and spending by local government.[2]

Table 11-1 provides a summary of the stages in the transmission mechanism. There are two critical links between the change in real balances (i.e., the real money stock)

---

[1] The precise expression for the monetary policy multiplier is given in equation (11) in Chap. 10. If you have worked through the optional Sec. 10-5, you should use that equation to confirm the statements in this paragraph.

[2] Some analyses also include a mechanism by which changes in real balances have a direct effect on aggre-gate demand through the *real balance effect.* The real-balance-effect argument is that wealth affects con-sumption demand and that an increase in real (money) balances increases wealth and therefore consumption demand. The real balance effect is not very important empirically, because the relevant real balances are only a small part of wealth. The classic work on the topic is Don Patinkin, *Money, Interest and Prices* (New York: Harper & Row, 1965).

TABLE 11-1 The Transmission Mechanism

(1) →	(2) →	(3) →	(4)
Change in real money supply.	Portfolio adjustments lead to a change in asset prices and interest rates.	Spending adjusts to changes in interest rates.	Output adjusts to the change in aggregate demand.

and the ultimate effect on income. First, the change in real balances, by bringing about portfolio disequilibrium, must lead to a change in interest rates. Second, that change in interest rates must change aggregate demand. Through these two linkages, changes in the real money stock affect the level of output in the economy. But that outcome immediately implies the following: If portfolio imbalances do not lead to significant changes in interest rates, for whatever reason, or if spending does not respond to changes in interest rates, the link between money and output does not exist.[3] We now study these linkages in more detail.

THE LIQUIDITY TRAP

In discussing the effects of monetary policy on the economy, two extreme cases have received much attention. The first is the *liquidity trap,* a situation in which the public is prepared, at a given interest rate, to hold whatever amount of money is supplied. This implies that the *LM* curve is horizontal and that changes in the quantity of money do not shift it. In that case, monetary policy carried out through open market operations has no effect on either the interest rate or the level of income. In the liquidity trap, monetary policy is powerless to affect the interest rate.

The possibility of a liquidity trap at low interest rates is a notion that grew out of the theories of the great English economist John Maynard Keynes. Keynes himself did state, though, that he was not aware of there ever having been such a situation, nor are we today, 60 years later.[4] But the liquidity trap is a useful expositional device for understanding the consequences of a relatively flat *LM* curve.

BANKS' RELUCTANCE TO LEND?

In 1991 a different possibility arose to suggest that sometimes monetary policy actions by the Fed might have only a very limited impact on the economy. In step (3) in Table 11-1, investment spending should increase in response to lower interest rates. However, in 1991, as interest rates declined, banks were reluctant to increase their lending.

The underlying reason was that many banks had made bad loans at the end of the 1980s, especially to finance real estate deals. When the real estate market collapsed in

---

[3]We refer to the responsiveness of aggregate demand—rather than investment spending—to the interest rate because consumption demand may also respond to the interest rate. Higher interest rates may lead to more saving and less consumption at a given level of income. Empirically, it has been difficult to isolate such an interest rate effect on consumption.

[4]J. M. Keynes, *The General Theory of Employment, Interest and Money* (New York: Macmillan, 1936), p. 207.

BOX 11-1 Q: Does the Federal Reserve set the interest rate, or does it set the money supply?

A: Yes.

According to our discussion, the Federal Reserve sets the money supply, through open market operations, and this pins down the position of the *LM* curve. But one frequently reads that the Fed has either raised or lowered interest rates. How are the two connected? The answer is that, as long as the positions of the *IS* and *LM* curves are known to the Fed, the two are equivalent.*

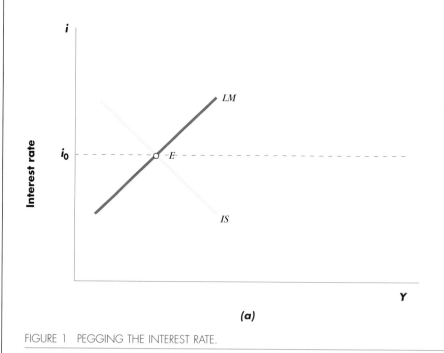

(a)

FIGURE 1   PEGGING THE INTEREST RATE.

*In practice the positions of the *IS* and *LM* curves are not known with absolute precision, and in the short run the difference between setting interest rates and setting the money supply is quite important. We investigate this question in detail in Chap. 16.

Suppose the Fed wishes to set the interest rate at a level i_0 and that the *IS* curve is positioned as shown in panel (*a*) of Figure 1. Rather than picking a value for the money supply and drawing a corresponding *LM* curve, you can draw an *LM* curve through point *E*—guaranteeing that the interest rate target i_0 is hit—and then work backward to find the money supply that will produce the *LM* curve drawn through *E*.

Suppose that, as illustrated in panel (*b*), the *IS* curve has shifted to the right. To keep the interest rate "pegged" at i_0, you would move the *LM* curve right to *LM'* and recompute the required money supply. So when the Fed pegs the interest rate, it is really adjusting the money supply to keep the *LM* intersecting the *IS* at the desired interest target.

At least in the short run, the Fed can peg the interest rate very effectively without actually carrying out calculations about the *IS-LM* equilibrium. Suppose the Fed wishes to peg the interest rate between 5.9 and 6 percent. The Fed, operating through its New York branch, offers to buy any amount of bonds at interest rates above 6 percent (promising unlimited open market purchases) and sell any amount at rates below 5.9 (promising unlimited open market sales). If interest rates start to veer above 6 percent, the Fed effectively increases the money stock, pushing interest rates back down. (And vice versa below 5.9 percent.)

Note that the Fed is *not* setting the interest rate by any sort of law or regulation. "Pegging the interest rate" is really just the use of open market operations on autopilot.

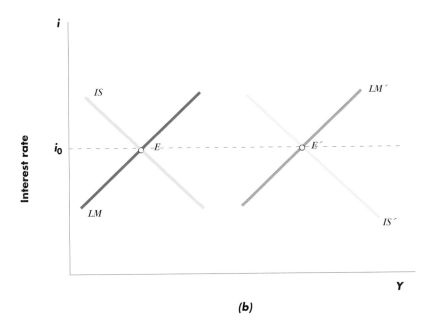

(b)

1990 and 1991, banks faced the prospect that a significant portion of their existing borrowers could not repay in full. Not surprisingly, banks showed little enthusiasm to lend more to new, perhaps risky, borrowers. Rather, they preferred to lend to the government, by buying securities such as Treasury bills. Lending to the U.S. government is as safe as any loan can be, because the U.S. government always pays its debts.[5]

If banks will not lend to firms, an important part of the transmission mechanism between a Fed open market purchase and an increase in aggregate demand and output is put out of action. Careful study suggested that banks were lending less to private firms than usual for this stage of the business cycle.[6] However, many argued that further open market operations, leading to further cuts in interest rates, would get the economy moving again. That is, they were arguing that if a given dose of Fed medicine had less effect on bank lending than usual, the dose should be increased. They appear to have been right, and by 1992, bank lending was picking up.

THE CLASSICAL CASE

The polar opposite of the horizontal *LM* curve—which implies that monetary policy cannot affect the level of income—is the vertical *LM* curve. The *LM* curve is vertical when the demand for money is entirely unresponsive to the interest rate.

Recall from Chapter 10 [equation (7)] that the *LM* curve is described by

$$\frac{\overline{M}}{P} = kY - hi \tag{1}$$

If *h* is zero, then corresponding to a given real money supply, $\overline{M}/P$, there is a unique level of income, which implies that the *LM* curve is vertical at that level of income. (Sneak a look ahead at Figure 11-6.)

The vertical *LM* curve is called the *classical case*. Rewriting equation (1), with *h* set equal to zero and with *P* moved to the right-hand side, we obtain

$$\overline{M} = k(\overline{P} \times Y) \tag{2}$$

We see that the classical case implies that nominal GDP, $P \times Y$, depends only on the quantity of money. This is the classical *quantity theory of money,* which argues that the level of nominal income is determined solely by the quantity of money. The quantity theory was originally motivated by the belief that people would hold money in a quantity proportional to total transactions, $P \times Y$, irrespective of the interest rate. As we will see in Chapter 15, money does respond to the interest rate; nonetheless, the quantity theory remains useful for expositional purposes—and a sophisticated version of the quantity theory is still espoused by monetarists.

---

[5]In 1995, the United States came close to suspending debt repayment while the president and Congress played a game of "chicken" over the federal budget. In the end, no payments were actually missed. (For readers unfamiliar with American slang, "chicken" is a game in which two male adolescents with more hormones than intelligence drive cars head-on at one another at high speed. The first one to turn aside is said to "chicken out"—to show cowardice. If neither turns aside, the results are much like the results of the U.S. government's failing to pay its debt.

[6]See, for example, Ben Bernanke and Cara Lown, "The Credit Crunch," *Brookings Papers on Economic Activity* 2 (1991).

When the *LM* curve is vertical, a given change in the quantity of money has a maximal effect on the level of income. Check this by moving a vertical *LM* curve to the right and comparing the resultant change in income with the change produced by a similar horizontal shift of a nonvertical *LM* curve.

By drawing a vertical *LM* curve, you can also see that shifts in the *IS* curve do not affect the level of income when the *LM* curve is vertical. *Thus, when the LM curve is vertical, monetary policy has a maximal effect on the level of income, and fiscal policy has no effect on income.* The vertical *LM* curve, implying the comparative effectiveness of monetary over fiscal policy, is sometimes associated with the view that "only money matters" for the determination of output. Since the *LM* curve is vertical only when the demand for money does not depend on the interest rate, the interest sensitivity of the demand for money turns out to be an important issue in determining the effectiveness of alternative policies. The evidence, to be reviewed in Chapter 15, is that the interest rate does affect the demand for money.

11-2

FISCAL POLICY AND CROWDING OUT

This section shows how changes in fiscal policy shift the *IS* curve, the curve that describes equilibrium in the goods market. Recall that the *IS* curve slopes downward because a decrease in the interest rate increases investment spending, thereby increasing aggregate demand and the level of output at which the goods market is in equilibrium. Recall also that changes in fiscal policy shift the *IS* curve. Specifically, a fiscal expansion shifts the *IS* curve to the right.

The equation of the *IS* curve, derived in Chapter 10, is repeated here for convenience:

$$Y = \alpha_G(\overline{A} - bi) \qquad \alpha_G = \frac{1}{1 - c(1 - t)} \tag{3}$$

Note that $\overline{G}$, the level of government spending, is a component of autonomous spending, $\overline{A}$, in equation (3). The income tax rate, t, is part of the multiplier. Thus both government spending and the tax rate affect the *IS* schedule.

AN INCREASE IN GOVERNMENT SPENDING

We now show, in Figure 11-4, how a fiscal expansion raises equilibrium income and the interest rate. At unchanged interest rates, higher levels of government spending increase the level of aggregate demand. To meet the increased demand for goods, output must rise. In Figure 11-4, we show the effect of a shift in the *IS* schedule. At each level of the interest rate, equilibrium income must rise by α_G times the increase in government spending. For example, if government spending rises by 100 and the multiplier is 2, equilibrium income must increase by 200 at each level of the interest rate. Thus the *IS* schedule shifts to the right by 200.

If the economy is initially in equilibrium at point E and government spending rises by 100, we would move to point E'' *if the interest rate stayed constant*. At E'' the goods market is in equilibrium in that planned spending equals output. But the money market

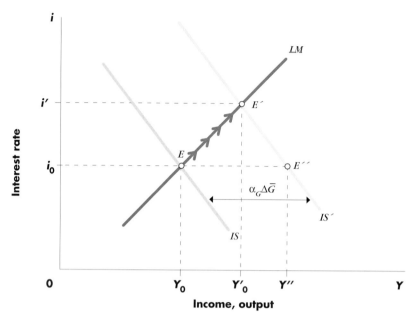

FIGURE 11-4   EFFECTS OF AN INCREASE IN GOVERNMENT SPENDING.

Increased government spending increases aggregate demand, shifting the IS curve to the right.

is no longer in equilibrium. Income has increased, and therefore the quantity of money demanded is higher. Because there is an excess demand for real balances, the interest rate rises. Firms' planned investment spending declines at higher interest rates, and thus aggregate demand falls off.

What is the complete adjustment, taking into account the expansionary effect of higher government spending and the dampening effects of the higher interest rate on private spending? Figure 11-4 shows that only at point E' do both the goods *and* money markets clear. Only at point E' is planned spending equal to income and, at the same time, the quantity of real balances demanded equal to the given real money stock. Point E' is therefore the new equilibrium point.

CROWDING OUT

Comparing E' to the initial equilibrium at E, we see that increased government spending raises both income and the interest rate. But another important comparison is between points E' and E'', the equilibrium in the goods market at unchanged interest rates. Point E'' corresponds to the equilibrium we studied in Chapter 9, when we neglected the impact of interest rates on the economy. In comparing E'' and E', it becomes clear that the adjustment of interest rates and their impact on aggregate demand dampen the expansionary effect of increased government spending. Income, instead of increasing to level Y'', rises only to Y'_0.

The reason that income rises only to Y'_0 rather than to Y'' is that the rise in the interest rate from i_0 to i' reduces the level of investment spending. We say that the increase in government spending *crowds out* investment spending. Crowding out occurs when expansionary fiscal policy causes interest rates to rise, thereby reducing private spending, particularly investment.

What factors determine how much crowding out takes place? In other words, what determines the extent to which interest rate adjustments dampen the output expansion induced by increased government spending? By drawing for yourself different *IS* and *LM* schedules, you will be able to show the following:

- Income increases more, and interest rates increase less, the flatter the *LM* schedule.
- Income increases less, and interest rates increase less, the flatter the *IS* schedule.
- Income and interest rates increase more the larger the multiplier, α_G, and thus the larger the horizontal shift of the *IS* schedule.

In each case the extent of crowding out is greater the more the interest rate increases when government spending rises.

To illustrate these conclusions, we turn to the two extreme cases we discussed in connection with monetary policy, the liquidity trap and the classical case.

THE LIQUIDITY TRAP

If the economy is in the liquidity trap, and thus the *LM* curve is horizontal, an increase in government spending has its full multiplier effect on the equilibrium level of income. There is no change in the interest rate associated with the change in government spending, and thus no investment spending is cut off. There is therefore no dampening of the effects of increased government spending on income.

You should draw your own *IS-LM* diagrams to confirm that if the *LM* curve is horizontal, monetary policy has no impact on the equilibrium of the economy and fiscal policy has a maximal effect. Less dramatically, if the demand for money is very sensitive to the interest rate, and thus the *LM* curve is almost horizontal, fiscal policy changes have a relatively large effect on output and monetary policy changes have little effect on the equilibrium level of output.

THE CLASSICAL CASE AND CROWDING OUT

If the *LM* curve is vertical, an increase in government spending has *no* effect on the equilibrium level of income and increases only the interest rate. This case, already noted when we discussed monetary policy, is shown in Figure 11-5a, where an increase in government spending shifts the *IS* curve to *IS'* but has no effect on income. If the demand for money is not related to the interest rate, as a vertical *LM* curve implies, there is a unique level of income at which the money market is in equilibrium.

Thus, with a vertical *LM* curve, an increase in government spending cannot change the equilibrium level of income and raises only the equilibrium interest rate. But if government spending is higher and output is unchanged, there must be an offsetting reduction in private spending. In this case, the increase in interest rates crowds out an amount of private (particularly investment) spending equal to the increase in government spending. Thus there is full crowding out if the *LM* curve is vertical.[7]

---

[7]Note that, in principle, consumption spending could be reduced by an increase in the interest rate, so both investment and consumption would be crowded out. Further, as we will see in Chap. 12, fiscal expansion can also crowd out net exports.

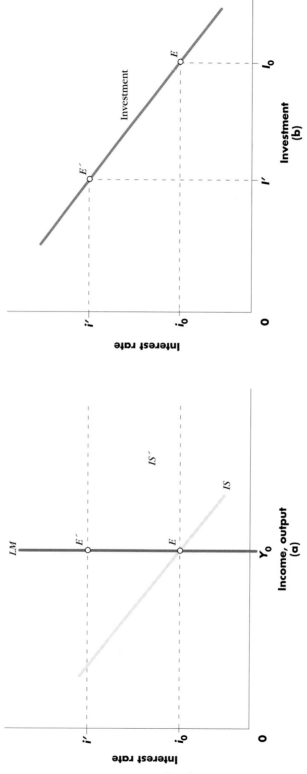

FIGURE 11-5 FULL CROWDING OUT.

With a vertical LM schedule, a fiscal expansion shifting out the IS schedule raises interest rates, not income. Government spending displaces, or crowds out, private spending, dollar for dollar.

In Figure 11-5 we show the crowding out in panel (*b*), where the investment schedule of Figure 10-4 is drawn. The fiscal expansion raises the equilibrium interest rate from i_0 to i' in panel (*a*). In panel (*b*), as a consequence, investment spending declines from the level I_0 to I'.

Is Crowding Out Important?

How seriously must we take the possibility of crowding out? Here three points must be made. The first point is also an important warning. In this chapter, as in the two preceding, we are assuming an economy with prices given, in which output is below the full-employment level. In these conditions, when fiscal expansion increases demand, firms can increase the level of output by hiring more workers. But in fully employed economies, crowding out occurs through a different mechanism. In such conditions an increase in demand will lead to an increase in the price level. The increase in price reduces *real* balances. (An increase in $\overline{P}$ reduces the ratio $\overline{M/P}$.) This reduction in the real money supply moves the *LM* curve to the left, raising interest rates until the initial increase in aggregate demand is fully crowded out.

The second point, however, is that in an economy with unemployed resources there will *not* be full crowding out because the *LM* schedule is not, in fact, vertical. A fiscal expansion will raise interest rates, but income will also rise. Crowding out is therefore a matter of degree. The increase in aggregate demand raises income, and with the rise in income, the level of saving rises. This expansion in saving, in turn, makes it possible to finance a larger budget deficit without *completely* displacing private spending.

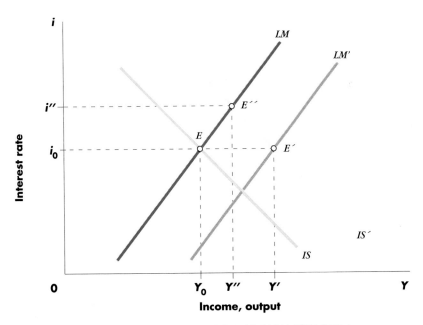

FIGURE 11-6   MONETARY ACCOMMODATION OF FISCAL EXPANSION.

The third point is that with unemployment and, thus, a possibility for output to expand, interest rates need not rise at all when government spending rises, and there need not be any crowding out. This is true because the monetary authorities can *accommodate* the fiscal expansion by an increase in the money supply. Monetary policy is accommodating when, in the course of a fiscal expansion, the money supply is increased in order to prevent interest rates from increasing. *Monetary accommodation* is also referred to as *monetizing budget deficits,* meaning that the Federal Reserve prints money to buy the bonds with which the government pays for its deficit. When the Fed accommodates a fiscal expansion, both the *IS* and the *LM* schedules shift to the right, as in Figure 11-6. Output will clearly increase, but interest rates need not rise. Accordingly, there need not be any adverse effects on investment.

11-3

THE COMPOSITION OF OUTPUT AND THE POLICY MIX

Table 11-2 summarizes our analysis of the effects of expansionary monetary and fiscal policy on output and the interest rate, provided the economy is not in a liquidity trap or in the classical case. Since the liquidity trap and the classical case represent, at best, extremes useful for expositional purposes, it is apparent that policy makers can, in practice, use either monetary or fiscal policy to affect the level of income.

What difference does it make whether monetary or fiscal policy is used to control output? The choice between monetary and fiscal policies as tools of stabilization policy is an important and controversial topic. One basis for decision is the flexibility and speed with which these policies can be implemented and take effect.

Here we do not discuss speed and flexibility; rather, we look at what these policies do to the components of aggregate demand, that is, to investment, consumption, and government spending, respectively. In that respect, there is a sharp difference between monetary policy and fiscal policy.[8] Monetary policy operates by stimulating interest-responsive components of aggregate demand, primarily investment spending. There is strong evidence that the earliest effect of monetary policy is on residential construction.

Fiscal policy, by contrast, operates in a manner that depends on precisely what goods the government buys or what taxes and transfers it changes. Choices include government purchases of goods and services such as defense spending or a reduction

---

[8]The two types of policy differ also in their impact on exports, as we shall see in Chap. 12.

TABLE 11-2 Policy Effects on Income and Interest Rates

POLICY	EQUILIBRIUM INCOME	EQUILIBRIUM INTEREST RATES
Monetary expansion	+	−
Fiscal expansion	+	+

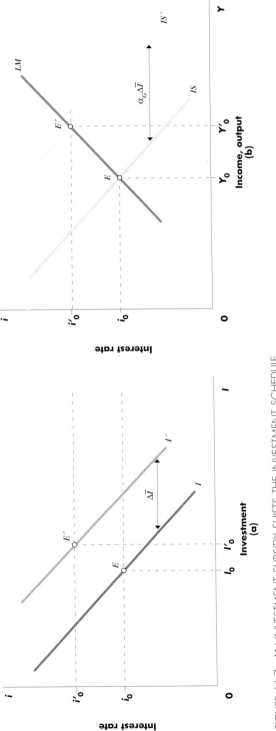

FIGURE 11-7   AN INVESTMENT SUBSIDY SHIFTS THE INVESTMENT SCHEDULE.

in the corporate profits tax, sales taxes, or social security contributions. Each policy affects the level of aggregate demand and causes an expansion in output, but the composition of the increase in output depends on the specific policy. An increase in government spending raises consumption spending along with government purchases. An income tax cut has a direct effect on consumption spending. An investment subsidy, discussed below, increases investment spending. All expansionary fiscal policies will raise the interest rate if the quantity of money is unchanged.

AN INVESTMENT SUBSIDY

Both an income tax cut and an increase in government spending raise the interest rate and reduce investment spending. However, it is possible for the government to raise investment spending through an *investment subsidy,* as shown in Figure 11-7. In the United States, the government has sometimes subsidized investment through an *investment tax credit,* whereby a firm's tax payments are reduced when it increases its investment spending. For instance, President Clinton proposed an investment tax credit in his 1993 fiscal package.

When the government subsidizes investment, it essentially pays part of the cost of each firm's investment. An investment subsidy shifts the investment schedule in panel (*a*) of Figure 11-7. At each interest rate, firms now plan to invest more. With investment spending higher, aggregate demand increases.

In panel (*b*), the *IS* schedule shifts by the amount of the multiplier times the increase in autonomous investment brought about by the subsidy. The new equilibrium is at point E', where goods and money markets are again in balance. But note now that although interest rates have risen, we see, in panel (*a*), that investment is higher. Investment is at the level I_0', up from I_0. The interest rate increase dampens but does not reverse the impact of the investment subsidy. This is an example in which both consumption, induced by higher income, and investment rise as a consequence of expansionary fiscal policy.

Table 11-3 summarizes the impacts of different types of fiscal policy on the composition of output, as well as on output and the interest rate.

THE POLICY MIX

In Figure 11-8 we show the policy problem of reaching full-employment output, Y^*, for an economy that is initially at point E, with unemployment. Should we choose a fiscal expansion, moving to point E_1 with higher income and higher interest rates? Or should we choose a monetary expansion, leading to full employment with lower interest rates at point E_2? Or should we pick a policy mix of fiscal expansion and accommodating monetary policy, leading to an intermediate position?

TABLE 11-3   Alternative Fiscal Policies

	INTEREST RATE	CONSUMPTION	INVESTMENT	GDP
Income tax cut	+	+	−	+
Government spending	+	+	−	+
Investment subsidy	+	+	+	+

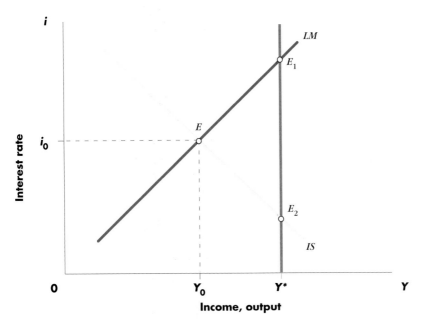

FIGURE 11-8   EXPANSIONARY POLICIES AND THE COMPOSITION OF OUTPUT.

Once we recognize that all the policies raise output but differ significantly in their impact on different sectors of the economy, we open up a problem of political economy. Given the decision to expand aggregate demand, who should get the primary benefit? Should the expansion take place through a decline in interest rates and increased investment spending, or should it take place through a cut in taxes and increased personal spending, or should it take the form of an increase in the size of government?

Questions of speed and predictability of policies apart, the issues have been settled by political preferences. Conservatives will argue for a tax cut anytime. They will favor stabilization policies that cut taxes in a recession and cut government spending in a boom. Over time, given enough cycles, the government sector becomes very small, as a conservative would want it to be. The counterpart view belongs to those who believe that there is a broad scope for government spending on education, the environment, job training and rehabilitation, and the like, and who, accordingly, favor expansionary policies in the form of increased government spending and higher taxes to curb a boom. Growth-minded people and the construction lobby argue for expansionary policies that operate through low interest rates or investment subsidies.

The recognition that monetary and fiscal policy changes have different effects on the composition of output is important. It suggests that policy makers can choose a *policy mix*—a combination of monetary and fiscal policies—that will not only get the economy to full employment but also make a contribution to solving other policy problems. We now discuss the policy mix in action.

11-4

THE POLICY MIX IN ACTION

In this section we review the U.S. monetary-fiscal policy mix of the 1980s, the economic debate over how to deal with the U.S. recession in 1990 and 1991, and the policy decisions made in Germany in the early 1990s as the country struggled with the macroeconomic consequences of the reunification of East and West Germany.

This section serves not only to discuss the issue of the policy mix in the real world but also to reintroduce the problem of inflation. The assumption that the price level is fixed is a useful expositional simplification for the theory of this chapter, but of course the real world is more complex. Remember that policies that reduce aggregate demand, such as reducing the growth rate of money or government spending, tend to reduce the inflation rate along with the level of output. An expansionary policy increases inflation together with the level of output. Inflation is unpopular, and governments will generally try to keep inflation low and prevent it from rising.

THE 1980S RECESSION AND RECOVERY

Economic policy in the United States in the early 1980s departed radically from the policies of the previous two decades. First, tight money was implemented at the end of 1979 to fight an inflation rate that had reached record peacetime levels. Then, in 1981, an expansionary fiscal policy was put in place as President Reagan's program of tax cuts and increased defense spending began.

FIGURE 11-9 INFLATION, UNEMPLOYMENT, AND THE INTEREST RATE.

(Source: DRI/McGraw-Hill Macroeconomic Database.)

Figure 11-9 shows the unemployment, inflation, and interest rates between 1972 and 1996. In 1973 the United States and the rest of the world were hit by the first oil shock, in which the oil-exporting countries raised the price of oil fourfold. The oil price increase raised other prices and, in the United States, helped create inflation and also a recession in which unemployment increased to the then post-World War II record rate of 8.9 percent. The recession ended in 1975. Economic policy under the Carter administration (1977–1981) was generally expansionary; by 1979 unemployment was below 6 percent and thus close to the full-employment level. Inflation increased with the expansionary policies of the period, and in 1979 the inflation rate jumped as the second oil shock hit and the price of oil doubled.

The rising inflation was extremely unpopular, and it was clear that some policy changes had to be made. In October 1979 the Fed acted, turning monetary policy in a highly restrictive direction. The monetary squeeze was tightened in the first half of 1980, at which point the economy went into a minirecession. After a brief recovery, 1982 brought the deepest recession since the Great Depression.

The reason for the sharp decline in activity was tight money. Because inflation was still above 10 percent and the money stock was growing at only 5.1 percent in 1981, the real money supply was falling. Interest rates continued to climb (see Table 11-4). Not surprisingly, investment, especially construction, collapsed. The economy was dragged into a deep recession with a trough in December 1982.

Table 11-4 also shows the second component of the early 1980s policy mix: The full-employment deficit increased rapidly from 1981 to 1984. The 1981 tax bill cut tax rates for individuals, with the cuts coming into effect over the next 3 years, and increased investment subsidies for corporations. The full-employment deficits in those years are the largest in peacetime U.S. history.

With a policy mix of easy fiscal and tight monetary policies, the analysis of Figure 11-8 tells us to expect a rise in the interest rate. With investment subsidies increased, Figure 11-7 tells us to look for the possibility that investment increases along with the interest rate.

The first element—a rise in the interest rate—indeed occurred. That may be a surprise if you look only at the Treasury bill rate in Table 11-4. But when there is inflation, the correct interest rate to consider is not the *nominal* rate but the *real* rate. The *real*

TABLE 11-4 The 1982 Recession and the Recovery
(Percent)

	1980	1981	1982	1983	1984
Nominal interest rate*	11.5	14.0	10.7	8.6	9.6
Real interest rate†	2.0	4.0	4.5	4.5	5.2
Full-employment deficit	.4	-0-	1.1	2.1	3.0
Unemployment rate	7.0	7.5	9.5	9.5	7.4
GDP gap	6.4	7.1	11.6	10.4	6.2
Inflation‡	9.5	10.0	6.2	4.1	4.4

*Three-month Treasury bill rate.

†Three-month Treasury bill rate less inflation rate of the GDP deflator.

‡GDP deflator.

Source: DRI/McGraw-Hill.

interest rate is the nominal (stated) rate of interest minus the rate of inflation. Over the period 1981–1984 the real interest rate increased sharply even as the nominal rate declined. The real cost of borrowing went up although the nominal cost went down. Investment spending responded to both the increased interest rates and the recession, falling 13 percent between 1981 and 1982, and the investment subsidies and prospects of recovery, increasing 49 percent between 1982 and 1984.

The unemployment rate peaked at over 11 percent in the last quarter of 1982 and then steadily declined under the impact of the huge fiscal expansion. Further fiscal expansion in 1984 and 1985 pushed the recovery of the economy forward, and the expansion continued throughout the 1980s.

THE RECESSION OF 1990–1991

The policy mix in the early 1980s featured highly expansionary fiscal policy and tight money. The tight money succeeded in reducing the inflation of the late 1970s and very early 1980s, at the expense of a serious recession. Expansionary fiscal policy then drove a recovery during which real interest rates increased sharply.

The recovery and expansion continued through the 1980s. By the end of 1988, the economy was close to full employment, and the inflation rate was nearing 5 percent. Fearing a continuing increase in inflation, the Fed tightened monetary policy, sharply raising the Treasury bill rate throughout 1988 and into 1989. Despite this, by early 1989 the unemployment rate touched its low for the decade, 5 percent.

The Fed kept nominal interest rates high—though declining—through 1989 (see Figure 11-9), and for a while it seemed to have put just the right amount of pressure on the brakes. The growth of real GDP slowed through 1989, inflation declined a bit, and unemployment slowly rose.

But by the middle of 1990, it was clear that the economy was heading for a recession. The recession was later determined to have begun in July 1990.[9] By the time the 1982–1990 recovery ended, it was the longest peacetime expansion on record.

The recession started before the Iraqi invasion of Kuwait in August. The price of oil jumped when Iraq invaded, and for a time the Fed was faced with the quandary of deciding whether to keep monetary policy tight by holding interest rates up, in order to fight inflation, or pursue an expansionary policy, in order to fight the recession. It compromised, letting interest rates fall slowly, but not much. The oil price rise turned out to be quite short-lived, and by the end of the year it was clear that the recession was the big problem.[10]

It was also clear that it was up to the Fed to fight the recession, because fiscal policy was immobilized. Why? First, the budget deficit (see Table 11-5) was already large, and was expected to rise, and no one was enthusiastic about increasing it. And second,

[9]The dates of peaks and troughs in the business cycle are determined *after the fact* by a committee of economists at the National Bureau of Economic Research in Cambridge, Massachusetts. They delay their decisions to be sure that enough evidence is in to distinguish a genuine change in the business cycle from a mere temporary blip. See Robert E. Hall, "The Business Cycle Dating Process," *NBER Reporter,* Winter 1991/92, and Victor Zarnovitz, *Business Cycles: Theory, History, Indicators and Forecasting* (Chicago: University of Chicago Press, 1991).

[10]Stephen McNees, "The 1990–91 Recession in Historical Perspective," Federal Reserve Bank of Boston *New England Economic Review,* January–February 1992, presents comparative data on this and earlier recessions.

TABLE 11-5   The 1990–1991 Recession
(Percent)

| | YEAR AND QUARTER | | | | | | |
| | 1990 | | 1991 | | | | 1992 |
	3	4	1	2	3	4	1
GDP growth	−1.6	−3.9	−3.0	1.7	1.2	.6	2.7
Inflation rate*	4.7	3.9	5.3	3.5	2.4	2.4	3.1
Unemployment rate	5.6	6.0	6.5	6.8	6.8	7.0	7.2
Treasury bill rate	7.5	7.0	6.0	5.6	5.4	4.5	3.9
Budget deficit/GDP	2.6	3.5	2.6	3.7	3.7	4.2	4.9
Full-employment deficit, GDP†	–0–	.5	1.0	1.8	1.8	2.4	3.0

*GDP deflator.

†Calculated by DRI/McGraw-Hill.

Source: DRI/McGraw-Hill.

for the political economy reasons we mentioned earlier, the Bush administration and the Democratic Congress fundamentally disagreed on the type of fiscal policy changes that should be made.

From the end of 1990, the Fed began to cut interest rates aggressively. The economy showed signs of recovering in the second quarter of 1991 but faltered in the fourth quarter (see Table 11-5). The political and economic talk turned to the possibility of a double-dip recession. The Fed, fearing that Congress and the president would agree on a fiscal policy change that would raise the budget deficit even more, cut the interest rate very sharply at the end of 1991, pushing it lower than it had been since 1972. In retrospect, this was sufficient to ward off a recession.

By spring 1991, a recovery, very moderate by past standards, had begun. And the Fed's aggressive action had probably helped prevent an expansionary fiscal policy change. Nonetheless, with the benefit of hindsight, it is clear that the Fed should have moved much more rapidly to cut interest rates during the early part of 1991. Of course, there is a bias in the way we evaluate policy makers. The Fed played an active part in helping to keep the expansion going as long as it did during the 1980s, but we focus on the recession. The Fed rarely receives credit for doing things right, but it certainly gets the blame for its mistakes. As the recovery continued through the mid-1990s with modest, but positive, growth and with low inflation, the Fed began to receive greater appreciation on Wall Street and in Washington.

THE GERMAN POLICY MIX, 1990–1992

When East Germany and West Germany were reunited in 1990, the West German government accepted the obligation to attempt to raise living standards in the eastern part of Germany rapidly. This required an immediate increase in government spending, in East German infrastructure, and in transfer payments to the residents of the former East Germany.

For political reasons, the German government did not want to raise taxes much. In effect, the government decided to run a loose fiscal policy, reflected in the increase

BOX 11-2 Anticipatory Monetary Policy

In February 1994, with the unemployment rate at 6.6 percent and inflation below 3 percent per annum, the Federal Reserve raised the discount rate from 4.75 to 5.25 percent. Given that unemployment was above most estimates of the natural rate and that inflation was still low, many observers were surprised at and critical of the Fed's decision—wasn't this killing economic growth even before it had a chance to get going?

However, the Fed—in an example of *anticipatory monetary policy*—was reacting not to the current state of aggregate demand and inflationary pressures but to the inflation that it feared would occur if the economy grew too rapidly.

In the event, the Fed seems to have done the right thing. The economy did grow very rapidly during 1994, at an annual rate of 3.5 percent, with the unemployment rate declining from 6.7 percent in January 1994 to 5.7 percent in January 1995. Despite the rapid growth, inflation stayed low. If the Fed had not raised interest rates, the economy would have grown even more rapidly and inflation would most likely have risen.

Critics who argued that the Fed should have waited until inflation was actually rising, rather than acting preemptively, were giving advice that would probably have forced the Fed to raise interest rates more in 1995 than it did in 1994—because inflation in 1995 would have been higher than it actually was.

The bottom line: It pays to look ahead when setting monetary policy.

in the budget deficit seen in Table 11-6. If aggregate demand and inflation were to be kept in check, it was up to the German central bank, the Bundesbank.

The Bundesbank is widely regarded as the most anti-inflationary of all central banks, and it was certainly not going to accommodate the increase in government spending. Accordingly, it kept money tight and allowed interest rates in Germany to rise to levels that had not been seen in that country for a decade. While the German nominal interest rate of 9.2 percent in 1991 does not look especially high, it is worth noting that the real interest rate in Germany in 1991 was well above that in the United States.[11]

The Bundesbank kept money tight through 1992, all the time expressing great unhappiness about the government's loose fiscal policy and the inflation that it had un-

---

[11]In the end-of-chapter problems, we ask you to calculate the real interest rates in Germany and the United States in 1991. This can be done using Tables 11-5 and 11-6.

TABLE 11-6 Macroeconomic Consequences of German Unification

	(Percent)			
	1989	1990	1991	1992
GDP growth	3.8	4.5	.9	1.8
Inflation rate	2.6	3.4	5.1	5.3
Budget deficit/GDP	.2	−1.7	−2.8	−3.2
Nominal interest rate	7.1	8.5	9.2	9.2

Source: International Monetary Fund.

leashed. In many countries, the German inflation rate in 1991 and 1992, under 5 percent, would be regarded as a miracle of low inflation. But in Germany, where desire for low inflation is part of the national consensus, inflation at that rate is a matter for real concern.[12]

The German policy mix of the early 1990s was like that of the United States in the early 1980s: easy fiscal policy and tight monetary policy. The consequences in both countries were also similar: high interest rates and a deficit in the current account of the balance of payments.

In the next chapter we add international trade to our basic model. We will see there that the inclusion of foreign trade modifies but does not fundamentally alter the analysis of the impacts of monetary and fiscal policy on the economy. We will also see that the combination of tight monetary policy and easy fiscal policy tends to produce a deficit in the balance of payments.

SUMMARY

1. Monetary policy affects the economy, first, by affecting the interest rate and then by affecting aggregate demand. An increase in the money supply reduces the interest rate, increases investment spending and aggregate demand, and thus increases equilibrium output.
2. There are two extreme cases in the operation of monetary policy. In the classical case the demand for real balances is independent of the rate of interest. In that case monetary policy is highly effective. The other extreme is the liquidity trap, the case in which the public is willing to hold *any* amount of real balances at the going interest rate. In that case changes in the supply of real balances have no impact on interest rates and therefore do not affect aggregate demand and output.
3. Taking into account the effects of fiscal policy on the interest rate modifies the multiplier results of Chapter 9. Fiscal expansion, except in extreme circumstances, still leads to an income expansion. However, the rise in interest rates that comes about through the increase in money demand caused by higher income dampens the expansion.
4. Fiscal policy is more effective the smaller the induced changes in interest rates and the smaller the response of investment to these interest rate changes.
5. The two extreme cases, the liquidity trap and the classical case, are useful to show what determines the magnitude of monetary and fiscal policy multipliers. In the liquidity trap, monetary policy has no effect on the economy, whereas fiscal policy has its full multiplier effect on output and no effect on interest rates. In the classical case, changes in the money stock change income, but fiscal policy has no effect on income—it affects only the interest rate. In this case there is complete crowding out of private spending by government spending.
6. A fiscal expansion, because it leads to higher interest rates, displaces, or crowds out, some private investment. The extent of crowding out is a sensitive issue in assessing the usefulness and desirability of fiscal policy as a tool of stabilization policy.
7. The question of the monetary-fiscal policy mix arises because expansionary monetary policy reduces the interest rate while expansionary fiscal policy increases the interest rate. Accordingly, expansionary fiscal policy increases output while

[12]Runaway German inflation after World War I contributed to Hitler's rise to power.

reducing the level of investment; expansionary monetary policy increases output and the level of investment.

8. Governments have to choose the mix in accordance with their objectives for economic growth, or increasing consumption, or from the viewpoint of their beliefs about the desirable size of the government.

KEY TERMS

open market operations	quantity theory of money	investment tax credit
transmission mechanism	crowding out	policy mix
portfolio disequilibrium	monetary accommodation	real interest rate
liquidity trap	monetizing budget deficits	anticipatory monetary
classical case	investment subsidy	policy

PROBLEMS

Conceptual

1. In the text we describe the effect of an open market purchase by the Fed.
    a. Define an open market sale by the Fed.
    b. Show the impact of an open market sale on the interest rate and output. Show both the immediate and the longer-term impacts.

2. Discuss the circumstances under which the monetary and fiscal policy multipliers are each, in turn, equal to zero. Explain in words why this can happen and how likely you think this is.

3. What is a liquidity trap? If the economy was stuck in one, would you advise the use of monetary or fiscal policy?

4. What is crowding out, and when would you expect it to occur? In the face of substantial crowding out, which will be more successful—fiscal or monetary policy?

5. What would the *LM* curve look like in a classical world? If this really were the *LM* curve that we thought best characterized the economy, would we lean toward the use of fiscal policy or monetary policy? (You may assume your goal is to affect output.)

6. What happens when the Fed monetizes a budget deficit? Is this something it should *always* try to do? (*Hint:* Outline the benefits and costs of such a policy over time.)

7. "We can have the GDP path we want equally well with a tight fiscal policy and an easier monetary policy, or the reverse, within fairly broad limits. The real basis for choice lies in many subsidiary targets, besides real GDP and inflation, that are differentially affected by fiscal and monetary policies." What are some of the subsidiary targets referred to in the quote? How would they be affected by alternative policy combinations?

Technical

1. The economy is at full employment. Now the government wants to change the composition of demand toward investment and away from consumption without, however, allowing aggregate demand to go beyond full employment. What is the required policy mix? Use an *IS-LM* diagram to show your policy proposal.

2. Suppose the government cuts income taxes. Show in the *IS-LM* model the impact of the tax cut under two assumptions: (1) The government keeps interest rates constant through an accommodating monetary policy. (2) The money stock remains unchanged. Explain the difference in results.

3. Consider two alternative programs for contraction. One is the removal of an investment subsidy; the other is a rise in income tax rates. Use the *IS-LM* model and the investment sched-

ule, as shown in Figure 11-7, to discuss the impact of these alternative policies on income, interest rates, and investment.

4. In Figure 11-8 the economy can move to full employment by an expansion in either money or the full-employment deficit. Which policy leads to E_1 and which to E_2? How would you expect the choice to be made? Who would most strongly favor moving to E_1? versus E_2? What policy would correspond to "balanced growth"?

CHAPTER 12

International Linkages

CHAPTER HIGHLIGHTS

- Economies are linked internationally through trade in goods and through financial markets. The exchange rate is the price of a foreign currency in terms of the dollar.

- Under fixed exchange rates, central banks buy and sell foreign currency to peg the exchange rate. Under floating exchange rates, the market determines the value of one currency in terms of another.

- In the very long run, exchange rates adjust so as to equalize the real cost of goods across countries.

- With perfect capital mobility and fixed exchange rates, fiscal policy is powerful. With perfect capital mobility and floating exchange rates, monetary policy is powerful.

As the twentieth century draws to a close, national economies are becoming more closely interrelated, and the notion of *globalization*—that we are moving toward a single global economy—is increasingly accepted. Economic influences from abroad already have powerful effects on the U.S. economy. And U.S. economic policies have even more substantial effects on foreign economies.

Whether the U.S. economy grows or moves into recession makes a big difference to Mexico or even to Japan, and whether other industrial countries shift to fiscal stimulus or stringency makes a difference to the U.S. economy. A tightening of U.S. monetary policy that raises domestic interest rates both affects interest rates worldwide and changes the value of the dollar relative to other currencies, and thus affects U.S. competitiveness and worldwide trade and GDP.

In this chapter we present the key linkages among *open economies*—economies that trade with others—and introduce some first pieces of analysis. We present more details on international aspects of macroeconomics in Chapter 21.

Any economy is linked to the rest of the world through two broad channels: trade (in goods and services) and finance. The *trade* linkage means that some of a country's production is exported to foreign countries, while some goods that are consumed or invested at home are produced abroad and imported. In 1995, U.S. exports of goods and services amounted to 9.7 percent of GDP, while imports were equal to 10.9 percent of GDP. Compared with other countries, the United States engages in relatively little international trade—it is a relatively closed economy. At the other extreme is the Netherlands—a very open economy—whose imports and exports each amount to about 60 percent of GDP.

Trade linkages are nonetheless important for the United States. Spending on imports escapes from the circular flow of income, in the sense that part of the income spent by U.S. residents is not spent on domestically produced goods; by contrast, exports appear as an increase in the demand for domestically produced goods. Thus the basic *IS-LM* model of income determination must be amended to include international effects.

In addition, the prices of U.S. goods relative to those of our competitors have direct impacts on demand, output, and employment. A decline in the dollar prices of our competitors, relative to the prices at which U.S. firms sell, shifts demand away from U.S. goods toward goods produced abroad. Our imports rise and exports fall. This is precisely what happened in the United States between 1980 and 1985, when the value of the dollar increased to record levels relative to foreign currencies, imports became cheap, and foreigners found U.S. goods very expensive. Conversely, when the value of the dollar declines relative to other currencies, U.S.-produced goods become relatively cheaper, demand here and abroad shifts toward our goods, exports rise, and imports decline.

There are also strong international links in the area of *finance.* U.S. residents, whether households, banks, or corporations, can hold U.S. assets such as Treasury bills or corporate bonds, or they can hold assets in foreign countries, say, in Canada or Germany. Most U.S. households hold almost exclusively U.S. assets, but that is certainly not true for banks or large corporations. Portfolio managers shop around the world for the most attractive yields, and they may well conclude that German government bonds, yen bonds issued by the Japanese government, or Argentine government bonds offer a better yield—all things considered—than U.S. bonds.

TABLE 12-1 The U.S. Balance of Payments
(Billions of dollars)

	1993	1994	1995
Current account	−99.9	−148.4	−148.2
Goods and services balance	−72.0	−166.1	−173.4
Capital account			
Net private capital*	−14.0	89.4	16.9
Balance of payments	−113.9	−5.9	−133.3

*Including statistical discrepancy.

Source: Federal Reserve Bulletin, January 1997.

As international investors shift their assets around the world, they link asset markets here and abroad, and thereby affect income, exchange rates, and the ability of monetary policy to affect interest rates. We show in this chapter how the *IS-LM* analysis has to be modified to take international trade and finance linkages into account. The first step is to discuss exchange rates and the balance of payments.

12-1

THE BALANCE OF PAYMENTS AND EXCHANGE RATES

The *balance of payments* is the record of the transactions of the residents of a country with the rest of the world. There are two main accounts in the balance of payments: the current account and the capital account. Table 12-1 shows recent data for the United States.

The *current account* records trade in goods and services, as well as transfer payments. Services include freight, royalty payments, and interest payments. Services also include *net investment income,* the interest and profits on our assets abroad less the income foreigners earn on assets they own in the United States. Transfer payments consist of remittances, gifts, and grants. The *trade balance* simply records trade in goods. Adding trade in services and net transfers to the trade balance, we arrive at the current account balance.

The simple rule for balance-of-payments accounting is that any transaction that gives rise to a payment by a country's residents is a deficit item in that country's balance of payments. Thus, for the United States, imports of cars, gifts to foreigners, a purchase of land in Spain, or a deposit in a bank in Switzerland—all are deficit items. Examples of surplus items, by contrast, would be U.S. sales of airplanes abroad, payments by foreigners for U.S. licenses to use American technology, pensions from abroad received by U.S. residents, and foreign purchases of U.S. assets.

The current account is in *surplus* if exports exceed imports plus net transfers to foreigners, that is, if receipts from trade in goods and services and transfers exceed payments on this account.

The *capital account* records purchases and sales of assets, such as stocks, bonds, and land. There is a U.S. capital account surplus—also called a net capital inflow—when our receipts from the sale of stocks, bonds, land, bank deposits, and other assets exceed our payments for our own purchases of foreign assets.

EXTERNAL ACCOUNTS MUST BALANCE

The central point of international payments is very simple: Individuals and firms have to pay for what they buy abroad. If a person spends more than her income, her deficit needs to be financed by selling assets or by borrowing. Similarly, if a country runs a deficit in its current account, spending more abroad than it receives from sales to the rest of the world, the deficit needs to be financed by selling assets or by borrowing abroad. This selling or borrowing implies that the country is running a capital account surplus. Thus any current account deficit is of necessity *financed* by an offsetting capital inflow:

$$\text{Current account deficit} + \text{net capital inflow} = 0 \qquad (1)$$

Equation (1) makes a drastic point: If a country has no assets to sell, if it has no foreign currency reserves to use up, and if nobody will lend to it, the country *has* to achieve balance in its current account, however painful and difficult that may be.

It is often useful to split the capital account into two separate parts: (1) the transactions of the country's private sector and (2) official reserve transactions, which correspond to the central bank's activities. A current account deficit can be financed by private residents selling off assets abroad or borrowing abroad. Alternatively, or as well, a current account deficit can be financed by the government, which runs down its reserves of foreign exchange,[1] selling foreign currency in the foreign exchange market. Conversely, when there is a surplus, the private sector may use the foreign exchange revenues it receives to pay off debt or buy assets abroad; alternatively, the central bank can buy the (net) foreign currency earned by the private sector and add that currency to its reserves.

The increase in official reserves is also called the overall *balance-of-payments surplus.* We can summarize our discussion in the following statement:

Balance-of-payments surplus = increase in official exchange reserves

= current account surplus + net private capital inflow[2]

$$(1a)$$

If both the current account and the private capital account are in deficit, then the overall balance of payments is in deficit; that is, the central bank is losing reserves. When one account is in surplus and the other is in deficit to precisely the same extent, the overall balance of payments is zero—neither in surplus nor in deficit.[3]

As Table 12-1 shows, the U.S. current account was in deficit during 1993–1995 (as it has been since 1982). In 1993 there was a net outflow of capital, as compared to

---

[1]All governments hold some amounts of foreign currency and of other assets such as gold. These are the country's *official reserves.*

[2]The term "net private capital inflow" is not entirely correct. Included here are also official capital flows unrelated to the exchange market operations. For example, the purchase of a new embassy building in Kiev would be an official capital account transaction, which would be put into the category "net private capital inflow." For our purposes, the broad distinctions are enough.

[3]Balance-of-payments data are poor. Changes in official reserves are generally accurately reported, trade flow data are reasonably good, data on service flows are poor, and capital flow data are extremely poor. For example, in the second quarter of 1995, there was a statistical discrepancy of positive $34 billion—followed the next quarter by a statistical discrepancy of negative $42 billion!

1994 and 1995 when there was a net inflow. In all three years the balance of payments was negative. Accordingly, the United States was running down reserves by selling foreign exchange.

FIXED EXCHANGE RATES

We focus now on how central banks, through their official transactions, finance, or provide the means of paying for, balance-of-payments surpluses and deficits. At this point we distinguish between fixed and floating exchange rate systems.

In a *fixed exchange rate system* foreign central banks stand ready to buy and sell their currencies at a fixed price in terms of dollars. The major countries had fixed exchange rates against one another from the end of World War II until 1973. Today, some countries fix their exchange rates, but others don't.

In the 1960s, for example, the German central bank, the Bundesbank, would buy or sell any amount of dollars at 4 deutsche marks (DM) per U.S. dollar. The French central bank, the Banque de France, stood ready to buy or sell any amount of dollars at 4.90 French francs (FF) per U.S. dollar. The fact that the central banks were prepared to buy or sell *any* amount of dollars at these fixed prices, or exchange rates, meant that market prices would indeed be equal to the fixed rates. Why? Because nobody who wanted to buy U.S. dollars would pay more than 4.90 francs per dollar when francs could be purchased at that price from the Banque de France. Conversely, nobody would part with dollars in exchange for francs for less than 4.90 francs per dollar if the Banque de France, through the commercial banking system, was prepared to buy dollars at that price.[4]

Intervention

Foreign central banks hold *reserves*—inventories of dollars and gold that they can sell for dollars—to sell when they want to or have to intervene in the foreign exchange market. *Intervention* is the buying or selling of foreign exchange by the central bank.

What determines the amount of intervention that a central bank has to do in a fixed exchange rate system? We already have the answer to that question. The balance of payments measures the amount of foreign exchange intervention needed from the central banks. For example, if the United States were running a deficit in the balance of payments vis-à-vis Germany, and thus the demand for marks in exchange for dollars exceeded the supply of marks in exchange for dollars from Germans, the Bundesbank would buy the excess dollars, paying for them with marks.[5]

---

[4]Would the Bundesbank and the Banque de France also have to set a mark-franc exchange rate? Not really, because if there are 4.90 francs to the dollar and 4 marks to the dollar there must be 1.225 (= 4.90/4) francs to the mark.

[5]Which central bank in fact intervenes in the foreign exchange market in the fixed rate system? If there was an excess supply of dollars and an excess demand for marks, either the Bundesbank could buy dollars in exchange for marks or the Fed could sell marks in exchange for dollars. In practice, during the fixed rate period, each foreign central bank undertook to *peg* (fix) its exchange rate vis-à-vis the dollar, and most foreign exchange intervention was undertaken by the foreign central banks. The Fed was nonetheless involved in the management of the exchange rate system, since it frequently made dollar loans to foreign central banks that were in danger of running out of dollars.

Fixed exchange rates thus operate like any other price support scheme, such as those in agricultural markets. Given market demand and supply, the price fixer has to make up the excess demand or take up the excess supply. In order to be able to ensure that the price (exchange rate) stays fixed, it is obviously necessary to hold an inventory of foreign currencies, or foreign exchange, that can be provided in exchange for the domestic currency.

As long as the central bank has the necessary reserves, it can continue to intervene in the foreign exchange markets to keep the exchange rate constant. However, if a country persistently runs deficits in the balance of payments, the central bank eventually will run out of reserves of foreign exchange and will be unable to continue its intervention.

Before that point is reached, the central bank is likely to decide that it can no longer maintain the exchange rate, and it will devalue the currency. In 1967, for instance, the British devalued the pound from $2.80 per pound to $2.40 per pound. That meant it became cheaper for Americans and other foreigners to buy British pounds, and the devaluation thus affected the balance of payments by making British goods relatively cheaper.

Since 1979, several European countries have tried to keep their mutual exchange rates constant through the *European exchange rate mechanism* (ERM). In 1999 the European Union intends to go even further, by replacing national currencies among countries joining the *European Monetary Union (EMU)* with a single European currency, the *Euro*. This is a highly controversial and historically important change, and it has been the dominant economic issue in European countries which are candidates for joining the EMU. (Both the ERM and the EMU are discussed in greater detail in Box 12-1.)

FLEXIBLE EXCHANGE RATES

Under fixed exchange rates, the central banks have to provide whatever amounts of foreign currency are needed to finance payments imbalances. In a *flexible exchange rate system,* by contrast, the central banks allow the exchange rate to adjust to equate the supply and demand for foreign currency. If the exchange rate of the dollar against the deutsche mark were 65 cents per mark and German exports to the United States increased, thus increasing the demand for marks by Americans, the Bundesbank could simply stand aside and let the exchange rate adjust. In this particular case, the exchange rate could move from 65 cents per mark to a level such as 67 cents per mark, making German goods more expensive in terms of dollars and thus reducing the demand for them by Americans. Later in this chapter we shall examine the way in which changes in exchange rates under floating rates affect the balance of payments. The terms *flexible rates* and *floating rates* are used interchangeably.

FLOATING, CLEAN AND DIRTY

In a system of *clean floating,* central banks stand aside completely and allow exchange rates to be freely determined in the foreign exchange markets. Since the central banks do not intervene in the foreign exchange markets in such a system, official reserve transactions are, accordingly, zero. That means the balance of payments is zero in a system of clean floating: the exchange rate adjusts to make the current and capital accounts sum to zero.

BOX 12-1 The ERM and the EMU

Beginning in 1979, several European countries, including Germany, France, and Italy, pledged to keep their mutual exchange rates essentially fixed within the *European exchange rate mechanism*, or ERM, for short. (Figure 1 shows exchange rates for the Italian lira and the French franc relative to the German deutsche mark.) The ERM rules allow limited flexibility of exchange rates, within a narrow band around a centrally agreed exchange rate or *parity*. For example, the Italian lira was originally allowed a 6 percent band around its parity; in 1990 the band was narrowed to 2.5 percent.

By 1992 the ERM system had broken into pieces: Britain, Spain, and Italy dropped out. For those remaining, notably the core members Germany and France, *target-zone* margins were widened to a large 15 percent on either side of the central parity. The ERM is now becoming a transition mechanism, on the way to full-fledged monetary union in Europe.*

The *Maastricht Treaty* of 1991 set out a blueprint for monetary union—the accession criteria and the institutions to govern the new money. In both respects great care was taken to make sure that the new money would be a good money.

CRITERIA

Partnership in the union requires that a candidate for accession meet several key criteria:

- The candidate's budget deficits have to be below 3 percent of GDP.
- Its public debt to GDP ratio has to be less than 60 percent.
- The country wishing to join must have an inflation rate no higher than 1.5 percent above the average of the three lowest-inflation countries.
- Long-term interest rates (as a measure of inflationary expectations) in the candidate country must not exceed by more than 2 percentage points the rates in, at most, the three best-performing countries in terms of price stability.
- The candidate must not have experienced devaluation of its currency for at least 2 years.

INSTITUTIONS

The treaty established the *European Monetary Institute (EMI)* as a transition institution to prepare the ground for the *European Central Bank (ECB)*. The EMI is already in operation, located in Frankfurt, and is charting the transition, including the nitty-gritty of how the ECB will operate.

Independence of the ECB from national political influence is firmly on the books and beyond tinkering. The governing board cannot seek or accept instructions from national governments. The structure of the ECB is modeled on the Bundesbank. Financing of public sector deficits by the ECB is prohibited; there is an explicit "no-bailout clause" for public

---

*See Peter Kenen (ed.), *Making EMU Happen: Essays in International Finance*, (Princeton, N.J.: Princeton University Press, 1996). See also Daniel Gross and Neils Thygessen, *European Monetary Integration* (London: St. Martin's Press, 1992), and Horst Ungerer et al., *The European Monetary System: Development and Perspectives*, International Monetary Fund Occasional Paper No. 73 (Washington, D.C.: IMF, 1990.)

FIGURE 1   EUROPEAN EXCHANGE RATES: ITALIAN LIRA AND FRENCH FRANC TO GERMAN DEUTSCHE MARK, 1985–1996 (INDEX: 1985 = 100).

debts. The mandate, narrower than that of the Fed or the Bundesbank, is price stability, plain and simple.

The name of the new currency has been chosen: *Euro.*

TIMETABLE

The Maastricht Treaty provides for a stepwise transition to a common money. The key dates on the horizon are the following:

- *Early 1998:* Determine which countries, on the basis of 1997 data, meet the criteria and thus can move on to monetary union. The executive board of the ECB will be appointed.
- *January 1999:* Establish *irrevocably* fixed exchange rates and common monetary policy for the group of EMU countries. National currencies will continue to exist but with fixed rates. Monetary policy will be conducted by the ECB for the member countries from day 1.
- *January 2002* (at the latest): Put Euro notes and coins in circulation and withdraw national currencies. Within 6 months national currencies will lose legal-tender status.

Over the next decade, the transition faces two major issues:

- *The big question:* When a new money is created, how can we be sure that it is a hard money? If not, what happens? If the new money is inflation-prone because it is dominated by political influence rather than an independent central bank with

BOX 12-1 continued

TABLE 1   Who Meets the Maastricht Targets?
(OECD forecasts for 1997)

	DEBT*	DEFICIT*	INFLATION**
Belgium	127.2	2.9	1.9
Denmark	70.4	0.4	2.5
France	56.6	3.2	1.3
Germany	63.2	3.4	1.5
Ireland	76.0	1.1	2.0
Italy	122.9	3.7	2.5
Netherlands	76.0	2.3	2.1
Portugal	67.6	2.9	2.6
Spain	68.9	3.4	2.9
United Kingdom	56.5	3.7	2.5

*As a percent of GDP.

**Percent per year.

Source: *OECD Economic Outlook*, December 1996.

a strong anti-inflation mandate, the currency is bound to weaken in world markets. Thus, whether the Euro will be strong or weak relative to the U.S. dollar is a key issue of the next decade.

- *The problem:* When countries do away with the exchange rate as an adjustment mechanism, what takes its place? Suppose a country's prices have gotten out of line. Wages must do the adjusting, or else there is risk of an increase in unemployment. But Europe has very little flexibility in labor markets, and that is the chief problem of the forthcoming EMU. It is not a problem that is easily remedied, particularly in a context of high unemployment.

    In practice, the flexible rate system, in effect since 1973, has not been one of clean floating. Instead, the system has been one of *managed,* or *dirty, floating.* Under managed floating, central banks intervene to buy and sell foreign currencies in attempts to influence exchange rates. Official reserve transactions are, accordingly, not equal to zero under managed floating. The reasons for central bank intervention under floating rates are discussed in Chapter 21.

TERMINOLOGY

Exchange rate language can be very confusing. In particular, the terms "depreciation" and "appreciation" and "devaluation" and "revaluation" recur in any discussion of international trade and finance. Because the exchange rate is the price of one currency in terms of another, it can be quoted two ways, for example, either 1.50 deutsche marks per dollar or 67 cents per deutsche mark. The foreign exchange markets generally settle on one way of quoting each rate. For example, the deutsche mark is typically quoted in deutsche marks per dollar, the British pound in dollars per pound. In

FIGURE 12-1   THE DOLLAR–DEUTSCHE MARK EXCHANGE RATE, 1958–1996.

(Source: DRI/McGraw-Hill Macroeconomic Database.)

academic economics the convention is that the exchange rate is a price in terms of domestic currency. For example, a quote for the dollar–deutsche mark exchange rate is
given in dollars per deutsche mark, say, $0.67 per deutsche mark—just as a pound of
bananas might cost 67 cents. So if the exchange rate falls, the domestic currency is
worth *more*; it costs fewer dollars to buy a unit of the foreign currency.[6]

Figure 12-1 shows the dollar–deutsche mark (DM) exchange rate since 1958. We
use the figure to clarify some points of terminology. The vertical axis shows the exchange rate measured as deutsche marks per U.S. dollar. First note that we show two
subperiods: the fixed rate period, throughout the 1960s and lasting until 1972, and the
flexible rate regime. During the fixed rate period the dollar price of the mark remained
constant for lengthy periods. It was constant, or pegged at a constant level by the
Bundesbank, except for two revaluations, in 1960 and 1970.

A *devaluation* takes place when the price of foreign currencies under a fixed rate
regime is increased by official action. A devaluation thus means that foreigners pay
less for the devalued currency and that residents of the devaluing country pay more for
foreign currencies. The opposite of a devaluation is a *revaluation.*

A change in the price of foreign exchange under flexible exchange rates is referred
to as *currency depreciation* or *appreciation.* A currency *depreciates* when, under floating rates, it becomes less expensive in terms of foreign currencies. For instance, if the

---

[6]Of course, this is only a convention, and in some countries, including Britain, economic theory uses the
other convention (just like driving on the left side of the road).

exchange rate of the pound sterling changes from $1.80 per pound to $1.75 per pound, the pound is depreciating. By contrast, currency *appreciates* when it becomes more expensive in terms of foreign money.

For example, in Figure 12-1 we see that in 1994–1995 the deutsche mark was depreciating, meaning that it took fewer and fewer dollars to buy a mark. By contrast, in 1992–1993 the deutsche mark was appreciating. Although the terms "devaluation/revaluation" and "depreciation/appreciation" are used in fixed and flexible rate regimes, respectively, there is no economic difference. These terms describe the *direction* in which an exchange rate moves.

RECAP

- The balance-of-payments accounts are a record of the transactions of the economy with other economies. The capital account describes transactions in assets, while the current account covers transactions in goods and services, as well as transfers.
- Any payment to foreigners is a deficit item in the balance of payments. Any payment from foreigners is a surplus item. The balance-of-payments deficit (or surplus) is the sum of the deficits (or surpluses) on current and capital accounts.
- Under fixed exchange rates, central banks stand ready to meet all demands for foreign currencies at a fixed price in terms of the domestic currency. They *finance* the excess demands for, or supplies of, foreign currency (i.e., the balance-of-payments deficits or surpluses, respectively) at the pegged (fixed) exchange rate by running down, or adding to, their reserves of foreign currency.
- Under flexible exchange rates, the demands for and supplies of foreign currency are equated through movements in exchange rates. Under clean floating, there is no central bank intervention and the balance of payments is zero. But central banks sometimes intervene in a floating rate system, engaging in so-called dirty floating.

12-2

THE EXCHANGE RATE IN THE LONG RUN

A government or central bank can peg the value of its currency, that is, fix the exchange rate, for a period of time. But in the long run, the exchange rate between a pair of countries is determined by the relative purchasing power of currency within each country. For example, if a hot dog costs 25 Danish kroner (DKr) at a *polsevogn*[7] in Copenhagen and $2.50 from a street vendor in Philadelphia, one might reasonably expect that the dollar–krone exchange rate would be $0.10. This illustrates the theory of *purchasing power parity,* or *PPP.* Two currencies are at purchasing power parity when a unit of domestic currency can buy the same basket of goods at home or abroad. The relative purchasing power of two currencies is measured by the *real exchange rate.*

The real exchange rate is the ratio of foreign to domestic prices, measured in the same currency. It measures a country's competitiveness in international trade. The real exchange rate, *R,* is defined as

[7]"Sausage wagon."

$$R = \frac{eP_f}{P} \qquad (2)$$

where P and P_f are the price levels here and abroad, respectively, and e is the dollar price of foreign exchange. Note that since P_f represents foreign prices, for example, prices measured in Danish kroner, and the exchange rate is measured as so many dollars per Danish kroner, the numerator expresses prices abroad measured in dollars; with the domestic price level, measured in this case in dollars, in the denominator, the real exchange rate expresses prices abroad relative to those at home.

If the real exchange rate equals 1, currencies are at purchasing power parity. A real exchange rate above 1 means that goods abroad are more expensive than goods at home. Other things equal, this implies that people—both at home and abroad—are likely to switch some of their spending to goods produced at home. This is often described as an increase in the competitiveness of our products. As long as R is greater than 1, we expect the relative demand for domestically produced goods to rise. Eventually, this should either drive up domestic prices or drive down the exchange rate, moving us closer to purchasing power parity.

Market forces prevent the exchange rate from moving *too* far from PPP or from remaining away from PPP indefinitely. However, pressures to move to PPP work only slowly. In the mid-1990s, the dollar–krone exchange rate was closer to 18 cents than to 10 cents and the real cost of hot dogs was nearly twice as much in Copenhagen as in Philadelphia. There are several reasons for slow movement toward PPP. The first reason is that market baskets differ across countries. Americans and Danes do not consume the same bundle of goods.[8] The second reason for slow movement toward PPP is that there are many barriers to the movement of goods between countries. Some are natural barriers—transportation costs are one obvious extra cost—while others, tariffs for example, are imposed by governments. Sometimes movement of final goods isn't enough: workers and capital would have to move. It isn't likely that Americans would commute to Denmark to sell hot dogs. Third, and probably of greatest importance, many goods—land is the classic example—are "nontraded" and cannot move.

Figure 12-2 shows the cost of barley in England relative to that in Holland over a *really* long span of time. Barley is a relatively homogenous commodity which is reasonably transportable. You can see in Figure 12-2 that the real barley exchange rate tended toward equalization. But you can also see that there have been long periods of substantial deviation from equality. The best current estimate, for modern times, is that it takes about 4 years to reduce deviations from PPP by half.[9] So while PPP holds in the long run, over a period of months and even years, it is only one of the determinants of the exchange rate.

Since both P_f and P in the formula for the real exchange rate represent baskets of goods specific to each country, PPP does not necessarily imply that the real exchange

---

[8]Hot dogs in Copenhagen are served on high-quality rolls—what Americans would call "French bread." Franks in Philadelphia are served on soft white buns, which Americans think of as the proper container for a hot dog but which most Danes wouldn't appreciate. Contrariwise, Danish *polse* are served with mayonnaise instead of with mustard and sauerkraut as in Philadelphia.

[9]J. Frankel and A. Rose, "A Panel Project on Purchasing Power Parity," *Journal of International Economics,* February 1996.

FIGURE 12-2 LOG RELATIVE ENGLISH TO DUTCH BARLEY PRICES, 1367–1985.

Price is silver price. (Source: Kenneth A. Froot, Michael Kim, and Kenneth Rogoff, "The Law of One Price over 700 Years," NBER Working Paper 5132, 1996.)

rate should be equal to 1. Rather, in practice, PPP is taken to mean that in the long run the real exchange rate will return to its average level. (This is sometimes called *relative PPP.*) Thus, if the real exchange rate is above its long-run average level, PPP implies that the exchange rate will fall.

12-3

TRADE IN GOODS, MARKET EQUILIBRIUM, AND THE BALANCE OF TRADE

With the basic concepts of international trade and finance in hand, we can now study the effects of trade in goods on the level of income and the effects of various disturbances on both income and the trade balance—which, in this section, we use as shorthand for the current account. We do not include the capital account at this stage, so for the present the current account and the balance of payments are the same.

In this section we fit foreign trade into the *IS-LM* framework. We assume that the price level is given and that the output demanded will be supplied. It is both conceptually and technically easy to relax the fixed-price assumption, and we shall do so in Chapter 21. But because it is important to be clear on how the introduction of trade modifies the analysis of aggregate demand, we start from the familiar and basic level of the *IS-LM* model.

DOMESTIC SPENDING AND SPENDING ON DOMESTIC GOODS

In an open economy, part of domestic output is sold to foreigners (exports) and part of spending by domestic residents purchases foreign goods (imports). We have to modify the *IS* curve accordingly.

The most important change is that domestic spending no longer determines domestic output. Instead, *spending on domestic goods* determines domestic output. Some spending by domestic residents is on imports, for instance, purchases of imported beer. Demand for domestic goods, by contrast, includes exports or foreign demand along with part of spending by domestic residents.

The effect of external transactions on the demand for domestic output was examined in Chapter 2. Define A to be spending *by* domestic residents; then:

$$\text{Spending by domestic residents} = A = C + I + G \tag{3}$$

$$\text{Spending on domestic goods} = A + NX = (C + I + G) + (X - Q)$$
$$= (C + I + G) + NX \tag{4}$$

where X is the level of exports, Q is imports, and $NX \equiv X - Q$ is the trade (goods and services) surplus. Spending on domestic goods is total spending by domestic residents less their spending on imports *plus* foreign demand or exports. Since exports minus imports is the trade surplus, or net exports (NX), spending on domestic goods is spending by domestic residents plus the trade surplus.

With this clarification we can return to our model of income determination. We will assume that domestic spending depends on the interest rate and income, so

$$A = A(Y,i) \tag{5}$$

NET EXPORTS

Net exports, or the excess of exports over imports, depend on our income, which affects import spending; on foreign income, Y_f, which affects foreign demand for our exports; and on the real exchange rate, R. A rise in R or a real depreciation improves our trade balance as demand shifts from goods produced abroad to those produced at home:[10]

$$NX = X(Y_f, R) - Q(Y, R) = NX(Y, Y_f, R) \tag{6}$$

We can immediately state three important results:

- A rise in foreign income, other things being equal, improves the home country's trade balance and therefore raises aggregate demand.
- A real depreciation by the home country improves the trade balance and therefore increases aggregate demand.
- A rise in home income raises import spending and hence worsens the trade balance.

[10]Note two points about net exports in equation (6). First, we measure net exports in terms of domestic output. To do so, we must measure imports (Q) in terms of their value in our currency. Second, we *assume* that a real appreciation worsens the trade balance and a real depreciation (a rise in R) improves the trade balance. This is a matter of assumption since there are opposing effects of changes in volume and in price. We return to this point in Chap. 21.

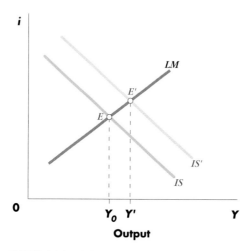

FIGURE 12-3   THE EFFECT OF A RISE IN FOREIGN INCOME.

GOODS MARKET EQUILIBRIUM

The increase in import demand caused by a $1 increase in income is called the *marginal propensity to import*. The marginal propensity to import measures the fraction of an extra dollar of income spent on imports. The fact that part of income will be spent on imports (rather than on domestic goods) implies that the *IS* curve will be steeper than it would be in a closed economy. For a given reduction in interest rates it takes a smaller increase in output and income to restore goods market equilibrium.

The open economy *IS* curve includes net exports as a component of aggregate demand. Therefore, the level of competitiveness, as measured by the real exchange rate *R,* affects the *IS* curve. A real depreciation increases the demand for domestic goods, shifting the *IS* curve out and to the right. Likewise, an increase in foreign income and, with it, an increase in foreign spending on our goods will increase net exports or demand for our goods. Thus we have

$$IS \text{ curve:} \quad Y = A(Y, i) + NX(Y, Y_f, R) \tag{7}$$

Since the equilibrium level of income will now depend on both foreign income and the real exchange rate, we have to ask how disturbances in foreign income, or real exchange rate changes, affect the equilibrium level of income.

Figure 12-3 shows the effect of a rise in foreign income. The higher foreign spending on our goods raises demand and hence, at unchanged interest rates, requires an increase in output. This is shown by the rightward shift of the *IS* schedule. The full

TABLE 12-2   Effects of Disturbance on Income and Net Exports

	INCREASE IN HOME SPENDING	INCREASE IN FOREIGN INCOME	REAL DEPRECIATION
Income	+	+	+
Net exports	−	+	+

TABLE 12-3 Effects of a 10 Percent Dollar Depreciation

IMPACT ON	YEAR 1	YEAR 2
Real GDP, %	0.5	0.6
CPI, %	0.4	1.3
Current account, ($ billions)	15	38

Source: Federal Reserve, unpublished model-based simulation.

effect of an increase in foreign demand thus is an increase in interest rates and an increase in domestic output and employment. It is easy to go through the opposite change. A weakening of foreign economies reduces their imports and hence pulls down domestic demand. Equilibrium income at home would fall as would our interest rates.

Figure 12-3 can also help explain the effect of a real depreciation. As we saw, a real depreciation raises net exports at each level of income and hence shifts the *IS* schedule up and to the right. A real depreciation therefore leads to a rise in our equilibrium income.

Table 12-2 summarizes the effects of different disturbances on the equilibrium levels of income and net exports. Each of these examples can be worked out using the *IS* schedule in conjunction with the net export schedule.

REPERCUSSION EFFECTS

In an interdependent world, our policy changes affect other countries as well as ourselves, and then feed back on our economy. When we increase government spending, our income rises; part of the increase in income will be spent on imports, which means that income will rise abroad, too. The increase in foreign income will then raise foreign demand for our goods, which in turn adds to the domestic income expansion brought about by higher government spending, and so on.

These *repercussion effects* can be important in practice. When the United States expands, it tends, like a locomotive, to pull the rest of the world into an expansion. Likewise, if the rest of the world expands, we share in the expansion.

Repercussion effects also arise in response to exchange rate changes. In Table 12-3 we show empirical estimates of the impact of changes in real exchange rates on U.S. real GDP. The table reports the effect of a 10 percent dollar depreciation against all other currencies. The U.S. level of output expands strongly; abroad, by contrast, real GDP falls. The reason is that the increase in U.S. net exports raises income at home while lowering demand and output abroad.

Note that whereas an expansionary fiscal policy increases both our GDP and that of other countries, a depreciation of our exchange rate increases our income while reducing foreign incomes.

12-4

CAPITAL MOBILITY

One of the striking facts about the international economy is the high degree of integration, or linkage, among financial, or capital, markets—the markets in which bonds and stocks are traded. In most industrial countries today there are no restrictions on holding assets abroad. U.S. residents, or residents in Germany or the United Kingdom, can hold their wealth either at home or abroad. They therefore search around the world for the highest return (adjusted for risk), thereby linking together yields in capital markets in different countries. For example, if rates in New York rose relative to those in Canada, investors would turn to lending in New York, while borrowers would turn to Toronto. With lending up in New York and borrowing up in Toronto, yields would quickly fall into line.

In the simplest world, in which exchange rates are fixed forever, taxes are the same everywhere, and foreign asset holders never face political risks (nationalization, restrictions on transfer of assets, default risk by foreign governments), we would expect all asset holders to pick the asset that has the highest return. That would force asset returns into strict equality everywhere in the world capital markets because no country could borrow for less.

In reality, though, none of these three conditions exists. There are tax differences among countries; exchange rates can change, perhaps significantly, and thus affect the payoff in dollars of a foreign investment; and, finally, countries sometimes put up obstacles to capital outflows or simply find themselves unable to pay. These are some of the reasons that interest rates are not equal across countries.

However, interest rate differentials among major industrialized countries, adjusted to eliminate the risk of exchange rate changes, are quite small in practice. Consider the case of the United States and Canada. Once interest rates are measured on a "covered" basis, so that the exchange risk is eliminated, they should be exactly the same.[11] In fact the differential is very small, averaging less than .5 percent, a result primarily of tax differences. We take this evidence to support the view that capital is very highly mobile across borders, as we assume henceforth.

Our working assumption from now on is that capital is *perfectly mobile.* Capital is perfectly mobile internationally when investors can purchase assets in any country they choose, quickly, with low transaction costs, and in unlimited amounts. When capital is perfectly mobile, asset holders are willing and able to move large amounts of funds across borders in search of the highest return or lowest borrowing cost.

The high degree of capital market integration implies that any one country's interest rates cannot get too far out of line without bringing about capital flows that tend to restore yields to the world level. To return to the previous example, if Canadian yields fell relative to U.S. yields, there would be a capital outflow from Canada because lenders would take their funds out of Canada and borrowers would try to raise funds in Canada. From the point of view of the balance of payments, this implies that a relative decline in interest rates—a decline in our rates relative to those abroad—will tend to worsen the balance of payments because of the capital outflow resulting from lending abroad by U.S. residents.

The recognition that interest rates affect capital flows and the balance of payments has important implications for stabilization policy. First, because monetary and fiscal

---

[11]Cover, or protection, against the risk of exchange rate changes can be obtained by buying a futures contract, which promises (of course, at a cost) to pay a given amount of one currency in exchange for a specified amount of another currency at a given future date. There are, in practice, simpler ways of obtaining foreign exchange risk cover, but the essential mechanism is the same.

policies affect interest rates, the policies have an effect on the capital account and therefore on the balance of payments. The effects of monetary and fiscal policies on the balance of payments are *not* limited to the trade balance effects discussed above but extend to the capital account. The second implication is that the way in which monetary and fiscal policies work in affecting the domestic economy and the balance of payments changes when there are international capital flows.

THE BALANCE OF PAYMENTS AND CAPITAL FLOWS

We introduce the role of capital flows within a framework in which we assume that the home country faces a given price of imports and a given export demand. In addition, we assume that the world rate of interest, i_f (i.e., the rate of interest in foreign capital markets), is given. Moreover, with perfect capital mobility, capital flows into the home country at an unlimited[12] rate if our interest rate is above that abroad (from now on, until further notice, we assume that exchange risk is absent). Conversely, if our rate is below that abroad, capital outflows will be unlimited.

Next we look at the balance of payments. The balance-of-payments surplus, *BP*, is equal to the trade surplus, *NX*, plus the capital account surplus, *CF*:

$$BP = NX(Y, Y_f, R) + CF(i - i_f) \tag{8}$$

Equation (8) shows the trade balance as a function of domestic and foreign income and the real exchange rate, and it shows the capital account as depending on the *interest differential.*[13] An increase in income worsens the trade balance, and an increase in the interest rate above the world level pulls in capital from abroad and thus improves the capital account. It follows that when income increases, even the tiniest increase in interest rates is enough to maintain an overall balance-of-payments equilibrium. The trade deficit would be financed by a capital inflow.

POLICY DILEMMAS: INTERNAL AND EXTERNAL BALANCE

The potential for capital flows to finance a current account deficit is extremely important. Countries frequently face policy dilemmas, in which a policy designed to deal with one problem worsens another problem. In particular, there is sometimes a conflict between the goals of external and internal balance.

External balance exists when the balance of payments is close to balance. Otherwise, the central bank is either losing reserves—which it cannot keep on doing—or gaining reserves—which it does not want to do forever.[14] *Internal balance* exists when output is at the full-employment level.

---

[12]"Unlimited" is a very strong word. Capital flows are very large compared to the American economy, so the Fed needs to watch them carefully when changing interest rates. For other countries, capital flows can be so large in comparison to their economy that the word "unlimited" really is appropriate.

[13]When capital mobility is perfect, the domestic and foreign interest rates cannot get out of line, so in equilibrium we will find that $i = i_f$; however, we write the capital flows equation with i potentially not equal to i_f in order to demonstrate the forces at work—including potentially massive capital flows—that produce equilibrium.

[14]However, some governments (e.g., Taiwan) do seem to want to have very large current account surpluses in order to be able to run capital account deficits that allow them to buy large amounts of foreign assets.

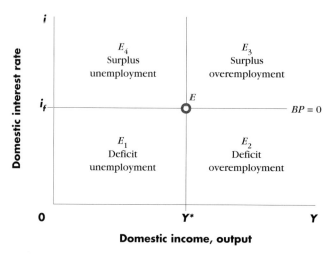

FIGURE 12-4   INTERNAL AND EXTERNAL BALANCE UNDER FIXED EXCHANGE RATES.

In Figure 12-4 we show the schedule $BP = 0$, derived from equation (8), along which we have balance-of-payments equilibrium. Our key assumption—perfect capital mobility—forces the $BP = 0$ line to be horizontal. Only at a level of interest rates equal to that of rates abroad can we have external balance: if domestic interest rates are higher, there is a vast capital account and overall surplus; if they are below foreign rates, there is an unlimited deficit.

Thus $BP = 0$ must be flat at the level of world interest rates. Points above the $BP = 0$ schedule correspond to a surplus, and points below to a deficit. We have also drawn, in Figure 12-4, the full-employment output level, Y^*. Point E is the only point at which both internal balance and external balance are achieved. Point E_1, for example, corresponds to a case of unemployment and a balance-of-payments deficit. Point E_2, by contrast, is a case of deficit and overemployment.

We can talk about policy dilemmas in terms of points in the four quadrants of Figure 12-4. For instance, at point E_1, there is a deficit in the balance of payments, as well as unemployment. An expansionary monetary policy would deal with the unemployment problem but worsen the balance of payments, thus apparently presenting a dilemma for the policy maker. The presence of interest-sensitive capital flows suggests the solution to the dilemma: if the country can find a way of raising the interest rate, it would obtain financing for the trade deficit.

That means that both monetary and fiscal policies would have to be used to achieve external and internal balance simultaneously. Each point in Figure 12-4 can be viewed as an intersection of the *IS* and *LM* curves. Each curve has to be shifted, but how? How the adjustment takes place depends critically on the exchange rate regime.

We are now ready to extend the analysis of output determination to the open economy with perfect capital mobility. In the next section we assume the exchange rate is fixed. In Section 12-6 we consider output determination with flexible exchange rates.

12-5

THE MUNDELL-FLEMING MODEL: PERFECT CAPITAL MOBILITY
UNDER FIXED EXCHANGE RATES

The analysis extending the standard *IS-LM* model to the open economy under perfect capital mobility has a special name, the *Mundell-Fleming model.* Robert Mundell, now a professor at Columbia University, and the late Marcus Fleming, who was a researcher at the International Monetary Fund, developed this analysis in the 1960s, well before flexible exchange rates came into operation.[15] Although later research has refined their analysis, the initial Mundell-Fleming formulation discussed here remains essentially intact as a way of understanding how policies work under high capital mobility.

Under perfect capital mobility the slightest interest differential provokes infinite capital flows. It follows that with perfect capital mobility, central banks cannot conduct an independent monetary policy under fixed exchange rates. To see why, suppose a country wishes to raise interest rates. It tightens monetary policy, and interest rates rise. Immediately, portfolio holders worldwide shift their wealth to take advantage of the new rate. As a result of the huge capital inflow, the balance of payments shows a gigantic surplus; foreigners try to buy domestic assets, tending to cause the exchange rate to appreciate and forcing the central bank to intervene to hold the exchange rate constant. It buys the foreign money, in exchange for domestic money. This intervention causes the home money stock to increase. As a result, the initial monetary contraction is reversed. The process comes to an end when home interest rates have been pushed back down to the initial level.

The conclusion is this: *Under fixed exchange rates and perfect capital mobility, a country cannot pursue an independent monetary policy.[16] Interest rates cannot move out of line with those prevailing in the world market. Any attempt at independent monetary policy leads to capital flows and a need to intervene until interest rates are back in line with those in the world market.*

Table 12-4 shows the steps in the argument. The commitment to a fixed rate involves step 5. With the exchange rate tending to appreciate because foreigners are trying to buy the domestic currency, the central bank has to provide the domestic currency. Just as in an open market operation the central bank buys and sells bonds for money, so in intervention in the foreign exchange market the monetary authority buys and sells foreign money (yen, deutsche marks, or Canadian dollars) for domestic money.

---

[15]Mundell's work on international macroeconomics has been extraordinarily important. The adventurous student should certainly consult his two books: *International Economics* (New York: Macmillan, 1967) and *Monetary Theory* (Pacific Palisades, Calif.: Goodyear, 1971). For more recent discussions, see D. MacDonald and M. Taylor, "Exchange Rate Economics: A Survey," *IMF Staff Papers,* 1992, and Peter Kenen (ed.), *Understanding Interdependence: The Macroeconomics of the Open Economy* (Princeton, N.J.: Princeton University Press, 1995).

[16]"Fixed exchange rates and perfect capital mobility" is a pretty good description of much of the industrialized world from the early 1960s through 1973—except for the United States. The U.S. economy was then so much larger than others that the U.S. was able to conduct a relatively, but not completely, independent monetary policy.

TABLE 12-4 Payments Imbalances, Intervention, and the Money Supply with Fixed Exchange Rates and Perfect Capital Mobility

1 Tightening of money
2 Increased interest rates
3 Capital inflow, payments surplus
4 Pressure for currency appreciation
5 Intervention by selling home money and buying foreign money
6 Monetary expansion due to intervention lowers interest rate
7 Back to initial interest rates, money stock, and payments balance

Thus the money supply is linked to the balance of payments. Surpluses imply *automatic* monetary expansion; deficits imply monetary contraction.

MONETARY EXPANSION

It is worthwhile looking at this point in terms of the open economy *IS-LM* model. In Figure 12-5 we show the *IS* and *LM* schedules as well as the *BP* = 0 schedule, which now, because of perfect capital mobility, is a horizontal line. Only at a level of interest rates equal to those abroad, $i = i_f$, can the country have payments balance. At any other interest rate, capital flows are so massive that the balance of payments cannot be in equilibrium, and the central bank has to intervene to maintain the exchange rate. This intervention shifts the *LM* schedule.

Consider specifically a monetary expansion that starts from point *E*. The *LM* schedule shifts down and to the right, and the economy moves to point *E'*. But at *E'* there is a large payments deficit and hence pressure for the exchange rate to depreciate. The central bank must intervene, selling foreign money and receiving domestic money in exchange. The supply of domestic money therefore declines. As a result, the *LM* schedule shifts back up and to the left. The process continues until the initial equilibrium at *E* is restored.

Indeed, with perfect capital mobility the economy never even gets to point *E'*. The response of capital flows is so large and rapid that the central bank is forced to reverse the initial expansion of the money stock as soon as it attempts it. Conversely, any attempt to contract the money stock would immediately lead to vast reserve losses, forcing an expansion of the money stock and a return to the initial equilibrium.

FISCAL EXPANSION

While monetary policy is essentially infeasible, fiscal expansion under fixed exchange rates with perfect capital mobility is, by contrast, extremely effective. We describe the effects in terms of the *IS-LM* model, but we do not draw the diagram, leaving that for one of the end-of-chapter problems.

With the money supply initially unchanged, a fiscal expansion moves the *IS* curve up and to the right, tending to increase both the interest rate and the level of output. The higher interest rate sets off a capital inflow that would lead the exchange rate to appreciate. To maintain the exchange rate, the central bank *has* to expand the money supply, thus increasing income further. Equilibrium is restored when the money supply has increased enough to drive the interest rate back to its original level, $i = i_f$. In this

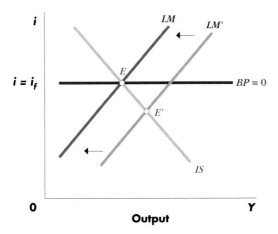

FIGURE 12-5 MONETARY EXPANSION UNDER FIXED RATES AND PERFECT CAPITAL MOBILITY.

case, with an endogenous money supply, the interest rate is effectively fixed, and the simple Keynesian multiplier of Chapter 9 applies for a fiscal expansion.

THE ENDOGENOUS MONEY STOCK

Although the assumption of perfect capital mobility is extreme, it is a useful benchmark case that in the end is not too far from reality for many countries. The essential point is that *the commitment to maintain a fixed exchange rate makes the money stock endogenous* because the central bank has to provide the foreign exchange or domestic money that is demanded at the fixed exchange rate. Thus, even when capital mobility is less than perfect, the central bank has only limited ability to change the money supply without having to worry about maintaining the exchange rate.

Box 12-2 describes the effects of the fiscal expansion set off by German unification, and the consequences for Germany's neighbors whose exchange rates were fixed against the deutsche mark.

12-6

PERFECT CAPITAL MOBILITY AND FLEXIBLE EXCHANGE RATES

In this section we use the Mundell-Fleming model to explore how monetary and fiscal policy works in an economy that has fully flexible exchange rates and perfect capital mobility. We assume here that domestic prices are fixed, even though the exchange rate is flexible. In Chapter 21 we examine how flexible exchange rates work when domestic prices are flexible.[17]

---

[17]The reason it is not misleading to examine the behavior of a system with flexible exchange rates and fixed domestic prices is that, in practice, exchange rates change much more quickly than do prices in most industrialized countries. The analysis of this section would not apply in cases in which the nominal exchange rate changes and domestic prices rise in the same proportion, so the real exchange rate is unchanged.

BOX 12-2   German Unification and External Problems

In fall 1989, the Berlin Wall came down and soon the unification of West and East Germany was under way. The West German government began transferring large amounts of resources to East Germany. The fiscal program included massive investment in East Germany's infrastructure, investment in industry, and an extensive income support program for the unemployed and for those working in loss-making firms.

The large fiscal expansion helped moderate the economic collapse in East Germany. But it came at the expense of a massive budget deficit. The expansionary fiscal policy brought with it a deterioration of the current account, higher interest rates, and an appreciation of the deutsche mark, as the Mundell-Fleming model predicts.

While Germany had been a net lender in world markets, starting in 1991 there was a deficit in the current account. German resources were being redirected from supplying the world market to reconstructing East Germany.

The German fiscal expansion had undesirable side effects on Germany's European trading partners, with whom Germany has a fixed exchange rate. In West Germany the economy overheated since demand from the East fell mostly on West German goods. In response to the overheating, the Bundesbank tightened monetary policy, raising interest rates sharply.

Countries like France or Italy in principle faced the choice of devaluing within the European monetary system or allowing their interest rates to increase along with German interest rates. Because they valued stable exchange rates, they defended their currencies by raising interest rates to match those in Germany. Without the benefit of a fiscal expansion, as had occurred in Germany, their economies slowed down sharply. Germany's trading partners kept urging the Bundesbank to cut interest rates, but the Bundesbank argued that it had to keep on fighting inflation. The episode makes the point that fixed exchange rates are hard to maintain when countries' policies go in opposite directions or when they face disturbances that are not the same for everyone.

TABLE 1   German Unification
(Percent of GNP)

	1989	1990	1991	1992
Current account	4.8	3.3	−1.1	−1.1
Budget deficit	−.1	2.1	3.3	2.8
Interest rate	7.1	8.5	9.2	9.5

Source: OECD, *Economic Outlook*, December 1995.

Under fully flexible exchange rates the central bank does not intervene in the market for foreign exchange. The exchange rate must adjust to clear the market so that the demand for and supply of foreign exchange balance. Without central bank intervention, therefore, the balance of payments must be equal to zero.

Under fully flexible exchange rates the absence of intervention implies a zero balance of payments. Any current account deficit must be financed by private capital inflows: a current account surplus is balanced by capital outflows. Adjustments in the exchange rate ensure that the sum of the current and capital accounts is zero.

A second implication of fully flexible exchange rates is that the central bank can set the money supply at will. Since there is no obligation to intervene, there is no longer any link between the balance of payments and the money supply.

Perfect capital mobility implies that there is only one interest rate at which the balance of payments will balance:[18]

$$i = i_f \tag{9}$$

At any other interest rate, capital flows are so large that the balance of payments cannot be zero. We show this in Figure 12-6 by the line $i = i_f$.

From equation (7) we know that the real exchange rate is a determinant of aggregate demand and, therefore, that changes in the real exchange rate shift the IS schedule. Given prices P and P_f, a depreciation makes the home country more competitive, improves net exports, and hence shifts the IS schedule to the right. Conversely, a real appreciation means our goods become relatively more expensive; hence the trade

---

[18]Equation (9) assumes that investors do not expect the exchange rate to change. Otherwise, nominal interest rates differ among countries by an amount that reflects expected changes in the exchange rate, in a way to be described in Chap. 21.

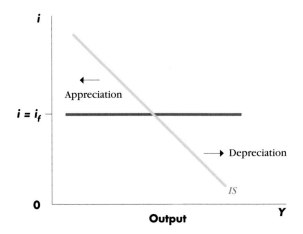

FIGURE 12-6 THE EFFECT OF EXCHANGE RATES ON AGGREGATE DEMAND.

balance worsens and demand for domestic goods declines, so the *IS* schedule shifts to the left.

The arrows in Figure 12-6 link the movement of aggregate demand to the interest rate. If the home interest rate were higher than i_f, capital inflows would cause currency appreciation. At any point above the $i = i_f$ schedule, the exchange rate is appreciating, our goods are becoming relatively more expensive, and aggregate demand is falling. Thus the *IS* schedule will be shifting to the left. Conversely, any point below the $i = i_f$ schedule corresponds to depreciation, improving competitiveness, and increasing aggregate demand. The *IS* schedule will therefore be shifting to the right. We now see how various disturbances affect output and the exchange rate.

ADJUSTMENT TO A REAL DISTURBANCE

Using our model, represented by equations (7), (8), and (9), we want to know how various changes affect the level of output, the interest rate, and the exchange rate. The first change we look at is an exogenous rise in the world demand for our goods, or an increase in exports.

Starting from an initial equilibrium at point E in Figure 12-7, we see that the increase in foreign demand implies an excess demand for our goods. At the initial interest rate, exchange rate, and output level, demand for our goods now exceeds the available supply. For goods market equilibrium at the initial interest rate and exchange rate, we require a higher level of output. Accordingly, the *IS* schedule shifts out and to the right, to *IS'*.

Now consider for a moment point E', at which the goods and money markets clear. Here output has increased to meet the increased demand. The rise in income has increased money demand and thus raised equilibrium interest rates. But point E' is not an equilibrium, because the balance of payments is not in equilibrium. In fact, we would

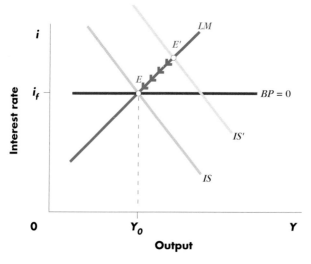

FIGURE 12-7   EFFECTS OF AN INCREASE IN THE DEMAND FOR EXPORTS.

not reach point E' at all. The tendency for the economy to move in that direction, as we now show, will bring about an exchange rate appreciation that will take us all the way back to the initial equilibrium at E.

THE ADJUSTMENT PROCESS

Suppose, then, that the increase in foreign demand takes place and that, in response, there is a tendency for output and income to increase. The induced increase in money demand will raise interest rates and thus bring us out of line with international interest rates. The resulting capital inflows immediately put pressure on the exchange rate. The capital inflows cause our currency to appreciate.

The exchange appreciation means, of course, that import prices fall and domestic goods become relatively more expensive. Demand shifts away from domestic goods, and net exports decline. In terms of Figure 12-7, the appreciation implies that the IS schedule shifts back from IS' to the left. Next, we have to ask how far the exchange appreciation will go and to what extent it will dampen the expansionary effect of increased net exports.

The exchange rate will keep appreciating as long as our interest rate exceeds the world level. This implies that the exchange appreciation must continue until the IS schedule has shifted back all the way to its initial position. This adjustment is shown by the arrows along the LM schedule. Only when we return to point E will output and income have reached a level consistent with monetary equilibrium at the world rate of interest.

We have now shown that under conditions of perfect capital mobility, an expansion in exports has no lasting effect on equilibrium output. With perfect capital mobility the tendency for interest rates to rise, as a result of the increase in export demand, leads to currency appreciation and thus to a complete offset of the increase in exports. Once we return to point E, net exports are back to their initial level. The exchange rate has, of course, appreciated. Imports will increase as a consequence of the appreciation, and the initial expansion in exports is, in part, offset by the appreciation of our exchange rate.

FISCAL POLICY

We can extend the usefulness of this analysis by recognizing that it is valid for disturbances other than an increase in exports. The same analysis applies to a fiscal expansion. A tax cut or an increase in government spending would lead to an expansion in demand in the same way as does increased exports. Again, the tendency for interest rates to rise leads to appreciation and therefore to a fall in exports and increased imports. There is, accordingly, complete crowding out. The crowding out takes place not, as in Chapter 11, because higher interest rates reduce investment but because the exchange appreciation reduces net exports.

The important lesson here is that real disturbances to demand do not affect equilibrium output under flexible rates with perfect capital mobility. We can drive the lesson home by comparing a fiscal expansion under flexible rates with the results we derived for the fixed rate case. In the previous section, we showed that with a fixed exchange rate, fiscal expansion under conditions of capital mobility is highly effective

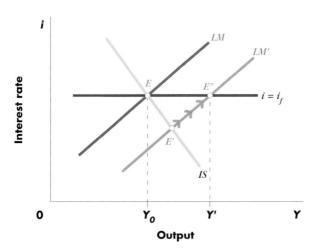

FIGURE 12-8   EFFECTS OF AN INCREASE IN THE MONEY STOCK.

in raising equilibrium output. For flexible rates, by contrast, a fiscal expansion does not change equilibrium output. Instead, it produces an offsetting exchange rate appreciation and a shift in the composition of domestic demand toward foreign goods and away from domestic goods.

This analysis helps in understanding developments in the U.S. economy in the early 1980s, when a fiscal expansion was accompanied by a current account deficit.

ADJUSTMENT TO A CHANGE IN THE MONEY STOCK

We now analyze a change in the money stock and show that it leads, under flexible exchange rates, to an increase in income and a depreciation of the exchange rate. Using Figure 12-8, we start from an initial position at point E and consider an increase in the nominal quantity of money, $\overline{M}$. Since prices are given, we have an increase in the real money stock, $\overline{M}/P$. At E there will be an excess supply of real balances. To restore equilibrium, interest rates would have to be lower or income would have to be larger. Accordingly, the LM schedule shifts down and to the right to LM'.

We ask once again whether the economy is in equilibrium at point E'. At E', the goods and money markets are in equilibrium (at the initial exchange rate), but interest rates have fallen below the world level. Capital outflows therefore put pressure on the exchange rate, leading to a depreciation. The exchange depreciation caused by the capital outflows leads import prices to increase, domestic goods become more competitive, and the demand for our output expands. The IS curve shifts out and to the right, and it continues doing so until exchange depreciation has raised demand and output to the level indicated by point E''. Only at E'' do we have goods market and money market equilibrium compatible with the world rate of interest. Consequently, there is no further tendency for exchange rates and relative prices, and hence demand, to change.[19]

---

[19]In the problem set at the end of this chapter we ask you to show that the current account improves between E' and E'', even though the increased level of income increases imports.

TABLE 12-5   Effects of U.S. Policy Actions
(Percent increase in GNP)

	FISCAL EXPANSION*	MONETARY EXPANSION†
United States	2.7	5.3
Japan	.4	−.6
Germany	.5	−.8

*A 5 percent of GNP increase in government spending.

†A 10 percent increase in the money supply target.

Source: Paul Masson et al., "Multimod Mark II: A Revised and Extended Model," IMF Occasional Paper 71, 1990, tables 9 and 10.

We have now shown that a monetary expansion leads to an increase in output and a depreciation of the exchange rate under flexible rates. One way of thinking about this result is that with $\bar{P}$ fixed, an increase in $\bar{M}$ increases $\bar{M}/\bar{P}$. The demand for real balances (L) is, from Chapter 10, equal to $L(i, Y)$. Since i cannot differ from the world rate of interest, Y has to rise to equate the demand for money to the supply. The exchange depreciation raises net exports, and the increase in net exports, in turn, sustains the higher level of output and employment. One interesting implication of our analysis, then, is the proposition that monetary expansion improves the current account through the induced depreciation.

How do our results compare with those in a fixed exchange rate world? Under fixed rates, the monetary authorities cannot control the nominal money stock, and an attempt to expand money will merely lead to reserve losses and a reversal of the increase in the money stock. Under flexible rates, by contrast, the central bank does not intervene, and so the money stock increase is *not* reversed in the foreign exchange market. The depreciation and expansion in output actually do take place, given the assumed fixed prices. The fact that the central bank *can* control the money stock under flexible rates is a key aspect of that exchange rate system.

Table 12-5 shows estimates of the quantitative impact of U.S. fiscal and monetary expansions on GNP in the United States and abroad, under flexible exchange rates. The table reports the percentage change in GNP over the first 2 years (on average) in response to two experiments. One is a sustained increase in government spending equal to 5 percent of GNP. The other is a monetary expansion of 10 percent. Note that, as expected, U.S. GNP expands in each case (although the estimated fiscal policy multiplier is relatively small). In line with our model, a U.S. fiscal expansion raises foreign output. By contrast, a U.S. monetary expansion reduces output abroad. The reason is that the dollar depreciates and that makes the rest of the world less competitive.

BEGGAR-THY-NEIGHBOR POLICY AND COMPETITIVE DEPRECIATION

We have shown that a monetary expansion in the home country leads to exchange depreciation, an increase in net exports, and therefore an increase in output and employment. But our increased net exports correspond to a deterioration in the trade balance abroad. The domestic depreciation shifts demand from foreign goods toward domestic goods. Abroad, output and employment decline. It is for this reason that a depreciation-induced change in the trade balance has been called a *beggar-thy-neigh-bor policy*—it is a way of exporting unemployment or of creating domestic employment at the expense of the rest of the world.

Recognition that exchange depreciation is mainly a way of shifting demand from one country to another, rather than changing the level of world demand, is important. It implies that exchange rate adjustment can be a useful policy when countries find themselves in different stages of the business cycle—for example, one in a boom (with overemployment) and the other in a recession. In that event, a depreciation by the country experiencing a recession would shift world demand in its direction and thus work to reduce divergence from full employment in each country.

By contrast, when countries' business cycles are highly synchronized, such as in the 1930s or in the aftermath of the oil shock of 1973, exchange rate movements will not contribute much toward worldwide full employment. If total world demand is at the wrong level, exchange rate movements do not correct the level of aggregate demand but essentially affect only the allocation of a *given* world demand among countries.

Similarly, exchange rate changes within a group of countries experiencing similar shocks can only move demand among them and have a beggar-thy-neighbor quality. This is one of the reasons Europeans are moving toward monetary union.

Nevertheless, from the point of view of an individual country, exchange depreciation works to attract world demand and raise domestic output. If every country tried to depreciate to attract world demand, we would have *competitive depreciation* and a shifting around of world demand rather than an increase in the worldwide level of spending. And if everyone depreciated to roughly the same extent, we would end up with exchange rates about where they started. Coordinated monetary and/or fiscal policies rather than depreciations are needed to increase demand and output in each country when worldwide aggregate demand is at the wrong level.

SUMMARY

1. The balance-of-payments accounts are a record of the international transactions of the economy. The current account records trade in goods and services as well as transfer payments. The capital account records purchases and sales of assets. Any transaction that gives rise to a payment by a U.S. resident is a deficit item for the United States.

2. The overall balance-of-payments surplus is the sum of the current and capital accounts surpluses. If the overall balance is in deficit, we have to make more payments to foreigners than they make to us. The foreign currency for making these payments is supplied by central banks.

3. Under fixed exchange rates, the central bank holds constant the price of foreign currencies in terms of the domestic currency. It does this by buying and selling foreign exchange at the fixed exchange rate. It has to keep reserves of foreign currency for that purpose.

4. Under floating, or flexible, exchange rates, the exchange rate may change from moment to moment. In a system of clean floating, the exchange rate is determined by supply and demand without central bank intervention. Under dirty floating, the central bank intervenes by buying and selling foreign exchange in an attempt to influence the exchange rate.

TABLE 12-6 Effects of Monetary and Fiscal Policy Under Perfect Capital Mobility

POLICY	FIXED EXCHANGE RATES	FLEXIBLE EXCHANGE RATES
Monetary expansion	No output change; reserve losses equal to money increase	Output expansion; trade balance improves; exchange depreciation
Fiscal expansion	Output expansion; trade balance worsens	No output change; reduced net exports; exchange appreciation

5. The introduction of trade in goods means that some of the demand for our output comes from abroad and that some spending by our residents is on foreign goods. The demand for our goods depends on the real exchange rate as well as on the levels of income at home and abroad. A real depreciation or increase in foreign income increases net exports and shifts the *IS* curve out to the right. There is equilibrium in the goods market when the demand for domestically produced goods is equal to the output of those goods.

6. The introduction of capital flows points to the effects of monetary and fiscal policy on the balance of payments through interest rate effects on capital flows. An increase in the domestic interest rate relative to the world interest rate leads to a capital inflow that can finance a current account deficit.

7. When capital mobility is perfect, interest rates in the home country cannot diverge from those abroad. This has major implications for the effects of monetary and fiscal policy under fixed and floating exchange rates. These effects are summarized in Table 12-6.

8. Under fixed exchange rates and perfect capital mobility, monetary policy is powerless to affect output. Any attempt to reduce the domestic interest rate by increasing the money stock would lead to a huge outflow of capital, tending to cause a depreciation which the central bank would then have to offset by buying domestic money in exchange for foreign money. This reduces the domestic money stock until it returns to its original level. Under fixed exchange rates with capital mobility, the central bank cannot run an independent monetary policy.

9. Fiscal policy is highly effective under fixed exchange rates with complete capital mobility. A fiscal expansion tends to raise the interest rate, thereby leading the central bank to increase the money stock to keep the exchange rate constant, reinforcing the expansionary fiscal effect.

10. Under floating rates, monetary policy is highly effective and fiscal policy is ineffective in changing output. A monetary expansion leads to depreciation, increased exports, and increased output. Fiscal expansion, however, causes an appreciation and completely crowds out net exports.

11. If an economy with floating rates finds itself with unemployment, the central bank can intervene to depreciate the exchange rate and increase net exports and thus aggregate demand. Such policies are known as beggar-thy-neighbor policies because the increase in demand for domestic output comes at the expense of demand for foreign output.

KEY TERMS

globalization	intervention	purchasing power parity
open economy	European exchange rate	(PPP)
trade	mechanism (ERM)	real exchange rate
finance	European Monetary Union	marginal propensity to
balance of payments	(EMU)	import
current account	target zone	repercussion effects
net investment income	flexible (floating) exchange	perfect capital mobility
trade balance	rate	interest differential
capital account	clean floating	external balance
balance-of-payments	managed (dirty) floating	internal balance
surplus	devaluation/revaluation	Mundell-Fleming model
fixed exchange rate system	currency depreciation	beggar-thy-neighbor policy
reserves	currency appreciation	competitive depreciation

PROBLEMS

Conceptual

1. It is sometimes said that a central bank is a necessary element for a balance-of-payments deficit. What is the explanation for this argument?

*2. Consider a country that is in a position of full employment and balanced trade. The exchange rate is fixed, and capital is not mobile. Which of the following types of disturbance can be remedied with standard aggregate demand tools of stabilization? Indicate in each case the impact on external and internal balance as well as the appropriate policy response.
   a. A loss of export markets
   b. A reduction in saving and a corresponding increase in demand for domestic goods
   c. An increase in government spending
   d. A shift in demand from imports to domestic goods
   e. A reduction in imports with a corresponding increase in saving

3. Explain how and why monetary policy retains its effectiveness when there is perfect mobility of capital.

4. a. If the dollar-pound exchange rate rises, has the dollar depreciated or appreciated?
   b. What has happened to the pound?

5. What is the difference between depreciation and devaluation?

6. Explain the purchasing power parity theory of the long-run behavior of the exchange rate. Indicate whether there are any circumstances under which you would *not* expect the PPP relationship to hold.

7. Why do economists care whether or not PPP holds?

8. When is a country in external balance? Internal balance? Should either or both of these be policy goals?

9. According to the Mundell-Fleming model, when exchange rates are fixed and capital is perfectly mobile, will fiscal or monetary policy be more successful? Explain.

10. Your country is in recession. You feel that a policy of exchange rate depreciation will stimulate aggregate demand and bring the country out of the recession.
   a. What can be done to trigger this depreciation?

*An asterisk denotes a more difficult problem.

    b. How might other countries react?

    c. When would this be a beggar-thy-neighbor policy?

Technical

1. Assume that capital is perfectly mobile, the price level is fixed, and the exchange rate is flexible. Now let the government increase purchases. Explain first why the equilibrium levels of output and the interest rate are unaffected. Then show whether the current account improves or worsens as a result of the increased government purchases of goods and services.

2. In 1990–1992 Finland fell into serious difficulties. The collapse of exports to the Soviet Union and a dramatic fall in the prices of pulp and paper—important export items—led to both a recession and a current account deficit. What adjustment policies would you recommend for such a case?

3. Suppose you expect the pound to depreciate by 6 percent over the next year. Assume that the U.S. interest rate is 4 percent. What interest rate would be needed on pound securities, such as government bonds, for you to be willing to buy those securities with your dollars today and then sell them in a year in exchange for dollars?

4. Illustrate, graphically, the effects of a fiscal expansion when capital is mobile and both prices and exchange rates are fixed. Over what horizon is the assumption of fixed prices a valid one? Explain.

5. What is the effect of a fiscal expansion on output and interest rates when exchange rates are fixed and capital is perfectly mobile? Show this rigorously, using the model developed in Section 12-5.

*6. This question is concerned with the repercussion effects of a domestic expansion once we recognize that, as a consequence, output abroad will expand. Suppose that at home there is an increase in autonomous spending, $\Delta \overline{A}$, that falls entirely on domestic goods. (Assume constant interest rates throughout this problem.)

    a. What is the effect on income, disregarding repercussion effects? What is the impact on our imports? Denote the increase in imports by ΔQ.

    b. Using the result for the increase in imports, consider what happens abroad. Our increase in imports means that foreign countries experience an increase in their exports and therefore an increase in the demand for their goods. In response, their output expands. Assuming the foreign marginal propensity to save is s^* and the foreign propensity to import is m^*, by how much will a foreign country's income expand as a result of an increase in its exports?

    c. Now combine the pieces by writing the familiar equation for equilibrium in the domestic goods market: change in supply, ΔY, equals the total change in demand, $\Delta \overline{A} + \Delta X - m\Delta Y + (1 - s)\Delta Y$, or

$$\Delta Y = \frac{\Delta \overline{A} + \Delta X}{s + m}$$

        Noting that our increase in exports, ΔX, is equal to foreigners' increase in imports, we can replace ΔX with the answer to part **(b)** to obtain a general expression for the multiplier with repercussions.

    d. Substitute your answer to part **(b)** in the formula for the change in our exports, $\Delta X = m^*\Delta Y^*$.

    e. Calculate the complete change in our income, including repercussion effects. Now compare your result with the case in which repercussion effects are omitted. What difference do repercussion effects make? Is our income expansion larger or smaller with repercussion effects?

f. Consider the trade balance effect of a domestic expansion with and without repercussion effects. Is the trade deficit larger or smaller once repercussion effects are taken into account?

4
Behavioral Foundations

CHAPTER 13

Consumption and Saving

- Consumption is a large, but relatively stable, fraction of GDP.

- Modern theories of consumption behavior link lifetime consumption to lifetime income. These theories suggest that the marginal propensity to consume out of transitory income should be small.

- Empirical evidence suggests that both modern theories and simple Keynesian "psychological rule-of-thumb" models contribute to explaining consumption.

- The savings rate in the United States is lower than the savings rate in many other countries.

Consumption accounts for more than 60 percent of aggregate demand, more than all other sectors combined. Fluctuations in consumption are proportionately smaller than fluctuations in GDP. These two facts—that consumption makes up a large fraction of GDP and that it is relatively stable—give the focus for this chapter.

We seek to understand what drives consumption, and we particularly wish to understand the dynamic link between consumption and income. In Chapter 9, we modeled consumption as a simple function of current income. Here we study several more advanced theories of consumption. The central finding is that lifetime consumption is linked to lifetime income, but the link between *this* year's consumption and *this* year's income is fairly weak.

The debate about different consumption theories can be viewed as a debate over whether the marginal propensity to consume (*MPC*) is large or small. Early Keynesian "psychological rule-of-thumb" models suggested a high *MPC,* while modern theories based on rational consumer decisions sometimes indicate a very low *MPC.* In introductory macromodels, the marginal propensity to consume, *c,* directly determines "the multiplier", $1/(1 - c)$. Even in more sophisticated models, a high *MPC* causes a large multiplier. The modern theories discussed below assign different values to the marginal propensity to consume out of income changes expected to persist for different lengths of time. The *MPC* out of income expected to be permanent is high, just as in earlier models, but the *MPC* out of transitory income is close to zero.

Figures 13-1 to 13-3 tell the story of the underlying concepts of this chapter. Figure 13-1 plots both changes in per capita consumption and changes in per capita

FIGURE 13-1   CHANGES IN PER CAPITA CONSUMPTION AND DISPOSABLE INCOME, 1947–1995.

Changes in per capita disposable income and changes in per capita consumption are closely related, although the latter is less volatile than the former. Consumption does not respond much to positive or negative income spikes (short-term swings in income). (Source: DRI/McGraw Hill Macroeconomic Database.)

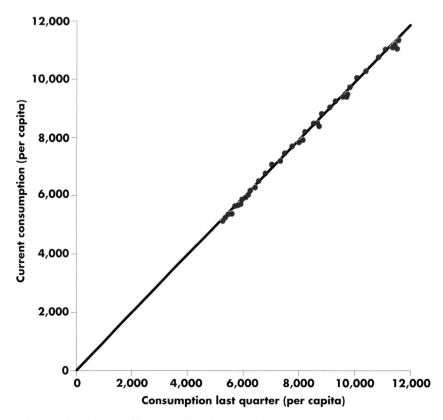

FIGURE 13-2   CURRENT AND LAGGED CONSUMPTION.

Consumption is almost perfectly predicted by consumption the previous period plus an allowance for growth. (Source: DRI/McGraw Hill Macroeconomic Database.)

disposable income.[1] Income swings that last 5 or 10 years have roughly matching consumption swings. But consumption doesn't respond much to income spikes—1958, 1975, and 1978 are examples. Long-term income swings generate changes in consumption, but short-term spikes don't; in other words, the long-run *MPC* is high, but the short-run *MPC* is low.

Figure 13-2 compares consumption this quarter with consumption the previous quarter. The formula for the line drawn through the scatter diagram is $C_t = \$16.34 + 1.002C_{t-1}$. So consumption this quarter is almost perfectly predicted by consumption last quarter plus a small allowance for growth. In Section 13-2 we will see that this relation is an outcome of the link between current consumption and expected future income.

---

[1]Consumption accounts are broken down into nondurables (e.g., food), services (haircuts), and durables (refrigerators). The consumption theory we study and the data we show apply to nondurables and services. Durable-goods "consumption" is in large part a form of *investment* on the part of a household, but it is not treated as investment in the national income accounts.

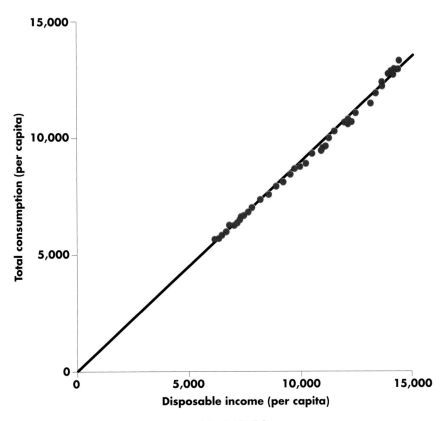

FIGURE 13-3 THE CONSUMPTION–INCOME RELATION.

There is a close relation, in practice, between consumption spending and disposable income. Consumption rises on average by 94 cents for each additional dollar of disposable income. (Source: DRI/McGraw Hill Macroeconomic Database.)

Modern consumption theory needs to explain Figures 13-1 and 13-2. Early Keynesian theories, looking at the kind of data shown in Figure 13-3, had current consumption and current income moving in lockstep without trying to separate temporary versus permanent changes in income.[2] In previous chapters we assumed that consumption (C) is determined by disposable income (YD) in the simple linear relation

$$C = \overline{C} + cYD \qquad 1 > c > 0 \tag{1}$$

The estimated values for the parameters for the line in Figure 13-3 are $\overline{C} = -478$ and $c = .94$. In other words, the traditional, measured consumption function is $C = -478 + .94\ YD$, and the measured value of the *MPC*, .94, is quite high.

---

[2]For reasons of tradition, the consumption measurement for Fig. 13-3 includes durable goods as well as nondurables and services.

We begin by presenting modern theory and then turn to modern empirical evidence. The life-cycle and permanent income theories do well at explaining Figures 13-1 and 13-2, but empirical evidence, examined below, indicates that the traditional view depicted in Figure 13-3 is still useful and that there is much merit in the earlier, psychological rule-of-thumb theories.

13-1

THE LIFE-CYCLE–PERMANENT-INCOME THEORY OF CONSUMPTION AND SAVING

Modern consumption theory emphasizes lifetime decision making. Originally, the *life-cycle* hypothesis emphasized choices about how to maintain a stable standard of living in the face of changes in income over the course of life, while *permanent income* theory focused on forecasting the level of income available to a consumer over a lifetime. Today, these two theories have largely merged.

LIFE-CYCLE THEORY

The consumption function [equation (1)] assumes that individuals' consumption behavior in a given period is related to their income in that period. The *life-cycle hypothesis* views individuals, instead, as planning their consumption and savings behavior over long periods with the intention of allocating their consumption in the best possible way over their entire lifetimes. Instead of relying on a single value (based on a psychological rule of thumb) for the marginal propensity to consume, life-cycle theory (based on maximizing behavior) implies different marginal propensities to consume out of permanent income, transitory income, and wealth. The key assumption is that most people choose stable lifestyles—not, in general, saving furiously in one period to have a huge spending spree in the next but, rather, consuming at about the same level in every period. In its simplest form, the assumption is that individuals try to consume the same amount each year.

A numerical example illustrates the theory: Suppose that a person starts life at age 20, plans to work until 65, and will die at 80 and that annual labor income, YL, is $30,000. Lifetime resources are annual income times years of working life ($WL = 65 - 20 = 45$)—in this example, $30,000 \times 45 = 1,350,000$.[3] Spreading lifetime resources over the number of years of life ($NL = 80 - 20 = 60$) allows for annual consumption of $C = 1,350,000/60 = 22,500$. The general formula is

$$C = \frac{WL}{NL} \times YL$$

So the marginal propensity to consume is WL/NL. Figure 13-4 illustrates the pattern of consumption and saving. (Note that once we have a theory of consumption, we also have a theory of saving, since saving is just income minus consumption.)

---

[3]Note that as a simplification we ignore the effect of interest earned on saving.

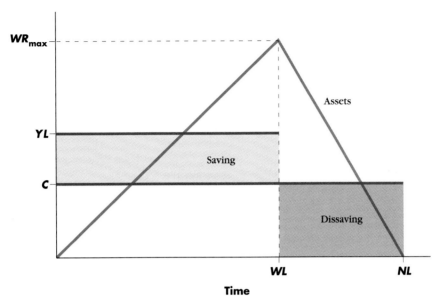

FIGURE 13-4 LIFETIME INCOME, CONSUMPTION, SAVING, AND WEALTH IN THE LIFE-CYCLE MODEL.

Consumption is constant throughout lifetime. During the working life, lasting WL years, the individual saves, accumulating assets. At the end of the working life, the individual begins to live off these assets, dissaving for the remaining years (NL − WL) of life such that assets equal exactly zero at the end of life.

Continuing with the numerical example, we can compute marginal propensities to consume by considering variations in the income stream. Suppose income were to rise permanently by $3,000 per year. The extra $3,000 times 45 working years spread over 60 years of life would increase annual consumption by $3,000 × (45/60) = $2,250. In other words, the *marginal propensity to consume out of permanent income* would be $WL/NL = 45/60 = .75$. In contrast, suppose income were to rise by $3,000 but only in 1 year. The extra $3,000 spread over 60 years would increase annual consumption by $3,000 × (1/60) = $50. In other words, the *marginal propensity to consume out of transitory income* would be $1/NL = 1/60 \approx .017$. While the exact examples are slightly contrived, the clear message is that the *MPC* out of *permanent income* is large and the *MPC* out of *transitory income* is small, fairly close to zero.

The life-cycle theory implies that the marginal propensity to consume out of wealth should equal the *MPC* out of transitory income and, therefore, be very small. The reasoning is that spending out of wealth, like spending out of transitory income, is spread out over the remaining years of life. The *MPC* out of wealth is used to link changes in the value of assets to current consumption. For example, an increase in the value of the stock market will increase current consumption. Changes in the value of the stock market can be very large in comparison to income changes, so even

BOX 13-1 Linking Demography and Consumption

Life-cycle theory helps link consumption and savings behavior to demographic considerations, especially to the age distribution of the population. Note that the marginal propensity to consume out of permanent income, WL/NL, changes with age. In the text example, the MPC out of permanent income at age 20 is 45/60. As a person ages, both the number of working years and the number of years of life decline. By age 50, for example, the MPC would have declined to 15/30. (The exact argument holds only for labor income, since WL isn't relevant to income from investments.) The MPC out of transitory income would rise from 1/60 at age 20 to 1/30 at age 50.

The economy is a mix of people of many different ages and life expectancies, so the MPC for the economy is a mix of corresponding MPCs. As a result, economies with different age mixtures have different overall marginal propensities to save and consume.

though the *MPC* out of wealth is small, the effect of a large dollar change in the stock market multiplied by a small *MPC* can generate a significant change in consumption.

PERMANENT-INCOME THEORY

Like the life-cycle hypothesis, the permanent-income theory of consumption argues that consumption is related not to current income but to a longer-term estimate of income, which Milton Friedman, who introduced the theory, calls "permanent income." Friedman provides a simple example: Consider a person who is paid or receives income only once a week, on Fridays. We do not expect that person to consume only on Friday, with zero consumption on the other days of the week. People prefer a smooth consumption flow rather than plenty today and scarcity tomorrow or yesterday.

The idea that consumption spending is geared to long-term, or average or permanent, income is appealing and essentially the same as the life-cycle theory. *Permanent income* is the steady rate of consumption a person could maintain for the rest of his or her life, given the present level of wealth and the income earned now and in the future.

In its simplest form the theory argues that consumption is proportional to permanent income:

$$C = cYP \tag{2}$$

where *YP* is permanent (disposable) income.

To think about the measurement of permanent income, imagine someone trying to figure out what her permanent income is. The person has a current level of income and has formed some idea of the level of consumption she can maintain for the rest of her life. Now income goes up. The person has to decide whether the increase is

BOX 13-2   Life-Cycle Consumption and Permanent-Income Theory: Why Can't Economists Ever Agree?

Modern consumption theory is due largely to Franco Modigliani of M.I.T. (life-cycle theory) and Milton Friedman of the University of Chicago (permanent-income theory), both of whom have won Nobel Prizes. Modigliani is a leading Keynesian, and Friedman is the "father of modern monetarism." Their theories are quite similar. (So much so that economists frequently call the combination the life-cycle–permanent-income hypothesis, abbreviated *LC-PIH*.) Like much of good macroeconomics, both theories pay careful attention to microeconomic foundations. While the theories differed in their developmental stage, the two have largely merged and today are largely accepted by all economists.

The history of these theories offers an important methodological lesson. Economists seem to derive enjoyment from disagreeing with one another. This is a good thing, because progress comes from examining disputes, not from singing as a chorus. As disputes are resolved, the frontier moves on. What people often don't see is that this process leads economists to agree on 90 percent of how the economy works, even while still fiercely contesting the frontiers of the science.

permanent or merely transitory or temporary. In any particular case, an individual may know whether an increase is permanent or transitory. An associate professor who is promoted to professor and given a raise will think that the increase in income is permanent; a worker who has exceptionally high overtime in a given year will likely regard that year's increased income as transitory. But in general a person is not likely to be so sure whether a change is permanent or transitory. A good Christmas bonus might be due to a change in your employer's compensation scheme (permanent) or it might signal that your firm had an unusually good year (transitory). The difference matters because transitory income is assumed not to have any substantial effect on consumption. (Note that the weak link between consumption and transitory income parallels the worked-out example, above, for the *MPC* out of transitory income.)

According to the LC-PIH, consumption should be *smoother* than income because spending out of transitory income is spread over many years. Figure 13-1 shows that this prediction is largely correct. In particular, the really large up-and-down spikes in income generate only modest consumption response. (The traditional consumption function, in contrast, predicts that income spikes should be matched by consumption spikes.)

BOX 13-3 Durable-Goods Consumption

The LC-PIH makes sense for consumption of nondurables and services, things from which we derive pleasure around the time of purchase. Durable goods, such as cars, refrigerators, and stereos, provide a stream of utility long after the purchase. The LC-PIH model explains the stream of utility, not the expenditure pattern. The theory of durable-goods purchases is really the theory of investment applied to households instead of firms. This has two implications for durable-goods expenditures. First, they are not smoothed out the way purchases of nondurables and services are. Second, durable-goods purchases are quite sensitive to interest rates, at least in countries like the United States and Canada, where consumer finance is readily available. Automobiles and household appliances are examples of goods that respond positively to swings in GDP and negatively to interest rates.

BOX 13-4 Misleading-Introspection Alert!

Tonight, the good economics fairy will surprise you with ten $100 bills—an event that will surely not happen more than once in your life! How will you spend this windfall? According to the LC-PIH, you should adjust your consumption by buying something like one extra can of soda pop every week for the rest of your life. In case this wasn't the first thing that popped into your mind, how do some alternatives stack up to the theory? Suppose, being a thrifty sort, you choose to pay back part of your student loan. Colloquially, we'd call this "spending," but in economic terms paying off a debt is a form of saving. So this fits the theory perfectly. Suppose, being more of a spendthrift, you decide to buy a really nice television. You'll really be buying the ability to watch shows over the next several years (see Box 13-3) so this too fits the theory.

BOX 13-5 The LC-PIH and Tax Policy

In 1968, President Johnson and Congress passed a temporary (1-year) income tax surcharge. The goal at the time was to cool down an economy temporarily overheated by spending for the Vietnam war. A temporary tax for temporary overheating sounds logical. But the LC-PIH predicts that a temporary tax increase, and therefore a temporary decrease in disposable income, will have very little effect on consumption and therefore very little effect on aggregate demand. The LC-PIH worked—and the tax cut didn't.

13-2

CONSUMPTION UNDER UNCERTAINTY—THE MODERN APPROACH

If permanent income were known exactly, then according to the LC-PIH, consumption would never change.[4] The modern version of the LC-PIH emphasizes the link between income uncertainty and changes in consumption and takes a more formal approach to consumer maximization. According to this newer version, changes in consumption arise from *surprise* changes in income. Absent income surprises, consumption this period should be the same as consumption last period. In Figure 13-2 we saw that this prediction is well supported by the data.

The modern approach to the LC-PIH begins by formally stating the lifetime utility maximization problem of a representative consumer. In a particular period, a consumer enjoys utility from consumption in that period, $u(C_t)$. *Lifetime utility* is the sum of period-by-period utilities, and the *lifetime budget constraint* is the sum of period-by-period consumption:[5]

$$\text{lifetime utility} = u(C_t) + u(C_{t+1}) + \ldots + u(C_{T-1}) + u(C_T)$$
$$\text{subject to } C_t + C_{t+1} + \ldots + C_{T-1} + C_T$$
$$= \text{wealth} + YL_t + YL_{t+1} + \ldots + YL_{T-1} + YL_T \tag{3}$$

Consumers choose consumption each period to maximize lifetime utility subject to total lifetime consumption equaling lifetime resources. The optimal choice is the consumption path which equates the *marginal utility of consumption* across periods, $MU(C_{t+1}) = MU(C_t)$, and so on. Why? Consider the alternative: If marginal utility were a little higher in period t than in period $t+1$, lifetime utility could be increased by shifting consumption into t from $t+1$ because the gain from the former would outweigh the gain from the latter. (By definition, marginal utility is the increase in utility from a small increase in consumption.)

Now add considerations of uncertainty. The consumer cannot actually implement an equate-marginal-utilities rule because future marginal utility, $MU(C_{t+1})$, is uncertain at time t. The consumer *can* equate marginal utility today with her best guess of marginal utility at time $t+1$, so the modified rule is to equate today's marginal utility with the expected value of tomorrow's marginal utility, $E[MU(C_{t+1})] = MU(C_t)$.[6]

---

[4]If a consumer knew total lifetime resources in advance, she could figure out once and for all how to spread consumption evenly. However, saying that "consumption would never change" is not quite right, because the statement ignores the effects of impatience and the financial return to saving. See footnote 5.

[5]*(Optional)* Equation (3) leaves out two factors. People prefer to consume now rather than later, so a high rate of time preference, represented by the parameter δ, moves consumption earlier. Counteracting this effect, deferred spending accrues interest at rate r, allowing greater consumption if one is patient. Measuring both δ and r in percent per period, a more fully specified version of equation (3) is

$$\text{lifetime utility} = u(C_t) + (1+\delta)^{-1}u(C_{t+1}) + \ldots + (1+\delta)^{-T}u(C_T)$$
$$\text{subject to } C_t + (1+r)^{-1}C_{t+1} + \ldots + (1+r)^{-T}C_T$$
$$= \text{wealth} + YL_t + (1+r)^{-1}YL_{t+1} + \ldots + (1+r)^{-T}YL_T$$

[6]*(Optional)* To fully account for the rate of time preference and the interest rate, the equate-expected-marginal-utilities rule needs to be modified to read

$$E[MU(C_{t+1})] = \left(\frac{1+\delta}{1+r}\right)MU(C_t)$$

Marginal utility functions aren't observable, but in this simple case the functions will be equal only if their arguments are equal, so the rule can be rewritten as $E(C_{t+1}) = C_t$. Expected values aren't observable either, but in the late 1970s Robert Hall realized that rational expectations theory could be applied to the problem—and in so doing, he revolutionized macroeconometrics.[7] Observed consumption can be written as expected consumption plus a surprise, $C_{t+1} = E(C_{t+1})$ + surprise. According to rational expectations theory, the surprise is truly random and unpredictable. Combining this rational expectations formula with the equate-expected-consumption rule, $E(C_{t+1}) = C_t$, leads to Hall's famous *random-walk model*[8]

$$C_{t+1} = C_t + \epsilon$$

which states that consumption tomorrow should equal consumption today plus a truly random error, $\epsilon = C_{t+1} - C_t$. Can such a strong implication of the LC-PIH possibly hold in the real world? Look again at Figure 13-2, which plots one period's consumption against the previous period's. The model appears to work nearly perfectly.[9] The random-walk model predicts that the line relating C_{t+1} to C_t should have an intercept of zero and a slope of 1. The actual equation has an intercept of $16 (compared to a mean consumption of $8,000) and a slope of 1.002, so these predictions of the random-walk model fail only in the third decimal place.

THE LC-PIH—THE TRADITIONAL MODEL STRIKES BACK

Based in rational consumer behavior, the LC-PIH is very attractive to economists. However, empirical evidence suggests that both the traditional rule-of-thumb consumption function and the LC-PIH contribute to explaining consumption behavior.[10] The actual behavior of consumption exhibits both *excess sensitivity* and *excess smoothness*. The former means that consumption responds too strongly to predictable changes in income; the latter, that it responds too little to surprise changes in income.[11] John Campbell and Greg Mankiw have developed a clever way of combining the LC-PIH and the traditional consumption function in order to test for excess sensitivity.[12] According to the

---

[7]Robert E. Hall, "Stochastic Implications of the Life Cycle–Permanent Income Hypothesis: Theory and Evidence," *Journal of Political Economy,* December 1978.

[8]At the time of Hall's discovery, everyone "knew" that consumption adjusted with long lags. Hall himself initially expected to *disprove* the LC-PIH. The random-walk model was so outlandish that Hall was the subject of much ribbing and good-natured abuse from his colleagues and his students—until everyone realized that he had found exactly the right approach to the problem.

[9]For those curious about formal statistical measures, 99.96 percent of the variance of C_{t+1} in Fig. 13-2 is explained by C_t. (In the language of statistics, $R^2 = .9996$.)

[10]The first crack in the LC-PIH wall was discovered by one of Hall's students, now a professor at the University of California–San Diego, Marjorie Flavin. See her article, "The Adjustment of Consumption to Changing Expectations about Future Income," *Journal of Political Economy,* October 1981.

[11]To see how this works in a formal model, see David Romer, *Advanced Macroeconomics* (New York: McGraw-Hill, 1996) chap. 7.

[12]John Y. Campbell and N. Gregory Mankiw, "Consumption, Income, and Interest Rates: Reinterpreting the Time Series Evidence," *NBER Macroeconomics Annual,* 1989. For earlier evidence on the same topic, see Robert E. Hall and Frederic S. Mishkin, "The Sensitivity of Consumption to Transitory Income: Estimates from Panel Data on Households," *Econometrica,* March 1982.

LC-PIH, the change in consumption equals the surprise element, ϵ, so $\Delta C_{LC\text{-}PIH} = \epsilon$. According to the traditional theory, $C = \bar{C} + cYD$, so $\Delta C_{\text{trad}} = c\Delta YD$. If λ percent of the population behaves in accordance with the traditional model and the remaining $1 - \lambda$ follow the LC-PIH, the total change in consumption is

$$\Delta C = \lambda\Delta C_{\text{trad}} + (1 - \lambda)\Delta C_{\text{LC-PIH}} = \lambda c\Delta YD + (1 - \lambda)\epsilon$$

Empirically estimating this equation yields

$$\Delta C = .486\Delta YD$$

suggesting that half of consumption behavior is explained by current income rather than permanent income.[13]

LIQUIDITY CONSTRAINTS AND MYOPIA

Why might a theory so elegant as the LC-PIH miss explaining so much of consumption behavior? Two explanations are *liquidity constraints* and *myopia*. The first argues that when permanent income is higher than current income, consumers are unable to borrow to consume at the higher level predicted by the LC-PIH. The second suggests that consumers simply aren't as forward-looking as the LC-PIH suggests.

A liquidity constraint exists when a consumer cannot borrow to sustain current consumption in the expectation of higher future income. Students in particular should appreciate the possibility that liquidity constraints exist. Most students can look forward to a much higher income in the future than they receive as students. The life-cycle theory holds that they should be consuming on the basis of their lifetime incomes, which means they should be spending much more than they currently earn. To do that, they would have to borrow. They can borrow to some extent, through student loan plans. But it is entirely possible that they cannot borrow enough to support consumption at its permanent level.

Such students are liquidity-constrained. When they leave college and take jobs, their incomes will rise and their consumption will rise, too. According to the life-cycle theory, consumption should not rise much when income rises, as long as the increase in income was expected. In fact, because the liquidity constraint is relieved, consumption will rise a lot when income rises. Thus consumption will be more closely related to *current* income than is implied by the LC-PIH. Similarly, individuals who cannot borrow when their incomes decline temporarily would be liquidity-constrained.[14]

---

[13](*Optional*) This equation was estimated by an advanced version of regression called *instrumental variables*. Consumption with lags 2 through 5 were used as instruments. The t statistic was 3.73. (Promise: This footnote will *not* be on the exam.)

[14]Estimates of the importance of liquidity constraints in the United States are presented in Marjorie Flavin, "Excess Sensitivity of Consumption to Current Income: Liquidity Constraints or Myopia?" *Canadian Journal of Economics,* February 1985; Stephen P. Zeldes, "Consumption and Liquidity Constraints: An Empirical Investigation," *Journal of Political Economy,* April 1989; and Tullio Jappelli, "Who Is Credit Constrained in the U. S. Economy?" *Quarterly Journal of Economics,* February 1989.

Even in developing countries, where the paucity of financial institutions makes borrowing difficult for the typical consumer, people try to smooth out their consumption in the face of income fluctuations. See the articles by Anne Case, Robert M. Townsend, Jonathan Morduch, and Timothy Besley in "Symposium on Consumption Smoothing in Developing Countries," *Journal of Economic Perspectives,* Summer 1995.

The alternative explanation for the sensitivity of consumption to current income—that consumers are myopic—is hard to distinguish in practice from the liquidity constraints hypothesis. For instance, David Wilcox of the Federal Reserve Board of Governors has shown that the announcement that social security benefits will be increased (which always happens at least 6 weeks before the change) does not lead to a change in consumption *until the benefit increases are actually paid.*[15] Once the increased benefits are paid, recipients certainly do adjust spending—primarily on durables. The delay could be either because recipients do not have the assets to enable them to adjust spending before they receive higher payments (liquidity constraints), or because they fail to pay attention to the announcements (myopia), or perhaps because they do not believe the announcements.

UNCERTAINTY AND BUFFER-STOCK SAVING

The life-cycle hypothesis is that people save largely to finance retirement. However, additional savings goals also matter. The evidence on bequests suggests that some saving is done to provide inheritances for children. There is also a growing amount of evidence to support the view that some saving is *precautionary,* undertaken to guard against rainy days. In other words, savings are used as a *buffer stock,* added to when times are good in order to maintain consumption when times are bad.

One piece of evidence for these other motives is that old people rarely actually dissave. They tend to live off the income (e.g., interest and dividends) from their wealth—not to draw down wealth, as predicted by the LC-PIH. One explanation is that the older they are, the more they fear having to pay large bills for medical care and, therefore, the more reluctant they are to spend. Evidence from surveys of consumers, who were asked why they are saving, also indicates that saving is undertaken to meet emergency needs.

This evidence is consistent with a version of the life-cycle model in which uncertainty about future income and future needs is explicitly included.[16] Recent work by Christopher Carroll uses these ideas to explain why the LC-PIH may be off the mark for the typical consumer.[17] Income fluctuations create considerable downside risk for the consumer, because the pain caused by a large drop in spending is greater than the pleasure caused by an equal-size increase in spending. One way consumers can avoid having to cut their consumption sharply in bad times is to save up a buffer stock of assets, which they can draw upon in emergencies. On the other hand, most consumers are impatient; they would prefer to spend now rather than save for the future. Under these conditions, consumers will have a "target" wealth level. The target will be the point where impatience exactly balances the precautionary (or buffer-stock) saving motive.

[15]David W. Wilcox, "Social Security Benefits, Consumption Expenditure, and the Life Cycle Hypothesis," *Journal of Political Economy,* April 1989.

[16]For example, Stephen Zeldes, "Optimal Consumption with Stochastic Income: Departures from Certainty Equivalence," *Quarterly Journal of Economics,* May 1989.

[17]See C. Carroll, "Buffer-Stock Saving and the Life Cycle/Permanent Income Hypothesis," *Quarterly Journal of Economics,* forthcoming. Carroll writes, "It seems plausible that many consumers ensure that retirement is taken care of by joining a pension plan, buy a house, and then subject the post-pension-plan, post-mortgage-payment income and consumption streams to buffer-stock saving rules."

If the wealth is below the target, the precautionary saving motive will be stronger than impatience and the consumer will try to build up wealth toward the target; if wealth is above the target, impatience will be stronger than caution and the consumer will dissave. These effects lead to a much higher *MPC* than would be predicted by the standard LC-PIH model.

13-3

FURTHER ASPECTS OF CONSUMPTION BEHAVIOR

CONSUMPTION, SAVING, AND INTEREST RATES

Anyone who saves receives a return in the form of interest or of dividends and capital gains (an increase in the price) on stocks. It seems, then, that the natural way to raise saving is to raise the return available to savers. Think of someone saving and receiving an interest rate of 5 percent each year for each dollar saved. Surely an increase in the rate to, say, 10 percent would make that person save more. This thinking has at times influenced tax policy in the United States. For instance, the interest received on savings in individual retirement accounts is exempt from the payment of taxes.[18] This means the return received by the saver is higher than it would be if the return were taxed.

But should we really expect an increase in the interest rate to increase saving? It is true that when the interest rate rises, saving is made more attractive. But it is also made less necessary. Consider someone who has decided to save an amount which will ensure that $10,000 per year will be available for retirement. Suppose the interest rate is now 5 percent, and the person is saving $1,000 per year. Now let the interest rate rise to 10 percent. With such a high interest rate, the individual needs to save less to provide the given $10,000 per year during retirement. It may be possible to provide the same retirement income by saving only about $650 a year. Thus an increase in the interest rate might reduce saving.[19]

What do the facts show? Does saving rise when the interest rate increases because every dollar of saving generates a higher return? Or does saving fall because there is less need to save to provide a given level of future income? The answers from the data are ambiguous. Many researchers have examined this question, but few have found strong positive effects of interest rate increases on saving. Typically, research suggests that the effects of interest rates on saving are small and hard to find.[20]

---

[18]R. Glenn Hubbard and Jonathan S. Skinner, in "Assessing the Effectiveness of Savings Incentives" (Washington, DC: AEI Press, 1996), suggest that the tax incentives of IRA accounts have a significant effect on increasing saving.

[19]These offsetting factors are called *substitution* and *income* effects. The substitution effect means that higher interest rates make consumption later more attractive. The offsetting income effect is that higher interest rates raise permanent income and encourage more consumption now.

[20]The best-known study finding positive interest rate effects is that by Michael Boskin, chairman of the President's Council of Economic Advisors from 1989 to 1993. See his "Taxation, Saving, and the Rate of Interest," *Journal of Political Economy,* part 2, April 1978. For more typical negative results, see Campbell and Mankiw, "Consumption, Income, and Interest Rates."

TABLE 13-1   Government and Private Gross Savings Rates, 1980s
(Percent)*

	UNITED STATES	JAPAN	GERMANY	UNITED KINGDOM	CANADA
Gross national saving	16.3	31.6	22.5	16.6	20.7
Government saving	−2.1	4.9	2.0	.1	−1.6
Private saving	18.5	26.8	20.5	16.4	22.2

*All data are gross saving relative to GNP. Components may not sum to totals, due to rounding error.

Source: OECD, *Annual National Accounts.*

INTERNATIONAL DIFFERENCES IN SAVINGS RATES

The U.S. savings rate is lower than that in other major countries, as Table 13-1 shows. The low savings rate is of great concern because, as we saw in Chapters 3 and 4, a low savings rate means a lower standard of living in the future. This international comparison is especially striking when we look at *net* savings rates, net saving (i.e., total saving minus depreciation) as a share of NNP. The net savings rate is a measure of the rate at which a country is adding to its wealth, and the very low rate of national saving in the United States causes concern because other countries are increasing their wealth at a higher rate.

It is useful to look at the different sectors of the economy that save, starting with the *government* and *private* sectors:

Gross national saving = government saving + private saving

The government saves when it spends less than it receives, that is, when it runs a budget surplus. Table 13-1 shows that the large government budget deficit helps account for the low savings rate in the United States. For example, the difference between the private savings rates of Germany and the United States was only 2 percent of GNP, while the German government saved 4 percent of GNP more than the U.S. government. *It seems that one way to raise the U.S. savings rate is to reduce government budget deficits.*[21]

Next we look at the difference between business and personal saving in the United States:

Private saving = business saving + personal saving

Business saving consists of retained earnings, that amount of profits not paid out to the owners of the business. A business saves when it does not pay income to its owners but, rather, keeps those funds to plow back into the business.

___

[21]Two points: (1) The government sector in Table 13-1 consists of federal, state, and local governments. All three levels need to be included for a valid comparison. In the United States, deficit spending is largely limited to the federal level, as most state constitutions prohibit borrowing (except for capital projects). In other nations arrangements for local versus national finance differ. Canadian provinces, for example, sometimes run very large deficits. (2) In Chap. 20 we look at an argument, under the topic of Ricardian equivalence, which holds that an increase in government spending would be completely offset by a reduction in private saving.

TABLE 13-2 Composition of U.S. Saving, 1981–1990*

Gross national saving rate	15.1
Government saving	−2.5
Business saving	13.0
Household saving	4.6

*All ratios are sectoral saving as a percentage of GNP.

Source: *Economic Report of the President*, 1992.

The fact that business saving is three times as large as personal saving in the United States (see Table 13-2) has not received the attention it should. That is partly because, for a long time, it seemed that households treated business saving as if it were being done on their behalf—that is, they "pierced the corporate veil"—and reduced their own saving exactly enough to offset any increased business saving. The more recent evidence is that households reduce their saving by only about 50 cents for every extra dollar of saving done by business.[22]

---

[22]James Poterba, "Tax Policy and Corporate Savings," *Brookings Papers on Economic Activity* 2 (1987).

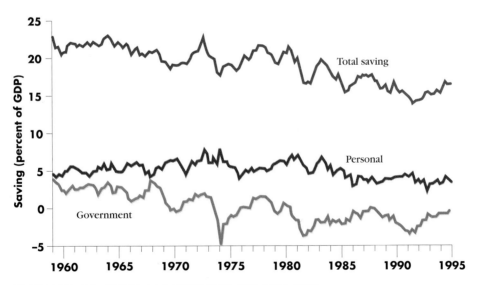

FIGURE 13-5 U.S. SAVING AS A PERCENT OF GDP, 1959–1995.

The diagram shows personal saving, government saving, and total U.S. saving. Total saving includes government saving, personal saving, and business saving. (Source: DRI/McGraw Hill Macroeconomic Database.)

Private saving in the United States trended up in the early postwar period but drifted sharply downward in the 1980s and early 1990s (Figure 13-5).[23] There has been no convincing single explanation for this trend. Nonetheless, we can observe that personal (nonbusiness) saving has been roughly steady, while business and government saving has turned downward.

So why does the United States save less than other countries? First, the U.S. government runs large deficits, while many other governments don't—a few even run surpluses. Second, demographic factors such as a large senior-citizen population account for some of the remaining difference. A third reason is that it is easier to borrow in the United States than in most other countries. In many countries, people have to save in order to make major purchases, such as a house or a car, whereas in the United States they can borrow for that purpose.

These factors do not fully account for international differences in savings rates. Some economists argue that there may simply be differences in national attitudes toward saving, but most still hope to find economic explanations for those underlying attitudes.

SUMMARY

1. The life-cycle–permanent-income hypothesis predicts that the marginal propensity to consume out of permanent income is large and that the marginal propensity to consume out of transitory income is very small. Modern theories of consumption assume that individuals want to maintain relatively smooth consumption profiles over their lifetimes. Their consumption behavior is geared to their long-term consumption opportunities—permanent income or lifetime income plus wealth. With such a view, current income is only one of the determinants of consumption spending. Wealth and expected income play a role, too.

2. Observed consumption is much smoother than the simple Keynesian consumption function predicts. Current consumption can be very accurately predicted from last period's consumption. Both these observations accord well with the LC-PIH.

3. The LC-PIH is a very attractive theory, but it does not give a complete explanation of consumption behavior. Empirical evidence shows that the traditional consumption function appears to also play a role.

4. The life-cycle hypothesis suggests that the propensities of an individual to consume out of disposable income and out of wealth depend on the person's age. It implies that saving is high (low) when income is high (low) relative to lifetime average income. It also suggests that aggregate saving depends on the growth rate of the economy and on such variables as the age distribution of the population.

5. The rate of consumption, and thus of saving, could in principle be affected by the interest rate. But the evidence, for the most part, shows little effect of interest rates on saving.

6. The U.S. savings rate is very low by international standards. Most private saving in the United States is done by the business sector.

---

[23]See also "The Saving Mystery, or Where Did the Money Go?" by Lynn Elaine Browne, *New England Economic Review,* September–October 1996.

KEY TERMS

life-cycle hypothesis
permanent-income hypothesis
lifetime utility
lifetime budget constraint
marginal utility of
    consumption

random-walk model of
    consumption
excess sensitivity
excess smoothness
liquidity constraint
myopia

buffer-stock saving
government saving
private saving
business saving
personal saving

PROBLEMS

Conceptual

1. The text implies that the ratio of consumption to accumulated saving declines over time until retirement.
   a. Why? What assumption about consumption behavior leads to this result?
   b. What happens to this ratio after retirement?

2. a. Suppose you earn just as much as your neighbor but are in much better health and expect to live longer than she does. Would you consume more or less than she does? Why? Derive your answer using the equation from the text, $C = (WL/NL) \times YL$.
   b. According to the life-cycle hypothesis, what would be the effect of the social security system on your average propensity to consume out of (disposable) income? Is the credibility of the social security system an issue here?

3. In terms of the permanent-income hypothesis, would you consume more of your Christmas bonus if *(a)* you knew there would be a bonus every year, or *(b)* this was the only year the bonus would be given?

4. Explain why successful gamblers (and thieves) might be expected to live very well even in years when they don't do well at all.

5. What are the similarities between the life-cycle and the permanent-income hypotheses? Do they differ in their approaches to explaining why the long-run *MPC* is greater than the short-run *MPC?*

6. The United States, during the 1980s, found its rate of personal saving to be particularly low. It also, during that time, had a demographic "blip"—the "baby-boomer" generation, then in its late twenties to early thirties.
   a. Does the life-cycle hypothesis suggest a reason that these two facts might be connected?
   b. What does this hypothesis suggest we should see as this generation ages?

7. Rank the following marginal propensities to consume:
   a. marginal propensity to consume out of permanent income
   b. marginal propensity to consume out of transitory income
   c. marginal propensity to consume out of permanent income when consumers are liquidity-constrained
   d. marginal propensity to consume out of transitory income when consumers are liquidity-constrained

8. What is a random walk? How is Hall's random-walk model of consumption related to the life-cycle and permanent-income hypotheses?

9. What are the problems of excess sensitivity and excess smoothness? Does their existence disprove or invalidate the LC-PIH? Explain.

10. What assumption(s) regarding consumers' knowledge and behavior in the life-cycle–permanent-income hypothesis do we need to change in order for it to explain the presence of

precautionary, or buffer-stock, saving? Do these assumptions, in your opinion, bring the model closer to or further from the world as you know it?

11. a. Explain why the interest rate might affect saving.

   b. Has this relationship been confirmed empirically?

Technical

1. Suppose that permanent income is calculated as the average of income over the past 5 years; that is,

$$YP = 1/5(Y + Y_{-1} + Y_{-2} + Y_{-3} + Y_{-4}) \tag{P1}$$

Suppose further that consumption is given by $C = .9YP$.

   a. If you have earned $20,000 per year for the past 10 years, what is your permanent income?

   b. Suppose that next year (period $t + 1$) you earn $30,000. What is your new YP?

   c. What is your consumption this year and next year?

   d. What is your short-run marginal propensity to consume? Long-run MPC?

   e. Assuming you continue to earn $30,000 starting in period $t + 1$, graph the value of your permanent income in each period, using equation (P1).

2. The graph below shows the lifetime earnings profile of a person who lives for four periods and earns incomes of $30, $60, and $90 in the first three periods of the life cycle. There are no earnings during retirement. Assume that the interest rate is 0.

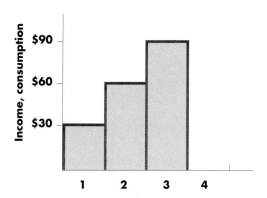

   a. Determine the level of consumption, compatible with the budget constraint, for someone who wants an even consumption profile throughout the life cycle. Indicate in which periods the person saves and dissaves and in what amounts.

   b. Assume now that, contrary to part *(a)*, there is no possibility of borrowing. The credit markets are closed to the individual. Under this assumption, what is the flow of consumption the individual will pick over the life cycle? In providing an answer, continue to assume that, if possible, an even flow of consumption is preferred. (*Note:* You are assuming here that there are liquidity constraints.)

   c. Assume next that the person described in *(b)* receives an increase in wealth, or non-labor income. The increase in wealth is equal to $13. How will that wealth be allocated over the life cycle with and without access to the credit market? How would your answer differ if the increase in wealth were $23?

3. Suppose that 70 percent of a country's population, as a consequence of liquidity constraints, behaves in accordance with the traditional model of consumption and thus consumes, every period, a given fraction of its disposable income. The other 30 percent of the population behaves in accordance with the LC-PIH.

   a. If the *MPC* in the traditional model is .8 and disposable income changes by $10 million (you may assume that this change is due entirely to a change in transitory income), by how much will consumption change?

   b. What if 70 percent of the population behaves in accordance with the LC-PIH, and 30 percent behaves in accordance with the traditional model?

   c. What if 100 percent of the population behaves in accordance with the LC-PIH?

4. Suppose the real interest rate has increased from 2 to 4 percent.

   a. What will happen to the opportunity cost of consuming a set of goods today, as opposed to tomorrow? Explain how this will affect the fraction of income you choose to save.

   b. Now suppose that you save only to finance your retirement and that your goal is to have $1 million tucked away by the time you're 70. Explain how your rate of saving will respond to the rise in the interest rate in *this* context.

   c. Can you make a prediction regarding the net effect of this increase in *r* on the rate of saving? Why, or why not?

5. Let's say that your goal is to raise the rate of saving in the United States by 3 percentage points. What are the various ways you could accomplish this? Which of your solutions do you favor?

CHAPTER 14

Investment Spending

CHAPTER HIGHLIGHTS

◆ Investment is the most volatile sector of aggregate demand.

◆ The demand for capital depends on interest rates, output, and taxes.

◆ Investment reflects the adjustment of the existing capital stock to the current demand for capital.

◆ Investment spending is the primary link from monetary policy to aggregate demand.

Investment spending is a central topic in macroeconomics for two reasons. First, investment spending is very volatile and thus responsible for much of the fluctuation of GDP across the business cycle. Second, investment spending is a primary link through which interest rates, and therefore monetary policy, affect the economy. In addition, tax policies affecting investment, under the control of Congress and the president, are important tools of fiscal policy. This chapter focuses on understanding fluctuations in investment, but you should remember that the average level of investment is also interesting because it determines the long-run rate at which the economy adds to its stock of physical capital and thus it helps determine long-run growth.[1]

Figure 14-1 illustrates the volatility of investment by comparing U.S. GDP (left scale) and investment (right scale). Investment averages about 16 percent of GDP, but it is relatively very volatile. (Note that the left and right scales differ by a ratio of 5 to 1.) Dips in total output are associated with much larger proportional dips in investment.

Figure 14-2 demonstrates the volatility of each of the three investment subsectors: *business fixed investment, residential investment,* and *inventory investment.* Fluctuations are on the order of several percent of GDP. Business fixed investment is the largest of the three, but all three subsectors undergo swings that are substantial fractions of swings

---

[1]Faster-growing countries, including Japan and Germany in the early postwar period and the Asian Tigers today, generally invest a higher share of their GDP than do slower-growing countries. In 1995 gross fixed capital as a fraction of GDP was 14 percent for the United States, compared with 36 percent for Korea and 34 percent for Singapore.

FIGURE 14-1   RELATIONSHIP OF PRIVATE INVESTMENT TO GDP, 1959–1995.

Investment averages about 16 percent of GDP, but it is relatively very volatile. (Source: DRI/McGraw Hill Macroeconomic Database.)

BOX 14-1 Why Investment is Volatile— The Back-of-an-Envelope Explanation

The flow of investment "tops off" the stock of capital to bring that stock to its desired level. The flow of investment is normally a very small percentage of the capital stock, so a small proportional change to desired capital results in a large proportional change to investment.

Stocks and flows are often compared using a bathtub metaphor, with the level of the bathwater playing the role of the stock of capital and the flow from the spigot being analogous to the flow of investment. A small change in demand for the level of bathwater can call forth a large change in the flow from the spigot.

We can easily rough out expected magnitudes for changes in investment. In the United States, private capital is roughly 2.5 years' GDP. Investment is about one-sixth of GDP. So the stock of capital is approximately 15 years' worth of investment. If the demand for capital were to drop 1 percent, the investment-GDP ratio would have to drop from around 16 percent of GDP to around 13.5 percent to satisfy the drop within 1 year. Put differently, a 1 percent drop in the capital stock is produced by a 15 percent drop in annual investment flow.

FIGURE 14-2   COMPONENTS OF INVESTMENT AS A PERCENTAGE OF GDP, 1959–1995.

The three different types of investment are shown: residential investment, business fixed investment, and inventory investment. The latter is very small and sometimes negative, but it is also relatively very volatile. (Source: DRI/McGraw Hill Macroeconomic Database.)

Box 14-2 Investment: Gross, Net, and More Inclusive Concepts

The distinction between *gross* and *net* investment is essential even though the difference, depreciation, is hard to measure. Depreciation is more than just the physical wear and tear that results from use and age. A piece of capital may become economically obsolete, for instance, because input prices change—as gas-guzzlers became obsolete when oil prices increased. Economic depreciation may be much more rapid than physical depreciation. Technological obsolescence may also cause rapid economic depreciation. This is particularly true of computers, for which quality improvements have been dramatic.

The rate of depreciation depends on the type of capital. For example, structures have a useful life of decades, while office equipment has a life of only a few years. This has an important implication: If investment shifts toward capital goods with a short life (e.g., computers), then those goods make up a larger share of the capital stock and, as a result, the overall rate of depreciation will rise. This is what happened in the United States in the 1980s, as can be seen in Table 1. Net investment declined by more than gross investment because depreciation increased.

Although it is traditional, the focus on private sector additions to the capital stock in this chapter takes a too-restricted view of investment, in two respects. First, it ignores *government investment*. As anyone who attends a public school or travels on the public highways can tell, government investment also contributes to economic productivity. There has

in GDP. Inventory investment is considerably smaller than the other two portions, but as you can see, it is particularly volatile.

Before getting down to business, we have to clarify terminology. In common usage, "investment" often refers to *buying* existing financial or physical assets. For example, we say someone "invests" in stocks, bonds, or a house when he or she buys the asset. In macroeconomics, "investment" has a more narrow, technical meaning: *Investment* is the flow of spending that adds to the physical stock of capital.

In this chapter we develop investment theories for business fixed investment, residential investment, and inventory investment. The theories are all alike in that they emphasize two elements: the demand for capital, and investment as a flow which adjusts the level of the *capital stock*. Capital is a *stock*, the given dollar value of all the buildings, machines, and inventories at a point in time. Both GDP and investment refer to spending *flows*. Investment is the amount spent by businesses to *add* to the stock of capital over a given period. The capital stock has been created by past investment and is always being reduced by depreciation, so some investment spending is needed just to keep the capital stock from declining.[2]

---

[2]The distinction between gross and net investment was drawn in Chap. 2.

TABLE 1 Gross and Net Investment
(Percent of GDP)

	1960–1980	1980–1990
Gross investment	18.1	17.6
Less depreciation	−11.5	−12.1
Net investment	6.6	5.5

Source: OECD, *Historical Statistics*, 1992.

been much recent work on the productivity of government capital, and there is no question that government investment should be included in aggregate investment. Estimates are that the government capital stock is about 15 to 20 percent of the private capital stock; therefore, the U.S. capital stock and investment are 15 to 20 percent larger than the magnitudes discussed in this chapter.

Second, individuals invest not only in physical capital but also in *human capital*, in increasing the productive capacity of people, through schooling and training. Robert Eisner of Northwestern University estimates that the stock of human capital in the United States is almost as large as the stock of physical capital.* There is much evidence that this investment, like that in physical capital, yields a positive real return; indeed, the return on human capital typically exceeds that on physical capital.

In thinking about investment as spending that increases future productivity, we should look beyond just private sector gross investment.

*See Eisner's comprehensive work, *Total Incomes System of Accounts* (Chicago: University of Chicago Press, 1989).

14-1

FIXED INVESTMENT:

THE NEOCLASSICAL APPROACH

Figure 14-2 shows fixed investment as a share of GDP. In a recession or shortly before, the share of investment in GDP falls sharply; then investment begins to rise as the recovery gets under way. The cyclical relationships extend much further back in history. For instance, gross investment fell to less than 4 percent of GDP in the Great Depression years 1932 and 1933. Understanding investment, then, will go a long way toward helping us understand the business cycle.

In this section, we provide a foundation for the essential component of the simple investment function of Chapter 10—that investment demand is reduced by increases in the interest rate—and, also, go beyond that investment function by discussing the roles of output, financial constraints, and taxes in determining investment. We also examine how investment spending can be affected by policy. Our focus here is on business decisions to add to the stock of equipment or structures. We leave for the next section the discussion of housing or residential investment.

The theory of business fixed investment is the theory of the desired demand for the *stock* of producer capital and the *flow* of investment which moves us from the current to the desired stock. Our analysis proceeds in two stages. First, we ask how much capital firms would like to use, given the costs and returns of using capital and the level of output they expect to produce. That is, we ask what determines the *desired capital stock*. The desired capital stock is the capital stock that firms would like to have in the long run, abstracting from the delays they face in adjusting their use of capital. Because it takes time to order new machines, build factories, and install the machines, firms cannot instantly adjust the stock of capital used in production. Second, therefore, we discuss the rate at which firms adjust from their existing capital stock toward the desired level over the course of time. Investment spending thus depends on two considerations: where we want to go, and how fast we want to get there.

THE DESIRED CAPITAL STOCK: OVERVIEW

Firms use capital, along with labor, to produce goods and services for sale. Their goal is, of course, to maximize profits. In deciding how much capital to use in production, firms have to balance the contribution that more capital makes to their revenues against the cost of using more capital. The *marginal product of capital* is the increase in output produced by using 1 more unit of capital in production. The *rental (user) cost of capital* is the cost of using 1 more unit of capital in production. (Note that both concepts are *flows*.) Whether a firm actually buys its own capital or leases it, the rental cost is the right measure of the *opportunity cost*.[3] As long as the value of the marginal product of capital is above the rental cost, it pays the firm to add to its capital stock. Thus the firm will keep investing until the value of the output produced by adding 1 more unit of capital is equal to the cost of using that capital—the rental cost of capital.

To derive the rental cost of capital, we think of the firm as financing the purchase of the capital by borrowing, at an interest rate i. In the presence of inflation, the nominal dollar value of capital rises over time, so the real cost of using capital over a year is the nominal interest payment less the nominal capital gain. At the time that a firm makes an investment, the nominal interest rate is known, but the inflation rate over the *coming* year is not. So the firm must base its decision on the *expected inflation rate, π^e*. In other words, the real cost of borrowing is the *expected real interest rate $r = i - \pi^e$*. Of course, capital also wears out over time, so the cost of depreciation must be added. A conventional assumption is that depreciation is d percent per year. Thus the complete formula for rental cost is $rc = r + d = i - \pi^e + d$. (Taxes matter too. They're discussed below.)

Firms desire to add capital until the marginal return to the last unit added drops to the rental cost of capital. *Diminishing marginal product* of capital means that the *marginal* product of capital drops as capital is increased. Figure 14-3 shows a *marginal-product-of-capital schedule*. A high rental cost can be justified only by a high marginal product. So an increase of the rental cost from rc_0 to rc_1 decreases the desired capital stock from K_0^* to K_1^*.

---

[3]Even if the firm finances the investment out of profits it has made in the past—retained earnings—it should still think of the interest rate as the basic cost of using the new capital, since it could have lent those funds and earned interest on them or paid them out as dividends to shareholders.

BOX 14-3 The Real Rate of Interest

The distinction between the *real* and *nominal* interest rates is essential here. The *real interest rate* is the nominal (stated) rate of interest minus the rate of inflation.

Think of capital as seed corn. Suppose 100 bushels of seed corn grow into 105 bushels in 1 year's time if strewn into a field and left unattended (i.e., pretend corn grows without the need for any labor). The real return to corn would be 5 percent per year. Absent inflation, a farmer would plant corn if she could borrow for less than 5 percent per year.

Now suppose that the price of corn rises from $1 per bushel at planting to $1.10 per bushel at harvest. An initial $100 investment will yield $115, so the farmer will plant if she can borrow for less than 15 percent per year.* The *real* return on corn is unchanged, but the nominal return includes a 10 percent inflation factor.

Since interest rates are generally quoted in nominal terms, our farmer wishes to subtract inflation from the nominal rate to get a real rate that can be compared to the real return on planting corn. Unfortunately, inflation over the coming year is not known with certainty, so the best the farmer can do is subtract expected inflation from the nominal interest rate to calculate the *expected real* rate of interest for comparison with the return on corn.

The real rate of interest is

$$r = i - \pi^e$$

which states that the real rate of interest is the nominal interest rate minus the expected rate of inflation.

The nominal rate can be a very misleading guide to the cost of borrowing. If the expected rate of inflation is zero and the nominal interest rate is 5 percent, the real interest rate is 5 percent. By contrast, if the nominal interest rate is 10 percent and the expected inflation rate is 10 percent, the real interest rate is zero. Other things equal, the desired capital stock in this example would be higher with the nominal interest rate of 10 percent than with the nominal rate of 5 percent.

Investment spending tends to be higher when the rental cost of capital is lower. But because of the distinction between real and nominal interest rates, that is *not* the same as saying that investment tends to be higher when the nominal rate of interest is lower.

*Note that 105 × $1.10 actually equals $115.50. Technically, when we approximate 15.5 percent by 15 percent, we are ignoring a second-order term.

An increase in the size of the economy moves the entire marginal-product-of-capital schedule to the right, as in Figure 14-4. The rightward shift increases the demand for capital at any given rental cost.

The general relationship among the desired capital stock, K^*, the rental cost of capital, rc, and the level of output is given by

$$K^* = g(rc, Y) \tag{1}$$

where an increase in the rental cost decreases K^* and an increase in GDP increases K^*.

FIGURE 14-3   MARGINAL PRODUCT OF CAPITAL IN RELATION TO THE CAPITAL STOCK.

Given the marginal-product-of-capital schedule, a higher rental cost of capital corresponds to a lower desired capital stock.

FIGURE 14-4   SHIFT OF THE MARGINAL-PRODUCT SCHEDULE.

An increase in the size of the economy shifts the marginal-product schedule to the right, increasing the desired capital stock at any given rental cost.

BOX 14-4 The Demand for Capital: A Cobb-Douglas Example

The generic formula for the production function is $Y = AF(K,N)$. If you prefer to follow the discussion with a specific formula, you can use the *Cobb-Douglas production function*, $Y = AK^\theta N^{1-\theta}$, which, with $\theta \approx .25$, gives a very good approximation to the production function in the United States. Using the Cobb-Douglas, the marginal product of capital is $MPK = \theta AK^{\theta-1} N^{1-\theta} = \theta A(K/N)^{-(1-\theta)} = \theta Y/K$. We find the demand-for-capital function by setting marginal product equal to rental cost, $\theta Y/K = rc$, and solving for K. So for the Cobb-Douglas production function, the demand for capital can be written $K^* = g(rc, Y) = \theta Y/rc$.

Expected Output

Equation (1) shows that the desired capital stock depends on the level of output. But that must be the level of output for some future period, during which the capital will be in production. For some investments the future time at which the output will be produced is a matter of months or only weeks. For other investments, such as power stations, the future time at which the output will be produced is years away.

This suggests that the notion of permanent income (in this case, permanent output) introduced in Chapter 13 is relevant to investment as well as consumption. The firm's demand for business fixed capital, which depends on the normal or permanent level of output, thus depends on expectations of future output levels, rather than the current level of output. However, current output is likely to affect expectations of permanent output.

Taxes and the Rental Cost of Capital

In addition to interest and depreciation, the rental cost of capital is affected by taxes. The two main tax variables are the corporate income tax and the investment tax credit. The corporate income tax is essentially a proportional tax on profits; that is, the firm pays a proportion, say, t, of its profits in taxes. Since the mid-1980s the corporate tax rate in the United States has been 34 percent, down from 46 percent in the early 1980s.

Surprisingly, a good argument can be made that the corporate income tax has no effect on the desired stock of capital. In the presence of the corporate income tax, the firm will want to equate the *after-tax* value of the marginal product of capital with the *after-tax* rental cost of capital in order to ensure that the marginal contribution of the capital to profits is equal to the marginal cost of using it. The key to understanding the impact of the corporate income tax is the fact that interest payments are deducted from the firm's income before its taxes are calculated.

Now consider the following example: Suppose there is no corporate income tax, no inflation, no depreciation, and an interest rate of 10 percent. The desired capital stock will be that level of the capital stock, say, K_0^*, such that the marginal product of

BOX 14-5 Temporary Investment Tax Credit Carries a Big Punch

It's natural to think that permanent changes to fiscal policy have bigger impacts than do temporary changes. But the temporary investment tax credit provides an interesting counterexample. Imagine that, faced with a recession, the government decided to provide an investment tax credit. What is the effect of a temporary, as contrasted with permanent, investment tax credit?

Suppose, as a firm manager, you were told you could get a 10 percent tax credit, *but only this year.* You would rush all your near-future capital spending plans into the current year. So a temporary credit gives a big boost to current investment. (Of course, the next few years might see substantially decreased investment, as the capital spending pipeline had been emptied.) In this way a temporary investment tax credit can be a particularly effective policy tool for boosting current investment spending. Unfortunately, governments are rarely able to so finely time tax changes.

capital is 10 percent. Next suppose that the corporate income tax rises to 34 percent and the interest rate remains constant. At the capital stock K_0^*, the after-tax marginal product of capital is now 6.6 percent (since 34 percent of the profits are paid in taxes). But if the interest rate stays at 10 percent and the firm gets to deduct 34 percent of its interest payments from taxes, the after-tax cost of capital will be 6.6 percent too. In this example, the desired capital stock is unaffected by the rate of corporate taxation.

However, this sharp message is no longer true when investment is financed in part by equity, as it often is. When dividends are paid out to equity holders, they are not deducted from the firm's income for tax purposes. *This means that the cost of capital tends to rise with the corporate tax rate.*

The second tool of investment tax policy, the investment tax credit, was in place in the United States for most of the period 1962–1986 but was discontinued in 1986. It allowed firms to deduct from their taxes a fraction, say, 10 percent, of their investment expenditures in each year. Thus a firm spending $1 million for investment purposes in a given year could deduct 10 percent of the $1 million, or $100,000, from the taxes it would otherwise have to pay the federal government. The investment tax credit reduces the price of a capital good to the firm, since the Treasury returns to the firm a proportion of the cost of each capital good. The investment tax credit therefore reduces the rental cost of capital.

The Effects of Fiscal and Monetary Policy on the Desired Capital Stock

Equation (1) states that the desired capital stock increases when the expected level of output rises and when the rental cost of capital falls. The rental cost of capital, in turn, falls when the real interest rate and the rate of depreciation fall and when the investment tax credit rises. An increase in the corporate tax rate is likely, through the equity route, to reduce the desired capital stock.

The major significance of these results is that they imply that monetary and fiscal policy affect the desired capital stock. Fiscal policy exerts an effect through both the corporate tax rate and the investment tax credit.

Fiscal policy also affects capital demand by its overall effects on the position of the *IS* curve and thus on the interest rate. A high-tax–low government-spending policy keeps the real interest rate low and encourages the demand for capital. A low-tax–high government-spending policy that produces large deficits raises the real interest rate and discourages the demand for capital.

Monetary policy affects capital demand by affecting the market interest rate. A lowering of the nominal interest rate by the Federal Reserve (given the expected inflation rate) induces firms to desire more capital. This expansion in capital demand, in turn, will affect investment spending.

The Stock Market and the Cost of Capital

Rather than borrowing, a firm can also raise the financing it needs to pay for its investment by selling shares, or equity. The people buying the shares expect to earn a return from dividends and/or, if the firm is successful, from the increase in the market value of their shares, that is, *capital gains.*

When its share price is high, a company can raise a lot of money by selling relatively few shares. When stock prices are low, the firm has to sell more shares to raise a given amount of money. The owners of the firm, the existing shareholders, will be more willing to have the firm sell shares to raise new money if it has to sell few shares to do so, that is, if the price is high. Thus we expect corporations to be more willing to sell equity to finance investment when the stock market is high than when it is low. That is why a booming stock market is good for investment.

The q Theory of Investment   The *q theory of investment* emphasizes this connection between investment and the stock market. The price of a share in a company is the price of a claim on the capital in the company. The managers of the company can, then, be thought of as responding to the price of the stock by producing more new capital— that is, investing—when the price of shares is high and as producing less new capital or not investing at all when the price of shares is low.

What is q?[4] It is an estimate of the value the stock market places on a firm's assets relative to the cost of producing those assets. In its simplest form, q is the ratio of the market value of a firm to the replacement cost of capital. When the ratio is high, firms will want to produce more assets, so investment will be rapid. In fact, the most simple version of this theory has a stronger prediction than "high q means high investment." Whenever q is greater than 1 a firm should add physical capital because for each dollar's worth of new machinery, the firm can sell stock for q dollars and pocket

---

[4]You will often see q referred to as "Tobin's q." Nobel Prize–winner James Tobin first put forth this way of connecting the stock market and investment.

a profit $q - 1$. This implies a flood of investment whenever $q > 1$. In reality, adjustment costs make such a flood inefficient, so investment rises moderately with q.

FROM DESIRED CAPITAL STOCK TO INVESTMENT

Equation (1) specifies the desired capital stock. The actual capital stock will often differ from the capital stock firms would like to have. At what speed do firms invest to move toward the desired capital stock? We begin by looking at the *flexible accelerator model,* a rule-of-thumb model for going from capital stock to investment flow.[5] We then discuss further considerations in the timing of investment.

Since it takes time to plan and complete an investment project, and because investing quickly is likely to be more expensive than gradual adjustments of the capital stock, firms do not try to adjust their capital stocks to the long-run desired level instantaneously. Very rapid adjustment of the capital stock would require expensive crash programs that would interfere with regular production. Thus, firms generally plan to adjust their capital stocks gradually over a period of time rather than immediately.

Capital Stock Adjustment

There are a number of hypotheses about the speed at which firms plan to adjust their capital stock over time; we single out the *flexible accelerator model.* The basic notion behind this model is that *the larger the gap between the existing capital stock and the desired capital stock, the more rapid a firm's rate of investment.*

According to the flexible accelerator model, firms plan to close a fraction, λ, of the gap between the desired and actual capital stocks each period. Denote the capital stock at the end of the last period by K_{-1}. The gap between the desired and actual capital stocks is $(K^* - K_{-1})$. The firm plans to add to last period's capital stock K_{-1} a fraction λ of the gap $(K^* - K_{-1})$ so that the actual capital stock at the end of the current period K will be

$$K = K_{-1} + \lambda(K^* - K_{-1}) \tag{2}$$

To increase the capital stock from K_{-1} to the level of K indicated by equation (2), the firm has to achieve the amount of net investment, $I \equiv K - K_{-1}$, indicated by equation (2). We can therefore write net investment as

$$I = K - K_{-1} = \lambda(K^* - K_{-1}) \tag{3}$$

which is the gradual adjustment formulation of net investment.[6]

In Figure 14-5 we show how the capital stock adjusts from an initial level of K_1 to the desired level K^*. The upper panel shows the stock of capital and the lower shows the corresponding flow of investment. The assumed speed of adjustment is $\lambda = .5$. Starting from K_1, one-half the gap between target capital and current actual capital is made up in every period. First-period net investment is therefore $.5(K^* - K_{-1})$. In the second period, investment will be one-half the previous period's rate, since the gap has

---

[5]The flexible accelerator model can be given a rigorous justification as a response to adjustment costs, but we don't pursue this avenue.

[6]Gross investment, as opposed to the net investment described in equation (3), includes, in addition, depreciation. Thus, gross investment is $I + dK_{-1}$, where d is again the rate of depreciation.

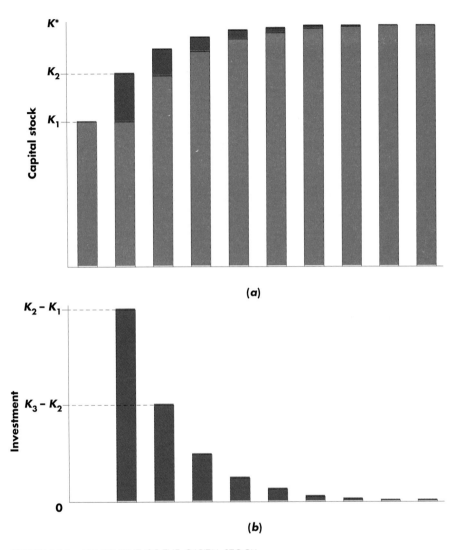

FIGURE 14-5   ADJUSTMENT OF THE CAPITAL STOCK.

If the desired capital stock changes, the capital stock adjusts to the new desired level over time, with investment in each period determined by the speed-of-adjustment parameter, λ.

been reduced by half. Investment continues until the actual capital stock reaches the level of target capital. The larger λ is, the faster the gap is reduced.

In equation (3), we have reached our goal of deriving an investment function that shows current investment spending determined by the desired stock of capital, K^*, and the actual stock of capital, K_{-1}. Any factor that increases the desired capital stock increases the rate of investment. Therefore, an increase in expected output, a reduction in the real interest rate, or an increase in the investment tax credit will each increase the rate of investment. The flexible accelerator demonstrates that investment contains

TABLE 14-1 Sources of Funds, U.S. Manufacturing Firms, 1970–1984

	SOURCE OF FUNDS,* % OF TOTAL					
FIRM SIZE	SHORT-TERM BANK DEBT	LONG-TERM BANK DEBT	OTHER LONG-TERM BANK DEBT	RETAINED EARNINGS	PERCENT OF LONG-TERM DEBT FROM BANKS	AVERAGE RETENTION RATIO, %
All firms	0.6	8.4	19.0	71.1	29.6	60
Asset class:						
Under $10 million	5.1	12.8	6.2	75.9	67.3	79
Over $1 billion	−0.6	4.8	27.9	67.9	14.7	52

*Minus sign indicates that firms have net assets (rather than liabilities) in this category.

Source: Steven M. Fazzari, R. Glenn Hubbard, and Bruce C. Petersen, "Financing Constraints and Corporate Investment," *Brookings Papers on Economic Activity* 1 (1988).

aspects of *dynamic behavior*—that is, behavior that depends on values of economic variables in periods other than the current period. Empirical evidence shows that the dynamics of the flexible accelerator are somewhat too rigid—for example, investment takes about 2 years to peak after a change in capital demand—but the basic principle of gradual adjustment is clear.

The Timing of Investment

Credit Rationing and Internal Sources of Finance Table 14-1 shows the sources of manufacturing firms' funding in the United States during the period 1970–1984. The predominance of retained earnings as a source of financing stands out. Firms of all sizes use outside funding from banks, bond markets, and equity only to a limited extent.[7] Instead, they rely on retained earnings, profits that they do not pay out to stockholders, to finance investment. As the last column of the table shows, retained earnings exceeds 50 percent of earnings for all firms and is relatively most important for the smallest firms.

What do these facts mean for the investment decision? They suggest that there is a close link between the earnings of firms and their investment decisions. If firms cannot readily obtain funding from outside sources when they need it, the amount of assets they have on hand will affect their ability to invest. This would mean that the state of a firm's balance sheet, and not just the cost of capital, is a financial determinant of investment decisions.

Box 14-6 describes the important phenomenon of *credit rationing,* which occurs when individuals cannot borrow even though they are willing to do so at the existing interest rates. There are good reasons for credit rationing, all stemming from the risk that the borrower will not repay the lender, for instance, because the borrower goes bankrupt. These arguments suggest that credit rationing is more likely for small firms

---

[7]Equity funding is excluded from the table, but independent evidence, noted in the article by Fazzari, Hubbard, and Petersen (cited in Table 14-1) shows that it provides very little financing for firms, especially small ones.

BOX 14-6 Credit Rationing

In the *IS-LM* model, interest rates are the only channel of transmission between financial markets and aggregate demand. Credit rationing is an important additional channel of transmission of monetary policy.* Credit rationing takes place when lenders limit the amount individuals can borrow, even though the borrowers are willing to pay the going interest rate on their loans.

Credit rationing can occur for two different reasons. First, a lender often cannot tell whether a particular customer (or the project the customer is financing) is good or bad. A bad customer will default on the loan and not repay it. Given the risk of default, the obvious answer seems to be to raise the interest rate.

However, raising interest rates works the wrong way: honest or conservative customers are deterred from borrowing because they realize their investments are not profitable at higher interest rates. But customers who are reckless or dishonest will borrow because they do not in any case expect to pay if the project turns out badly. However carefully they try to evaluate their customers, the lenders cannot altogether escape this problem. The answer is to limit the amount lent to any one customer. Most customers get broadly the same interest rate (with some adjustments), but the amount of credit they are allowed is rationed, according to both the kind of security the customer can offer and the prospects for the economy.

When times are good, banks lend cheerfully because they believe that the average customer will not default. When the economy turns down, credit rationing intensifies—and this may happen even though interest rates decline.

Credit rationing provides another channel for monetary policy. If lenders perceive that the Fed is shifting to restraint and higher interest rates to cool down the economy, lenders fearing a slowdown will tighten credit. Conversely, if they believe policy is expansionary and times will be good, they ease credit, via both lower interest rates and expanded credit rationing.[†]

A second type of credit rationing can occur when the central bank imposes credit limits on commercial banks and other lenders. Banks are then not allowed to expand their loans during a given period by more than, say, 5 percent or even less. Such a credit limit can bring a boom to an abrupt end. A striking example occurred in the United States in early 1980. Concerned with the risk of double-digit inflation, the Fed clamped on credit controls. In no time the economy fell into a recession, with output falling at an annual rate of 9 percent.

Credit controls thus are an emergency brake for the central bank. They work, but they do so in a very blunt way. For that reason their use is very infrequent and remains reserved for occasions when dramatic, fast effects are desired.

---

[*]For a comprehensive survey on credit rationing, see Dwight Jaffee and Joseph Stiglitz, "Credit Rationing" in Ben Friedman and Frank Hahn (eds.), *Handbook of Monetary Economics* (Amsterdam: North-Holland, 1990).

[†]Frederick Mishkin provides a readable introduction to the transmission mechanism between monetary policy and the private economy in "Symposium on the Monetary Transmission Mechanism," *Journal of Economic Perspectives*, Fall 1995. In the same issue see also John B. Taylor, "The Monetary Transmission Mechanism: An Empirical Framework," Ben S. Bernanke and Mark Gertler, "Inside the Black Box: The Credit Channel of Monetary Policy Transmission," and Allan H. Meltzer, "Monetary, Credit (and Other) Transmission Processes: A Monetarist Perspective."

without an established reputation than for large firms with a track record. The fact that the retention ratio in Table 14-1 declines with firm size is consistent with this implication. These data, as well as the experience of firms that want to borrow, are consistent with the assumption that firms are rationed in their access to funding.[8]

Under such conditions, firms' investment decisions will be affected not only by the interest rate but also by the amount of funds the firms have saved out of past earnings and by their current profits. The cost of capital must still affect the investment decision, because firms that retain earnings have to consider the alternative of holding financial assets and earning interest rather than investing in plant and equipment. There is indeed evidence that the rate of investment is affected by the volume of retained earnings and by profits, as well as by the cost of capital.

In the early 1990s, in the aftermath of severe banking problems due to losses in real estate, credit rationing was held responsible for the slow—despite low short-term interest rates—rate of investment in the United States. Banks were lending very little, especially to small- and medium-size firms. The problem was especially severe in depressed regions, because small businesses can only borrow locally, from banks, but banks in a depressed region are especially unwilling to lend.

Irreversibility and the Timing of Investment Decisions   Beneath the stock-demand-for-capital-leads-to-investment-flow model lies the idea that capital is "putty-putty." Goods are in a malleable form that can be transformed into capital by investment and then easily transformed back into general goods. Much capital is better described as "putty-clay." Once capital is built, it can't be used for much except its original purpose. A warehouse (putty-putty) may have high-valued alternative uses as a factory or an office building. A jetliner (putty-clay) isn't of much use except for flying. The essence of putty-clay investment is that it is *irreversible*. An irreversible investment will be executed not when it becomes merely profitable but, rather, when it does not pay to wait for any further improvement in profitability.[9]

◆ O P T I O N A L ◆

The Business Investment Decision: The View from the Trenches

Businesspeople making investment decisions typically use *discounted cash flow analysis*.[10] The principles of discounting are described in Chapter 17. Consider a businessperson deciding whether to build and equip a new factory. The first step is to figure out how much it will cost to get the factory into working order and how much revenue the factory will bring in each year after it starts operation.

---

[8]In "Is There a Broad Credit Channel for Monetary Policy," Federal Reserve Bank of San Francisco *Economic Review* 1 (1996), Stephen D. Oliner and Glenn D. Rudebusch present evidence showing that internal sources of funds are especially important for small firms and especially important in downturns.

[9]This statement is based on a sophisticated argument in terms of financial option theory. See Robert Pindyck, "Irreversible Investment, Capacity and Choice and the Value of the Firm," *American Economic Review,* December 1988, and Avinash K. Dixit and Robert S. Pindyck, *Investment under Uncertainty* (Princeton, N.J.: Princeton University Press, 1993).

[10]Discounted cash flow analysis and the rental-cost-equals-marginal-product-of-capital models are simply different ways of thinking about the same decision process. You will sometimes hear businesspeople discussing what we call the marginal product of capital as the "internal rate of return."

TABLE 14-2 Discounted Cash Flow Analysis and Present Value
                (Dollars)

	YEAR 1	YEAR 2	YEAR 3	PRESENT DISCOUNTED VALUE
Cash or revenue	-100	$+50$	$+80$	
Present value of $1	1	$1/1.12 = 0.893$	$1/1.12^2 = 0.797$	
Present value of costs or revenue	-100	50×0.893 $= 44.65$	80×0.797 $= 63.76$	$-100 + 44.65 + 63.76$ $= 8.41$

For simplicity, consider a very short lived project, one that costs $100 to set up in the first year and then generates $50 in revenue (after paying for labor and raw materials) in the second year and a further $80 in the third year. By the end of the third year the factory has disintegrated.

Should the project be undertaken? Discounted cash flow analysis says that the revenues received in later years should be *discounted* to the present in order to calculate their present value. If the interest rate is 10 percent, $110 a year from now is worth the same as $100 now. (See Chapter 17 for a more extended discussion.) Why? Because if $100 is lent out today at 10 percent, a year from now the lender will end up with $110. To calculate the value of the project, the firm calculates the project's present discounted value at the interest rate at which it can borrow. If the present value is positive, the project is undertaken.

Suppose that the relevant interest rate is 12 percent. The calculation of the present discounted value of the investment project is shown in Table 14-2. The $50 received in year 2 is worth only $44.65 today: $1 a year from now is worth $1/1.12 = 0.893 today, and so $50 a year from now is worth $44.65. The present value of the $80 received in year 3 is calculated similarly. The table shows that the present value of the net revenue received from the project is positive ($8.41); thus the firm should undertake the project.

Note that if the interest rate had been much higher—say, 18 percent—the decision would have been *not* to undertake the investment. We thus see that *the higher the interest rate, the less likely the firm will be to undertake any given investment project.*

At any time, each firm has an array of possible investment projects and estimates of the costs and revenues from those projects. Depending on the level of the interest rate, the firm will want to undertake some of the projects and not undertake others. Adding the investment demands of all the firms in the economy, we obtain the total demand for investment in the economy at each interest rate.

14-2

RESIDENTIAL INVESTMENT

Figure 14-6 shows residential investment spending as a percentage of GDP, together with the nominal mortgage interest rate. Residential investment is low when mortgage interest rates are high, and it declines in all recessions.

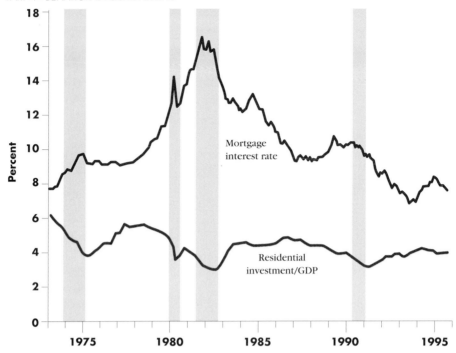

FIGURE 14-6   RESIDENTIAL INVESTMENT AND MORTGAGE INTEREST RATES, 1973–1995.

Residential investment spending as a percentage of GDP is low when nominal mortgage rates are high. Residential investment declines in recessions. (Source: DRI/McGraw Hill Macroeconomic Database.)

Residential investment consists of the building of single-family and multifamily dwellings, which we call *housing* for short. Housing is distinguished as an asset by its long life. Consequently, investment in housing in any one year tends to be a very small proportion—about 3 percent—of the existing stock of housing. The theory of residential investment starts by considering the demand for the existing *stock* of housing.

In Figure 14-7 we show the demand for the stock of housing in the downward-sloping DD_0 curve. The lower the price of housing (P_H), the greater the quantity demanded. The position of the demand curve itself depends on a number of economic variables. First, the more wealthy individuals are, the more housing they desire to own. Thus an increase in wealth would shift the demand curve from DD_0 to DD_1. Second, the demand for housing as an asset depends on the real return on other assets. If returns on other forms of holding wealth—such as bonds—are low, then housing looks like a relatively attractive form in which to hold wealth. A reduction in the return on other assets, such as bonds or common stock, shifts the demand curve from DD_0 to DD_1.

Third, the demand for the housing stock depends on the net real return obtained by owning housing. The gross return—before taking costs into account—consists either of rent, if the housing is rented out, or of the implicit return that the homeowner receives by living in the home plus capital gains arising from increases in the value of the housing. In turn, the costs of owning the housing consist of interest costs, typically the mortgage interest rate, plus any real estate taxes and depreciation. These costs are deducted from the gross return and, after tax adjustments, constitute the net return. An

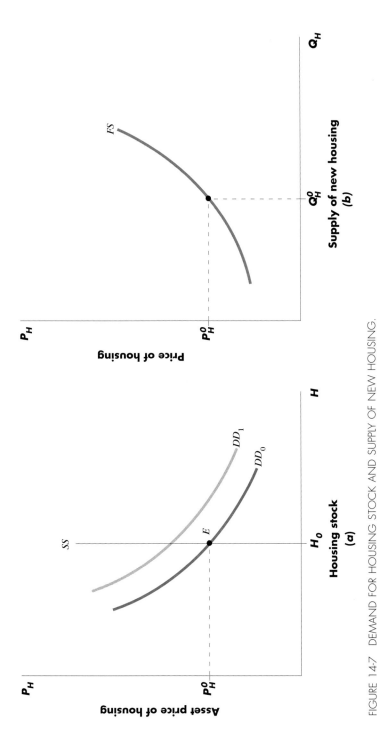

FIGURE 14-7   DEMAND FOR HOUSING STOCK AND SUPPLY OF NEW HOUSING.

Panel (a) shows the demand relationship for housing, which can be shifted by changes such as an increase in the wealth of individuals or a decrease in the return on other assets. The line SS indicates the fixed stock of housing at a point in time. Panel (b) shows the flow supply curve for new housing as a function of the price of housing. The quantity of new housing supplied in a period adds to the stock of housing.

increase in the net return on housing, caused, for example, by a reduction in the mortgage interest rate, makes housing a more attractive form in which to hold wealth and shifts the demand curve for housing from DD_0 to DD_1.

The price of housing is determined by the interaction of this demand with the stock supply of housing. At any time the stock supply is fixed—there is a given stock of housing that cannot be changed quickly. The supply curve of the stock of housing is therefore the *SS* curve of Figure 14-7a. The equilibrium *asset price of housing, P_H^0,* is determined by the intersection of the supply and demand curves. The asset price of housing is the price of a typical house or apartment. At any one time, the market for the stock of housing determines the asset price of housing.

THE RATE OF HOUSING INVESTMENT

We now consider the determinants of the rate of investment in housing, and for that purpose turn to Figure 14-7b. The *FS* curve represents the supply of new housing as a function of the price of housing. This curve is the same as the regular supply curve of any industry. The supply curve shows the amount of a good that suppliers want to sell at each price. In this case, the good being supplied is new housing. The position of the *FS* curve is affected by the costs of factors of production used in the construction industry and by technological factors affecting the cost of building.

The *FS* curve is sometimes called the *flow* supply curve, since it represents the flow of new housing into the market in a given time period. In contrast, the *stock* supply curve, *SS,* represents the total amount of housing in the market at a moment of time.

Given the price of housing established in the asset market, P_H^0, building contractors supply the amount of new housing, Q_H^0, for sale at that price. The higher the asset price, the greater the supply of new housing. Thus, the supply of new housing is nothing other than gross investment in housing—total additions to the housing stock. Figure 14-7 thus represents our basic theory of housing investment.

Any factor affecting the demand for the existing stock of housing will affect the asset price of housing, P_H, and thus the rate of investment in housing. Similarly, any factor shifting the flow supply curve, *FS,* will affect the rate of investment.

Suppose the interest rate—the rate that potential homeowners can obtain by investing elsewhere—rises. Then the asset demand for housing falls and the price of housing falls; that, in turn, induces a decline in the rate of production of new housing, or a decline in housing investment. Or suppose that the mortgage interest rate rises. Once again there is a fall in the asset price of housing and a reduction in the rate of construction.

Because the existing stock of housing is so large relative to the rate of investment in housing, we can ignore the effects of the current supply of new housing on the price of housing in the short run. However, over time, as new construction increases the housing stock, it shifts the *SS* curve of panel (*a*) to the right. The long-run equilibrium in the housing industry would be reached, in a nongrowing economy, when the housing stock became constant. Constancy of the housing stock requires that gross investment be equal to depreciation or net investment be equal to zero. The asset price of housing would have to be at the level at which the rate of construction was just equal to the rate of depreciation of the existing stock of housing in long-run equilibrium. If population or income and wealth were growing at a constant rate, the long-run equilibrium would be one in which the rate of construction was just sufficient to cover depreciation and the steadily growing stock demand. In an economy subjected to continual, nonsteady changes, that long-run equilibrium is not necessarily ever reached.

Minor qualifications to the basic theoretical structure arise chiefly because new housing cannot be constructed immediately in response to changes in P_H. Thus, the supply of new housing responds not to the actual price of housing today but to the price expected to prevail when the construction is completed. However, the lags are quite short; it takes less than a year to build a typical house. Another qualification stems from that same construction delay. Since builders have to incur expenses before they sell their output, they need financing during the construction period. They frequently obtain mortgages to provide the needed funds. Hence, the position of the flow supply curve is affected by the mortgage interest rate as well as the amount of lending undertaken by mortgage lenders.

MONETARY POLICY AND HOUSING INVESTMENT

Monetary policy has powerful effects on housing investment. Part of the reason is that most houses are purchased with mortgages. Since the 1930s, a mortgage in the United States has typically been a debt instrument of very long maturity, 20 to 30 years, with fixed monthly repayments until maturity.[11]

Monetary policy has powerful effects on housing investment because the demand for housing is sensitive to the interest rate. There is sensitivity to both the *real* and the *nominal* interest rates. The reason for this sensitivity can be seen in Table 14-3, which shows the monthly payment that has to be made by someone borrowing $100,000 through a conventional mortgage at different interest rates. All these interest rates have existed at some time during the last 35 years: 5 percent at the beginning of the 1960s, 10 percent at the end of the seventies and end of the eighties, 15 percent in 1981 and 1982, and 8 percent in the mid-1990s. The monthly repayment by the borrower approximately doubles when the interest rate doubles. Thus an essential component of

[11]Adjustable rate mortgages (ARMs) were introduced in the United States in the 1970s. The interest rate on such mortgages is adjusted in accordance with some reference rate, such as the 1-year Treasury-bill rate. Both fixed rate mortgages and ARMs are now used to finance housing. Arrangements for housing finance differ significantly across countries. Five-year renewable mortgages are common in Canada. In Japan and Korea, home buyers (and family) provide more housing funding than is common in the United States.

TABLE 14-3 Monthly Payments on Mortgages*

	CIRCA 1960	CIRCA 1988	CIRCA 1982	CIRCA 1996
Nominal interest rate, %	5	10	15	8
Inflation rate, %	0	5	10	3
Real interest rate, %	5	5	5	5
Monthly payment, $	537	878	1,264	774
After-tax payment, $	376	614	885	514
Real after-tax payment, $	376	198	52	264

*The assumed mortgage is a loan for $100,000 paid back over 30 years, with equal monthly payments throughout the 30 years. A 30 percent tax rate is assumed and real after-tax payments assume capital gains are effectively untaxed.

the cost of owning a home rises almost proportionately with the interest rate. It is therefore not surprising that the demand for housing is very sensitive to the interest rate.

Table 14-3 also shows the effect of taxes and inflation on housing costs. In the United States, interest payments on a principal residence are deductible from the personal income tax. The deduction, not available in many other countries, is part of a deliberate attempt to encourage individual homeownership. A further feature of the U.S. tax system is that nominal interest payments are deductible and nominal capital gains due to inflation are essentially untaxed. This means that the combination of high nominal rates and high inflation strongly encourages housing investment. Consider payments on a $100,000 mortgage when the nominal interest rate is 15 percent and the inflation rate is 10 percent. Annual interest is approximately $15,000. For a homeowner in the 30 percent marginal tax bracket, the mortgage interest deduction is $4,500, so the after-tax interest cost is approximately $10,500. But at 10 percent inflation, this cost is offset by a $10,000 increase in the nominal value of the house. In effect, the real cost of capital for the house is nearly zero.

Despite this analysis, high nominal interest rates do discourage home ownership because of two kinds of liquidity effects. First, the homeowner has to make the full nominal payments up front and receives the offsetting capital gain far in the future. Second, banks use rules of thumb to qualify mortgage applicants (e.g., that payments can be no more than 28 percent of income) that don't adjust very much in periods of high inflation. Both these liquidity effects depend on the nominal, not real, interest rate.

14-3

INVENTORY INVESTMENT

Inventories consist of raw materials, goods in the process of production, and completed goods held by firms in anticipation of the products' sale. The ratio of manufacturing inventories to sales in the United States has been in the range of 10 to 15 percent over the past 40 years. The trend has been declining in the 1990s.

Firms hold inventories for several reasons:

- Sellers hold inventories to meet future demand for goods, because goods cannot be instantly manufactured or obtained to meet demand.
- Inventories are held because it is less costly for a firm to order goods less frequently in large quantities than to order small quantities frequently—just as the average householder finds it is useful to keep several days' worth of groceries in the house to avoid having to visit the supermarket daily.
- Producers may hold inventories as a way of smoothing their production. Since it is costly to keep changing the level of output on a production line, producers may produce at a relatively steady rate even when demand fluctuates, building up inventories when demand is low and drawing them down when demand is high.
- Some inventories are held as an unavoidable part of the production process. There is an inventory of meat and sawdust inside the sausage machine during the manufacture of sausage, for example.

Firms have a desired ratio of inventories to final sales that depends on economic variables. The smaller the cost of ordering new goods and the greater the speed with which such goods arrive, the smaller the inventory-sales ratio. The inventory-sales ratio may also depend on the level of sales, with the ratio falling with sales because there is relatively less uncertainty about sales as sales increase.

Finally, there is the *interest rate.* Since firms carry inventories over time, the firms must tie up resources in order to buy and hold the inventories. There is an interest cost involved in such inventory holding, and the desired inventory-sales ratio should be expected to fall with increases in the interest rate.

THE ACCELERATOR MODEL

All these considerations notwithstanding, inventory investment can be explained surprisingly well with the simple *accelerator model.* The accelerator model asserts that investment spending is proportional to the change in output and is not affected by the cost of capital, $I = \alpha(Y - Y_{-1})$.[12] Figure 14-8 compares inventory investment to the change in GDP. Much, but not all, inventory investment can be explained this way. The connection of the *level* of inventory investment to the *change* in output is an important channel adding to the overall volatility of the economy.

---

[12]The accelerator model is actually a special case of the flexible accelerator. (The former came first.) To see this, ignore the role of the rental cost and set $\lambda = 1$ in the formula for the flexible accelerator.

FIGURE 14-8   CHANGE IN GDP AND THE LEVEL OF INVENTORY INVESTMENT.

(Source: DRI/McGraw Hill Macroeconomic Database.)

ANTICIPATED VS. UNANTICIPATED INVENTORY INVESTMENT

Inventory investment takes place when firms increase their inventories. The central aspect of inventory investment lies in the distinction between anticipated (desired) and unanticipated (undesired) investment. Inventory investment could be high in two circumstances. First, if sales are unexpectedly low, firms would find unsold inventories accumulating on their shelves; that constitutes unanticipated inventory investment. Second, inventory investment could be high because firms plan to build up inventories; that is anticipated or desired investment.

The two circumstances obviously have very different implications for the behavior of aggregate demand. Unanticipated inventory investment is a result of unexpectedly low aggregate demand. By contrast, planned inventory investment adds to aggregate demand. Thus rapid accumulation of inventories could be associated with either rapidly declining aggregate demand or rapidly increasing aggregate demand.

INVENTORIES IN THE BUSINESS CYCLE

Inventory investment fluctuates proportionately more in the business cycle than any other component of aggregate demand. In every post-World War II recession in the United States there has been a decline in inventory investment between peak and trough. As a recession develops, demand slows down and firms add involuntarily to the stock of inventories. Thus the inventory-sales ratio rises. Then production is cut, and firms meet demand by selling goods from inventories. At the end of every recession, firms were reducing their inventories, meaning that inventory investment was negative in the final quarter of every recession.

The role of inventories in the business cycle is a result of a combination of unanticipated and anticipated inventory change. Figure 14-9 illustrates the combination using

FIGURE 14-9 SALES AND OUTPUT IN RECESSION AND RECOVERY, 1981–1983.

The shaded area marks the period of recession. (Source: DRI/McGraw-Hill.)

data from the deep recession at the start of the 1980s. Before the 1981–1982 recession began, GDP increased rapidly, recovering from the previous recession. That meant firms were running down their inventories. From the beginning of 1981 firms began to accumulate inventories, as output exceeded their sales. Firms were probably anticipating high sales in the future and decided to build up their stocks of goods for future sale. Thus there was *intended* inventory accumulation.

Final sales turned down at the beginning of 1981, but GDP stayed high until the third quarter. Thus the first half of 1981 was a period of *unintentional* inventory accumulation. Then firms realized their inventories were too high, and they cut production to get them back in line. In the first quarter of 1982, firms cut output way back and finally were successfully and *intentionally* reducing their inventories; hence, in that quarter sales exceeded output. This stage, in which output falls sharply as firms intentionally cut back production to get inventories back in line, has been typical in post-World War II recessions. Finally, inventories were built up *intentionally* as the recovery got under way in 1983.

To understand the *inventory cycle,* consider the case of a hypothetical automobile dealer who sells, say, thirty cars per month and holds an average of 1 month's sales—namely, thirty cars—in inventory. As long as sales stay steady at thirty cars per month, the dealer will be ordering thirty cars each month from the factory. Now suppose sales drop to twenty-five cars per month, and it takes the dealer 2 months to respond to the change. During those 2 months inventory will have climbed to forty cars. In the future the dealer will want an inventory of only twenty-five cars on hand. Thus, when responding to the fall in demand, the dealer cuts the order from the factory from thirty cars to ten in the third month to get the inventory back to 1 month's sales. After the desired inventory-sales ratio has been restored, the order will be twenty-five cars per month. We see in this extreme case how the drop in demand of five cars, instead of leading to a simple drop in car output of five cars per month, causes a drop in output of twenty cars in 1 month, followed by the longer-run drop in output of five cars per month.

Just-in-Time Inventory Management

If inventories could be kept more closely in line with sales, or aggregate demand, fluctuations in inventory investment and in GDP would be reduced. As business methods are improving all the time, the hope is often expressed that new methods of management will enable firms to keep tighter control over their inventories and thus that the prospects for steadier growth can be improved. *"Just-in-time" inventory management* techniques, imported from Japan, emphasize the synchronization of suppliers and users of materials, thereby allowing firms to operate with small inventories, so production is "lean" in inventories. These improved methods help account for the downward trend in inventories. Indeed, in the 1990–1991 recession, the inventory–final sales ratio increased very little, much less than in previous recessions.

14-4

INVESTMENT AROUND THE WORLD

This chapter focuses on investment as a component of aggregate demand and on the role investment plays in the business cycle. But, because the capital stock is a key

TABLE 14-4   Ratio of Investment to Output
(Percent)

COUNTRY	1975	1995
United States	17.6	17.2
Canada	24.4	17.3
Japan	32.5	28.6
Korea	24.9	53.7
Singapore	35.1	34.4
Bangladesh	5.5	16.1
Tanzania	18.6	27.5

Source: International Financial Statistics Yearbook 1996, ratio of gross fixed capital formation to GDP.

determinant of productivity, investment also affects long-run aggregate supply. One reason that high-growth countries *are* high-growth countries is because they devote a substantial fraction of their output to investment. Table 14-4 shows the ratio of gross fixed capital formation to GDP for several countries. The investment ratios are determined by both the demand for capital, as studied in this chapter, and the supply of savings.

Table 14-4 suggests that high rates of investment occur in rapidly growing countries but not necessarily in countries that have already become very wealthy. In both 1975 and 1995, the United States and Canada were wealthy countries with moderate growth rates. In 1975, Japan was a moderately well off country with a high growth rate. Over this period both Singapore and Korea grew very rapidly, due in part to their high rates of investment, but had not yet reached the income levels of the United States. In 1975, the two poor countries shown, Bangladesh and Tanzania, had investment rates too low to support rapid growth. By 1995, although both countries remained relatively poor, their investment rates had picked up considerably.

The relatively low rates of investment in the United States and Canada, compared to their international competitors, are a source of long-run concern to policy makers.

SUMMARY

1. Investment is spending that adds to the capital stock. Investment usually constitutes less than 17 percent of aggregate demand in the United States, but fluctuations in investment account for a large share of business cycle movements in GDP. We analyze investment in three categories: business fixed investment, residential investment, and inventory investment.

2. The neoclassical theory of business fixed investment sees the rate of investment being determined by the speed with which firms adjust their capital stocks toward the desired level. The desired capital stock is bigger the larger the *expected* output the firm plans to produce and the smaller the rental or user cost of capital.

3. The real interest rate is the nominal (stated) interest rate minus the inflation rate.

4. The rental cost of capital is higher the higher the real interest rate, the lower the price of the firm's stock, and the higher the depreciation rate of capital. Taxes also

affect the rental cost of capital, in particular through the investment tax credit. The investment tax credit is, in effect, a government subsidy for investment.

5. In practice, firms decide how much to invest using discounted cash flow analysis. This analysis gives answers that are consistent with those of the neoclassical approach.

6. The accelerator model of investment is a special case of the gradual adjustment model of investment. It predicts that investment demand is proportional to the *change* in GDP.

7. Because credit is rationed, firms' investment decisions are affected also by the state of their balance sheets, and thus by the amount of earnings they have retained.

8. Empirical results show that business fixed investment responds with long lags to changes in output. The accelerator model, which does not take into account changes in the rental cost of capital, does almost as good a job of explaining investment as the more sophisticated neoclassical model.

9. The theory of housing investment starts from the demand for the *stock* of housing. Demand is affected by wealth, the interest rates available on alternative investments, and the mortgage rate. The price of housing is determined by the interaction of the stock demand and the fixed stock supply of housing available at any given time. The rate of housing investment is determined by the rate at which builders supply housing at the going price.

10. Housing investment is affected by monetary policy because housing demand is sensitive to the mortgage interest rate (real and nominal). Credit availability also plays a role.

11. Monetary policy and fiscal policy both affect investment, particularly business fixed investment and housing investment. The effects take place through changes in real (and nominal, in the case of housing) interest rates and through tax incentives for investment.

12. There are substantial lags in the adjustment of investment spending to changes in output and other determinants of investment. Such lags are likely to increase fluctuations in GDP.

13. Inventory investment fluctuates proportionately more than any other class of investment. Firms have a desired inventory-to-sales ratio. The ratio may get out of line if sales are unexpectedly high or low, and then firms change their production levels to adjust inventories. For instance, when aggregate demand falls at the beginning of a recession, inventories build up. Then when firms cut back production, output falls even more than did aggregate demand. This is the inventory cycle.

KEY TERMS

business fixed investment	real interest rates	inventory cycle
residential investment	*q* theory of investment	just-in-time inventory
inventory investment	flexible accelerator model	management
investment capital stock	credit rationing	
desired capital stock	discounted cash flow	
marginal product of capital	analysis	
rental (user) cost of capital	accelerator model	

PROBLEMS

Conceptual

1. If an economy has achieved its desired capital stock and wishes merely to maintain it, should any investment occur? If not, why not? If so, how much?

2. What effect has the recent shift toward investment in high-tech capital goods had on the rate of depreciation? Do you think there is a rate of depreciation associated with the stock of human capital?

3. If a firm invests out of retained profits rather than borrowed funds, will its investment decisions still be affected by the changes in the interest rate? Explain.

4. The neoclassical model of business fixed investment examines the benefits and costs to firms of owning capital goods. Its basic conclusion is that firms will increase their capital stock as long as the marginal product of their capital exceeds the marginal cost. What is Tobin's q, and how does it relate to this neoclassical model?

5. According to the description of business fixed investment in this chapter, how would you expect a firm's investment decisions to be affected by a sudden increase in the demand for its product? What factors would determine the speed of its reaction?

6. The number of small firms in the U.S. economy has grown substantially over the last decade. If small firms do, indeed, encounter more credit rationing than large firms, what effect might this have on output fluctuations (business cycles) in the United States?

7. **a.** Give at least two reasons why higher profits may increase the rate of investment.
   b. Explain why lenders may ration the quantity of credit rather than merely charge higher interest rates to more risky borrowers.

8. **a.** Explain why the housing market usually prospers when the (real) mortgage rates are low.
   b. In some states, usury laws prohibit (nominal) mortgage rates in excess of a legal maximum. Explain how this could lead to an exception to the conclusion in (**a**).

9. What is the relationship between the accelerator model of inventory investment and the flexible accelerator model of capital accumulation?

10. Can changes in inventories predict movements in the business cycle? Why does it matter whether these changes are planned or unplanned?

11. In the 1990–1991 recession, the inventory-sales ratio did not rise appreciably. How do you explain this fact?

12. Why should (or shouldn't) policy makers be concerned about the relatively low levels of U.S. investment that have prevailed in the last decade?

Technical

1. Describe how a car rental agency would calculate the price at which it rents cars, and relate your description to the equation for rental cost which is given in the text.

2. The cash flows for an investment project are listed below. The firm will invest if the present value of the cash flows is positive.

YEAR 1	YEAR 2	YEAR 3
− 200	100	120

Should the firm undertake this project:
   a. If the interest rate is 5 percent?
   b. If the interest rate is 10 percent?

3. Suppose that an explicitly temporary tax credit is enacted. The tax credit is at the rate of 10 percent and lasts only 1 year.

   a. What is the effect of this tax measure on investment in the long run (say, after 4 or 5 years)?

   b. What is the effect in the current year and in the following year?

   c. How would your answers in (**a**) and (**b**) differ if the tax credit were permanent?

4. Using Figure 14-7, trace carefully the step-by-step effects on the housing market of an increase in interest rates. Explain each shift and its long-run and short-run effects.

5. a. Explain how final sales and output can differ.

   b. In Figure 14-9, point out periods of planned and unplanned inventory investment and drawing down.

   c. During a period of slow but steady growth, how would you expect final sales and output to be related? Explain. Draw a hypothetical figure like Figure 14-9 for such a period.

6. Given the following information, calculate Tobin's q statistic: Let's suppose that a company has 1 million outstanding shares of stock, each valued at $25. Let us suppose also that the replacement cost of its physical capital stock is $18 million.

   a. Should this firm invest (net) in more physical capital?

   b. Would your answer change if the replacement cost of its physical capital stock at this time was $25,000,000? $28,000,000?

7. (*Optional*) For this question use the Cobb-Douglas production function and the corresponding desired capital stock given by $K^* = g(rc,Y) = \theta Y/rc$. Assume that $\gamma = .3$, $Y = 5 trillion, and $rc = .12$.

   a. Calculate the desired capital stock, K^*.

   b. Now suppose that Y is expected to rise to $6 trillion. What is the corresponding desired capital stock?

   c. Suppose that the capital stock was at the desired level before the change in income was expected. Suppose further that $\lambda = .4$ in the gradual adjustment model of investment. What will the rate of investment be in the first year after expected income changes? In the second year?

   d. Does your answer in (**c**) refer to gross or net investment?

CHAPTER 15

The Demand for Money

CHAPTER HIGHLIGHTS

◆ Money is whatever asset is used in transactions. This varies over time and place.

◆ Money demand is a demand for *real balances*, the number of dollars divided by the price level.

◆ The demand for money rises with higher income and falls with higher interest rates.

What is "money" and why does anyone want it?

This question is less frivolous than it appears, because economists use the term "money" in a special technical sense. By "money" we mean the medium of exchange, the stuff you use to pay for things—cash, for example. In colloquial use "money" sometimes means "income" ("I made a lot of money last year") or "wealth" ("That guy has a lot of money"). When economists speak of the "demand for money," we are asking about the stock of assets held as cash, checking accounts, and closely related assets, specifically *not* generic wealth or income. Our interest is in why consumers and firms hold money as opposed to an asset with a higher rate of return. The interaction between the demand for money and the supply of money provides the link through which the monetary authority, the Federal Reserve in the United States, affects output and prices.

Money is the means of payment or medium of exchange. More informally, money is whatever is generally accepted in exchange. In the past, seashells or cocoa or gold coins served as money in different places. In the United States, *M*1, consisting of currency plus checkable deposits, comes closest to defining the means of payment. At the end of 1996, *M*1 was about $4,200 per person. There is lively debate today concerning whether a broader group of monetary assets—*M*2, or even *M*3 (both discussed below)—might better meet the definition of money in a modern payments system.

Which assets constitute money? Discussions of the meaning of money are fluid for a simple reason: In the past, money was the means of payment generally accepted in exchange, but it also had the characteristic that it did not pay interest. Thus the sum of currency and demand deposits (which did not earn interest in the United States) was the accepted definition of money for a long time. This aggregate is now known as *M*1. In the course of the 1980s, however, a widening range of interest-bearing assets also became checkable. That has forced an ongoing review on where to draw the line between assets that form part of our definition of money and those that are just financial assets and not money proper. The issue is important not only conceptually but also for the evaluation of which monetary aggregate the Fed should try to control.

15-1

COMPONENTS OF THE MONEY STOCK

There is a vast array of financial assets in any economy, from currency to complicated claims on other financial assets. Which part of these assets is called money? In the United States, there are four main monetary aggregates: currency, *M*1, *M*2, *M*3, and *L*. Box 15-1 describes the components of the different measures of money.

*M*1 comprises those claims that can be used *directly, instantly,* and *without restrictions* to make payments. These claims are *liquid*. An asset is liquid if it can immediately, conveniently, and cheaply be used for making payments. *M*1 corresponds most closely to the traditional definition of money as the means of payment. *M*2 includes, in addition, claims that are not instantly liquid—withdrawal of time deposits, for example, may require notice to the depository institution; money market mutual funds may set a minimum on the size of checks drawn on an account. But with these qualifications, these additional claims also fall into a broader category of money. In *M*3 we include items that most people never see, namely, large negotiable deposits and

BOX 15-1 Components of the Monetary Aggregates

We briefly describe here the components of the monetary aggregates.

1. *Currency:* Consists of coins and notes in circulation.
2. *Demand deposits:* Non-interest-bearing checking accounts at commercial banks, excluding deposits of other banks, the government, and foreign governments.
3. *Traveler's checks:* Only those checks issued by nonbanks (such as American Express). Traveler's checks issued by banks are included in demand deposits.
4. *Other checkable deposits:* Interest-earning checking accounts, with a variety of legal arrangements and marketing names.

$$M1 = (1) + (2) + (3) + (4)$$

5. *Money market mutual fund (MMMF) shares:* Interest-earning checkable deposits in mutual funds that invest in short-term assets. Some MMMF shares are held by institutions; these are excluded from $M2$ but included in $M3$.
6. *Money market deposit accounts (MMDAs):* MMMFs run by banks, with the advantage that they are insured up to $100,000. They were introduced at the end of 1982 to allow banks to compete with MMMFs.
7. *Savings deposits:* Deposits at banks and other thrift institutions that are not transferable by check and are often recorded in a separate passbook kept by the depositor.
8. *Small time deposits:* Interest-bearing deposits with a specific maturity date. Before

repurchase agreements. These are held primarily by corporations but also by wealthy individuals. Finally, L includes several liquid assets that are close substitutes for, but which are not themselves, money.

As we move from the top to the bottom of the list in Box 15-1, the liquidity of the assets decreases, while their interest yield increases. Currency earns zero interest, checking accounts earn less than money market deposit accounts, and so on. This is a typical economic tradeoff—in order to get more liquidity, asset holders have to give up yield.

$M2$ AND OTHER MONETARY AGGREGATES

All the assets described in Box 15-1 are to some extent substitutes for one another, and there is therefore no clear point at which to draw the line in defining money. $M2$ adds to $M1$ assets that are close to being usable as a medium of exchange. The largest part of $M2$ consists of savings and small (less than $100,000) time deposits at banks and thrift institutions. These can be used with little difficulty for making payments. In the case of a savings deposit, the bank has to be notified to transfer funds from the savings deposit to a checking account; for time deposits, it is in principle necessary to wait until the time deposit matures or else to pay an interest penalty.

The second-largest category of assets in $M2$ consists of money market mutual funds and deposit accounts. A money market mutual fund (MMMF) invests its assets that date they can be used only if a penalty is paid. "Small" means less than $100,000.

$$M2 = M1 + (5) + (6) + (7) + (8)$$

9. *Repurchase agreements (RPs):* Transactions in which a bank borrows from a non-bank customer. The bank sells a security (e.g., a Treasury bill) to the customer to-day and promises to buy it back at a fixed price tomorrow. That way the bank gets to use the amount borrowed for a day.

10. *Eurodollars:* Deposits that pay interest and mature the next day, held in overseas, typically Caribbean, branches of U.S. banks.

11. *Large-denomination time deposits:* Interest-earning deposits of more than $100,000 denomination. The total excludes amounts held by MMMFs or MMDAs (and some other institutions) to make sure the same asset is not counted twice in the monetary aggregates.

12. *Institutional holdings of MMMFs.*

$$M3 = M2 + (9) + (10) + (11) + (12)$$

13. *Savings bonds:* U.S. government bonds, typically sold to small savers.

14. *Banker's acceptances:* Orders to pay a specific amount at a specific time that are obligations of banks. They arise largely in international trade.

15. *Commercial paper:* Short-term liabilities of corporations.

16. *Short-term Treasury securities:* Securities issued by the U.S. Treasury that have less than 12 months to maturity.

$$L = M3 + (13) + (14) + (15) + (16)$$

Source: Federal Reserve Bulletin, which reports the data and definition in each monthly issue.

---

in short-term interest-bearing securities, such as negotiable certificates of deposit (CDs) and Treasury bills.[1] MMMFs pay interest and permit the owner of the account to write checks against the account. Money market deposit accounts (MMDAs) are MMMFs held in commercial banks. A limited number of checks can be written against MMDAs each month. Obviously, MMDAs and MMMFs are close to being checkable deposits—but they also serve as financial investments.

Until 1987, $M1$ was the most closely watched money stock, both because it comes closest to the theoretical definition of money as a medium of exchange and because its demand function was reasonably stable. But after the demand for $M1$ became difficult to predict,[2] many economists, including those on the Federal Reserve Board, began to pay more attention to the behavior of $M2$. Since the early 1990s, the behavior of $M2$ has also become unpredictable, and $M3$ is not much better. Unpredictability of the demand for the monetary aggregates complicates the task of monetary policy, as we shall see in Chapter 16.

---

[1]Negotiable CDs are liabilities of the banks that can be bought and sold in the open market like other se-curities. Typically they come in large denominations of $100,000 or more.

[2]Yoshihisa Baba, David Hendry, and Ross Starr provide a detailed investigation of the instability of $M1$ in "The Demand for $M1$ in the U.S.A., 1960–1988," *Review of Economic Studies,* January 1992.

BOX 15-2 Who's Got the Cash?

A 1984 survey of cash holdings of U.S. households, undertaken for the Federal Reserve System, showed that the average amount of currency held per person surveyed then was about $100.* At that time, total currency outstanding divided by population was $675. Thus the vast majority of the currency outstanding is not held by U.S. households—or at least they do not admit to holding it. Some currency is held by legitimate businesses, but large amounts must be held to finance illegal activities, particularly drug-related ones, or are held outside the United States. In many countries undergoing severe financial distress, U.S. currency circulates in preference to local currency.

Since 1990, there has been a dramatic upswing in the proportion of U.S. currency held outside the United States. Richard Porter and Ruth Judson estimate that over $8 billion per year in currency now flows abroad.†

*"The Use of Cash and Transaction Accounts by American Families," *Federal Reserve Bulletin,* February 1986.

†Richard D. Porter and Ruth A. Judson, "The Location of U.S. Currency: How Much Is Abroad?" *Federal Reserve Bulletin,* October 1996.

FINANCIAL INNOVATION

Changes in the definitions of the monetary aggregates followed financial innovations, frequently a result of attempts to get around government regulations. For instance, thrifts, which pay interest on deposits and had been forbidden to have checkable accounts, invented NOW accounts as a way of getting around the prohibition. A NOW, a negotiable order of withdrawal, looks and smells like a check but is not, legally speaking, a check. Similarly, money market mutual funds were invented only in 1973. Until 1982, banks were not allowed to issue money market deposit accounts, but as soon as they were permitted to do so, there was a rapid inflow of such deposits to banks: MMDA deposits rose from zero in November 1982 to $320 billion in March 1983.

Clearly, there is no unique set of assets that will always constitute the money supply, nor are present definitions beyond question. For instance, there is a question of whether credit cards should be regarded as a means of making payment. And there are even arguments for using a *less* broad definition than M1—for example, should $1,000 bills, which are not easily used to buy groceries, be included? What is certain is that over the course of time, the particular assets that serve as a medium of exchange, or means of payment, will change further, and so will the definitions of the monetary aggregates.

15-2

THE FUNCTIONS OF MONEY

Money is so widely used that we rarely step back to think how remarkable a device it is. It is impossible to imagine a modern economy operating without the use of money or something very much like it. In a mythical barter economy in which there is no money, every transaction has to involve an exchange of goods (and/or services) on both sides of the transaction. The examples of the difficulties of barter are endless. The economist wanting a haircut would have to find a barber wanting to listen to a lecture on economics; the actor wanting a suit would have to find a tailor wanting to watch a performance; and so on. Without a medium of exchange, modern economies could not operate. Money, as a *medium of exchange,* makes it unnecessary for there to be a "double coincidence of wants," such as the barber and economist bumping into each other at just the right time.

There are four traditional functions of money, of which medium of exchange is the first.[3] The other three are store of value, unit of account, and standard of deferred payment. These stand on a different footing from the medium-of-exchange function.

A *store of value* is an asset that maintains value over time. Thus, an individual holding a store of value can use that asset to make purchases at a future date. If an asset were not a store of value, it would not be used as a medium of exchange. Imagine trying to use ice cream as money in the absence of refrigerators. There would hardly ever be a good reason for anyone to give up goods for money (ice cream) if the money were sure to melt within the next few minutes. To be useful as money, an asset must be a store of value, but there are many stores of value other than money—such as bonds, stocks, and houses.

The *unit of account* is the unit in which prices are quoted and books kept. Prices are quoted in dollars and cents, and dollars and cents are the units in which the money stock is measured. Usually, the money unit is also the unit of account, but that is not essential. In many high-inflation countries, dollars become the unit of account even though the local money continues to serve as the medium of exchange.

Finally, as a *standard of deferred payment,* money units are used in long-term transactions, such as loans. The amount that has to be paid back in 5 or 10 years is specified in dollars and cents. Dollars and cents are acting as the standard of deferred payment. Once again, though, it is not essential that the standard of deferred payment be the money unit. For example, the final payment of a loan may be related to the behavior of the price level, rather than being fixed in dollars and cents. This is known as an indexed loan. The last two of the four functions of money are, accordingly, functions that money *usually* performs but not functions that it *necessarily* performs. And the store-of-value function is one that many assets perform.

There is one final point we want to reemphasize. *Money is whatever is generally accepted in exchange.* In the past an astounding variety of monies have been used: simple commodities such as seashells, then metals, pieces of paper representing claims on gold or silver, pieces of paper that are claims only on other pieces of paper, and then paper and electronic entries in banks' accounts.[4] However magnificently a piece of paper may be engraved, it is not money if it is not accepted in payment. And however unusual the material of which it is made, anything that is generally accepted in payment is money. There is thus an inherent circularity in the acceptance of money. Money

---

[3]For the classic statement of the functions of money, see W. S. Jevons, *Money and the Mechanism of Exchange* (London: Kegan Paul, 1875).

[4]See Glyn Davies, *A History of Money from Ancient Times to the Present* (Aberystwyth: University of Wales Press, 1994).

is accepted in payment only because of the belief that it will later also be accepted in payment by others.

15-3

THE DEMAND FOR MONEY: THEORY

In this section we review the three major motives underlying the demand for money, and we concentrate on the effects of changes in income and the interest rate on money demand. Before we take up the discussion, we must make an essential point about money demand: The demand for money is a demand for *real balances*. In other words, people hold money for its purchasing power, for the amount of goods they can buy with it. They are not concerned with their *nominal* money holdings, that is, the number of dollar bills they hold. Two implications follow:

1. *Real* money demand is unchanged when the price level increases, and *all* real variables, such as the interest rate, real income, and real wealth, remain unchanged.
2. Equivalently, *nominal* money demand increases in proportion to the increase in the price level, given the real variables just specified.

In other words, we are interested in a money demand function which tells us the demand for real balances, M/P, not nominal balances, M. There is a special name for the behavior described here. An individual is free from *money illusion* if a change in the level of prices, holding all real variables constant, leaves the person's real behavior, including real money demand, unchanged.

The theories we are about to review correspond to Keynes's famous three motives for holding money:[5]

- The *transactions motive,* which is the demand for money arising from the use of money in making regular payments
- The *precautionary motive,* which is the demand for money to meet unforeseen contingencies
- The *speculative motive,* which arises from uncertainties about the money value of other assets that an individual can hold

In discussing the transactions and precautionary motives, we are mainly discussing $M1$, whereas the speculative motive refers more to $M2$ or $M3$, as we shall see.[6]

These theories of money demand *are built around a tradeoff between the benefits of holding more money versus the interest costs of doing so.* Money ($M1$, that is, currency and some checkable deposits) generally earns no interest or less interest than

---

[5]J. M. Keynes, *The General Theory of Employment, Interest and Money* (New York: Macmillan, 1936), chap. 13.

[6]Although we examine the demand for money by looking at the three motives for holding it, we cannot separate a particular person's money holdings, say, $500, into three neat piles of, say, $200, $200, and $100, each being held from a different motive. Money being held to satisfy one motive is always available for another use. The person holding unusually large balances for speculative reasons also has those balances available to meet an unexpected emergency, so they serve, too, as precautionary balances. All three motives influence an individual's holdings of money.

other assets. The higher the interest loss from holding a dollar of money, the less money we expect the individual to hold. In practice, we can measure the cost of holding money as the difference between the interest rate paid on money (perhaps zero) and the interest rate paid on the most nearly comparable other asset, such as a savings deposit or, for corporations, a certificate of deposit or commercial paper. The interest rate on money is referred to as the *own* rate of interest, and the *opportunity cost* of holding money is equal to the difference between the yield on other assets and the own rate.

TRANSACTIONS DEMAND

The transactions demand for money arises from the use of money in making regular payments for goods and services. In the course of each month, an individual makes a variety of payments for rent or a mortgage, groceries, the newspaper, and other purchases. In this section we examine how much money an individual would hold to finance these purchases.

The tradeoff here is between the amount of interest an individual forgoes by holding money and the costs and inconveniences of holding a small amount of money. To make the problem concrete, consider someone who is paid, say, $1,800 each month. Assume the person spends the $1,800 evenly over the course of the month, at the rate of $60 per day. Now at one extreme, the individual could simply leave the $1,800 in cash and spend it at the rate of $60 per day. Alternatively, on the first day of the month the individual could take $60 to spend that day and put the remaining $1,740 in a daily-interest savings account. Then every morning the person could go to the bank and withdraw that day's $60 from the savings account. By the end of the month the depositor would have earned interest on the money retained each day in the savings account. That would be the *benefit* of keeping the money holdings down as low as $60 at the beginning of each day. The *cost* of keeping money holdings down is simply the cost and inconvenience of the trips to the bank to withdraw the daily $60.

The greater the number of trips to the bank, the larger the amount earning interest in the savings account. With one trip—everything taken as cash on the first day—no interest is earned. The cash balance falls smoothly from $1,800 on the first day to $0 at the end of the month for an average balance of ($1,800 − $0)/2 = $900, forgoing interest of $i \times$ $900. For two trips, the cash balance falls from $1,800/2 to zero at midmonth and then repeats, for an average cash balance of ($1,800/2 − $0)/2 = $450. We show in the appendix to this chapter that this generalizes so that starting with income Y, if n trips are made, the average cash balance is $Y/2n$. If each trip costs tc, the combined cost of trips plus forgone interest is $(n \times tc) + i \times (Y/2n)$. Choosing n to minimize costs and computing the implied average money holdings leads to the famous square-root Baumol-Tobin formula for the demand for money:[7]

$$\frac{M}{P} = \sqrt{\frac{tc \times Y}{2i}} \qquad (1)$$

[7]The theory has quite general applicability for determining optimal inventories of goods as well as money. This inventory-theoretical approach to the demand for money is associated with the names of William Baumol and James Tobin: William Baumol, "The Transactions Demand for Cash: An Inventory Theoretic Approach," *Quarterly Journal of Economics,* November 1952; James Tobin, "The Interest Elasticity of Transactions Demand for Cash," *Review of Economics and Statistics,* August 1956.

BOX 15-3 A Back of the Envelope Calculation Using Income Elasticity

You are now the monetary authority of the small country of Baumol-Tobania. Real growth reliably averages 3 percent per year. How fast should you increase the money supply to stabilize the price level?

According to equation (1), 3 percent growth in GDP raises money demand 1.5 percent per year. If you increase the nominal money supply by the same 1.5 percent, real money supply and demand will stay in balance with a constant price level. If you had thought the income elasticity was 1 instead of ½, you would have created money at 3 percent per year, in the erroneous belief that money demand was rising 3 percent per year, leading to a small but steady inflation.

Equation (1) shows that the demand for money decreases with the interest rate and increases with the cost of transacting. Money demand increases with income, but less than proportionately, and with the level of income, but also less than proportionately. This point is sometimes put in different words by saying that there are *economies of scale* in cash management.

Equation (1) makes two very strong predictions: The income elasticity of money demand is ½, and the interest elasticity is $-½$.[8] Empirical evidence supports the signs of these predictions but suggests that the income elasticity is somewhat closer to 1 and that the interest elasticity is somewhat closer to zero.

THE PRECAUTIONARY MOTIVE

In discussing the transactions demand for money, we focused on transactions costs and ignored uncertainty. In this section, we concentrate on the demand for money that arises because people are uncertain about the payments they might want, or have, to make.[9] Realistically, an individual does not know precisely what payments she will be receiving in the next few weeks and what payments will have to be made. The person might decide to have a hot-fudge sundae, or need to take a cab in the rain, or have to pay for a prescription. If the person does not have money with which to pay, she will incur a loss.

The more money an individual holds, the less likely he or she is to incur the costs of illiquidity (that is, not having money immediately available). But the more money the person holds, the more interest he or she is giving up. We are back to a tradeoff similar to that examined in relation to the transactions demand. The added consideration is that greater uncertainty about receipts and expenditures increases the demand for money.

[8]Meaning that if income rises 1 percent, money demand should rise ½ of 1 percent, etc. Be careful about the definition of percentage change with interest rates. If the interest rate goes from 10 percent per year to 10.5 percent per year, it has gone up by 5 percent of its original level, so money demand should drop by 2.5 percent.

[9]See Edward H. Whalen, "A Rationalization of the Precautionary Demand for Cash," *Quarterly Journal of Economics*, May 1966.

THE SPECULATIVE DEMAND FOR MONEY

The transactions demand and the precautionary demand for money emphasize the medium-of-exchange function of money, for each refers to the need to have money on hand to make payments. Each theory is most relevant to the $M1$ definition of money, though the precautionary demand could certainly explain some of the holding of savings accounts and other relatively liquid assets that are part of $M2$. Now we move over to the store-of-value function of money and concentrate on the role of money in the investment portfolio of an individual.

An individual who has wealth has to hold that wealth in specific assets. Those assets make up a *portfolio.* One would think an investor would want to hold the asset that provides the highest returns. However, given that the return on most assets is uncertain, it is unwise to hold the entire portfolio in a single *risky asset.* You may have the hottest tip that a certain stock will surely double within the next 2 years, but you would be wise to recognize that hot tips are far from infallible. The typical investor will want to hold some amount of a safe asset as insurance against capital losses on assets whose prices change in an uncertain manner. Money is a safe asset in that its nominal value is known with certainty.[10] In a famous article, James Tobin argued that money would be held as the safe asset in the portfolios of investors.[11] The title of the article, "Liquidity Preference as Behavior towards Risk," explains the essential notion. In this framework, the demand for money—the safest asset—depends on the expected yields as well as on the riskiness of the yields on other assets. Tobin shows that an increase in the expected return on other assets—an increase in the opportunity cost of holding money (that is, the return lost by holding money)—lowers money demand. By contrast, an increase in the riskiness of the returns on other assets increases money demand.

An investor's aversion to risk certainly generates a demand for a safe asset. However, that asset is not likely to be $M1$. From the viewpoint of the yield and risks of holding money, it is clear that time or savings deposits or MMDAs have the same risks as currency or checkable deposits. However, the former generally pay a higher yield. Given that the risks are the same, and with the yields on time and savings deposits higher than those on currency and demand deposits, portfolio diversification explains the demand for assets such as time and savings deposits, which are part of $M2$, better than the demand for $M1$.

15-4

EMPIRICAL EVIDENCE

This section examines the empirical evidence—the studies made using actual data—on the demand for money. We know from Chapter 10 that the *interest elasticity* of the demand for money plays an important role in determining the effectiveness of monetary and fiscal policies. We showed in Section 15-3 that there are good theoretical reasons

---

[10]Of course, when the rate of inflation is uncertain, the real value of money is also uncertain, and money is no longer a safe asset. Even so, the uncertainties about the values of equity are so much larger than the uncertainties about the rate of inflation that money can be treated as a relatively safe asset (countries at risk of hyperinflation excepted).

[11]James Tobin, "Liquidity Preference as Behavior towards Risk," *Review of Economic Studies,* February 1958.

for believing that the demand for real balances should depend on the interest rate. The empirical evidence supports that view. Empirical studies have established that the demand for money is negatively related to the interest rate.

The theory of money demand also predicts that the demand for money should depend on the level of income. The response of the demand for money to the level of income, as measured by the *income elasticity* of money demand, is also important from a policy viewpoint. As we shall see below, the income elasticity of money demand provides a guide for the Fed as to how fast to increase the money supply in order to support a given rate of GDP growth without changing the interest rate.

LAGGED ADJUSTMENT

The empirical work on the demand for money has introduced one complication that we did not study in the theoretical section—that the demand for money adjusts to changes in income and interest rates *with a lag*. When the level of income or the interest rate changes, there is first only a small change in the demand for money. Then, over the course of time, the change in the demand for money increases, slowly building up to its full long-run change.

There are two basic reasons for these lags. First, there are costs of adjusting money holdings; second, money holders' expectations are slow to adjust. The costs of adjustment include the costs of figuring out the new best way to manage money and the cost of opening up a new type of account if that is needed. On the expectations side, if people believe that a given change in the interest rate is temporary, they may be unwilling to make a major change in their money holdings. As time passes and it becomes clearer that the change is not transitory, they are willing to make a larger adjustment.

EMPIRICAL RESULTS FOR *M*1 DEMAND

A comprehensive 1973 study by the late Stephen Goldfeld of Princeton University describes the standard *M*1 demand-for-money function.[12]

Table 15-1 summarizes Goldfeld's results. In the short run (one quarter), the elasticity of demand with respect to real income is .19. This means that a 1 percent increase in real income raises money demand by .19 percent, which is considerably less than proportionately. The table shows that an increase in interest rates reduces money demand. The short-run interest elasticities are quite small. An increase in the rate on time deposits from 4 to 5 percent, that is, a 25 percent increase (5/4 = 1.25), reduces the demand for money by only 1.12 percent (= .045 × .25). An increase in the rate on commercial paper (an alternative asset for firms to hold) from 4 to 5 percent would reduce money demand by only .47 percent.

The long-run elasticities exceed the short-run elasticities by a factor of more than 3, as Table 15-1 shows. The long-run real income elasticity is .68, meaning that in the

---

[12]This work, along with a vast amount of more recent material, is summarized in Stephen Goldfeld and Daniel Sichel, "The Demand for Money," in B. M. Friedman and F. H. Hahn (eds.), *Handbook of Monetary Economics,* vol. 1 (Amsterdam: North-Holland, 1990), chap. 8. See also the comprehensive review of theory and empirical work in David Laidler, *The Demand for Money: Theories, Evidence, and Problems,* 3d ed. (New York: HarperCollins, 1990).

TABLE 15-1 Elasticities of Real M1 Money Demand

	Y	i_{TD}	i_{CP}
Short run	.19	−.045	−.019
Long run	.68	−.160	−.067

Source: S. Goldfeld, "The Demand for Money Revisited," *Brookings Papers on Economic Activity* 3 (1973).

long run the increase in real money demand occurring as a result of a given increase in real income is only 68 percent as large as the proportional increase in income. Real money demand thus rises less than proportionately to the rise in real income. The long-run interest elasticities sum to a little over .2, meaning that an increase in both i_{TD} *and* i_{CP} from 4 to 5 percent would reduce the demand for money by less than 6 percent.[13]

This early work by Goldfeld established four essential properties of money demand that continue to hold:

- The demand for real money balances responds negatively to the rate of interest. An increase in interest rates reduces the demand for money.
- The demand for money increases with the level of real income.
- The short-run responsiveness of money demand to changes in interest rates and income is considerably less than the long-run response. The long-run elasticities are estimated to be over 3 times the size of the short-run elasticities.
- The demand for nominal money balances is proportional to the price level. There is no money illusion; in other words, the demand for money is a demand for *real* balances.

Until 1973 the demand for real money balances was considered one of the best understood and most highly stable equations in the U.S. macroeconomy, and indeed in other countries too. Since then, *M*1 demand has been shifting and has not yet settled down to the extent that there is agreement on the empirically correct form of the money demand function. However, there is general agreement on the fact that money demand is affected primarily by income and interest rates.

*M*2 MONEY DEMAND

Innovation in the financial system has made it easier to move back and forth between *M*1 and other assets. For example, automatic teller machines typically allow cash withdrawals from savings accounts. We would say that savings accounts are now better substitutes for *M*1 than they were in the past. When money flows between savings accounts and cash, as an example, *M*1 changes but *M*2 does not. For this reason, financial innovation has made the demand for *M*2 more stable than the demand for *M*1.[14]

---

[13]Recent work on *M*1 demand by Baba, Hendry, and Starr ("The Demand for *M*1") estimates long-run elasticities fairly close to those suggested by Goldfeld.

[14]See the discussion in David Small and Richard Porter, "Understanding the Behavior of *M*2 and *V*2," *Federal Reserve Bulletin,* April 1989. See also Robert Hetzel and Yash Mehra, "The Behavior of Money Demand in the 1980s," *Journal of Money, Credit and Banking,* November 1989, and R. W. Hafer and Dennis Jansen, "The Demand for Money in the United States: Evidence from Cointegration Tests," *Journal of Money, Credit and Banking,* May 1991.

BOX 15-4 Money Demand and High Inflation

The demand for real balances depends on the alternative cost of holding money. That cost is normally measured by the yield on alternative assets, say, Treasury bills, commercial paper, or money market funds. But there is another margin of substitution. Rather than holding their wealth in financial assets, households or firms can also hold real assets: stocks of food or houses or machinery. This margin of substitution is particularly important in countries in which inflation is very high and capital markets do not function well. In that case it is quite possible that the return on holding goods can even be higher than that on financial assets.

Consider a household deciding whether to hold $100 in currency or a demand deposit or to hold its wealth in the form of groceries on the shelf. The advantage of holding groceries is that, unlike money, they maintain their real value. Rather than having the purchasing power of money balances eroded by inflation, the household gets rid of money, buying goods and thus avoiding a loss.

This *flight out of money* occurs systematically when inflation rates become high. In a famous study of hyperinflations (defined in the study as inflation rates of more than 50 percent *per month*), Phillip Cagan of Columbia University found large changes in real balances taking place as inflation increased.* In the most famous hyperinflation, that in Germany in 1922–1923, the quantity of real balances at the height of the hyperinflation had fallen to one-twentieth of its preinflation level. The increased cost of holding money leads to a reduction in real money demand and, with it, to changes in the public's payment habits as everybody tries to pass money on like a hot potato.

In well-developed capital markets, interest rates will reflect expectations of inflation, and hence it will not make much difference whether we measure the alternative cost of holding money by interest rates or inflation rates. But when capital markets are not free because interest rates are regulated or have ceilings, it is often appropriate to use inflation, not interest, rates as the measure of the alternative cost. Franco Modigliani has offered the following rule of thumb: The right measure of the opportunity cost of holding money is the higher of the two, interest rates or inflation.

*Phillip Cagan, "The Monetary Dynamics of Hyperinflation," in Milton Friedman (ed.), *Studies in the Quantity Theory of Money* (Chicago: University of Chicago Press, 1956).

We would expect real money demand to depend negatively on the opportunity cost of holding *M*2, the difference between a market interest rate, such as the Treasury-bill rate, and a weighted average of the interest rates paid on various kinds of deposits constituting *M*2. We also expect real *M*2 money demand to depend positively on the level of income.

These hypotheses are, indeed, confirmed by the empirical evidence. An estimate with quarterly data for the period 1953–1991 yields the elasticities shown in Table 15-2. The table confirms that the elasticity with respect to the opportunity cost is negative. The short-run elasticities are smaller than the long-run elasticities.

The long-run income elasticity of *M*2 is clearly positive and is approximately equal to unity. This implies that, other things equal, the ratio of real balances, measured by *M*2, to real GNP will remain constant over time.

TABLE 15-2 Elasticities of Real *M2* Money Demand, 1953–1991

	Y	Opportunity Cost*
Short run	.39	−.017
Long run	.98	−.08

*Six-month commercial paper rate less own rate on *M2*.

Source: Yash P. Mehra, "The Stability of the *M2* Demand Function: Evidence from an Error-Correction Model," *Journal of Money, Credit, and Banking*, August 1993.

15-5

THE INCOME VELOCITY OF MONEY AND THE QUANTITY THEORY

The *income velocity of money* is the number of times the stock of money is turned over per year in financing the annual flow of income. It is equal to the ratio of nominal GDP to the nominal money stock. Thus in 1995 GDP was about \$7,248 billion, the *M2* money stock averaged \$3,580 billion, and *M2* velocity was therefore about 2. The average dollar of *M2* money balances financed \$2.02 of spending on final goods and services, or the public held an average of 50 cents of *M2* per dollar of income.

Income velocity (from now on, we shall refer to "velocity" rather than "income velocity")[15] is defined as

$$V \equiv \frac{P \times Y}{M} = \frac{Y}{M/P} \tag{2}$$

that is, the ratio of nominal income to the nominal money stock or, equivalently, the ratio of real income to real balances.

The concept of velocity is important largely because it is a convenient way of talking about money demand. Let the demand for real balances be written $M/P = L(i,Y)$. Substituting into equation (2), velocity can be rewritten as $V = Y/L(i,Y)$. This is especially convenient if money demand is proportional to income, as is roughly true for long-run *M2* demand, so money demand can be written as $L(i,Y) = Y \times l(i)$. In this case equation (2) is simply $V = 1/l(i)$, so velocity is a quick way to summarize the effect of interest rates on money demand—remembering that high velocity means low money demand.[16]

Figure 15-1 shows *M2* velocity (left scale) and the Treasury-bill interest rate (right scale). *M2* velocity is relatively stable—the left-hand scale is only between 1.6 and 2.1 over a 35-year period—and velocity has a strong tendency to rise and fall with market interest rates.

---

[15]Why do we say "income velocity" and not plain "velocity"? There is another concept, transactions velocity, which is the ratio of *total transactions* to money balances. Total transactions far exceed GDP for two reasons. First, many transactions involving the sale and purchase of assets do not contribute to GDP. Second, a particular item in final output typically generates total spending on it that exceeds the contribution of that item to GDP. For instance, a dollar's worth of wheat generates transactions as it leaves the farm, as it is sold by the miller, and so forth. Transactions velocity is thus higher than income velocity.

[16]In fact, while academic economists use velocity and money demand more or less interchangeably, "Wall Street" tends to focus directly on velocity as a measure.

FIGURE 15-1   VELOCITY OF MONEY (LEFT SCALE) AND TREASURY-BILL RATES (RIGHT SCALE).

THE QUANTITY THEORY

The *quantity theory of money* provides a very simple way to organize thinking about the relation between money, prices, and output:

$$M \times V = P \times Y \tag{3}$$

Equation (3) is the famous *quantity equation,* linking the price level and the level of output to the money stock. The quantity equation became the *(classical) quantity theory* of money when it was argued that both V, the income velocity of money, and Y, the level of output, were fixed. Real output was taken to be fixed because the economy was at full employment, and velocity was assumed not to change much. Neither of these assumptions holds in fact, but it is, nonetheless, interesting to see where they lead. *If both V and Y are fixed, it follows that the price level is proportional to the money stock.* Thus the classical quantity theory was a theory of inflation.

The classical quantity theory is the proposition that the price level is proportional to the money stock:

$$P = \frac{V \times M}{Y} \tag{3a}$$

If V is constant, changes in the money supply translate into proportional changes in *nominal GDP*, $P \times Y$. When the *classical case* (vertical) supply function examined in Chapter 5 applies, Y is fixed and changes in money translate into changes in the overall price level, P.

SUMMARY

1. The demand for money is a demand for real balances. It is the purchasing power, not the number of dollar bills, that matters to holders of money.

2. The money supply, $M1$, is made up of currency and checkable deposits. A broader measure, $M2$, also includes savings and time deposits at depository institutions as well as some other interest-bearing assets.

3. The chief characteristic of money is that it serves as a means of payment. The three classic reasons to hold money are for transactions purposes ($M1$) and for precautionary ($M1$ and $M2$) and speculative reasons ($M2$ and $M3$).

4. Decisions to hold money are based on a tradeoff between the liquidity of money and the opportunity cost of holding it when other assets have a higher yield.

5. The inventory-theoretic approach shows that an individual will hold a stock of real balances that varies inversely with the interest rate but increases with the level of real income and the cost of transactions. According to the inventory approach, the income elasticity of money demand is less than unity, implying that there are economies of scale.

6. Uncertainty about payments and receipts in combination with transactions costs gives rise to a precautionary demand for money. Precautionary money holdings are higher the greater the variability of net disbursements, the higher the cost of illiquidity, and the lower the interest rate.

7. Some assets that are in $M2$ form part of an optimal portfolio because they are less risky than other assets—their nominal value is constant. Because they earn interest, assets such as savings or time deposits and MMMF shares dominate currency and demand deposits for portfolio diversification purposes.

8. The empirical evidence provides support for a negative interest elasticity of money demand and a positive income elasticity. Because of lags, short-run elasticities are much smaller than long-run elasticities.

9. The demand function for $M1$ started showing instability in the mid-1970s. The demand function for $M2$ appears to be more stable, showing a unit income elasticity, a positive elasticity with respect to the own rate, and a negative elasticity with respect to the commercial paper rate.

10. The income velocity of money is defined as the ratio of income to money or the rate of turnover of money. The behavior of velocity is closely tied to the demand for money, so an increase in the opportunity cost of holding money leads to an increase in velocity.

11. The velocity of $M2$ has been roughly constant over long periods of time. The constancy is a reflection of small changes in the opportunity cost of holding money and of a unit income elasticity of demand for $M2$.

12. Inflation implies that money loses purchasing power, and inflation thus creates a cost of holding money. The higher the rate of inflation, the lower the amount of real balances that will be held. Hyperinflations provide striking support for this prediction. Under conditions of very high expected inflation, money demand falls dramatically relative to income. Velocity rises as people use less money in relation to income.

KEY TERMS

money	standard of deferred	risky asset
M1	payment	interest elasticity
M2	real balances	income elasticity
M3	money illusion	flight out of money
liquidity	transactions motive	income velocity
medium of exchange	precautionary motive	quantity theory of money
store of value	speculative motive	quantity equation
unit of account	portfolio	classical quantity theory

PROBLEMS

Conceptual

1. What is money, and why does anyone want it?
2. To what extent would it be possible to design a society in which there was no money? What would the problems be? Could currency at least be eliminated? How? (Lest all this seem too unworldly, you should know that some people are beginning to talk of a "cashless economy" in the next century.)
3. Do you think credit card credit limits should be counted in the money stock? Why or why not?
4. Discuss the various factors that go into an individual's decision regarding how many traveler's checks to take on a vacation.
5. Explain the concept of the opportunity cost of holding money.
6. The demand for nominal balances rises with the price level. At the same time, inflation causes the real demand to fall. Explain how these two assertions can both be correct.
7. "Muggers favor deflation." Comment.

Technical

1. Evaluate the effects of the following changes on the demand for M1 and M2. Which of the functions of money do they relate to?
   a. "Instant-cash" machines that allow 24-hour withdrawals from savings accounts at banks
   b. The employment of more tellers at your bank
   c. An increase in inflationary expectations
   d. Widespread acceptance of credit cards
   e. Fear of an imminent collapse of the government
   f. A rise in the interest rate on time deposits
2. a. Is velocity high or low relative to trend during recessions? Why?
   b. How can the Fed influence velocity?

The next two questions are related to the material in the appendix.

*3. The transactions demand-for-money model can also be applied to firms. Suppose a firm sells steadily during the month and has to pay its workers at the end of the month. Explain how the firm would determine its money holdings.
*4. a. Determine the optimal strategy for cash management for a person who earns $1,600 per month, can earn .5 percent interest per month in a savings account, and has a transaction cost of $1. (*Hint:* Integer constraints matter here.)
   b. What is the individual's average cash balance?
   c. Suppose income rises to $1,800. By what percentage does the individual's demand for money change?

*An asterisk denotes a more difficult problem.

◆ O P T I O N A L ◆

APPENDIX: THE BAUMOL-TOBIN TRANSACTIONS DEMAND MODEL

The assumptions of the Baumol-Tobin transactions demand model are set out in the text and summarized here. An individual receives a payment, Y, at the beginning of each month and spends it at an even pace during the month. He or she can earn interest at the rate i per month by holding money in a savings account (equivalently, bonds). There is a cost of tc per transaction for moving between bonds and money. We denote by n the number of transactions per month between bonds and money, and we assume, for convenience, that monthly income is paid into the savings account or paid in the form of bonds.

The individual minimizes the cost of money management during the month. Those costs consist of the transactions cost, $(n \times tc)$, plus the interest forgone by holding money instead of bonds during the month. The interest cost is $(i \times M)$, where M is the average holdings of money during the month.

M, the average holdings of money, depends on n, the number of transactions. Suppose that each time the individual makes a transaction, she transfers amount Z from bonds into money.[17] If the individual makes n equal-size withdrawals during the month, the size of each transfer is Y/n, since a total of Y has to be transferred. Thus

$$nZ = Y \qquad \text{(A1)}$$

Now, how is the *average* cash balance related to n? Figure 15A-1 helps answer the question. In Figure 15A-1*a*, the average cash balance held during the month is $Y/2 = Z/2$, since the cash balance starts at Y and runs down in a straight line to zero.[18] In the case of Figure 15A-1*b*, the average cash balance for the first half of the month is $Y/4 = Z/2$, and the average cash balance for the second half of the month is also $Z/2$. Thus, the average cash balance for the entire month is $Y/4 = Z/2$, as you might want to confirm by drawing diagrams similar to Figure 15A-1 for $n = 3$ or other values of n. Using equation (A1), it follows that the average cash balance is $Y/2n$.

The total cost of cash management is accordingly

$$\text{Total cost} = (n \times tc) + \frac{iY}{2n} \qquad \text{(A2)}$$

The optimum number of transactions is found by minimizing total cost with respect to n.[19] That implies

$$n^* = \sqrt{\frac{iY}{2n}} \qquad \text{(A3)}$$

where n^* is the optimal number of transactions. As we should expect, the individual makes more transactions the higher the interest rate, the higher the income, and the lower the transactions cost.

---

[17]With simple interest being paid on the savings account, the individual's transactions between bonds and cash should be evenly spaced over the month.

[18]The average cash balance is the average of the amount of cash the individual holds at each moment during the month. For instance, if the balance held is $400 for 3 days and zero for the rest of the month, the average cash balance would be $40, or one-tenth (3 days ÷ 30 days) of the month times $400.

[19]If you can handle calculus, derive equation (A3) by minimizing the total cost with respect to n in equation (A2).

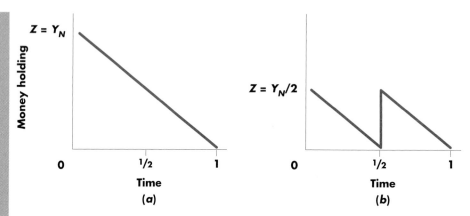

FIGURE 15A-1   AMOUNT OF CASH HELD BY THE PUBLIC RELATED TO NUMBER OF
TRANSACTIONS.

The Baumol-Tobin result, equation (1) in the text, is obtained using equation (A3) and the
fact that $M = iY/2n$.

In addition to deriving the square-root formula, we want also to show why for many people, it is optimal to make only one transaction between bonds and money. Consider the example in the text of an individual who receives $1,800 per month. Suppose that the interest rate on
deposits is as high as .5 percent per month. The individual cannot avoid making one initial transaction, since income is paid into the savings account to start with. Does it pay to make a second transaction? For $n = 2$, the average cash balance is $1,800/2n = $450, so interest earned
would be (.005 × $450) = $2.25.

If the transaction cost exceeds $2.25, the individual will not bother to make more than one
transaction. And $2.25 is not an outrageous cost in terms of the time and nuisance of making a
transfer between bonds (or a savings account) and money.

For anyone making only one transaction, the average cash balance is half his or her income.
That means the interest elasticity of money demand for that person is zero—up to the point that
the interest rate becomes high enough to make a second transaction worthwhile. And the income
elasticity is 1, up to the point that income rises high enough to make a second transaction worthwhile. Since for some people the income elasticity is 1 and for others the Baumol-Tobin formula is closer to applying, we expect the income elasticity to be between ½ and 1; similarly,
since for some the interest elasticity is zero while for others it is closer to −½, we expect the interest elasticity to be between −½ and zero.

CHAPTER 16

The Fed, Money, and Credit

CHAPTER HIGHLIGHTS

◆ The Federal Reserve provides the monetary base (bank reserves and currency) upon which the money supply (currency and deposits) is built.

◆ The primary tool for controlling the money supply is open market purchases, purchases of bonds paid for with newly printed money.

◆ The Federal Reserve chooses both intermediate and ultimate targets. The key consideration in choosing targets is uncertainty about different kinds of economic shocks.

In the recession of 1990–1991 and in 1992, the Fed cut interest rates twenty-three times to try to revive growth. Some critics said that the Fed acted too late and too little and that the slow rates of growth of $M2$ and $M3$ (see Table 16-1) proved it. Other critics emphasized the slow growth of *credit* as a sign that monetary policy was not expansionary enough.[1] The Fed said that it had acted prudently and decisively and that the rapid declines in interest rates proved it.

Judged by the outcome—recession and slow growth—the critics were right. But it is always easy to be right after the event, and the data in Table 16-1 raise difficult questions. Should the Fed have been guided more by monetary targets or by interest rates? Why did bank credit grow so slowly? Should the Fed have cut interest rates more rapidly? Could the Fed have made $M2$ grow faster if it had wanted to? And what precisely does the Fed do to cut interest rates?

16-1

MONEY STOCK DETERMINATION—THE MONEY MULTIPLIER

The money supply consists mostly of deposits at banks,[2] which the Fed does not control directly. In this section we develop the details of the process by which the money supply is determined, and particularly the role of the Fed. The key concept to understand is *fractional reserve banking*. In a world in which only gold coins were money and in which the king reserved to himself the right to mint coins, the money supply

---

[1]Credit consists of loans, short- and long-term, to firms, households, and the government.

[2]We refer to all deposit-taking institutions, including savings and loan associations, mutual savings banks, and credit unions, as "banks."

TABLE 16-1 Monetary Policy 1988–1992
(Percent per annum)

	1988	1989	1990	1991	1992
Growth rate of $M1$	4.9	.9	4.0	8.7	14.2
Growth rate of $M2$	5.5	5.1	3.5	3.0	2.3
Growth rate of $M3$	6.6	3.5	1.3	1.4	.4
Growth rate of debt	9.3	8.0	6.8	4.2	4.3
Growth rate of bank loans	9.1	7.7	4.4	−.1	−.3
Treasury-bill rate	6.7	8.1	7.5	5.4	3.8
10-year bond rate	8.9	8.5	8.6	7.9	7.3
Real GDP growth	3.9	2.5	1.0	−.7	2.1
Inflation (GDP deflator)	3.9	4.4	4.1	3.7	2.5

Note: Money growth rates for 1989–1992 are for December relative to previous December; interest rates are averages for the period shown.

Source: DRI/McGraw-Hill.

FIGURE 16-1   RELATIONSHIP BETWEEN HIGH-POWERED MONEY AND THE MONEY STOCK.

would equal the number of coins minted. Contrast this with a futuristic cashless society in which all payments are made by electronic transfers through banks and in which the law requires (here's where the "fractional reserve" part comes in) banks to hold gold coins equal to 20 percent of their outstanding deposits. In this latter case, the money available to the public would be 5 times the number of gold coins (coins/.20). The coins would not be used as money. Rather, the coins would form a "base" supporting deposits available through the banking system. The real money supply is determined by a blend of these two fictional systems.

High-powered money (or the monetary base) consists of currency (notes and coins) and banks' deposits at the Fed. The part of the currency held by the public forms part of the money supply. The currency in bank vaults and the banks' deposits at the Fed are used as reserves backing individual and business deposits at banks. The Fed's control over the monetary base is the main route through which it determines the money supply.

Before going into details, we want to think briefly about the relationship between the money stock and the stock of high-powered money (see Figure 16-1). At the top of the figure we show the stock of money. At the bottom we show the stock of high-powered money, also called the *monetary base.* Money and high-powered money are related by the *money multiplier.* The money multiplier is the ratio of the stock of money to the stock of high-powered money. The money multiplier is larger than 1. It is clear from the diagram that the larger deposits are as a fraction of the money stock, the larger the multiplier is. That is true because currency uses up a dollar of high-powered money per dollar of money. Deposits, by contrast, use up only a fraction of a dollar of high-powered money (in reserves) per dollar of money stock. For instance, if the reserve ratio is 10 percent, every dollar of the money stock in the form of deposits uses up only 10 cents of high-powered money. Equivalently, each dollar of high-powered money held as bank reserves can support $10 of deposits.

The Federal Reserve has direct control over high-powered money, H. We are interested in the supply of money, M. The two are linked by the money multiplier, *mm.* We ignore the distinction between various kinds of deposits (and thus the distinction between different M's) and consider the money supply process as if there were only a uniform class of deposits, D. Using this simplification, the money supply consists of currency, CU, plus deposits:

$$M = CU + D \tag{1}$$

High-powered money consists of currency plus reserves:

$$H = CU + \text{reserves} \tag{2}$$

We summarize the behavior of the public, the banks, and the Fed in the money supply process by three variables: the *currency-deposit ratio*, $cu \equiv CU/D$; the *reserve ratio*, $re \equiv \text{reserves}/D$; and the stock of high-powered money. Rewrite equations (1) and (2) as $M = (cu + 1)D$ and $H = (cu + re)D$. In this way we can express the money supply in terms of its principal determinants, re, cu, and H:

$$M = \frac{1 + cu}{re + cu} H \equiv mm \times H \tag{3}$$

where mm is the money multiplier given by

$$mm \equiv \frac{1 + cu}{re + cu}$$

- The money multiplier is larger the smaller the reserve ratio, re.
- The money multiplier is larger the smaller the currency-deposit ratio, cu. That is because the smaller the cu, the smaller the proportion of the high-powered money stock that is being used as currency (which translates high-powered money only one for one into money) and the larger the proportion that is available to be reserves (which translates much more than one for one into money).

We turn now to the determinants of the reserve-deposit and currency-deposit ratios.

THE CURRENCY-DEPOSIT RATIO

The payment habits of the public determine how much currency is held relative to deposits. The currency-deposit ratio is affected by the cost and convenience of obtaining cash; for instance, if there is a cash machine nearby, individuals will on average carry less cash with them because the costs of running out are lower. The currency-deposit ratio has a strong seasonal pattern, being highest around Christmas.

THE RESERVE-DEPOSIT RATIO

Bank reserves consist of deposits banks hold at the Fed and "vault cash," notes and coin held by banks. In the absence of regulation, banks would hold reserves to meet (1) the demands of their customers for cash and (2) payments their customers make by checks that are deposited in other banks. However, in the United States banks hold reserves primarily because the Federal Reserve requires them to. In addition to these *required reserves*, banks hold some *excess reserves* in order to meet unexpected withdrawals. Because reserves earn no interest, banks try to minimize excess reserves. When market interest rates are high, banks try especially hard to keep excess reserves to a

BOX 16-1 Deposit Insurance and Bank Runs

Many banks failed in the 1930s; that is, they were unable to meet the demands of their depositors for cash. If you have a deposit in a failed bank, you cannot "get your money out." Anyone who believes his or her bank may run out of cash will rush to the bank to try to withdraw money before the other depositors. A *run on a bank* occurs when depositors rush to try to withdraw cash because they believe others will also try to do so. There may be good reasons for the running investors to worry about the bank's safety, but it is even possible that a run on a fundamentally sound bank may occur precisely because its depositors believe that a run on the bank is likely to occur.*

Bank runs have both microeconomic and macroeconomic effects. The former takes the form of *disintermediation*. Having lost deposits, banks are no longer able to make loans to support business investment and purchases of private homes. The latter takes the form of an increase in *cu* and, therefore, a drop in the money multiplier. Unless the central bank offsets this by increasing the monetary base, the macroeconomic effect is a drop in the money supply.

The massive bank failures of the 1930s, as a consequence of runs on banks, gave rise to an important institutional reform, the creation of the *Federal Deposit Insurance Corporation (FDIC)*. That institution insures bank deposits, so depositors get paid even if a bank fails. That means there is no reason to worry about losing your money if your bank fails; as a result, bank runs have been rare since the 1930s.† Bank failures virtually disappeared between 1940 and 1979, but in the 1980s they became a more serious problem. Still, the scale today is much less than in the early 1930s, and—because of the FDIC—the economic consequences are much less serious now.

*The notion of self-justifying runs on banks has both intuitive appeal and historical support. It has been formalized in an ingenious but very difficult article by Douglas Diamond and Philip Dybvig, "Bank Runs, Deposit Insurance and Liquidity," *Journal of Political Economy*, June 1983. A less technical example appears in the movie *It's a Wonderful Life*, with Jimmy Stewart.

†In the 1980s there were runs on thrift institutions in Ohio and Rhode Island whose deposits were not covered by federal insurance.

minimum. So while *re* is mostly determined by regulation,[3] high interest rates do to a limited extent reduce *re*.

Banks have to keep reserves in the form of notes and coin because their customers have a right to currency on demand. They keep accounts at the Fed mainly to make payments among themselves. Thus, when I pay you with a check drawn on my bank account, which you deposit in your bank, my bank makes the payment by transferring money from its account at the Fed to your bank's account at the Fed.[4] Banks can also

[3]This is so in the United States. In Canada and the United Kingdom, for example, reserve requirements are not set by regulation.

[4]Many banks, particularly small ones, hold their reserves in the form of deposits at other banks. These *interbank deposits* serve the same function as reserves but are not included in the U.S. measure of reserves. They are excluded from the definitions of the money stock.

use their deposits at the Fed to obtain cash; the Fed sends the cash over in an armored truck on request.

16-2

THE INSTRUMENTS OF MONETARY CONTROL

The Federal Reserve has three instruments for controlling the money supply: *open market operations, the discount rate, and the required-reserve ratio.* As a practical matter, open market operations are nearly always the tool of choice.

AN OPEN MARKET PURCHASE

The method by which the Fed most often changes the stock of high-powered money is an open market operation. We examine the mechanics of an open market *purchase,* an operation in which the Fed buys, say $1 million of government bonds from a private individual. An open market purchase *increases* the monetary base.

The accounting for the Fed's purchase is shown in Table 16-2. The Fed's ownership of government securities rises by $1 million, which is shown in the "Government securities" entry on the assets side of the balance sheet. How does the Fed pay for the bond? It writes a check on itself. In return for the bond, the seller receives a check instructing the Fed to pay (the seller) $1 million. The seller takes the check to his or her bank, which credits the depositor with the $1 million and then deposits the check at the Fed. That bank has an account at the Fed; the account is credited with $1 million, and the "Bank deposits at Fed" entry on the liabilities side of the balance sheet rises by $1 million. The commercial bank has just increased its reserves by $1 million, which are held in the first instance as a deposit at the Fed.

The only unexpected part of the story is that the Fed can pay for the securities it bought by giving the seller a check on itself. The eventual owner of the check then has a deposit at the Fed. That deposit can be used to make payments to other banks, or it can be exchanged for currency. Just as the ordinary deposit holder at a bank can obtain currency in exchange for deposits, the bank deposit holder at the Fed can acquire currency in exchange for its deposits. When the Fed pays for the bond by writing a check on itself, it creates high-powered money with a stroke of the pen. The striking result is that the Fed can create high-powered money at will merely by buying assets, such as government bonds, and paying for them with its own liabilities.

TABLE 16-2 Effects of an Open Market Purchase on the Fed Balance Sheet
(Millions of dollars)

ASSETS		LIABILITIES	
Government securities	+1	Currency	0
All other assets	0	Bank deposits at Fed	+1
Monetary base (sources)	+1	Monetary base (uses)	+1

TABLE 16-3 Simplified Form of the Fed Balance Sheet, Showing Sources and Uses of High-Powered Money, February 1996
(Billions of dollars)

ASSETS (SOURCES)			LIABILITIES (USES)		
Gold and foreign exchange		$ 21.2	Currency		$412.5
Federal reserve credit		408.6	Held by the public	377.2	
Loans and discounts	1.2		Vault cash	35.3	
Government securities	376.7		Bank deposits at the Fed		16.7
Net other credit	30.7				
			Plus		
			Net other liabilities		0.6
Monetary base (sources)		429.8	Monetary base (uses)		429.8

Source: *Federal Reserve Bulletin*, May 1996.

THE FED BALANCE SHEET

We turn now to the Fed balance sheet, shown in Table 16-3, and start by examining the asset side. As we have just seen, the purchase of assets generates high-powered money. The gold that the Fed owns was acquired in the past, when the Fed paid for it, too, by writing checks on itself. There is, accordingly, almost no difference between the way in which an open market purchase of gold or, as we shall see, of foreign currency affects the balance sheet and the way in which an open market purchase of bonds affects the balance sheet.[5]

FOREIGN EXCHANGE AND THE BASE

The Fed sometimes buys or sells foreign currencies in an attempt to affect exchange rates. These purchases and sales of foreign exchange—*foreign exchange market intervention*—affect the base. Note from the balance sheet that if the central bank buys gold or foreign exchange, there is a corresponding increase in high-powered money, as the Fed pays with its own liabilities for the gold or foreign exchange that is purchased. Thus foreign exchange market operations affect the base.[6]

LOANS AND DISCOUNTS

A bank that runs short of reserves can borrow to make good the deficiency. It may borrow either from the Fed or from other banks that have spare reserves. The cost of borrowing from the Fed is the *discount rate*. The discount rate is the interest rate charged by the Fed to banks that borrow from it to meet temporary needs for reserves.

[5]The Fed's 1996 holdings of gold were about $11 billion, valued at $42 an ounce. The market value of the gold is much higher, since the market price of gold is far above $42 per ounce. In the problem set, you are asked to show how the balance sheet would be affected if the Fed decided to value its gold at the free-market price. For that purpose you will have to adjust the item "Net other liabilities" appropriately.

[6]Details of this impact may be complicated by the fact, which we do not pursue, that the Fed and the Treasury usually collaborate in foreign exchange intervention.

BOX 16-2 The Fed as Lender of Last Resort

An important function assigned to central banks since the nineteenth century is to act as "lender of last resort." When financial panic threatens the collapse of the financial system, swift action by the central bank can restore confidence and avoid a systemwide run on financial intermediaries, a freezing of credit lines, or, worse, a widespread calling in of loans. The Fed does act in this role whenever major financial institutions go under or whenever there is a serious risk of instability, as when the stock market fell 20 percent on one day in the October 1987 collapse.

The need for a lender of last resort emerges from the following consideration: The credit system is by its very nature *illiquid,* though not *insolvent*—various debtors can repay their loans given time but cannot do so on demand. But many liabilities, for example, bank deposits or large CDs of banks and corporations, have very short maturities. If all creditors ask for their assets, many of the debtors would not be able to pay and would have to default.

Now imagine that a major financial institution, say First Bank of Nowhere (First, for short) has payment difficulties. Other financial institutions may well have lent to First and will want to recover their money before anyone else. A bank run starts. Other financial institutions are aware that *some* institutions have lent to First, cannot recover their loans, and are therefore vulnerable themselves, as are their creditors in turn. There arises a general uncertainty as to who lent to whom and who is in trouble because someone (or many) in the many layers of credit and intermediation cannot meet redemption demands. As a result, *all* credit freezes; nobody wants to lend to anyone because everyone is afraid of being pulled into the default. But if nobody wants to lend, short-term credit lines cannot be rolled over, and many institutions become illiquid. The process deteriorates in a 1930s-style financial collapse as assets are liquidated to recover liquidity.

The Fed enters in such a situation by *isolating* the center of the storm, guaranteeing the liabilities of the individual financial institution (beyond the guarantees of the FDIC). The guarantee assures everybody that third parties will not suffer losses and hence not become a risk.* Thus the lender-of-last-resort function prevents spillover effects to the credit market of individual payment difficulties. But the function also comes into its own when there is a marketwide problem. Walter Bagehot (1826–1877) in his famous 1873 book, *Lombard Street,* gave the classic prescription: *"During crisis discount freely!"*

Milton Friedman and Anna Schwartz, in their *A Monetary History of the United States,* blamed the Fed for not responding to the systemwide problems induced by the stock market crash of 1929, thus violating Bagehot's prescription. But during the stock market crash of 1987, the lesson had been learned. Fed chairman Alan Greenspan did not hesitate. He announced that the Fed stood behind the banking system. The Fed immediately reduced interest rates, providing much needed liquidity that would help stem the risk of a credit collapse.

*Knowing that the Fed stands ready to bail them out in case of trouble, bank managers have an incentive to take too many risks. To discourage such behavior, the Fed often fires bank managers and eliminates stockholder equity when bailing out a bank.

BOX 16-3 The Discount Rate Is *Not* Itself a Component of a Bank's Cost of Funds

It is often thought that banks obtain funds primarily from the Fed and that, as a result, changes in the discount rate directly change the banks' cost of funds. Changes in the discount rate sometimes affect market interest rates through the money supply mechanism, but the amount banks borrow from the Fed is completely trivial as a component of costs. For example, at the beginning of 1996 borrowing from the Fed equaled about 1/1,000 of 1 percent of loans and securities at commercial banks.

Discount rate changes serve two principal functions: (1) They signal the Fed's intentions; (2) they affect the free-market federal funds rate.

In some countries other than the United States, the central bank is a more significant source of funds for the banking system.

The discount rate is the explicit cost of Fed borrowing, but there is also an implicit cost, since the Fed frowns on banks that try to borrow from it too often.

The cost of borrowing from other banks is the *federal funds rate.* Federal funds are reserves that some banks have in excess and others need. The federal funds rate varies together with other market rates and can be affected by the Fed.

The Fed's role as a lender is reflected by the "Loans and discounts" item in Table 16-3. The Fed provides high-powered money to banks that need it by lending to them at the discount rate. Banks' willingness to borrow from the Fed is affected by the discount rate, which accordingly influences the volume of borrowing. Since borrowed reserves are also part of high-powered money, the Fed's discount rate has some effect on the monetary base. However, the real role of the discount rate is as a signaling mechanism of Fed intentions. When the Fed increases the discount rate, banks and financial markets take this as a signal that the Fed intends to reduce the money supply and increase market interest rates. The Fed often needs to change the discount rate simply to keep it in line with other interest rates. In these cases, the Fed actually announces this need as the reason in order to make it clear that it is *not* sending a signal.

THE RESERVE RATIO

Looking at the money multiplier in equation (3), it is easy to see that the Fed can increase the money supply by reducing the required-reserve ratio. However, this has not been done in recent years. Reserves pay no interest, and so are a kind of interest-free loan from banks to the Fed—a sort of implicit tax. Therefore, changes in reserve requirements have undesirable side effects on bank profits.

FINANCING FEDERAL DEFICITS

The U.S. Treasury maintains an account at the Fed and makes payments to the public by writing checks on its Fed account. The relationship between the Fed and the Treasury helps clarify the financing of government budget deficits.

Budget deficits can be financed by the Treasury's borrowing from the public. In that case, the Treasury sells bonds to the public. The public pays for the bonds with checks, which the Treasury deposits in an account it holds in a commercial bank, thereby making sure it does not affect the stock of high-powered money. When the Treasury uses the proceeds of the bond sales to make a payment, it moves the money into its Fed account just before making the payment. As a result, the monetary base is not affected by the Treasury's deficit financing, except for the short time between which the Treasury moves the money into its Fed account and then pays it out.

Alternatively, the Treasury can finance its deficit by borrowing from the Fed. It is simplest to think of the Treasury's selling a bond to the Fed instead of to the public. When the bond is sold, the Fed's holdings of government securities increase and, simultaneously, the asset "Net other assets" falls because Treasury deposits, a liability of the Fed, have risen. But then when the Treasury uses the borrowed money to make a payment, the stock of high-powered money rises. Accordingly, when a budget deficit is financed by the Treasury's borrowing from the Fed, the stock of high-powered money is increased.

We often talk of central bank financing of government deficits as financing through the printing of money. Typically, the deficit is not literally financed by the central bank through the printing of money, but central bank financing increases the stock of high-powered money, which comes to much the same thing.

In some countries the central bank automatically finances the treasury and may be subordinated to the treasury. In the United States, by contrast, the Federal Reserve answers to Congress and is not legally obliged to finance government deficits by buying bonds. Thus it still retains its ability to control the stock of high-powered money even when the Treasury is running a budget deficit.

16-3

THE MONEY MULTIPLIER AND BANK LOANS

We now present an alternative way of describing the workings of the money multiplier by showing how adjustments by banks and the public following an increase in the monetary base produce a multiple expansion of the money stock.

A Fed open market purchase increases the monetary base. To start with, the increase in the base shows up as an increase in bank reserves. This is because the Fed pays for the securities by writing a check on itself, which the seller of the securities deposits in his or her bank account. The bank in turn presents the check for collection to the Fed and will be credited with an increase in its reserve position at the Fed.

The bank in which the original check was deposited now has a reserve ratio that is too high. Its reserves and deposits have gone up by the same amount. Therefore, its ratio of reserves to deposits has risen. To reduce the ratio of reserves to deposits, it increases its lending.

When the bank makes a loan, the person receiving the loan gets a bank deposit. At this stage, when the bank makes a loan, *the money supply has risen by more than the amount of the open market operation.* The person who sold the security to the Fed has increased his or her holdings of money by the value of the bonds sold. The person receiving the loan has a new bank deposit and thus the process has already generated a multiple expansion of the money stock.

In the subsequent adjustment, part of the increase in high-powered money finds its way into the public's holdings of currency and part serves as the basis for an expansion of lending by the banking system. When banks lend, they do so by crediting the deposits of their loan customers with the loan. Banks therefore create money whenever they make loans.

The expansion of loans, and hence money, continues until the reserve-deposit ratio has fallen to the desired level and the public again has achieved its desired currency-deposit ratio. The money multiplier summarizes the total expansion of money created by a dollar increase in the monetary base.

16-4

CONTROL OF THE MONEY STOCK AND CONTROL OF THE INTEREST RATE

We make a simple but important point in this section: *The Fed cannot simultaneously set both the interest rate and the stock of money at any given target levels that it may choose.*

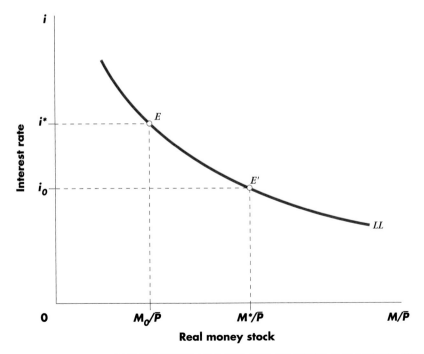

FIGURE 16-2   RELATIONSHIP BETWEEN THE REAL MONEY STOCK AND INTEREST RATES.

Figure 16-2 illustrates this point. Suppose that the Fed, for some reason, wants to set the interest rate at a level $i*$ and the money stock at a level $M*$ and that the demand-for-money function is as shown by LL. The Fed can move the money supply function around, but it cannot move the money demand function around. It can set only the combinations of the interest rate and the money supply that lie along LL. At interest rate $i*$, it can have money supply M_0/P. At target money supply $M*/P$, it can have interest rate i_0. But it cannot have both $M*/P$ and $i*$.

The point is sometimes put more dramatically, as follows: When the Fed decides to set the interest rate at some given level and keep it fixed—a policy known as *pegging* the interest rate—it loses control over the money supply. If the money demand curve were to shift, the Fed would have to supply whatever amount of money was demanded at the pegged interest rate.

The Fed in its day-to-day operations can more accurately control interest rates than the money stock. The Fed buys and sells government securities through its *open market desk* at the New York Fed every day. If it wants to raise the price of government securities (lower the interest rate), it can buy the securities at that price. If it wants to reduce the price of government securities (raise the interest rate), it can sell a sufficient amount of securities from its large portfolio. Thus, on a day-to-day basis, the Fed can determine the market interest rate quite accurately.[7]

These are *technical* reasons why the Fed cannot hit the target stock of money exactly even if it wants to. But over a slightly longer period, the Fed can determine the money supply fairly accurately. As data on the behavior of the money stock and the money multiplier become available, the Fed can make midcourse corrections to its setting of the base. For example, if the Fed were aiming for monetary growth of 5 percent over a given period, it might start the base growing at 5 percent. If it found halfway into the period that the multiplier had been falling, and the money stock therefore growing by less than 5 percent, the Fed would step up the growth rate of the base to compensate.

The main reasons the Fed does not hit its money growth targets are not technical but, rather, have to do with its having both interest rate *and* money stock targets, and as we have seen in this section, it cannot hit them both at the same time.

16-5

MONEY STOCK AND INTEREST RATE TARGETS

Over the period since the 1950s, the emphasis the Fed has placed on controlling the interest rate versus controlling the money supply has changed. Initially the emphasis was almost entirely on interest rates—indeed, it was not until 1959 that the Fed even began to publish money stock data. Until 1982 the emphasis on monetary targets increased more or less steadily. Since then the emphasis has shifted back increasingly toward interest rates and to a more eclectic approach to monetary policy.[8]

[7]For a description of techniques of monetary control, see Daniel Thornton, "The Borrowed Reserves Operating Procedure: Theory and Evidence," Federal Reserve Bank of St. Louis *Review*, January–February 1988.

[8]See Ann-Marie Meulendyke, "A Review of Federal Reserve Policy Targets and Operating Guides in Recent Decades," Federal Reserve Bank of New York *Quarterly Review*, Autumn 1988.

In this section we discuss the issues involved in the choice between interest rate and money stock targets. The analysis we present here is based on a classic article by William Poole.[9]

We assume that the Fed's aim is to have the economy reach a particular level of output. The analysis, which uses the *IS-LM* model, applies to a short period such as 3 to 9 months. In Figure 16-3, the *LM* curve labeled *LM(M)* is the *LM* curve that exists when the Fed fixes the money stock. The *LM* curve labeled *LM(i)* describes money market equilibrium when the Fed fixes the interest rate. It is horizontal at the chosen level of the interest rate, i^*.

The problem for policy is that the *IS* and *LM* curves shift unpredictably. When they shift, output ends up at a level different from the target level. In Figure 16-3a we show two alternative positions for the *IS* curve: IS_1 and IS_2. We assume that the Fed does not know in advance which will be the true *IS* curve: the position depends, for instance, on investment demand, which is difficult to predict. The Fed's aim is to have income come out as close as possible to the target level, Y^*.

In Figure 16-3a we see that the level of output stays closer to Y^* if the *LM* curve is *LM(M)*. In that case the level of output will be Y_1 if the *IS* curve is IS_1 and Y_2 if the *IS* curve is IS_2. If policy had kept the interest rate constant, we would in each case have a level of income that is further from Y^*: Y'_1 instead of Y_1, and Y'_2 instead of Y_2.

Thus we have our first conclusion: *If output deviates from its equilibrium level mainly because the IS curve shifts about, output is stabilized by keeping the money stock constant. The Fed should, in this case, have monetary targets.*

We can see from Figure 16-3a why it is more stabilizing to keep *M* rather than *i* constant. When the *IS* curve shifts to the right and the *LM(M)* curve applies, the interest rate rises, thereby reducing investment demand and moderating the effect of the shift. But if the *LM(i)* curve applies, there is no resistance from monetary policy to the effects of the *IS* shift. Monetary policy is thus automatically stabilizing in Figure 16-3a when the *IS* curve shifts and the money stock is held constant.

In Figure 16-3b we assume that the *IS* curve is stable. Now the uncertainty about the effects of monetary policy results from shifts in the *LM* curve. Assuming that the Fed can fix the money stock, the *LM* curve shifts because the money demand function shifts. When it sets the money stock, the Fed does not know what the interest rate will be. The *LM* curve could end up being either LM_1 or LM_2. Alternatively, the Fed could simply fix the interest rate at level i^*. That would ensure that the level of output is Y^*.

If the Fed were to fix the money stock, output could be either Y_1 or Y_2. If it fixes the interest rate, output will be Y^*. Thus we have our second conclusion: *If output deviates from its equilibrium level mainly because the demand-for-money function shifts about, the Fed should operate monetary policy by fixing the interest rate.* That way it automatically neutralizes the effects of the shifts in money demand. In this case the Fed should have interest rate targets.

The Poole analysis helps explain why the Fed stopped specifying $M1$ targets from 1987 on, while continuing to target $M2$ (and $M3$ and total nonfinancial debt). The increasing instability of the demand for $M1$ limited its usefulness as a monetary target.

[9]W. Poole, "Optimal Choice of Monetary Policy Instruments in a Simple Stochastic Macro Model," *Quarterly Journal of Economics*, May 1970.

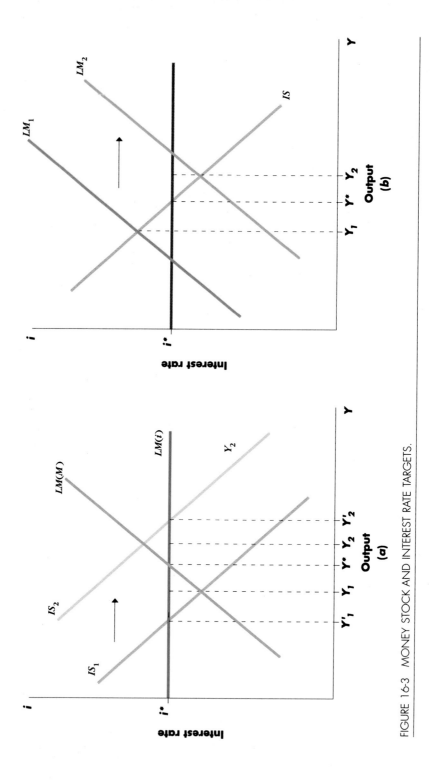

FIGURE 16-3 MONEY STOCK AND INTEREST RATE TARGETS.

Similarly, the unpredictability of the growth of all the monetary aggregates in the last few years has led to the increasing weight on interest rates.

THE SHORT RUN AND THE LONG RUN

It is important to note that the Poole argument discusses Fed targeting over short periods. The Fed is *not* to be thought of as announcing or desiring that the interest rate will be, say, 8 percent forever. Rather, the Fed should readjust its targets in light of the changing behavior of the economy: the target interest rate might be 5 percent at the bottom of a recession and 15 percent when the economy is overheating. Similarly, the money growth targets could also be adjusted in response to the state of the economy.

Monetarist proponents of money stock targeting might agree with the technical details of the Poole analysis but still argue that it is a mistake to target interest rates rather than money. They argue that increases in the money stock lead eventually to inflation and that the only way to avoid inflation in the long run is by keeping money growth moderate. The problem with focusing on interest rates, they suggest, is that while the Fed keeps its eye on interest rates, the growth rate of money and the inflation rate often tend to increase.[10] This argument appears to fit the facts of the 1960s and 1970s well.

However, that experience has led the Fed to watch inflationary trends very closely and to tighten policy when inflation threatens. That experience, and the monetarist analysis, has also led the Fed to set monetary targets for itself and, when it misses the targets, to appraise carefully the reasons why. At the same time, it pays attention to interest rates in case its monetary targets lead in the short run to recession or inflation if there are shifts in money demand.

16-6

MONEY, CREDIT, AND INTEREST RATES

The Fed targets not only $M2$ and $M3$ but also the increase in the total *debt* of the non-financial sectors, that is, the debt of the government, households, and firms other than financial firms. Their debt is equal to the credit (lending) that has been extended to them. Thus the Fed can also be described as having *credit targets*.

Why? In the first instance, this is a very old approach of the Fed, which had credit targets in the 1950s. The Fed returned to them in 1982 in part because of econometric evidence, presented by Benjamin Friedman of Harvard, showing that there was a tighter link between the volume of debt and GNP than between money and nominal GNP.[11]

At a fundamental level, proponents of the credit view, such as Ben Bernanke of Princeton and Mark Gertler of New York University, argue for the importance of the

---

[10]Another argument for money targeting arises from the distinction between real and nominal interest rates. The nominal interest rate can rise because inflation is expected. If the Fed fights this increase in the nominal rate by increasing the money stock, it is only feeding the inflation. We examine this argument in more detail in Chap. 19.

[11]B. Friedman, "The Roles of Money and Credit in Macroeconomic Analysis," in James Tobin (ed.), *Macroeconomics, Prices, and Quantities* (Washington, D.C.: The Brookings Institution, 1983).

BOX 16-4 Money Growth, Interest Rates, and Credit in the 1990–1991 Recession

In the 1990–1991 recession, fiscal policy was completely immobilized by the size of the budget deficit. The burden of dealing with the recession therefore fell on monetary policy, which ran into severe difficulties as banks appeared unwilling to lend and the different monetary aggregates grew at very different rates.

The starting point for the 1990–1991 recession was the gradually rising inflation rate at the end of the 1980s. From a low of 1.9 percent in 1986, the CPI inflation rate reached 4.8 percent in 1989. With the unemployment rate in 1989 at 5.2 percent, perhaps even below the natural rate, the Fed's main concern was to fight inflation.

The main indicators of monetary policy showed a tightening in 1989 (see Table 16-1). The most visible sign was the rise in the Treasury-bill rate from an average of 6.7 percent in 1988 to 8.1 percent in 1989; in addition, the growth rate of each of the monetary aggregates and of debt declined between 1988 and 1989—though M1 growth virtually collapsed while M2 fell very little. The Fed entered 1990 with inflation on its mind, viewing the 2.5 percent GDP growth in 1989 as being at about the sustainable rate.

The recession dates from July 1990, before the Iraqi invasion of Kuwait. We know now that GDP fell in both the third and fourth quarters of 1990, though the third-quarter decline showed up only in revised data in July 1992. But the Fed, then preoccupied with the question of how to deal with the 40 percent rise in the price of oil that followed the Iraqi invasion, held its interest rates constant through the end of the year. Then, as the re-

extent of financial intermediation—the volume of lending and borrowing through financial institutions—in the economy. Financial intermediation occurs when financial institutions channel funds from savers to investors, as banks do when they lend funds deposited with them to borrowers who want to invest. Bernanke's research suggests that a large part of the decline in output in the Great Depression was the result of the breakdown of the financial system and the collapse in the quantity of credit, rather than the decline in the quantity of money.[12] The slow growth of credit in 1989–1991 has also been blamed for the 1990–1991 recession (see Box 16-4).

Proponents of the central role of credit also argue that *credit rationing* makes interest rates an unreliable indicator of monetary policy. Credit is rationed when individuals

---

[12]Ben Bernanke, "Non-Monetary Effects of the Financial Crisis in the Propagation of the Great Depression," *American Economic Review*, June 1983. See, too, Ben Friedman, "Monetary Policy without Quantity Variables," *American Economic Review*, May 1988, and Anil Kashyap, Jeremy Stein, and David Wilcox, "Monetary Policy and Credit Conditions: Evidence from the Composition of External Finance," *American Economic Review*, March 1993. For more recent work on the operation of the credit channel, see Stephen D. Oliner and Glenn D. Rudebusch, "Is There a Broad Credit Channel for Monetary Policy," Federal Reserve Bank of San Francisco *Economic Review* 1 (1996).

cession continued, the Fed kept reducing the interest rate, very slowly through 1991, always concerned not to go too far in case it reignited inflation.

At the end of 1991, with the recession probably already over, the data again began to show signs of weakening production and output. There was much talk of a *double-dip recession*. This time the Fed moved decisively, cutting the discount rate from 4.5 to 3.5 percent. Treasury-bill rates moved to their lowest level in 20 years, and then as growth continued sluggish, they fell to their lowest level in 30 years. Interestingly though, long-term interest rates were very slow to come down, as can be seen by looking at the 10-year bond rate in Table 16-1. The explanation is that markets believed that inflation would soon return.

It is striking that in the 1990–1992 period, the Fed conducted monetary policy almost entirely with reference to interest rates. The reason can be seen in Table 16-1: the growth rates of the different monetary aggregates diverged wildly.

There was one other special feature of the recession: the view that credit was unusually difficult to get. Even before the recession began, business executives and policy makers were complaining about the difficulty of getting loans. The credit crunch—the reluctance of banks and thrifts to lend—seemed to worsen as the recession continued. The volume of bank loans declined in the recession, confirming the existence of the problem.*

Why was there a crunch? Bank regulators, worried about bank failures, were tightening their standards, trying to make sure the banks did not make bad loans. Banks, in response, tended to move to safety, holding government securities rather than making loans to businesses.

*Ben Bernanke and Cara Lown, "The Credit Crunch," *Brookings Papers on Economic Activity* 2 (1991). See also the special issue on the credit slowdown published by the Federal Reserve Bank of New York *Quarterly Review,* Spring 1993.

---

cannot borrow as much as they want at the going interest rate. Credit is rationed because lenders fear that borrowers who are willing to borrow may not be able to repay. But if credit is rationed at a given interest rate, that interest rate does not fully describe the impact of monetary policy on investment and aggregate demand. Proponents of the credit view argue that the Fed should focus directly on the volume of credit to see what impact monetary policy is having on demand.

16-7

WHICH TARGETS FOR THE FED?

We are now ready to set monetary policy in a broader perspective by discussing the targets of monetary policy. There are three points to note before we get down to the details:

1. A key distinction is between *ultimate targets* of policy and *intermediate targets.* Ultimate targets are variables such as the inflation rate and the unemployment rate (or real output) whose behavior matters. The interest rate or the rate of growth of

money or credit are intermediate targets of policy—targets the Fed aims at so that it can hit the ultimate targets more accurately. The discount rate, open market operations, and reserve requirements are the *instruments* the Fed has with which to hit the targets.[13]

2. It matters how often the intermediate targets are reset. For instance, if the Fed were to commit itself to 5.5 percent money growth over a period of several years, it would have to be sure that the velocity of money was not going to change unpredictably; otherwise, the actual level of GDP would be far different from the targeted level. If the money target were reset more often, as velocity changed, the Fed could come closer to hitting its ultimate targets.

3. The need for targeting arises from a lack of knowledge. If the Fed had the right ultimate goals and knew exactly how the economy worked, it could do whatever was needed to keep the economy as close to its ultimate targets as possible.[14]

Intermediate targets give the Fed something concrete and specific to aim for in the next year. That enables the Fed itself to focus on what it should be doing. It also helps the private sector know what to expect. If the Fed announces and will stick to its targets, firms and consumers have a better idea of what monetary policy will be.

Another benefit of specifying targets for monetary policy is that the Fed can then be held *accountable* for its actions. It has a job to do. By announcing targets, the Fed makes it possible for outsiders to discuss whether it is aiming in the right direction and then later to judge whether it succeeded in its aims.

The ideal intermediate target is a variable that the Fed can control exactly and that, at the same time, has an exact relationship with the ultimate targets of policy. For instance, if the ultimate target could be expressed as some particular level of nominal GDP, and if the money multiplier and velocity were both constant, the Fed could hit its ultimate target by having the money base as its intermediate target.

In practice, life is not so simple. Rather, *in choosing intermediate targets, the Fed has to trade off between those targets it can control exactly and those targets that are most closely related to its ultimate targets.*

TARGETING THE MONETARY BASE

Sometimes proposed, at one extreme, is *monetary-base targeting.*[15] The Fed can essentially control the monetary base exactly. If that were the intermediate target, the Fed would have no trouble hitting the bull's-eye. Further, it could certainly be held accountable for not hitting the target, since it could not plausibly blame factors beyond its control for any failures.

The problem with monetary-base targeting is that the Fed might be hitting the bull's-eye on the money-base target while completely missing the ultimate targets of

---

[13]See Benjamin Friedman, "Targets and Indicators of Monetary Policy," in B. Friedman and F. Hahn (eds.), *Handbook of Monetary Economics* (Amsterdam: North-Holland, 1991).

[14]See the discussions of lags and of multiplier uncertainty in Chap. 18.

[15]See Bennett T. McCallum, "Could a Monetary Base Rule Have Prevented the Great Depression?" *Journal of Monetary Economics,* August 1990, and "Monetary Policy Rules and Financial Stability," NBER Working Paper 4692, April 1994.

policy. Unpredictable changes in the money multiplier and in velocity break the tight link between the money base and nominal GDP.

INFLATION TARGETING

Inflation targeting is at the other end of the tradeoff. The Fed could reduce money growth whenever inflation appears to be developing. Inflation targeting has the very considerable attraction that the Fed clearly has the ability to keep inflation at a permanently low average level, even if it can't hit an inflation target precisely each quarter. The disadvantage, also considerable, is that inflation targeting eliminates the Fed's ability to smooth fluctuations in real output and employment. Indeed, in the case of an adverse supply shock which raises prices and reduces output, inflation targeting may lead the Fed to reduce the money supply at a time when the economy is already in a recession. Nonetheless, inflation targeting has become increasingly popular as a method by which central banks can emphasize their long-term commitment to price stability.[16]

TARGETING NOMINAL GDP

Under *nominal GDP targeting,* the Fed would announce a target path for nominal GDP—for instance, that it wants nominal GDP to grow by 10 percent. But since the Fed does not directly control nominal GDP, it would have to calculate, each period, the money stock or money base that would enable it to come closest to hitting the GDP target. Relative to money stock targeting, nominal GDP targeting implies that the Fed automatically adjusts money targets for velocity shifts.

By targeting nominal GDP growth, the Fed builds in an automatic policy trade-off between inflation and output. If inflation turns out high, the nominal income growth target implies that the Fed will be aiming for a lower level of output growth than it would have otherwise.[17]

With nominal GDP targeting, the Fed might well not be to blame if the target is missed—fiscal policy or supply shocks could be just as responsible as monetary policy. Thus those who believe the main problem in monetary policy is controlling the Fed typically argue for monetary-base or money stock rules. Those who believe that the Fed can be trusted to do the right thing tend to prefer nominal GDP targeting.

Beyond the issue of trusting the Fed lie questions of whether the economy would be more stable if, over periods of a year or so, nominal GDP growth were held constant or if money-base growth or interest rates were held constant. There are no simple

[16]Stanley Fischer, "Why Are Central Banks Pursuing Long-Run Price Stability?" *Achieving Price Stability* (Federal Reserve Bank of Kansas City, 1996) and, by the same author, "Modern Central Banking," in *The Future of Central Banking: The Tercentenary Symposium of the Bank of England* (Cambridge, England: Cambridge University Press, 1994). See also Robert G. King and Alexander L. Wolman, "Inflation Targeting in a St. Louis Model of the 21st Century," Federal Reserve Bank of St. Louis *Review,* May–June 1996; William T. Gavin, "The FOMC in 1995: A Step Closer to Inflation Targeting?" Federal Reserve Bank of St. Louis *Review,* September–October 1996; and Ben S. Bernanke and Frederic S. Mishkin, "Inflation Targeting: A New Framework for Monetary Policy?" NBER Working Paper 5893, January 1997.

[17]See Michael D. Bradley and Dennis W. Jansen, "Understanding Nominal GNP Targeting," Federal Reserve Bank of St. Louis *Review,* November–December 1989. See, too, Jeffrey A. Frankel with Menzie Chinn, "The Stabilizing Properties of a Nominal GNP Rule in an Open Economy," *Journal of Money, Credit, and Banking,* May 1995, for an extension of the analysis to the open economy.

answers at this stage: the answer depends on what shocks are likely to hit the economy, as the Poole analysis above illustrates.

Which targets should the Fed have? The Fed should have and announce ultimate targets for monetary policy, such as the path of nominal GDP it would like to attain over the next few years. At the same time, it should announce money stock targets for the next year and explain why those targets are consistent with its ultimate targets of policy. It should be willing to adjust the intermediate targets as velocity and the shocks hitting the economy change.

What do we conclude? That targeting has an important role in monetary policy, that public discussion about monetary policy is important, and that—because the economy is always evolving unpredictably—the Federal Reserve Board cannot avoid using its judgment in deciding which targets to follow and which to change.

SUMMARY

1. The stock of money is determined by the Fed through its control of the monetary base (high-powered money); by the public, through its preferred currency-deposit ratio; and by the banks, through their preferred reserve-holding behavior.

2. The money stock is larger than the stock of high-powered money because part of the money stock consists of bank deposits, against which the banks hold less than 1 dollar of reserves per dollar of deposits.

3. The money multiplier is the ratio of the money stock to high-powered money. It is larger the smaller the reserve-deposit ratio and the smaller the currency-deposit ratio.

4. The Fed creates high-powered money in open market purchases when it buys assets (e.g., Treasury bills, gold, foreign exchange) by creating liabilities on its balance sheet. These purchases increase banks' reserves held at the Fed and lead, through the multiplier process, to an increase in the money stock which is larger than the increase in high-powered money.

5. The money multiplier builds up through an adjustment process in which banks make loans (or buy securities) because deposits have increased their reserves above desired levels.

6. The Fed has three basic policy instruments: open market operations, the discount rate, and required reserves for depository institutions.

7. The Fed cannot control both the interest rate and the money stock exactly. It can only choose combinations of the interest rate and money stock that are consistent with the demand-for-money function.

8. The Fed operates monetary policy by specifying target ranges for both the money stock and the interest rate. In order to hit its target level of output, the Fed should concentrate on its money targets if the *IS* curve is unstable or shifts about a great deal. It should concentrate on interest rate targets if the money demand function is the major source of instability in the economy.

9. The Fed targets not only *M*2 and *M*3 and interest rates but also total nonfinancial debt, or the volume of credit, in the economy.

10. In choosing targets for monetary policy, the Fed faces a tradeoff between targets that it can hit exactly but that may be far from the ultimate targets of policy and targets that are closer to ultimate targets but are more difficult to hit. Critics of

the Fed argue that, in addition, the Fed should choose targets on which it can be held accountable for its actions—this suggests the Fed's selecting intermediate targets that it can hit quite accurately.

KEY TERMS

credit	Federal Deposit Insurance	federal funds rate
fractional reserve banking	Corporation (FDIC)	credit targets
high-powered money	required reserves	credit rationing
monetary base	excess reserves	ultimate target
money multiplier	open market operation	intermediate target
currency-deposit ratio	discount rate	instrument(s)
reserve ratio	required-reserve ratio	monetary-base targeting
bank run	foreign exchange market	inflation targeting
disintermediation	intervention	nominal GDP targeting

PROBLEMS

Conceptual

1. The Fed wants to increase the money supply. What are the main instruments available to it, and how can each, specifically, increase the money supply? (*Hint:* There are three.)
2. Can the Fed affect the currency-deposit ratio?
3. Under what circumstances should the Fed conduct monetary policy by targeting mainly *(a)* interest rates or *(b)* the money stock?
4. **a.** What is a bank run?
   b. Why might one occur?
   c. If the Fed took no action in the face of a bank run, what would be the effects on the money supply and on the money multiplier?
   d. How does the existence of the FDIC help prevent this problem?
5. **a.** Why does the Fed not stick more closely to its target paths for money?
   b. What are the dangers of targeting nominal interest rates?
6. Categorize each of the following as either an ultimate or intermediate target or an instrument of monetary policy:
   a. Nominal GDP
   b. The discount rate
   c. The monetary base
   d. $M1$
   e. The Treasury-bill rate
   f. The unemployment rate
7. What might be the danger in using interest rates as targets for monetary policy when credit rationing is taking place?
8. Why might the Fed choose intermediate targets for its monetary policy, as opposed to directly pursuing its ultimate targets? What are the benefits and the dangers of using these intermediate targets?
9. "The Fed's target for monetary policy should be to produce constant growth of real GDP at a rate of 3.5 percent per year." Discuss.

Technical

1. Show how an open market sale affects the Fed's balance sheet and also the balance sheet of the commercial bank of the purchaser of the bond sold by the Fed.

2. When the Fed buys or sells gold or foreign exchange, it automatically offsets, or *sterilizes,* the impact of these operations on the monetary base by compensating open market operations. What it does is to buy gold and at the same time sell bonds from its portfolio. Show the effects on the Fed balance sheet of a purchase of gold and a corresponding sterilization through an open market sale.

3. A proposal for "100 percent banking" involves a reserve-deposit ratio of unity. Such a scheme has been proposed for the United States in order to enhance the Fed's control over the money supply.

    a. Indicate why such a scheme would help monetary control.

    b. Indicate what bank balance sheets would look like under this scheme.

    c. Under 100 percent money, how would banking remain profitable?

4. You, as chair of the Fed (congratulations), are considering whether the monetary base or the interest rate should be used as a target. What information do you need to have to make an informed decision? When would each be a good (or bad!) choice?

CHAPTER 17

Financial Markets

CHAPTER HIGHLIGHTS

◆ We can understand how the returns on two different investments are related by asking what sort of returns would make investors willing to hold both.

◆ The term structure of interest explains how long-term interest rates relate to short-term interest rates.

◆ In a well-functioning stock market, stock price changes are largely unpredictable.

◆ Changes in exchange rates can be explained in part as reflecting international differences in interest rates.

Financial markets link macroeconomic shocks and government policy directly to the lives of everyday people. Changes in interest rates affect our ability to finance a home or a car. The movements of the stock market determine the value of pensions for many people. The rates of return in financial markets also feed back into the goods markets by affecting the level of investment and consumption. In this chapter, we examine the behavior of three important financial markets: the bond market, the stock market, and the foreign exchange market. In each case, the analysis begins with two ideas:

- Markets are forward-looking.
- Key relations depend on the idea of *arbitrage*—in equilibrium, prices must make investors equally willing to buy or sell an asset: any other price will place everyone on only one side of the market.

17-1

INTEREST RATES—LONG-TERM AND SHORT

Through much of the text we represent interest rates with the single symbol *i,* as if there were only one interest rate in the economy. In fact, since an interest rate summarizes

FIGURE 17-1   INTEREST RATES ON TREASURY BILLS AND BONDS, 1970–1996.

(Source: DRI/McGraw-Hill Macroeconomic Database.)

the promised repayment terms on a bond or loan, interest rates differ according to the creditworthiness of the issuer, tax treatments, and other factors. The factor of greatest interest here is the length of time the interest rate covers—the *term* of the bond. The interest rate on a 10-year bond is usually, but not always, greater than the interest rate on a 1-year bond. The relation between interest rates of different *maturities* is called the *term structure of interest.*

Figure 17-1 shows interest rates for U.S. Treasury securities with maturities from 3 months to 30 years. Three patterns emerge. First, interest rates of different maturities mostly go up and down together. Rates were all relatively high in 1981 and low in 1992. Second, the gap between long-term rates and short-term rates varies. In 1989, the interest rate on 30-year bonds and the interest rate on 3-month Treasury bills were about equal, but in 1994 the 30-year rate was about 4 percentage points higher. Third, long-term rates are usually higher than short-term rates. Between 1970 and 1995 the 30-year rate averaged about 1.9 percentage points more than the 3-month rate. The theory of the term structure explains these three patterns.

As a concrete example, let's examine the relation between the 1-year rate and the 3-year rate. Pretend that today's date is January 1, 2000. On the financial page of "today's" newspaper you can read the current 1-year rate, $_1i_{2000}$; that is the rate on money lent at the beginning of the year 2000 to be repaid at the beginning of 2001. You can also read the current 3-year rate covering a bond to be repaid at the beginning of the year 2003, $_3i_{2000}$. (The "frontscripts" indicate the length of the investment and the subscripts in their usual spot indicate the date the investment is made.) You have the option of making a 3-year investment today and earning $_3i_{2000}$ each year or of investing for 1 year, reinvesting for another year at the rate prevailing at the beginning of 2001, and then reinvesting for a final year at the rate prevailing in 2002. Figure 17-2 illustrates the two alternatives.

If all the rates shown in Figure 17-2 were known in advance, the total return from one 3-year investment would have to equal the return from the series of three 1-year investments. If the total returns were not equal, everyone would choose the alternative with the higher return, completely abandoning the other path. For both long-term and short-term investments to coexist when the rates of return are known in advance, the total returns from long and short investments must be equal. This argument illustrates the idea of *arbitrage:* 3 years of returns at the 3-year rate must equal the total of three single-year returns, $_3i_{2000} + {}_3i_{2000} + {}_3i_{2000} = {}_1i_{2000} + {}_1i_{2001} + {}_1i_{2002}$. Note that

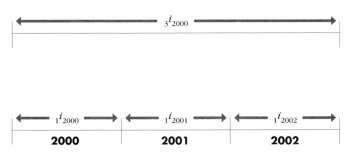

FIGURE 17-2   ALTERNATIVE INVESTMENTS.

BOX 17-1 Compound Interest

$100 invested at 5 percent earns $5 the first year and in the second year earns . . .? No, not another $5, but $5 additional interest on the principal plus 5 percent of the interest earned the first year ($5 × 0.05 = $0.25), for a second-year total of $5.25. Interest on money invested for multiple periods compounds. Thus $100 invested at 5 percent grows to $100 × 1.05 = $105.00 after 1 year and ($100 × 1.05) × 1.05 = $110.25 after 2 years. In general, an amount P invested at rate i for t years grows to $P(1 + i)^t$.

Because interest rates multiply rather than add, our term structure equation should really rely on geometric rather than arithmetic averages. Under certainty, a more accurate version of the term structure equation given in the text is $(1 + {}_3i_{2000})^3 = (1 + {}_1i_{2000})(1 + {}_1i_{2001})(1 + {}_1i_{2002})$. For example, if the three short-term interest rates were 5, 10, and 15 percent, the exact 3-year rate would be 9.924 percent, rather than 10 percent. You can see that this difference doesn't matter for understanding the term structure but would be worth paying attention to if you were investing hundreds of millions of dollars.

the subscripts on the 3-year rate all indicate that this is the rate agreed to at the beginning of 2000.

We can rewrite the arbitrage condition as ${}_3i_{2000} = ({}_1i_{2000} + {}_1i_{2001} + {}_1i_{2002})/3$. This brings us to our first simple, model of the term structure: The long-term interest rate equals the average of current and future short-term interest rates. (But see Box 17-1.)

The only problem with this theory is that at the beginning of the year 2000 we can't know either ${}_1i_{2001}$ or ${}_1i_{2002}$ with certainty, although we can make an educated guess. Uncertainty about future short-term rates necessitates two modifications to our simple theory. First, today's long-term rate depends on the current short-term rate and the *expected* future short-term rates. Second, uncertainty implies risk, and long-term investments command a *term premium, PR,* to compensate for this risk. Putting these into our example, we would write the term structure equation as

TABLE 17-1 Average Term Premiums above 3-Month Treasury Bill

?M	PREMIUM
ths	—
?s	.13
	.79
	1.14
	1.28
	1.53
	70
	9

$$_3i_{2000} = \frac{_1i_{2000} + _1i^e_{2001} + _1i^e_{2002}}{3} + PR \qquad (1)$$

where the e superscripts indicate the expectation of the future short-term interest rate. Written this way, equation (1) shows the *expectations theory of the term structure.* Term premiums vary over time but are generally higher for longer-term rates. The higher-term premiums in part reflect the higher risk associated (for reasons discussed below) with the greater price volatility of longer-term bonds. Table 17-1 shows average term premiums based on the interest rates shown in Figure 17-1.

THE YIELD CURVE

Interest rates for different maturities are shown on the *yield curve,* a snapshot of the opportunities available on a particular day. Figure 17-3 shows two such yield curves, one for January 1994 and one for January 1981. Because long rates are generally higher than short rates, the yield curve usually rises with maturity, as it did in January 1994. Occasionally, the yield curve slopes down, meaning that short rates are above long rates. The expectations theory of the term structure implies that a downward-sloping yield curve means that financial markets expect interest rates to fall.

FIGURE 17-3   COMPARISON OF TWO YIELD CURVES.

(Source: DRI/McGraw-Hill Macroeconomic Database.)

BOX 17-2 Present Value and Arbitrage

Congratulations, you've won $10 million in the state lottery! Well . . . actually you've won $500,000 a year for 20 years. If you were to ask really nicely, would the state let you have the $10 million in a lump sum instead? No. In fact, the state probably contracted with a private firm to cover the stream of 20 payments—at an upfront cost of around $5.6 million. So the "$10 million" prize is really worth only a bit more than half the stated amount.

Why is the *present value* of a payment due in the future less than the stated payment, for example, $5.6 versus $10 million? We can find the answer through an arbitrage argument: two different ways to make a future payment must have the same value or only one will be used.

Suppose you owe a store $100, due 1 year from now. What is the value *today* of the debt due in 1 year? One way to value the debt is to ask how much you would need to invest today in order to pay the debt when due. We call the amount needed to invest today the *present value* of the debt, or *PV*. The amount due in the future—"$100 in 1 year"—we call the *future value* of the debt, or *FV*.

Suppose you have the $100 in hand now. While you could discharge the debt today, you could also invest some, but not all, of the $100 for 1 year and then use the investment plus accumulated interest to pay off the debt in a year's time. With this procedure, you will not only cover the debt but will also have enough money left over for a small pizza and the legal beverage of your choice. The amount you need to invest is less than *FV* since part of the debt will be covered by accumulated interest. Since *FV*-in-a-year and *PV*-today-plus-interest both discharge the debt, they must have the same value: $FV = PV + i \times PV$. We can turn this around to figure out the present value of a future debt, that is, how much needs to be set aside today:

$$PV = \frac{FV}{1 + i}$$

The same argument can be extended to payments due more than 1 year in the future. For a debt due in 2 years we have $PV = FV/(1 + i)^2$, and for a debt due in T years we have $PV = FV/(1 + i)^T$. If you owe FV_1 due in 1 year and FV_2 due in 2 years, then to cover both debts, you would need to set aside

$$PV = \frac{FV_1}{(1 + i)^1} + \frac{FV_2}{(1 + i)^2}$$

By the way, another common name for "present value" is *net present value*, or *NPV*.

(Since the long rate is an average of current and future short rates, the long rate can be below the current short rate only if future short rates are expected to be below the current short rate.)

A downward-sloping yield curve is often, but not always, a recessionary signal.

BOX 17-3 The Math of Net Present Value, Prices, and Yield

Formally, the price of a bond equals the *net present value (NPV)* of coupons plus face value at current interest rates. If a bond makes T annual coupon payments and returns face value F at the end of year T, its price must be

$$P = \frac{c}{1 + i} + \frac{c}{(1 + i)^2} + \cdots + \frac{c}{(1 + i)^T} + \frac{F}{(1 + i)^T}$$

Using an algebraic theorem about geometric series, this can be rewritten

$$P = \frac{c}{i}\left[1 - \frac{1}{(1 + i)^T}\right] + \frac{F}{(1 + i)^T}$$

Note two useful facts. First, if $i = c/P$, then $P = F$. For example, a bond with a $100 face value and a $5 coupon is, unsurprisingly, worth $100 when the interest rate is 5 percent. Second, the formula for a bond that lasts forever, called a *consol* or a *perpetuity*, is simply $P = c/i$. A very long-term bond with a $5 coupon is worth $100 when the interest rate is 5 percent but the price drops to $50 if the interest rate rises to 10 percent. Consols exist in Canada and the United Kingdom, but they are rarely traded in the United States. However, the consol formula gives a reasonable approximation to the pricing of common long-term bonds such as 30-year U.S. government bonds.

BOND PRICES AND YIELDS

Bond prices are inversely related to interest rates. If a bond is to pay $100 a year from now and has an interest rate i, then its price, P, must be such that $P(1 + i) = 100$ or $P = 100/(1 + i)$. For example, a $100 bond will have a 5 percent yield if its price is $95.24 [$95.24 = $100/(1 + 0.05)$].

Most bonds in the United States make a periodic payment called a *coupon* (because once upon a time there were actual coupons that had to be clipped and mailed in to receive payment) and then return the bond's *face value* at maturity. For example, a bond priced at $100 with a $5 coupon at the end of year 1 and again at the end of year 2, plus a $100 return of principal at the end of year 2, would have a 5 percent yield: $100 \times (1.05)^2 = $5 \times (1.05) + $5 + 100. When a bond price equals its face value, the bond is said to trade "at par."

In order to see how changes in market interest rates affect bond prices, suppose that an instant after you bought the bond just described the market interest rate rose from 5 to 10 percent. In order to sell the bond, you would have to lower the price sufficiently to compensate the buyer for receiving $5 coupons instead of the $10 available with a brand-new bond: $P \times (1.10)^2 = $5 \times (1.10) + $5 + 100, or $P = 91.32. The longer the remaining term of the bond, the greater the required change in the price to compensate for a change in the interest rate. For this reason, long-term bonds are subject to considerable price fluctuations. The same interest rate change applied to a 30-year bond would drop the bond's price to $52.87.

17-2

THE RANDOM WALK OF STOCK PRICES

Surely, one of the best-established facts in economics is that changes in stock prices are essentially unpredictable. And just as surely, this fact is one of the least believed and most disliked. After all, one objective of the study of economics is the ability to explain and predict market behavior. What we show in this section is that it is exactly the fact that the stock market is well understood that makes stock price changes hard to predict.

Figure 17-4 plots an index of Canadian stock prices against the same prices lagged 1 month.[1] The central stylized fact of the plot is that the data is tightly scattered around a 45° line which intersects the vertical axis a smidgen above the point (0, 0). We can write the equation for the 45° line as $P_{t+1} \approx P_t + \epsilon$ or, to account for the small vertical displacement, as

$$P_{t+1} = a + P_t + \epsilon \tag{2}$$

[1] Actually, the plot shows the natural logarithm of the price.

FIGURE 17-4   RELATIONSHIP OF CANADIAN STOCK PRICES TO THEIR PAST VALUES.

(Source: DRI/McGraw-Hill Macroeconomic Database.)

where a is quite small and represents the expected return to holding stocks. In either formulation ϵ represents the surprise change in the stock price.

Why should an innocuous equation like (2) be so controversial?[2] First, equation (2) implies that aside from the very small a component, the change in the stock price, $\Delta P = a + \epsilon$, is unpredictable. Second, equation (2) states that following a shock, stock prices *do not* have a tendency to return to a "normal" level. Rather, changes to stock prices are independent over time. If stocks did well last month, they are no more likely to either do well or do poorly this month than at any other time. The process described by equation (2) is called a *random walk*.[3] A random walk is a sign of market efficiency. Using just two assumptions, we can show that a random walk is just what we should expect from a well-functioning market:

- The price of a stock is the net present value of expected dividends.
- New information changes expectations of future dividends but only by surprise, since if it's not a surprise, it's not *new* information.

Suppose that at date t we expect to start receiving dividends in k periods at levels $d_{t+k}, d_{t+k+1}, d_{t+k+2}$, and so on. The stock price at date t will equal the net present value of these expected dividends, discounted at a rate r. (The discount rate r will be higher than the interest rate on Treasury bills in order to compensate for the riskiness of stock investment.) We can write the relation as

$$P_t = \frac{d_{t+k}}{(1+r)^k} + \frac{d_{t+k\,1}}{(1+r)^{k+1}} + \frac{d_{t+k+2}}{(1+r)^{k+2}} + \ldots \tag{3}$$

At date $t + 1$ the same relation will apply, but with dividends discounted by one less interest factor since it will be closer to their receipt:

$$P_{t+1} = \frac{d_{t+1+(k-1)}}{(1+r)^{k-1}} + \frac{d_{t+1+(k)}}{(1+r)^k} + \frac{d_{t+1+(k+1)}}{(1+r)^{k+1}} + \ldots \tag{4}$$

Multiply both sides of equation (3) by $(1 + r)$ to make the right-hand side look just like the right-hand side of equation (4). For example, the first term becomes

$$\frac{d_{t+k}}{(1+r)^k} \times (1+r) = \frac{d_{t+k}}{(1+r)^k} \times \frac{1}{(1+r)^{-1}} = \frac{d_{t+k}}{(1+r)^{k-1}} = \frac{d_{t+1+(k-1)}}{(1+r)^{k-1}}.$$ Equating P_{t+1} with P_t times $(1 + r)$ we have

$$P_{t+1} = (1+r)P_t \tag{5}$$

In practice, our expectations of future dividends are likely to change between periods t and $t + 1$, so the effect of this news must be added to equation (5), as in

$$P_{t+1} = (1+r)P_t + \epsilon \tag{6}$$

which is pretty much what Figure 17-4 shows.[4]

---

[2]"Controversial" is a funny term here. Economists *all* agree that equation (2) gives an excellent description of the behavior of major stock markets.

[3]The classic—and readable—book on the subject is Burton Malkiel's *A Random Walk Down Wall Street: Updated for the 1990s Investor* (New York: Norton 1991).

[4]More precisely we could write $P_{t+1} = (1+r)P_t \times \epsilon$ and then, taking logarithms of both sides, write $\ln P_{t+1} = \ln(1+r) + \ln P_t + \ln \epsilon$. The log of P is what's actually shown in Figs. 17-4 and 17-5. Note that the "small intercept," a, should approximately equal the expected return to stocks, r.

Not all stock markets are "efficient" in the sense of the market following a random walk, but the really major markets do follow random walks. Figure 17-5 shows the same picture of tomorrow's price versus today's as does Figure 17-4, only for U.S. rather than Canadian data.

Figure 17-5 is based on the Standard & Poor's (S&P) 500 index, an index of the stocks of 500 large companies in the U.S. stock market. The equation behind the line in Figure 17-5, estimated using monthly data from 1947 through 1996, is

$$\ln P_{t+1} = 0.0068 + 0.999905 \ln P_t$$

which corresponds extraordinarily well with the theoretical prediction.

Theory and data are in agreement, but is it *really* true that stock returns are unpredictable? The answer is no, yes, and no.

Figure 17-6 shows a plot of the 3-month Treasury-bill interest rate shown in Figure 17-1, along with the return to the S&P 500. The return to the stock market is extraordinarily volatile compared to interest rates, but it is also substantially higher on average. So the first "no" is because the return is predictably higher *on average* than the return on less volatile investments. The "yes" is because while mean return is higher,

FIGURE 17-5   RELATIONSHIP OF S&P 500 INDEX TO PAST VALUES.

The diagram shows the close correspondence of the index to its value from the previous month.
(Source: DRI/McGraw-Hill Macroeconomic Database.)

BOX 17-4 Linking the Bond Market and Stock Market

The stock market is heavily influenced by long-term interest rates, as stock prices fall when interest rates rise. One easy way to understand the connection is to pretend that a stock is expected to pay a dividend, d, forever, making the stock much like a consol. The present value formula in equation (3) would simplify to $P = d/r$. A very small change in r will cause a very large change in P.

As an example, a rise in long-term interest rates from 5 to 5.05 percent would be enough to drop the entire stock market 1 percent in this formulation. A .05 interest rate change is—outside financial markets—too small too notice. A .1 percent drop in the stock market is certainly large enough to make the headlines of the business section of the newspaper.

FIGURE 17-6   COMPARISON OF TREASURY-BILL RATE TO S&P 500 INDEX, 1947–1996.

(*Source: DRI/McGraw-Hill Macroeconomic Database.*)

the timing of swings is unpredictable, as random-walk theory predicts. The final "no" arises because there are a few findings of return predictability, particularly over very long horizons.[5] Nonetheless, the random-walk model is probably a $99\,^{44}/_{100}$ percent accurate description of stock market behavior.

17-3

EXCHANGE RATES AND INTEREST RATES

Arbitrage arguments also link exchange rate changes to international interest rate differentials. Consider the following two investment strategies for an American wishing to invest $100 for 1 year:

Strategy 1: Invest in the United States.

Strategy 2: Convert $100 to Canadian dollars, and invest in Canada for 1 year. At the end of the year convert back to U.S. dollars.

The end result of strategy 1 is straightforward; the investor ends the year with $100 \times (1 + i)$ dollars. If the interest rate in the United States, i, is 10 percent, the investor will end up with US$110.

Executing strategy 2 involves several steps. First, U.S. dollars are converted to Canadian dollars. Suppose the exchange rate, e_t, is CDN$0.75 per US$1.00. (In other words, the Canadian dollar is worth 75 U.S. cents.) The conversion gives the investor $100/e_t$ Canadian dollars (in this example, CDN$133.33). If the Canadian interest rate is i^*, then after a year the investor will have $(100/e_t) \times (1 + i^*)$ Canadian dollars. (Suppose the Canadian interest rate is 12 percent. At the end of the year, the investor has CDN$149.33.) Canadian dollars can be converted back to U.S. dollars at the exchange rate prevailing at the end of the year, e_{t+1}, for a final end-of-the-year U.S. value of $e_{t+1} \times [(100/e_t) \times (1 + i^*)]$. For strategy 1 and strategy 2 to have equal returns, we need $(1 + i) = (e_{t+1}/e_t) \times (1 + i^*)$. (In other words, both Americans and Canadians should have invested only in Canada if $e_{t+1} > .737$ or only in the United States if $e_{t+1} < .737$.) This relation can be closely approximated by

$$\frac{e_{t+1} - e_t}{e_t} = i - i^* \tag{7}$$

which is sometimes called *uncovered interest parity*—"uncovered" because e_{t+1} is not known with certainty at the time the investment is made. However, e_{t+1} should turn out to be higher than the prediction in equation (7) about half the time and lower about half the time. Since there is an inherent risk, equation (7) may not hold exactly, even on average.

---

[5]Because billions of dollars are invested in the stock market, even extremely small deviations from the random-walk model are of interest. Economists actively search for such deviations and, being selfless sorts, publish their results when they find apparent profit opportunities.

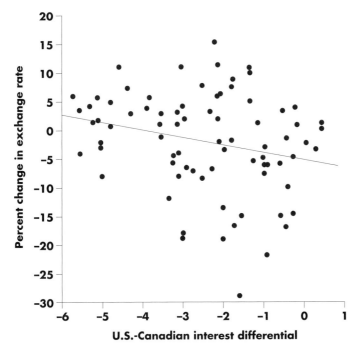

FIGURE 17-7   RELATIONSHIP OF THE CHANGE IN THE U.S.-CANADIAN EXCHANGE RATE TO U.S.-CANADIAN INTEREST RATE DIFFERENTIALS.

(Source: DRI/McGraw-Hill Macroeconomic Database.)

The vertical axis in Figure 17-7 shows changes in the Canadian dollar—the horizontal axis shows interest rate differentials.[6] Unsurprisingly, e_{t+1} is frequently much higher or much lower than might have been expected at time t. During the period shown, the exchange rate change averaged .13 percent per year more than the U.S.-Canadian interest rate differential. The relation between interest rate differentials and exchange rate changes is roughly, but not perfectly, as predicted. Uncovered interest parity provides a good first approximation to the data we see in the world.

SUMMARY

1. Financial markets are forward-looking. We can understand the 1: ent and future by considering arbitrage opportunities and of uncertainty.
2. Long-term interest rates equal the average of current an term interest rates plus a term premium.

[6]More precisely, the vertical is 400 times the percentage change in e at 90-day in axis is the difference in the U.S. and Canadian 3-month interest rate (Source: Data

3. The behavior of stock prices is accurately described as a random walk.
4. Changes in exchange rates depend on international differences in interest rates.

KEY TERMS

maturity (or term) of bond	yield curve	random walk
term structure of interest	net present value	uncovered interest parity
arbitrage	coupon	
term premium	face value	
expectations theory of the	consol (or perpetuity)	
term structure		

PROBLEMS

Conceptual

1. What role do financial markets play in the economy? Why do we, as macroeconomists, study them?
2. What is arbitrage? What makes the concept of arbitrage so central to our understanding of financial markets?
*3. Suppose you observe that short-term interest rates are higher than long-term interest rates.
    a. What expectations must people have regarding future interest rates?
    b. Why might the above relationship signal a recession? Why might it not?
    c. What will the yield curve for this problem look like?
4. Why is the fact that stock prices follow a random walk a signal of stock market efficiency? What would have to be true if stock prices did not follow a random walk?
5. Explain why an increase in U.S. interest rates relative to Canadian interest rates would affect the U.S.-Canadian dollar exchange rate.

Technical

1. a. What is the relationship between the rates of interest on a 10-year bond and on the series of 1-year bonds covering the same period? Assume, for the moment, that all interest rates are known in advance, so there is no uncertainty.
    b. Suppose the interest rate on the 10-year bond is 12 percent and that the interest rates on 1-year bonds, for the next 10 years, are expected to remain at 10 percent. What must the term premium be on the 10-year bond?
2. a. Suppose a 10-year bond is to be issued at par, so its price is equal to its $100 face value. Suppose also that the prevailing rate of interest on the bond is 10 percent. How big would the bond's coupon have to be to induce people to hold it?
    b. Now suppose that, just after this bond has been issued [its coupon is now fixed at the rate you found in part (a)], interest rates on all 10-year bonds fall to 5 percent. What will happen to the bond's price? If you happened to be holding this bond, would this help you, hurt you, or not affect you at all?
*3. Suppose that Japanese interest rates increase 5 percentage points and those in the United States remain fixed. What will happen to the relative value of this period's versus next period's dollar-yen exchange rate? [*Hint:* Use equation (7).]

*An asterisk denotes a more difficult problem.

CHAPTER 18

Stabilization Policy: Prospects and Problems

CHAPTER HIGHLIGHTS

◆ Uncertainty and policy lags make successful stabilization difficult.

◆ Modern macroeconomics grew out of the Great Depression.

◆ Our imperfect knowledge of the economy calls for caution in the application of economic policy.

◆ Democracies face the difficult problem of structuring policy-making bodies so as to avoid temptation toward an inflationary bias.

Stabilization policy seems easy to design and implement according to the macroeconomic models set out in Chapters 5 to 17: in recession, use expansionary monetary and fiscal policy; in booms and when inflation is too high, use contractionary policy. If stabilization policy were that simple, recessions would be rare and brief and inflation would always be low. Evidently stabilization policy is not so simple. In part that is because the goals of keeping both inflation and unemployment low sometimes conflict, as we discussed in Chapters 5 to 7. In this chapter we discuss problems that arise in using stabilization policies even with a single agreed-upon goal.

The modern approach to stabilization policy developed out of the Great Depression, knowledge of which is still, over 60 years later, essential to understanding both modern economics and the U.S. economy.[1] We start by describing the events of the Great Depression and the New Economics that it spawned, with its emphasis on the potential for active policy, particularly fiscal policy, to help stabilize the economy.

Then we turn to technical problems in policy making, which imply that policy cannot be expected to always keep the economy close to full employment with low inflation. In a nutshell, we will argue that a policy maker who (1) observes a disturbance,

---

[1] A nice historical perspective is given in J. Bradford De Long, "Keynesianism, Pennsylvania Avenue Style: Some Economic Consequences of the Employment Act of 1946," *Journal of Economic Perspectives,* Summer 1996.

OUTPUT, PRICES, AND UNEMPLOYMENT IN THE GREAT DEPRESSION, 1929–1939.

Department of Commerce, The National Income and Product Accounts of ...tes, *1929–1974;* Economic Report of the President, *1957; Revised Bureau ...stics data taken from Michael Darby, "Three-and-a-Half Million U.S. Em- ...Been Mislaid, Or, an Explanation of Unemployment, 1934–1941,"* Journal ...conomy, *February 1976.)*

TABLE 18-1 **Economic Statistics of the Great Depression**

	(1)	(2)	(3)	(4)	(5)	(6)	(7)	(8)	(9)	(10)
Year	GNP, 1992 \$, billions	I/GNP, %	G, 1992 \$, billions	Un-employ-ment rate, %	CPI, 1929 = 100	Com-mercial paper rate, %	AAA rate, %	Stock market index*	M1, 1929 = 100	Full-employ-ment surplus/Y*, % †
1929	938.1	17.8	121.9	3.2	100.0	5.9	4.7	83.1	100.0	−.8
1930	850.2	13.5	133.0	8.7	97.4	3.6	4.6	67.2	96.2	−1.4
1931	784.9	9.0	137.7	15.9	88.7	2.6	4.6	43.6	89.4	−3.1
1932	676.1	3.5	131.2	23.6	79.7	2.7	5.0	22.1	78.0	−.9
1933	662.1	3.8	127.6	24.9	75.4	1.7	4.5	28.6	73.5	1.6
1934	713.7	5.5	145.2	21.7	78.0	1.0	4.0	31.4	81.4	.2
1935	777.4	9.2	148.5	20.1	80.1	.8	3.6	33.9	96.6	−.1
1936	882.7	10.9	174.4	16.9	80.9	.8	3.2	49.4	110.6	−1.1
1937	923.5	12.8	167.8	14.3	83.3	.9	3.3	49.2	114.8	1.8
1938	885.7	8.1	182.7	19.0	82.3	.8	3.2	36.7	115.9	.6
1939	953.0	10.5	190.2	17.2	81.0	.6	3.0	38.5	127.3	−.1

*Stock market index is Standard & Poor's composite index, which includes 500 stocks; September 1929 = 100.

†Y*denotes full-employment output.

Source: Cols. 1, 2, 3: U.S. Department of Commerce, *The National Income and Product Accounts of the United States, 1929–1974.* Col. 4: Revised Bureau of Labor Statistics data taken from Michael Darby, "Three-and-a-Half Million U.S. Employees Have Been Mislaid: Or, an Explanation of Unemployment , 1934–1941," *Journal of Political Economy,* February 1976. Cols. 5, 6, 7: *Economic Report of the President,* 1957. Col. 8: Standard & Poor's Statistical Service, *Security Price Index Record,* 1978. Col. 9: Milton Friedman and Anna J. Schwartz, *A Monetary History of the United States, 1867–1960* (Princeton, N.J.: Princeton University Press, 1963), table A1, col. 7. Col. 10: E. Cary Brown, "Fiscal Policy in the Thirties: A Reappraisal," *American Economic Review,* December 1956, table 1, cols. 3, 5, and 19.

(2) does not know whether it is permanent or not, and (3) takes time to develop a policy that (4) takes still more time to affect behavior and (5) has uncertain effects on aggregate demand is very unlikely to do a perfect job of stabilizing the economy. When the economy is far from full employment, stabilization policy has a clear target and is bound to work. Near full employment, however, policies intended to stabilize the economy can easily go wrong.

18-1

THE GREAT DEPRESSION: THE FACTS

The *Great Depression* shaped many institutions in the economy, including the Fed and modern macroeconomics. The essential facts about the Depression are shown in Figure 18-1 and in Table 18-1.

The best-known event of the Great Depression is the stock market crash. Between September 1929 and June 1932, the market fell by 85 percent, which means that stocks worth \$1,000 at the stock market peak were worth only \$150 at the bottom of the market in 1932. The Depression and the stock market crash are popularly thought of as almost the same thing. In fact, the economy started turning down in August 1929, before the stock market crash, and continued falling until 1933.

Between 1929 and 1933, GNP fell by nearly 30 percent and the unemployment rate rose from 3 to 25 percent. Until early 1931, the economy was suffering from a very severe depression, but not one that was out of the range of the experience of the previous century.[2] It was in the period from early 1931 until Franklin Roosevelt became president in March 1933 that the Depression became "Great." More than anything else, the Great Depression is remembered for the mass unemployment that it brought. During the 10 years 1931 to 1940, the unemployment rate averaged 18.8 percent, ranging between a low of 14.3 percent in 1937 and a high of 24.9 percent in 1933.[3] By contrast, the post-World War II high, reached in 1982, was under 11 percent.

Investment collapsed in the Great Depression; indeed, net investment was negative from 1931 to 1935. The consumer price index fell nearly 25 percent from 1929 to 1933.

In the recovery, from 1933 to 1937, real GNP grew at a rapid annual rate of nearly 9 percent, but even that did not get the unemployment rate down to normal levels. Then, in 1937–1938 there was a major recession within the Depression, pushing the unemployment rate back up to nearly 20 percent. In the second half of the decade, short-term interest rates, such as the commercial paper rate, were near zero.

The two most important questions raised by these events are: Why did this happen, and could it have been prevented? Whenever the economy is in recession economists are asked—and they ask themselves—Could "it" happen again?

ECONOMIC POLICY

What was economic policy during this period? The money stock had already declined nearly 4 percent from 1929 to 1930, and then it fell rapidly in 1931 and 1932 and continued falling through April 1933.

The fall in the money stock was in part the result of large-scale bank failures. Banks failed because they did not have the reserves with which to meet customers' cash withdrawals,[4] and in failing they destroyed deposits and hence reduced the money stock. But the failures went further in reducing the money stock, because they led to a loss of confidence on the part of depositors and hence to an increase in the desired currency-deposit ratio. Furthermore, banks that had not yet failed adjusted to the possibility of a run by increasing reserve holdings relative to deposits. The rise in the currency-deposit ratio and the reserve-deposit ratio reduced the money multiplier and hence sharply contracted the money stock.

---

[2]The classic work by Milton Friedman and Anna J. Schwartz, *A Monetary History of the United States, 1867–1960* (Princeton, N.J.: Princeton University Press, 1963), gives a very detailed account of the Great Depression, comparing it with other recessions and emphasizing the role of the Fed.

[3]Michael Darby, "Three-and-a-Half Million U.S. Employees Have Been Mislaid: Or, an Explanation of Unemployment, 1934–1941," *Journal of Political Economy*, February 1976. Darby argues that unemployment has been mismeasured after 1933 because those on government work relief programs are counted as unemployed. Adjusted for those individuals, the unemployment rate falls rapidly from 20.6 percent in 1933 to below 10 percent in 1936. See also Thomas Mayer, "Money and the Great Depression: A Critique of Professor Temin's Thesis," *Explorations in Economic History*, April 1978, and Karl Brunner (ed.), *The Great Depression Revisited* (Boston: Martinus Nijhoff, 1981).

[4]We discussed bank runs in Chap. 16.

BOX 18-1 Black Tuesday and Black Monday

On Tuesday, October 29, 1929, the New York stock market crashed, with the Dow Jones Average falling by 12 percent. The "Great Crash" has remained fixed in the popular mind as the genesis of the Great Depression.

The crash of 1987, on Monday, October 19, was far worse in terms of the stock market. On that day the Dow dropped 22.6 percent. The next day, stock markets around the world also fell sharply. But perhaps those who learn from history are blessed not to repeat it. In 1987, the Fed and other central banks acted instantly, promising to flood the market with unlimited liquidity if necessary to prevent a panic. (The Fed allowed the federal funds rate—the interest rate on 1-day loans—to drop massively, from 7.56 percent on the 19th to 6.87 on the 20th and then to 6.50 percent on the 21st.) After a few jittery days, investors and the general public regained confidence and both the stock market and the economy continued to prosper.

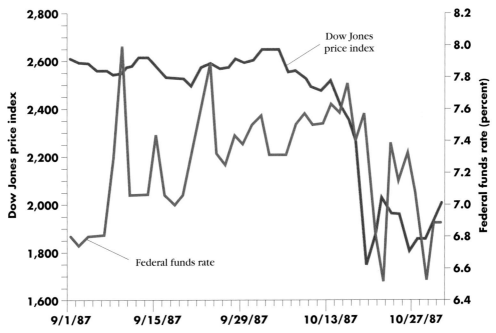

FIGURE 1   THE DOW JONES INDUSTRIAL AVERAGE AND THE INTEREST RATE ON FEDERAL FUNDS, SEPTEMBER AND OCTOBER 1987.

(Source: Datastream International.)

TABLE 18-2   Government Spending and Revenue 1929–1939
(Percent)

	TOTAL GOVERNMENT*		FEDERAL GOVERNMENT		
	(1)	(2)	(3)	(4)	(5)
	EXPEN-	ACTUAL	EXPEN-	ACTUAL	TOTAL GOVERNMENT*:
	DITURE/	SURPLUS/	DITURE/	SURPLUS/	FULL-EMPLOYMENT
YEAR	GNP	GNP	GNP	GNP	SURPLUS/Y*†
1929	10.0	1.0	2.5	1.2	−.8
1930	12.3	−.3	3.1	.3	−1.4
1931	16.4	−3.8	5.5	−2.8	−3.1
1932	18.3	−3.1	5.5	−2.6	−.9
1933	19.2	−2.5	7.2	−2.3	1.6
1934	19.8	−3.7	9.8	−4.4	.2
1935	18.6	−2.8	9.0	−3.6	−.1
1936	19.5	−3.8	10.5	−4.4	−1.1
1937	16.6	.3	8.2	.4	1.8
1938	19.8	−2.1	10.2	−2.5	.6
1939	19.4	−2.4	9.8	−2.4	−.1

*Includes federal, state, and local.

†$Y*$ denotes full-employment output.

Source: Cols. 1, 2, 3, 4: *Economic Report of the President,* 1972, tables B1 and B70. Col. 5: E. Cary Brown, "Fiscal Policy in the Thirties: A Reappraisal," *American Economic Review,* December 1956, table 1, cols. 3, 5, and 19.

The Fed took very few steps to offset the fall in the money supply. For a few months in 1932 it did undertake a program of open market purchases, but otherwise seemed to acquiesce in bank closings and certainly failed to act vigorously to prevent the collapse of the financial system.[5]

Fiscal policy, too, was weak. The natural impulse of politicians then was to balance the budget in times of trouble, and both major presidential candidates campaigned on balanced-budget platforms in 1932. In fact, as Table 18-2 shows, the federal government ran large deficits, particularly for that time, averaging 2.6 percent of GNP from 1931 to 1933 and even more later. (But these deficits are lower as a percentage of GNP than those in the early 1990s.) The belief in budget balancing was more than rhetoric, however, for state and local governments raised taxes to match their expenditures, as did the federal government, particularly in 1932 and 1933. President Roosevelt tried seriously to balance the budget—he was no Keynesian. The full-employment surplus shows fiscal policy (combined state, local, and federal) to have been most expansionary in 1931 and to have moved to a more contractionary level from 1932 to 1934. In fact, the full-employment surplus was positive in 1933 and 1934, despite the actual deficits. Of course, the concept of the full-employment surplus had not yet been invented in the 1930s.

Economic activity recovered in the period from 1933 to 1937, with fiscal policy becoming more expansionary and the money stock growing rapidly. The growth of the

---

[5]Friedman and Schwartz (*A Monetary History*) speculate on the reasons for the Fed's inaction; the whodunit or who didn't do it on pp. 407–419 of their book is fascinating.

money stock was based on an inflow of gold from Europe. This provided high-powered money for the monetary system. It was in the 1930s that the Fed acquired most of its current holdings of gold.

INSTITUTIONAL CHANGE

The period from 1933 to 1937 also saw substantial legislative and administrative action—the *New Deal*—from the Roosevelt administration. The Fed was reorganized, and the Federal Deposit Insurance Corporation (FDIC) was established to insure deposits and supervise banks. A number of regulatory agencies were also created, most notably the Securities and Exchange Commission, which regulates the securities industry. Its purpose was to prevent speculative excesses that were thought to be largely responsible for the stock market crash.

The Social Security Administration was set up so that the elderly would not have to rely on their own savings to ensure themselves a minimally adequate standard of living in retirement. By the mid-1990s, such social welfare payments would be the biggest single item in the federal budget. The Roosevelt administration also believed that the route to recovery lay in increasing wages and prices, so it encouraged trade unionization, as well as price-raising and price-fixing schemes by business, through the National Recovery Administration.

INTERNATIONAL ASPECTS

The Great Depression was virtually worldwide. To some extent, this was the result of the collapse of the international financial system.[6] It resulted, too, from the mutual adoption by many countries (including the United States) of high-tariff policies, which were intended to keep out foreign goods in order to protect domestic producers.

The policies were called "beggar-thy-neighbor" strategies (see Chapter 12) since they attempted to "export" unemployment by improving one country's trade position and hence demand for its goods at the expense of its trading partners. And, of course, if each country keeps out foreign goods, the volume of world trade declines, providing a contractionary influence on the world economy. Table 18-3 documents the decline in *world* production and in world trade.

Almost every country suffered a deep recession in the 1930s, but some countries did better than the United States. Sweden began an expansionary policy in the early

---

[6]This aspect of the Depression is emphasized by Charles Kindleberger, *The World in Depression, 1929–1939* (Berkeley: University of California Press, 1986), and Gottfried Haberler, *The World Economy, Money and the Great Depression* (Washington, D.C.: American Enterprise Institute, 1976).

TABLE 18-3   World Production and Trade, 1929–1935
(1929 = 100)

	1929	1932	1933	1935
Production	100	69	78	95
Trade				
Volume	100	75	76	82
Price	100	53	47	42

Source: League of Nations, *World Economic Survey, 1935/36.*

1930s and reduced its unemployment relatively quickly in the second half of the decade. Britain's economy suffered high unemployment in both the 1920s and the 1930s. In 1931, Britain went off the gold standard and the ensuing devaluation of the pound sterling set the stage for at least some improvement. Germany grew rapidly after Hitler came to power and expanded government spending. China escaped the recession until after 1931, essentially because it had a floating exchange rate.[7]

In 1939, real GNP in the United States rose above its 1929 level for the first time in the decade. But it was not until 1942, after the United States formally entered World War II, that the unemployment rate finally fell below 5 percent.

18-2

THE GREAT DEPRESSION: THE ISSUES AND IDEAS

The Depression was the greatest economic crisis the Western world had experienced. In the 1930s, by contrast with the 1990s, it was the economy of the Soviet Union that was booming while Western economies seemed to be collapsing. The questions of what caused the Great Depression, whether it could have been avoided, and whether it could happen again have therefore to be taken seriously.

The classical economics of the time had no well-developed theory that would explain persistent unemployment nor any policy prescriptions to solve the problem. Many economists then did, in fact, recommend government spending as a way of reducing unemployment, but they had no macroeconomic theory by which to justify their recommendations.

Keynes wrote his great work, *The General Theory of Employment, Interest and Money,* in the 1930s, after Britain had suffered during the 1920s from a decade of double-digit unemployment and while the United States was in the depths of its Depression. He was fully aware of the seriousness of the issues. As the late Don Patinkin of the Hebrew University put it:

> . . . the period was one of fear and darkness as the Western world struggled with the greatest depression that it had known. . . . [T]here was a definite feeling that by attempting to achieve a scientific understanding of the phenomenon of mass unemployment, one was not only making an intellectual contribution, but was also dealing with a critical problem that endangered the very existence of Western civilization.[8]

Keynesian theory explained what had happened, what could have been done to prevent the Depression, and what could be done to prevent future depressions. The explanation soon became accepted by most macroeconomists, in the process described

---

[7]A particularly valuable source on the international experience is Barry Eichengreen, *Golden Fetters* (New York: Oxford University Press, 1992). The central thesis of this book is that adherence to the gold standard forced countries into deflation and only after gold was abandoned could recovery start. The devaluation of sterling in 1931 is also discussed in Alec Cairncross and Barry Eichengreen, *Sterling in Decline* (Oxford, England: Basil Blackwell, 1983).

[8]Don Patinkin, "The Process of Writing *The General Theory:* A Critical Survey," in Don Patinkin and J. Clark Leith (eds.), *Keynes, Cambridge and the General Theory* (Toronto: University of Toronto Press, 1978), p. 3. For a biography of Keynes, see D. E. Moggridge, *John Maynard Keynes* (New York: Macmillan, 1990).

as the *Keynesian revolution,* even though the Keynesian revolution did not have much impact on economic policy making in the United States until the 1960s.

THE KEYNESIAN EXPLANATION

The essence of the Keynesian explanation of the Great Depression is contained in the simple aggregate demand model. Growth in the 1920s, in this view, was based on the mass production of the automobile and radio and was fueled by a housing boom. The collapse of growth in the 1930s resulted from the drying up of investment opportunities and a downward shift in investment demand. The collapse of investment, shown in Table 18-1, fits in with this picture. Some researchers also believe there was a downward shift in the consumption function in 1930.[9] Poor fiscal policy, as reflected in the perverse behavior of the full-employment surplus from 1931 to 1933, shares the blame, particularly for making the Depression worse.

It was also widely believed that the experience of the Depression showed that the private economy was inherently unstable—that recessions could begin spontaneously as a result of self-fulfilling prophecy. The experience of the 1930s was, implicitly or explicitly, the basis for the belief that an active stabilization policy was needed to maintain good economic performance.

The Keynesian model not only offered an explanation of what had happened but also suggested policy measures that could have been taken to prevent the Depression and that could be used to prevent future depressions. Vigorous use of countercyclical fiscal policy was the preferred method for reducing cyclical fluctuations. If a recession ever showed signs of deteriorating into a depression, the cure would be to cut taxes and increase government spending. And those policies would, too, have prevented the Depression from being as deep as it was.

What about monetary factors in the Depression? The Fed argued in the 1930s that there was little it could have done to prevent the Depression, because interest rates were already as low as they could possibly go. A variety of sayings of the type, "You can't push on a string," were used to explain that further reductions in interest rates would have had no effect if there was no demand for investment. Investment demand was thought to be very unresponsive to the rate of interest—implying a very steep *IS* curve. At the same time, the *LM* curve was believed to be quite flat, though not necessarily reaching the extreme of a liquidity trap. In this situation, monetary expansion would be relatively ineffective in stimulating demand and output.

There is nothing in the *IS-LM* model developed in Chapter 10 that suggests that fiscal policy is more useful than monetary policy for stabilization of the economy. Nonetheless, it is true that until the 1950s, Keynesians tended to give more emphasis to fiscal than to monetary policy.

THE MONETARIST CHALLENGE

The Keynesian emphasis on fiscal policy, and its downplaying of the role of money, was challenged by Milton Friedman and his coworkers during the 1950s.[10] They

---

[9]Peter Temin, *Did Monetary Forces Cause the Great Depression?* (New York: Norton, 1976).

[10]See, in particular, Milton Friedman (ed.), *Studies in the Quantity Theory of Money* (Chicago: University of Chicago Press, 1956).

emphasized the role of monetary policy in determining the behavior of both output and prices.

If monetary policy was to be given an important role, though, it was necessary to dispose of the view that monetary policy had been tried in the Great Depression and had failed. In other words, the idea that "you can't push on a string" had to be challenged.

The view that monetary policy in the thirties had been impotent was attacked in 1963 by Friedman and Schwartz in their *Monetary History*. They argued that the Depression, far from showing that money does not matter, "is in fact a tragic testimonial to the importance of monetary factors."[11] They argued, with skill and style, that the failure of the Fed to prevent bank failures and the decline of the money stock from the end of 1930 to 1933 was largely responsible for the recession's being as serious as it was. This monetary view, in turn, came close to being accepted as the orthodox explanation of the Depression.[12]

SYNTHESIS

Both the Keynesian and the monetarist explanations of the Great Depression fit the facts, and both provide answers to the questions of why it happened and how to prevent it from happening again. Both inept fiscal and inept monetary policies made the Great Depression severe. If there had been prompt, strong, expansive monetary and fiscal policy, the economy would have suffered a recession but not the trauma it did.

There is general agreement that the Great Depression could not happen today, except, of course, in the event of truly perverse government policy. But that is less likely now than it was then. For one thing, we have history to help us avoid its repetition. Taxes would not again be raised in the middle of a depression, nor would attempts be made to balance the budget. The Fed would seek actively to keep the money supply from falling and not allow bank failures to reduce the money stock. In addition, the government now has a much larger role in the economy than it did then, and automatic stabilizers, including the income tax and unemployment insurance, reduce the size of the multiplier and hence the impact of demand shocks on output.

If, as we argue, there is no inherent conflict between the Keynesian and monetarist explanations of the Great Depression, why has there been controversy over its causes? The reason is that the 1930s are seen as the period that set the stage for massive government intervention in the economy. Those opposed to an active role for government have to explain away the debacle of the economy in the 1930s. If the Depression occurred because of, and not despite, the government (particularly the Fed), the case for an active government role in economic stabilization is weakened. Further, the 1930s are a period in which the economy behaved in such an extreme way that competing theories have to be subjected to the test of whether they can explain that period.

[11]Friedman and Schwartz, *A Monetary History*, p. 300.

[12]Ben Bernanke, in "Nonmonetary Effects of the Financial Crisis in the Propagation of the Great Depression," *American Economic Review*, June 1983, takes issue with the monetary view, arguing instead that the destruction of the financial system made it difficult for borrowers to obtain funds needed for investment. However, there is no conflict between that argument and the view that more decisive monetary policy by the Fed in 1930 and 1931 would have mitigated the Depression.

18-3

THE NEW ECONOMICS

After the 1930s and the writing of Keynes and his followers, Keynesian economics was rapidly accepted by most macroeconomists, but it was adopted by policy makers more slowly. The budget was used as a countercyclical policy tool in Britain in the entire post–World War II period. In the United States, the Employment Act of 1946 required that the government follow policies to produce high employment. Nonetheless, it was not until the Kennedy administration in the early 1960s that a U.S. administration began to follow avowedly Keynesian policies.

The approach was described as the *New Economics*. The analytical approach of the New Economics consisted of the aggregate supply–aggregate demand plus growth theory model we have studied, with a less-than-modern understanding of the importance of expectations. The philosophy characterizing that approach to economics is a mix of activism and optimism. It is well characterized by an excerpt from the 1962 *Economic Report of the President:*[13]

> Insufficient demand means unemployment, idle capacity, and lost production. Excessive demand means inflation—general increases in prices and money incomes, bringing forth little or no gains in output and real income. The objective of stabilization policies is to minimize these deviations, i.e., to keep overall demand in step with the basic production potential of the economy.

> Stabilization does not mean a mere leveling off of peaks and troughs in production and employment. . . . It means minimizing deviations from a rising trend, not from an unchanging average. In a growing economy, demand must grow in order to maintain full employment of labor and full utilization of capacity at stable prices. The economy is not performing satisfactorily unless it is almost continuously setting new records of production, income, and employment.

In the 1930s, policy groped, and badly, for some way to get the economy moving again. The Roosevelt administration did run budget deficits, but most unwillingly, and it had no concept of the full-employment surplus. In the 1960s, by marked contrast, policy makers came into a not very difficult economic situation with well-thought-out theories and policies to apply. Those policies were based on the Keynesian analysis that developed in the 1930s and on the experience of that decade. The Kennedy-Johnson administration made the concept of the full-employment budget a central tenet of fiscal policy. It called for a tax cut in 1963–1964 even though the budget was already in deficit, and it sold the policy to a skeptical Congress.

We briefly review the basic analytical concepts of the New Economics before concluding this section by discussing what was new in the New Economics.

POTENTIAL OUTPUT AND THE GNP GAP

To focus attention on the target of full employment and for use as an operating guide to policy, the *Council of Economic Advisors (CEA),* and particularly the late Arthur

---

[13]President Kennedy's Council of Economic Advisors was served by many distinguished economists, among them three who later won the Nobel Prize: James Tobin of Yale, Kenneth Arrow of Stanford, and Robert Solow of M.I.T. A fourth Nobel Prize winner, Paul Samuelson, served as an unofficial adviser.

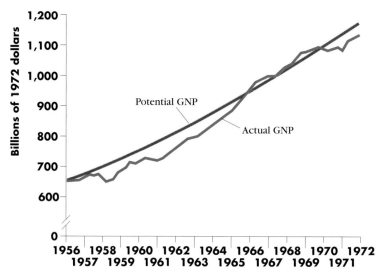

FIGURE 18-2   ACTUAL AND POTENTIAL GNP, 1956–1971.

(Source: Survey of Current Business, *April 1982 and 1983; DRI/McGraw-Hill.)*

Okun, developed and stressed the concept of *potential output.* Potential output or full-employment output, introduced in Chapters 1 and 2, measures the level of real GNP the economy can produce with full employment. The full-employment rate of unemployment used in defining potential output in the 1960s was about 4 percent, below the rates of 5 to 6 percent used more recently. Figure 18-2 shows potential output for the 1956–1971 period.

Along with the concept and measurement of potential output went the notion of the *GNP gap.*[14] The gap is the difference between actual and potential real output. For the years 1961–1965, actual GNP was below its potential level, and the GNP gap was therefore positive. At the beginning of 1961, the GNP gap was more than 7 percent of GNP. A gap of that magnitude clearly called for expansionary monetary or fiscal policy to raise aggregate demand to a level closer to the economy's potential.

Although the notions of potential output and the GNP gap seem very simple, they dramatize the costs of unemployment in easily understood terms—and that is very important in the political context in which economic policy decisions are made.

THE FULL-EMPLOYMENT BUDGET SURPLUS

The *full-employment budget* concept is important and useful because it directs attention away from the automatic effect of the business cycle on the actual budget. In recessions there are deficits in the actual budget, but that should not be an obstacle to antirecessionary stimulus.

The New Economists planned to use fiscal policy as the instrument with which to close the GNP gap. It was important for them to get across to Congress and the public the idea of the full-employment surplus because the federal budget was in ac-

---

[14]Until 1992, the United States used GNP rather than GDP as its basic measure of output.

tual deficit. Herbert Stein, chairperson of the CEA under President Nixon, reviewed the progress toward the major policy measure of the early 1960s, the 1964 tax cut, in his book *The Fiscal Revolution in America*.[15] He shows how both the Kennedy administration and Congress had to get accustomed to the idea that a tax cut that increased the budget deficit during a recession was not necessarily a step toward fiscal irresponsibility.

The contrast between the scope for fiscal policy in the sluggish economies of the early 1960s and in the 1990s is very clear. In the early 1960s, the full-employment budget was in surplus, so a tax cut was very plausible. By the early 1990s, while unemployment was high, the full-employment budget had been in deficit for a decade, and the easy arguments of the 1960s could no longer be marshaled to support further fiscal stimulus. (See Table 18-4.)

GROWTH AND INFLATION

The New Economics emphasized economic growth in two ways. First, aggregate demand needed to grow in order to achieve full employment. In that respect, growth was a matter of achieving full employment and maintaining it. Second, there was an emphasis on achieving a high rate of growth of potential output itself. The focus was on investment spending to encourage growth in productive potential—a supply-side emphasis. To that end the administration introduced an investment tax credit in 1962.

The New Economics emphasized the behavior of money wages in affecting the rate of inflation. Early in the Kennedy-Johnson years, in 1962, the CEA set up *guideposts* for the behavior of money wages.[16] The basic guidepost was that money wages should not grow faster than the average rate at which labor productivity was increasing in the economy. Labor productivity is the ratio of output to labor input.

[15]University of Chicago Press, 1969.

[16]For an interesting, and sometimes amusing, discussion of the guideposts, see George P. Shultz (a University of Chicago economist and later secretary of state) and Robert Z. Aliber (eds.), *Guidelines* (Chicago: University of Chicago Press, 1966).

TABLE 18-4 Budget Deficits, 1985–1995
(Percent of GDP)

	ACTUAL DEFICIT	FULL-EMPLOYMENT DEFICIT	UNEMPLOYMENT RATE, %
1985	3.9	4.8	7.2
1986	4.0	4.7	7.0
1987	2.7	2.8	6.2
1988	2.4	3.0	5.5
1989	2.1	2.8	5.3
1990	2.7	2.9	5.6
1991	3.3	3.1	6.9
1992	4.5	3.5	7.5
1993	3.9	3.5	6.9
1994	2.7	2.8	6.1
1995	2.2	2.7	5.6

Source: DRI/McGraw-Hill Macroeconomic Database; Congressional Budget Office.

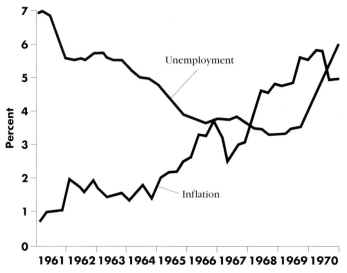

FIGURE 18-3   INFLATION AND UNEMPLOYMENT, 1961–1970.

(Source: DRI/McGraw-Hill.)

When productivity is growing, less labor is being used to produce the same amount of goods. Thus, if wages are growing as fast as productivity, the labor costs of producing a good are constant. Assuming, as the New Economics did, that prices are set as a markup on labor costs, prices would not rise if wages were rising no faster than productivity. This argument also implies that more rapid investment—which contributes to productivity increases—can help reduce inflation from the supply side.

What was new in the New Economics was not the analysis, which was by then standard macroeconomics, but rather the active and successful use of that analysis in the operation of U.S. macroeconomic policy.

THE NEW ECONOMICS AND THE ECONOMY

The most ambitious and successful policy action of the Kennedy-Johnson administration was the tax cut of 1964.[17] The tax cut kept the economy growing rapidly through the mid-1960s, thus reducing the unemployment rate. At the same time, as Figure 18-3 shows, the inflation rate stayed below 3 percent per year.

Through the middle of the 1960s, the economy was behaving as well as it ever has. Productivity growth was high, output was growing fast, unemployment was falling, and the inflation rate was low. It is little wonder that there was considerable optimism about the possibilities of the New Economics.

Things began to go wrong in the late 1960s. Much of the problem was political. Government spending for the Vietnam war was rising rapidly, but President Johnson feared that a tax increase would make the war more unpopular. In 1966 and 1967, it was left to monetary policy to fight the increasing expansionary pressure of fiscal pol-

---

[17]The classic analysis of the tax cut is presented in Arthur Okun's paper, "Measuring the Impact of the 1964 Tax Reduction," in his book *Economics for Policymaking* (Cambridge, Mass.: M.I.T. Press, 1983).

icy. Only in 1968 was the Johnson administration willing to ask Congress for a tax increase to try to contain the expansionary pressure of military spending.

A temporary tax increase was enacted, but the contractionary effect was less than expected and the impact on inflation negligible.[18] Thus by 1969, the inflation rate exceeded 5 percent. To be sure, the unemployment rate was below 4 percent, and the economy was still in the longest economic expansion on record.

The record of the 1960s is one of full employment, expansion, and rising inflation. Keynesian economics, or the New Economics, received the popular credit for the expansion of the mid-1960s following the tax cut. Similarly, it received the blame for the rising inflation. The rising inflation that accompanied the expansion in output opened up the question of whether active monetary and fiscal policy could be used successfully to control the economy, to which we now turn.

18-4

LAGS IN THE EFFECTS OF POLICY

Suppose that the economy is at full employment and has been affected by an aggregate demand disturbance that will reduce the equilibrium level of income below full employment. Suppose further that there was no advance warning of this disturbance and that, consequently, no policy actions were taken in anticipation of its occurrence. Policy makers now have to decide *whether to respond at all* and *how* to respond to the disturbance.

The first concern is to distinguish whether a disturbance is *permanent,* or at least very persistent, or *transitory* and short-lived. Suppose the disturbance is only transitory, such as a one-period reduction in consumption spending. When the disturbance is transitory, so that consumption rapidly reverts to its initial level, the best policy may be to do nothing at all. Provided suppliers or producers do not mistakenly interpret the decrease in demand as permanent but, rather, perceive it as transitory, they will absorb it by production and inventory changes rather than by capacity adjustments. The disturbance will affect income in this period but will have very little permanent effect. Since today's policy actions take time to have an effect, today's actions would be hitting an economy that would otherwise have been close to full employment, and they would tend to move the economy *away* from the full-employment level. Thus, if a disturbance is temporary and has no long-lived effects and policy operates with a lag, the best policy is to do nothing.

Figure 18-4 illustrates the main issue. Assume that an aggregate demand disturbance reduces output below potential, starting at time t_0. Without active policy intervention, output declines for a while but then recovers and reaches the full-employment level again at time t_2. Consider next the path of GDP under an active stabilization policy, but one that works with the disadvantage of lags. Thus, expansionary policy might be initiated at time t_1 and start taking effect some time after. Output now tends to re-

---

[18]For an explanation, which relies on the fact that a temporary tax increase has only a small effect on permanent income and therefore on consumption, see Robert Eisner, "What Went Wrong?" *Journal of Political Economy,* May–June 1971.

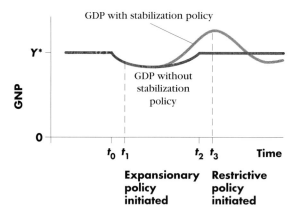

FIGURE 18-4   LAGS AND DESTABILIZING POLICY.

cover faster as a consequence of the expansion but, because of poor dosage and/or timing, actually overshoots the full-employment level. By time t_3, restrictive policy is initiated, and some time after, output starts turning down toward full employment and may well continue cycling for a while. In this example, "stabilization" policy may actually *destabilize* the economy.

One of the main difficulties of policy making is establishing whether or not a disturbance is temporary. It was clear enough in the case of World War II that a high level of defense expenditures would be required for some years. However, in the case of the OPEC oil embargo of 1973–1974, it was not at all clear how long the embargo would last or whether the high prices for oil that were established in late 1973 would persist. At the time, there were many who argued that the oil cartel would not survive and that oil prices would soon fall—that is, that the disturbance was temporary. "Soon" turned out to be 12 years.

Let us suppose, however, that it is known that the disturbance will have effects that will last for several quarters and that the level of income will, without intervention, be below the full-employment level for some time. What lags do policy makers encounter?

We now consider the steps required before action can be taken after a disturbance has occurred, and then we examine the process by which that policy action affects the economy. There are delays, or lags, at every stage, and these can be divided into two stages: an *inside lag,* which is the time period it takes to undertake a policy action—such as a tax cut or an increase in the money supply—and an *outside lag,* which describes the timing of the effects of the policy action on the economy. The inside lag, in turn, is divided into recognition, decision, and action lags.

THE RECOGNITION LAG

The *recognition lag* is the period that elapses between the time a disturbance occurs and the time the policy makers recognize that action is required. This lag could, in principle, be *negative* if the disturbance can be predicted and appropriate policy actions considered *before* it even occurs. For example, we know that seasonal factors affect behavior. Thus it is known that at Christmas the demand for currency is high. Rather than allow this to exert a restrictive effect on the money supply, the Fed will accommodate this seasonal demand by an expansion in high-powered money.

In general, however, the recognition lag is positive, so time elapses between the disturbance and the recognition that active policy is required. Kareken and Solow have studied the history of policy making and concluded that on average the recognition lag has been about 5 months.[19] The lag was found to be somewhat shorter when the required policy was expansionary and somewhat longer when restrictive policy was required. The speed with which tax cuts follow sharp increases in unemployment was clearly evident in both 1975 and 1980.

THE DECISION AND ACTION LAGS

The *decision lag*—the delay between the recognition of the need for action and the policy decision—differs between monetary and fiscal policy. The Federal Reserve System's Open Market Committee meets frequently to discuss and decide on policy. Thus, once the need for a policy action has been recognized, the decision lag for monetary policy is short. Further, the *action lag*—the lag between the policy decision and its implementation—for monetary policy is also short. The major monetary policy actions take the form of open market operations. These policy actions can be undertaken almost as soon as a decision has been made. Thus, under the existing arrangements of the Federal Reserve System, the decision lag for monetary policy is short and the action lag practically zero.

However, fiscal policy actions are less rapid. Once the need for a fiscal policy action has been recognized, the administration has to prepare legislation for that action. Next, the legislation has to be considered and approved by both houses of Congress before the policy change can be made. That may be a lengthy process. Even after the legislation has been approved, the policy change has still to be put into effect. If the fiscal policy takes the form of a change in tax rates, it may be some time before the change in tax rates begins to be reflected in paychecks—that is, there may be an action lag. On occasion, though, as in early 1975 when taxes were reduced, the fiscal decision lag may be short; in 1975 it was about 2 months.

BUILT-IN STABILIZERS

The existence of the inside lag in policy making focuses attention on the built-in or automatic stabilizers that we discussed in Chapter 9. One of the major benefits of automatic stabilizers is that their inside lag is zero. The most important automatic stabilizer is the income tax. It stabilizes the economy by reducing the multiplier effects of any disturbance to aggregate demand. The multiplier for the effects of changes in autonomous spending on GDP is inversely related to the income tax rate. Unemployment compensation is another automatic stabilizer. When workers become unemployed and reduce their consumption, that reduction in consumption demand tends to have multiplier effects on output. Those multiplier effects are reduced when a worker receives unemployment compensation because disposable income is reduced by less than the loss in earnings.

---

[19]See John Kareken and Robert Solow, "Lags in Monetary Policy," in *Stabilization Policies,* prepared for the Commission on Money and Credit (Englewood Cliffs, N.J.: Prentice-Hall, 1963).

Although built-in stabilizers have desirable effects, they cannot be carried too far without also affecting the overall performance of the economy. The multiplier could be reduced to 1 by increasing the tax rate to 100 percent, and that would appear to be a stabilizing influence on the economy. But with 100 percent marginal tax rates, the desire to work, and consequently the level of GDP, would be reduced. Thus there are limits on the extent to which automatic stabilizers are desirable.[20]

THE OUTSIDE LAG

The inside lag of policy is a *discrete lag*—so many months—from recognition to decision and implementation. The outside lag is generally a *distributed lag*: once the policy action has been taken, its effects on the economy are spread over time. There may be a small immediate effect of a policy action, but other effects occur later.

The idea that policy operates on aggregate demand and income with a distributed lag is illustrated by the dynamic multiplier in Figure 18-5. There we show the effects over time of a once-and-for-all increase in bank reserves in period zero. The impact is initially very small, and it continues to increase over a long period of time. The lags of monetary policy are represented by the fact that any significant impact of money on spending and output takes several quarters and builds up only gradually.

What are the policy implications of the distributed lag encountered in the outside lag? If it were necessary to increase the level of employment rapidly to offset a demand disturbance, a large open market purchase would be necessary. But in later quarters, the large initial open market purchase would build up large effects on GDP, and those effects would probably overcorrect the unemployment, leading to inflationary pressures. It would then be necessary to reverse the open market purchase and conduct open market sales to avoid the inflationary consequences of the initial open market purchase.

[20]For a discussion of the history of automatic stabilizers, see Herbert Stein, *The Fiscal Revolution in America* (Chicago: University of Chicago Press, 1969).

FIGURE 18-5 MONETARY POLICY MULTIPLIER FROM THE DRI MODEL.

Why are there such long outside lags? Consider the example of monetary policy. Because aggregate demand depends heavily on lagged values of income, interest rates, and other economic variables, an open market purchase initially has effects mainly on interest rates and not on income. The interest rates, in turn, affect investment with a lag, and also affect consumption by affecting the value of wealth. When aggregate demand is ultimately affected, the increase in spending itself produces a series of induced adjustments in output and spending. When policy acts slowly, with the impacts of policy building up over time as in Figure 18-5, considerable skill is required of policy makers if their own attempts to correct an initially undesirable situation are not to lead to problems that themselves need correcting.

MONETARY VERSUS FISCAL POLICY LAGS

Fiscal policy—and certainly changes in government spending, which act directly on aggregate demand—affect income more rapidly than monetary policy. However, while fiscal policy has a shorter outside lag, it has a considerably longer inside lag. The long inside lag makes fiscal policy less useful for stabilization and means that fiscal policy tends to be used relatively infrequently to try to stabilize the economy.

Our analysis of lags indicates clearly one difficulty in undertaking stabilizing short-term policy actions: It takes time to set the policies in action, and then the policies themselves take time to affect the economy. But that is not the only difficulty. Further difficulties arise because policy makers cannot be certain about the size and the timing of the effects of policy actions.

18-5

EXPECTATIONS AND REACTIONS

Uncertainty about the effects of policies on the economy arise because policy makers do not know the precise values of multipliers.[21] The government is always uncertain about how the economy will react to policy changes. In practice, governments work with econometric models of the economy in estimating the effects of policy changes. An *econometric model* is a statistical description of the economy or some part of it.

Government uncertainty about the effects of policy arises partly because the government does not know the true model of the economy and partly because it does not know what expectations firms and consumers have. In this section we concentrate on the role of expectations.

REACTION UNCERTAINTIES

Suppose that in early 1999, because of weakness in the economy, the government decides to cut taxes. Because the deficit is so large, the tax cut is meant to be strictly temporary—a brief shot in the arm to get the economy moving and nothing more.

---

[21]Elsewhere we have discussed uncertainty due to unforecastable shocks. Such shocks effect the equilibrium of the economy but not necessarily the *marginal* responses, and so not necessarily the multipliers.

BOX 18-2 How Good Are Macroeconomic Forecasts?

In business and finance and in government, knowing what will happen in the economy next quarter and next year is critical as an ingredient for planning, for portfolio selection, and for policy making. The demand for forecasts is met by a broad group of professional forecasters. The methods used range from informal, almost back-of-the-envelope, calculations to the use of sophisticated macroeconometric models where literally thousands of equations representing the economy are the basis of the outlook.*

How good are the forecasts? Table 1 shows the forecasts and the actual results from three sources. The first is the Congressional Budget Office (CBO), which uses macroeconometric models as the background for revenue and outlay projections. The second is the administration forecasts. The third source is the Blue Chip forecast, a consensus of private forecasters. The projections in the table are obviously sometimes off—the forecasters missed low growth in 1990–1991. From 1993 through 1995, in contrast, the forecasts were right on target.

How can forecasters go wrong? They may not predict disturbances (the Gulf war, for example); they may misread the current state of the economy and hence base their forecasts on a wrong picture of the present situation; and they may misjudge the timing or vigor of the government's monetary and fiscal responses to booms or recessions. The fact is that forecasting has not reached perfection, particularly at major turning points in the economy, as illustrated in the table.†

*To learn about a large-scale econometric model, see F. Brayton and P. A. Tinsley, "A Guide to FRB/US: A Macroeconomic Model of the United States," Board of Governors of the Federal Reserve System, October 1996.

†Stephen K. McNees "How Large Are Economic Forecast Errors?" *New England Economic Review,* July–August 1992, provides detailed examination of the historical record of forecasters and identifies what they are good at and what they seemingly do not do so well. Also by Stephen K. McNees, "An Assessment of the 'Official' Economic Forecasts," *New England Economic Review,* July–August 1995, compares a variety of government and private forecasts.

TABLE 1   How Accurate Are Macroeconomic Forecasts? Actual Versus Forecast 2-Year Average Growth Rates

	ACTUAL	CBO	ADMINISTRATION	BLUE CHIP
1976–1977	5.3	6.2	5.9	—
1986–1987	2.8	3.1	3.7	3.0
1990–1991	.2	2.0	2.8	1.9
1993–1994	2.9	2.9	2.9	3.0
1994–1995	2.7	2.8	2.9	2.8

Source: *The Economic and Budget Outlook: An Update,* table A-1, Congressional Budget Office, August 1996.

In figuring out how big a tax cut is needed, the government has to guess how the public will react to a temporary tax cut. One possible answer is that the tax cut raises permanent income by very little and hence leads to only a very small increase in spending. That suggests that to be useful, a temporary tax cut would have to be large. Alternatively, perhaps consumers will believe that the tax cut will last much longer than the government says—after all, the public knows that raising taxes is difficult. In this case the marginal propensity to spend out of a tax cut announced as temporary would be larger. A smaller tax cut would be enough to raise spending a lot. If the government is wrong in its guess about consumers' reactions, it could destabilize rather than stabilize the economy.

CHANGES IN POLICY REGIME

A special problem emerges when the government changes the way it has traditionally responded to disturbances. For example, a government that has typically cut taxes in recessions and now no longer does so (e.g., because the deficit is large) may find that the cut had been expected and that there is an extra drop in demand when consumers realize taxes will not be cut this time.

It is particularly important to consider the effects of a given policy action itself on expectations, since it is possible that a new type of policy will affect the way in which expectations are formed.[22] Suppose that the Federal Reserve System announced that from now on its policy would be aimed *solely* at maintaining price stability and that in response to any price-level increase it would reduce the money supply (and vice versa). If people believed the announcement, they would not base expectations of money growth and inflation on the past behavior of the inflation rate.

However, people are not likely to fully believe such an announcement immediately. The policy makers are likely to lack full *credibility*. Policy makers have credibility when their announcements are believed by economic agents. Typically, policy makers have to earn credibility, by behaving consistently over long periods, so that people learn to believe what they say.

Earning credibility is likely to be costly. Consider what happens if the Fed announces it will keep inflation low and is not believed. Then the expected inflation rate is above the actual inflation rate, and—as the Phillips curve shows—a recession follows. Only over time, as the new policies are understood, is credibility earned.

As an example, credibility issues are always a problem when governments promise to keep exchange rates fixed. In the 1980s, governments in the European Monetary System of quasi-fixed exchange rates announced that they would no longer respond to increases in wages and prices with devaluations. Initially, the policy makers lacked credibility, and inflation stayed high. But eventually, by holding fast, and with the aid of recessions, policy makers gained credibility and inflation came down. Then in 1992, under the macroeconomic impact of German unification, major devaluations were forced on reluctant governments, and their credibility was seriously dented.

---

[22]The interactions of policy and expectations have been the focus of the rational expectations approach to macroeconomics, introduced in Chap. 8. For a very early statement, see Thomas J. Sargent and Neil Wallace, "Rational Expectations and the Theory of Economic Policy," *Journal of Monetary Economics,* April 1976.

ECONOMETRIC POLICY EVALUATION CRITIQUE

The public's reactions to changes in income, interest rates, or exchange rates depend on what people expect will be happening in the economy and what the policy responses of the government will be. This poses an acute dilemma for policy research. We would like to know what the public will do in response to this or that new policy. But we cannot find the answer from historical relationships between variables and policies unless we know what expectations people held about policy.

This difficulty has been identified by Robert Lucas, of the University of Chicago, in a challenge to stabilization policy. Lucas argues in his *econometric policy evaluation critique* that existing macroeconometric models cannot be used to study the effects of policy changes because the way private agents (firms and consumers) respond to changes in income and prices depends on the types of policy being followed.[23]

Lucas claims that problems of this sort are pervasive in macroeconometric models. He does not argue that it will never be possible to use econometric models to study policy—only that existing models cannot be used for that purpose.

Accordingly, the Lucas critique is not one that rules out the use of econometric models.[24] It suggests, rather, that very careful modeling of the responses of consumers and firms to changes in income and prices, and particularly to changes in policy, is necessary for serious policy analysis.

18-6

UNCERTAINTY AND ECONOMIC POLICY

Uncertainty about the expectations of firms and consumers is one reason that policy makers can go wrong in using active stabilization policy. Another reason is that it is difficult to forecast disturbances, such as changes in the price of oil, that might disturb the economy before policy takes effect.

A third reason is that economists and therefore policy makers do not know enough about the true structure of the economy. We distinguish between uncertainty about the correct model of the economy and uncertainty about the precise values of the parameters or coefficients within a given model of the economy, even though the distinction is not watertight.

First, there is considerable disagreement and therefore uncertainty about the correct model of the economy, as evidenced by the large number of macroeconometric models. Reasonable economists can and do differ about what theory and empirical evidence suggest are the correct behavioral functions of the economy. Generally, each economist will have reasons for favoring one particular form and will use that form. But, being reasonable, the economist will recognize that the particular formulation being used may not be the correct one and will thus regard its predictions as subject to

---

[23]See "Econometric Policy Evaluation: A Critique," in R. E. Lucas, Jr., *Studies in Business Cycle Theory* (Cambridge, Mass.: M.I.T. Press, 1981).

[24]The attempt of real business cycle theorists to uncover "deep parameters," as studied in Chap. 8, arose in part as a response to the Lucas critique.

a margin of error. In turn, policy makers will know that there are different predictions about the effects of a given policy, and they will want to consider the range of predictions that are being made in deciding on policy.

Second, even within a given model there is uncertainty about the values of parameters and multipliers. The statistical evidence does allow us to say something about the likely range of parameters or multipliers, so we can at least get some idea of the type of errors that could result from a particular policy action.[25]

Uncertainty about the size of the effects that will result from any particular policy action—whether because of uncertainty about expectations or about the structure of the economy—is known as *multiplier uncertainty.* For instance, our best estimate of the multiplier of an increase in government spending might be 1.2. If GDP has to be increased by $60 billion, we would increase government spending by $50 billion. But the statistical evidence might be better interpreted as saying only that we can be quite confident that the multiplier is between .9 and 1.5. In that case, when we increase government spending by $50 billion, we expect GDP to rise by some amount between $45 and $75 billion.

How should a policy maker react in the face of these uncertainties? The more precisely policy makers are informed about the relevant parameters, the more activist the policy can afford to be. Conversely, if there is a considerable range of error in the estimate of the relevant parameters—in our example, the multiplier—then policy should be more modest. With poor information, very active policy runs a large danger of introducing unnecessary fluctuations in the economy.

THE POLICY PORTFOLIO UNDER UNCERTAINTY

Consider the choice between monetary policy and fiscal policy when both monetary and fiscal policy multipliers are uncertain. According to *IS-LM* analysis, when policy multipliers are known, either monetary policy or fiscal policy may be used to hit an output target, although one policy may be preferred over the other because of side effects on interest rates, exchange rates, or the budget deficit. We have, however, just argued that no policy should be used "full-strength" when there is multiplier uncertainty.

The best procedure is to employ a *portfolio* of policy instruments—use a weaker dose of both monetary and fiscal policies. The reason for practicing *diversification* in this way is that there is at least a chance that the errors in estimating one multiplier will be offset by the errors in estimating the other.[26] With good luck, errors in setting policy will partially cancel one another. Even if we are unlucky, we are no worse off than if we had relied fully on one instrument.[27]

---

[25]We are discussing here confidence intervals about estimates of parameters; see Robert Pindyck and Daniel Rubinfeld, *Econometric Models and Economic Forecasts* (New York: McGraw Hill, 1991), for further discussion.

[26]If you have studied finance, you will be familiar with the notion of picking a *portfolio* of investments in order to reduce risk through *diversification.* The choice of words here is no coincidence—the principles of choosing a policy portfolio are the same as those involved in choosing an investment portfolio.

[27]The practice of coordinating monetary and fiscal policies has an interesting downside for macroeconomists. We are, of course, very interested in separating the effects of one type of policy from those of another. But if two policies are generally used in concert, it is very difficult to use historical data to know which policy was responsible for the observed results.

◆ OPTIONAL ◆

MULTIPLIER UNCERTAINTY AND POLICY: A FORMAL ANALYSIS

Multipliers measure the quantitative effect of policy. The argument that the less certain we are about the size of a multiplier, the more cautious we should be in application of the associated policy instrument is intuitively plausible. This intuition was first given formal expression by William Brainard.[28] We present a simplified version here.

Suppose that our entire knowledge of the effect of monetary policy on the economy can be boiled down to one equation:

$$Y = \beta M \tag{1}$$

where Y is output, M is the money stock, and β is the monetary policy multiplier. Y^* is the target for output. Because we may not be able to hit the target precisely, we need a rule for evaluating the success of policy that measures the damage done when we miss the target. While we hope that Y will hit Y^* exactly, we recognize there will generally be some gap between actual and target outcomes, $Y - Y^*$. We "keep score"; that is, we measure the damage attributable to a "miss" with the *loss function*:

$$L = \tfrac{1}{2}(Y - Y^*)^2 \tag{2}$$

Note that this loss function puts a much larger penalty on large losses than on small losses. We evaluate the success of a policy choice, M, by substituting βM for the realized value of output, Y, in equation (2). The *marginal loss function*, with respect to changes in the policy instrument M, is

$$ML(M) = (\beta M - Y^*) \times \beta \tag{3}$$

and, as usual in economics, one way to think about minimizing losses is to set the marginal loss to zero.

We now work out an example, first when the multiplier is known and then when it is uncertain. Suppose that our target is $Y^* = 3$ and that we somehow know the multiplier is exactly $\beta = \bar{\beta} = 1$. The appropriate policy is obviously to set $M = 3$, but to carry out the formal analysis, we set the marginal loss equal to zero in equation (4) and solve for the optimal policy in equation (5):

$$ML(M) = 0 = (\bar{\beta}M - Y^*) \times \bar{\beta} = (Y - Y^*) \times \bar{\beta} \tag{4}$$

$$M = \frac{Y^*}{\bar{\beta}} \tag{5}$$

So we choose $M = 3/1 = 3$; observe $Y = 1 \times 3 = 3 = Y^*$; hit the target exactly; and according to the rating from equation (2), achieve a perfect, zero-loss, score.

Now, suppose instead that β is either .5 or 1.5, with a 50 percent chance for either value. The average value of β remains $\bar{\beta} = (0.5 + 1.5)/2 = 1.0$, just as in the previous example; the difference is that we have introduced uncertainty. Suppose basing policy on this average value, we again set policy at $M = 3$. (This is called the *certainty-equivalence policy*.) If β is actually .5, we will undershoot the target; if β equals 1.5, we will overshoot. However, we can do a little better by shading in the direction of

---

[28]William Brainard, "Uncertainty and the Effectiveness of Policy," *American Economic Review,* May 1967.

undershooting rather than overshooting, because a low value of β means that the marginal impact of the policy is lower.

We can work out the optimal choice for M in this case by weighting the marginal loss function with equal chances for each value of β. The weighted marginal loss function is

$$ML(M) = 0 = 50\% \times [(0.5M - Y^*) \times 0.5] + 50\% \times [(1.5M - Y^*) \times 1.5] \quad (6)$$

$$M = \frac{Y^*}{1.25} \quad (7)$$

Equation (7) tells us to set M to 2.4 instead of 3—we are more conservative in our use of policy than we would be under certainty equivalence. Thus Brainard's analysis affirms our intuition that uncertainty should lead to caution.

18-7

ACTIVIST POLICY

We started this chapter by asking why there are any fluctuations in the American economy when the policy measures needed to iron out those fluctuations seem to be so simple. The list of difficulties in the way of successful policy making that we have outlined may have raised the opposite question: Why should one believe that policy can do *anything* to reduce fluctuations in the economy?[29]

Indeed, considerations of the sort spelled out in the previous four sections have led Milton Friedman and others to argue that there should be no use of active countercyclical monetary policy and that monetary policy should be confined to making the money supply grow at a constant rate. The precise value of the constant rate of money growth, Friedman suggests, is less important than the fact that monetary growth should be constant and that policy should *not* respond to disturbances. At various times, he has suggested growth rates for money of 2 or 4 or 5 percent. As Friedman has expressed it, "By setting itself a steady course and keeping to it, the monetary authority could make a major contribution to promoting economic stability. By making that course one of steady but moderate growth in the quantity of money, it would make a major contribution to avoidance of either inflation or deflation of prices."[30] Friedman thus advocates a simple monetary rule in which the Fed does not respond to the condition of the economy. Policies that respond to the current or predicted state of the economy are called *activist policies*. Interestingly, Friedman does make an exception to this rule in the face of extreme disturbances.

In discussing the desirability of activist monetary and fiscal policy, we want to distinguish between policy actions taken in response to major disturbances to the economy and *fine tuning*, in which policy variables are continually adjusted in response to small disturbances in the economy. We see no case for arguing that monetary and fis-

---

[29]An excellent discussion of the issues is Steven Sheffrin, *The Making of Economic Policy* (Oxford, England: Basil Blackwell, 1989).

[30]Milton Friedman, "The Role of Monetary Policy," *American Economic Review,* March 1968. See also his book, *A Program for Monetary Stability* (New York: Fordham University Press, 1959).

BOX 18-3 Fine Tuning and Monetary Policy in the 1980s and 1990s

At the same time as the analytic arguments against fine tuning and discretionary policy were being refined in the 1980s and 1990s, the Fed under the chairmanship first of Paul Volcker (1979–1987) and then Alan Greenspan (1987–present), was implementing one of the most successful periods of monetary policy in its history—and the policies were clearly discretionary.

What happened? Through the 1970s, inflation had been rising from business cycle to business cycle; in each cycle, the peak inflation rate was higher than it had been in the previous cycle. Paul Volcker's priority as chairman was to bring inflation under control. That goal was achieved, albeit at the cost of the recession of 1981–1982, during which the unemployment rate hit the highest level of the post-World War II period, 10.8 percent.

When Alan Greenspan took over in August 1987, the inflation rate was 4.6 percent and the economy was fundamentally at full employment. Two months later, the new chairman of the Fed was faced with a potentially massive crisis, when the stock market crashed on October 19, 1987. The Fed rose to the challenge by providing enough liquidity to make sure there was no financial panic.

Perhaps partly as a result of that injection of liquidity, inflationary pressures continued to rise through the end of the decade, and the Fed accordingly tightened monetary policy by raising interest rates. Eventually, in July 1990, a recession began. However, the recession was shallow, with unemployment rising to a maximum of only 7.7 percent. Once the recession was clearly recognized, the Fed cut interest rates, slowly and repeatedly. The recession ended in March 1991, and the recovery continued as inflation declined.

By the end of 1994, the economy was back at full employment, but inflation stayed low. And during the following 2 years the Fed succeeded in keeping both inflation and unemployment low.

There can be no doubt that in the 1990s active and discretionary Fed policy, a

cal policy should not be used actively in the face of major disturbances to the economy. Most of the considerations of the previous sections of this chapter indicate some uncertainty about the effects of policy, but sometimes there can be no doubt about which direction to move policy.

For instance, an administration coming to power in 1933 should not have worried about the uncertainties associated with expansionary policy that we have outlined. The economy does not move from 25 percent unemployment to full employment in a short time. Thus, expansionary measures, such as a rapid growth of the money supply, increased government expenditures, tax reductions, or all three, would have been appropriate policy since there was no chance that the economy would have "overshot" into a boom. They would have an impact only after the economy was at full employment. Similarly, contractionary policies for private demand are called for in wartime. In the

FIGURE 1   INFLATION, UNEMPLOYMENT, AND THE FEDERAL FUNDS INTEREST RATE, 1978–1996.

fine-tuning policy, has helped keep the economy operating better than at any time in the last 30 years. Of course, the Fed was not perfect, and in particular has been criticized for cutting interest rates too slowly during the 1990–1991 recession. But, on balance, the Fed has done an excellent job.

event of large disturbances in the future, activist monetary and/or fiscal policy should once again be used.

Fine tuning presents more complicated issues. In the case of fiscal policy, the long inside lags make discretionary fine tuning virtually impossible, though automatic stabilizers are in fact fine tuning all the time. But with monetary policy decisions being made frequently, fine tuning of monetary policy is indeed possible. The question, then, is whether a small increase in the unemployment rate should lead to a small increase in the growth rate of money or whether policy should not respond until the increase in unemployment becomes large, say more than 1 percent.

The problem is that the disturbance that caused the increase in unemployment may be either transitory or permanent. If it is transitory, nothing should be done. If it is permanent, policy should react to a small disturbance in a small way. Given uncertainty over the nature of the disturbance, the technically correct response is a small one, between the zero that is appropriate for a transitory shock and the full response that is appropriate for a permanent disturbance. Accordingly, fine tuning is appropriate provided that policy responses are always kept small in response to small disturbances.

What does this say about the problems of discretionary policy? First, the inflationary bias of policy noted in the text can be reduced by having an independent central bank, charged with the task of maintaining the value of the currency or low inflation. Second, good policy makers make a difference. So does a good staff—and the Fed has an excellent professional staff.

However, the case for fine tuning is a controversial one. The major argument against it is that in practice policy makers do not in fact behave as suggested—making only small adjustments in response to small disturbances. If allowed to do anything, they may do too much. Instead of merely trying to offset disturbances, policy makers shift toward fine tuning to keep the economy always exactly at full employment, with the risk of overdoing a good thing. The "full-employment bias" in policies risks creating inflation.

The major lesson is not that policy is impossible but that overly ambitious policy is risky. The lesson is to proceed with extreme caution, always bearing in mind the possibility that policy itself may be destabilizing.

RULES VERSUS DISCRETION

If there is a risk that policy makers react to disturbances in unpredictable ways, and in a dosage that is excessively influenced by the perception of the day, and if all this is possibly one of the reasons for macroeconomic instability, why not put policy on automatic pilot? This is the issue of *rules versus discretion*. Should the monetary authority and also the fiscal authority conduct policy in accordance with preannounced rules that describe precisely how their policy variables will be determined in all future situations, or should they be allowed to use their discretion in determining the values of the policy variables at different times?

One example of a rule is the constant-growth-rate rule, say at 4 percent, for monetary policy. The rule is that no matter what happens, the money supply will be kept growing at 4 percent. Another example would be a rule stating that the money supply growth rate will be increased by 2 percent per year for every 1 percent unemployment in excess of, say, 5.5 percent. Algebraically, such a rule would be expressed as

$$\frac{\Delta M}{M} = 4.0 + 2(u - 5.5) \tag{8}$$

where the growth rate of money $\Delta M/M$ is an annual percentage rate, and u is the percentage unemployment rate.

The activist monetary rule of equation (8) implies that at 5.5 percent unemployment, monetary growth is 4 percent. If unemployment rises above 5.5 percent, monetary growth is *automatically* increased. Thus, with 7.5 percent unemployment, monetary growth would be 8 percent, using equation (8). Conversely, if unemployment dropped below 5.5 percent, monetary growth would be lowered below 4 percent. The rule therefore gears the amount of monetary stimulus to an indicator of the business cycle. By linking monetary growth to the unemployment rate, an activist, anticyclical monetary policy is achieved, but this is done without any discretion.

BOX 18-4 Fiscal Policy and Fine Tuning— the Side Effects

Fiscal policy can be an inappropriate tool with which to tune the economy because of its side effects. Presumably the best tax rate is one which pays for the government while introducing minimal distortions in private decisions. Presumably the level of unemployment compensation is set so as to balance fairness to the unemployed against lost incentives to work. There is little reason that such choices will coincidentally be just the right ones to move the economy out of a recession.

So even if purely macroeconomic considerations argue for the use of fiscal rather than monetary policy, the existence of side effects limits the availability of fiscal policy for short-run stabilization.

The issue of rules versus discretion has been clouded by the fact that most proponents of rules have been nonactivists, whose preferred monetary rule is a constant-growth-rate rule. Consequently, the argument has tended to center on whether activist policy is desirable or not. The fundamental point to recognize is that we can design *activist rules*. We can design rules that have countercyclical features without, at the same time, leaving any discretion about their actions to policy makers. The point is made by equation (8), which is an activist rule because it expands money supply when unemployment is high and reduces it when unemployment is low. The equation leaves no room for policy discretion and in this respect is a rule.

Given that both the economy and our knowledge of it are changing over time, there is no economic case for stating permanent policy rules that would tie the hands of the monetary and fiscal authorities permanently.[31] Two practical issues, then, arise in the rules-versus-discretion debate. The first is where the authority to change the rule is located. At one extreme, the growth rate of money could be prescribed by the Constitution. At the other it is left to the Fed or the "Fisc" (the equivalent fiscal policy-making body). In each case policy can be changed, but changing the Constitution takes longer than it takes the Fed to change its policy. In the tradeoff between certainty about future policy and flexibility of policy, activists place a premium on flexibility, and those in favor of rules that are difficult to change place a premium on the fact that the Fed has often made mistakes in the past. Because the financial system responds very quickly to shocks and is so interconnected, we believe it essential that the Fed have considerable discretion and thus flexibility to respond to disturbances. But that is far from a universal judgment.

The second issue is whether the policy makers should announce in advance the policies they will be following for the foreseeable future. Such announcements are in principle desirable because they help private individuals to forecast future policy. In fact, the chairperson of the Fed is required to announce to Congress the Fed's mone-

---

[31]For evidence on this point, see John B. Taylor, "Discretion and Policy Rules in Practice," *Carnegie-Rochester Conference Series on Public Policy,* December 1993.

tary targets. In practice, however, these announcements have not been a great help because the Fed does not stick to its targets. If the Fed is able to keep output close to potential and inflation low by departing from announced policy, it helps private individuals forecast the variables in which they are really interested—their future incomes and, in the case of firms, the demand for their goods—rather than those, like the money supply, that they need know only as an intermediate step in forecasting.

18-8

DYNAMIC INCONSISTENCY AND RULES VERSUS DISCRETION

The case for modest, activist, discretionary policy seems clear. Why then do countries, such as the United States, which follow such procedures sometimes seem to have a bias toward too much inflation? Is there any way to restructure stabilization policy to avoid this bias? The answer to these questions is found in an examination of the idea of *dynamic inconsistency.* Essentially, the argument is that policy makers who have discretion will be tempted to take short-run actions that are inconsistent with the economy's best long-run interests.[32] What's more, this is the natural outcome with rational, well-intentioned, policy makers. In fact, the analysis of dynamic inconsistency begins with the assumption that the policy maker shares the public's dislike of both inflation and unemployment.

The key to understanding dynamic inconsistency lies in remembering that there is a short-run tradeoff between inflation and unemployment given by the short-run Phillips curve but there is no long-run tradeoff because of the adjustment of inflationary expectations. The best long-run position for the economy is full employment with zero (or at least low) inflation. However, if the policy maker announces a full-employment—zero-inflation policy, she will immediately be led to "cheat" by seeking lower unemployment and slightly higher inflation. It is this split between announced and executed plans that gives rise to the name "dynamic inconsistency."

One can model the interaction between policy maker and the economy as occurring in three sequential steps:

1. The policy maker announces a policy, say 0 percent inflation.
2. Economic decision makers choose a level of anticipated inflation consistent with the announced policy, implying the economy will be positioned on the short-run Phillips curve at full employment.
3. The policy maker implements the best possible policy. Since the short-run Phillips curve is now fixed, the policy maker can reduce unemployment at the expense of a little inflation. This policy is *optimal,* although it is *inconsistent* with the policy announced in step 1.

---

[32]The basic reference is Finn Kydland and Edward Prescott, "Rules Rather than Discretion: The Inconsistency of Optimal Plans," *Journal of Political Economy,* June 1977. This is very difficult reading. See also V. V. Chari, "Time Consistency and Optimal Policy Design," Federal Reserve Bank of Minneapolis *Quarterly Review,* Fall 1988. See also Robert J. Barro and David B. Gordon, "A Positive Theory of Monetary Policy in a Natural Rate Model," *Journal of Political Economy,* August 1983, and "Rules, Discretion and Reputation in a Model of Monetary Policy," *Journal of Monetary Economics,* July 1983.

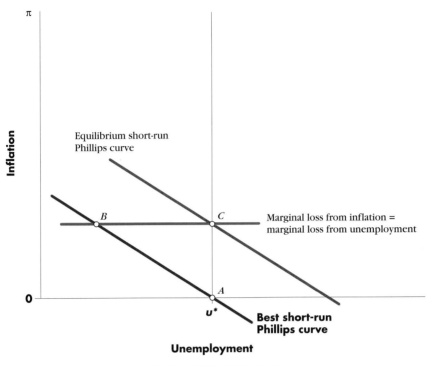

FIGURE 18-6 THE PHILLIPS CURVE AND ECONOMIC POLICY.

We use Figure 18-6 to illustrate the interactions between the policy maker and economic decision makers. The figure shows the Phillips curve tradeoff between unemployment and inflation. Everyone, policy maker and public, prefers to be at point *A,* with full employment and zero inflation. At point *A,* the policy maker promises and the public expects zero inflation, so the economy operates on the blue short-run Phillips curve. Suppose, through good fortune, that the economy reached the preferred point, *A.* What will the policy maker do? At zero inflation, everyone, policymaker and public, is willing to accept a small amount of increased inflation in order to reduce unemployment. So the right thing for the policy maker to do is to increase inflation a little in order to reduce unemployment, sliding up and to the left along the blue short-run Phillips curve. The policy maker will push the economy to point *B,* where inflation is just high enough so that the marginal loss from more inflation equals the marginal benefit from lower unemployment.

At point *B,* inflation is greater than anticipated. Decision makers will come to anticipate higher inflation, and the short-run Phillips curve will move up to the Phillips curve shown in red. Eventually, the economy reaches equilibrium at point *C,* at full employment but with positive inflation. (At point *C,* the marginal loss from inflation is high enough that the policy maker is unwilling to increase inflation further to reduce unemployment; that is, there is no temptation to move further to the left along the red Phillips curve.)

In equilibrium, the economy ends up with high inflation at point *C,* even though everyone prefers point *A.* The policy maker will gladly promise to return to zero in-

BOX 18-5 Central Bank Independence and Democracy—without Further Comment

I know there's the myth of the autonomous Fed . . . [short laugh] and when you go up for confirmation some Senator may ask you about your friendship with the President. Appearances are going to be important, so you can call Ehrlichman to get messages to me, and he'll call you.

—*Richard Nixon to about-to-be Fed chairman Arthur Burns*

Source: Cited in J. Bradford De Long, "America's Only Peacetime Inflation: The 1970s," NBER Historical Paper 84, May 1996, referencing John Ehrlichman, *Witness to Power* (New York: Simon & Schuster, 1982).

flation and stay at point *A*, but the promise isn't *credible*, because if the economy returned to point *A, everyone* would again agree to inflate back to *B*. It would be better if the policy maker kept her promises, but as soon as low-inflation promises are believed, it is then in everyone's best interest to "cheat."

How can the temptation to engage in dynamic inconsistency be avoided, or at least minimized? First, a forward-looking policy maker will realize the value of maintaining a *reputation* for consistency. The difficulty is that there will always be outside pressures pushing for a short-run inflationary bias. Second, the government can choose a policy maker whose personal tastes are more anti-inflationary than those of the public at large, so that the policy maker will lean against inflationary pressures. In terms of Figure 18-6, this means finding a policy maker with a green line lower than society's green line. Third, the policy maker can be given a contract with payments that reward low inflation. Fourth, low-inflation "rules" can be adopted to prevent the policy maker from making the "discretionary" choices that lead to dynamic inconsistency. All these ideas have merit and all have been used to some extent. The problem remains that in a democracy there is always a temptation to lower unemployment at the cost of higher inflation "just this one time."

THE INDEPENDENCE OF THE CENTRAL BANK

One solution to the problem of dynamic inconsistency is to require that the central bank follow a monetary rule, for instance, to increase the money supply at a low, constant rate. However, because the monetary rule may be wrong and because there are good reasons for monetary policy to respond to some shocks, such as a supply shock, no country has adopted a rigid form of rule.

Another solution to the inflationary bias of discretionary policy is to set up a central bank that is independent of the electoral cycle and that has a clear mandate to fight inflation. The Fed is in principle independent of the administration, though it does report to Congress.[33] In Germany, the central bank, the Bundesbank, is fiercely independent, and it is a fierce inflation fighter. There is strong empirical evidence showing that the more independent the central bank, the lower the inflation rate in a country.[34]

The question of the optimal degree of independence of the central bank is a complicated one. There *are* short-run tradeoffs, and there is always a question of just how fast a central bank should try to reduce inflation. Thus central banks end up exercising judgment, which ultimately depends on their evaluation of what the public's real interests are. But there is no way of knowing what those interests are without some democratic input. Whenever the Fed shows its independence, typically by refusing to expand as fast as the administration or Congress wants—for example, in 1991—there are calls to clip its wings. This is one way the Fed gets the message.

◆ OPTIONAL ◆

DYNAMIC INCONSISTENCY—A FORMAL APPROACH

In this section we present an algebraic version of the model of dynamic inconsistency illustrated in Figure 18-6. We assume that the policy maker chooses the level of inflation, although in practice the policy maker actually chooses monetary or fiscal policy and inflation is a result rather than a direct choice. The choice of inflation leads to the unemployment rate given by the short-run Phillips curve in equation (9):

$$\pi = \pi^e + \epsilon(u^* - u) \qquad (9)$$

The policy maker, and the public, prefers low unemployment and zero inflation. We "keep score" by specifying a loss function for the policymaker in equation (10):

$$L = a(u - u^*) + \pi^2 \qquad (10)$$

The loss function in equation (10) says that high unemployment is bad and that any deviation from zero inflation is bad. The higher the coefficient a, the greater the relative weight given to lowering unemployment.

The three steps in the "game" played by the policy maker are (1) the policy maker chooses and announces an inflation policy (point A in Figure 18-6); (2) "the economy" picks anticipated policy, π^e (point B); (3) the policy maker implements an actual policy, π, that minimizes the loss function in equation (10) (point C). In step 2, the decision makers look forward, guessing what the policy maker will do in step 3. In step 1, the policy maker is also looking forward, guessing what the economy will do in step 2 as it looks toward step 3. So early choices by the policy maker must anticipate later stages, which themselves depend on the choices made earlier. Decision makers work out their choices by starting at the end and working backward. This choice method is a simple example of *dynamic programming*.

---

[33]See Alan S. Blinder, "Central Banking in a Democracy," Federal Reserve Bank of Atlanta *Economic Quarterly*, Fall 1996.

[34]Vittorio Grilli, Donato Masciandaro, and Guido Tabellini, in "Political and Monetary Institutions and Public Financial Policies in the Industrial Countries," *Economic Policy*, October 1991, show this result as well as results on the relationship between institutions and fiscal policy.

The final "score" is calculated by inserting the actual policy, π, and anticipated inflation, π^e, into the loss function using the Phillips curve relation to compute the deviation of unemployment from the natural rate. The final score is

$$L(\pi) = a\left[-\frac{1}{\epsilon}(\pi - \pi^e)\right] + \pi^2 \tag{11}$$

The policy maker minimizes the loss in equation (11) by setting the marginal loss function in (12) equal to zero, giving the green line in Figure 18-6:

$$ML(\pi) = -\frac{a}{\epsilon} + 2\pi = 0 \tag{12}$$

So the optimal policy is

$$\pi = \frac{a}{2\epsilon} \tag{13}$$

Note that the result in equation (13) holds for *any* level value of π^e.

Everyone desires zero inflation, but in the last stage of the game it always "pays" for the policy maker to choose a positive inflation rate. In fact, since anticipated inflation equals $a/2\epsilon$, if the policy maker chooses in the last step to set inflation below $a/2\epsilon$, a recession will result. The problem is that society has no way to *commit* to zero inflation.

Note, in equation (13), that a loss function weighted heavily against unemployment—one with a high a—results in more inflation. This perverse result occurs because a high a increases the incentive in the last step to raise inflation to lower unemployment. But if society can cede power to a policy maker who cares less about unemployment, one with a lower a, lower inflation will result.

SUMMARY

1. Despite the apparent simplicity of policies needed to maintain continuous full employment, the historical record of recessions and unemployment implies that successful stabilization policy is difficult to carry out.

2. The Great Depression shaped both modern macroeconomics and many of the economy's institutions. The extremely high unemployment and the length of the Depression led to the view that the private economy was unstable and that government intervention was needed to maintain high employment levels.

3. Keynesian economics succeeded because it seemed to explain the causes of the Great Depression—a collapse of investment demand—and because it pointed to expansionary fiscal policy as a means of preventing future depressions.

4. Keynesian views did not much affect economic policy making in the United States until the New Economics of the Kennedy-Johnson administration. The greatest success of the New Economics was the tax cut of 1964. The New Economics is perceived by the public as having been responsible for increasing inflation during the 1960s. As confidence in the New Economics declined, its emphasis on active stabilization policy was reexamined.

5. The potential need for stabilizing policy actions arises from economic disturbances. Some of these disturbances, such as changes in money demand, con-

sumption spending, or investment demand, arise from within the private sector. Others, such as wars, may arise for noneconomic reasons.

6. The three key difficulties of stabilization policy are that (*a*) policy works with lags; (*b*) the outcome of policy depends very much on private sector expectations, which are difficult to predict and which may react to policy; and (*c*) there is uncertainty about both the structure of the economy and the shocks that hit the economy.

7. There are clearly occasions on which active monetary and fiscal policy actions should be taken to stabilize the economy. These are situations in which the economy has been affected by major disturbances.

8. Fine tuning—continuous attempts to stabilize the economy in the face of small disturbances—is more controversial. If fine tuning is undertaken, it calls for small policy responses in an attempt to moderate the economy's fluctuations, rather than to remove them entirely. A very active policy in response to small disturbances is likely to destabilize the economy.

9. In the rules-versus-discretion debate, it is important to recognize that activist rules are possible. The two important issues in the debate are how difficult it should be to change policy and whether policy should be announced as far ahead as possible. There is a tradeoff between the certainty about future policy that comes from rules and the flexibility of the policy makers in responding to shocks.

10. Central bank independence is one avenue democracies use to add to the credibility of policy and to help mitigate the problem of dynamic inconsistency.

KEY TERMS

Great Depression	action lag	marginal loss function
New Deal	discrete lag	activist policies
Keynesian revolution	distributed lag	fine tuning
New Economics	econometric model	rules vs. discretion
potential output	credibility	activist rules
GDP gap	Lucas (econometric policy	dynamic inconsistency
full-employment budget	evaluation) critique	dynamic programming
inside lag	multiplier uncertainty	
outside lag	diversification of policy	
recognition lag	instruments	
decision lag	loss function	

PROBLEMS

Conceptual

1. **a.** What do "Keynesians" believe caused the Great Depression?
   b. What do "monetarists" believe caused the Great Depression?
   c. Are these explanations mutually exclusive?
   d. Why are macroeconomists so interested in explaining the causes of the Great Depression?

*2. Suppose there was a small, negative shock to demand. You—a policy maker—have a stack of papers in front of you detailing the magnitude of the shock and its devastating effects upon

*An asterisk denotes a more difficult problem.

the people of your country. You are tempted to use an active policy to offset these effects. Your advisers have estimated its impact on the economy, in both the long and short runs. What questions should you ask yourself before committing to this course of action? Why?

3. **a.** What is an inside lag?
    b. We can divide inside lags into three smaller, sequential lags. What are these, and in what order do they occur?
    c. Which has the smaller inside lag—fiscal or monetary policy? Why?
    d. What is the inside lag for automatic stabilizers?

4. **a.** What is an outside lag?
    b. Why does it generally take the form of a distributed lag?
    c. Which has the smaller outside lag—fiscal or monetary policy?

5. Which would you recommend be used to offset the effect of a temporary shock to output—fiscal or monetary policy? Why?

6. **a.** What is an econometric model?
    b. How might one be used?
    c. There is always some uncertainty with respect to predictions based on such models. Why? What is the source of this uncertainty?

7. What role do expectations play in Lucas's critique of econometric policy evaluation?

8. Evaluate the argument that monetary policy should be determined by a rule rather than discretion. How about fiscal policy?

9. Evaluate the arguments for a constant-growth-rate rule for money.

10. What is dynamic inconsistency? Explain intuitively how it might arise in the case of the short-run tradeoff between inflation and unemployment.

Technical

1. It is sometimes said that the Great Depression would have been a severe recession if it had stopped in 1931 but would not have been the calamity it was.
    a. From Table 18-1 calculate the rate at which GNP was falling from 1929 to 1931.
    b. How does that rate compare with the rate at which real GDP fell during the 1990–1991 recession?
    c. Do you agree with the first sentence in this question? Explain.

2. Using Table 18-2, explain why concentration on the actual budget deficit might have given a misleading impression of fiscal policy at some stages between 1929 and 1933.

3. Suppose that GDP is $40 billion below its potential level. It is expected that next-period GDP will be $20 billion below potential and that two periods from now it will be back at its potential level. You are told that the multiplier for government spending is 2 and that the effects of the increased government spending are immediate. What policy actions can be taken to put GDP back on target each period?

4. The basic facts about the path of GDP are as in question 3. But there is now a one-period outside lag for government spending. Decisions to spend today are translated into actual spending only tomorrow. The multiplier for government spending is still 2 in the period that the spending takes place.
    a. What is the best that can be done to keep GDP as close to target as possible each period?
    b. Compare the path of GDP in this question with the path in problem 3 after policy actions have been taken.

5. Life has become yet more complicated. Government spending works with a distributed lag. Now when $1 billion is spent today, GDP increases by $1 billion this period and $1.5 billion next period.
   a. What happens to the path of GDP if government spending rises enough this period to put GDP back to its potential level this period?
   b. Suppose fiscal policy actions are taken to put GDP at its potential level this period. What fiscal policy will be needed to put GDP on target next period?
   c. Explain why the government has to be so active in keeping GDP on target in this case.

6. Suppose that you knew that the multiplier for government spending was between 1 and 2.5 but that its effects ended in the period in which spending was increased. How would you run fiscal policy if GDP would, without policy, behave as in problem 3?

*7. Suppose that, as the chair of the Fed, you decided to "put policy on automatic pilot" and require that monetary policy follow an established rule. When might each of the following two rules be appropriate? (*a*) Maintain a constant interest rate. (*b*) Maintain a constant money supply. Show this rigorously, using an *IS-LM* framework. (*Hint:* See Chapter 16.)

8. (*Optional*) Check the *Federal Reserve Bulletin,* where the forecasts of the Federal Reserve Board are presented twice a year following the February and July monetary policy report to Congress.
   a. How well did the Fed anticipate the economic performance of 1996?
   b. Explain why econometric forecasts are not totally accurate.

5

Inflation, Budget Deficits, and International Adjustments

CHAPTER 19

Money, Deficits, and Inflation: Evidence and Policy Issues

CHAPTER HIGHLIGHTS

◆ Money and inflation are tightly linked in the long run but are not always so tightly linked in the short run.

◆ Money and inflation are tightly linked in very high inflation countries but are less tightly linked in countries with moderate inflation rates.

◆ Large budget deficits typically play a role in the extensive money creation that generates hyperinflations.

In this chapter we concentrate on the effects of money growth on inflation and interest rates. We take up four main topics. We begin by examining the monetarist proposition that inflation is a monetary phenomenon, which means that inflation is entirely, or at least primarily, due to excessive money growth. We then study the linkages among interest rates, inflation, and money growth. Next, we look at the links between budget deficits and money growth, asking whether or under what circumstances budget deficits cause money growth. Finally, we describe hyperinflations—extremely high inflations—and the role of money growth in them.

We will show that high inflation is indeed primarily a monetary phenomenon in the sense that inflation could not continue without continued money growth. But, typically, high budget deficits underlie the rapid money growth. Such was the case, for instance, in the high inflations or hyperinflations in Israel, Bolivia, Argentina, and Brazil in the 1980s. We will also see that in conditions of high inflation nominal interest rates become very high, as expected inflation becomes incorporated into nominal rates.

However, money plays a less singular role when inflation rates are lower, in the single-digit or low-double-digit range; in this situation supply shocks may well play a relatively larger role. We will also see that, in comparison to situations of hyperinflation, more moderate budget deficits, such as those in the United States in the early 1990s, do not necessarily lead to higher money growth and inflation.

MONEY, INFLATION, AND INTEREST RATES

Our study of money demand and the long-run aggregate supply curve has shown the following:

- A sustained increase in the growth rate of money will, in the long run when all adjustments have taken place, lead to an equal increase in the rate of inflation. In the long run, the inflation rate is equal to the growth rate of money adjusted for trend growth in real income.
- A sustained increase in money growth will have no long-run effects on the level of output: there is no long-run tradeoff between inflation and output.

This is consistent with the monetarist claim that inflation is caused by money growth, *in the long run.*[1] But as one moves away from the long run, disturbances other than changes in the money stock—such as supply shocks—affect inflation and, conversely, changes in the money stock do have real effects.

We also recall the relationship between money growth and interest rates:

- In the short run, increased money growth will reduce the real interest rate. But in the long run, after all adjustments have taken place, the *real* interest rate will return to its initial level.

Since the nominal interest rate equals the real interest rate plus the inflation rate, once the real rate has returned to its initial level, the nominal interest rate will have increased by the amount of the increase in the inflation rate. This pass-through of inflation into the nominal interest rate is the *Fisher effect,* which we now consider more carefully.

---

[1]See, for instance, Milton Friedman, "Monetarism in Rhetoric and Practice," Bank of Japan *Monetary and Economic Studies,* October 1983.

19-1

INTEREST RATES AND INFLATION: THE FISHER EQUATION

We have noted at various points in this book the relationship between nominal interest rates, real rates, and the expected rate of inflation. The (expected) real rate of interest is the nominal rate less the expected rate of inflation:[2]

$$r^e = i - \pi^e \tag{1}$$

Equation (1) is the Fisher equation, named after Irving Fisher (1867–1947), the most famous American economist of the first third of this century, who analyzed the inflation–interest rate linkage.[3]

The Fisher equation draws attention to an important finding about money growth, inflation, and interest rates. In the long run the real interest rate converges to its full-employment level, r^*, and actual and expected inflation are equal. Using these two facts ($r^e = r^*$, $\pi^e = \pi$), we express the long-run relationship as

$$i \equiv r^* + \pi \tag{2}$$

With r^* given, equation (2) implies a key result: In the long run when all adjustments have occurred, an increase in inflation is reflected fully in nominal interest rates. Nominal interest rates rise one for one with the increase in inflation. The reason we have such a strong inflation–nominal interest rate link is that in the long run the real interest rate is unaffected by monetary disturbances, which do affect the inflation rate.

Of course, the constancy of the real interest rate holds only in long-run equilibrium. During the adjustment process the real interest rate does change and short-run changes in the nominal interest rate reflect both changes in real rates and changes in inflationary expectations.

Figure 19-1 shows interest rates, measured by the 3-month Treasury-bill rate, and inflation, measured as the change in the GDP deflator over the previous year. You can see the very strong long-run tendency for the two to move together, but you can also see that the real interest rate, the vertical distance between the lines, does change in the short run.

As can be seen in Figure 19-1, there were several episodes of negative real rates in the 1970s, particularly in 1974–1975, when inflation, in green, increased sharply and exceeded the interest rate, in blue, by a significant margin. By contrast, in the period since 1980 the real rate of interest has been *persistently* positive, and in most years by a good margin. This is a quite new experience if we look back only a few years, but it certainly has precedents in U.S. experience in the past 100 years, during which real interest rates were significantly positive in several decades, as shown in Table 19-1.

---

[2]You may wish to review Box 14-3 on the relation between real and nominal interest rates.

[3]See Irving Fisher, *The Rate of Interest* (New York: Macmillan, 1907). Fisher taught at Yale and was an effective and sophisticated developer of the quantity theory of money. He had other interests, too; he was the inventor of the card index file still used for keeping addresses and was a health food enthusiast who wrote several books on the subject. Fisher was an early, if long forgotten, discoverer of the Phillips curve. See the reprinted version of his 1926 article, "A Statistical Relation between Unemployment and Price Changes," under the heading "Lost and Found," *Journal of Political Economy,* March–April 1973, pp. 496–502.

FIGURE 19-1   INTEREST RATES AND INFLATION, 1960–1996.

Interest rates are depicted by the 3-month Treasury-bill rate, and inflation is based on the GDP deflator.
(Source: DRI/McGraw-Hill Macroeconomic Database.)

Table 19-2 presents international evidence on the interest rate–inflation link. Two features stand out. First, the countries with high inflation, such as Italy and Mexico, tend to have higher *nominal* interest rates. This is especially true when the inflation rate is very high, as for Mexico and Brazil. Second, real interest rates vary widely across countries.

The evidence is thus that inflation and nominal interest rates tend to move together, within a country over time and across countries. But the data do not support a very strict

TABLE 19-1   The Real Interest Rate, United States
(Average annual percent)

PERIOD	RATE	PERIOD	RATE
1860–1869	1.5	1930–1939	3.6
1870–1879	9.8	1940–1949	−4.6
1880–1889	7.2	1950–1959	.4
1890–1899	4.2	1960–1969	2.1
1900–1909	2.3	1970–1979	−.2
1910–1919	−3.6	1980–1989	4.1
1920–1929	−6.0	1990–1995	1.7

Source: Lawrence Summers, "The Non-Adjustment of Nominal Interest Rates: A Study of the Fisher Effect," in J. Tobin (ed.), *Macroeconomics, Prices and Quantities* (Washington, D.C.: The Brookings Institution, 1983), updated by the authors.

TABLE 19-2 Interest Rates and Inflation, 1995*

COUNTRY	INTEREST RATE, % PER ANNUM	INFLATION RATE
Argentina	12.6	3.4
Brazil	52.2†	84.4
Canada	5.7	2.2
Finland	5.8	1.0
Germany	4.5	1.8
Italy	10.5	5.2
Mexico	50.5	35.0
United Kingdom	6.0	3.4
United States	5.8	2.8

*Interest rates are short-term (money market rate except where noted); inflation rate is percent change in the CPI over the previous year.

†Rate on savings deposits.

Source: International Financial Statistics, 1996; Datastream.

Fisher effect. Real interest rates are tied to the productivity of capital. This tie limits the range of possible values for real interest rates. Inflation rates, in contrast, can vary widely—as instances of hyperinflation show. Therefore, moderate swings in the nominal interest rate may be due to changes in either the real interest rate or the inflation rate, but huge swings are predominantly the result of changes in the inflation rate. The Fisher equation is primarily a guide to nominal interest rates when inflationary disturbances are large relative to all other factors determining interest rates.

19-2

EMPIRICAL EVIDENCE

What is the evidence on the links between money growth and inflation?

THE MONEY-INFLATION LINK

In examining the links between inflation and money growth, it is convenient to use the *quantity theory of money.* The quantity theory relates the level of nominal income (PY), the money stock (M), and the velocity of money (V):

$$MV = PY \tag{3}$$

Recall that the *velocity* of money is the number of times the money stock turns over each year in financing payments made to purchase the economy's output.

The quantity equation can also be written in terms of the percentage change over time of each of the four terms in equation (3):

$$m + v = \pi + y \tag{4}$$

Putting the inflation rate on the left, we obtain the central result:

$$\pi = m - y + v \tag{5}$$

FIGURE 19-2   MONEY GROWTH AND INFLATION, 1960–1996.

Money growth is based on M2 and inflation on the GDP deflator.
(Source: DRI/McGraw-Hill Macroeconomic Database.)

where m is money growth, v is the percentage change in velocity, π is the inflation rate, and y is the growth rate of output.

Equation (5) can be used to account for the sources of inflation, that is, for what part is due to velocity changes or to money growth or to output growth. The monetarist claim that inflation is predominantly a monetary phenomenon implies that velocity and output changes are small.

Now we turn to the data. Figure 19-2 shows annual $M2$ growth and the inflation rate of the GDP deflator for the United States. We see that the inflation rate and the growth rate of money have broadly moved together. Both trend upward until the late 1970s and trend downward from sometime in the 1980s to the present. But the relationship is *very* rough, with large gaps between the growth lines which persist for several years. As equation (5) shows, that means that changes in output growth and/or velocity changes were affecting inflation.

In Table 19-3 we examine the link between money growth and inflation over longer periods, specifically decades, and also adjust for growth in output. The growth adjustment is made by subtracting the growth rate of output from the growth of money, as implied by equation (5).[4]

---

[4]In making this adjustment for output growth, we are assuming that velocity is not systematically related to income. That means we are assuming a unit income elasticity of money demand (see Chap. 15). In general, the inflation rate is equal to money growth minus the product of the income elasticity of money demand and the growth rate of output.

TABLE 19-3   Money, Inflation, and Output Growth
(Percent per year)

	M1	M2	Inflation*	GDP Growth
1960–1969	3.8	7.0	2.5	4.0
1970–1979	6.4	9.6	7.6	3.2
1980–1989	7.4	7.7	3.5	2.7
1990–1996	6.3	2.9	3.2	2.1
1960–1996	5.9	7.4	4.5	3.2

*Based on the GDP deflator.

Source: DRI/McGraw-Hill Macroeconomic Database.

In Table 19-3, inflation is closely related to the growth rate of $M2$.[5] For example, in the 1960s money growth less real growth was 3 percent and actual inflation averaged 2.5 percent, not far off the mark. Likewise, for the 1970s equation (5) predicts 6.4 percent whereas actual inflation was 7.6 percent. And the same close forecast is evident once more in the 1980s, with a predicted inflation rate of 5 percent versus an actual rate of 4.5 percent.

The relationship between money growth and inflation is much looser for $M1$. This is a reflection of the instability of $M1$ money demand, especially in the 1980s. To obtain a stable relationship between money growth and inflation, we need a stable real money demand or, equivalently, stable velocity.

Fluctuations of Velocity

If the 10-year average $M2$ growth-inflation relation in Table 19-3 works well, why is the year-to-year relationship in Figure 19-2 much looser? One reason, of course, is that we have adjusted for output growth in Table 19-3. But the more important reason is fluctuations in velocity.

Figure 19-3 shows year-to-year percentage changes in $M2$ velocity—the v term in equation (5). Velocity frequently shifts by 3 to 4 percent per year, thus adding considerable short-run variability to the money growth–inflation relationship.

Since velocity is a shortcut for thinking about money demand, fluctuations in velocity arise from the same factors that shift money demand—variations in output and interest rates and innovations to the financial system. For example, because the *short-run* income elasticity is much less than unity, a fall in real income will reduce velocity. Similarly, a rise in interest rates will raise velocity. Indeed, shifts in interest rates or income that result in velocity changes could even be caused by changes in the money stock itself. The other critical factor affecting velocity is financial innovation.

---

[5]In Chap. 15 we saw that the demand for real money balances ($M2$) has a long-run income elasticity of about unity. Thus the long-run relationship between $M2$ growth and inflation should be approximately 1:1 except for changes in velocity unrelated to income growth.

FIGURE 19-3   QUARTERLY CHANGE IN VELOCITY OF MONEY, 1960–1996.

The graph shows the percentage change in the velocity of M2.
(Source: DRI/McGraw-Hill Macroeconomic Database.)

If innovation introduces substitutes for the particular monetary aggregate we study, we expect a fall in real money demand and hence a rise in velocity. There are thus many potential causes of the short-run instability of velocity that is evident in Figure 19-3.

Finally, a warning is in order: Even the good long-run performance of the money (*M2*) growth–inflation relation may be the exception rather than the rule. There is no economic rule that says velocity in the long run must be constant. We regard a roughly constant velocity over long periods as therefore somewhat surprising and as deserving further examination.

Historical and International Trends

In the United States, the *M2* money-inflation link has not always been as tight as it was in the past three decades. In the end-of-chapter problems we provide data for decadal averages in the period 1860–1989 and ask you to investigate the money-inflation link for that period. There are clearly some outliers, for example, the 1890s, when money growth (adjusted for real income growth) was high but prices were falling.

International data, shown in Table 19-4, give the same impression as the data for the United States: generally, higher growth rates of money (adjusted for output growth) are associated with higher inflation, but the relationship is not 1:1. For some countries, such as the United Kingdom, inflation is well below the "predicted" rate (the growth rate of money minus output growth), while for others, such as Italy, the converse is true. Once again the reasons the relationship is not exact include shifts in

BOX 19-1 Monetarism and Modern Macroeconomics

In the early 1960s, monetarists began a serious challenge to the Keynesian macroeconomics that had dominated the field since the Great Depression. Many leading economists, Nobel laureate Milton Friedman foremost,* have propounded the basic message of monetarism, that money is extremely important for macroeconomics.

Three decades later, many of the positions originally associated with monetarism are part of the agreed-upon core of macroeconomics, while others remain controversial. Here they are, along with the chapters in which they are discussed:

1. *Money.* Money matters (this chapter).
2. *A monetary growth rule.* Monetary policy would be better conducted by a rule—that is, that money should grow at a constant rate—than by discretion (Chapter 18).
3. *Money targets.* Monetary policy is better conducted by setting money targets rather than interest rate targets (Chapter 16).
4. *Long and variable lags.* Monetary policy affects the economy with lags that are both long and variable (Chapter 18).

There are two other monetarist positions that should be noted:

5. *The inherent stability of the private sector.* Monetarists argue that the private sector is inherently stable and that most disturbances to the economy are caused by mistaken government policy. They believe that less government is better than more and that governments have an inherent tendency to grow. (Some of these issues are discussed in Chapter 20.)
6. *Flexible exchange rates.* In the 1950s Milton Friedman was the outstanding proponent of the view that exchange rates should be flexible rather than fixed. Although this view is not necessarily monetarist—in the sense that it is independent of the argument that money matters—most monetarists (along with many other macroeconomists) accept it, regarding the exchange rate as just another price that markets should be free to set and that governments are likely to get wrong (Chapter 21).

Where does the profession come out on the issues? As Nobel laureate Franco Modigliani of M.I.T. has said, "We are all monetarists now," in the sense that we all believe that *some* stock of money has major impacts on the economy, that sustained rapid money growth leads to inflation, and that inflation cannot be kept low unless money growth is low. While other monetarist positions are generally more controversial, there is no question that monetarism has had major successes, including the adoption of money growth targets in the 1980s in many countries—a success that turned out to be temporary, as some of the countries that adopted money growth targets have now abandoned them in the light of the instability of money demand.

*For a recent account of Friedman's views, see his *Monetarist Mischief* (New York: Harcourt Brace Jovanovich, 1992). Among the prominent monetarists are Anna J. Schwartz of the National Bureau of Economic Research, Friedman's coauthor of (among other books and articles) the magisterial *A Monetary History of the United States, 1867–1960* (Princeton, N.J.: Princeton University Press, 1963), and the late Karl Brunner of the University of Rochester, Allan Meltzer and Bennett McCallum of Carnegie-Mellon, Phillip Cagan of Columbia University, David Laidler and Michael Parkin of the University of Western Ontario, William Poole of Brown University, and many leading economists around the world.

TABLE 19-4 Money and Inflation in International Perspective, 1960–1990
(Percent per year)

	MONEY GROWTH*	OUTPUT GROWTH	"PREDICTED" INFLATION	ACTUAL INFLATION
Canada	8.9	2.8	6.1	5.9
United States	8.9	3.2	5.7	4.8
Japan	13.8	6.3	7.5	5.4
Germany	8.6	3.1	5.5	3.5
France†	9.8	2.1	7.7	7.0
Italy	11.3	2.4	8.9	10.9
United Kingdom	14.5	2.4	12.1	7.7

*$M1$ plus quasi-money.

†For 1979–1990 only, previous data being unavailable for broad monetary aggregates.

Source: OECD, *Historical Statistics,* 1992.

money demand, perhaps caused by financial deregulation, changes in interest rates that affect velocity, and income elasticities of money demand that are different from unity.[6]

Summary: Is Inflation a Monetary Phenomenon?

The answer to the question of whether inflation is a monetary phenomenon *in the long run* is yes. No major inflation can take place without rapid money growth, and rapid money growth will cause rapid inflation. Further, any policy that determinedly keeps the growth rate of money low will lead eventually to a low rate of inflation. However, in the short run neither the quantity theory nor the Fisher effect holds exactly.

19-3

ALTERNATIVE STRATEGIES TO REDUCE INFLATION

Suppose the inflation rate in the economy is 10 percent and the government decides to reduce inflation rates to 2 or 3 percent. This is the decision that was made in the United States in 1979. By the mid-1980s the inflation rate was down to the 3 to 4 percent range, but in the meantime the economy went through two recessions, in 1980 and again in 1981–1982. The problem of how to disinflate is one that faces governments recurrently—and occasionally the problem is how to end a hyperinflation in which the *monthly* inflation rate is well into the double digits.

The key question for any government contemplating disinflation is how to disinflate as cheaply as possible—that is, with as small a recession as possible. In this section we consider alternative strategies for disinflation. The basic method of disinflation should be clear from Chapter 7: it is to reduce the growth rate of aggregate demand. That can be done by cutting back on money growth and, in the short run, by using fiscal policy. In this section we consider only monetary policy.

[6]Definitions of monetary aggregates differ substantially among countries. The term "money" in Table 19-4 describes the closest aggregate corresponding to $M2$ in the United States.

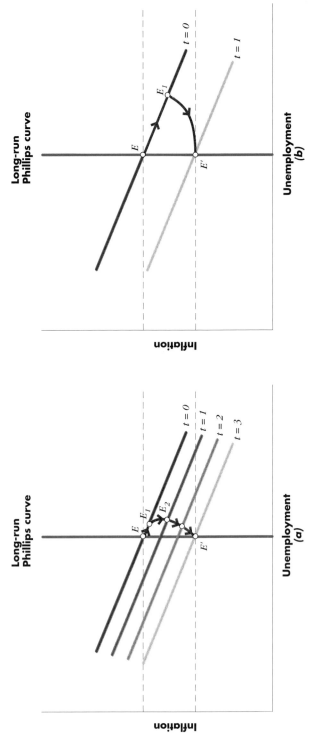

FIGURE 19-4 GRADUALISM VS. COLD TURKEY: EFFECTS OF POLICY CHOICE ON THE PHILLIPS CURVE.

GRADUALISM VERSUS COLD TURKEY

Figure 19-4 shows the choices. A policy of *gradualism* attempts a slow and steady return to low inflation. The gradualist policy, shown in Figure 19-4*a,* begins with a small reduction in the money growth rate that shifts the economy to the right along the short-run Phillips curve, from E to E_1. In response to the lower inflation at E_1, the short-run Phillips curve shifts downward to the Phillips curve marked $t = 1$. A further small cut in the money growth moves the economy to E_2, the aggregate supply curve shifts down again, and the process continues.

Eventually output returns to its potential level, at point E', at a lower inflation rate. There is no massive recession during the adjustment process, although unemployment is above normal throughout.

Panel (*b*) of Figure 19-4 shows the *cold-turkey* alternative. The cold-turkey strategy tries to cut the inflation rate fast. The strategy starts with an immediate sharp cutback in money growth, shifting the economy far out to the right along the short-run Phillips curve and moving the economy from E to E_1. The immediate recession is larger than that under gradualism.

By creating a larger fall in the inflation rate than would result from the gradualist policy, the cold-turkey strategy causes the short-run Phillips curve to move down faster than it does in Figure 19-4*a.* The cold-turkey strategy keeps up the pressure by holding the rate of money growth low. Eventually the rate of inflation falls enough that output and employment begin to grow again. The economy returns to point E' with full employment and a lower rate of inflation.

Figure 19-5 presents the gradualist and cold-turkey strategies in an alternative form. In the gradualist strategy the growth rate of money is initially reduced only slightly, and the economy never strays very far from the natural rate of unemployment. But the inflation rate comes down only slowly. The cold-turkey strategy, by contrast, starts with a massive cut in the growth rate of money and a large recession. The recession is much worse than it ever is with the gradualist strategy, but the reduction in inflation is more rapid.

Which strategy should be chosen? Is moderate unemployment with higher inflation preferable to higher unemployment with lower inflation? U.S. policy makers in 1981–1982 chose a policy closer to cold turkey than to gradualism.

CREDIBILITY

The cold-turkey strategy has one major point in its favor. It is much more clear in the case of cold turkey than it is in gradualism that a decisive policy change has been made, with the firm aim of driving down the inflation rate. Thus people forming their expectations rationally will be more likely to believe policy has changed under the cold-turkey strategy than under gradualism: the cold-turkey policy is more *credible* than a gradualist policy.[7] A credible policy is one that the public believes will be maintained and will succeed.

---

[7]In the European context, Thomas Egebo and Steven Englander have investigated whether the European exchange rate system of quasi-fixed rates helped reduce the costs of disinflation. See their article "Institutional Commitments and Policy Credibility: A Critical Survey and Empirical Evidence from the ERM," *OECD Economic Studies,* Spring 1992.

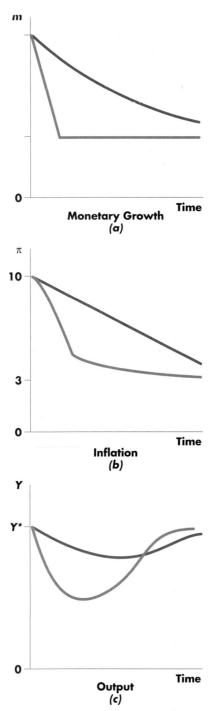

FIGURE 19-5   GRADUALISM VS. COLD TURKEY: EFFECTS OF POLICY CHOICE ON MONETARY GROWTH, INFLATION, AND OUTPUT.

A belief that policy has changed will by itself drive down the expected rate of inflation and for that reason cause the short-run Phillips curve to shift down. Thus a credible policy earns a *credibility bonus* in the fight against inflation.

Throughout the period of disinflation in the United States, starting with the Fed's change in policy in October 1979, there was strong emphasis on the credibility of policy. Some proponents of rational expectations even believed that if policy could only be made credible, it would be possible to disinflate practically without causing any recession at all.[8]

The argument went like this: The expectations-augmented aggregate supply curve is

$$\pi = \pi^e + \lambda(Y - Y^*) \tag{6}$$

If the policy is credible, people adjust their expectations of inflation when a new, lower money growth rate is adjusted, and the short-run aggregate supply curve therefore moves down immediately. Accordingly, if policy is credible and if expectations are rational, the economy can move immediately to a new long-run equilibrium when there is a change in policy. In other words, if policy is credible, π can be reduced by lowering π^e while suffering less from low $(Y - Y^*)$.

The experience of the United States in the early 1980s—the worst recession since the Great Depression—casts doubt on the relevance of this optimistic scenario; even more so does the experience of Britain in the same period, when the unmistakably tough-minded Thatcher government was pursuing a resolute anti-inflationary policy but still reached a 13 percent unemployment rate.

There are two possible reasons the simple credibility–rational expectations argument does not work. First, credibility may be very difficult to obtain; second, the economy has, at any time, an overhang of past contracts embodying past expectations, and the contract renegotiations take time. Thus, because of *inflationary inertia,* a rapid return to lower inflation in economies experiencing inflation rates in the 10 to 20 percent range is unlikely.

It is easiest to change the inflation rate when there are no long-term contracts that embody the ongoing inflation—for instance, by building in high rates of wage increase for the next several years—in the economy. There will be very few such contracts if inflation is high, for instance, in a hyperinflation. Under such conditions negotiators will not want to sign an agreement in nominal terms because they will be gambling too much on the future behavior of the price level. Long-term nominal contracts disappear, and wages and prices are frequently reset. In these circumstances, a credible policy will have rapid effects. But such rapid success cannot be expected in an economy in which the structure of contracts has not yet been destroyed by extreme inflation.

It remains true, though, that whatever the structure of contracts, the more credible a policy that aims to disinflate the economy is, the more successful that policy will be.

DISINFLATION AND THE SACRIFICE RATIO

Inflation reduction almost always costs a recession, but what exactly is the tradeoff? How much output is lost through different methods of disinflation, such as cold turkey and grad-

---

[8]See John Fender, *Inflation* (Ann Arbor: University of Michigan Press, 1990), and Dean Croushore, "What Are the Costs of Disinflation?" Federal Reserve Bank of Philadelphia *Business Review,* May–June 1992.

BOX 19-2 The Rational Expectations School, Monetarism, and Hyperinflation

The *rational expectations school* in macroeconomics accepts many monetarist positions, including a preference for rule and the belief that government intervention usually makes the situation worse. Indeed, many of the leaders of the rational expectations school were students of Friedman. Some, including Robert Lucas, studied under Friedman at the University of Chicago; others, such as Robert Barro and Thomas Sargent, studied his works while they were graduate students at other universities.

Rational expectations views include:

1. The market-clearing rational expectations approach to the Phillips curve (Chapter 8)
2. Rational expectations as a theory of expectations (Chapter 8)
3. An emphasis on the credibility of policy makers (Chapter 18 and this chapter)
4. A preference for policy-making rules rather than discretion (Chapter 18)

Most of these views can be seen as extensions of the monetarist approach. However, the monetarist and rational expectations schools differ on one key issue: Whereas monetarists, like Keynesians, see the economy as reacting to disturbances and policy changes slowly and with long and variable lags and are willing to allow the possibility that markets may not clear, the rational expectations school generally insists that markets clear rapidly. (In the simplest case, monetarists think monetary policy has real effects for several quarters to several years; the rational expectations school does not.) Obviously, we do not share

ualism? Discussion of the costs of disinflation makes extensive use of the concept of the *sacrifice ratio.*[9] The sacrifice ratio is the ratio of the cumulative percentage loss of GDP (as a result of a disinflation policy) to the reduction in inflation that is actually achieved.

Thus, suppose a policy reduces the inflation rate from 10 to 4 percent over a 3-year period, at the cost of levels of output that are 10 percent below potential in the first year, 8 percent below potential in the second year, and 6 percent below potential in the third year. The total loss of GDP is 24 percent (10 + 8 + 6), the reduction in inflation is 6 percent (10 − 4), and the sacrifice ratio is 4.

Before the disinflation of the 1980s, economists estimated sacrifice ratios that would apply if a disinflation program were undertaken. Estimates ranged between 5 and 10. The Reagan-Volcker disinflation and recession shocked the economy with high unemployment but succeeded in reducing inflation. Laurence Ball estimates that the sacrifice ratio was 1.83—well below then-existing estimates.[10] The fact that the sacri-

---

[9]See Chap. 7 for more on the sacrifice ratio.

[10]Laurence Ball, "How Costly Is Disinflation? The Historical Evidence," Federal Reserve Bank of Philadelphia *Business Review,* November–December 1993.

the latter view, nor does much of the profession. However, as we noted in Chapter 8, the rational expectations approach to expectations is widely shared. So is the emphasis on the *credibility* of policy makers.

Though the rational expectations approach started influencing macroeconomic theory in the early 1970s, the single most influential article in the macroeconomic policy debate was Thomas Sargent's "The Ends of Four Big Inflations."* In this article, written while the United States was suffering from double-digit inflation, Sargent argued that the major European hyperinflations had, as a result of a *credible* reform of monetary and fiscal policy, ended rapidly and at very little cost in terms of forgone output. By implication, he suggested that the United States could do the same.

Critics of this view argue that it was one thing to end a hyperinflation in an economy that had broken down and another to end an inflation that was just barely in the double digits. In any event, the United States ended its inflation only after the deep recession of 1981–1982. Further research has shown that even the European hyperinflations did not end costlessly.†

All experience suggests that credibility is difficult to earn and difficult to keep and that the structure of contracts that exist in an economy has to be taken into account in analyzing the effects of policy changes. Thus while we do not doubt that credibility is an important aspect of policy making, we believe that its role has been exaggerated by proponents of rational expectations, and we are suspicious of policy arguments in which credibility is the main reason for pursuing a policy that otherwise makes little economic sense.

*In Robert E. Hall (ed.), *Inflation: Causes and Effects* (Chicago: University of Chicago Press, 1982). For a general overview of twentieth-century hyperinflations, see Perre Siklos (ed.), *Great Inflations of the 20th Century* (Brookfield, Vt.: Edgar Elger, 1995), in particular the article by Carlo Vegh, "Stopping High Inflation."

†See Elmus Wicker, "Terminating Hyperinflation in the Dismembered Habsburg Monarchy," *American Economic Review,* June 1986; see also the articles on modern high inflations in Michael Bruno et al. (eds.), *Lessons of Economic Stabilization and Its Aftermath* (Cambridge, Mass.: M.I.T. Press, 1991).

fice ratio was low suggests that the economy benefited from the credible position of the Fed chairman and the president as inflation fighters.

IS THERE A BETTER WAY?

The treatments for the inflation summarized in Figure 19-5 are painful and have led to a search for better ways. The most frequent alternative involves an attempt to control prices and wages directly.

Incomes Policy (or Wage and Price Controls)

Inflation stabilization takes time and involves unemployment because that is what is needed to get the rate of wage change down. *Incomes policies* are policies that attempt to reduce the rate of wage and price increases by direct action. Either wages and prices are controlled by law, or the government tries to persuade labor leaders and businesses to raise wages and prices more slowly than they otherwise would. Incomes policies, if successful, shift the short-run aggregate supply curve down.

Wage and price controls are common in wartime and were also used in the United States in the period 1971–1974. The 1971 controls were imposed in an effort to break the back of an inflation that for 2 years had shown little sign of responding to restrictive monetary and fiscal policies.

As we have seen in Chapters 6 and 18, reducing inflation causes a recession because reductions in inflationary expectations lag behind reductions in actual inflation. In other words, the economy moves along the short-run Phillips curve into higher unemployment. Freezing wages and prices forces companies and workers to act in a sense *as if* they expected low inflation. In other words, the short-run Phillips curve moves down so that low inflation is consistent with full employment. If aggregate demand policy is then made consistent with low inflation, a low-inflation–full-employment equilibrium is *ratified*. It is then possible to remove the wage and price controls without suffering from pent-up inflationary pressures.

A wage-price freeze certainly brings the inflation rate down. So why not get rid of inflation that way? The reason is that wages and prices have to be flexible if resources are to be allocated efficiently in the economy. Anti-inflationary policy has to try to reduce the average rate of price increase without interfering with the role of prices in allocating resources. However, all attempts to control inflation through direct means run into the difficulty that relative wages and prices in the economy do have to change if the price mechanism is to work. Thus these policies cannot be effective except during short transitional periods.

One reason incomes policies have rarely been successful is that governments often fail to implement restrictive aggregate demand policies to accompany them.[11] Wage and price controls can be used successfully when the right monetary and fiscal policy measures are taken. For instance, in 1985, Israel put into place a policy package to reduce the inflation rate from several hundred percent per year to the low double digits. In addition to sharply cutting the budget deficit and tightening credit, the package involved controls on wages and prices. These controls contributed to the success of the disinflation, especially in making a rapid reduction in inflation possible without a big increase in unemployment. At the same time, though, a similar-looking program in Argentina failed when fiscal policy was not kept sufficiently tight.

In summary, price and wage controls can be useful in the short term when they are consistent with monetary and fiscal policies. Attempts to control prices directly, rather than control aggregate demand, are doomed to failure.

19-4

DEFICITS, MONEY GROWTH, AND THE INFLATION TAX

We have seen that a sustained increase in money growth ultimately translates into increased inflation. But that still leaves the question of what determines the money growth rate. A

---

[11]For a careful account of wage and price controls, see Hugh Rockoff, *Drastic Measures: A History of Wage and Price Controls in the United States* (London: Cambridge University Press, 1984).

frequent argument is that money growth is the result of government budget deficits. In this section we examine several possible relationships between the budget deficit and inflation.

THE GOVERNMENT'S BUDGET CONSTRAINT

The federal government as a whole, consisting of the Treasury plus the Fed, can finance its budget deficit in two ways. It can either sell bonds or "print money." The Fed "prints money" when it increases the stock of high-powered money, typically through open market purchases that buy up part of the debt that the Treasury is selling.

The *government budget constraint* is

$$\text{Budget deficit} = \text{sales of bonds} + \text{increase in money base} \qquad (7)$$

There are two types of possible links between budget deficits and money growth. First, in the short run, an increase in the deficit caused by expansionary fiscal policy will tend to raise nominal and real interest rates. If the Fed is targeting interest rates in any way, it may increase the growth rate of money in an attempt to keep the interest rate from rising. Second, the government may deliberately be increasing the stock of money as a means of obtaining government revenue over the long term.

We examine first the short-run links between money and deficits that come from central bank policy and then the use of money printing as a means of financing government budgets. Finally, we link the short- and long-run aspects.

THE FED'S DILEMMA

The Fed is said to *monetize* deficits whenever it purchases a part of the debt sold by the Treasury to finance the deficit. In the United States the monetary authorities enjoy independence from the Treasury and therefore can choose whether to monetize or not.[12]

The Fed faces a dilemma in deciding whether to monetize a deficit. If it does not finance the deficit, the fiscal expansion, not being accompanied by accommodating monetary policy, raises interest rates and thus crowds out private expenditure. There is accordingly a temptation for the Fed to prevent crowding out by buying securities, thereby increasing the money supply and hence allowing an expansion in income without a rise in interest rates.

But such a policy of accommodation, or *monetization,* runs a risk. If the economy is near full employment, the monetization feeds inflation. Often the Fed should *not* accommodate; that is, it should let the interest rate increase and keep the growth rate of money constant. An unwise fiscal expansion would be made even more potent by fueling it with a monetary expansion.

There are other circumstances, though, in which the risks of igniting inflation are much more remote. Certainly in a deep recession there is no reason to shy away from accommodating a fiscal expansion with higher money growth.

In any particular case, the Fed has to judge whether to pursue an accommodating monetary policy or whether to stay with an unchanged monetary target or even offset

---

[12]In other countries the central bank may enjoy much less independence; for instance, it might be under the control of the Treasury, and then it may simply be ordered to finance part or all of the deficit by creating high-powered money. It is noteworthy that the Maastricht Accord strictly prohibits the new European central bank from financing government deficits.

a fiscal expansion by a tightening of monetary policy. To make that decision, the Fed must decide what relative weight it attaches to inflation and to unemployment whenever expansionary policy threatens to cause inflation.

THE U.S. EVIDENCE

A number of studies have tried to determine how the Fed reacts to deficits in practice. The question here is whether there is a systematic link between monetary policy and the budget. Specifically, does the Fed allow money growth to rise when the budget deficit increases.

Figure 19-6 shows a scatter diagram of the change in the growth rate of the monetary base and the change in the budget deficit (expressed as a percent of GDP).[13] There is no notable pattern of accommodation.

More sophisticated empirical work provides some evidence that the Fed does react in the direction of accommodation, monetizing deficits at least in part. But the evidence is not conclusive because it is difficult to know whether the Fed is reacting to

[13]The monetary base is the relevant aggregate because the deficit can be financed either by the sale of bonds or by the creation of high-powered money (or monetary base).

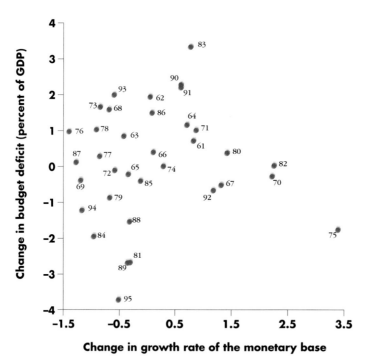

FIGURE 19-6   CHANGE IN MONEY GROWTH AND CHANGE IN THE BUDGET DEFICIT, 1960–1995.

The budget deficit is expressed as a percent of GDP.
(Source: DRI/McGraw-Hill Macroeconomic Database.)

the deficit itself or to other macroeconomic variables, specifically unemployment and the rate of inflation.[14]

THE INFLATION TAX

In discussing monetization of deficits in the United States, we paid no attention to the fact that financing government spending through the creation of high-powered money is an alternative to explicit taxation. For the United States, and for most of the industrialized economies, the creation of high-powered money is a fairly minor source of revenue. Other governments can—and some do—obtain significant amounts of resources year after year by printing money, that is, by increasing high-powered money. This source of revenue is sometimes known as *seigniorage,* which is the government's ability to raise revenue through its right to create money.

When the government finances a deficit by creating money, it in effect keeps printing money, period after period, which it uses to pay for the goods and services it buys. This money is absorbed by the public. But why would the public choose to increase its holdings of nominal money balances period after period?

The only reason, real income growth aside, for the public's adding to its holdings of nominal money balances would be to offset the effects of inflation. Assuming there is no real income growth, in the long run the public will hold a constant level of *real* balances. But if prices are rising, the purchasing power of a given stock of *nominal* balances is falling. To maintain the real value of its money balances constant, the public has to be adding to its stock of nominal balances at a rate that will exactly offset the effects of inflation.

When the public is adding to its stock of nominal balances in order to offset the effects of inflation on holdings of real balances, it is using part of its income to increase holdings of nominal money. Suppose a person has to add, say, $300 to a bank account just to maintain the real value of his or her money holdings. That $300 is not available for spending. The person seems to be saving $300 in the form of money holdings, but in fact all that person is doing is preventing his or her wealth from decreasing as a result of inflation.

Inflation acts just like a tax because people are forced to spend less than their income and pay the difference to the government in exchange for extra money.[15] The government thus can spend more resources, and the public less, just as if the government had raised taxes to finance extra spending. When the government finances its deficit by issuing money, which the public adds to its holdings of nominal balances to

---

[14]See Alan Blinder, "On the Monetization of Deficits," in Laurence Meyer, *The Economic Consequences of Government Deficits* (Norwell, Mass.: Kluwer-Hijhoff, 1983); Gerald Dwyer, "Federal Deficits, Interest Rates and Monetary Policy," *Journal of Money, Credit and Banking,* November 1985; and Douglas Joines, "Deficits and Money Growth in the United States: 1872–1983," *Journal of Monetary Economics,* November 1985.

[15]There is one complication in this analysis. As noted above, the amount that is received by the government is the increase in the stock of *high-powered* money, because the Fed is buying Treasury debt with high-powered money. But the public is increasing its holdings of both bank deposits and currency, and thus part of the increase in the public's holdings of money does not go to the government to finance the deficit. This complication in no way changes the essence of the analysis.

BOX 19-3 Real Balances and Inflation

A sustained increase in money growth and in inflation ultimately leads to a reduction in the real money stock.

Here is a very important result that might seem a bit puzzling: Increased *nominal* money growth reduces the long-run *real* money stock. Conversely, reduced nominal money growth raises the long-run real money stock. The reason is that higher inflation raises the nominal interest rate and hence raises the opportunity cost of holding money. Hence money holders will reduce the amount of real balances they choose to hold. This reduction in real balances is an important part of the adjustment process to an increase in money growth. It means that, on average, in the period of adjustment to an increase in money growth, prices must rise faster than money.

Higher money growth means higher inflation in the long run, and therefore higher interest rates and lower real money balances, $\overline{M}/P$. For $\overline{M}/P$ to drop, P must at some point grow faster than M grows. During this transition, inflation is higher than the long-run inflation rate. Empirically, this extra "transitional" inflation can be quite high.

maintain the real value of money balances constant, we say the government is financing itself through the *inflation tax.*[16]

How much revenue can the government collect through the inflation tax? The amount of revenue produced is the product of the tax rate (the inflation rate) and the object of taxation (the real monetary base):

[16]Inflation is often referred to as the "cruelest tax." This refers not to the above analysis of the inflation tax but, rather, to the redistribution of wealth and income associated particularly with unanticipated inflation, which was discussed in Chap. 7.

TABLE 19-5   Inflation and Inflation Tax, 1983–1988
(Percent)

	AVERAGE 1983–1988		
COUNTRY	INFLATION TAX, % OF GDP	ANNUAL INFLATION RATE	PEAK-YEAR INFLATION TAX, % OF GDP
Argentina	3.7	359	5.2
Bolivia	3.5	1,797	7.2
Brazil	3.5	341	4.3
Chile	.9	21	1.1
Colombia	1.9	22	2.0
Mexico	2.6	87	3.5
Peru	4.7	382	4.5

Source: M. Selowsky, "Preconditions Necessary for the Recovery of Latin America's Growth," World Bank, June 1989 (mimeographed).

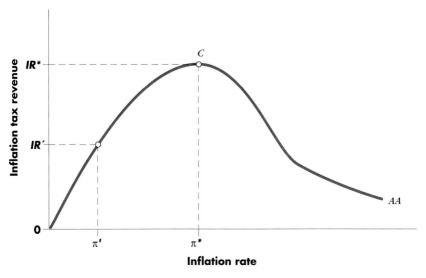

FIGURE 19-7 THE INFLATION TAX.

$$\text{Inflation tax revenue} = \text{inflation rate} \times \text{real money base} \qquad (8)$$

Table 19-5 shows data on the inflation tax for Latin American countries in the 1983–1988 period.[17] Clearly the amounts are very significant, as are the inflation rates at which these amounts of revenue are obtained by the government.

The amount of revenue the government can raise through the inflation tax is shown by curve AA in Figure 19-7. When the inflation rate is zero, the government gets no revenue from inflation.[18] As the inflation rate rises, the amount of inflation tax received by the government increases. But, of course, as the inflation rate rises, people reduce their real holdings of the money base—because the base is becoming increasingly costly to hold. Individuals hold less currency, and banks hold as few excess reserves as possible. Eventually the real monetary base falls so much that the total amount of inflation tax revenue received by the government falls. That starts to happen at point C and signifies that there is a maximum amount of revenue the government can raise through the inflation tax; the maximum is shown as amount IR^* in the figure. There is a corresponding inflation rate, denoted π^*: the inflation rate at which the inflation tax is at its maximum.[19]

---

[17]Hyperinflation has been a frequent plague for much of Latin America. For more information on both the monetary and real sides of Latin American economies, see Eliana Cardoso and Ann Helwege, *Latin America's Economy: Diversity, Trends, and Conflicts* (Cambridge, Mass.: M.I.T. Press, 1995).

[18]When the economy is growing, the government obtains some revenue from seigniorage even if there is no inflation. That is because when the demand for the real monetary base is growing, the government can create some base without producing inflation.

[19]Miguel A. Keguel and Pablo Andres Neumeyer, in "Seigniorage and Inflation: The Case of Argentina," *Journal of Money, Credit and Banking,* August 1995, consider whether Argentina went past the revenue-maximizing point in the 1980s. They estimate that the revenue-maximizing inflation rate was in the range of 20 to 30 percent per month. With the exception of spring 1989, inflation in Argentina was generally below these levels.

Suppose that in Figure 19 7, the economy is initially in a situation where there is no deficit and no printing of money. Inflation is zero and the economy is at point 0 in the figure. Now the government cuts taxes and finances the deficit by printing money. We assume that the deficit is equal to amount IR' in Figure 19-7, and thus it can be financed entirely through the inflation tax. Money growth is permanently increased, and inflation in the long run moves to the rate π', corresponding to the inflation tax revenue IR'.

It is clear from Figure 19-7 that the more revenue the government wishes to raise through the inflation tax, the higher the inflation rate must be—as long as the economy is on the rising part of the curve. The figure raises the question of what happens if the government tries to finance a deficit larger than IR^* by printing money. That cannot be done. We take up that issue in Section 19-5, on hyperinflation.

INFLATION TAX REVENUE

The amounts of inflation tax revenue obtained in the high-inflation developing countries in Table 19-5 are very large. In the more industrialized economies, in which the real money base is small relative to the size of the economy, the government obtains only small amounts of inflation tax revenue. For instance, in the United States the base is about 6 percent of GDP. At a 5 percent inflation rate the government would, from equation (8), be collecting about .3 percent of GDP in inflation tax revenue. That is not a trivial amount, but it is not a major source of government revenue either.[20] It is hard to believe that the inflation rate in the United States is set with the revenue aspects of inflation as the main criterion. Rather, the Fed and the administration choose policies to influence the inflation rate on the basis of an analysis of the costs and benefits of inflation, along the lines presented in Chapter 7.

In countries in which the banking system is less developed and in which people therefore hold large amounts of currency, the government obtains more revenue from inflation and is more likely to give much weight to the revenue aspects of inflation in setting policy. And, as we will see in the next section, under conditions of high inflation in which the conventional tax system breaks down, the inflation tax revenue may be the government's last resort to keep paying its bills. But whenever the inflation tax is used on a large scale, inflation invariably becomes extreme.

19-5

HYPERINFLATION

Large budget deficits were inevitably part of the extreme inflations of 50 to 100 to 500 percent per year that took place in the mid-1980s in Latin America and Israel. They are also part of the even more extreme cases of *hyperinflation*. Although there is no

---

[20]A measure of seigniorage different from the value of the printing of high-powered money is sometimes used in the United States. It is the value of the interest payments the Fed earns on its portfolio. Since the Fed's securities were obtained through open market purchases that increased the high-powered money stock, this is a measure of how much interest the Treasury saves (since the Fed pays its profits to the Treasury) as a result of *previous* Fed money printing. The printing of high-powered money is a measure of the current command over resources obtained as a result of money printing this period.

precise definition of the rate of inflation that deserves the star ranking of "hyperinflation" rather than "high inflation," a working definition is that a country is in hyperinflation when its annual inflation rate reaches 1,000 percent per annum.[21] Table 19-6 shows recent extreme inflation experiences.[22] Note that in the 1990s many Latin American countries successfully stabilized the inflation rate at nonhyperinflationary levels. In contrast, several of the countries emerging out of the former Eastern bloc saw very high rates of inflation.

It seems difficult to believe that countries can function for any length of time with inflation rates of several hundred percent or more. In fact, they do not function well, and sooner or later they will stabilize a high inflation simply because the economy turns chaotic. Thus, Israel successfully stabilized in 1985, as did Bolivia (see Box 19-4). However, such experiences do not seem to prevent other countries from entering hyperinflations.[23]

In a hyperinflationary economy, inflation is so pervasive and such a problem that it completely dominates daily economic life. People spend significant amounts of resources minimizing the inflationary damage. They have to shop often so as to get to the stores before the prices go up; their main concern in saving or investing is how to protect themselves against inflation; they reduce holdings of real balances to a remarkable extent to avoid the inflation tax but have to compensate by going to the bank more often—daily or hourly instead of weekly, for example,—to get currency. Wages are paid very often—at the end of the German hyperinflation, several times a day.

---

[21]When inflation becomes very high, it is reckoned in terms of *monthly* rates, not inflation per year. The power of compound interest is apparent when we look at the correspondence between monthly inflation rates and the same rate annualized. For example, a 20 percent inflation per month corresponds to an annualized rate of 791 percent.

[22]Hyperinflation is not a contemporary invention. Extreme experience with inflation can be found in history. See Edwin Seligman, *Currency Inflation and Public Debts: An Historical Sketch* (New York: Equitable Trust Company, 1921). There was a wave in the 1920s, notably in Austria, Hungary, Germany, and Poland, and again in the 1940s. The most famous experience is that in Germany in the 1920s; see Steven Webb, *Hyperinflation and Stabilization in Weimar Germany* (Oxford, England: Oxford University Press, 1989.)

[23]The classic hyperinflations have taken place in the aftermath of wars or the breakup of empires. The most famous of all—though not the most rapid—was the German hyperinflation of 1922–1923. The average inflation rate during the hyperinflation was 322 percent *per month*. The highest rate of inflation was in October 1923, just before the end of the hyperinflation, when prices rose by over 29,000 percent. In dollars that means that something that cost $1 at the beginning of the month would have cost $290 at the end of the month. The most rapid hyperinflation was that in Hungary at the end of World War II: The *average* rate of inflation from August 1945 to July 1946 was 19,800 percent per month, and the maximum monthly rate was 41.9 quadrillion percent. (At least, so we think. The price level rose 41.9×10^{15} percent in July 1946.) Data are from Phillip Cagan, "The Monetary Dynamics of Hyperinflation," in Milton Friedman (ed.), *Studies in the Quantity Theory of Money* (Chicago: University of Chicago Press, 1956). This classic paper contains data on seven hyperinflations. For additional historical perspective, see Forrest H. Capie (ed.), *Major Inflations in History* (Brookfield, VT.: Edgar Elger, 1991).

Keynes, in a masterful description of the hyperinflation process in Austria after World War II, tells of how people would order two beers at a time because the beer grew stale at a rate slower than that at which the price was rising. [See John Maynard Keynes, *A Tract on Monetary Reform* (New York: Macmillan, 1923), which remains one of the most readable accounts of inflation.] The story is also told of a woman who carried her (almost worthless) currency in a basket and found that when she set it down for a moment, the basket was stolen but the money left behind.

BOX 19-4 Bolivian Hyperinflation and Stabilization

In the 1920s, Europe experienced hyperinflation, and the experience is reviewed in an important paper by Thomas Sargent.* Latin America followed in the 1980s. In 1985 Bolivia experienced a full-fledged hyperinflation, as can be seen in Figure 1. At the peak, in mid-1985, inflation was, at an annual rate, 35,000 percent!

There were three main reasons for the Bolivian hyperinflation. First, like other Latin American countries, Bolivia had overborrowed in the 1970s. When, in the early 1980s, interest rates increased in world markets, it could no longer service its debt by taking out new loans for the purpose of paying the interest on the old loans. But without borrowing, the country did not have the budgetary resources to service the debt. The attempt to do so strained the budget and led to high rates of money creation. Second, commodity prices, especially of tin, fell sharply. For Bolivia this meant a large fall in real income and in revenues for the government. Third, substantial political instability led to capital flight. The combination of factors set off an inflationary spiral that forced increasing depreciation of

*See Thomas Sargent, "The End of Four Big Inflations," in R. Hall (ed.), *Inflation* (Chicago: University of Chicago Press, 1982).

FIGURE 1   BOLIVIAN HYPERINFLATION, 1984–1988.

(Source: Banco Central de Bolivia.)

TABLE 1   The Bolivian Hyperinflation

	1980–1983	1984	1985	1986
Budget deficit*	11.9	26.5	10.8	3.0
Tax collection†	6.7	2.3	3.1	6.6
Inflation	123.0	1,282.0	11,750.0	276.0

*Percent of GDP.

†Percent per year.

Source: World Bank and Banco Central de Bolivia.

the currency and opened an ever-wider gap between government outlays and revenues. Tax collection sharply dropped by more than half, as can be seen in Table 1.

By 1984–1985 the government was attempting to finance nearly 25 percent of GNP with money creation. But, of course, by this time the demand for real balances had fallen to negligible levels because of the hyperinflation. It took ever-larger rates of inflation to finance the ever-growing deficit.

In August–September 1985 a new government came into power and, in a short time, imposed a drastic stabilization plan. By stopping external debt service and raising taxes, the drain in the budget was brought under control; money creation was reduced from the extreme rates of the past years; and the exchange rate was stabilized. Within half a year the inflation rate had come down to less than 50 percent. Moreover, because the decrease in the budget deficit was maintained and reinforced, the gain in disinflation continued; by 1989, inflation rates had fallen to less than 10 percent per year.

The Bolivian stabilization is a good example of how a sharp turn toward fiscal stabilization can stop a major inflation.† But there should be no illusion about the costs. As a result of austerity (and of poor export prices), Bolivian per capita income in 1989 was 35 percent less than it had been 10 years earlier, at its peak. Inflation had been brought under control, but confidence was not sufficient to bring back growth on a significant scale.

While Bolivia succeeded in controlling inflation, inflation was exploding in several other Latin American countries. An important question for these countries was whether *heterodox* programs, combining wage-price controls with the *orthodox* medicine of fiscal austerity, would reduce the costs of stabilization. The stabilization attempts, undertaken several times in 1985–1989 in Argentina and Brazil, were long on price controls and short on fiscal contraction. As might have been predicted, wage-price controls without fiscal and monetary reform were ineffective.‡

†See Juan A. Morales, "Inflation Stabilization in Bolivia," in M. Bruno et al. (eds.), *Inflation Stabilization* (Cambridge, Mass.: M.I.T. Press, 1988), and J. Sachs, "The Bolivian Hyperinflation and Stabilization," *American Economic Review,* May 1987.

‡See E. Helpman and L. Leiderman, "Stabilization in High Inflation Countries: Analytical Foundations of Recent Experience," *Carnegie-Rochester Conference Series on Public Policy* 28 (1988); M. Kiguel and N. Liviatan, "Inflationary Rigidities and Orthodox Stabilization Policies: Lessons from Latin America," *The World Bank Economic Review* 3 (1988); M. Blejer and N. Liviatan, "Fighting Hyperinflation," *IMF Staff Papers,* September 1987; and Bruno et al. (eds.), *Lessons from Stabilization and Its Aftermath* (Cambridge, Mass.: M.I.T. Press, 1991).

TABLE 19-6   Recent High-Inflation Experiences
(Percent per year)

	1985	1986	1987	1988	1989	1990	1991	1992	1993	1994	1995
Argentina	672	90	131	343	3,080	2,314	172	25	11	4	3
Bolivia	11,750	276	15	16	15	17	21	12	9	8	10
Brazil	227	145	230	682	1,287	2,938	441	1,009	2,148	2,669	84
Czech Republic	—	—	—	—	—	—	—	—	210	232	253
Israel	305	48	20	16	20	17	19	12	11	12	10
Mexico	58	86	132	114	20	27	23	16	10	7	35
Nicaragua	220	681	912	10,205	4,770	7,485	2,945	24	20	8	11
Peru	163	78	86	667	3,399	7,482	410	74	49	24	11
Russia	—	—	—	—	—	—	—	—	875	307	236
Ukraine	—	—	—	—	—	—	—	—	4,735	891	377

Source: International Financial Statistics, 1996.

DEFICITS AND HYPERINFLATION

The hyperinflationary economies all suffered from large budget deficits. In several cases the origin of the budget deficit was wartime spending, which generated large national debts and also destroyed the tax-gathering apparatus of the country.

But there is a two-way interaction between budget deficits and inflation. Large budget deficits can lead to rapid inflation by causing governments to print money to finance the deficit. In turn, high inflation increases the measured deficit. There are two main mechanisms through which inflation increases budget deficits: tax collection effects and increases in nominal payments on the national debt.

As the inflation rate rises, the real revenue raised from taxation falls. The reason is that there are lags in both the calculation and payment of taxes. Suppose, to take an extreme example, that people pay taxes on April 15 on the income they earned the previous year. Consider someone who earned $50,000 last year and has a tax bill of $10,000 due on April 15. If prices have in the meantime gone up by a factor of 10, as they might in hyperinflation, the real value of the taxes is only one-tenth of what it should be. The budget deficit can rapidly get out of hand.[24]

The measured budget deficit includes the interest payments on the national debt. Since the nominal interest rate tends to rise when inflation increases, higher inflation generally increases the *nominal* interest payments that are made by the government, and the measured deficit therefore increases. Accordingly, economists in high-inflation countries often calculate the *inflation-adjusted deficit:*

Inflation-adjusted deficit = total deficit − (inflation rate × national debt)   (9)

The inflation adjustment removes that component of interest payments on the debt that is attributed directly to inflation, and gives a more accurate picture of what the budget situation would be at a very low inflation rate than does the actual deficit.

---

[24]This impact of inflation on the real value of tax revenues is called the *Tanzi-Olivera effect,* so named after two economists who independently documented it, Vito Tanzi of the IMF and Julio Olivera of the University of Buenos Aires.

STOPPING HYPERINFLATIONS

All hyperinflations come to an end. The dislocation of the economy becomes too great for the public to bear, and the government finds a way of reforming its budget process. Often a new money is introduced, and the tax system is reformed. Typically, too, the exchange rate of the new money is pegged to that of a foreign currency in order to provide an anchor for prices and expectations. Frequently, there are unsuccessful attempts at stabilization before the final success.

The presence of so many destabilizing factors in inflation, particularly the collapse of the tax system as the inflation proceeds, together with an economy that is extremely dislocated by inflation, raises the fascinating possibility that a coordinated attack on inflation may stop the inflation with relatively little unemployment cost. Monetary, fiscal, and exchange rate policies are combined with incomes policies in this *heterodox approach* to stabilization. This approach was used in Argentina and Israel in 1985 and in Brazil in 1986, when the governments froze wages and prices. That stopped the inflation at a single blow.

The Israeli stabilization succeeded, while the Argentinean and Brazilian did not. The difference, as noted above, was fiscal policy. The Israelis corrected their fiscal deficit, whereas the two others did not. Wage and price controls alone cannot keep inflation in check if the underlying fundamentals of fiscal and monetary policy are not consistent with low inflation.[25]

SUMMARY

1. A monetary expansion typically expands output in the short run. In the long run sustained higher money growth is translated fully into inflation.

2. A sustained change in money growth ultimately raises the nominal interest rate by the same amount. This positive association between inflation and nominal interest rates is called the Fisher effect.

3. A sustained monetary expansion ultimately raises nominal interest rates and hence reduces the demand for real balances. That means that prices must on average rise faster than money in the transition to the new long-run equilibrium.

4. In the U.S. economy, broad trends in money growth and in inflation do coincide. Money growth does affect inflation, but the effects occur with a lag that is not very precise. In the short term, inflation is affected by other than monetary shocks, for example, fiscal policy changes and supply shocks.

5. Nominal interest rates tend to reflect the rate of inflation in the U.S. economy. But the real interest rate is definitely not constant. In the early 1980s the real rate increased sharply compared with the levels of the 1970s and long-term average rates.

6. When fiscal policy turns expansionary, the Fed has to decide whether to monetize the deficit, printing money in order to prevent a rise in interest rates and crowding

---

[25]One more important feature of the stabilizations should be brought out. *Money growth rates following stabilization are very high.* Why? Because as people expect less inflation, nominal interest rates decline and the demand for real balances rises. With the demand for real balances increasing, the government can create more money without creating inflation. Thus at the beginning of a successful stabilization there may be a bonus for the government: it can temporarily finance part of the deficit through the printing of money, without renewing inflation. But it certainly cannot do so for very long periods without reigniting inflation.

out; to keep the growth rate of money constant; or even to tighten monetary policy. If the government monetizes the deficit, it runs the risk of increasing the inflation rate. The evidence on deficit monetization in the United States remains ambiguous.

7. Inflation is a tax on real balances. To keep constant the purchasing power of holdings of money in the face of rising prices, a person has to add to nominal balances. In this fashion resources are transferred from money holders to money issuers, specifically the government.

8. Hyperinflations have generally taken place in the aftermath of wars. Large budget deficits are typical in hyperinflations. Governments can use the inflation tax to finance deficits to a limited extent, but if too large a deficit has to be financed, inflation explodes.

9. There is a two-way interaction between inflation and budget deficits. Higher deficits tend to cause higher inflation, since they are typically financed in part by money printing. As well, higher inflation causes higher deficits, by reducing the real value of tax collection. Higher nominal interest rates raise the measured deficit by increasing the value of nominal interest payments in the budget. The inflation-corrected deficit adjusts for this effect.

10. Money growth rates are very high following a successful inflation stabilization, as people increase their holdings of real balances.

KEY TERMS

Fisher effect	inflationary inertia	seigniorage
quantity theory of money	sacrifice ratio	inflation tax
velocity of money	rational expectations school	hyperinflation
gradualism	incomes policies	inflation-adjusted deficit
cold-turkey strategy	government budget	heterodox approach to
credible policy	constraint	stabilization
credibility bonus	monetization	

PROBLEMS

Conceptual

1. Is inflation a monetary phenomenon? Be sure to distinguish, in your answer, between the long run and the short run.

2. **a.** Evaluate the strengths and weaknesses of gradual versus cold-turkey strategies of inflation reduction.

    b. Why is the credibility of anti-inflationary policy important?

3. How does the presence of long-term contracts hamper our ability to quickly and costlessly reduce inflation?

4. **a.** Can wage and price controls be an effective strategy for stabilizing a hyperinflation? Explain.

    b. Are there side effects of employing such a strategy that might be troublesome in themselves? Discuss.

5. Are budget deficits a problem? Why or why not?

6. When should, and shouldn't, the Fed monetize deficits?

7. How do the monetarist and rational expectations schools of thought differ in their beliefs regarding the short-term effects of monetary policy?
8. How can inflation create government revenue?
9. At the height of the German hyperinflation, the government was covering only 1 percent of its spending with taxes.
   a. How could the German government have financed the remaining 99 percent of its spending?
   b. Explain how, after the end of hyperinflation, it was possible for the nominal money stock in Germany to increase by a factor of nearly 20 without restarting the inflation.
*10. The classic hyperinflations have occurred in the aftermath of wars or major social upheavals. What factors lay behind the high rates of Russian inflation in the early 1990s? (For more information regarding events in Russia during this period, see the section "Reform and Growth in Eastern Europe" in Chapter 4.)

Technical

1. a. Show graphically the effects of a reduction in the growth rate of money on output and inflation.
   b. Show also how the real interest rate adjusts over time.
2. Suppose the money base is 10 percent of GDP. Suppose also that the government is considering raising the inflation rate from 0 to 10 percent per annum and believes that doing so will increase government revenue by 1 percent of GDP. Explain why the government must be overestimating the revenue it will receive from the resulting inflation tax.
3. Calculate the inflation-adjusted deficit when the national debt is 30 percent of GDP, the inflation rate is 7 percent per annum, and the total budget deficit is 4 percent of GDP.

*An asterisk denotes a more difficult problem.

TABLE 19-7

	MONEY GROWTH, %*	OUTPUT GROWTH, %†	INFLATION, %†
1870–1879	2.3	5.5	−3.0
1880–1889	6.6	1.4	−1.1
1890–1899	5.0	3.7	−2.2
1900–1909	7.3	4.0	1.9
1910–1919	9.8	3.5	6.6
1920–1929	3.3	4.2	2.2
1930–1939	.8	1.5	−1.9
1940–1949	11.5	3.4	5.6
1950–1959	3.8	3.3	2.5
1960–1969	7.1	4.0	2.7
1970–1979	9.8	2.8	7.1
1980–1989	8.0	2.6	5.4

*Money refers to M2.

†Inflation refers to the GNP deflator.

Source: Data for 1870 to 1959 are from Milton Friedman and Anna Schwartz, *Monetary Trends in the United States and the United Kingdom* (Chicago: University of Chicago Press, 1982); data for 1960 to 1989 are from DRI/McGraw Hill.

TABLE 19-8

	NOMINAL INTEREST RATE, %*	INFLATION RATE, %†
Argentina	86.5‡	92.3
Brazil	690.0§	468.4
Canada	7.4	5.6
Finland	13.1	4.1
Germany	8.8	3.5
Italy	12.2	6.4
Mexico	19.3	22.7
United Kingdom	11.8	5.9
United States	5.7	4.3

*Interest rates are 1991 short-term market rates.

†The inflation rate is for the CPI, from December 1990 through December 1991.

‡Average of deposit and lending rates.

§Rate on savings deposits.

Source: International Financial Statistics, various issues.

4. Table 19-7 shows the growth rate of *M2*, the rate of inflation, and the rate of growth in output for the United States in decade averages, starting with the 1870s. Discuss the extent to which money growth, adjusted for output growth, helps explain inflation in recent U.S. history. (*Note:* This question is discussed briefly in Section 19-2.)

5. Calculate real interest rates for the countries in Table 19-8. How might you explain the difference in real interest rates across countries? Remember that these are open economies where investors are concerned about returns in a common currency.

CHAPTER 20

Budget Deficits and the Public Debt

CHAPTER HIGHLIGHTS

◆ Since the 1980s, the United States has run large budget deficits of a magnitude unprecedented during peacetime.

◆ According to one school of thought, deficits do not burden future generations because an increased deficit is offset by increased saving by current generations.

◆ The future of the social security system has become a major economic issue around the world. There are important questions of both intergenerational equity and economic efficiency.

During the 1980s, the United States experienced the largest sustained budget deficits in its peacetime history. Although politicians regularly made fine speeches about the need to reduce the deficit, cutting spending or raising taxes was not politically popular. Gradually, in the 1990s, the deficit began to be brought under control, and towards the end of the decade Congress and the president agreed that the budget should be balanced by the early part of the next century.

In Europe, members of the European Union have agreed that countries must cut budget deficits below 3 percent of GDP as one of the criteria for joining the common currency (the euro) area planned for 1999. Reaching this deficit target has been difficult for almost every European country. In 1997, the pressure was on for countries to cut deficits, if necessary using accounting tricks to make it under the 3 percent wire.

In this chapter we discuss the role of government debt and deficits in the economy.[1] We begin by looking at the facts about the federal debt. We ask how budget deficits are measured and whether the national debt is a burden on the public. We conclude with a brief examination of the social security system—a major source of intergenerational transfers—a current "hot-button" topic in many industrialized countries.

Several important issues in this discussion center on a surprising question: Does it make any difference whether the government pays for its expenditures by raising taxes or by issuing debt? Classical economists emphasize the *Barro-Ricardo* view, which holds that, since borrowing today means higher future taxes to service the debt, there is no fundamental difference between tax (current taxes) and debt (future taxes) financing of deficits. We will discuss that view, which stands in sharp contrast to the argument made in earlier chapters that the size of the deficit does matter—tax increases lower aggregate demand and spending increases raise aggregate demand.

We start with an overview of federal public finances.

20-1

FEDERAL GOVERNMENT FINANCES: FACTS AND ISSUES

In this section we review the facts about the composition of and trends in U.S. government spending and revenues, the deficit and the public debt. Historically, the United States ran large deficits during wartime and slowly paid off the deficits while at peace.

As Figure 20-1 shows, for two decades the United States has run deficits regularly. The main question is, Why did the U.S. deficit reach such high levels?

OUTLAYS

Table 20-1 shows the outlays of the federal government since 1960. The table introduces some special terminology. There is a distinction between *mandatory* and *discretionary* outlays. The former are outlays that are made under *entitlement programs,* for which the law specifies that a person meeting certain requirements is automatically entitled to receive payments. Examples of entitlement programs are Medicaid and so-

---

[1]Discuss explicitly, that is. Of course, much of our study of government policy has had implications for the deficit. For a recent article tying the deficit to other macroeconomic questions, see Laurence Ball and N. Gregory Mankiw, "What Do Budget Deficits Do?" NBER Working Paper 5263, September 1995.

FIGURE 20-1   U.S. BUDGET DEFICITS WITH AND WITHOUT INTEREST PAID ON THE DEBT, 1960–1996.

(Source: DRI/McGraw Hill-Macroeconomic Database.)

cial security. Discretionary spending, by contrast, is governed by the congressional appropriation process and includes, for example, defense expenditures and foreign aid.

Three points stand out in Table 20-1. First, defense expenditures have declined significantly as a fraction of GDP. Second, entitlement programs have nearly doubled. Third, interest payments by the government have become an important part of government outlays. The share of federal interest payments in GDP has nearly tripled over the past 30 years.

TABLE 20-1   Federal Government Outlays
(Percent of GDP; fiscal years; period average)

	1962–1969	1970–1979	1980–1989	1990–1995
National defense	8.6	5.9	5.8	4.7
Entitlements and other mandatory spending	6.3	9.5	10.8	11.3
Nondefense discretionary spending	3.9	4.5	4.1	3.8
Net interest	1.3	1.5	2.8	3.2
Total outlays*	18.8	20.1	22.3	21.9

*Column totals do not match total outlays because "offsetting receipts" and deposit insurance figures are excluded.

Source: Congressional Budget Office, *The Economic and Budget Outlook,* July 1996.

TABLE 20-2   Sources of Federal Revenue
(Percent of GDP; fiscal years; period average)

	1960–1969	1970–1979	1980–1989	1990–1995
Individual income tax	7.8	8.2	8.5	8.0
Corporate income tax	3.8	2.7	1.7	1.8
Social insurance taxes and contributions	3.5	5.0	6.4	6.7
Other*	2.8	2.1	1.8	1.6
Total revenue	17.9	18.0	18.4	18.2

*Includes excise (sales) taxes, estate and gift taxes, customs duties, and miscellaneous receipts.

Source: Congressional Budget Office, *The Economic and Budget Outlook,* July 1996.

Government spending consists of *purchases* of goods and services and *transfer payments.*[2] By the mid-1990s only one-third of federal government outlays (less than 10 percent of GDP) represented spending on goods and services, while transfer payments accounted for two-thirds.

RECEIPTS

Most of the federal government's revenues come from taxes. The sources of revenue and the total are shown in Table 20-2. The revenue sources are self-explanatory, except perhaps for social insurance taxes. These are taxes on wages paid by employers and by wage earners.

Total federal government revenue as a share of GDP has changed very little over the past 30 years. However, there has been a shift in the sources of revenue. Social security taxes and contributions have become a substantially higher source of revenue, corporate income taxes have declined by more than half, and personal income taxes have remained mostly unchanged.

THE BUSINESS CYCLE AND DEFICITS

The distinction between the actual and the *structural* deficit is widely used. The *structural* deficit, or the *full-employment* or *high-employment* or *cyclically adjusted* deficit, is the level at which the deficit would be if output were at its full-employment level. The *cyclical* deficit is the difference between the actual and the structural deficit.

If the budget were, on average, balanced over long periods, we would expect budget deficits in recessions and surpluses in boom years because tax collections rise and fall with economic output. That used to be the case, but there has been a gradual increase in the structural deficit over time. Now there are large deficits even at business cycle peaks. Indeed, the cyclically adjusted budget was last balanced in 1963.

---

[2]Purchases are a component of aggregate demand—the G term in $Y = C + I + G$—whereas transfer payments affect aggregate demand indirectly, via changes in disposable income.

MEASURING THE DEFICIT

Government Assets

The U.S. government traditionally kept its books in a most bizarre fashion. It measured the deficit by simply subtracting current revenues from current spending, as if the government had heard neither of capital acquisition nor of depreciation. So in the years that Grand Coulee Dam was built, the government added the construction cost to those years' deficits.[3] It is important to recognize that the government has assets as well as debts. The real capital—Grand Coulee Dam—acquired by the government should be treated as an offset against the debt issued to pay for its construction.

The United States has recently started to track government investment and depreciation of government assets. Including government investment raises estimates of total investment from about 15 to about 18 percent of GDP. Government expenditure is now split into "government investment" and "government consumption expenditures." This long-awaited revision has changed measures of the budget deficit by as much as $30 billion.

In public discussions it is often forgotten that government spending is not all consumption or transfers. Robert Eisner of Northwestern University has strongly emphasized this point in presenting government balance sheets in which both government debts and assets are listed.[4] For example, in 1990 the federal government owned reproducible assets (valued at replacement cost) of $834 billion but had debts of $2,687 billion. Thus the government had a net debt of $1,853 billion, far less than the size the official debt numbers would suggest. If additional adjustment were made for holdings of land, the net debtor position would be even far lower.[5] However, these adjustments do not change the conclusion that the deficit is relatively larger today than in the past.

Interest Payments versus the Primary Deficit

Measuring the federal deficit is complicated by the fact that most of the deficit can be accounted for by interest payments on the national debt. So most of the deficit represents not the excess of current spending over revenues but the legacy of past deficits. We distinguish between two components of the budget deficit: the *primary,* or *noninterest, deficit* and interest payments on the public debt:

$$\text{Total deficit} \equiv \text{primary deficit} + \text{interest payments} \tag{1}$$

The primary deficit (or surplus) represents all government outlays, except interest payments, minus all government revenue. The primary deficit is also called the noninterest deficit.

[3]*Economic Report of the President,* February 1996, Box 2-3; "Preview of the Comprehensive Revision of the National Income and Product Accounts: Recognition of Government Investment and Incorporation of a New Methodology for Calculating Depreciation," *Survey of Current Business,* September 1995; "Improved Estimates of the National Income and Product Accounts for 1959–1995: Results of the Comprehensive Revision," *Survey of Current Business,* January–February 1996.

[4]See Robert Eisner, *How Real Is the Federal Deficit?* (New York: Free Press, 1986), and "Budget Deficits: Rhetoric and Reality," *Journal of Economic Perspectives,* Spring 1989.

[5]See the data series on the economy's capital stock in *Survey of Current Business,* January 1992.

The blue line in Figure 20-1 shows the primary deficit. The primary deficit has clearly been higher in the 1980s and 1990s than it was during the 1960s, but the increase is less striking than is the increase in the overall deficit.

When interest payments are large, as they are in the United States, proper measurement of the deficit is complicated by the distinction between real and nominal interest rates. Since the nominal interest rate equals the real interest rate plus inflation, interest payments on the debt can be divided into real payments and payments due to inflation. The latter do not cost the government anything in real terms, because they are exactly offset by the decrease in the real value of the nominal debt.[6] During periods of high inflation most of the interest payments are offset by inflation. Even during periods of low inflation, nearly half the interest payments may be offset in this way.

20-2

THE BURDEN OF THE DEBT

As deficits continue, the national debt piles up. The U.S. (gross) national debt at the end of 1996 exceeded $5 trillion, an amount that is enough to get anyone worried. In per capita terms, the national debt amounts to about $20,000 per person. Do we actually have to pay off this debt? It is the notion that every person in the country owes a large debt that makes the existence of the debt seem so serious.

However, by and large, we owe the national debt to ourselves. Each individual shares in the obligation to repay the public debt, but many individuals own the national debt in the form of Treasury bonds held directly or indirectly through financial intermediaries. As a first step, one could think of the liability that the debt represents as canceling out the asset that the debt represents to the individuals who hold claims on the government. In this case, the debt would not be a net burden on society. However, this argument is limited by the fact that a large portion of the debt is owned by foreigners. The portion of the debt owned by foreigners does represent a future tax burden to be borne by U.S. taxpayers.

A more important sense in which the debt may be a burden is through the potential long-run effects of the deficit and debt on the capital stock. We saw earlier that debt financing increases the interest rate and reduces investment. Hence the capital stock will be lower with debt financing than otherwise, and output will be lower as a result of debt financing of a deficit. This *is* a real burden.

Thus, if the debt is a burden, it is a burden for reasons very different from those suggested by the statement that every person in the United States has a debt of $20,000 as a share of the national debt. The major source of burden arises from the possible effects of the national debt on the country's net national worth: an increase in the national debt can reduce the capital stock and/or increase the nation's external debt.

---

[6]See Mario Blejer and Adrienne Cheasty, "The Measurement of Fiscal Deficits: Analytical and Methodological Issues," *Journal of Economic Literature,* December 1991.

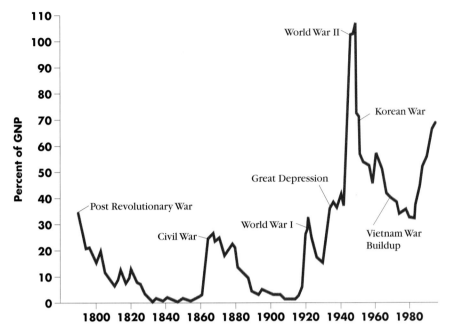

FIGURE 20-2 THE U.S. DEBT-TO-INCOME RATIO IN HISTORICAL PERSPECTIVE.

(Source: Congressional Budget Office, from material cited in James R. Barth and Stephen O. Morrell, "A Primer on Budget Deficits," Federal Reserve Bank of Atlanta Economic Review, August 1982; DRI/McGraw-Hill Macroeconomic Database.)

DEBT, GROWTH, AND INSTABILITY

The national debt in the United States has risen almost every year for the past 50 years. Does that mean the government budget is bound to get out of hand, with interest payments rising so high that taxes have to keep rising, until eventually something terrible happens? The answer is no, because the economy has been growing.

Figure 20-2 shows the U.S. public debt as a fraction of GNP for a long stretch of time, starting in the early nineteenth century.[7] The most striking fact is that the debt rises sharply as a result of large wartime deficits. Then, in each postwar period, it declines. Over most of the period from World War II to 1974 the debt-income ratio was falling even though the debt itself was rising as the result of budget deficits.

How could this happen? It is helpful to look at the definition of the *debt-income ratio:*

$$\text{Debt ratio} = \frac{\text{debt}}{PY} \tag{2}$$

where PY represents nominal GDP. The ratio of debt to GDP falls when nominal GDP grows more rapidly than the debt. To see this point, it is useful to look separately at the numerator and denominator of the debt-GDP ratio. The numerator, the debt, grows

---

[7]Since GNP and GDP are almost the same for the United States, it does not make a difference whether we discuss the debt-to-GNP or debt-to-GDP ratio. Only debt-GNP data is available for earlier years.

because of deficits. The denominator, nominal GDP, grows as a result of both inflation and real GDP growth.

Why is it useful to look at the ratio of debt to income rather than at the absolute value of the debt? The reason is that GDP is a measure of the size of the economy, and the debt-GDP ratio is thus a measure of the magnitude of the debt relative to the size of the economy. A national debt of $5 trillion would have been overwhelming in 1929 when U.S. GDP was about $100 billion: even if the interest rate had been only 1 percent, the government would have had to raise 50 percent of GDP in taxes to pay interest on the debt. But when GDP is over $7.5 trillion, a $5 trillion debt is large—but certainly not overwhelming.

GENERATIONAL ACCOUNTING

There is no hard-and-fast economic principle that describes what is fair and not fair in allocating burdens among generations. Nonetheless, politicians and nonpoliticians have strong views on how burdens should be shared across generations. Such decisions have, of course, to be based on an accounting of just how much current policies impose burdens on different generations. *Intergenerational accounting* evaluates the costs and benefits of the entire fiscal (tax and spending) system for various age groups in society.

Laurence Kotlikoff of Boston University has made a systematic estimate of the intergenerational redistribution involved in U.S. fiscal policies. He comes up with a stark and controversial finding:[8]

> The big winners from fiscal policy in the 1980s were Americans over forty at the time. Americans under forty were hurt by the policies. Young women were particularly hard hit by the decline in real welfare benefits and the rise in excise taxation.

As the last sentence of the quotation suggests, Kotlikoff arrives at his unexpected conclusion by taking into account not only the future tax burdens imposed by the growing debt but also the burdens and benefits different generations derive from government tax and spending programs.

THE SIZE-OF-GOVERNMENT DEBATE

There has been a worldwide trend over the last 30 years toward an increased share of government in GDP. In the United States, government (all levels) outlays were 23 percent of GDP in 1960 and 33 percent in 1995 (see Figure 20-3). This increase reflects in large measure the broadening of government social programs, especially the growth of transfer programs. Since 1981, growth in spending has been under sharp attack.

How large should the government be? That is, of course, a difficult question to answer. Clearly, some government programs are widely regarded as desirable; for instance, relatively few dispute the need for an adequate national defense. Other programs, such as social security, also command wide support, though just how large such programs should be is controversial. To conservatives government is far too large, and hence the deficit—and the pressures it puts on interest rates and financial stability—is desirable. Deficit pressure, in this view, is the best way to get spending cuts.

In practice, of course, the issue of how much government spending there should be is handled by the political process. In the 1930s and in the 1960s the rules and traditions

---

[8]Laurence Kotlikoff, *Generational Accounting* (New York: Free Press, 1992), p. 184.

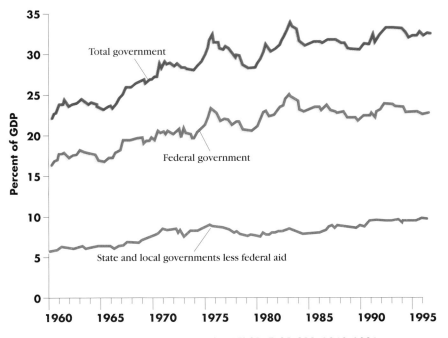

FIGURE 20-3 GOVERNMENT SPENDING AS A PERCENT OF GDP, 1960–1996.

(Source: DRI/McGraw-Hill Macroeconomic Database.)

of fiscal policy were changed by activist government policy in pursuit of full employ-ment and widening social objectives. Today there is widespread sentiment that things have gone too far and need to be brought under control by a return to "sound fiscal pol-icy." The fiscal revolt reflects a disagreement in society on how best to use resources. At the same time, there is a strand of thinking that calls for a resumption of government ac-tivity from infrastructure to education. The debate is not over, and the acute fiscal prob-lem is bound to keep the difficult tradeoffs involved at the forefront of the discussion.

20-3

THE BARRO-RICARDO PROBLEM

Does the size of the deficit matter? That is, given the size of government spending, does it matter whether sufficient taxes are levied to pay for what we spend? The traditional aggregate supply–aggregate demand model gives a clear answer: Lower taxes mean higher aggregate demand, higher interest rates, more crowding out, and less investment for the future. New classical economists, led by Robert Barro,[9] give a surprisingly dif-ferent answer: Deficits don't matter. The logic behind this answer is simple and goes as follows: Suppose first that government spending increases $100 per family and that

---

[9]See Robert Barro, "The Neoclassical Approach to Fiscal Policy," in R. Barro (ed.), *Modern Business Cy-cle Theory* (Cambridge, Mass.: Harvard University Press, 1989).

taxes also increase $100. Each family has $100 less in lifetime resources to allocate and makes choices to reduce lifetime spending accordingly. Suppose, instead, that the government had raised spending $100 per family but had left taxes unchanged and borrowed the $100. Just as in the first case, the "representative family" has $100 less in allocable resources *today,* but now it is because the family has loaned the money to the government. Since the family is in the same financial position in this $100-deficit case as it would be in the zero-deficit case, the family will make the same decisions. The deficit doesn't matter.

There is one *apparent* difference in the $100-deficit case: the family now owns a $100 government bond. However, the family also realizes that at the time its bond comes due, the government will find it has to raise taxes to pay off the principal and interest due on the bonds it issued to finance the deficit. So ownership of the bond does not affect the family's decisions because the value of the bond is exactly offset by the value of its implicit future tax liability.

The issue raised by this argument is sometimes posed as the question, *Are government bonds net wealth?* The question goes back at least to the classical English economist David Ricardo. Renewed by Robert Barro,[10] it is known as the *Barro-Ricardo equivalence proposition,* or *Ricardian equivalence.* The proposition is that debt financing by bond issue merely postpones taxation and therefore, in many instances, is strictly equivalent to current taxation. (Incidentally, after raising this as a theoretical possibility, Ricardo rejected its practical significance.)

The strict Barro-Ricardo proposition that government bonds are not net wealth turns on the argument that people realize their bonds will have to be paid off with future increases in taxes. If so, an increase in the budget deficit unaccompanied by cuts in government spending should lead to an increase in saving that precisely matches the deficit.

There are two main theoretical objections to the Barro-Ricardo proposition. First, given that people have finite lifetimes, different people will pay off the debt than those who are receiving the tax cut today. This argument assumes that people now alive do not take into account the higher taxes their descendants will have to pay in future. Second, it is argued that many people cannot borrow, and so do not consume according to their permanent income. They would like to consume more today, but because of *liquidity constraints*—their inability to borrow—they are constrained to consuming less than they would want according to their permanent income. A tax cut for these people eases their liquidity constraint and allows them to consume more.[11]

These theoretical disagreements mean that the Barro-Ricardo hypothesis has to be settled by examining the empirical evidence. The sharp decline of the U.S. private savings rate in the 1980s in the face of increased public deficits is one piece of evidence

---

[10]The original article is Robert Barro, "Are Government Bonds Net Wealth?" *Journal of Political Economy,* December 1974. See also, by the same author, "The Ricardian Approach to Budget Deficits," *Journal of Economic Perspectives,* Spring 1989. Theoretical challenges to the Barro-Ricardo view include Olivier Blanchard, "Debts, Deficits and Finite Horizons," *Journal of Political Economy,* April 1985, and Douglas Bernheim, "A Neoclassical Perspective on Budget Deficits," *Journal of Economic Perspectives,* Spring 1989.

[11]Barro himself pointed out another qualification to the equivalence proposition. Changes in marginal tax rates change tax-induced distortions in private decision making. Deficits which allow low tax rates today at the expense of high tax rates in the future may create greater overall distortion than would a constant-over-time medium tax rate.

against the proposition. Less casual empirical research continues in an attempt to settle the issue of whether the debt is wealth.[12] We believe the evidence to date is, on balance, unfavorable to the Barro-Ricardo proposition, but we recognize that the issue has not yet been decisively settled.

◆ O P T I O N A L ◆

BARRO-RICARDO EQUIVALENCE MORE FORMALLY

We present here a more formal demonstration of the Ricardian equivalence theorem. The demonstration emphasizes that the theorem relies on the absence of liquidity constraints and the presence of an *operational bequest motive,* that is, parents' desire to leave a bequest to their children. To make the example concrete, suppose a father and son, Alan and Larry, consume C_{Alan} and C_{Larry} respectively. We look at the father's decision problem about how to allocate resources between his own consumption and a bequest, B, to Larry. Larry's utility depends on his own consumption. Alan's utility depends on his own consumption and on Larry's welfare. Let T be the amount of taxes Alan pays.

The key to the effect of deficit financing lies in writing out Alan and Larry's budget constraints. Larry's consumption equals his income plus the value of the bequest:

$$C_{\text{Larry}} = Y_{\text{Larry}} + B \qquad (3)$$

Alan leaves a bequest equal to his saving plus accrued interest. Saving equals disposable income, income less taxes, minus his consumption:

$$B = (1 + r)[(Y - T) - C_{\text{Alan}}] \qquad (4)$$

Alan chooses consumption, C_{Alan}, to maximize his utility consistent with his budget constraint, trading off his own consumption against the pleasure he gets from knowing Larry's utility rises with the extra consumption a bequest allows.[13]

Suppose now that rather than impose a tax on the current generation, the government practices deficit finance, borrowing the amount L, $L = T$, and promising to pay off the loan with interest, $(1 + r)L$, by imposing a tax, $(1 + r)T$, in the future. Larry's consumption will be reduced by the taxes he must pay:

$$C_{\text{Larry}} = [Y_{\text{Larry}} - (1 + r)T] + B \qquad (5)$$

Alan now leaves a bequest which includes the principal and interest repayment on his loan to the government. Because he pays no taxes, his disposable income has risen, but in addition to consuming, he uses some of his money to make a loan to the government:

$$B = (1 + r)[Y - (L + C_{\text{Alan}})] + (1 + r)L \qquad (6)$$

---

[12]See, for example, Joseph J. Altonji, Fumio Hayashi, and Laurence Kotlikoff, "Is the Extended Family Altruistically Linked? Direct Tests Using Micro Data," *American Economic Review,* December 1992, and John J. Seater, "Ricardian Equivalence," *Journal of Economic Literature,* March 1993.

[13]If one can imagine that Larry might also have an interest in intergenerational transfers and plan himself to leave a bequest, we get a more sophisticated argument that Alan gets pleasure out of Larry's happiness, which is due in part to money left to grandchildren—and future generations.

The question to be answered is how does Alan's consumption choice under deficit spending compare to the choice he made under the tax-as-you-go system above. Can Alan still follow the same plan? Yes! Alan can set consumption at the same level by taking the money previously paid in taxes and lending it to the government. This allows Alan to increase his bequest by the eventual proceeds from the loan repayment, $(1 + r)L$. The increase in the bequest will provide Larry with just enough extra funds to pay *his* extra taxes, while leaving C_{Larry} unchanged. Thus Alan and Larry will have the same consumption levels as before. All that has happened is that Alan has increased his private saving, in the form of the loan to the government, by just enough to offset the decrease in public saving, in the form of the increased deficit.

There is an implicit assumption in this analysis that the intergenerational bequest motive is operative—meaning that Alan *wants* to leave money to Larry. If he doesn't, then deficit finance allows Alan to spend more and leave a tax bill for Larry.

20-4

SOCIAL SECURITY

The typical American pays more to the federal government in social security taxes than in income tax. Most of the people reading this textbook can expect to make large contributions to the social security system, while wondering whether the system will have enough funds to pay them pensions after they retire. In this section we consider two aspects of the social security system: intergenerational transfers and economic efficiency. The key to understanding both is that in most countries, and certainly in the United States, social security is a *pay-as-you-go system,* whereby taxes on the currently working generation are used to fund payments to retirees.[14]

SOCIAL SECURITY AS AN INTERGENERATIONAL TRANSFER

A pay-as-you-go social security system may transfer resources from the young to the old for three reasons: (1) because of population growth, (2) because of real income growth, and (3) because of the political process. We deal with each in turn. As a benchmark, we ask first what would benefits and payments look like in a no-resource-transfer system?

Suppose the typical person works and makes contributions to the social security system from age 26 through 65 and receives benefits from age 66 through 75. Since there are 40 years of work for 10 years of retirement, there will be four active contributors for each active beneficiary.[15] This means that the social security system budget

---

[14]"Pay as you go" is a bit of an oversimplification. Currently, taxes exceed payments in the United States, so the balance in the Social Security Trust Fund is rising. However, obligations to pay future benefits are larger than the fund balance. Under current law, social security will run out of money in 2029.

[15]We pick a round number, four, for purposes of illustration. Real social security systems have more complicated rules for computing taxes and benefits.

TABLE 20-3 The Ratio of Working-Age Population to Retirement-Age Population

YEAR	CANADA	FRANCE	GERMANY	ITALY	JAPAN	UNITED KINGDOM	UNITED STATES
1960	7.7	5.3	6.3	7.5	10.5	5.6	6.5
1990	5.9	4.7	4.5	4.7	5.8	4.3	5.3
2010	4.7	4.1	2.8	3.9	3.4	4.5	5.3
2030	3.5	3.3	3.0	3.4	3.0	3.9	4.9
2040	2.6	2.6	2.1	2.4	2.6	3.0	3.1

Source: Patricia S. Pollard, "How Will Demographics Affect Social Security," Federal Reserve Bank of St. Louis *International Economic Trends,* August 1996, based on OECD data.

will balance if each beneficiary receives the payments of four workers. And, since each worker pays in for 4 times the number of years she receives benefits, over a lifetime her contributions and benefits will balance.

Intergenerational Transfers because of Population Growth
Growing populations have a higher ratio of young to old than do stable populations. The higher ratio arises simply because each succeeding generation is larger than the one before it. For example, if population growth is 2 percent a year, the ratio of the working-age to retirement-age population in the example above will be 7 to 1 instead of 4 to 1. Thus the benefit-contribution ratio can be much higher in a growing population than in a stable population.

Taking advantage of population growth to increase the benefit-contribution ratio is understandably politically attractive. The problem with such a setup is that one day population growth may end. To maintain expected benefits, contributions by the working generations will have to increase drastically. (In the example we've been using, contributions would have to nearly double, increasing by a ratio of 7 to 4.) This is exactly what has happened as most of the world's industrialized countries have moved toward zero population growth (ZPG).

Table 20-3 gives projections of the working-age to retirement-age population for seven industrialized countries. You can see that in the future in all these countries pay-as-you-go social security will have to either increase contributions from each worker or cut benefits to each retiree.[16]

Intergenerational Transfers because of Income Growth
Younger generations have a higher standard of living than older generations that is simply due to economic growth.[17] Suppose that contributions are set at a certain percentage of income, rather than a fixed dollar level. In a pay-as-you-go system, retired workers

[16]For projections on the effect of possible social security reforms in the major industrial countries, see "Fiscal Challenges Facing Industrial Countries," *World Economic Outlook* (International Monetary Fund), May 1996.

[17]Not every member of every generation is better off than his or her parents, of course. For example, in the United States today, young workers with low levels of education generally have a standard of living no higher than that of their parents.

receive benefits higher than their own contributions because the source of the contributions is the higher income of the younger generation. At reasonable levels of productivity growth, this effect allows benefits to be much higher than would otherwise be possible. If long-run economic growth were to falter, the system would collapse. But as long as economic growth continues, each generation can count on receiving extra benefits based on the productivity of the young.

Intergenerational Transfers because of the Political Process

Social security systems are in trouble in many countries. Put simply, social security has been set up to pay out more in benefits than can be supported by the level of contributions, even considering population and income growth. This worked to the advantage of early recipients, but, the day of reckoning having arrived, young people today can expect to receive a far lower benefit per dollar of contribution than did their parents. This situation has a political, rather than purely economic, explanation. Older people vote more than younger people, and current generations can vote for benefit programs without consulting the not-yet-born generations who will be required to pay for them. Older generations are, at least sometimes, in a position to enforce intergenerational transfers through the political system.

SOCIAL SECURITY AND ECONOMIC EFFICIENCY

There is a strong economic argument in favor of a social security system. As a society, there is a minimal standard of living we find acceptable for the elderly. Social security is a roundabout way of forcing everyone to undertake at least some saving for old age. Without a social security system, we would have to choose between seeing some of the elderly go hungry and having younger generations support older generations who had insufficient savings.

Unfortunately, in a pay-as-you-go system, society as a whole does not save for the future. Since contributions are immediately disbursed, no productive capital is created. (The so-called Social Security Trust Fund consists of IOUs from one generation to another. Unlike private pension plans, it isn't backed by any real investment.) So while social security forces some people to "save" who otherwise would not, it also reduces the effectiveness of investment by those who would have saved anyway by a remarkable amount.

In a pay-as-you-go system, $100 in contributions produces $100 in benefits. In our pay-in-40-year/take-out-10-year example, a worker would pay in $25 per year to sustain a $100 per year benefit level. Contrast this return with the compound return on real investment. At 5 percent interest, $25 per year in contributions sustains a $391 per year benefit level.[18] The difference between the $391 per year and the $100 per year benefit level is the economic cost of society's forgoing productive investment.[19]

---

[18]This calculation is sensitive to the real interest rate used in the calculation. We use 5 percent per year, a number commonly used by universities in computing a rate at which endowments may be drawn on. At 2 percent annual interest, the benefit would be $168; at 8 percent the benefit would be $965.

[19]You can also think of the efficiency argument in terms of the effect of lower saving reducing economic growth and lowering very long run output. We studied this point in Chaps. 3 and 4.

Social security contributions almost certainly do not crowd out private (productive) retirement savings one for one. But each dollar of private saving which is displaced significantly reduces the size of society's nest egg.

POLICY RESPONSES

Finding a "fix" for social security is a hot political problem. Avoiding a crunch in the future requires making hard decisions today—and political systems are not good at making current sacrifices for future benefits. Reforms are being considered to attack both the insolvency and the inefficiency aspects of social security.[20] The solution to insolvency necessarily requires increasing taxes or cutting benefits, at least indirectly. Suggested reforms include:[21]

- Increase the age at which one becomes eligible for benefits.
- Tax all benefits received in excess of contributions.
- Reduce cost-of-living increases by changing the way inflation is measured.[22]

Suggested reforms to reduce the inefficiency associated with pay-as-you-go social security involve investing part of the Social Security Trust Fund in productive investments rather than government IOUs.[23] Two specific suggestions are:

- Invest part of the trust fund in a wide variety of stocks and corporate bonds.
- Allow individuals to substitute investment in private retirement accounts in place of part of their social security contributions.

Investments in the private sector earn higher returns than investments in the government bonds which now back the social security system. Thus, allowing productive investment also helps solve the insolvency problem.

SUMMARY

1. Federal government expenditures are financed through taxes and borrowing.
2. Federal government receipts come chiefly from the individual income tax and from social insurance taxes and contributions. The share of the last category has increased rapidly in the postwar period, especially since the 1960s.

---

[20]For readable-but-technical articles on social security reform, see Edward Gramlich, "Different Approaches for Dealing with Social Security," Olivia S. Mitchell and Stephen P. Zeldes, "Social Security Privatization: A Structural Analysis," Laurence J. Kotlikoff, "Privatizing Social Security at Home and Abroad," and Sylvester J. Schieber and John B. Shoven, "Social Security Reform: Around the World in 80 Ways," all in *American Economic Association Papers and Proceedings,* May 1996.

[21]Suggestions for reforms, some of which have been implemented, have been made by a series of study commissions. Doubtlessly, new commissions and new ideas will continue to appear. As an example of some of the difficulties reformers face, look at the headline story about the Advisory Council on Social Security, "Panel in Discord on the Financing of Social Security: A Baby-Boom Shortage," *New York Times,* Dec. 8, 1996.

[22]As we discussed in Chap. 2, there is good reason to believe current statistics overstate the true inflation rate.

[23]See Edward M. Gramlich, "Different Approaches for Dealing with Social Security," and Peter A. Diamond, "Proposals to Restructure Social Security," both in *Journal of Economic Perspectives,* Summer 1996.

3. Federal government expenditures are chiefly for defense and transfer payments to individuals. The share of defense in federal expenditure has fallen over the past 30 years, while the shares of transfers and interest have risen.

4. The debt-income ratio rises if the growth rate of debt—determined by interest payments and the primary deficit—exceeds the growth rate of nominal income.

5. The major sense in which the national debt may be a burden is that it may lead to a decline in the capital stock in the long run.

6. Large U.S. deficits over more than a decade were in large part financed by external borrowing. This external borrowing increases the net external debt of the United States and gives rise to a debt burden.

7. The Barro-Ricardo equivalence proposition notes that debt represents future taxes. It asserts that debt-financed tax cuts will not have any effect on aggregate demand.

8. Social security is financed on a pay-as-you-go system. Social security systems around the world have become vulnerable as population growth has slowed.

9. To the extent social security displaces private saving and investment, the productive capital stock is substantially reduced.

KEY TERMS

mandatory outlays	primary (or noninterest)	operational bequest motive
discretionary outlays	deficit	pay-as-you-go social secu-
entitlement programs	debt-income ratio	rity system
government purchases	intergenerational accounting	
transfer payments	Ricardian (or Barro-	
structural deficit	Ricardo) equivalence	
cyclical deficit	liquidity constraints	

PROBLEMS

Conceptual

1. **a.** What is the structural deficit?
    b. What is the cyclical deficit?
    c. Why is it useful to split the deficit into these two components?

2. **a.** How does the U.S. government measure its deficit?
    b. How can this measure be misleading?
    c. What adjustments might we want to make to it, and why?

3. **a.** To what extent do we need to worry about the component of our total deficit which consists of interest payments on the public debt? (*Hint:* Ask yourself how much of this component is a real cost to the government.)
    b. To what extent do we need to worry about the national debt? In what way or ways is it a burden on society?

4. Should we require that the budget be balanced? Discuss.

5. Why is it more useful to look at the ratio of debt to GDP than at the absolute value of the debt?

6. **a.** In the Barro-Ricardo view, does it make any difference whether the government pays for its expenditures by raising taxes or issuing debt?
    b. Why?
    c. What are the two main theoretical objections to the Barro-Ricardo view?

7. German unification involved massive expenditures for infrastructure in the east, as well as transfer payments to many former East Germans. Should such expenditures have been financed by (*a*) money creation because of their transitory, exceptional nature, (*b*) debt, or (*c*) taxes? Justify your answer.

8. **a.** Why might a pay-as-you-go social security system transfer resources from the young to the old?

   b. What are the consequences of such a system on economic efficiency?

   *c. Are there other ways to structure a social security system that might alleviate some of the problems associated with this one? Explain.

Technical

1. Table 20-1 shows how the U.S. government's spending has changed over the last several decades.

   a. Calculate how much total spending as a percentage of GDP has increased since the 1960s.

   b. In the 1960s (due largely to spending for the war in Vietnam) defense spending was the single largest component of total outlays. What has been the largest component since then?

   c. What types of outlays does the table suggest are responsible for growth in total spending since the 1960s?

2. Table 20-2 shows how the U.S. government's income has changed over the last several decades.

   a. Calculate how much total revenues have increased since the 1960s.

   b. The individual income tax was the largest component of federal revenue in the 1960s and remains the largest today. The second-largest component has changed dramatically, however. What was it in the 1960s, and what has it been since?

   c. What types of income does the table suggest are responsible for growth in total revenues as a percentage of GDP since the 1960s?

3. Use the data in Tables 20-1 and 20-2 to find an estimate of the U.S. budget deficit as a percentage of GDP during each of the decades represented. How much has it increased since the 1960s?

4. If the growth rate of output averaged roughly 4 percent a year and the growth rate of the national debt averaged 5 percent, what would happen to the ratio of debt to GDP over time? Why?

5. Use equation (2) to show how the ratio of debt to GDP should move (if at all) over the business cycle. You may assume, for simplicity, that the debt is fixed at some number.

6. Analyze the difference in the impact on the interest rate, investment, and the price level of a temporary change in government spending financed by borrowing rather than taxes. State explicitly the assumptions you are making. (That is, are you assuming Ricardian equivalence? Be aware of the way this will change your answer.)

*7. Standard Keynesian theory predicts that tax increases will lower aggregate demand and, in the short run, decrease output.

   a. What elements of standard theory come together to yield this prediction?

   b. In making an argument for Ricardian equivalence, do we have to discard any standard theory?

*An asterisk denotes a more difficult problem.

c. Using an *IS-LM* framework and assuming the Barro-Ricardo point of view, show what happens to output when taxes are increased.

CHAPTER 21

International Adjustment and Interdependence

CHAPTER HIGHLIGHTS

◆ National economies are linked through trade flows, exchange rates, and interest rates.

◆ Failure to keep exchange rates in line with prices ultimately leads to a devaluation crisis.

◆ The monetary approach to the balance of payments emphasizes the connection between changing the domestic money supply and the level of the balance of payments.

International economic issues are increasingly prominent on the macroeconomic scene. Countries are interdependent: booms or recessions in one country spill over to other countries through trade flows, and changes in interest rates in any major country cause immediate exchange or interest rate movements in other countries.

In 1991–1993, for example, German interest rates were at the center of European and international controversy. As a result of massive government spending to finance German unification, the German economy began to boom and inflation rose. The German central bank, the Bundesbank, fought the inflation by sharply raising interest rates. Countries such as Britain and France either had to match the German interest rate increase, even though their economies were not booming, or had to accept a depreciation of their currencies. The British wanted to do neither, and as a result, there was a major European currency crisis in September 1992.

We introduced the basic facts and models of international linkages in Chapter 12. Now we explore the issues of international interdependence further. In the first three sections of this chapter we discuss aspects of the mechanisms through which a country with a fixed exchange rate adjusts to balance-of-payments problems. This discussion helps clarify current international economic issues even though exchange rates among the dollar, yen, and other major currencies have been flexible since 1973; the fixed exchange rate mechanisms remain relevant because some smaller countries still operate with fixed exchange rates and also because exchange rates are fixed among countries in the European Monetary System (EMS).[1] In addition, an understanding of the adjustment mechanisms that operate under fixed exchange rates helps in grasping the operation of flexible exchange rates.

In the rest of the chapter we take up aspects of the behavior of the current flexible exchange rate system.[2]

21-1

ADJUSTMENT UNDER FIXED EXCHANGE RATES

Adjustment to a balance-of-payments problem can be achieved in two ways. One is to change economic policy; the second is through *automatic adjustment mechanisms.* There are two automatic mechanisms: payments imbalances affect the money supply and hence spending, and unemployment affects wages and prices and thereby competitiveness. Policy measures, by contrast, include monetary and fiscal policy, and also tariffs or devaluation.

THE ROLE OF PRICES IN THE OPEN ECONOMY

We start the analysis by bringing prices explicitly into our analysis of the open economy. In Chapter 12 we assumed that the price level was constant. With fixed prices and a given exchange rate the *real* exchange rate is also fixed. Recall the definition of the real exchange rate:

---

[1]As discussed in Box 12-1, exchange rates among many European countries will become irrevocably fixed when the EMU goes into effect—an event scheduled for January 1, 1999.

[2]For an extensive review of recent work on both theory and evidence, see Mark Taylor, "The Economics of Exchange Rates," *Journal of Economic Literature,* March 1995.

$$R = \frac{eP_f}{P} \tag{1}$$

Here e is the nominal exchange rate, P_f the foreign price level, and P the domestic price level. We now abandon the assumption of a fixed domestic price level but, for the time being, take the exchange rate and foreign prices as given.

How does the openness of the economy affect the aggregate demand curve? In the closed economy version of the model, aggregate demand declines when the price level rises: a higher price level implies lower real balances, higher interest rates, and lower spending. In an open economy with a fixed exchange rate, an increase in the price level reduces demand for an additional reason: an increase in our prices makes our goods less competitive with (more expensive relative to) foreign-produced goods. Given the exchange rate, when the prices of goods produced at home rise, our goods become more expensive for foreigners to buy and their goods become *relatively* cheaper for us to buy. An increase in our price level thus shifts demand away from our goods toward imports and also reduces exports.

In Figure 21-1 we show the downward-sloping demand schedule for our goods, AD. Demand is equal to aggregate spending by domestic residents plus net exports, or $AD \equiv A + NX$, and now there are two reasons for the aggregate demand curve to slope down.

The demand for domestic goods, AD, is drawn for a given level of foreign prices, a given nominal money supply, given fiscal policy, and an exchange rate that is fixed. An increase in the nominal money stock shifts the schedule upward, as does expansionary fiscal policy. We show, too, the short-run aggregate supply schedule, AS, and the full-employment level of output, Y^*. Initial equilibrium is at point E, at which we have unemployment.

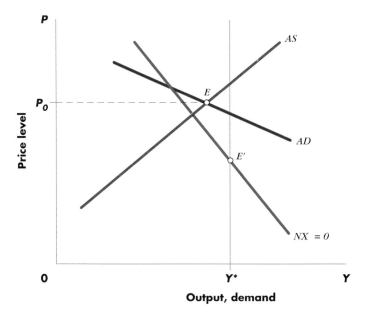

FIGURE 21-1   OPEN ECONOMY EQUILIBRIUM WITH PRICE ADJUSTMENT.

Next we look at the trade balance equilibrium schedule, $NX = 0$. An increase in our income raises imports and worsens the trade balance. To restore trade balance equilibrium, domestic prices would have to be lower. This would make the home country more competitive, raise exports, and reduce imports. Thus we show the trade balance equilibrium schedule as downward-sloping.[3] We assume that it is steeper than the demand schedule for domestic goods. The schedule is drawn for a given level of prices abroad.

FINANCING AND ADJUSTMENT

At point E the home country has a trade deficit. Our prices are too high or our income is too high to have exports balance imports. To achieve trade balance equilibrium, we would have to become more competitive, thus exporting more and importing less. Alternatively, we could reduce our level of income in order to reduce import spending.

What does a country with a current account deficit, like that at E, do? In a fixed exchange rate system, it is possible for the central bank to use its reserves to finance temporary imbalances of payments—that is, to meet the excess demand for foreign currency at the existing exchange rate arising from balance-of-payments deficits. Alternatively, a country experiencing balance-of-payments difficulties can borrow foreign currencies abroad.

A current account deficit cannot be financed by borrowing from abroad without raising the question of how the borrowing will be repaid. If the foreign lenders are convinced the country can repay—for instance, because the cause of the current account deficit is temporary or because they believe the borrowings will be used to increase the country's ability to export—the loans will be available. However, problems may well arise in repaying the foreign debt if borrowing is used to finance consumption spending.

But maintaining and financing current account deficits indefinitely or for very long periods of time is impossible. The economy has to find some way of *adjusting* the deficit, that is, of getting rid of or at least reducing it. Again, that can happen automatically or through policy. We examine first the important automatic adjustment mechanisms.

AUTOMATIC ADJUSTMENT

First we look at the aggregate demand side. When a country runs a balance-of-payments deficit, the demand for foreign exchange is by definition larger than the amount being supplied by the private markets, and the central bank has to sell the difference. When the central bank sells foreign exchange, it reduces domestic high-powered money and therefore the money stock—unless it *sterilizes* its foreign exchange intervention by buying bonds as it sells foreign exchange. Ruling out that possibility, the deficit at point E implies that the central bank is pegging the exchange rate, selling foreign exchange to keep the exchange rate from depreciating, and reducing the domestic money stock. It follows immediately that over time the aggregate demand schedule (which is drawn for a given money supply) will be shifting downward and to the left.

---

[3]We assume that a decline in domestic prices improves the trade balance. This requires that exports and imports be sufficiently responsive to prices. There is a possibility that a reduction in our price level (which reduces the prices of our exports) lowers our revenue from exports—because the increased sales are not sufficient to compensate for the lower prices. We assume that this possibility does not occur. We assume, too, that import spending does not depend on the interest rate.

Turning now to the aggregate supply side: point E in Figure 21-1 is also a point of unemployment. Unemployment leads to declines in wages and costs, which are reflected in a downward-shifting aggregate supply schedule. Over time, therefore, the short-run equilibrium point, E, moves downward as both demand and supply schedules shift (not shown). The points of short-run equilibrium move in the direction of point E', and the process will continue until that point is reached. (The approach may be cyclical, but that is not of major interest here.)

Once point E' is reached, the country has automatically achieved long-run equilibrium. Because the trade balance is in equilibrium, there is no pressure on the exchange rate and therefore no need for exchange market intervention, so there are no further changes in the money supply. On the supply side, wages and costs are constant, so the supply schedule is not shifting. Thus at E' the country has successfully and automatically adjusted to the initial balance-of-payments deficit: it has achieved trade balance equilibrium combined with full employment.

This is the *classical adjustment process.* It relies on price adjustments and an adjustment in the money supply based on the trade balance. The adjustment process "works," *but* it may take a very long time and require a very long recession.[4] The alternative to waiting for the automatic adjustment mechanisms to do the whole job is to make explicit policy changes to move the economy more rapidly toward balance.

POLICIES TO RESTORE BALANCE: EXPENDITURE SWITCHING AND REDUCING

Because of their side effects, policies to restore external balance must generally be combined with policies to achieve full employment: policies to create employment will typically worsen the external balance, and policies to create a trade surplus will affect employment. In general it is necessary to combine *expenditure-switching policies,* which shift demand between domestic and imported goods, and *expenditure-reducing* (or *expenditure-increasing*) *policies* in order to cope with the two targets of *internal balance* and *external balance.* This point is of general importance and continues to apply when we take account of capital flows and other phenomena omitted in this section.

One method of adjusting a current account deficit is by imposing *tariffs*—taxes on imports. However, tariffs cannot be freely used to adjust the balance of trade, partly because there are international organizations and agreements such as the *World Trade Organization (WTO)* and the *International Monetary Fund (IMF)* that outlaw, or at least frown on, the use of tariffs. Tariffs have generally fallen in the post-World War II period as the industrialized world has moved to desirably freer trade between countries.

Another way of adjusting a current account deficit is to use policies to reduce aggregate demand. These are expenditure-reducing policies. In this regard, it is worth repeating that a trade deficit reflects an excess of expenditure over income. The identities in Chapter 2 imply that

$$NX \equiv Y - (C + I + G) \tag{2}$$

where NX is the trade surplus and I is investment. Thus, a balance-of-trade deficit can

---

[4]Olivier Blanchard and Pierre-Alain Muet, in "Competitiveness through Disinflation: An Assessment of French Macro Policy," *Economic Policy,* April 1993, show that it took France almost a decade to achieve such an adjustment, starting in 1983.

BOX 21-1 Why Are Devaluations So Often Delayed?

Countries that have fixed their exchange rates often delay devaluing until they have no choice—and when they reach that point, the government is perceived to have suffered a major defeat. This was certainly the case in Mexico in 1994; earlier it was the case in the United Kingdom and Italy, which were forced to devalue in 1992.

Why do countries wait too long? First, the economic reasons: For a devaluation to be effective, for it to reduce the balance-of-payments deficit, it has to make imported goods more expensive so that domestic residents buy fewer of them. When Mexico devalued, American candies (and many more important imports) became more expensive, and the living standards of Mexicans fell accordingly. But it is not only the prices of imports that rise; so do the prices of goods that use imported raw materials in their production.

Devaluations are unpopular because they reduce the domestic standard of living. In addition, the increases in prices of imports sometimes set off more general price rises, or inflation, which is also unpopular.

There is another reason that governments often delay devaluations too long. Devaluations are in many ways self-fulfilling prophecies: the expectation that a country will devalue increases the probability that it will do so.* (Why? Because if you expect the currency to devalue, e.g., if you expect the peso to fall from 3.5 to the dollar to 6 to the dollar, you will buy dollars as soon as possible for only 3.5 pesos, expecting that you will later make a profit in pesos by selling the dollars at a higher (peso) price. But as you buy dollars, you deplete the country's peso reserves and make it harder to maintain the exchange rate.) Accordingly, especially when the public begins to fear that a devaluation is likely, government officials often make stirring statements to the effect that there will under no circumstances be a devaluation. For a while that may reassure the public, and thus help prevent the devaluation. But when devaluation becomes necessary, the government officials look foolish and defeated—and that is another reason they delay too long.

*See Paul Krugman, "Self-Fulfilling Currency Crises," *NBER Macro Annual*, 1996, and Norbert Funke, "Vulnerability of Fixed Exchange Rate Regimes: The Role of Fundamentals," *OECD Economic Studies* 26 (1996).

be reduced by reducing spending ($C + I + G$) relative to income (Y) through restrictive monetary and/or fiscal policy.

The link between the external deficit and budget deficits is shown in equation (2a):[5]

$$NX \equiv (S - I) + [TA - (G + TR)] \tag{2a}$$

where S denotes *private* saving and $TA - (G + TR)$ is the government budget surplus.

[5]To derive equation (2a), we combine equation (2) with the accounting identities $Y \equiv YD + (TA - TR)$ and $YD \equiv C + S$.

Equation (2*a*) shows an immediate relation between the budget and the external balance. If saving and investment were constant, then changes in the budget would translate, one for one, into changes in the external balance; budget cutting would bring about equal changes in the external deficit. But budget cutting will affect saving and investment, and therefore we need a more complete model to explain how budget cuts affect the external balance.

Devaluation

The unemployment that typically accompanies automatic adjustment and the desirability of free trade, which argues against the use of tariffs, both suggest the need for an alternative policy for restoring internal and external balance. The major policy instrument for dealing with payments deficits is *devaluation,* which usually has to be combined with restrictive monetary and/or fiscal policy. A devaluation is an increase in the domestic currency price of foreign exchange. Given the nominal prices in two countries, devaluation increases the relative price of imported goods in the devaluing country and reduces the relative price of exports from the devaluing country. Devaluation is primarily an expenditure switching policy.

How does a devaluation work? Consider first the special case of a country that has been in full employment with balance-of-trade equilibrium and is at point *E* in Figure 21-2. Now let there be an exogenous decline in export earnings, so the *NX* = 0 schedule shifts to the left to *NX'* = 0. With a lower demand for exports and with a fixed exchange rate, output would decline. The *AD* schedule moves to the left as a result of the fall in exports. The lower level of income reduces imports but not enough to make up for the loss of export revenue. The net effects are therefore unemployment and a trade deficit.

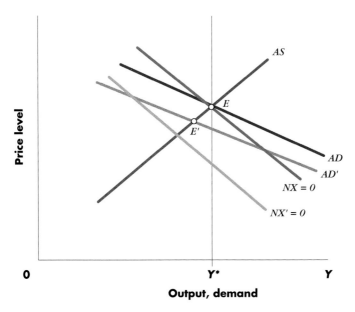

FIGURE 21-2 EFFECTS OF A LOSS OF EXPORT REVENUE.

BOX 21-2   Mexico's External Balance

In the 1980s Mexico went through a deep crisis. The country had borrowed too much in world markets and under the pressure of high world interest rates in the early 1980s found it impossible to service its external debt. Borrowing abroad became impossible from one day to the next. Mexico had to rebuild its economy, starting by depreciating its currency, reducing import tariffs and quotas, privatizing state-owned firms, and reducing government regulation of the economy. By the end of the 1980s these reforms bore fruit: the Mexican economy was growing again.*

With the return of growth and especially with a domestic investment boom, the current account worsened sharply. There was no trouble financing the current account deficit, because foreign firms and investors were investing heavily in Mexico. The question that arose was whether the Mexican government should allow the deficit to continue and even grow or, rather, cut the deficit by devaluation and a reduction in domestic spending. Table 1 shows how large the Mexican capital account surplus was. Much of the surplus went to the Mexican private sector. But capital inflows far exceeded the borrowings of Mexican private residents. A large part of the inflow was bought by the Mexican central bank, to add to its foreign exchange reserves. Such a situation is possible when, as in the Mexican case, the rest of the world decides that a country has outstanding profit opportunities and, as a result, invests in that country's stock market or in high-yield government bonds. Mexico in 1990–1992 offered that attraction and thus had no trouble attracting large capital flows.

The problem, of course, is that when borrowing in world markets is too easy, a country may overborrow—as Mexico certainly did in the 1970s. In the face of a current ac-

*On the Mexican experience in the 1980s, see Pedro Aspe, *Economic Transformation: The Mexican Way* (Cambridge, Mass.: M.I.T. Press, 1993). An annual account is given in *The Mexican Economy,* published by Mexico's central bank, Banco de Mexico.

The automatic adjustment mechanism would work, but slowly, to restore equilibrium. Alternatively, the country can devalue its currency. This has the obvious advantage that it does not require a protracted recession to reduce domestic costs. The adjustment is done by the stroke of a pen—a devaluation of the currency. Why would a devaluation achieve the adjustment? *Given* prices of foreign goods in terms of foreign currency (e.g., the mark prices of German goods), a devaluation raises the relative price of foreign goods. Imports fall, and exports rise.

The case we have just considered is special, however, in one important respect. The economy was initially in balance-of-trade equilibrium at full employment. The disturbance to the economy took place in the trade account. Accordingly, if we could move the $NX' = 0$ locus back to the full-employment level of income—as we could with a devaluation—both internal and external balance would be attained. Put differently, the reason there was unemployment in Figure 21-2 was the reduction in exports

TABLE 1   Mexico's External Balance
(Billions of U.S. dollars)

	1989	1990	1991
Current account	−6,050	−7,114	−13,283
Trade balance	−404	−882	−6,930
Capital account	6,050	7,114	13,283
Private*	5,564	3,881	5,777
Increase in reserves	396	3,233	7,506

*Including errors and omissions.

count deficit of almost $20 billion in 1992, that question emerged once again. Was it not a more prudent policy choice to say no to foreign investors, reduce demand by a tightening of fiscal policy, and perhaps even devalue the peso to make Mexican goods more competitive in world trade and imports more expensive in Mexico?

Countries rarely adjust early because tightening policy before that step becomes inevitable is politically difficult. That is what happened in 1982. A crisis emerged when foreign lenders and investors lost confidence in Mexico and were no longer willing to buy Mexican assets and when the Mexican private sector sent its capital abroad. A huge financing gap emerged. For a while the central bank met the financing gap by running down its reserves. Ultimately the process ended in a major devaluation and a deep recession. Many observers in 1992 were conscious of just how destructive it would be to go through the same cycle once more.

The argument against doing so was that devaluation would be disruptive to confidence in capital markets and to the attempt to reduce inflation. Moreover, it was argued, the deficit in the current account primarily reflected a high level of Mexican investment, which would generate the revenues with which to pay off the borrowing. In a few years, it was argued, the deficit would go down, and in the meantime it could be financed without grave risk. *A good story, but for how long?*

---

and consequent external balance problem. Both problems could thus be cured through devaluation.

In general, though, a country cannot secure both external and internal balance following a disturbance by using just one instrument of policy. A general rule of policy making is that we need to use as many policy instruments as we have policy targets.

Finally, a comment on the role of the exchange rate in a fixed rate system: in a fixed rate system, the exchange rate is an *instrument of policy*. The central bank can change the exchange rate for policy purposes, devaluing when the current account looks as though it will be in for a prolonged deficit. In a system of clean floating, by contrast, the exchange rate moves freely to equilibrate the balance of payments. In a system of dirty floating, the central bank attempts to manipulate the exchange rate while not committing itself to any given rate. The dirty floating system is thus intermediate between a fixed rate system and a clean floating system.

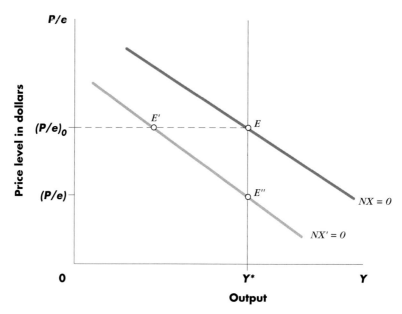

FIGURE 21-3   COMPETITIVENESS AND ADJUSTMENT.

An adverse external shock can be shown as a leftward shift of the NX schedule.

EXCHANGE RATES AND PRICES

A devaluation that takes place when domestic and foreign prices are constant will succeed in reducing the relative price of a country's goods and will thus improve the trade balance. However, the price level typically changes along with the exchange rate. The essential issue when a country devalues is whether it can achieve a *real devaluation*. A country achieves a real devaluation when a devaluation reduces the price of the country's own goods relative to the price of foreign goods.

Recalling the definition of the real exchange rate, eP_f/P, and taking the foreign price level (P_f) as given, a real devaluation occurs when e/P rises, or *when the exchange rate increases by more than the price level.*

We use Figure 21-3, and the example of Mexico, to illustrate the problem of securing a real devaluation. Let $P_{U.S.}$ be the price level in the United States, P the Mexican price level, and e Mexico's exchange rate, that is, the number of pesos per dollar. (So the analysis treats Mexico as the home country and the United States as "abroad.") Mexico's competitiveness then is measured by U.S. prices relative to Mexican prices, both measured in dollars: $P_{U.S.}/(P/e)$ ($= eP_{U.S.}/P$). We assume that the U.S. price level is given and show P/e, the Mexican price level measured in dollars, on the vertical axis in Figure 21-3. For a given U.S. price level, a rise in Mexican dollar prices (P/e) worsens Mexico's net exports. Accordingly, points to the right of $NX = 0$ correspond to deficits.

Consider now the problem of adjustment to external shocks. Suppose that an oil price fall in world markets reduces Mexico's export earnings at each price level and thus creates a deficit. (Mexico is a major oil exporter.) Initially we were at E, with internal and external balance, and now external balance only prevails along $NX' = 0$.

BOX 21-3 Balance of Payments Crises Are Pretty Well Understood

We have intentionally left Box 21-2 untouched from the last edition, except for italicizing the last sentence, *"A good story, but for how long?"* According to our notes, the text has been unchanged since October 14, 1992.

In 1994 and 1995, Mexico underwent the exchange rate drop foreseen in the previous edition of this text. The exchange rate began to fall early in 1994. Starting in December 1994, shortly after a new president took office in Mexico City, the peso went into free fall. The peso recovered slightly, assisted by massive American and IMF loans (since repaid) and then fell further through 1995.*

While predicting the precise timing or even the depth of an exchange rate crisis is difficult, the need for a policy change—voluntary or market-driven—was both predictable and predicted.

*To learn more about what happened in the Mexican crisis and why, see Jeffrey Sachs, Aaron Tornell, and Andrés Velasco, "The Collapse of the Mexican Peso: What Have We Learned?" *Economic Policy*, April 1996.

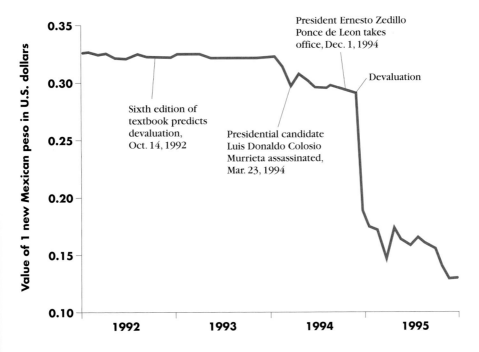

FIGURE 1   VALUE OF THE MEXICAN PESO, 1992–1996.

(Source: DRI/McGraw-Hill Macroeconomic Database.)

BOX 21-4 Debt Crises Are Not a New Phenomenon

The loans from the creditor country begin with a modest amount and proceed crescendo. They are likely to be made in exceptionally large amounts toward the culminating stage of a period of activity and speculative upswing, and during that stage become larger from month to month so long as the upswing continues. With the advent of a crisis, they are at once cut down sharply, even cease entirely. . . . A sudden reversal takes place in the debtor country's international balance sheet; it feels the consequences abruptly, in an immediate need of increased remittances to the creditor country, in a strain on its banks, high rates of discount, falling prices. And this train of events may ensue not only once.

—Harvard economist Frank Taussig writing on speculation and repeated debt crises . . . in 1927!

Source: Frank Taussig, *International Trade,* (New York: MacMillan, 1927), p. 130.

In the short run a country might absorb an external shock by staying at point *E*, borrowing abroad to finance the external deficit. But that is not possible forever; the country has somehow to return to point *E″*. It could do that slowly, through the automatic mechanisms. Or it can devalue the currency and move directly to point *E″*.

But the devaluation can be frustrated if it is offset by an increase in domestic prices. What matters is that a country with an external deficit (say, Mexico) succeeds in reducing its prices in dollars, *P/e*. If devaluation leads to a rise in domestic prices, there is no gain in competitiveness.

Mexico undertook exchange rate devaluations in 1982, in 1985–1986, and in 1994 that sharply reduced the dollar prices of Mexican goods. But the gains in competitiveness did not last after the first two of these three devaluations. Inflation in Mexico soon raised prices relative to the exchange rate; by 1992 the *real* exchange rate was less than it had been in 1987. Failure to keep exchange rates in line with prices—that is, to maintain competitiveness—ultimately results in devaluation crises, as happened in December 1994.[6] In Boxes 21-2 and 21-3 we discuss Mexican adjustment.[7]

[6]See Paul Krugman, *Currencies and Crises* (Cambridge, Mass: M.I.T. Press, 1992), and Pierre-Richard Agenor, Jagdeep Bhandari, and Robert Flood, "Speculative Attacks and Models of Balance of Payments Crises," *IMF Staff Papers,* June 1992. The problem of postponed adjustment is not peculiar to developing countries, as the European currency crisis of 1992 in countries including Italy, Finland, and the United Kingdom demonstrates.

[7]For more on the Mexican peso crisis, see the January–February 1996 issue of the Federal Reserve Bank of Atlanta *Economic Review.* For more on currency management, see Robert Bartley, "Mexico's Money Theorists Need a Tip from Hong Kong," and David Malpass, "Currency Stability on the March," both in the *Wall Street Journal,* Dec. 20, 1996.

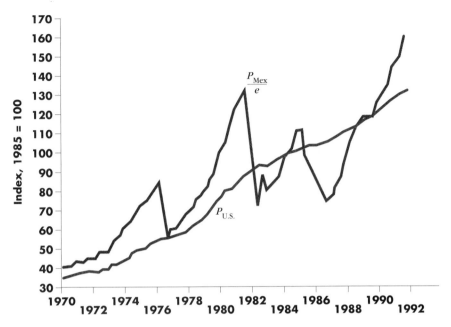

FIGURE 21-4   DOLLAR PRICE LEVELS: UNITED STATES AND MEXICO, 1970–1992.

Crawling-Peg Exchange Rates

When a country experiences inflation above the rate of its trading partners, holding the exchange rate fixed would imply a steady loss in competitiveness. In order to avoid the widening deficits, many countries follow a *crawling-peg* exchange rate policy. Under a crawling peg exchange rate policy, the exchange rate is depreciated at a rate roughly equal to the inflation differential between the country and its trading partners. The idea of a crawling peg is to maintain the *real* exchange rate, $R = P_f/(P/e)$, constant by raising e at the same rate as (P/P_f) is rising.

It is clear from Figure 21-4 that for lengthy periods, for example, in 1989–1992, Mexico failed to offset the impact of its inflation on competitiveness. The exchange rate was not depreciated fast enough to maintain the real exchange rate. As a result, competitiveness fell and foreign exchange problems remained.

Countries are often and easily tempted to use the exchange rate to slow inflation. When the exchange rate is held constant, the prices of imports stay constant (assuming foreign prices are not rising), and therefore the prices of some of the goods that enter the consumer price index are not increasing. This slows inflation. But the reduction in inflation is bought by steadily reducing competitiveness. Often such a strategy ultimately brings about a foreign exchange crisis. In the end, inflation has to be stopped by monetary and fiscal policy; exchange rate policy is at best a supplementary tool—at times a very valuable one,[8] but it cannot do most of the work in disinflation.

---

[8]For example, as discussed in Chap. 19, when it is necessary to stop an extreme inflation.

21-2

EXCHANGE RATE CHANGES AND TRADE ADJUSTMENT: EMPIRICAL ISSUES

In this section we take up two important empirical issues related to the possibility of adjusting current account imbalances by changes in the exchange rate.[9] The first is whether nominal devaluations do usually succeed in achieving real devaluations or whether, as Figure 21-4 suggests, that may be unusual.

The second issue is whether changes in relative prices, if they occur, do improve the current account. We have explicitly assumed here that a decline in the relative price of our goods improves the current account. But a perverse reaction is possible. When import prices rise, import demand may not decline sufficiently to compensate for the higher prices of imports, and thus total import spending (price times quantity) may actually increase. We turn our attention now to these two issues.

EXCHANGE RATES AND RELATIVE PRICE ADJUSTMENT

In studying the flexible wage-price model, we assumed that wages and prices adjust to achieve full employment. But in practice prices are based on labor cost or wages. Now suppose that wages are inflexible in real terms, because labor wants to maintain the purchasing power of wages. This may be reflected in the formal indexation of wages to the consumer price index, or it may be the outcome of the bargaining between firms and workers. In such a world, changes in the cost of living triggered by a devaluation would lead to changes in money wages, which would feed back into prices, which could offset the effects of the nominal devaluation.

A process in which changes in prices feed back into wages and from there into prices is a *wage-price spiral* that may produce considerable volatility in the price level. Small disturbances can set off quite large changes in the price level. Suppose, first, that the real wage is fixed in terms of the consumer price index, which includes both domestic goods and imports, so changes in the consumer price index are fully passed on into wages. Assume, second, that changes in wages are fully passed on into increased domestic prices.

Now suppose that the country has to devalue to try to restore the trade balance. The devaluation raises import prices and thereby raises consumer prices. To maintain the real wage, workers demand higher money wages, which firms grant and pass on by raising prices. Where are we after the process ends? Real wages are constant, which means wages and the price level (a weighted average of the prices of domestic and imported goods) have risen in the same proportion; wage increases have been fully passed on, which means that real wages *in terms of domestic output* are also unchanged. The two results imply that relative prices are unchanged and that *the nominal devaluation has had no effect on the real exchange rate.*

Of course, this is not the whole story, because we have to ask how the higher price level affects aggregate demand. If the government did not increase the money stock, the higher prices reduce real balances and aggregate demand; with income down, the

---

[9]For a comprehensive survey on the response of trade flows, see P. Hooper and J. Marquez, "Exchange Rates, Prices and External Adjustment in the United States and Japan," in Peter Kenen (ed.), *Understanding Interdependence: The Macroeconomics of the Open Economy* (Princeton, N.J.: Princeton University Press, 1995).

current account improves. The spiral will take place only if, when wages rise, the government raises the money stock so as not to create unemployment. Hence, in this context of a devaluation, it is crucial that the central bank not accommodate nominal price increases if it wants to achieve a real devaluation.

A second context in which the idea of *sticky real wages* (wages that are difficult to change) is important is that of real disturbances. Suppose our export demand declines permanently because of, say, the introduction of superior technology abroad. To return to full employment, the relative price of our goods must fall to encourage foreign demand. But how can the relative price fall? If we devalue, and workers succeed in restoring their real wages, and prices are marked up on wages, there will be no change in the relative price of our goods. Then the only way to reduce the real wage would be protracted unemployment.

The empirical question, then, is, How flexible are real wages? That is, to an important extent, a question of institutional arrangements. In small, open economies with substantial cost-of-living indexation in wage agreements, it may indeed be very difficult to change real wages and relative prices through exchange rate changes. In general, countries that devalue have to use restrictive aggregate demand policies to make sure that induced increases in prices do not simply undo the real effects of the nominal devaluation.

RELATIVE PRICES AND THE TRADE BALANCE: THE J CURVE

We come now to the second issue, the effect of changes in relative prices on the trade balance and the possibility that a depreciation *worsens* the trade balance. To make this point clear, we write out the trade balance, measured in terms of domestic goods, as

$$NX = X - \frac{eP_f}{P}Q \tag{3}$$

where X denotes the foreign demand for our goods or exports and Q denotes our own import quantity. The term $(eP_f/P)Q$ thus measures the *value* of our imports in terms of domestic goods.

Suppose that we now have an exchange depreciation and that, in the first instance, domestic and foreign prices, P and P_f, are unchanged. Then the relative price of imports, eP_f/P, rises. This leads to two effects. First, if the physical *volume* of imports does not change, their *value* measured in domestic currency unambiguously increases because of the higher price. This means higher import spending (measured in terms of the domestic currency) and thus a worsening of the trade balance. This is the source for the potentially perverse response of the trade balance to exchange depreciation.

However, there are two *volume* responses that run in the opposite direction: Exports should rise because our goods are now cheaper for foreigners to buy, and the volume of imports should decline because imports are more expensive.

The question, then, is whether the volume effects on imports and exports are sufficiently strong to outweigh the price effect, that is, whether depreciation raises or lowers net exports. The empirical evidence on this question is quite strong and shows the following result:[10] *The short-term volume effects, say, within a year, are quite small*

---

[10]See Ellen Meade, "Exchange Rate Adjustment and the J Curve," *Federal Reserve Bulletin,* October 1988, and Paul Krugman, "The J-Curve, the Fire Sale and the Hard Landing," *American Economic Review,* May 1989.

and thus do not outweigh the price effect. The long term volume effects, by contrast, are quite substantial, and certainly enough to make the trade balance respond in the normal fashion to a relative price change.

Why does this pattern of responses take place? First, the low short-term and high longer-term volume effects result from the length of time consumers and producers take to adjust to changes in relative prices. Some of these adjustments may be instantaneous, but it is clear that tourism patterns, for example, may take 6 months to a year to adjust and that relocation of production internationally in response to changes in relative costs and prices may take years. A case in point is increased foreign direct investment in the United States—say, Toyota's moving from Japan to California. In the long term, such direct investment leads to reduced imports by the United States, and thus to an improved trade balance, but such an adjustment takes years, not weeks or months.

The lag in the adjustment of trade flows to changes in relative prices is thus quite plausible. What do these lags imply about the impact of relative price changes on the trade balance? Suppose that at a particular time, starting with a deficit, we have a depreciation that raises the relative price of imports. The short-term effects result primarily from increased import prices with very little offsetting volume effects. Therefore, the trade balance initially worsens. Over time, as trade volume adjusts to the changed relative prices, exports rise and import volume progressively declines. The volume effects come to dominate, and in the long run the trade balance shows an improvement. This pattern of adjustment is referred to as the *J-curve effect,* because diagrammatically the response of the trade balance looks like a "J."

The J-curve effect could be seen in the behavior of the U.S. current account after 1985. Despite a rapid depreciation of the dollar starting in February 1985, the current account continued to worsen for the next year. But the current account began to improve in 1987 and continued improving in 1988.

The medium-term problem of sticky real wages and the J-curve effect provides important clues for the interpretation of macroeconomic experiences across countries, particularly in showing why depreciations typically do not lead to improvements in the current account in the short term.

Hysteresis Effects of Overvaluation

A further complication has been suggested in the aftermath of the large and persistent overvaluation of the dollar in 1980–1985, namely, *hysteresis effects.* Such effects are present, in the case of the exchange rate, when a change in the exchange rate that is later exactly reversed nonetheless leaves a long-term impact on the trade account. In the early 1980s, the U.S. dollar was very strong. This put U.S. firms at a sharp disadvantage in world trade and in the U.S. market. The dollar prices of imports declined, and in foreign markets, U.S. firms lost out because their relative prices increased.

These are the normal effects of a currency appreciation. The hysteresis argument is that when exchange rate changes are very large and long-lasting, they will lead to a relatively permanent change in trade patterns.[11] Once foreign firms have become es-

---

[11]See Richard Baldwin and Paul Krugman, "Persistent Trade Effects of Large Exchange Rate Shocks," *Quarterly Journal of Economics,* November 1989, and by the same authors, "The Persistence of the U.S. Trade Deficit," *Brookings Papers on Economic Activity* (1987).

tablished in the United States and consumers have become accustomed to their goods, even a reversal of the exchange rate to the initial level will not be enough to enable U.S. firms to recapture their share of the market. Similarly, when U.S. firms have lost foreign market share and even left some foreign markets entirely, going back to the initial exchange rate will not be enough to bring U.S. firms back. To return to the initial trade pattern, exchange rates would have to overshoot in the opposite direction, making it profitable to incur the costs of starting up export operations and competing with foreign firms that supply imports.

The evidence on these hysteresis effects remains tentative, but the idea is certainly plausible. The continued higher share of imports into the U.S. market and the failure of the U.S. external balance to correct itself fully, even after the 1985–1988 depreciation brought the real exchange rate back close to its 1980 level, support the idea that the damage of overvaluation may be a lasting one.

21-3

THE MONETARY APPROACH TO THE BALANCE OF PAYMENTS

It is frequently suggested that external balance problems are monetary in nature and that, in particular, balance-of-payments deficits are a reflection of an excessive money supply.

There is a simple first answer to that claim. It is obviously true that, for any given balance-of-payments deficit, a sufficient contraction of the money stock will restore external balance. The reason is that a monetary contraction, by raising interest rates and reducing spending, reduces income and therefore imports. It is equally true that this result could be achieved by tight fiscal policy, and so there is nothing especially monetary about this interpretation of remedies for external imbalance.

A more sophisticated interpretation of the problem recognizes the links among the balance-of-payments deficit, foreign exchange market intervention, and the money supply in a fixed exchange rate system. The automatic mechanism is for a sale of foreign exchange—as arises in the case of a balance-of-payments deficit—to reduce the stock of high-powered money and hence the money stock. In a surplus country the central bank increases the outstanding stock of high-powered money when it buys foreign exchange, thereby expanding the money stock. Given this link between the money supply and the external balance, it is obvious that this adjustment process must ultimately lead to the right money stock so that external payments will be in balance. This is the adjustment process discussed in Section 21-1.

STERILIZATION

The only way the automatic adjustment process can be suspended is through *sterilization operations*. Central banks frequently offset, or sterilize, the impact of foreign exchange market intervention on the money supply through open market operations. Thus, a deficit country that is selling foreign exchange and correspondingly reducing its

TABLE 21-1   Balance Sheet of the Monetary Authorities

ASSETS	LIABILITIES
Net foreign assets (*NFA*)	High-powered money (*H*)
Domestic credit (*DC*)	

money supply may offset this reduction by open market purchases of bonds that restore the money supply.[12]

With sterilization, persistent external deficits are possible because the link between the external imbalance and the equilibrating changes in the money stock is broken. It is in this sense that persistent external deficits are a monetary phenomenon: by sterilizing, the central bank actively maintains the stock of money too high for external balance.

THE MONETARY APPROACH AND THE IMF

The emphasis on monetary considerations in the interpretation of external balance problems is called the *monetary approach to the balance of payments*.[13] The monetary approach has been used extensively by the IMF in its analysis and design of economic policies for countries in balance-of-payments trouble. We give the flavor of the approach by describing typical IMF procedure in analyzing a balance-of-payments problem.

We start with the balance sheet of the monetary authority, usually the central bank, as in Table 21-1. The monetary authority's liabilities are high-powered money. But on the asset side it can hold both foreign assets—including foreign exchange reserves, gold, and claims on other central banks or governments—and domestic assets, or *domestic credit*. Domestic credit consists of the monetary authority's holdings of claims on the public sector—government debt—and on the private sector—usually loans to banks.

From the balance sheet identity, we have

$$\Delta NFA = \Delta H - \Delta DC \tag{4}$$

where ΔNFA denotes the change in net foreign assets, ΔH the change in high-powered money, and ΔDC the change in the central bank's extension of domestic credit. In words, the change in the central bank's holdings of foreign assets is equal to the change in the stock of high-powered money minus the change in domestic credit.

---

[12]*Currency boards,* such as those set up in Lithuania and Estonia, fix their country's exchange rate and permit high-powered money to be created only if it is fully backed by holdings of foreign currency. Currency boards amount to a fixed exchange rate system strictly without sterilization. Because sterilization is ruled out, adjustment is automatic, though of course not painless. Excellent references on currency boards include Steve Hanke and K. Schuler, *Currency Boards for Developing Countries* (San Francisco: International Center for Economic Growth, 1994), and Anna Schwartz, "Currency Boards: Their Past, Present, and Possible Future Role," *Carnegie-Rochester Conference on Public Policy,* December 1993.

[13]For a collection of essays on this topic, see Jacob Frenkel and Harry G. Johnson (eds.), *The Monetary Approach to the Balance of Payments* (London: Allen & Unwin, 1976). See also IMF, *The Monetary Approach to the Balance of Payments* (Washington, D.C.: International Monetary Fund, 1977), and Nadeem Haque, Kajal Lahiri, and Peter Montiel, "A Macroeconometric Model for Developing Countries," *IMF Staff Papers,* September 1990.

The important point about equation (4) is that ΔNFA is the balance of payments: official reserve transactions, which are all that ΔNFA is, are equal to the balance of payments.

The first step in developing a monetary-approach type of stabilization policy package is to decide on a balance-of-payments target, ΔNFA^*. The IMF asks how much of a deficit the country can afford and then suggests policies to make the projected deficit no larger. The target is based largely on the availability of loans and credit from abroad and the possibility of drawing down existing reserves or the need to add revenues.

The next step is to ask how much the demand for money in the country will increase. The planned changes in the stock of high-powered money, ΔH^*, will have to be just sufficient to produce, via the money multiplier process, the right increases in the stock of money to meet the expected increase in demand. Then, given ΔNFA^* and ΔH^*, equation (4) tells the monetary authority how much domestic credit it can extend consistent with its balance-of-payments target and expected growth in money demand. Typically, a stabilization plan drawn up by the IMF will include a suggested limit on the expansion of domestic credit.

The limit provides a *ceiling on domestic credit expansion.* The adoption of such a ceiling helps the central bank avoid the temptation of expanding its loans to the government or private sector in the face of rising interest rates or government budget deficits.

HOW DOES IT WORK?

The simplicity of equation (4) raises an obvious question. Since all it takes to improve the balance of payments is a reduction in the rate of domestic credit expansion, why not balance payments immediately and always? To answer this question, we need to understand the channels through which the curtailment of domestic credit improves the balance of payments.

Controlling domestic credit means operating tight monetary policy. Consider an economy that is growing and has some inflation, so demand for nominal balances is rising. If domestic credit expansion is slowed, an excess demand for money develops. This, in turn, causes interest rates to rise and spending to decline. The increase in interest rates leads to a balance-of-payments improvement. That is, the monetary approach as used by the IMF relies on restrictive monetary policy to control the balance of payments. There is, though, a subtle difference between domestic credit ceilings and ordinary tight money. In an open economy with fixed exchange rates, the money stock is endogenous. The central bank cannot control the money stock, since it has to meet whatever demand arises for foreign currency. But it can make "money" tight by reducing the growth of domestic credit. That will imply that the only source of money growth becomes an increase in foreign exchange reserves or foreign borrowing. The economy has to go through enough of a recession or rise in interest rates to generate a balance-of-payments surplus.

The use of domestic credit ceilings is a crude but easy-to-understand policy to improve the balance of payments. But the simplicity of the conceptual framework, and the apparent definiteness of the policy recommendations to which it leads, frequently makes it the best policy tool available, particularly if dramatic action is needed and the credibility of the government's policies needs to be restored.

THE MONETARY APPROACH AND DEPRECIATION

Proponents of the monetary approach have argued that depreciation of the exchange rate cannot improve the balance of payments except in the short run. The argument is that in the short run the depreciation does improve a country's competitive position and that this very fact gives rise to a trade surplus and therefore to an increase in the money stock. Over the course of time, the rising money supply raises aggregate demand and therefore prices until the economy returns to full employment and external balance. Devaluation thus exerts only a transitory effect on the economy, which lasts as long as prices and the money supply have not yet increased to match fully the higher import prices.

The analysis of the monetary approach is entirely correct in its insistence on a longer-run perspective in which, under fixed exchange rates, prices and the money stock adjust and the economy achieves internal and external balance. It is also correct in arguing that monetary or domestic credit restraint will improve the balance of payments. Typically, the tight money policy produced by slow domestic credit growth produces a recession.

The monetary approach is misdirected when it suggests that exchange rate policy cannot, even in the short run, affect a country's competitive position. More importantly, exchange rate changes frequently arise from a position of deficit and unemployment. In that case, a devaluation can be used to speed up the adjustment process.

We return now to the world of flexible exchange rates.[14]

21-4

FLEXIBLE EXCHANGE RATES, MONEY, AND PRICES

In studying flexible exchange rates, we assume, as in Chapter 12, that capital is perfectly mobile. The only difference from that earlier treatment is that now prices are allowed to change. We examine how output, the exchange rate, and prices respond to monetary and fiscal policies and how that response evolves over time. Our starting point is a discussion of the adjustment of prices and the exchange rate to the state of the economy.

THE ADJUSTMENT PROCESS

Figure 21-5 shows the interest rate and output, with full employment at Y^*. The assumption of perfect international capital mobility is reflected in the horizontal BB schedule. Only at an interest rate $i = i_f$ will the balance of payments be in equilibrium. If the interest rate were higher, there would be net inflows of capital. Conversely, with a lower domestic interest rate, capital would flow out and the balance of payments would turn toward a deficit position.

We make two strategic assumptions to describe the adjustment process: First, prices are rising whenever output exceeds the full-employment level. Second, because capital is highly mobile, the interest rate in Figure 21-5 is always moving toward the BB schedule—our interest rate cannot diverge far from that in the rest of the world.

---

[14]See Ronald MacDonald and Mark Taylor, "Exchange Rate Economics: A Survey," *IMF Staff Papers,* March 1992, for a broad discussion of models of exchange rate determination and the empirical evidence.

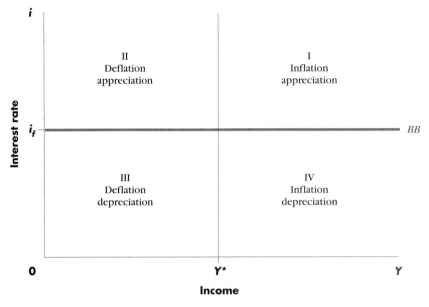

FIGURE 21-5   ADJUSTMENT OF EXCHANGE RATES AND PRICES.

There is a complicated set of adjustments in the background as the economy moves toward *BB*. For instance, say there is a monetary expansion that causes a decline in interest rates. Capital flows out, which means that people try to sell our currency to buy foreign currencies. Our currency depreciates, exports and income increase, money demand rises, and so do interest rates, thus moving us back toward *BB*. This mechanism works in reverse if domestic interest rates tend to rise because of a monetary tightening or fiscal expansion.

With these assumptions we can study the adjustment process using Figure 21-5. Anywhere to the right of Y^*, prices are rising; to the left, prices are falling. Points above *BB* lead to capital inflows and appreciation; points below, to capital outflows and depreciation. Moreover, with extremely high capital mobility, the exchange rate will adjust very rapidly, so we are always close to or on the *BB* schedule.

A MONETARY EXPANSION: SHORT- AND LONG-RUN EFFECTS

With given prices a monetary expansion under flexible rates and perfect capital mobility leads to depreciation and increased income. We ask how that result is modified once we take adjustments in prices into account. The answer is that the output adjustment is now only transitory. In the long run a monetary expansion leads to an exchange depreciation and to higher prices with no change in competitiveness.

In Figure 21-6 we start at point E with full employment, a payments balance, monetary equilibrium, and equilibrium in the domestic goods market. Now a monetary expansion takes place and shifts the *LM* schedule to *LM′*. The new goods and money market equilibrium at $E′$ involves an interest rate below the world level, and therefore the exchange rate immediately depreciates, raising home competitiveness and thus shifting

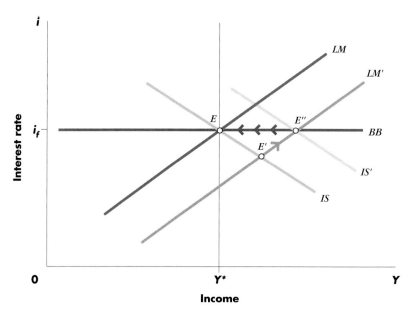

FIGURE 21-6   SHORT- AND LONG-RUN EFFECTS OF A MONETARY EXPANSION.

the *IS* schedule to *IS'*. The economy moves rapidly from *E* via *E'* to *E"*. Output has risen, the exchange rate has depreciated, and the economy has thereby gained in external competitiveness. But that is not the end of the story.

At *E"* output is above the full-employment level. Prices are therefore rising, and that implies that real balances are falling. As the real money stock, M/P, declines because of rising prices, the *LM* schedule starts shifting to the left. Interest rates tend to rise, capital tends to flow in, and the resulting appreciation leads now to a decline in competitiveness that also shifts the *IS* schedule back toward the initial equilibrium. Both the *IS* and *LM* schedules thus move back toward point *E*. The process continues until point *E* is reached again.

What adjustments have taken place once the economy is back to point *E?* At point *E,* interest rates have returned to their initial level and so have relative prices, eP_f/P. In moving from *E* to *E'* the exchange rate depreciated immediately, ahead of the rise in prices. But when prices increased and real balances fell, some of that depreciation was reversed. Over the whole adjustment process, prices and exchange rates rose in the same proportion, leaving relative prices, eP_f/P, and therefore aggregate demand unchanged. In the long run, money was therefore *entirely neutral.* Table 21-2 summarizes these results. By the end of the adjustment process, nominal money, prices, and the exchange rate have all increased in the same proportion, so the real money stock and relative prices—including the real exchange rate—are unchanged.

EXCHANGE RATE OVERSHOOTING

The analysis of monetary policy under flexible exchange rates, given above, leads to an important insight about the adjustment process. The important feature of the adjustment

TABLE 21-2   Short- and Long-Run Effects of a Monetary Expansion

	M/P	e	P	eP_f/P	Y
Short run	+	+	0	+	+
Long run	0	+	+	0	0

process is that *exchange rates and prices do not move at the same rate.* When a monetary expansion pushes interest rates down, the exchange rate adjusts immediately but prices adjust only gradually. Monetary expansion therefore leads in the short run to an immediate and abrupt change in relative prices and competitiveness.

Figure 21-7 shows time paths of nominal money, the exchange rate, and the price level implied by the analysis of Figure 21-6. For each of these variables we show an index that is initially equal to 100. The economy starts at long-run equilibrium. Then, at time T_0, the money stock is increased by 50 percent and stays at that higher level, as shown by the red schedule. The exchange rate immediately depreciates. In fact the exchange rate index rises more than money does, say, from the initial level of 100 at point A to a new level of 170 at point A'. Prices, by contrast, do not move rapidly.

Following the impact effect at time T_0, further adjustments take place. Because the gain in competitiveness at time T_0 has raised output above potential, there is now inflation. Prices are rising and, at the same time, the exchange rate is appreciating, thus undoing part of the initial, sharp depreciation. Over time, prices rise to match the increase in money, and the exchange rate will also match the higher level of money and

FIGURE 21-7   EXCHANGE RATE OVERSHOOTING.

prices. In the long run, real variables are unchanged. The adjustment pattern for the exchange rate seen in Figure 21-7 involves *overshooting*. The exchange rate overshoots its new equilibrium level when, in response to a disturbance, it first moves *beyond* the equilibrium it ultimately will reach and then gradually returns to the long-run equilibrium position. Overshooting means that changes in monetary policy produce large changes in exchange rates.

Those who believe that exchange rate overshooting introduces an undesirable instability into the economy argue that governments should intervene in foreign exchange markets to avoid large, excessive exchange rate fluctuations. The sharp dollar appreciation in 1980–1985 strongly reinforced the call for such intervention. In 1985 the major countries agreed in principle that they would intervene to try to prevent exchange rate instability. The agreement notwithstanding, major exchange rate movements continue to occur. For instance, in 1995, the yen reached an exchange rate of 80 yen to the dollar. The major industrial countries agreed that the yen was overvalued and should depreciate. This declaration, and intervention by the Bank of Japan, moved the exchange rate to 110 yen to the dollar within a year. Accordingly, although the current flexible rate system emerged because the Bretton Woods system of fixed rates broke down in 1973,[15] it is not viewed as the last word, and reform of the international monetary system is always on the agenda.

PURCHASING POWER PARITY (PPP)

In the preceding analysis, the exchange rate rose by precisely the right amount to offset the effects of domestic inflation on the real exchange rate. That is, the exchange depreciation maintained the *purchasing power* of our goods in terms of foreign goods between the initial and the final equilibrium points.

An important view of the determinants of the exchange rate is the theory that exchange rates move primarily as a result of differences in price-level behavior between the two countries in such a way as to maintain the terms of trade constant. This is the *purchasing power parity (PPP)* theory. The purchasing power parity theory of the exchange rate argues that exchange rate movements primarily reflect differences in inflation rates between countries. Examining the real exchange rate, eP_f/P, the theory maintains the following: When P_f and/or P changes, e changes in such a way as to maintain eP_f/P constant.[16]

PPP is a plausible description of the trend behavior of exchange rates, especially when inflation differentials between countries are large. In particular, we have seen that the PPP relationship does hold in the case of an increase in the money stock. If price-level movements are caused by monetary changes—as they are likely to be if the inflation rate is high—we should expect PPP relationships to hold in the long term.

But qualifications are necessary. First, even a monetary disturbance affects the real exchange rate in the short run. Exchange rates tend to move quite rapidly relative to prices, and thus in the short term of a quarter or a year we should not be at all surprised

---

[15]This is the system of fixed exchange rates that prevailed from the end of World War II to 1973, so called because it was designed, in 1944, in a major international conference held in Bretton Woods, New Hampshire.

[16]Assuming, of course, that the initial level of the real exchange rate had equated purchasing power between the two countries.

to see substantial deviations of exchange rates from the rates implied by PPP even if the exchange rate change is caused by monetary policy.

The second important qualification concerns the role of nonmonetary disturbances in affecting exchange rates. For example, we saw that an increase in exports leads to currency appreciation at unchanged domestic prices. This example illustrates that, over time, adjustments to *real* disturbances will affect the *equilibrium* real exchange rate. In the longer run, exchange rates and prices do *not* necessarily move together, as they do in a world where all disturbances are monetary. On the contrary, we may have changes in relative prices, which run counter to the purchasing power parity view of exchange rates.

Consider Figure 21-8, which shows that the real exchange rate between the dollar and the deutsche mark ($eP_{Ger}/P_{U.S.}$) fluctuates a great deal over time. The figure also shows the nominal exchange rate. According to PPP, when the exchange rate index (DM/\$) changes, the real exchange rate should not—because according to PPP the exchange rate should be moving only because relative price levels change. However, the real exchange rate clearly moves roughly in parallel with the nominal exchange rate, showing that PPP does not hold in the case of Germany and the United States over the period since 1979. Nor is PPP a good description of the behavior of exchange rates among the major currencies over any recent period.

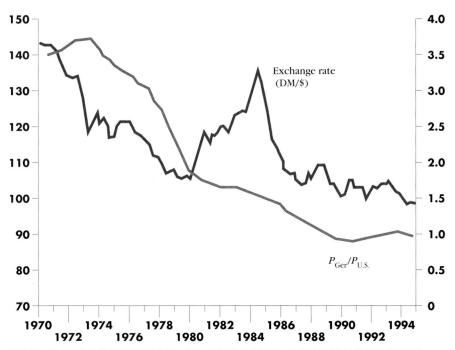

FIGURE 21-8 THE EXCHANGE RATE AND RELATIVE PRICES, GERMANY AND THE UNITED STATES, 1970–1995.

Note the different scales of the axes. The left axis shows relative prices, indexed to 1985 = 100. The right axis shows the number of deutsche marks per dollar.
(Source: DRI/McGraw-Hill Macroeconomic Database; International Financial Statistics Yearbook, 1996, IMF).

TABLE 21-3   Unit Labor Costs in Manufacturing
(Dollar index, 1992 = 100)

	UNITED STATES	GERMANY	JAPAN	CANADA
1960	—	11	11	32
1970	—	27	15	35
1985	90	42	50	70
1990	95	88	83	99
1995	97	113	140	85

Source: U.S. Department of Labor, *Monthly Labor Review,* November 1996.

EXTERNAL COMPETITIVENESS

PPP measures are closely related to the behavior of a country's competitiveness in external trade. A decline in a country's relative price level makes the country's goods relatively cheaper and thus more competitive. In Table 21-3 we show unit labor costs in manufacturing measured in U.S. dollars for several countries.

The data make it clear that nominal exchange rates affect unit labor costs in dollars. In 1985, when the dollar peaked, Germany and Japan had very low costs in dollars compared, say, to 1990, by which time the dollar had weakened considerably. Thus *nominal exchange rate movements clearly affect competitiveness.*

21-5

INTEREST DIFFERENTIALS AND EXCHANGE RATE EXPECTATIONS

A cornerstone of our theoretical model of exchange rate determination was international capital mobility. In particular, we argued that with capital markets sufficiently integrated, we would expect interest rates to be equated across countries. How does this assumption stand up to the facts?[17] In Figure 21-9 we show the U.S. federal funds rate and the money market rate in Germany. Obviously, these rates are not equal. How do we square this fact with our theory?

EXCHANGE RATE EXPECTATIONS

Our theoretical analysis was based on the assumption that capital flows internationally in response to nominal interest differentials. For example, if domestic interest rates were 6 percent and foreign rates were 10 percent, we would, according to the earlier sections, expect a capital outflow.

However, such a theory is incomplete in a world in which exchange rates can, do, and are expected to change.[18] For example, consider a situation in which the deutsche mark is expected to depreciate by 5 percent over the next year relative to the dollar. With a 5 percent deutsche mark depreciation, the return *in dollars* of investing in Germany is

[17]On capital mobility, see Jeffrey Frankel, "International Capital Mobility: A Review," *American Economic Review,* May 1991.

[18]You may wish to review the material in Chap. 17, "Financial Markets."

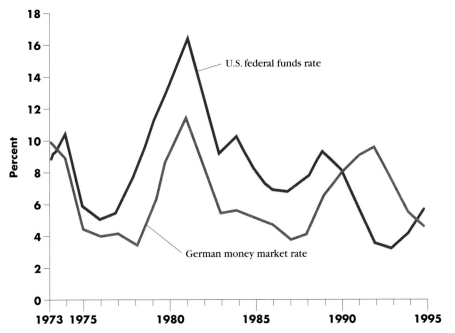

FIGURE 21-9 THE U.S. FEDERAL FUNDS RATE AND GERMAN MONEY MARKET RATE, 1973–1996.

(*Source:* International Financial Statistics Yearbook, *1996, IMF.*)

only 5 percent (= 10 percent − 5 percent). The natural preference is to invest in American bonds, even though the U.S. interest rate is below the German rate.

It is clear, therefore, that we must extend our discussion of interest rate equalization to incorporate expectations of exchange rate changes. Anyone who invests in domestic bonds earns the interest rate i. Alternatively, by investing in foreign bonds, the investor earns the interest rate on foreign bonds, i_f, *plus* whatever she earns from the appreciation of the foreign currency. The total return on foreign bonds, measured in our currency, is then

$$\text{Return on foreign bonds (in terms of domestic currency)} = i_f + \Delta e/e \qquad (5)$$

Of course, since the investor does not know at the time she makes her decision by how much the exchange rate will change, the term $\Delta e/e$ in equation (5) should be interpreted as the *expected* change in the exchange rate.

The introduction of exchange rate expectations modifies our equation for the balance of payments. Now capital flows are governed by the difference between our interest rate and the foreign rate adjusted for expected depreciation: $i - i_f - \Delta e/e$. An increase in foreign interest rates or an expectation of depreciation, given our interest rates, would lead to a capital outflow. Conversely, a rise in our rates or an expectation of appreciation would bring about a capital outflow. We thus write the balance of payments as

$$BP = NX\left(Y, \frac{eP_f}{P}\right) + CF\left(i - i_f - \frac{\Delta e}{e}\right) \qquad (6)$$

The adjustment for exchange rate expectations thus accounts for international differences in interest rates that persist even when capital is freely mobile among countries. When capital is completely mobile, we expect interest rates to be equalized, after adjusting for expected depreciation:

$$i = i_f - \Delta e/e \tag{6a}$$

Expected depreciation helps account for differences in interest rates among low- and high-inflation countries. When the inflation rate in a country is high, its exchange rate is expected to depreciate. In addition, the Fisher relationship suggests that the nominal interest rate in that country will be high.[19] Thus high-inflation countries tend to have high interest rates and depreciating currencies. This is an international extension of the Fisher equation, which relies on PPP to argue that inflation differentials internationally are matched by depreciation. Our long-term relation, then, is

$$\text{Inflation differential} \cong \text{interest differential} \cong \text{depreciation rate} \tag{7}$$

The $\cong$ means "approximately equal to." The relation is only approximate because exchange rates can move independently of prices and also because obstacles to capital flows may create long-term interest differentials.

SPECULATIVE CAPITAL FLOWS

Changes in exchange rate expectations can affect the actual exchange rate as well as the domestic interest rate and output. The point is made with the help of Figure 21-10,

[19]The Fisher relationship states that the nominal interest rate equals the expected real interest rate plus expected inflation, $i = r + \pi^e$.

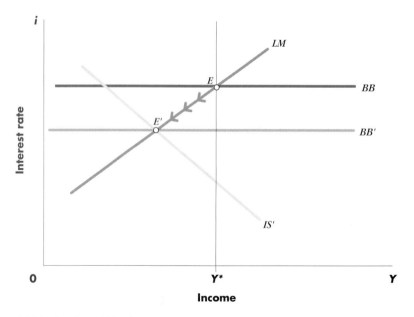

FIGURE 21-10   RESPONSE TO AN EXPECTED APPRECIATION OF CURRENCY.

which assumes perfect capital mobility, as specified in equation (6*a*). Here the *BB* schedule is drawn for a given foreign interest rate and a given expected rate of change of the exchange rate, say, zero.

Suppose that we start in full equilibrium at point *E* and that the market develops the expectation that the home currency will appreciate. This implies that even with a lower home interest rate, domestic assets are attractive, and so the *BB* schedule shifts downward by the amount of expected appreciation.

Point *E* is no longer an equilibrium, given the shift of the *BB* schedule to *BB'*, but rather a position of surplus with large-scale capital inflows motivated by the anticipation of appreciation. The surplus at *E* causes the exchange rate to start appreciating, and we move in a southwesterly direction, as indicated by the arrow. The speculative attack causes appreciation, a loss in competitiveness, and, consequently, falling output and employment. Thus the expectation of an exchange rate appreciation is *self-fulfilling*.

This analysis confirms that exchange rate expectations, through their impact on capital flows and thus on actual exchange rates, are a potential source of disturbance to macroeconomic equilibrium—something which policy makers who try to fix exchange rates when capital is fully mobile keep having to learn.

21-6

EXCHANGE RATE FLUCTUATIONS AND INTERDEPENDENCE

In the 1960s there was growing dissatisfaction with fixed exchange rates. The Bretton Woods system put in place at the end of World War II was called a "crisis system" because from time to time exchange rates would get out of line and expectations of exchange rate changes would mobilize massive capital flows that often precipitated the exchange rate changes that speculators expected. Is the system of flexible rates among the major currencies of the period since 1973 better? Is it less crisis-prone, and does it provide a better framework for macroeconomic stability? Before providing answers, we look briefly at how flexibly the system has, in fact, operated.

FOREIGN EXCHANGE MARKET INTERVENTION

When exchange rates are fully flexible, the government takes no action in the foreign exchange market. It stays out of the foreign exchange market, whatever happens to the exchange rate. Such a system is almost unheard of, although the United States did behave that way briefly in 1981–1982. More commonly, governments intervene in the foreign exchange market to a lesser or greater extent. *Foreign exchange market intervention* occurs when a government buys or sells foreign exchange in an attempt to influence the exchange rate.

The extent to which governments intervene in the foreign exchange markets varies substantially. They may try only to offset short-term fluctuations and buy or sell foreign exchange to maintain "orderly markets." But they also may try to keep an overvalued exchange rate from depreciating or an undervalued exchange rate from appreciating. *Dirty* (as opposed to clean) *floating* is the practice of using substantial intervention to try to maintain an exchange rate against the pressure of market forces.

For almost the entire period since 1973, exchange rate floating has been of the decidedly dirty variety. Governments have intervened on a very large scale. This leads naturally to the question of why a government would try to resist market forces to prevent an appreciation or a depreciation of the currency.

WHY GOVERNMENTS INTERVENE

Central banks intervene to affect exchange rates for several reasons.[20] Probably the main reason is the belief that many capital flows represent merely unstable expectations and that the induced movements in exchange rates cause unnecessary changes in domestic output. The second reason for intervention is a central bank's attempt to move the real exchange rate in order to affect trade flows. The third reason arises from the effects of the exchange rate on domestic inflation. Central banks sometimes intervene in the exchange market to prevent the exchange rate from depreciating, with the aim of preventing import prices from rising and thereby helping to slow inflation.

The basic argument for intervention (dirty floating) is that the central bank can intervene to smooth out fluctuations in exchange rates. The only—and overwhelming—objection to this argument is that there is no simple way of telling an erratic movement from a trend movement. How can we tell whether a current appreciation in the exchange rate is merely the result of a disturbance that will soon reverse itself or is the beginning of a trend movement in the exchange rate? There is no way of telling at the time a change occurs, although with the benefit of hindsight one can see which exchange rate movements were later reversed.

There is one circumstance under which central bank intervention might be desirable. It is clear from our earlier analysis that one of the key determinants of exchange rate behavior is expectations of economic policy. It may sometimes be possible to make it clear that there has been a change in policy only by intervening in the foreign exchange market. This is a case of putting your money where your mouth is.

STERILIZED VERSUS NONSTERILIZED INTERVENTION

In discussing intervention, it is important also to ask whether it works. For instance, does it make any difference to the exchange rate if the Bundesbank sells $1 billion from its foreign currency reserves?

To judge the effectiveness of intervention, we must distinguish between *sterilized* and *nonsterilized intervention,* discussed earlier in this chapter. In the case of sterilized intervention a central bank, say, buys foreign exchange, issuing domestic money. But then the increase in home money is reversed by an open market sale of securities. In the sterilized intervention case, therefore, the home money supply is kept unchanged. In the case of nonsterilization, by contrast, there is a change in the money stock equal to the amount of intervention.

It is widely agreed that nonsterilized intervention, because it changes the money supply, will affect exchange rates. There is widespread skepticism, however, about the

---

[20]Some academic critics oppose intervention. See, for instance, Milton Friedman, "Deja Vu in Currency Markets," *Wall Street Journal,* Sept. 22, 1992. Paul Volcker and Toyoo Gyohten, two prominent practitioners of intervention, discuss its merits in *Changing Fortunes: The World's Money and the Threat to American Leadership* (New York: Random House, 1992).

effectiveness of sterilized intervention. In 1978–1979 the U.S. dollar was depreciating in currency markets even though there was intervention on a massive scale. But that intervention was carefully sterilized. Only in late 1979, when the dollar depreciation began to alarm the Fed, did a change in policy take place. Monetary policy was tightened, and immediately the dollar depreciation was stopped and soon massively reversed.

That episode, and other evidence, strongly suggests the effectiveness of nonsterilized intervention and of intervention that is backed by credible policies. The earlier failure of sterilized intervention suggested that only unsterilized intervention could affect the exchange rate. But a more recent episode gives cause for rethinking that issue.

The very large appreciation of the dollar from 1980 to 1985, described in Box 21-5, was a major concern to policy makers in the United States, Europe, and Japan. Many policy makers thought that the markets had pushed the dollar too high and that only speculative forces were keeping it up. In September 1985 the finance ministers of the "Group of Five" (the United States, Japan, Germany, France, and the United Kingdom) announced their view that the dollar was too high, and their central banks went into action to sell dollars in order to drive the rate down. The dollar responded quickly, suggesting that concerted action can affect the exchange rate even if there is no obvious change in monetary policy. Such action is certainly not guaranteed to work, but it could work if there is widespread speculation in the markets about the future course of policy and if announcements and intervention suggest that future policy will try to move the exchange rate in a particular direction. By contrast, if policy makers are unwilling to use interest rates to defend their currency, as was the case in the United Kingdom in September 1992, even a $30 billion intervention cannot help the exchange rate.

INTERDEPENDENCE

It used to be argued that under flexible exchange rates countries could pursue their own national economic policies—monetary and fiscal policy and the inflation rate—without having to worry about the balance of payments. That is certainly correct, but it is also misleading. There are important linkages between countries *whatever the exchange rate regime.*[21]

These *spillover,* or *interdependence, effects* have been at the center of the discussion about flexible exchange rates. For instance, suppose the United States tightens monetary policy. As discussed earlier, U.S. interest rates rise and that attracts capital flows from abroad. The dollar appreciates, and foreign currencies depreciate. Table 21-4 shows the effects in other countries.

The U.S. appreciation implies a loss in competitiveness. World demand shifts from U.S. goods to those produced by our competitors. Therefore, at home, output and employment decline. Abroad, our competitors benefit from the depreciation of

---

[21]On interdependence, see Ralph C. Bryant et al., "Domestic and Cross-Border Consequences of U.S. Macroeconomic Policies," International Finance Discussion Paper 344, Board of Governors of the Federal Reserve System, March 1989; Jeffrey Shaffer, "What the U.S. Current Account Deficit Has Meant for Other OECD Countries," *OECD Studies,* Spring 1988; and Paul Masson et al., "Multimod Mark II: A Revised and Extended Model," IMF Occasional Paper 71, 1990.

BOX 21-5 Unsustainable Deficits and the Dollar Bubble

In the early 1980s there was very little concern about U.S. current account deficits. Following the 1982 world recession, the U.S. economy was growing much faster than others, and a deficit in the current account was seen as a by-product of a strong expansion. But increasingly the strong dollar added to the deficit by eroding U.S. competitiveness (see Figure 1).

By 1985 an ever-larger deficit and an ever-stronger dollar started raising questions: If the dollar remained at its 1985 level, would the deficit ever go away? And if the deficit did not decline, would the United States soon become a net foreign debtor and then, year after year, have to go increasingly into debt? And if debt and the interest that had to be paid on the debt were to grow for a long period, would that be consistent with a strong dollar?

THE DOLLAR AS A BUBBLE

The extreme rise of the dollar and the large deficit in 1985 led to the conclusion that the dollar was overvalued. Dollar depreciation on a major scale would have to take place at some time in order to trim the deficit and thus slow down the rate of increase in foreign indebtedness. But if a major dollar depreciation was inevitable, why were the foreign exchange markets still pushing the dollar up? If the foreign exchange markets anticipated a major dollar decline, traders would be quick to buy other currencies, trying to avoid being caught when the dollar fell. The attempt by everybody to sell would therefore bring about a very rapid alignment of the dollar.

Even as the discussion of an unsustainable dollar emerged, the dollar actually started its post-1985 decline. But that left unanswered the question of why it had risen so much in the first place. Explanations of tight U.S. monetary policy and fiscal expansion went some way in explaining the rise of the dollar, but that could not be the whole story; the timing did not match, since monetary policy had started easing already in fall 1982.

Some observers concluded that the dollar peak of 1985 had been a *speculative bubble*, a departure of the dollar from the level justified by the fundamental factors that should

their currency. They become more competitive, and therefore output and employment abroad expand. Our monetary tightening thus tends to promote employment gains abroad, which come, of course, at the expense of our own employment.

There are also spillover effects through prices. When our currency appreciates, import prices in dollars fall. Therefore, our inflation tends to decline quite rapidly when there is a sharp dollar appreciation. But abroad the opposite occurs. Foreign currencies depreciate, and therefore prices in those currencies tend to increase. Inflation abroad thus rises. Foreigners might welcome an increase in employment as a side effect of our

FIGURE 1 THE U.S. CURRENT ACCOUNT AS A PERCENTAGE OF GDP, 1970–1996.

(Source: DRI/McGraw-Hill Macroeconomic Database.)

determine its value: interest rates, the current account, and expected future current accounts. Once the bubble had burst, in part because of central bank cooperation in intervention, the dollar declined for 2 years to reach more realistic levels. The discussion of whether asset markets and, in particular, the foreign exchange market are or are not rational continues unresolved.*

*See Jeffrey Frankel and Ken Froot, "Using Survey Data to Test Standard Propositions Regarding Exchange Rate Expectations," *American Economic Review*, March 1987. Exchange rate expectations, and their rationality, are reviewed in Takatoshi Ito, "Foreign Exchange Rate Expectations: Micro Survey Data," *American Economic Review*, June 1990; Shinji Takagi, "Exchange Rate Expectations," *IMF Staff Papers*, March 1991; and Ken Froot and Richard Thaler, "Anomalies: Foreign Exchange," *Journal of Economic Perspectives*, Summer 1990.

monetary policy, but they certainly could do without the inflation that comes from currency depreciation.

In the same way, U.S. fiscal policies exert effects abroad. A U.S. fiscal expansion, such as the one in the 1980–1985 period, will lead to dollar appreciation and a loss in competitiveness. The direct increase in our spending and the deterioration in our competitiveness are the channels through which our expansion is shared abroad. When the United States has a fiscal expansion, the rest of the world shares via increased exports.

TABLE 21-4   Monetary and Fiscal Policy Effects with Interdependence

	U.S. MONETARY CONTRACTION		U.S. FISCAL EXPANSION	
	UNITED STATES	REST OF THE WORLD	UNITED STATES	REST OF THE WORLD
Exchange rate	$ appreciates		$ appreciates	
Output	−	+	+	+
Inflation	−	+	−	+

Table 21-4 also shows the effects of monetary and fiscal policy on inflation. Because fiscal expansion leads to appreciation, the decline in import prices helps reduce inflation in the expanding country. But abroad import prices will rise, and that means inflation will be increased. These impacts of exchange rate movements on inflation were important factors in changing inflation rates in industrial countries in the 1980–1985 period.

Policy makers abroad therefore must decide whether to accept the higher-employment–higher-inflation effects of our policies or whether they should change their own policies. If inflation is already a problem abroad, or if the rest of the world is highly averse to inflation, the policy response abroad to this *imported inflation* may well be to tighten money. If the dollar appreciation was caused by a tightening of U.S. monetary policy, it will also cause a monetary contraction abroad if foreign countries decide to fight imported inflation. That means our monetary tightening touches off worldwide tightening. This was substantially what happened in the worldwide recession of 1981–1982.

POLICY SYNCHRONIZATION

The large changes in exchange rates that occur when policies are not fully synchronized between countries pose a major threat to free trade. When import prices fall by 20 or 30 percent because of a currency appreciation, large shifts in demand will occur. Domestic workers become unemployed, and they have no trouble seeing that it is foreigners who gain the jobs they just lost. Accordingly, there will be pressure for protection—tariffs or quotas—to keep out imports that are "artificially cheap" due to the currency appreciation. In the United States in the 1980s repeated calls for protection in the automobile industry, in steel, and in many other industries reflected in large part the side effects of a dollar that appreciated sharply in response to tight money and easy fiscal policy.

The experience of the last 20 years offers an unambiguous answer to the question of whether flexible exchange rates isolate countries from shocks that originate abroad. Under flexible exchange rates there is as much or more interdependence as there is under fixed rates. Moreover, because exchange rates are so flexible and so ready to respond to policies (good or bad), macroeconomic management does not become easier. Further, to the extent that exchange rate overshooting causes sharp changes in competitiveness, it leads to protectionist sentiment.

On all counts then, flexible rates are far from being a perfect system. But there is no better system, for the Bretton Woods system collapsed. Therefore, we can ask only whether, through international coordination of interests and policies, we can make the system work better than it has in the recent past. Although the leaders of the major industrial countries have repeatedly recognized their interdependence and agreed to work toward more coordinated policies, there have been no major institutional changes to ensure coordination of economic policies.[22]

One major suggestion is to have *target zones*. In a target-zone arrangement central banks limit the fluctuations of exchange rates to a specified range. Target zones require policy coordination. Specifically, in an effective target-zone arrangement governments must synchronize both their monetary and their fiscal policies.[23] The unwillingness to give up this sovereignty stands in the way of more limited exchange rate fluctuations between the United States, Europe, and Japan. Even within Europe, as the discussion around the *Maastricht Treaty* that envisages the creation of a common European central bank shows, giving up monetary independence is not an easy step.[24]

SUMMARY

1. A monetary expansion in the long run increases the price level and the exchange rate, keeping real balances and the terms of trade constant. In the short run, though, the monetary expansion increases the level of output and reduces the interest rate, depreciating the exchange rate. The exchange rate overshoots its new equilibrium level.

2. External imbalances can be financed in the short term. In the long run they call for adjustment. Adjustment of the external balance calls for expenditure-reducing and expenditure-switching policies. The former change the level of spending; the latter affect the composition of spending between domestic goods and imports and exports.

3. Under fixed exchange rates, the automatic adjustment mechanism works through prices and money. Unemployment leads to a decline in prices, a gain in competitiveness, increased net exports, and a gain in employment. Money responds to trade imbalances, affecting the level of interest rates, spending, and hence the payments deficit.

4. Because trade flows respond only gradually to a change in the real exchange rate, we observe a J-curve: a real depreciation will worsen the trade balance in the short run but then will gradually improve it in later years as volume effects dominate.

5. The monetary approach to the balance of payments draws attention to the fact that a payments deficit is always a reflection of a monetary disequilibrium and is

[22]See Jacob A. Frenkel, Morris Goldstein, and Paul Masson, "Characteristics of a Successful Exchange Rate System," IMF Occasional Paper 82, July 1991, and Morris Goldstein, Peter Isard, Paul Masson, and Mark Taylor, "Policy Issues in the Evolving International Monetary System," IMF Occasional Paper 96, June 1992.

[23]For a proposal on target zones, see John Williamson and Marcus Miller, *Targets and Indicators: A Blueprint for the International Coordination of Economic Policy* (Washington, D.C.: Institute for International Economics, 1987); J. Williamson, "The Case for Roughly Stabilizing the Real Value of the Dollar," *American Economic Review,* May 1989; and Martin Feldstein, "The Case against Trying to Stabilize the Dollar," *American Economic Review,* May 1989. See, too, Jacob Frenkel and Morris Goldstein, "Exchange Rate Volatility and Misalignment: Evaluating Some Proposals for Reform," in Federal Reserve Bank of Kansas City, *Financial Market Volatility* (Kansas City, 1989).

[24]See Daniel Gros and Niels Thygesen, *European Monetary Integration: From the European Monetary System to European Monetary Union* (London: Longman, 1992); Paul de Grauwe, *The Economics of Monetary Integration* (Oxford, England: Oxford University Press, 1992); and Horst Ungerer et al., "The European Monetary System: Developments and Perspectives," IMF Occasional Paper 73, 1990.

always self-correcting. But the correction mechanism, because it involves unemployment, may be excessively painful compared with policy actions such as devaluation.

6. Exchange rate overshooting results from the rapid response of exchange rates to monetary policy and the sluggish adjustment of prices. A monetary expansion will lead to an immediate depreciation but only a gradual increase in prices. Exchange rate overshooting implies that real exchange rates are highly volatile.

7. Purchasing power parity (PPP) refers to the long-run tendency of exchange rates to offset divergent trends in national price levels. The currency of the country with the higher rate of inflation would tend to be depreciating at a rate equal to the inflation differential. If exchange rates follow PPP, nominal exchange rate movements have no effects on competitiveness. In the short run, exchange rates certainly do not follow a PPP pattern.

8. Capital moves internationally in response to yield differentials, taking into account anticipated exchange rate movements. Interest rates in a country with a depreciating currency have to be sufficiently high to compensate asset holders for the depreciation of the assets.

9. Changes in nominal exchange rates will affect relative prices only if there are no offsetting changes in wages and prices. The real exchange rate, $R = eP_f/P$, can change as a result of nominal exchange rate movements only if P_f/P does not move in a fully offsetting manner. Among industrialized countries stickiness of wages and prices ensures that real exchange rates change when nominal rates do.

10. Governments can intervene in exchange markets to limit the impact on output and prices of exchange rate fluctuations stemming from asset market disturbances. But intervention is problematic when the authorities cannot determine whether the exchange rate is moving on account of fundamentals or for purely speculative reasons.

11. Even under flexible exchange rates economies are closely tied to one another. A monetary expansion at home will lead to unemployment and disinflation abroad. A fiscal expansion will cause an expansion abroad along with inflation. These interdependence effects make a case for coordinating policies.

KEY TERMS

automatic adjustment mechanisms	International Monetary Fund (IMF)	exchange rate overshooting
sterilized intervention	devaluation	purchasing power parity (PPP)
classical adjustment process	real devaluation	self-fulfilling expectations
expenditure-switching policies	crawling peg	foreign exchange market intervention
expenditure-reducing (-increasing) policies	wage-price spiral	speculative bubble
internal and external balance	sticky real wages	spillover (interdependence) effects
tariff	J-curve effect	target zone
World Trade Organization (WTO)	hysteresis effects	Maastricht Treaty
	monetary approach	
	domestic credit	
	domestic credit ceiling	
	neutrality of money	

PROBLEMS

Conceptual

1. Consider a country that is in a position of full employment and balanced trade. Which of the following types of disturbance can be remedied with standard aggregate demand tools of stabilization? Indicate in each case the impact on external and internal balance as well as the appropriate policy response.

    a. A loss of export markets

    b. A reduction in saving and a corresponding increase in the demand for domestic goods

    c. An increase in government spending

    d. A shift in demand from imports to domestic goods

    e. A reduction in imports with a corresponding increase in saving

2. In relation to external imbalance, a distinction is frequently made between imbalances that should be "adjusted" and those that should be "financed." Give examples of disturbances that give rise, respectively, to imbalances that require adjustment and those that should more appropriately be financed.

3. Should countries intervene to stabilize the exchange rate?

4. What is a wage-price spiral, and how can a devaluation start one? Is it something undesirable? Explain. How can a wage-price spiral be avoided?

5. What is a target-zone arrangement? What are the benefits and costs of participating in one?

6. It is a consequence of our model of (flexible) exchange rate determination that, when capital markets are sufficiently integrated, interest rates across countries must be equated. Clearly, however, there *are* differences across countries. How can we reconcile this fact with our theory?

7. Equation (7) in Section 21-5 tells us that inflation differentials, interest differentials, and depreciation rates are all *approximately equal.* Why are they only approximately, as opposed to exactly, equal?

8. In the early 1970s, the United States moved from a system of fixed exchange rates to a system of floating ones. Is the current flexible system less crisis-prone, or does it provide a better framework for macroeconomic stability? Discuss.

9. Discuss the lures and dangers in exchange market intervention when exchange rates are flexible. Do you think such intervention is a good idea?

10. Is the importance of spillover effects larger or smaller under flexible exchange rates, as opposed to fixed ones? Is macroeconomic management easier under one regime than the other?

Technical

1. Assume that there is perfect mobility of capital. How does the imposition of a tariff affect the exchange rate, output, and the current account? (*Hint:* Given the exchange rate, the tariff reduces our demand for imports.)

2. Use the central bank balance sheet to show how a balance-of-payments deficit affects the stock of high-powered money under fixed exchange rates. Show, too, how sterilization operations are reflected in the central bank's balance sheet.

3. Consider a world with some capital mobility; the home country's capital account improves as domestic interest rates rise relative to the world rate of interest. Initially, the home country is in internal and external balance. (Draw the *IS, LM,* and *BB* schedules.) Assume now that the rate of interest abroad increases.

    a. Show the effect of the foreign interest rate increase on the BB schedule.

    b. What policy response would immediately restore internal and external balance?

    c. If the authorities took no action, what would be the adjustment process along the lines described by the monetary approach to the balance of payments?

4. Suppose your country's exports were to permanently increase. Explain how income, price adjustments, and adjustments to the real money supply would interact to lead it back to full employment and external balance.

5. What are the short- and long-term volume effects of an exchange depreciation? Does empirical evidence suggest that they are of sufficient size to outweigh price effects and therefore improve the trade balance?

6. Show, graphically, the short- and long-run effects of a monetary expansion when both exchange rates and prices are flexible and capital is perfectly mobile. What happens during the period of adjustment from the short to the long run?

*7. Consult the *Wall Street Journal* or some other newspaper that lists foreign exchange rates on its financial pages. For some countries, such as Britain and Germany, you should find futures prices listed. A futures price is the price to be paid today to receive 1 unit of the foreign currency in the future. A 30-day futures price for the pound sterling, say, is the price paid today to receive 1 pound 30 days from now. Explain why the futures prices are not generally equal to the spot price—the price paid today to receive the foreign currency today. See whether you can explain the difference between the relationship of spot and futures prices for the pound and deutsche mark, respectively.

*An asterisk denotes a more difficult problem.

INDEX

Note: Page numbers followed by *n*. indicate reference notes or source notes.

Selected Historical Series on Gross Domestic Product and Related Series
(Billions of 1992 dollars, except as noted)

YEAR	GDP (1992 DOLLARS)	GDP (CURRENT DOLLARS)	IMPLICIT PRICE DEFLATOR (1992 = 100)	PERSONAL CONSUMPTION EXPENDITURES	GROSS PRIVATE DOMESTIC INVESTMENT	GOVERNMENT EXPENDITURES	EXPORTS	IMPORTS	DISPOSABLE PERSONAL INCOME	SAVING AS A PERCENT OF DISPOSABLE PERSONAL INCOME
1929	790.9	103.8	13.12	593.9	92.4	105.4	35.6	46.3	635.3	4.3
1930	719.7	91.1	12.6	562.1	59.8	116.2	29.4	40.3	594.2	3.8
1931	674	76.4	11.34	544.9	37.6	121.2	24.4	35.2	573.5	3.5
1932	584.3	58.6	10.05	496.1	9.9	117.1	19.1	29.2	496.7	−1.4
1933	577.3	56.2	9.78	484.8	16.4	112.8	19.2	30.4	481.6	−2.1
1934	641.1	65.9	10.27	519	31.5	127.3	21.4	31.1	528.6	0.6
1935	698.4	73.1	10.46	550.9	58	131.3	22.6	40.7	578.9	3.7
1936	790	83.6	10.58	606.9	75.5	152.5	23.7	40.2	650.9	5.6
1937	831.5	91.8	10.96	629.7	94	147	29.9	45.3	673.5	5.3
1938	801.2	85.9	10.75	619.5	61.3	157.8	29.6	35.2	634.4	1.1
1939	866.5	91.9	10.61	654	79.5	171.6	31.2	36.9	687.9	3.7
1940	941.2	101.2	10.73	688	111.3	174.2	35.4	37.8	734.3	5
1941	1,101.80	126.7	11.43	737.1	137.3	288	36.4	46.5	845.6	11.7
1942	1,308.90	161.6	12.34	719.7	72.1	692	23.9	42.2	952.8	23.8
1943	1,523.00	198.3	13.03	739.5	41.9	1,032.20	19.9	53.3	995.8	25.2
1944	1,644.70	219.7	13.37	761	52.2	1,158.50	21.4	55.7	1,031.30	25.7
1945	1,626.70	223.2	13.72	808.4	68.8	1,012.00	30.3	59.3	1,016.80	19.9
1946	1,447.70	222.6	15.35	907.9	176.8	349	66	49.1	1,011.00	9.3
1947	1,430.70	244.6	17.08	926.2	169.9	290.3	75.4	46.6	974.1	3.9
1948	1,491.00	269.7	18.08	946.4	216	310.3	59.4	54.4	1,025.60	6.6
1949	1,479.80	267.8	18.09	972.2	163.2	345.8	58.8	52.5	1,031.60	4.6
1950	1,611.30	294.6	18.26	1,034.10	234.1	344.6	51.4	62	1,124.70	6.7
1951	1,734.00	339.7	19.51	1,049.20	235.2	468.6	63.1	64.5	1,157.30	8.1
1952	1,798.70	358.6	19.92	1,082.40	210.6	566.2	60.1	70.2	1,194.80	8.1
1953	1,881.40	379.7	20.18	1,135.00	220.4	605.2	56.1	76.8	1,254.30	7.9
1954	1,868.20	381.3	20.41	1,158.90	209.9	562.6	58.9	73	1,270.20	7.1
1955	2,001.10	415.1	20.71	1,242.60	261.9	541.3	65.1	81.8	1,355.60	6.6
1956	2,040.20	438	21.44	1,278.20	257.9	542.8	75.9	88.4	1,418.50	8
1957	2,078.50	461	22.18	1,308.20	246.1	566.8	82.5	92.1	1,452.60	8.1
1958	2,057.50	467.3	22.72	1,318.80	224.5	585.3	71.2	96.5	1,466.40	8.2
1959	2,210.20	507.2	22.95	1,394.60	271.7	618.5	71.9	106.6	1,533.90	7.2
1960	2,262.90	526.6	23.27	1,432.60	270.5	617.2	86.8	108.1	1,569.20	6.6
1961	2,314.30	544.8	23.54	1,461.50	267.6	647.2	88.3	107.3	1,619.40	7.7
1962	2,454.80	585.2	23.84	1,533.80	302.1	686	93	119.5	1,697.50	7.6
1963	2,559.40	617.4	24.12	1,596.60	321.6	701.9	100	122.7	1,759.30	7
1964	2,708.40	663	24.48	1,692.30	348.3	715.9	113.3	129.2	1,885.80	7.9
1965	2,881.10	719.1	24.95	1,799.10	397.2	737.6	115.6	143	2,003.90	7.8
1966	3,069.20	787.8	25.66	1,902.00	430.6	804.6	123.4	164.2	2,110.60	7.5
1967	3,147.20	833.6	26.48	1,958.60	411.8	865.6	126.1	176.2	2,202.30	8.7
1968	3,293.90	910.6	27.64	2,070.20	433.3	892.4	135.3	202.5	2,302.10	7.7
1969	3,393.60	982.2	28.94	2,147.50	458.3	887.5	142.7	214	2,377.20	7.2
1970	3,397.60	1,035.60	30.48	2,197.80	426.1	866.8	158.1	223.1	2,469.00	8.5
1971	3,510.00	1,125.40	32.05	2,279.50	474.9	851	159.2	235	2,568.30	8.8
1972	3,702.30	1,237.30	33.42	2,415.90	531.8	854.1	172	261	2,685.70	7.6
1973	3,916.30	1,382.60	35.3	2,532.60	595.5	848.4	209.6	272.6	2,875.20	9.5
1974	3,891.20	1,496.90	38.46	2,514.70	546.5	862.9	229.8	265.3	2,854.20	9.5
1975	3,873.90	1,630.60	42.09	2,570.00	446.6	876.3	228.2	235.4	2,903.60	9.3
1976	4,082.90	1,819.00	44.55	2,714.30	537.4	876.8	241.6	281.5	3,017.60	7.9
1977	4,273.60	2,026.90	47.42	2,829.80	622.1	884.7	247.4	311.6	3,115.40	6.9
1978	4,503.00	2,291.40	50.88	2,951.60	693.4	910.6	273.1	338.6	3,276.00	7.5
1979	4,630.60	2,557.50	55.22	3,020.20	709.7	924.9	299	344.3	3,365.50	7.7
1980	4,615.00	2,784.20	60.34	3,009.70	628.3	941.4	331.4	321.3	3,385.70	8.5
1981	4,720.70	3,115.90	66.01	3,046.40	686	947.7	335.3	329.7	3,464.90	9.4
1982	4,620.30	3,242.10	70.18	3,081.50	587.2	960.1	311.4	325.5	3,495.60	9.1
1983	4,803.70	3,514.50	73.16	3,240.60	642.1	987.3	303.3	366.6	3,592.80	7
1984	5,140.10	3,902.40	75.92	3,407.60	833.4	1,018.40	328.4	455.7	3,855.40	8.7
1985	5,323.50	4,180.70	78.53	3,566.50	823.8	1,080.10	337.3	485.2	3,972.00	7.2
1986	5,487.70	4,422.20	80.58	3,708.70	811.8	1,135.00	362.2	526.1	4,101.00	6.5
1987	5,649.50	4,692.30	83.06	3,822.30	821.5	1,165.90	402	558.2	4,168.20	5.3
1988	5,865.20	5,049.60	86.1	3,972.70	828.2	1,180.90	465.8	580.2	4,332.10	5.5
1989	6,062.00	5,438.70	89.72	4,064.60	863.5	1,213.90	520.2	603	4,416.80	5.1
1990	6,136.30	5,743.80	93.64	4,132.20	815	1,250.40	564.4	626.3	4,498.20	5.3
1991	6,079.40	5,916.70	97.32	4,105.80	738.1	1,258.00	599.9	622.2	4,500.00	6
1992	6,244.40	6,244.40	100	4,219.80	790.4	1,263.80	639.4	669	4,626.70	6.2
1993	6,386.10	6,553.00	102.62	4,339.50	857	1,261.00	658.2	730.2	4,682.00	4.8
1994	6,608.40	6,935.70	104.96	4,473.20	979.3	1,260.00	712	817.6	4,786.70	3.9
1995	6,742.20	7,253.80	107.57	4,577.80	1,009.40	1,260.20	775.4	883	4,943.30	4.6
1996	6,906.80	7,576.10	109.88	4,690.70	1,056.60	1,270.60	825.9	939.5	5,086.00	4.9

Source: Survey of Current Business, May 1997.

Real Net Stock of Fixed Reproducible Tangible Wealth, 1929–95

[Billions of chained (1992) dollars; yearend estimates]

YEAREND	TOTAL	FIXED PRIVATE CAPITAL					GOVERNMENT-OWNED FIXED CAPITAL			DURABLE GOODS OWNED BY CONSUMERS
		TOTAL	NONRESIDENTIAL			RESIDENTIAL	TOTAL	FEDERAL	STATE AND LOCAL	
			TOTAL	EQUIPMENT	STRUCTURES					
1929	3,392.3	2,933.8	1,530.1	281.5	1,309.1	1,397.9	446.5	84.3	361.2	154.3
1930	3,451.3	2,967.8	1,555.3	283.4	1,335.1	1,406.4	472.1	84.9	386.0	156.2
1931	3,465.7	2,963.5	1,547.2	275.0	1,339.8	1,410.4	498.6	86.7	410.9	153.7
1932	3,432.7	2,922.4	1,514.6	257.8	1,331.8	1,403.5	520.1	89.5	429.5	146.8
1933	3,389.4	2,873.7	1,476.7	241.3	1,316.4	1,394.5	535.2	95.4	438.7	140.4
1934	3,370.6	2,840.5	1,451.2	231.6	1,303.4	1,387.7	554.6	103.4	450.5	136.2
1935	3,377.5	2,825.6	1,437.4	228.5	1,292.7	1,387.5	575.8	114.4	460.9	135.4
1936	3,428.8	2,835.6	1,440.5	232.9	1,288.8	1,394.6	609.4	124.9	483.9	138.8
1937	3,490.3	2,861.5	1,457.0	242.1	1,292.6	1,403.7	637.2	134.2	502.4	143.7
1938	3,523.0	2,862.8	1,449.9	239.5	1,288.8	1,412.6	668.8	143.2	525.0	143.9
1939	3,581.4	2,878.9	1,448.9	240.2	1,286.3	1,430.1	704.8	151.7	552.5	148.3
1940	3,657.7	2,910.1	1,459.8	248.5	1,285.1	1,450.6	739.0	165.5	572.6	155.7
1941	3,791.4	2,957.9	1,484.3	261.8	1,291.7	1,473.9	822.1	237.4	584.3	160.7
1942	3,995.6	2,947.5	1,472.1	257.9	1,283.9	1,476.0	1,042.1	466.6	586.7	159.5
1943	4,226.9	2,921.6	1,453.6	252.7	1,270.7	1,468.7	1,315.0	767.4	583.1	155.2
1944	4,422.5	2,914.5	1,454.0	258.7	1,262.3	1,461.3	1,548.0	1,030.6	578.2	150.2
1945	4,514.9	2,930.4	1,477.5	278.1	1,261.2	1,454.5	1,640.4	1,138.0	574.5	148.7
1946	4,532.4	3,022.0	1,533.2	307.3	1,283.3	1,490.6	1,522.0	1,005.5	576.0	164.4
1947	4,594.8	3,142.9	1,600.3	349.9	1,302.1	1,544.6	1,411.9	875.4	583.5	186.5
1948	4,689.6	3,278.6	1,669.6	390.7	1,326.5	1,611.3	1,327.2	767.0	595.5	208.3
1949	4,812.5	3,388.2	1,720.5	416.7	1,349.0	1,669.9	1,299.0	713.3	615.3	230.6
1950	4,992.9	3,536.0	1,780.2	445.9	1,376.8	1,757.4	1,274.9	660.3	638.8	261.4
1951	5,191.8	3,664.2	1,840.4	472.9	1,407.9	1,825.3	1,319.9	681.8	663.0	280.8
1952	5,389.8	3,783.0	1,894.1	495.6	1,437.7	1,890.5	1,385.4	725.5	687.4	295.0
1953	5,615.0	3,912.9	1,956.6	522.0	1,472.4	1,957.9	1,458.3	774.0	714.5	314.6
1954	5,824.4	4,041.4	2,011.2	540.4	1,508.6	2,031.7	1,525.4	807.9	749.0	329.5
1955	6,074.2	4,198.2	2,078.3	566.6	1,548.3	2,121.4	1,584.0	828.8	786.8	355.6
1956	6,301.7	4,351.7	2,152.5	592.0	1,596.9	2,200.9	1,639.8	846.0	825.2	372.8
1957	6,515.5	4,496.3	2,224.7	617.4	1,643.1	2,273.3	1,695.7	860.0	866.4	386.9
1958	6,694.7	4,613.7	2,269.2	625.4	1,681.9	2,347.5	1,760.5	878.8	912.3	391.8
1959	6,933.2	4,766.8	2,326.4	642.4	1,722.6	2,445.4	1,835.3	907.4	958.8	405.9
1960	7,158.7	4,916.0	2,390.1	660.6	1,768.8	2,532.0	1,903.4	929.3	1,005.0	418.1
1961	7,380.2	5,059.3	2,449.3	675.1	1,815.3	2,617.4	1,984.3	960.5	1,055.3	424.8
1962	7,641.3	5,225.0	2,521.0	697.9	1,864.2	2,712.5	2,066.5	991.5	1,106.9	441.1
1963	7,926.6	5,409.9	2,598.3	725.1	1,913.4	2,821.6	2,144.3	1,012.1	1,163.8	462.8
1964	8,249.0	5,623.5	2,696.2	762.4	1,971.8	2,938.2	2,222.5	1,028.1	1,225.1	490.0
1965	8,616.0	5,866.5	2,827.6	816.7	2,045.0	3,048.9	2,300.3	1,038.9	1,290.8	527.4
1966	9,004.5	6,114.4	2,977.8	883.6	2,122.4	3,144.6	2,389.3	1,056.4	1,361.0	569.4
1967	9,364.1	6,338.8	3,110.7	939.8	2,194.9	3,234.7	2,481.4	1,072.2	1,435.5	606.3
1968	9,750.1	6,583.0	3,247.7	999.7	2,267.5	3,340.9	2,564.7	1,075.4	1,513.0	652.9
1969	10,131.1	6,840.6	3,395.8	1,065.5	2,345.0	3,449.7	2,637.2	1,073.2	1,584.4	694.9
1970	10,451.3	7,068.3	3,524.6	1,117.3	2,419.9	3,547.3	2,697.4	1,066.5	1,647.5	724.1
1971	10,797.2	7,319.9	3,641.8	1,162.5	2,490.7	3,682.7	2,745.3	1,051.0	1,706.3	763.8
1972	11,225.0	7,638.5	3,798.0	1,223.9	2,584.5	3,845.3	2,795.3	1,043.9	1,760.7	815.9
1973	11,668.1	7,969.7	3,969.2	1,313.2	2,664.8	4,005.1	2,836.7	1,029.6	1,814.1	878.7
1974	12,014.8	8,237.6	4,123.8	1,395.4	2,736.1	4,117.2	2,878.0	1,015.6	1,866.4	916.7
1975	12,283.2	8,430.7	4,228.3	1,441.4	2,794.0	4,205.1	2,919.6	1,004.7	1,916.3	949.7
1976	12,607.4	8,660.9	4,337.9	1,492.8	2,851.2	4,326.5	2,958.5	994.8	1,964.0	1,001.0
1977	13,002.6	8,957.4	4,477.0	1,568.2	2,912.8	4,484.8	2,991.5	985.7	2,005.9	1,062.3
1978	13,459.2	9,306.7	4,655.4	1,669.9	2,987.3	4,655.5	3,031.4	977.7	2,054.1	1,125.6
1979	13,916.7	9,665.2	4,855.3	1,778.2	3,077.3	4,814.0	3,076.7	972.2	2,105.3	1,176.9
1980	14,269.2	9,950.0	5,032.5	1,855.4	3,176.9	4,921.4	3,123.8	969.1	2,155.7	1,198.0
1981	14,609.5	10,227.4	5,217.7	1,928.1	3,289.3	5,012.4	3,165.5	969.8	2,196.4	1,220.0
1982	14,866.5	10,479.2	5,358.6	1,965.8	3,392.7	5,071.9	3,203.9	974.1	2,230.4	1,237.4
1983	15,195.5	10,664.4	5,479.0	2,008.0	3,470.9	5,186.7	3,249.0	985.2	2,264.3	1,285.6
1984	15,662.9	10,995.8	5,667.5	2,091.7	3,575.6	5,329.1	3,306.4	1,000.4	2,306.6	1,363.3
1985	16,178.0	11,346.5	5,875.6	2,177.9	3,697.5	5,471.1	3,378.2	1,022.2	2,356.6	1,455.0
1986	16,702.7	11,684.3	6,044.0	2,251.9	3,791.8	5,640.6	3,458.0	1,047.5	2,411.1	1,561.1
1987	17,200.7	12,003.0	6,194.7	2,311.4	3,883.1	5,808.4	3,541.4	1,075.8	2,466.2	1,656.2
1988	17,691.5	12,317.6	6,348.2	2,380.3	3,967.8	5,969.4	3,616.8	1,092.9	2,524.4	1,756.7
1989	18,160.3	12,616.8	6,502.0	2,450.7	4,051.3	6,114.8	3,693.2	1,109.1	2,584.4	1,850.0
1990	18,586.4	12,889.5	6,649.5	2,507.3	4,142.2	6,240.0	3,777.8	1,125.9	2,652.0	1,919.2
1991	18,883.1	13,077.6	6,742.8	2,537.5	4,205.3	6,334.9	3,855.5	1,138.6	2,717.0	1,950.0
1992	19,212.4	13,278.3	6,830.0	2,578.9	4,251.1	6,448.3	3,935.7	1,148.5	2,787.2	1,998.4
1993	19,609.5	13,533.4	6,946.5	2,649.1	4,297.9	6,586.6	4,009.9	1,149.9	2,860.5	2,066.7
1994	20,059.1	13,832.6	7,094.5	2,756.9	4,339.8	6,737.6	4,076.3	1,144.4	2,933.7	2,151.8
1995	20,555.5	14,170.8	7,279.8	2,885.5	4,399.1	6,890.9	4,147.2	1,136.7	3,013.8	2,240.9

Source: Reproduced from Table 15, Survey of Current Business, May 1997.